GEORGIA ADMISSIBILITY OF EXPERT TESTIMONY

2007 Edition

By
MARY DONNE PETERS
and
JAMES WILLIS STANDARD, JR.

THOMSON
™
WEST

Mat # 40550212

© 2006 Thomson/West

ISBN-13: 978-0-314-96684-1
ISBN-10: 0-314-96684-6

DEDICATION

This book is dedicated to my son, Jake Roeland and his dad Bob Roeland, and my friend and partner Mike Gorby.

Mary Donne Peters.

This book is dedicated to the memory of my parents, James Willis Standard and Carolyn Gilroy Standard.

James Willis Standard, Jr.

PREFACE

Sweeping tort reform measures adopted by the Georgia General Assembly in 2005 ushered in some of the most dramatic changes in Georgia evidentiary rules in almost a century. A long- standing state court rule that expert testimony was generally admissible in evidence was replaced with a new set of rules that require judges to perform a gatekeeping function for expert testimony in civil litigation. Georgia's new expert witness rules, which are codified at O.C.G.A. Section 24-9-67.1, specifically engraft a body of case law that has been developing in the federal court system for over a decade: Daubert v. Merrell Dow Pharmaceuticals, Inc., and its progeny. Essentially, state trial courts must now ensure that an expert's testimony is both reliable and relevant before it will be presented to the jury. In the federal system, the trial court is given broad power to determine the admissibility of expert testimony and the appellate courts will overturn the decision to admit or exclude expert testimony only for abuse of discretion-even if exclusion of the expert's opinion will result in dismissal of the case. This book is intended to help practitioners, judges and even experts understand the sweeping changes in Georgia law and to anticipate procedural issues and complications that may arise with respect to the timing and content of expert witness disclosures and challenges.

WESTLAW® ELECTRONIC RESEARCH GUIDE

Westlaw, Computer–Assisted Legal Research

Westlaw is part of the research system provided by Thomson/West. With Westlaw, you find the same quality and integrity that you have come to expect from West books. For the most current and comprehensive legal research, combine the strengths of West books and Westlaw.

Westlaw Adds to Your Library

Whether you wish to expand or update your research, Westlaw can help. For instance, Westlaw is the most current source for case law, including slip opinions and unreported decisions. In addition to case law, the online availability of statutes, statutory indexes, legislation, court rules and orders, administrative materials, looseleaf publications, texts, periodicals, news and business information makes Westlaw an important asset to any library. Check the online Westlaw Directory or the print Westlaw Database Directory for a list of available databases and services. Following is a brief description of some of the capabilities that Westlaw offers.

Natural Language Searching

You can search most Westlaw databases using WIN®, the revolutionary Natural Language search method. As an alternative to formulating a query using terms and connectors, WIN allows you to simply enter a description of your research issue in plain English:

> What is the government's obligation to warn military
> personnel of the danger of past exposure to radiation?

Westlaw then retrieves the set of documents that have the highest statistical likelihood of matching your description.

Retrieving a Specific Document

When you know the citation to a case or statute that is not in your library, use the Find service to retrieve the document on Westlaw. Access Find and type a citation like the following:

> 181 ne2d 520
> in st 27–1–12–1

Updating Your Research

You can use Westlaw to update your research in many ways:

- Retrieve cases citing a particular statute.

- Update a state or federal statute by accessing the Update service from the displayed statute using the Jump marker.

- Retrieve newly enacted legislation by searching in the appropriate legislative service database.

- Retrieve cases not yet reported by searching in case law databases.

- Read the latest U.S. Supreme Court opinions within an hour of their release.

- Update West digests by searching with topic and key numbers.

Determining Case History and Retrieving Citing Cases

KeyCite®, the citation research service developed by West and made available through the Westlaw computer-assisted legal research service, integrates all the case law on Westlaw, giving you the power to

- trace the history of a case;

- retrieve a list of all cases on Westlaw that cite a case; and

- track legal issues in a case.

Citing references from the extensive library of secondary sources on Westlaw, such as ALR® annotations and law review articles, are covered by KeyCite as well. You can use these citing references to find case discussions by legal experts.

In addition, KeyCite is completely integrated with West's Key Number System so that it provides the tools for navigating the case law databases on Westlaw. Only KeyCite combines the up-to-the-minute case-verification functions of an online citator service with the case-finding tools needed to find relevant case law.

Additional Information

For more detailed information or assistance, contact your Westlaw account representative or call 1–800–REF–ATTY (1–800–733–2889).

RELATED PRODUCTS FROM THOMSON/WEST

(Many of the following products are part of the highly respected
Harrison product line, now published by Thomson/West)

ALTERNATIVE DISPUTE RESOLUTION

Alternative Dispute Resolution: Practice and Procedure in Georgia
Douglas H. Yarn

Georgia Settlements Law and Strategies
H. Sol Clark and Fred S. Clark

BUSINESS/CORPORATIONS

Georgia Contracts—Law and Litigation
John K. Larkins, Jr.

***Kaplan's Nadler* Georgia Corporations, Limited Partnerships and Limited Liability Companies, with Forms**
Jerome L. Kaplan, B. Joseph Alley, Jr., Robert P. Finch, Scott A. Fisher, David A. Forehand, Jr., Hardy Gregory, Jr., David B. McAlister, Patricia T. Morgan, Shelli Willis de Roos

Georgia Securities Practice, with Forms
James S. Rankin, Jr.

CRIMINAL LAW

***Molnar's* Georgia Criminal Law, Crimes and Punishments**
Robert E. Cleary, Jr.

***Kurtz's* Criminal Offenses and Defenses in Georgia**
Robert E. Cleary, Jr.

***Daniel's* Georgia Criminal Trial Practice**
John J. Goger

***Daniel's* Georgia Criminal Trial Practice Forms**
John J. Goger

The Georgia DUI Trial Practice Manual
William C. Head

RELATED PRODUCTS FROM THOMSON/WEST

DAMAGES, REMEDIES AND COLLECTIONS

Georgia Legal Collections
Lewis N. Jones

Georgia Construction Mechanics' and Materialmen's Liens, with Forms
Daniel F. Hinkel

Georgia Law of Damages, with Forms
Eric James Hertz and Mark D. Link

Punitive Damages in Georgia
Eric James Hertz

Georgia Post–Judgment Collection, with Forms
Stuart Finestone

Dobb's Georgia Enforcement of Securities Interests in Personal Property, with Forms
James S. Rankin, Jr.

ELDER LAW

Elder Care and Nursing Home Litigation in Georgia with Forms/Long–Term Health Care
Michael S. Reeves

EVIDENCE

Georgia Rules of Evidence
Paul S. Milich

Courtroom Handbook on Georgia Evidence
Paul S. Milich

Daniel's Georgia Handbook on Criminal Evidence
Jack Goger

Herman and McLaughlin Admissibility of Evidence in Civil Cases—A Manual for Georgia Trial Lawyers
Michael E. McLaughlin

Green's Georgia Law of Evidence
Alexander Scherr

Agnor's Georgia Evidence
D. Lake Rumsey, Jr.

RELATED PRODUCTS FROM THOMSON/WEST

LANDLORD AND TENANT

Georgia Landlord and Tenant—Breach and Remedies, with Forms
William J. Dawkins

Georgia Landlord and Tenant—Leases, Forms and Causes
James A. Fleming

LITIGATION

Georgia Appellate Practice, with Forms
Christopher J. McFadden, Edward C. Brewer III and Charles R. Sheppard

Georgia Civil Discovery, with Forms
Wayne M. Purdom

***Davis and Shulman's* Georgia Practice and Procedure**
Richard C. Ruskell

Georgia Process and Service, with Forms
Phillip Weltner II

Trial Handbook for Georgia Lawyers
Ronald L. Carlson

PERSONAL INJURY AND TORTS

**Medical Torts in Georgia:
A Handbook on State and Federal Law**
C. Ashley Royal, Preyesh K. Maniklal, Gary C. Christy and
Jennifer Lewis Roberts

Premises Liability in Georgia, with Forms
Michael J. Gorby

Georgia Products Liability
Jane F. Thorpe, David R. Vanderbush and J. Kennard Neal

Soft Tissue Injuries in Georgia, Including Whiplash, with Forms
Houston D. Smith III

Georgia Law of Torts
Charles R. Adams III

Georgia Law of Torts—Forms
Eric James Hertz, Mark D. Link, Houston D. Smith III

Summary of Contents

Table of Contents

CHAPTER 7.   ACTIONS INVOLVING REAL PROPERTY

CHAPTER 8.   PSYCHOLOGICAL TESTIMONY AND RELATED MATTERS

CHAPTER 9.   MEDICAL MALPRACTICE

CHAPTER 10. MOTOR VEHICLE ACCIDENTS

CHAPTER 11. PERSONAL INJURY

CHAPTER 12. EXPERT TESTIMONY IN COMMERCIAL AND BUSINESS–RELATED DISPUTES

APPENDICES

Chapter 1

Overview Of Georgia And Federal Law And Recent Changes To Georgia Law

---

KeyCite⬥: Cases and other legal materials listed in KeyCite Scope can be researched through the KeyCite service on Westlaw⬥. Use KeyCite to check citations for form, parallel references, prior and later history, and comprehensive citator information, including citations to other decisions and secondary materials.

---

§ 1:1 Georgia law historically

"Experts" are a unique species of witness under the law. Conceptually, there is nothing especially complex about what an "expert" is. An "expert" is simply an individual who possesses knowledge—beyond that of an average juror—on an issue relevant in any particular case.[1] Given the virtually unlimited number of circumstances which may lead to an action at law, it is not surprising to find that experts come in an almost equal number of varieties. Depending on the issues involved in a case, an expert may hail from a wide variety of professions or

---

[Section 1:1]

[1]See Chapter 2, § 2:1.

disciplines involving esoteric concepts entirely alien to the average juror, such as neurology, epidemiology, biomechanical engineering, or forensic economics.

Expert witnesses are permitted broad latitude unavailable to other witnesses in offering testimony which is calculated to affect the outcome in any given case. Unlike an ordinary witness, whose testimony is generally limited to what that individual has perceived through his or her own senses,[2] one designated as an "expert" enjoys the ability to testify based upon matters not within his or her personal knowledge.[3] Moreover, unlike an ordinary witness, whose testimony is generally limited to describing the *facts* of which he or she has personal knowledge,[4] those designated as "experts" enjoy the ability to testify as to *opinions or inferences* derived from a set of facts.[5] Such opinions and inferences may even include opinions on the issue to be ultimately decided by a jury, such as whether a party's conduct fell below the applicable "standard of care" required of that party, or whether a party's conduct was the "cause" of another party's complained-of injuries.[6]

Georgia law has historically been very receptive to expert testimony. This liberal stance was reflected in, and indeed, commanded by O.C.G.A. § 24-9-67. Prior to 2005, this statute set the baseline for determining the admissibility of expert testimony in Georgia courts by providing, in pertinent part, that the

---

[2]Johnson v. Knebel, 267 Ga. 853, 485 S.E.2d 451 (1997); McCorkle v. Department of Transp., 257 Ga. App. 397, 571 S.E.2d 160 (2002).

[3]Williamson v. Harvey Smith, Inc., 246 Ga. App. 745, 749, 542 S.E.2d 151, 155 (2000); Blackburn v. State, 180 Ga. App. 436, 437, 349 S.E.2d 286, 288 (1986). See Chapter 2, § 2:8.

[4]Johnson v. Knebel, 267 Ga. 853, 856, 485 S.E.2d 451, 454 (1997) (observing that lay witness may render an opinion only if it is based on his or her own perception, and only insofar as the witness cannot adequately relate his or her perception without also conveying an opinion). In Dual S. Enterprises, Inc. v. Webb, 138 Ga. App. 810, 227 S.E.2d 418 (1976), the court explained that, due to practical limitations in language, it is often times difficult, if not impossible, to express a statement of fact without contemporaneously expressing an

opinion or conclusion.

[W]hen the subject matter of an inquiry relates to numerous facts perceived by the sense, to a series of instances passing under the observation of a witness, or to a variety of circumstances and a combination of appearances, which, under the limitations of language, cannot be adequately described and presented to the jury with the same force and clearness as they appeared to the witness, the witness may state his impressions drawn from, and opinions based upon, the facts and circumstances observed by him or the effect which they produced on his mind.

Dual S. Enterprises, Inc. v. Webb, 138 Ga. App. 810, 811, 227 S.E.2d 418 (1976).

[5]Smith v. State, 247 Ga. 612, 277 S.E.2d 678 (1981); Metropolitan Life Ins. Co. v. Saul, 189 Ga. 1, 5 S.E.2d 214 (1939).

[6]See generally Chapter 2, § 2:4.

"opinions of experts on any question of science, skill, trade or like questions shall always be admissible[.]"[7]

Despite the command that expert testimony "always be admissible," the admissibility of such testimony was not without its boundaries. While these limits and rules are discussed in greater detail elsewhere in this treatise, it is worth mentioning some general principles which have historically operated to limit the bounds of an expert's opinion testimony. First and foremost, the expert witness was required to be qualified, by virtue of education, skill, or experience, to provide testimony on the subject for which the expert was offered.[8] Second, the subject matter on which the expert's testimony was offered needed to be relevant to the issues in the case,[9] and beyond the ability of the jury to ascertain on its own, i.e. "helpful" to the jury in enabling it to better understand the issues in the case.[10] Third, the expert's opinion testimony was required to be based upon more than speculation and conjecture,[11] and based, at least in part, upon facts in evidence.[12] Finally, with respect to testimony based upon certain scientific procedures or techniques, the procedures and techniques had to be shown to be reliable, or in other words, to have reached a "scientific stage of verifiable certainty."[13]

In 1993, the United States Supreme Court decided the landmark case of *Daubert v. Merrell Dow Pharmaceuticals*.[14] In *Daubert*, the Supreme Court held that, before it is admitted to a jury, a trial judge has a duty to ensure that scientific testimony is based upon reliable principles and methods.[15] Several years later, the Court extended this ruling by making it applicable not only to expert testimony which was "scientific" in nature, but to all expert testimony.[16] In the year 2000, Rule 702 of the Federal Rules of Evidence was amended to specifically incorporate the principles enunciated in these cases.[17]

In 2005, the Georgia legislature enacted O.C.G.A. § 24–9–67.1(b), which, in the context of civil cases, substantially adopts the language of Rule 702 of the Federal Rules of Evidence. More-

---

[7]O.C.G.A. § 24–9–67.

[8]See Chapter 2, § 2:1.

[9]See Chapter 2, § 2:3.

[10]See Chapter 2, § 2:4.

[11]See Chapter 2, § 2:10.

[12]See Chapter 2, § 2:8.

[13]Harper v. State, 249 Ga. 519, 292 S.E.2d 389 (1982). See Chapter 2, § 2:11.

[14]Daubert v. Merrell Dow Pharmaceuticals, Inc., 509 U.S. 579, 113 S. Ct. 2786, 125 L. Ed. 2d 469 (1993).

[15]For a discussion of the *Daubert* case, see § 1:4 below.

[16]Kumho Tire Co., Ltd. v. Carmichael, 526 U.S. 137, 119 S. Ct. 1167, 143 L. Ed. 2d 238 (1999). For a discussion of the *Kumho Tire* case, see § 1:6 below.

[17]See § 1:7 below for a discussion of the year 2000 amendments to the Federal Rules of Evidence.

over, subsection (f) of this statute expressly states that, in construing this code section, Georgia courts "may draw from the opinions of the United States Supreme Court Daubert v. Merrell Dow Pharmaceuticals, Inc., 509 U.S. 579, 113 S. Ct. 2786, 125 L. Ed. 2d 469 (1993); General Elec. Co. v. Joiner, 522 U.S. 136, 118 S. Ct. 512, 139 L. Ed. 2d 508 (1997); Kumho Tire Co., Ltd. v. Carmichael, 526 U.S. 137, 119 S. Ct. 1167, 143 L. Ed. 2d 238 (1999); and other cases in federal courts applying the standards announced by the United States Supreme Court in these cases." Accordingly, before moving to a discussion of O.C.G.A. § 24–9–67.1, a brief overview of the relevant federal law is conducted below. While the federal case law following in the wake of *Daubert* and Rule 702 is legion, emphasis will be focused on the three Supreme Court cases explicitly cited to in O.C.G.A. § 24–9–67.1.

§ 1:2 Federal law—Historical overview of federal law

Prior to the 1993 decision of *Daubert v. Merrell Dow*, the predominant standard by which the admissibility of novel scientific evidence was determined was whether it had been "generally accepted" as reliable in the relevant scientific community.[1] This standard was first articulated in the 1923 case of *Frye v. United States*,[2] which dealt with the admissibility of evidence derived from a rudimentary form of a polygraph. In oft-quoted language, the *Frye* Court observed that:

> Just when a scientific principle or discovery crosses the line between experimental and demonstrable stages is difficult to define. Somewhere in this twilight zone the evidential force of the principle must be recognized, and while courts will go a long way in admitting expert testimony deduced from a well-recognized scientific principle or discovery, the thing from which the deduction is made must be sufficiently established to have gained general acceptance in the particular field in which it belongs.[3]

Over one-half a century following the *Frye* decision, the United States Congress, in 1975, enacted the Federal Rules of Evidence.[4] Rule 402 provided that, as a general rule and unless otherwise prohibited, "[a]ll relevant evidence is admissible[.]" Rule 702, applying specifically to expert testimony, provided that:

> [i]f scientific, technical, or other specialized knowledge will assist

---

[Section 1:2]

[1] Daubert v. Merrell Dow Pharmaceuticals, Inc., 509 U.S. 579, 584, 113 S. Ct. 2786, 2792, 125 L. Ed. 2d 469 (1993).

[2] Frye v. U.S., 293 F. 1013 (App. D.C. 1923).

[3] Frye v. U.S., 293 F. 1013, 1014 (App. D.C. 1923).

[4] Sarah Brew, Where the Rubber Hits The Road: Steering The Trial Court Through A Post–Kumho Tire Evaluation of Expert Testimony, 27 Wm. Mitchell L. Rev. 467, 470 (2000).

the trier of fact to understand the evidence or to determine a fact in issue, a witness qualified as an expert by knowledge, skill, experience, training, or education, may testify thereto in the form of an opinion or otherwise.[5]

As the United States Supreme Court has found significant, nothing in this text referred to the "general acceptance" test enunciated in *Frye*.[6]

Over the years, commentators were increasingly quick to point out that the *Frye* inquiry left many questions unanswered. For instance, *Frye* did not define who or what comprises the relevant field or community, nor did it define what quantum of acceptance within this community would constitute general acceptance.[7] Opponents of the *Frye* test argued that it was too restrictive, and led to the exclusion of relevant scientific evidence—sometimes on the cutting-edge of the field—simply because it was too "new," and therefore, had not yet attained general acceptance.[8] Critics of the *Frye* test contended that the *Frye* test's focus was on the mere "counting of heads," rather than on verifying the soundness of scientific principles as applied in any given case.[9] Other commentators argued that, notwithstanding the "general acceptance" test, scientific evidence which was utterly unreliable made its way before a jury. In this regard, one commentator observed, in language that has now entered into the lexicon of the debate: "the kind of expertise regularly accepted as admissible by courts was, frankly, 'junk' of scandalous lack of dependability."[10] The term "junk science" was thus coined.

---

[5]Daubert v. Merrell Dow Pharmaceuticals, Inc., 509 U.S. 579, 588, 113 S. Ct. 2786, 125 L. Ed. 2d 469 (1993).

[6]Daubert v. Merrell Dow Pharmaceuticals, Inc., 509 U.S. 579, 588, 113 S. Ct. 2786, 125 L. Ed. 2d 469 (1993).

[7]Henry F. Fradella, Lauren O'Neill and Adam Fogarty, The Impact of Daubert On Forensic Evidence, 31 PEPP. L. REV. 323, 326 (2004).

[8]Henry F. Fradella, Lauren O'Neill and Adam Fogarty, The Impact of Daubert On Forensic Evidence, 31 PEPP. L. REV. 323, 326 (2004); Sarah Brew, Where the Rubber Hits The

Road: Steering The Trial Court Through A Post–Kumho Tire Evaluation of Expert Testimony, 27 Wm. Mitchell L. Rev. 467, 470 (2000). See also Daubert v. Merrell Dow Pharmaceuticals, Inc., 509 U.S. 579, 585 n.4, 113 S. Ct. 2786, 125 L. Ed. 2d 469 (1993).

[9]Sarah Brew, Where the Rubber Hits The Road: Steering The Trial Court Through A Post–Kumho Tire Evaluation of Expert Testimony, 27 Wm. Mitchell L. Rev. 467, 470 (2000).

[10]Peter W. Huber, Galileo's Revenge: Junk Science in the Courtroom (New York, Basic Books 1991).

§ 1:3   Federal law—Daubert v. Merrell Dow

In 1993, the United States Supreme Court issued the seminal case of *Daubert v. Merrell Dow Pharmaceuticals, Inc.*[1] which addressed the continued vitality of the "general acceptance" test. Observing that nothing in the Federal Rules of Evidence established general acceptance as an "absolute prerequisite" to admissibility, the Court stated that such a "rigid" requirement "would be at odds with the 'liberal thrust' of the Federal Rules and their 'general approach of relaxing the traditional barriers to 'opinion' testimony.' "[2] At the same time, the Court observed that the Federal Rules of Evidence did place limits on the admissibility of scientific evidence, and that a trial judge has a duty to "ensure that any and all scientific testimony or evidence admitted is not only relevant, but reliable."[3]

In addressing the reliability prong of the test, the Court keyed in on the text of Rule 702, noting that the term "scientific" suggests "a grounding in the methods and procedures of science[,]" and the term " 'knowledge' connotes more than subjective belief or unsupported speculation."[4] Reading these two terms together, the Court held that "in order to qualify as 'scientific knowledge,' an inference or assertion must be derived by the scientific method. Proposed testimony must be supported by appropriate validation—i.e. 'good grounds,' based on what is known. In short, the requirement that an experts testimony pertain to 'scientific knowledge' establishes a standard of evidentiary reliability."[5]

In addressing the relevance prong of the test, the Court observed that the requirement that the expert evidence or testimony "assist the tier of fact" goes primarily to the issue of relevance, and that expert testimony must relate to the issues in the case.[6] Moreover, expert testimony which is not "sufficiently tied to the facts of the case" does not assist the jury in understanding the evidence or resolving a factual dispute, and is therefore

---

[Section 1:3]

[1]Daubert v. Merrell Dow Pharmaceuticals, Inc., 509 U.S. 579, 585, 113 S. Ct. 2786, 125 L. Ed. 2d 469 (1993).

[2]Daubert v. Merrell Dow Pharmaceuticals, Inc., 509 U.S. 579, 588, 113 S. Ct. 2786, 125 L. Ed. 2d 469 (1993) (quoting Beech Aircraft Corp. v. Rainey, 488 U.S. 153, 169, 109 S. Ct. 439, 450, 102 L. Ed. 2d 445 (1988)).

[3]Daubert v. Merrell Dow Pharmaceuticals, Inc., 509 U.S. 579, 589, 113 S. Ct. 2786, 2795, 125 L. Ed.

2d 469 (1993).

[4]Daubert v. Merrell Dow Pharmaceuticals, Inc., 509 U.S. 579, 590, 113 S. Ct. 2786, 2795, 125 L. Ed. 2d 469 (1993).

[5]Daubert v. Merrell Dow Pharmaceuticals, Inc., 509 U.S. 579, 590, 113 S. Ct. 2786, 2795, 125 L. Ed. 2d 469 (1993).

[6]Daubert v. Merrell Dow Pharmaceuticals, Inc., 509 U.S. 579, 591, 113 S. Ct. 2786, 2795, 125 L. Ed. 2d 469 (1993).

not relevant.[7] The Court described this concept as one of "fit,"[8] noting that the "helpfulness" requirement of Rule 702 "requires a valid scientific connection to the pertinent inquiry as a precondition to admissibility."[9]

The Court held that the trial court, when faced with a proffer of expert testimony, has the duty to determine whether the testimony is both reliable and relevant, and that this inquiry "entails a preliminary assessment of whether the reasoning or methodology underlying the testimony is scientifically valid and of whether that reasoning or methodology properly can be applied to the facts in issue."[10] The Court emphasized the fact that such an inquiry is required because expert witnesses, unlike ordinary lay witnesses, are permitted broad latitude to offer opinions, including opinions on matters which are based neither on firsthand knowledge nor upon personal observation.[11] The Court noted that such a "gatekeeping" duty is also indicated because "[e]xpert evidence can be both powerful and quite misleading because of the difficulty in evaluating it."[12] This "gatekeeping" role is not limited to "novel" or "unconventional" science; however, a scientific theory or technique which is "so firmly established as to have attained the status of scientific law" may be subject to being judicially noticed by the trial court.[13]

To aid trial courts in performing their "gatekeeping" function, the Court proposed a non-exhaustive checklist of factors which will bear upon the inquiry as to whether expert testimony is sufficiently reliable and relevant so as to be admitted into evidence. The first of these factors is whether a theory or technique can be,

---

[7]Daubert v. Merrell Dow Pharmaceuticals, Inc., 509 U.S. 579, 591, 113 S. Ct. 2786, 2795–2796, 125 L. Ed. 2d 469 (1993).

[8]The Court observed that "fit" is "not always obvious, and scientific validity for one purpose is not necessarily scientific validity for other, unrelated purposes. *Id. at 591.* By way of illustration, the Court observed that:

[t]he study of the phases of the moon, for example, may provide valid scientific "knowledge" about whether a certain night was dark, and if darkness is a fact in issue, the knowledge will assist the trier of fact. However (absent creditable grounds supporting such a link), evidence that the moon was full on a certain night will not assist the trier of fact in determining whether an individual was unusually likely to have behaved irrationally on that night. *Id.*

[9]Daubert v. Merrell Dow Pharmaceuticals, Inc., 509 U.S. 579, 591–592, 113 S. Ct. 2786, 2796, 125 L. Ed. 2d 469 (1993).

[10]Daubert v. Merrell Dow Pharmaceuticals, Inc., 509 U.S. 579, 592–593, 113 S. Ct. 2786, 2796, 125 L. Ed. 2d 469 (1993).

[11]Daubert v. Merrell Dow Pharmaceuticals, Inc., 509 U.S. 579, 592, 113 S. Ct. 2786, 2796, 125 L. Ed. 2d 469 (1993).

[12]Daubert v. Merrell Dow Pharmaceuticals, Inc., 509 U.S. 579, 595, 113 S. Ct. 2786, 2798, 125 L. Ed. 2d 469 (1993).

[13]Daubert v. Merrell Dow Pharmaceuticals, Inc., 509 U.S. 579, 592 n.11, 113 S. Ct. 2786, 2796, 125 L. Ed. 2d 469 (1993).

and has been, tested.[14] "Scientific methodology today is based on generating hypotheses and testing them to see if they can be falsified; indeed, this methodology is what distinguishes science from other fields of human inquiry."[15]

A second factor is whether the theory or technique has been subjected to "peer review and publication."[16] The Court noted that publication is not the "sine qua non" of admissibility, as some "well-grounded but innovative" theories may not have been published, and others may be of too limited interest to have been published.[17] Nonetheless, publication, or lack thereof, is a relevant, though non-dispositive factor, as "submission to the scrutiny of the scientific community is a component of 'good science,' in part because it increases the likelihood that substantive flaws in methodology will be detected."[18]

A third factor is the known or potential rate of error of a particular scientific technique.[19] A closely-related inquiry will pertain to the existence and maintenance of standards controlling the technique's operation.[20] Relevant to this inquiry is what the Court observed to be the scientific concepts of validity—"does the principle support what it purports to show?"—and reliability—"does application of the principle produce consistent results?"[21]

While the Court had rejected "general acceptance" as an "absolute prerequisite" to admissibility, the Court did identify it as a fourth factor with bearing on the inquiry.[22] A known technique which has been able to attract only "minimal support" within the scientific community "may be properly viewed with

---

[14]Daubert v. Merrell Dow Pharmaceuticals, Inc., 509 U.S. 579, 593, 113 S. Ct. 2786, 2796, 125 L. Ed. 2d 469 (1993).

[15]Daubert v. Merrell Dow Pharmaceuticals, Inc., 509 U.S. 579, 593, 113 S. Ct. 2786, 2796, 125 L. Ed. 2d 469 (1993).

[16]Daubert v. Merrell Dow Pharmaceuticals, Inc., 509 U.S. 579, 593, 113 S. Ct. 2786, 2797, 125 L. Ed. 2d 469 (1993).

[17]Daubert v. Merrell Dow Pharmaceuticals, Inc., 509 U.S. 579, 593, 113 S. Ct. 2786, 2797, 125 L. Ed. 2d 469 (1993).

[18]Daubert v. Merrell Dow Pharmaceuticals, Inc., 509 U.S. 579, 593–594, 113 S. Ct. 2786, 125 L. Ed. 2d 469 (1993).

[19]Daubert v. Merrell Dow Pharmaceuticals, Inc., 509 U.S. 579, 594, 113 S. Ct. 2786, 2797, 125 L. Ed. 2d 469 (1993).

[20]Daubert v. Merrell Dow Pharmaceuticals, Inc., 509 U.S. 579, 594, 113 S. Ct. 2786, 2797, 125 L. Ed. 2d 469 (1993).

[21]Daubert v. Merrell Dow Pharmaceuticals, Inc., 509 U.S. 579, 590 n.9, 113 S. Ct. 2786, 2795, 125 L. Ed. 2d 469 (1993).

[22]Daubert v. Merrell Dow Pharmaceuticals, Inc., 509 U.S. 579, 594, 113 S. Ct. 2786, 2797, 125 L. Ed. 2d 469 (1993).

skepticism."[23] In determining whether a theory has reached a level of general acceptance, the court may consider what constitutes the "relevant scientific community" and the "particular degree of acceptance within that community."[24]

The Court noted that the focus of this inquiry is "solely" on the principles and methodology employed, not the conclusions generated thereby.[25] Noting that this inquiry is a flexible one, the Court noted that other rules of evidence other than Rule 702 should also be considered. For example, if the expert is basing his testimony on hearsay, the facts or data that form the basis of his testimony must be "of a type reasonably relied upon by experts in the particular field in forming opinions or inferences upon the subject."[26] The Court also referred to the balancing test in Rule 403 of the Federal Rules of Evidence, which permits the exclusion of evidence when the probative value of the evidence is substantially outweighed by unfair prejudice, confusion of issues, or misleading of the jury.[27]

On a final note, while the *Daubert* opinion emphasized the trial court's gatekeeping role in screening and excluding expert testimony which does not meet a certain threshold of reliability, the Court reaffirmed the role of cross-examination in exposing weaknesses in "shaky," but otherwise reliable, expert testimony. "Vigorous cross-examination, presentation of contrary evidence, and careful instruction on the burden of proof are the traditional and appropriate means of attacking shaky but admissible evidence."[28]

§ 1:4 Federal law—General Electric Co. v. Joiner

Four years after *Daubert* was decided, the Supreme Court revisited its holding in the case of *General Elec. Co. v. Joiner.*[1] Originating out of the Federal District Court for the Northern District of Georgia, *Joiner* involved the issue of whether the

---

[23]Daubert v. Merrell Dow Pharmaceuticals, Inc., 509 U.S. 579, 594, 113 S. Ct. 2786, 2797, 125 L. Ed. 2d 469 (1993).

[24]Daubert v. Merrell Dow Pharmaceuticals, Inc., 509 U.S. 579, 594, 113 S. Ct. 2786, 2797, 125 L. Ed. 2d 469 (1993).

[25]Daubert v. Merrell Dow Pharmaceuticals, Inc., 509 U.S. 579, 595, 113 S. Ct. 2786, 2797, 125 L. Ed. 2d 469 (1993).

[26]Daubert v. Merrell Dow Pharmaceuticals, Inc., 509 U.S. 579, 595, 113 S. Ct. 2786, 125 L. Ed. 2d 469 (1993) (citing FED. R. EVID. 703).

[27]Daubert v. Merrell Dow Pharmaceuticals, Inc., 509 U.S. 579, 595, 113 S. Ct. 2786, 2798, 125 L. Ed. 2d 469 (1993).

[28]Daubert v. Merrell Dow Pharmaceuticals, Inc., 509 U.S. 579, 596, 113 S. Ct. 2786, 2798, 125 L. Ed. 2d 469 (1993).

[Section 1:4]

[1]General Elec. Co. v. Joiner, 522 U.S. 136, 118 S. Ct. 512, 139 L. Ed. 2d 508 (1997).

plaintiff's exposure to certain substances caused his lung cancer. The trial court had granted summary judgment to the defendants, in part because it had found that the plaintiff's experts had failed to show a causal link between the plaintiff's cancer and his exposure to certain chemicals. The Eleventh Circuit Court of Appeals reversed on the grounds that because the Federal Rules of Evidence "display a preference for admissibility, we apply a particularly stringent standard of review to the trial judge's exclusion of expert testimony."

The Court reversed the Eleventh Circuit, holding that "abuse of discretion is the proper standard by which to review a district court's decision to admit or exclude scientific evidence."[2] The Court held that a trial court's exercise of its gatekeeping role was subject to the abuse of discretion standard even though the exclusion of expert testimony was "outcome dispositive."[3]

The Court also took this opportunity to modify the holding in *Daubert* that the focus of the reliability inquiry is focused "solely on principles and methodology, not on the conclusions that they generate."[4] Noting that "conclusions and methodology are not entirely distinct from one another[,]" the Court went on to state:

> Trained experts commonly extrapolate from existing data. But nothing in either *Daubert* or the Federal Rules of Evidence requires a district court to admit opinion evidence that is connected to existing data only by the *ipse dixit* of the expert. A court may conclude that there is simply too great an analytical gap between the data and the opinion proferred.[5]

§ 1:5 Federal law—Kumho Tire Co. v. Carmichael

In *Daubert*, while recognizing that Rule 702 applied not only to "scientific" knowledge, but also to "technical or other specialized knowledge" as well, the Supreme Court nonetheless limited its discussion "to the scientific context because that [was] the nature

---

[2]General Elec. Co. v. Joiner, 522 U.S. 136, 146, 118 S. Ct. 512, 519, 139 L. Ed. 2d 508 (1997).

[3]General Elec. Co. v. Joiner, 522 U.S. 136, 144, 118 S. Ct. 512, 517, 139 L. Ed. 2d 508 (1997).

[4]General Elec. Co. v. Joiner, 522 U.S. 136, 146, 118 S. Ct. 512, 519, 139 L. Ed. 2d 508 (1997) (citing Daubert v. Merrell Dow Pharmaceuticals, Inc., 509 U.S. 579, 595, 113 S. Ct. 2786, 2797, 125 L. Ed. 2d 469 (1993)).

[5]General Elec. Co. v. Joiner, 522 U.S. 136, 146, 118 S. Ct. 512, 519, 139 L. Ed. 2d 508 (1997). On remand in

Daubert, the Ninth Circuit Court of Appeals issued a similar admonition that a court may not simply "take the expert at his word" in determining whether the expert's testimony is supported by sufficiently reliable science: "[T]he expert's bald assurance of validity is not enough. Rather, the party presenting the expert must show that the expert's findings are based on sound science, and this will require some objective, independent validation of the expert's methodology." Daubert v. Merrell Dow Pharmaceuticals, Inc., 43 F.3d 1311, 1316 (9th Cir. 1995).

of the expertise" at issue.[1] In the wake of this decision, the debate raged as to whether *Daubert's* principles were applicable to expert testimony which was not, strictly speaking, "scientific," but "technical or "specialized" in nature. Specifically, commentators on both sides of the debate argued that *Daubert* either was, or was not, applicable to the "soft" sciences, such as economics or psychology, "technical" fields, such as engineering, and other "non-scientific" testimony that was nonetheless "specialized."[2] A split developed among the federal circuit courts as to whether *Daubert* was applicable to "technical" and "other specialized" knowledge.[3] This debate was finally addressed by the Supreme Court in the 1999 case of *Kumho Tire Company, Ltd. v. Carmichael.*[4]

Kumho Tire involved a mechanical engineer's testimony that the cause of a tire "blow-out" on a minivan, leading to the serious injuries and death of the minivan's passengers, was caused by manufacturing or design defect in the tire. The defendants moved to exclude the engineer's testimony on the grounds that the engineer's conclusions were premised on unreliable methodology, and the trial court granted the motion. The Eleventh Circuit reversed, holding that *Daubert's* analysis applies only where the expert has relied upon the application of "scientific" principles, rather than "skill-or experience-based observation."

The Court again reversed the Eleventh Circuit, noting that *Daubert* had been limited to the issue of expert testimony that was "scientific" in nature only because that was the nature of the testimony at issue.[5] Observing that Rule 702 made no relevant distinction between knowledge which is "scientific," "technical," or "specialized," and instead, made it clear that any such knowledge may be the subject of expert testimony, the Court held that a trial court's duty to act as a gatekeeper to ensure the reliability

---

[Section 1:5]

[1]Daubert v. Merrell Dow Pharmaceuticals, Inc., 509 U.S. 579, 590, 113 S. Ct. 2786, 2795, 125 L. Ed. 2d 469 (1993).

[2]See, e.g. Shubha Ghosh, Federal and State Resolutions of The Problem of Daubert and "Technical or Other Specialized Knowledge," 22 AM. J. TRIAL ADVOC. 237 (Fall 1998); Edward J. Imwinkelried, The Escape Hatches From Frye and Daubert: Sometimes You Don't Need to Lay Either Foundation In Order To Introduce Expert Testimony! 23 AM. J. TRIAL ADVOC. 1 (1999); John V. Jansonius, and Andrew M. Gould, Expert Wit-

nesses In Employment Litigation: The Role of Reliability in Assessing Admissibility, 50 BAYLOR L. REV. 267, 321–325 (1998).

[3]John V. Jansonius, and Andrew M. Gould, Expert Witnesses In Employment Litigation: The Role of Reliability in Assessing Admissibility, 50 BAYLOR L. REV. 267, 321–23 (1998).

[4]Kumho Tire Co., Ltd. v. Carmichael, 526 U.S. 137, 119 S. Ct. 1167, 143 L. Ed. 2d 238 (1999).

[5]Kumho Tire Co., Ltd. v. Carmichael, 526 U.S. 137, 147–148, 119 S. Ct. 1167, 1174, 143 L. Ed. 2d 238 (1999).

of expert testimony applied to *all* expert testimony, whether based on "scientific," "technical," or "other specialized" knowledge.[6] The Court reasoned that experts whose testimony is based on technical or other specialized knowledge, just as experts whose testimony is based on scientific knowledge, will be testifying on experience "foreign" to that of the average juror, and are generally permitted latitude unavailable to other witnesses to express their opinions.[7] Moreover, the Court noted that, as a practical matter, given the fact that there is no "clear line" that divides one type of knowledge from the other, it would "prove difficult, if not impossible" to administer evidentiary rules, in a principled manner, that depended upon such fine and unclear distinctions.[8]

The Court further elaborated upon *Daubert* by holding that when the factual basis, data, principles, or methods underlying an expert's testimony, or their application to the facts at issue, are sufficiently called into question, the trial court must determine whether the expert's testimony has a sufficiently reliable basis so as to be admissible.[9] However, the Court also emphasized that a trial court must have "considerable leeway" in deciding *how* to determine whether particular expert testimony is reliable.[10] The "abuse of discretion" standard enunciated in *Joiner* applies just as much to the trial court's determination of *how* to assess the reliability of an expert's testimony as it does to the trial court's ultimate determination of whether to admit or exclude such testimony.[11] The Court noted that *Daubert* itself made it clear that the various factors outlined by the Court for use in a reliability assessment did not constitute a "definitive checklist," and that a reliability assessment will necessarily be a

---

[6]Kumho Tire Co., Ltd. v. Carmichael, 526 U.S. 137, 141, 147, 119 S. Ct. 1167, 143 L. Ed. 2d 238 (1999).

[7]Kumho Tire Co., Ltd. v. Carmichael, 526 U.S. 137, 148–149, 119 S. Ct. 1167, 1174, 143 L. Ed. 2d 238 (1999).

[8]Kumho Tire Co., Ltd. v. Carmichael, 526 U.S. 137, 148, 119 S. Ct. 1167, 1174, 143 L. Ed. 2d 238 (1999).

[9]Kumho Tire Co., Ltd. v. Carmichael, 526 U.S. 137, 149, 119 S. Ct. 1167, 1175, 143 L. Ed. 2d 238 (1999).

[10]Kumho Tire Co., Ltd. v. Carmichael, 526 U.S. 137, 152, 119 S. Ct. 1167, 1176, 143 L. Ed. 2d 238 (1999).

[11]Kumho Tire Co., Ltd. v. Carmichael, 526 U.S. 137, 152, 119 S. Ct. 1167, 1176, 143 L. Ed. 2d 238 (1999). The concurring opinion by Justice Scalia, who was joined by Justices O'Connor and Thomas, added on this point that while a trial court enjoys discretion as to the manner of testing the reliability of an expert's testimony, the trial court does not have discretion to abandon its gatekeeping function by failing to perform a reliability assessment. *Id. at 158–159.*

"flexible" inquiry.[12] The Court observed that, depending on the particular issues and facts involved in any given case, one or several of *Daubert's* factors may or may not apply.[13]

For instance, the fact that a certain contention of an expert witness has never been subjected to peer review may not be particularly undermining of the expert's opinion if the particular application has never been of widespread interest.[14] Similarly, the fact that an expert's contention enjoys general acceptance within a particular field may not be particularly helpful if the field itself is of suspect reliability.[15] Further, the Court observed that *Daubert's* factors may be helpful in evaluating the reliability of testimony which, rather being based on "science," is based on "experience," as might be the case in determining how often an engineer's experienced-based methodology has produced erroneous results and whether such a method is generally accepted in the relevant engineering community.[16]

In upholding the trial court's decision to exclude the engineer's testimony, the Court noted that at issue was not the reasonableness, in a *general* sense, of the expert's methodology, but rather, the way in which the expert had and had not applied an otherwise accepted methodology to the facts of this *particular* case.[17] In upholding the trial court's determination that an otherwise reliable methodology had not been reliably applied to the facts of this particular case, the Court shed further light on the trial court's gatekeeping role as envisioned under *Daubert*:

> It is to make certain that an expert, whether basing testimony upon professional studies or personal experience, employs in the courtroom the same level of intellectual rigor that characterizes the practice of an expert in the relevant field.[18]

§ 1:6   Federal law—The 2000 amendments to Federal Rule 702

In the year 2000, Rule 702 was amended in response to the

---

[12]Kumho Tire Co., Ltd. v. Carmichael, 526 U.S. 137, 150, 119 S. Ct. 1167, 1175, 143 L. Ed. 2d 238 (1999).

[13]Kumho Tire Co., Ltd. v. Carmichael, 526 U.S. 137, 151, 119 S. Ct. 1167, 1175, 143 L. Ed. 2d 238 (1999).

[14]Kumho Tire Co., Ltd. v. Carmichael, 526 U.S. 137, 151, 119 S. Ct. 1167, 1175, 143 L. Ed. 2d 238 (1999).

[15]Kumho Tire Co., Ltd. v. Carmichael, 526 U.S. 137, 151, 119 S.

Ct. 1167, 1175, 143 L. Ed. 2d 238 (1999).

[16]Kumho Tire Co., Ltd. v. Carmichael, 526 U.S. 137, 151, 119 S. Ct. 1167, 1176, 143 L. Ed. 2d 238 (1999).

[17]Kumho Tire Co., Ltd. v. Carmichael, 526 U.S. 137, 153–157, 119 S. Ct. 1167, 1176–1179, 143 L. Ed. 2d 238 (1999).

[18]Kumho Tire Co., Ltd. v. Carmichael, 526 U.S. 137, 152, 119 S. Ct. 1167, 1176, 143 L. Ed. 2d 238 (1999).

holding of *Daubert* and the many cases addressing the admissibility of expert testimony following in its wake, including *Kumho Tire*.[1] Tracing several of the principles enunciated in *Daubert* and *Kumho Tire*, Rule 702 was amended to provide:

> [i]f scientific, technical, or other specialized knowledge will assist the trier of fact to understand the evidence or to determine a fact in issue, a witness qualified as an expert by knowledge, skill, experience, training, or education, may testify thereto in the form of an opinion or otherwise, if (1) the testimony is based upon sufficient facts or data, (2) the testimony is the product of reliable principles and methods, and (3) the witness has applied the principles and methods reliably to the facts of the case.

In the Eleventh Circuit, including federal district courts sitting in Georgia, the following tri-part test has been developed as an outline for assessing the admissibility of expert testimony:

> 1) the expert is qualified to testify competently regarding the matters he intends to address; 2) the methodology by which the expert reaches his conclusions is sufficiently reliable as determined by the sort of inquiry mandated in *Daubert*; and 3) the testimony assists the trier of fact, through the application of scientific, technical, or specialized expertise, to understand the evidence or to determine a fact in issue.[2]

The Advisory Committee Notes to Rule 702 provide a useful guide to understanding Rule 702, and indeed, federal case law as it has developed under *Daubert* and its progeny. As can be seen from the very test of Rule 702, the 2000 amendment reaffirms the trial court's role under *Daubert* as a gatekeeper to ensure that expert testimony is both helpful and reliable.[3] Consistent with the admonition of *Kumho Tire*, the amendment does not distinguish between scientific and other types of expert testimony, and indeed, "rejects the premise that an expert's testimony should

---

[Section 1:6]

[1]Advisory Committee Notes to Rule 702.

[2]City of Tuscaloosa v. Harcros Chemicals, Inc., 158 F.3d 548, 562 (11th Cir. 1998). See also Club Car, Inc. v. Club Car (Quebec) Import, Inc., 362 F.3d 775 (11th Cir. 2004), cert. denied, 543 U.S. 1002, 125 S. Ct. 618, 160 L. Ed. 2d 461 (2004); U.S. v. Frazier, 387 F.3d 1244 (11th Cir. 2004), cert. denied, 544 U.S. 1063, 125 S. Ct. 2516, 161 L. Ed. 2d 1114 (2005); Hudgens v. Bell Helicopters/Textron, 328 F.3d 1329 (11th Cir. 2003); Williamson Oil Co., Inc. v. Philip Morris USA, 346 F.3d 1287 (11th Cir. 2003); U.S. v. Hansen, 262 F.3d 1217 (11th Cir. 2001); Toole v. Baxter Healthcare Corp., 235 F.3d 1307 (11th Cir. 2000); Maiz v. Virani, 253 F.3d 641 (11th Cir. 2001); Allison v. McGhan Medical Corp., 184 F.3d 1300 (11th Cir. 1999).

[3]Advisory Committee Notes to Rule 702.

be treated more permissively simply because it is outside the realm of science."[4]

The amendment codifies the general standards enunciated in *Daubert* and its progeny, which the trial court must use in assessing the reliability and helpfulness of an expert's proferred testimony.[5] As the Advisory Committee Notes explain, Rule 702 requires that an expert's testimony be premised upon a sufficient basis of information before the expert is permitted to testify.[6] Moreover, the trial court must "scrutinize not only the principles and methods used by the expert, but also whether those principles and methods have been properly applied to the facts of the case."[7] "[W]hen an expert purports to apply principles and methods in accordance with professional standards, and yet reaches a conclusion that other experts in the field would not reach, the trial court may fairly suspect that the principles and methods have not been faithfully applied."[8] The requirement that the expert's testimony be the product of reliable principles and knowledge is not limited to testimony of a scientific nature, and remains relevant when the testimony is based on technical or other specialized knowledge.[9] At the same time, recognizing that, in certain fields, experience provides the predominant basis for testimony, nothing in the amendment suggests that testimony based predominantly, or even solely, upon experience is unreliable.[10] However, where such is the case, Rule 702 contemplates that an expert be able to explain "how that experience leads to the conclusion reached, why that experience is a sufficient basis for the opinion, and how that experience is reliably applied to the facts. The trial court's gatekeeping function requires more than simply 'taking the expert's word for it.' "[11]

The amendment does not codify the specific factors enunciated

---

[4]Advisory Committee Notes to Rule 702, citing Watkins v. Telsmith, Inc., 121 F.3d 984, 991 (5th Cir. 1997) ("[I]t seems exactly backwards that experts who purport to rely on general engineering principles and practical experience might escape screening by the district court simply by stating that their conclusions were not reached by any particular method or technique.").

[5]Advisory Committee Notes to Rule 702.

[6]Advisory Committee Notes to Rule 702.

[7]Advisory Committee Notes to Rule 702, citing In re Paoli R.R. Yard PCB Litigation, 35 F.3d 717, 745 (3d Cir. 1994) ("any step that renders the analysis unreliable . . . renders the expert's testimony inadmissible. This is true whether the step completely changes a reliable methodology or merely misapplies that methodology.").

[8]Advisory Committee Notes to Rule 702, citing Lust By and Through Lust v. Merrell Dow Pharmaceuticals, Inc., 89 F.3d 594, 598 (9th Cir. 1996).

[9]Advisory Committee Notes to Rule 702.

[10]Advisory Committee Notes to Rule 702.

[11]Advisory Committee Notes to Rule 702, citing Daubert v. Merrell Dow Pharmaceuticals, Inc., 43 F.3d 1311, 1319 (9th Cir. 1995), and

in *Daubert* for ascertaining the reliability of an expert's testimony.[12] As was noted in *Daubert*, these factors are neither "exclusive nor dispositive[,]" and as was noted in *Kumho Tire*, not all of the factors will necessarily be applicable in every type of case.[13] As noted in *Daubert*, factors which a trial court may find helpful for assessing the reliability of an expert's testimony may include: 1) whether the technique or theory can be, or has been, tested; 2) whether the technique or theory has been subjected to peer review and publication; 3) the technique or theory's known or potential error rate; 4) the existence and maintenance of standards and controls for the theory or technique's operation; and 5) whether the theory or technique has been generally accepted in the relevant scientific community.[14] Surveying federal case law, the Advisory Committee Notes recognize other factors which various courts have found helpful in assessing the reliability of an expert's testimony, including:

1) "Whether experts are 'proposing to testify about matters growing naturally and directly out of research they have conducted independent of the litigation, or whether they have developed their opinions expressly for purposes of testifying.' "[15]

2) "Whether the expert has unjustifiably extrapolated from an accepted premise to an unfounded conclusion."[16]

3) "Whether the expert has adequately accounted for obvious alternative explanations."[17]

4) "Whether the expert 'is being as careful as he would in his regular professional work outside his paid litigation consulting.' "[18] and

---

O'Conner v. Commonwealth Edison Co., 13 F.3d 1090 (7th Cir. 1994) (expert testimony properly excluded where it was based on completely subjective methodology).

[12]Advisory Committee Notes to Rule 702.

[13]Advisory Committee Notes to Rule 702.

[14]Advisory Committee Notes to Rule 702.

[15]Advisory Committee Notes to Rule 702, citing Daubert v. Merrell Dow Pharmaceuticals, Inc., 43 F.3d 1311, 1317 (9th Cir. 1995).

[16]Advisory Committee Notes to Rule 702, citing General Elec. Co. v. Joiner, 522 U.S. 136, 146, 118 S. Ct. 512, 519, 139 L. Ed. 2d 508 (1997),

which observed that a trial court "may conclude that there is simply too great an analytical gap between the data and the opinion proferred."

[17]Advisory Committee Notes to Rule 702, citing Claar v. Burlington Northern R. Co., 29 F.3d 499 (9th Cir. 1994), where an expert's testimony was excluded when the expert had failed to consider other obvious causes of the plaintiff's condition, and comparing Ambrosini v. Labarraque, 101 F.3d 129 (D.C. Cir. 1996), where the court noted that provided the expert has considered and ruled out the most obvious causes, the possibility of some remaining uneliminated causes presents a question of weight and not admissibility).

[18]Advisory Committee Notes to

5) "Whether the field of expertise claimed by the expert is known to reach reliable results."[19]

The Advisory Committee Notes state that, while all of these factors remain relevant to the reliability inquiry under the amended Rule 702, other factors may also be relevant,[20] and "no single factor is necessarily dispositive[.]"[21] The Advisory Committee Notes caution that a finding that one expert's testimony is reliable does not necessarily require a finding that contradictory expert testimony is reliable, as the amendment "is broad enough to permit testimony that is the product of competing principles or methods in the same field of expertise."[22] Finally, the Advisory Committee Notes indicate the amendment does not contemplate

---

Rule 702, citing Sheehan v. Daily Racing Form, Inc., 104 F.3d 940, 942 (7th Cir. 1997). On this point, the Advisory Committee Notes also cite Kumho Tire's proposition that a trial court is to assure itself that the expert "employs in the courtroom the same level of intellectual rigor that characterizes the practice of an expert in the relevant field." Kumho Tire Co., Ltd. v. Carmichael, 526 U.S. 137, 152, 119 S. Ct. 1167, 1176, 143 L. Ed. 2d 238 (1999).

[19]Advisory Committee Notes to Rule 702, citing *Kumho Tire's* proposition regarding the fact that a theory or technique may be generally accepted in a particular discipline is of no avail in establishing the reliability of the theory or technique "where the discipline itself lacks reliability." Kumho Tire Co., Ltd. v. Carmichael, 526 U.S. 137, 152, 119 S. Ct. 1167, 1176, 143 L. Ed. 2d 238 (1999).

[20]Advisory Committee Notes to Rule 702, citing Kumho Tire Co., Ltd. v. Carmichael, 526 U.S. 137, 152, 119 S. Ct. 1167, 1176, 143 L. Ed. 2d 238 (1999) ("trial judge must have considerable leeway in deciding in a particular case how to go about determining whether particular expert testimony is reliable").

[21]Advisory Committee Notes to Rule 702, citing Heller v. Shaw Industries, Inc., 167 F.3d 146, 155 (3d Cir. 1999) ("not only must each stage of the expert's testimony be reliable, but each stage must be evaluated

practically and flexibly without bright-line exclusionary (or inclusionary) rules"), and Daubert v. Merrell Dow Pharmaceuticals, Inc., 43 F.3d 1311, 1317 (9th Cir. 1995) (observing that some expert disciplines "have the courtroom as a principal theatre of operations[,]" and with respect to those disciplines, "the fact that the expert has developed an expertise principally for purposes of litigation will obviously not be a substantial consideration.").

[22]Advisory Committee Notes to Rule 702, citing Heller v. Shaw Industries, Inc., 167 F.3d 146, 155 (3d Cir. 1999) (expert testimony should not be excluded simply because an expert employs one test over another where both tests are accepted in the field and produce reliable results); Ruiz–Troche v. Pepsi Cola of Puerto Rico Bottling Co., 161 F.3d 77, 85 (1st Cir. 1998) "Daubert neither requires nor empowers trial courts to determine which of several competing scientific theories has the best provenance."); Daubert v. Merrell Dow Pharmaceuticals, Inc., 43 F.3d 1311, 1318 (9th Cir. 1995) (expert testimony may be permitted where it is shown that methods employed also used by "a recognized minority of scientists in their field."); and In re Paoli R.R. Yard PCB Litigation, 35 F.3d 717, 744 (3d Cir. 1994) (proponent of expert testimony does "not have to demonstrate to the judge by a preponderance of evidence that their opinions are reliable. . . . The evidentiary require-

an automatic challenge to expert testimony in every case, and that the trial court's gatekeeping role is not intended to serve as a "replacement for the adversary system" in cases where an expert's testimony, although "shaky," is nonetheless sufficiently reliable.[23]

§ 1:7   Federal law—The 2000 amendments to Federal Rule 703

At the same time Rule 702 was amended in 2000, Rule 703, also applicable to expert testimony, was amended with the inclusion of the following italicized language:

> [t]he facts or data in the particular case upon which an expert bases an opinion or inference may be those perceived by or made known to the expert at or before the hearing. If of a type reasonably relied upon by experts in the particular field in forming opinions or inferences upon the subject, the facts or data need not be admissible in evidence in order for the opinion or inference to be admitted. *Facts or data that are otherwise inadmissible shall not be disclosed to the jury by the proponent of the opinion or inference unless the court determines that their probative value in assisting the jury to evaluate the expert's opinion substantially outweighs their prejudicial effect.*

As explained by the Advisory Committee Notes on Rule 703, this rule has historically recognized that the facts or data upon which an expert bases his opinion may be derived from three possible sources: 1) firsthand observation, as might be the case for a treating physician; 2) presentation at trial, as would be the case wherein an expert witness is posed with a hypothetical question; and 3) sources outside the expert's own perception, but only when of the sort "reasonably relied" upon by other experts in the field in formulating opinions.[1] Rule 702, when originally enacted, was intended to liberalize the admissibility of expert testimony based upon this last source of facts or data in order to "bring the judicial practice into line with the practice of experts themselves when not in court."[2] The Advisory Committee Notes indicate that Rule 703 was designed to obviate the need for a proponent of such evidence to expend the "time in producing and examining various

---

ment of reliability is lower than the merits standard of correctness.").

[23]Advisory Committee Notes to Rule 702, citing Kumho Tire Co., Ltd. v. Carmichael, 526 U.S. 137, 152, 119 S. Ct. 1167, 1176, 143 L. Ed. 2d 238 (1999); Daubert v. Merrell Dow Pharmaceuticals, Inc., 509 U.S. 579, 596, 113 S. Ct. 2786, 2798, 125 L. Ed.

2d 469 (1993); and U.S. v. 14.38 Acres of Land, More or Less Situated in Leflore County, State of Miss., 80 F.3d 1074, 1075 (5th Cir. 1996).

[Section 1:7]
[1]Advisory Committee Notes to Rule 703.
[2]Advisory Committee Notes to Rule 703.

authenticating witnesses" in order to secure the admissibility of the expert's opinion testimony based upon these sources.[3] By way of example, the Advisory Committee Notes reference physicians, who make "life-and-death" decisions based upon such sources, which may include reports and opinions from other providers, and that the physician's "validation, expertly performed and subject to cross-examination, ought to suffice for judicial purposes."[4]

The 2000 amendment was included "to emphasize that when an expert reasonably relies on inadmissible information to form an opinion or inference, the underlying information is not admissible simply because the opinion or inference is admitted."[5] It provides a presumption against the expert disclosing to the jury information which, while forming the basis of an expert's opinion, is not itself admissible for any substantive purpose.[6] When the information is reasonably relied upon by the expert, but is only admissible for the purpose of assisting the jury in evaluating the expert's opinion and not for any other substantive purpose, the amendment requires the trial court to weigh the probative value of the information in assisting the jury to evaluate the expert's opinion against the prejudice that may result from the jury's potential misuse of the information for substantive purposes.[7] The Rule does not prevent presentation of the facts or data when offered by an adverse party, and otherwise inadmissible information may become admissible on rebuttal when the adversary has "opened the door" to the use of such information.[8]

As construed in relation to Rule 702, Rule 703 is not geared toward addressing the admissibility of the expert's testimony.[9] As explained by the Advisory Committee Notes, Rule 702 addresses the "overarching requirement" of reliability, and the "sufficiency of the basis of an expert's testimony is to be decided under Rule 702."[10] Rule 703, by contrast, entails the "relatively narrow inquiry" of determining whether the information an expert has relied upon is of the sort reasonably relied upon by other experts

---

[3]Advisory Committee Notes to Rule 703.

[4]Advisory Committee Notes to Rule 703. By contrast, the Advisory Committee Notes state that this liberalized rule "would not warrant admitting in evidence the opinion of an 'accidentologist' as to the point of impact in an automobile collision based on statements of bystanders since [the requirement of 'reasonable reliance'] is not satisfied."

[5]Advisory Committee Notes to Rule 703.

[6]Advisory Committee Notes to Rule 703.

[7]Advisory Committee Notes to Rule 703.

[8]Advisory Committee Notes to Rule 703.

[9]Advisory Committee Notes to Rule 703.

[10]Advisory Committee Notes to Rule 702.

in the field; if so, the expert may rely on that information in reaching his opinion."[11] "However, the question whether the expert is relying on a sufficient basis of information—whether admissible or not—is governed by the requirements of Rule 702."[12]

§ 1:8 Georgia law post–Daubert

In several respects, Georgia case law, even before the enactment of O.C.G.A. § 24–9–67.1, paralleled federal law pertaining to expert testimony as enunciated in *Daubert* and its progeny, and as codified in Rule 702 of the Federal Rules of Evidence. For instance, in the seminal case of Harper v. State,[1] the Georgia Supreme Court had, a decade before *Daubert* was even decided, rejected the "general acceptance" test enunciated in Frye v. United States.[2] Instead, the *Harper* Court opted for a test wherein the trial court made the determination as to "whether the procedure or technique in question has reached a scientific stage of verifiable certainty."[3] This ruling parallels *Daubert* in two significant ways. First, it closely resembles the standard that the "reasoning or methodology underling the [expert's] testimony [be] scientifically valid[.]"[4] Second, the ruling contemplated that the trial judge would make this preliminary determination before admitting the testimony, which was a "gatekeeping" role as contemplated by *Daubert*.[5]

However, in many respects, Georgia law significantly deviated from federal law pertaining to the admissibility of expert testimony. As an initial matter, the Georgia courts consistently refused to apply a *Daubert*-like analysis, reasoning that *Daubert* involved the application of Rule 702 of the Federal Rules of Evi-

---

[11]Advisory Committee Notes to Rule 702.

[12]Advisory Committee Notes to Rule 702.

[Section 1:8]

[1]Harper v. State, 249 Ga. 519, 292 S.E.2d 389 (1982).

[2]Harper v. State, 249 Ga. 519, 525, 292 S.E.2d 389, 395 (1982) ("[W]e conclude that the Frye rule of 'counting heads' in the scientific community is not an appropriate way to determine the admissibility of a scientific procedure.").

[3]Harper v. State, 249 Ga. 519, 525, 292 S.E.2d 389, 395 (1982).

[4]Daubert v. Merrell Dow Pharmaceuticals, Inc., 509 U.S. 579, 592–593, 113 S. Ct. 2786, 2796, 125 L. Ed. 2d 469 (1993).

[5]Harper v. State, 249 Ga. 519, 525, 292 S.E.2d 389, 395 (1982). In *Harper*, the Court explained the trial court's "gatekeeping" role as follows: "The trial court may make this determination from evidence presented to it at trial by the parties; in this regard expert testimony may be of value. Or the trial court may base its determination on exhibits, treatises or the rationale of cases in other jurisdictions. . . . The significant point is that the trial court makes this determination based on the evidence available to him rather than by simply calculating the consensus in the scientific community." Harper v. State, 249 Ga. 519, 292 S.E.2d 389 (1982)

dence, a rule which had not been adopted in Georgia.[6] Courts often emphasized the rule enunciated in former O.C.G.A. § 24–9–67 that expert testimony was "always" admissible,[7] and that this rule was subject only to the expert being qualified in the field in which the expert was to provide testimony and that the facts upon which the expert was relying were admitted into evidence.[8]

When the test enunciated in *Harper* was employed, the Georgia Supreme Court ruled that it did not apply to all expert testimony, but only that which was "scientific" in nature.[9] Thus, the Georgia Supreme Court held that "expert testimony which deals simply with observations based on skill and expertise is not subject to the *Harper v. State* analysis."[10] Moreover, in further limiting the analysis to be conducted under *Harper*, the Georgia Supreme Court held that such an analysis is applicable only with respect to scientific "procedures or techniques," not scientific "principles."[11]

§ 1:9 O.C.G.A. § 24–9–67.1

In 2005, the General Assembly modified O.C.G.A. § 24–9–67, and enacted O.C.G.A. § 24–9–67.1. O.C.G.A. § 24–9–67 was modified to apply only in the context of criminal cases, and read as follows:

> In criminal cases, the opinions of experts on any question of science, skill, trade, or like questions shall always be admissible; and such opinions may be given on the facts as proved by other witnesses.

---

[6]See, e.g. Dailey v. State, 271 Ga. App. 492, 496, 610 S.E.2d 126, 129 (2005); Jones v. Chatham County Bd. of Tax Assessors, 270 Ga. App. 483, 487 n.10, 606 S.E.2d 673, 677 (2004); Bryant v. Hoffmann-La Roche, Inc., 262 Ga. App. 401, 408 n.4, 585 S.E.2d 723 (2003); Norfolk Southern Railway Co. v. Baker, 237 Ga. App. 292, 294, 514 S.E.2d 448, 451 (1999); Jordan v. Georgia Power Co., 219 Ga. App. 690, 693, 466 S.E.2d 601 (1995); Orkin Exterminating Co., Inc. v. McIntosh, 215 Ga. App. 587, 592–593, 452 S.E.2d 159, 165 (1994).

[7]Home Depot U.S.A., Inc. v. Tvrdeich, 268 Ga. App. 579, 581, 602 S.E.2d 297 (2004), cert. denied, (Oct. 25, 2004); Norfolk Southern Railway Co. v. Baker, 237 Ga. App. 292, 294, 514 S.E.2d 448, 451 (1999); Orkin Exterminating Co., Inc. v. McIntosh,

215 Ga. App. 587, 592, 452 S.E.2d 159, 165 (1994).

[8]Norfolk Southern Railway Co. v. Baker, 237 Ga. App. 292, 294, 514 S.E.2d 448, 451 (1999); Orkin Exterminating Co., Inc. v. McIntosh, 215 Ga. App. 587, 592, 452 S.E.2d 159, 165 (1994).

[9]Home Depot U.S.A., Inc. v. Tvrdeich, 268 Ga. App. 579, 602 S.E.2d 297 (2004), cert. denied, (Oct. 25, 2004).

[10]Home Depot U.S.A., Inc. v. Tvrdeich, 268 Ga. App. 579, 602 S.E.2d 297 (2004), cert. denied, (Oct. 25, 2004).

[11]Home Depot U.S.A., Inc. v. Tvrdeich, 268 Ga. App. 579, 602 S.E.2d 297 (2004), cert. denied, (Oct. 25, 2004); cf. concurring and dissenting opinions in this case.

While the statutory provision remained the same for the admissibility of expert testimony in criminal cases,[1] the legislature significantly modified the rule applicable in civil cases, as is discussed below.

§ 1:10   O.C.G.A. § 24–9–67.1—Georgia's adoption of Rule 702 and *Daubert*

O.C.G.A. § 24–9–67.1 governs the admissibility of expert testimony in all civil cases.[1] Subsection (b) of this statute embodies the 2000 amendments to Rule 702 of the Federal Rules of Evidence, providing as follows:

> If scientific, technical, or other specialized knowledge will assist the trier of fact in any cause of action to understand the evidence or to determine a fact in issue, a witness qualified as an expert by knowledge, skill, experience, training, or education may testify thereto in the form of an opinion or otherwise, if: (1) the testimony is based upon sufficient facts or data which are or will be admitted into evidence at the hearing or trial; (2) the testimony is the product of reliable principles and methods; and (3) the witness has applied the principles and methods reliably to the facts of the case.

Subsection (f) of the statute provides little doubt as to the intended construction of the statute, expressly providing that Georgia courts may draw from the opinions of *Daubert, Joiner, Kumho Tire*, "and other cases in federal courts applying the standards announced by the United States Supreme Court in these cases" in construing this statute. Subsection (f) goes on to expressly state that "[i]t is the intent of the legislature that, in all civil cases, the courts of the State of Georgia not be viewed as open to expert evidence that would not be admissible in other states."

Despite their similarity, there is at least one notable difference between Rule 702 and O.C.G.A. 24–9–67.1. Whereas the first prong of Rule 702's three part test only requires that the expert's testimony be based upon "sufficient facts or data," Georgia's version of this prong of its three part test requires that the expert's testimony be based upon "sufficient facts or data *which are or*

[Section 1:9]

[1]Note that O.C.G.A. § 24–9–67.1 applies in certain civil hearings that relate to criminal matters. In Carlson v. State, 634 S.E.2d 410 (Ga.App.2006), the Court of Appeals ruled that O.C.G.A. § 24–9–67.1 applies to civil actions to revoke a proba-

tion. It is also significant to note that the legislature specifically excluded from the Daubert standard expert testimony regards issues of just and adequate compensation. See O.C.G.A. § 22–1–14.

[Section 1:10]

[1]O.C.G.A. § 24–9–67.1.

will be admitted into evidence at the hearing or trial."[2] This requirement should be compared with Subsection (a) of the statute, discussed below, which provides that the facts or data upon which an expert relies in forming his opinion need not be admissible in evidence provided they are of a type "reasonably relied upon" by other experts in the field in formulating opinions.[3] Construed together, O.C.G.A. § 24–9–67.1(b)'s requirement that an expert's testimony be based not only on "sufficient facts or data," but sufficient facts and data "which are or will be admitted into evidence," would appear to require a certain quantum of the evidence upon which an expert relies in forming his opinions be evidence which has in fact been, or which will be, admitted into evidence. In other words, while an expert may rely upon some evidence which is otherwise inadmissible in forming his opinions, the expert nevertheless must base his opinion on a "sufficient" quantum of facts or data which are in fact in evidence.

The expert's opinions would need to be based, at least in part, on evidence which was or would be in evidence, such as an expert/medical doctor's personal knowledge derived from an examination of a patient, or the expert's review of the patient's medical records. Construed as such, this requirement obligates an expert to be able to demonstrate to the court those facts and data which form the basis of expert opinions, and prevents the expert from claiming that experience alone has informed the expert opinions. In other words, the "bald assurances," or *ipse dixit*, of an expert that methodologies are sound, or that opinions are reliable, are not enough to render them admissible.[4]

§ 1:11   O.C.G.A. § 24–9–67.1—Georgia's adoption of Rule 703

O.C.G.A. § 26–9–67.1(a) essentially embodies Rule 703 of the Federal Rules of Evidence by providing that the facts or data upon which an expert relies in forming his opinions need not be admissible in evidence provided the facts and data are of the sort which experts in the filed "reasonably rely upon" in forming opinions. In pertinent part, this subsection provides as follows:

---

[2]O.C.G.A. § 24–9–67.1(b)(1) (emphasis added).

[3]O.C.G.A. § 24–9–67.1(a).

[4]See, e.g. General Elec. Co. v. Joiner, 522 U.S. 136, 146, 118 S. Ct. 512, 519, 139 L. Ed. 2d 508 (1997) ("nothing in either Daubert or the Federal Rules of Evidence requires a district court to admit opinion evidence that is connected to existing data only by the ipse dixit of the expert."); Daubert v. Merrell Dow Pharmaceuticals, Inc., 43 F.3d 1311, 1316 (9th Cir. 1995) ("[T]he expert's bald assurance of validity is not enough. Rather, the party presenting the expert must show that the expert's findings are based on sound science, and this will require some objective, independent validation of the expert's methodology.").

The opinion of a witness qualified as an expert under this Code section may be given on facts as proved by other witnesses. The facts or data in the particular case upon which an expert bases an opinion or inference may be those perceived by or made known to the expert at or before the hearing or trial. If of a type reasonably relied upon by experts in the particular field in forming opinions or inferences on the subject, the facts or data need not be admissible in evidence in order for the opinion or inference to be admitted. Facts or data that are otherwise inadmissible shall not be disclosed to the jury by the proponent of the opinion or inference unless the court determines that their probative value in assisting the jury to evaluate the expert's opinion substantially outweighs their prejudicial effect.

As discussed in greater detail elsewhere,[1] the new statute is substantially similar to the law as it existed in Georgia prior to the 2005 enactment of the statute. While, historically, Georgia courts had not been receptive to expert opinion testimony which was based upon facts not in evidence such as hearsay,[2] Georgia courts have increasingly recognized that an expert's reliance on hearsay evidence did not necessarily require exclusion of the expert's opinion when the opinion was based only partially upon hearsay.[3]

§ 1:12   O.C.G.A. § 24–9–67.1—Pretrial hearings

O.C.G.A. § 24–9–67.1(d) provides a procedure by which a court may exercise its "gatekeeping" role under this code section. This subsection provides that, upon a party's motion, the court may hold a pretrial hearing for the purposes of determining: 1) whether a witness qualifies as an expert; and 2) an expert's testimony satisfies the requirements of O.C.G.A. § 24–9–67.1(a) and (b). This hearing, and any ruling upon this hearing, is to be completed no later than the final pretrial conference as provided for in O.C.G.A. § 9–11–16. This provision is analogous to Rule 104 of the Federal Rules of Evidence, which provides in pertinent part that "[p]reliminary questions concerning the qualification of a person to be a witness, . . . or the admissibility of evidence

---

[Section 1:11]

[1]See Chapter 2, § 2:8.

[2]See, e.g. Loper v. Drury, 211 Ga. App. 478, 482, 440 S.E.2d 32, 36 (1993) (noting that to allow an expert to base his testimony on a letter not in evidence "would permit the admission of hearsay, speculation and unsupported opinion, by the simple expedient of asking an expert to read the inadmissible matter into the record or testify to it while asserting that he relied

upon it.").

[3]See, e.g. Roebuck v. State, 277 Ga. 200, 586 S.E.2d 651 (2003); Roberts v. Baker, 265 Ga. 902, 463 S.E.2d 694 (1995); King v. Browning, 246 Ga. 46, 268 S.E.2d 653 (1980); Williamson v. Harvey Smith, Inc., 246 Ga. App. 745, 749, 542 S.E.2d 151, 155 (2000); McEver v. Worrell Enterprises, 223 Ga. App. 627, 478 S.E.2d 445 (1996); Blackburn v. State, 180 Ga. App. 436, 437, 349 S.E.2d 286, 288 (1986).

shall be determined by the court[.]" Such pretrial hearings were explicitly contemplated in *Daubert*.[1]

§ 1:13 O.C.G.A. § 24–9–67.1—Expert testimony requirements in professional negligence cases

In addition to the foregoing rules, O.C.G.A. § 24–9–67.1 provides specific rules pertaining to the qualifications of expert witnesses in professional negligence cases. While the statute does not specifically define what constitutes a "professional negligence" case, another statute—O.C.G.A. § 9–11–9.1—lists those professions for which an expert affidavit is required to be filed, subject to dismissal of the complaint, at the time of filing an action alleging professional negligence. O.C.G.A. § 24–9–67.1(e) makes specific reference to this other statute by providing that experts providing affidavits pursuant to the requirements of O.C.G.A. § 9–11–9.1 "must meet the requirements of [O.C.G.A. § 24–9–67.1] in order to be deemed qualified to testify as an expert by means of the affidavit." It would thus appear that a "professional negligence" case, as contemplated by O.C.G.A. § 24–9–67.1, would be those cases in which allegations of professional negligence are levied against those professions itemized in O.C.G.A. § 9–11–9.1.

Moreover, and in addition to the foregoing requirements applicable to all experts in civil cases, the opinion of an expert who is otherwise qualified to provide opinion testimony regarding the acceptable standard of conduct applicable to the professional whose conduct is at issue is admissible only if, at the time the act or omission is alleged to have occurred, the expert was licensed by an "appropriate regulatory agency to practice his or her profession in the state in which such expert was practicing or teaching in the profession at such time[.]"[1]

§ 1:14 O.C.G.A. § 24–9–67.1—Expert testimony requirements in medical negligence cases

In addition to the foregoing rules, including those applicable in professional negligence cases in general, more stringent requirements exist with respect to the qualifications of experts in medical malpractice actions. The expert must have had, at the time the act or omission is alleged to have occurred, "actual professional knowledge and experience in the area of practice or

---

[Section 1:12]

[1]Daubert v. Merrell Dow Pharmaceuticals, Inc., 509 U.S. 579, 592, 113 S. Ct. 2786, 2796, 125 L. Ed. 2d 469 (1993).

[Section 1:13]

[1]O.C.G.A. § 24–9–67.1(c)(1).

specialty in which the opinion is to be given[.]"[1] Such professional knowledge or experience must have been derived through either the practice of, or teaching in,[2] the profession for at least three of the past five years.[3] As is to be determined by the court, this practice or teaching must have been performed with "sufficient frequency" so as to establish an "appropriate level" of knowledge in "performing the procedure, diagnosing the condition, or rendering the treatment" at issue.[4]

Subject to certain exceptions, the expert must also generally be a member of the same profession as the person regarding whom the expert is providing standard of care testimony.[5] This requirement does not apply where a medical doctor is testifying as to the standard of care applicable to a doctor of osteopathy, or vice-versa.[6] Moreover, this requirement is not applicable where a physician is testifying as to the standard of care applicable to certain statutorily-enumerated health care providers, such as a nurse, provided that the physician "has knowledge of the standard of care of that health care provider under the circumstances at issue" as a result of having "supervised, taught, or instructed" such health care providers during at least three of the last five years immediately preceding the time of the alleged negligence.[7] These statutorily-enumerated health care providers may not, however, testify as to the standard of care applicable to a physician.[8]

Globally, these rules specific to experts in medical malpractice claims require that an expert possess adequate knowledge in the profession at issue before the expert is permitted to testify.[9] It would also appear that these rules seek to ensure that an expert witness possess a certain minimum amount of experience, and at the same time, that the expert's knowledge is sufficiently current and up-to-date. By requiring the expert to have had actual professional knowledge and experience "at the time the act or omission occurred," the statute tends to prohibit testimony from experts whose knowledge base might be perceived as "too new," or alternatively, may have become "too stale." By requiring the

---

[Section 1:14]

[1]O.C.G.A. § 24–9–67.1(c)(2).

[2]In the case where the expert's knowledge and experience is derived from teaching, the expert must have been an "employed member of the faculty of an educational institution accredited in the teaching of such profession[.]" O.C.G.A. § 24–9–67.1(c)(2)(B).

[3]O.C.G.A. § 24–9–67.1(c)(2)(A) and (B).

[4]O.C.G.A. § 24–9–67.1(c)(2)(A) and (B).

[5]O.C.G.A. § 24–9–67.1(c)(2)(C)(i).

[6]O.C.G.A. § 24–9–67.1(c)(2)(C)(ii) and (iii).

[7]O.C.G.A. § 24–9–67.1(c)(2)(D).

[8]O.C.G.A. § 24–9–67.1(c)(2)(D).

[9]For a more detailed discussion of the rules as applied in medical malpractice cases, see Chapter ___.

expert to have actual practice or teaching experience for three of the past five years, the statute tends to encourage experts whose knowledge base is informed by current knowledge and trends.

Chapter 2

General Principles Pertaining to Expert Testimony in Georgia

KeyCite[®]: Cases and other legal materials listed in KeyCite Scope can be researched through the KeyCite service on Westlaw[®]. Use KeyCite to check citations for form, parallel references, prior and later history, and comprehensive citator information, including citations to other decisions and secondary materials.

---

§ 2:1   Qualifications

Historically, an expert witness under Georgia law is "anyone who, through training, education, skill, or experience, has peculiar knowledge that the average juror would not possess as to 'any question of science, skill, trade, or like questions[.]' "[1]O.C.G.A.

[Section 2:1]

[1]In Interest of C.W.D., 232 Ga. App. 200, 206, 501 S.E.2d 232, 238 (1998) (citing O.C.G.A. § 24-9-67); see also Bryant v. Hoffmann-La Roche, Inc., 262 Ga. App. 401, 407, 585 S.E.2d 723, 729 (2003) ("A witness with such skill, knowledge, or experience in a field or calling as to be able to draw an inference that could not be drawn by the average layperson may be qualified as an expert witness."); Murray v. Department of Transp., 240 Ga. App. 285, 286, 523 S.E.2d 367, 368 (1999) (one is "competent to testify as an expert if he can show through education, training, or experience that he has special knowledge concerning the matters on which he is testifying."); Faubion v. Piedmont Engineering &

§ 24–9–67.1(b) substantially codifies this common law definition by providing that a witness may provide expert opinion testimony regarding "scientific, technical, or other specialized knowledge[,]" provided the witness has been qualified as an expert by virtue of "knowledge, skill, experience, training, or education[.]"

The question as to whether a witness qualifies as an expert is a legal determination for the court.[2] The decision as to whether a witness is qualified as an expert falls within the sound discretion of the trial court,[3] and a trial court's determination will not be disturbed absent a manifest abuse of discretion.[4] There is no rule of law which prevents a party to the litigation from being qualified as an expert.[5]

It has often been held that the requirements for a witness to qualify as an expert are "minimal."[6] The term "expert" is relative: "amongst any community of specialists, only a few are considered by others to be the real 'experts,' but to the rest of the world any of the specialists would be an 'expert' and would be considered one in a court of law."[7] Generally, all that is required in order to qualify as an expert is that the witness, by virtue of his education, training, or experience, possess knowledge in a particular field beyond that of the average juror.[8] However, a party's or witness' conclusory pronouncement of his or her familiarity with a

---

Const. Corp., 178 Ga. App. 256, 257, 342 S.E.2d 718, 719 (1986) ("An expert witness is one who through education, training or experience has peculiar knowledge concerning some matter of science or skill to which his testimony relates.").

[2]Williamson v. Harvey Smith, Inc., 246 Ga. App. 745, 748, 542 S.E.2d 151, 155 (2000); Carlson v. State, 240 Ga. App. 589, 589, 524 S.E.2d 283, 285 (1999); Faubion v. Piedmont Engineering & Const. Corp., 178 Ga. App. 256, 257, 342 S.E.2d 718, 719 (1986).

[3]Taylor v. State, 261 Ga. 287, 290, 404 S.E.2d 255, 259 (1991); Bryant v. Hoffmann-La Roche, Inc., 262 Ga. App. 401, 407, 585 S.E.2d 723, 729 (2003); Yount v. State, 249 Ga. App. 563, 564–565, 548 S.E.2d 674, 676 (2001).

[4]Dayoub v. Yates–Astro Termite Pest Control Co., 239 Ga. App. 578, 579, 521 S.E.2d 600, 602 (1999); Humphrey v. Alvarado, 185 Ga. App. 486, 487, 364 S.E.2d 618 (1988); Faubion v. Piedmont Engineering &

Const. Corp., 178 Ga. App. 256, 257, 342 S.E.2d 718, 719 (1986).

[5]Williamson v. Harvey Smith, Inc., 246 Ga. App. 745, 749, 542 S.E.2d 151, 155 (2000); Loving v. Nash, 182 Ga. App. 253, 255, 355 S.E.2d 448, 450 (1987) (defendant physician in medical malpractice action competent to offer standard of care opinion on his own behalf); Graves v. Jones, 184 Ga. App. 128, 129, 361 S.E.2d 19, 20 (1987) (defendant attorney in legal malpractice action competent to offer standard of care opinion on his own behalf).

[6]Hall v. State, 255 Ga. App. 631, 635, 566 S.E.2d 374, 379– 380 (2002); Manesh v. Baker Equipment Engineering Co., 247 Ga. App. 407, 410, 543 S.E.2d 61, 65 (2000); Dayoub v. Yates–Astro Termite Pest Control Co., 239 Ga. App. 578, 580, 521 S.E.2d 600, 602–603 (1999).

[7]Drummond v. Gladson, 219 Ga. App. 521, 522–523, 465 S.E.2d 687, 688 (1995).

[8]Bryant v. Hoffmann-La Roche, Inc., 262 Ga. App. 401, 407, 585 S.E.2d

particular field is insufficient to establish the witnesses' qualifications to testify as an expert, and this determination must be based upon evidence of the witness' education, training, or experience in the pertinent field.[9]

As is set forth in the statute itself, formal education may provide a sufficient basis for one to qualify as an expert in a particular matter, but formal education is not a prerequisite.[10] An expert may obtain the necessary expertise in a particular subject matter by other means, including experience in the pertinent field.[11] For instance, it has been held that a police officer, with no formal education in psychology, was competent to provide expert opinion testimony on the attributes of child victims of sexual abuse and child molesters given the officer's experience in investigating such crimes.[12] A police officer with no formal education in engineering has been held competent to provide expert testimony on the cause of a motor vehicle accident given the officer's training and experience in accident investigation.[13] Similarly, it has been held that a pathologist, who did not hold a medical degree, was competent to provide expert testimony regarding the time of a victim's death where he had a bachelor's degree in chemistry, several years of training in anatomy and pathology, and substantial experience in performing autopsies for the state.[14]

As a general proposition, a witness is not required to be licensed in the field or profession in which he or she is providing

---

723, 729 (2003); Williamson v. Harvey Smith, Inc., 246 Ga. App. 745, 749, 542 S.E.2d 151, 155 (2000); In Interest of C.W.D., 232 Ga. App. 200, 206, 501 S.E.2d 232, 238 (1998).

[9]Carlson v. State, 240 Ga. App. 589, 589–590, 524 S.E.2d 283, 285 (1999); Goodman v. Lipman, 197 Ga. App. 631, 632–633, 399 S.E.2d 255, 257 (1990).

[10]Taylor v. State, 261 Ga. 287, 290, 404 S.E.2d 255, 259 (1991); Bryant v. Hoffmann-La Roche, Inc., 262 Ga. App. 401, 407, 585 S.E.2d 723, 729 (2003); Dayoub v. Yates–Astro Termite Pest Control Co., 239 Ga. App. 578, 580, 521 S.E.2d 600, 602–603 (1999).

[11]Applebrook Country Dayschool, Inc. v. Thurman, 264 Ga. App. 591, 595, 591 S.E.2d 406, 410–411 (2003), cert. granted, (Apr. 27, 2004) and

rev'd, 278 Ga. 784, 604 S.E.2d 832 (2004) and opinion vacated in part, 613 S.E.2d 192 (Ga. Ct. App. 2005); Hall v. State, 255 Ga. App. 631, 635, 566 S.E.2d 374, 379–380 (2002); Manesh v. Baker Equipment Engineering Co., 247 Ga. App. 407, 410, 543 S.E.2d 61, 65 (2000); Williamson v. Harvey Smith, Inc., 246 Ga. App. 745, 749, 542 S.E.2d 151, 155 (2000); Dayoub v. Yates–Astro Termite Pest Control Co., 239 Ga. App. 578, 580, 521 S.E.2d 600, 602–603 (1999).

[12]Weeks v. State, 270 Ga. App. 889, 893, 608 S.E.2d 259, 264 (2004), cert. denied, (Apr. 26, 2005).

[13]Drummond v. Gladson, 219 Ga. App. 521, 522, 465 S.E.2d 687, 688 (1995).

[14]Barrow v. State, 235 Ga. 635, 639, 221 S.E.2d 416, 419–420 (1975).

expert testimony.[15] The fact as to whether a witness is licensed in
a particular profession or discipline is not a matter which goes to
whether the witness is qualified to offer expert opinion testimony,
but is a matter of weight and credibility a jury may give to the
expert's opinions.[16] An exception to this general rule has been
created by O.C.G.A. § 24–9–67.1(c), applicable to professional
malpractice actions.[17] This provision provides that an expert
testifying in a professional malpractice action must have been, at
the time the professional malfeasance is alleged to have occurred,
"licensed by an appropriate regulatory agency to practice his or
her profession in the state in which such expert was practicing or
teaching in the profession[.]"[18] This licensure requirement
represents a change in Georgia law, apparently designed to
ensure that an expert offering standard of care testimony regarding a professional's conduct has an appropriate level of knowledge regarding the standard of care applicable at the time of the
alleged malfeasance.[19] The statute does not require that the
expert have been licensed in Georgia, a requirement which the
courts have historically rejected.[20]

§ 2:2   Testifying within one's qualifications

While, as noted in the immediately preceding section, Georgia
courts have historically been fairly liberal as to what qualifica-

---

[15]Williamson v. Harvey Smith, Inc., 246 Ga. App. 745, 748, 542 S.E.2d 151, 155 (2000); Dayoub v. Yates–Astro Termite Pest Control Co., 239 Ga. App. 578, 580, 521 S.E.2d 600, 602 (1999).

[16]Dayoub v. Yates–Astro Termite Pest Control Co., 239 Ga. App. 578, 580, 521 S.E.2d 600, 602 (1999); In Interest of C.W.D., 232 Ga. App. 200, 206–207, 501 S.E.2d 232, 239 (1998).

[17]For a discussion of the specific rules applicable to expert witness qualifications in medical malpractice actions, see Chapter 10 below.

[18]O.C.G.A. § 24–9–67.1(c)(1).

[19]See, e.g. Goodman v. Lipman, 197 Ga. App. 631, 399 S.E.2d 255 (1990). In *Goodman,* a physician was offered to provide expert testimony that the defendant physician deviated from the applicable standard of care in treating the plaintiff's heart dis-ease. The defendant objected to the presentation of this testimony, argu-ing that the plaintiff's expert was not competent to opine on the standard of care applicable to the defendant at the time of his care of the plaintiff because the expert had not become licensed to practice medicine until five years after the alleged malfeasance, and indeed, had not even entered medical school at the time of the alleged malfeasance. In finding that the expert was quali-fied, the court noted that the mere fact that he was not licensed to practice medicine at the time of the alleged malfeasance "does not mean that the physician cannot become familiar with the applicable standard of care prac-ticed in the medical community at the time of the alleged malpractice." Goodman v. Lipman, 197 Ga. App. 631, 632, 399 S.E.2d 255 (1990).

[20]Dayoub v. Yates–Astro Termite Pest Control Co., 239 Ga. App. 578, 580, 521 S.E.2d 600, 602 (1999); In Interest of C.W.D., 232 Ga. App. 200, 206–207, 501 S.E.2d 232, 239 (1998) (expert held license to practice psy-chology in Virginia, but not Georgia).

tions are sufficient to confer one with the ability to offer expert opinion testimony, Georgia courts do require that an expert's opinion testimony be limited to his or her area of expertise. "While expert witnesses may give their opinions as to facts, principles and rules involved in the science in which they are learned, they are not, as to questions lying outside the domain of the science, art, or trade in which they are experts, exempt from the restriction of the rule which requires witnesses to state facts and not opinions."[1]

A witness with expertise in one area will not necessarily be qualified to offer expert opinion testimony on separate, albeit related, areas of inquiry.[2] Georgia courts have cautioned against assuming that merely because a witness has been conferred with a particular title or degree that the witness is competent to address matters only tangentially related to the scope of the witness' area of expertise.[3] Georgia courts allow experts to offer opinion testimony when the subject matter of the opinion falls

---

[Section 2:2]

[1]Johnson v. Knebel, 267 Ga. 853, 857–858, 485 S.E.2d 451, 455 (1997) (citing Chandler Exterminators, Inc. v. Morris, 262 Ga. 257, 416 S.E.2d 277 (1992)).

[2]See, e.g. Johnson v. Knebel, 267 Ga. 853, 857–858, 485 S.E.2d 451, 455 (1997) (professional engineer with experience in accident reconstruction was qualified to opine upon events leading to motor vehicle accident, but with no demonstrated training or experience in physiology or biomechanics, was not qualified to testify as to which of two collisions was the cause of the plaintiff's injuries); Chandler Exterminators, Inc. v. Morris, 262 Ga. 257, 257–258, 416 S.E.2d 277, 278 (1992) (neuropsychologist qualified to offer testimony regarding psychological condition of plaintiff, but not qualified to testify that plaintiff's condition was caused by inhalation of certain chemicals); Cromer v. Mulkey Enterprises, Inc., 254 Ga. App. 388, 392–393, 562 S.E.2d 783, 786–787 (2002) (biomechanicist qualified to testify regarding manner in which motor vehicle accident occurred and how passenger reacted in response to forces of collision, but not qualified to testify

whether accident caused herniation of plaintiff's disks).

[3]See, e.g. Johnson v. Knebel, 267 Ga. 853, 859 n.16, 485 S.E.2d 451, 456 (1997) (citing Southern Ry. Co. v. Cabe, 109 Ga. App. 432, 136 S.E.2d 438 (1964)); Lee v. North American Life & Cas. Co., 196 Ga. App. 792, 793, 397 S.E.2d 64, 66 (1990) (insurance industry expert's testimony excluded because witness had no expertise in the type of insurance at issue, and thus, the witness' testimony "constituted nothing more than his personal views on the case").

See also Southern Ry. Co. v. Cabe, 109 Ga. App. 432, 136 S.E.2d 438 (1964). At issue in this case was whether a professional engineer with degrees in mechanical and civil engineering, and who taught at Georgia Tech for 41 years, was qualified to testify that reason why injured railway worker did not evade injury caused by oncoming railcar was fact that worker was not able to perceive rate at which railcar approached him due to an optical illusion. In holding that the trial court erred in allowing such testimony, the court cautioned against the admission of expert opinion testimony merely by virtue of an expert's qualifications, and without regard to whether

within the expert's *demonstrated* area of expertise.[4] However, the proferred testimony clearly falls outside of the expert's field of expertise, or when there is insufficient evidence before the court to demonstrate that an expert possesses the qualifications so as to be able to offer opinion testimony on a particular matter, courts have not hesitated to disallow opinion testimony on the topic.[5]

the expert is qualified to offer opinion testimony on the precise matter before the court.

> In this modern day of specialized inquiry, the terms engineer, civil engineer, or surveyor cannot properly embrace expertise within the meaning of the law in every phase of science. The court cannot accord to those broad terms the requisite 'study' and 'experience' in every facet of knowledge or assume that every technical problem 'lies within the domain' of those callings.

Southern Ry. Co. v. Cabe, 109 Ga. App. 432, 442–443, 136 S.E.2d 438 (1964)

[4]See, e.g. Brown v. Hove, 268 Ga. App. 732, 603 S.E.2d 63 (2004), cert. denied, (Jan. 10, 2005) (neuroradiologist competent to testify that motor vehicle accident likely did not cause plaintiff's disc herniation where evidence established that neuroradiologist had acquired knowledge in field of biomechanics by review of radiological literature and in evaluating injuries depicted in radiographic films); Applebrook Country Dayschool, Inc. v. Thurman, 264 Ga. App. 591, 595, 591 S.E.2d 406, 411 (2003), cert. granted, (Apr. 27, 2004) and rev'd, 278 Ga. 784, 604 S.E.2d 832 (2004) and opinion vacated in part, 613 S.E.2d 192 (Ga. Ct. App. 2005) (insurance agent with experience in predicting client's future incomes qualified in offering testimony of plaintiff's lost future earnings); Dayoub v. Yates–Astro Termite Pest Control Co., 239 Ga. App. 578, 580, 521 S.E.2d 600, 602 (1999) (entomologist qualified to offer testimony on standard of care applicable to pest control technicians despite fact he was not a licensed pest control technician, given educational background and the fact that he had training and experience in the field and consulted with

pest control companies); In Interest of S.T., 201 Ga. App. 37, 38–39, 410 S.E.2d 312, 313–314 (1991) (social worker who was not clinical psychologist or psychiatrist qualified to testify with respect to plaintiff's mental health problems).

[5]Cromer v. Mulkey Enterprises, Inc., 254 Ga. App. 388, 392–393, 562 S.E.2d 783, 786–787 (2002) (biomechanicist's testimony that motor vehicle accident caused plaintiff's herniated disk excluded where no evidence presented showing that field of biomechanics enabled him to make this determination); Yount v. State, 249 Ga. App. 563, 564–565, 548 S.E.2d 674, 676 (2001) (expert with bachelor degree in chemistry who served as chief toxicologist for South Carolina law enforcement division qualified to testify on body's absorption and metabolizing of alcohol, but not qualified on use of infrared breath-testing machines to test for alcohol consumption absent evidence that expert was familiar with type of machine employed in Georgia and how such machines worked); Davis v. State, 209 Ga. App. 572, 574, 434 S.E.2d 132, 134 (1993) (police officer qualified as expert on narcotic investigations, but record failed to show officer was expert on drug use so as to enable him to testify that defendant possessed sufficient amount of heroine so as to infer that defendant intended to sell the drug, as opposed to using it for personal consumption); Goodman v. Lipman, 197 Ga. App. 631, 633–634, 399 S.E.2d 255, 257–258 (1990) (pharmacologist qualified to testify as to whether and how medications cause plaintiff's injuries, but not qualified as to whether physician deviated from standard of care in proscribing said medications to plaintiff); Faubion v. Piedmont

§ 2:3 Relevance of the expert's testimony

O.C.G.A. § 24–2–1 sets forth a benchmark for all evidence by providing that "[e]vidence must relate to the questions being tried by the jury and bear upon them either directly or indirectly. Irrelevant matter should be excluded." Evidence which does not have a reasonable tendency to make more or less probable the issues of fact in controversy is irrelevant, and thus, inadmissible.[1] This fundamental rule, or course, applies with equal force to expert testimony. O.C.G.A. § 24–9–67.1 requires that the expert's testimony assist the jury to "understand the evidence or to determine a fact in issue[.]" Not only must a witness be qualified as an expert to render an opinion, but the witness' particular expertise must be relevant to the issues to be decided in the case.[2] Moreover, the particular testimony to be provided by virtue of the witness' expertise must be relevant to the issues in the case, and "[i]f there is no relevant expert testimony to be given, there is no reason to recognize the witness as an expert regardless of how qualified he or she may be."[3]

Expert testimony is inadmissible when it bears no relation to the elements of, or defense to, a civil cause of action.[4] For instance, expert testimony regarding an attorney's breach of professional rules of conduct has been held irrelevant when the

Engineering & Const. Corp., 178 Ga. App. 256, 257, 342 S.E.2d 718, 719 (1986) (one with experience in purchasing component parts for business machines not necessarily qualified to provide testimony on the market for such parts in breach of contract action).

[Section 2:3]

[1]Horne v. State, 125 Ga. App. 40, 41, 186 S.E.2d 542, 543 (1971).

[2]Vaughn v. Protective Ins. Co., 243 Ga. App. 79, 84, 532 S.E.2d 159, 163 (2000); see also Bryant v. Hoffmann-La Roche, Inc., 262 Ga. App. 401, 408, 585 S.E.2d 723, 729 (2003).

[3]Davis v. State, 209 Ga. App. 572, 576, 434 S.E.2d 132 (1993) (dissenting opinion); see also Anthony v. Chambless, 231 Ga. App. 657, 500 S.E.2d 402 (1998) (expert testimony that patient could have survived aortic aneurysm if surgery had been performed within one hour of aneurysm irrelevant because no such treatment was available or even possible); Sosebee

v. State, 190 Ga. App. 746, 380 S.E.2d 464 (1989) (expert testimony regarding child's competence at time out of court statements held irrelevant because issue was child's competence to testify at time of trial).

[4]It is important to bear in mind that evidence, while irrelevant for one purpose, may be relevant for another purpose. See, e.g. Rose v. Figgie Intern., Inc., 229 Ga. App. 848, 495 S.E.2d 77 (1997) (psychiatrist's testimony that plaintiff suffered from syndrome causing her to exaggerate injuries and malinger not admissible for purposes of questioning credibility, but was relevant and admissible for disputing issues of causation and extent of plaintiff's injuries); Torrance v. Brennan, 209 Ga. App. 65, 432 S.E.2d 658 (1993) (expert testimony regarding dog's vicious conduct subsequent to attack at issue not relevant for purposes of demonstrating owner's knowledge of vicious propensities, but was relevant for purposes of showing vicious propensities themselves).

dispute at issue pertained to a simple breach of contract.[5] Expert testimony is irrelevant when it imposes standards greater than those which are imposed by law,[6] or when it addresses the violation of standards which was not causally related to the injuries complained of.[7] Expert testimony which is premised upon a calculation of damages greater than those allowed by law is similarly irrelevant.[8] In medical malpractice cases, in which the standard of care is measured by the medical profession generally as opposed to what an individual doctor thought advisable under the circumstances, an expert's testimony as to how he or she personally would have elected to treat a patient is irrelevant.[9]

Similarly, expert testimony is inadmissible when it is bears no relation to the elements of, or defense to, a crime for which a defendant has been charged.[10] For instance, where a defendant was charged with driving under the influence of alcohol despite the

---

[5]Mantegna v. Professional Auto Care, Inc., 204 Ga. App. 254, 419 S.E.2d 43 (1992).

[6]Rios v. Norsworthy, 266 Ga. App. 469, 473–474, 597 S.E.2d 421, 426–427 (2004) (expert testimony that driver was required to be "constantly aware" of surrounding vehicles and "maintain a constant vigil" imposed heightened standard of conduct greater than that imposed by law, and was thus irrelevant); Key v. Norfolk Southern Ry. Co., 228 Ga. App. 305, 491 S.E.2d 511 (1997) (expert testimony that steps were defectively designed irrelevant when evidence showed steps designed in conformity with federal regulations); see also Hyles v. Cockrill, 169 Ga. App. 132, 312 S.E.2d 124 (1983) (on other grounds, Ketchup v. Howard, 247 Ga. App. 54, 543 S.E.2d 371 (2000)) (expert testimony that defendant physician failed to disclose possible complications of procedure to patient irrelevant where law did not recognize the "informed consent" doctrine). It should be noted that Georgia now does recognize the "informed consent" doctrine. See, e.g. Ketchup v. Howard, 247 Ga. App. 54, 543 S.E.2d 371 (2000).

[7]Rios v. Norsworthy, 266 Ga. App. 469, 597 S.E.2d 421 (2004); Moore v. State, 258 Ga. App. 293, 574 S.E.2d 372 (2002) (expert testimony pertaining to driver's violation of federal motor carrier safety regulations irrelevant where violation of such standards was not a proximate cause of the collision at issue).

[8]DuBois v. DuBois, 240 Ga. 314, 240 S.E.2d 706 (1977) (in divorce action for child support, economist's testimony which including in its estimate of future child support funds for college expenses held irrelevant as parents under no legal obligation to provide for such expenses); Herron v. Metropolitan Atlanta Rapid Transit Authority, 177 Ga. App. 201, 338 S.E.2d 777 (1985) (in condemnation proceeding to acquire temporary easements over residential property for purpose of constructing a rapid transit system, economist's testimony which premised assessment of damages on property's proximity to rapid transit system held irrelevant where at issue in proceeding was damages occasioned by the easements).

[9]Johnson v. Riverdale Anesthesia Associates, P.C., 275 Ga. 240, 563 S.E.2d 431 (2002); McNabb v. Landis, 223 Ga. App. 894, 479 S.E.2d 194 (1996).

[10]See, e.g. Lee v. State, 262 Ga. 593, 423 S.E.2d 249 (1992), where a man of Chinese heritage shot to death his ex-wife's lover after being berated by the individual. The defendant sought to present an expert on Chinese culture to explain the defendant's

fact that he refused to submit himself to a field sobriety or breath test, expert testimony describing the unreliability of such tests in determining whether one is intoxicated was held to be irrelevant.[11] While the defendant claimed that such testimony helped explain his decision to refuse to submit to a sobriety test, the court observed that the crime for which the defendant was charged was driving under the influence, not refusing to take a sobriety test. Because one's state of mind is not relevant to the crime of driving under the influence, this testimony had no logical tendency to prove or disprove a material fact at issue in the case and was therefore inadmissible.[12]

A criminal defendant's state of mind is often invoked in support of a defense of self-defense or justification. In unique circumstances, expert testimony may be relevant for explaining why the defendant had a reasonable belief of imminent danger to his or her person, despite the absence of any actual imminent threat of harm. Such is the case with expert testimony on the so-called "battered person syndrome," which may be used to explain the reasonableness of a defendant's belief that he or she was in imminent danger when the defendant has been the victim of a long-term abusive relationship with the victim of the defendant's crime.[13] However, when there has been no abusive relationship between the defendant and the actual victim, expert testimony on such psychological syndromes has generally been found irrele-

---

state of mind at the time of the killing, including the effects of cultural influences on the Chinese male, the distinct roles between males and females in Chinese culture, and the concept of divorce within Chinese culture. Such testimony was excluded as irrelevant because the defendant had testified that he fired the first shot accidentally, and the second shot in self-defense, and the testimony would therefore not be probative on the issues to be decided by the jury. Lee v. State, 262 Ga. 593, 594, 423 S.E.2d 249 (1992)

[11]Lucas v. State, 192 Ga. App. 231, 384 S.E.2d 438 (1989).

[12]Lucas v. State, 192 Ga. App. 231, 233–234, 384 S.E.2d 438, 441 (1989). In *Lucas,* the court also noted that such expert testimony was irrelevant for the additional reason that the defendant had testified that he had based his decision not to submit to a

sobriety test on personal experience and unidentified articles he had read, not on the expert's own theories. Thus, the expert's testimony was found irrelevant on the witness' state of mind at the time he refused to take the test. Lucas v. State, 192 Ga. App. 231, 233-234, 384 S.E.2d 438, 441 (1989) See also Evans v. State, 253 Ga. App. 71, 558 S.E.2d 51 (2001) (defense expert testimony on the unreliability of chemical testing for blood alcohol content irrelevant because defendant, having refused to submit himself to such testing, had been charged with reckless driving, not with driving under the influence, and there was no reason to challenge the reliability of such tests).

[13]See, e.g. Bishop v. State, 271 Ga. 291, 519 S.E.2d 206 (1999); Mobley v. State, 269 Ga. 738, 739, 505 S.E.2d 722, 723 (1998); Smith v. State, 268 Ga. 196, 486 S.E.2d 819 (1997).

vant for explaining the reasonableness of a defendant's conduct with respect to the victim.[14]

§ 2:4 Helpfulness of expert testimony

O.C.G.A. § 24–9–67.1(b) provides that expert opinion testimony is admissible when it will "assist the trier of fact . . . to understand the evidence or to determine a fact in issue[.]" This statute essentially codifies the long-standing rule that, in order to be admissible, expert testimony must be "helpful" in assisting the jury to understand the evidence.[1] The concept of "helpfulness" is broad, and indeed, overlaps with other rules governing the admissibility of expert testimony, addressed elsewhere in this chapter. For instance, if expert testimony is not relevant to the issues to be decided by the jury, it will not assist the jury in deciding the issues before it.[2] Similarly, if the methodology employed by an expert in arriving at his conclusions is not reliable, such testimony will not assist the jury in evaluating the issues in the case. Three aspects of this "helpfulness" requirement are addressed in this section: expert testimony on the "ultimate issue," expert testimony amounting to "legal conclusions," and expert testimony bearing upon the credibility of other witnesses.

§ 2:5 Helpfulness of expert testimony—Expert testimony on the ultimate issue

As a general rule, witnesses are not permitted to express an opinion on the issue which is ultimately be decided by the jury,

---

[14]See, e.g. Blair v. State, 273 Ga. 668, 543 S.E.2d 685 (2001) (expert testimony pertaining to defendant's sexual abuse as a child irrelevant where defendant murdered his lover); Weems v. State, 268 Ga. 142, 485 S.E.2d 767 (1997) (expert testimony regarding defendant's "catastrophic reaction" after beating by drug dealers irrelevant where defendant fired gun into crowd, killing several unrelated persons); Johnson v. State, 266 Ga. 624, 469 S.E.2d 152 (1996) (expert testimony regarding defendant's "explosive rage" irrelevant where defendant killed unrelated person with whom he had no personal history).

[Section 2:4]

[1]See, e.g. Hall v. State, 261 Ga.

778, 782, 415 S.E.2d 158, 162 (1991) ("Expert testimony is admissible when the conclusion of the expert is one which jurors would not ordinarily be able to draw for themselves and when such testimony would be helpful or necessary to assist the jury.").

[2]See, e.g. Daubert v. Merrell Dow Pharmaceuticals, Inc., 509 U.S. 579, 591, 113 S. Ct. 2786, 2796, 125 L. Ed. 2d 469 (1993) ("Rule 702 further requires that the evidence or testimony 'assist the trier of fact to understand the evidence or to determine a fact in issue.' . . . 'Expert testimony which does not relate to any issue in the case is not relevant and, ergo, nonhelpful.' ").

as such an expression would "invade the province of the jury."[1] However, experts may offer opinions, even on such "ultimate issues," where the expert's conclusion is "beyond the ken" of the jury.[2] When the conclusion to be drawn from the facts is one which jurors would not ordinarily be able to reach on their own— "i.e., the conclusion is beyond the ken of the average layman"— expert opinion testimony is admissible to assist the jury in understanding and evaluating the evidence.[3] Stated slightly differently, such opinion testimony is admissible when the nature of the subject matter is "among those things shrouded in the mystery of professional skill or knowledge[.]"[4]

Application of this rule is commonly seen when expert testimony is employed to address various psychological syndromes.[5] For instance, "battered woman syndrome" describes characteristics of women who have been in an abusive relationship, and the reasons such women may act in a way which is seemingly counter-intuitive, such as remaining in the relationship or failing to report the abuse.[6] Expert testimony is commonly offered to describe this syndrome and the fact that a woman charged with killing an abusive mate exhibits characteristics consistent with this syndrome. This testimony is offered for the purpose of demonstrating the reasonableness of the woman's belief that she was in imminent danger when she killed her abusive mate despite the fact that no physical abuse was occurring or even imminent at the time of the homicide.[7] Expert opinion testimony on this syndrome has been routinely admitted because it addresses "a complex area of human response and behavior,"[8] and provides an "interpretation of the facts which differs from ordinary lay perception"[9] and "conclusions that jurors could not ordinarily draw for themselves."[10]

[Section 2:5]

[1]Lowery v. State, 260 Ga. App. 260, 262, 581 S.E.2d 593, 595 (2003); Amaechi v. State, 254 Ga. App. 490, 494, 564 S.E.2d 22, 26 (2002); Adams v. State, 231 Ga. App. 279, 285, 499 S.E.2d 105, 111 (1998).

[2]Smith v. State, 247 Ga. 612, 619, 277 S.E.2d 678, 683 (1981); Adams v. State, 231 Ga. App. 279, 285, 499 S.E.2d 105, 111 (1998).

[3]Smith v. State, 247 Ga. 612, 619, 277 S.E.2d 678, 683 (1981).

[4]Metropolitan Life Ins. Co. v. Saul, 189 Ga. 1, 5 S.E.2d 214 (1939);

see also Smith v. State, 268 Ga. 196, 486 S.E.2d 819 (1997).

[5]For a thorough discussion of expert testimony in this regard, see Chapter 9.

[6]Mobley v. State, 269 Ga. 738, 739, 505 S.E.2d 722, 723 (1998); Smith v. State, 268 Ga. 196, 486 S.E.2d 819 (1997).

[7]Mobley v. State, 269 Ga. 738, 739, 505 S.E.2d 722, 723 (1998); Smith v. State, 268 Ga. 196, 486 S.E.2d 819 (1997).

[8]Bishop v. State, 271 Ga. 291, 292, 519 S.E.2d 206 (1999); Smith v.

Similarly, "child sexual abuse accommodation syndrome" describes certain characteristics common to child victims of sexual abuse, including the fact that disclosure of the abuse may be delayed, equivocal, or retracted.[11] Expert testimony is commonly admitted to describe the syndrome, and the fact that the child exhibits characteristics or behaviors consistent with the syndrome, because "[l]aymen would not understand this syndrome without expert testimony, nor would they be likely to believe that a child who denied a sexual assault, or who was reluctant to discuss a sexual assault, in fact had been assaulted."[12] However, the bounds of the expert's testimony is not without limits, and while the expert may describe the syndrome and express an opinion as to whether the child exhibits symptoms "consistent with" the syndrome, the expert may not then take the "next step" and conclude that the child was therefore abused, as the jury, presented with the foregoing evidence, is capable of reaching this "ultimate" conclusion on its own.[13]

At the same time, a party may not simply "bolster his case as to the ultimate issue with expert testimony when the jury could reach the same conclusion independently of the opinion of others."[14] When "(a) the path from evidence to conclusion is not shrouded in the mystery of professional skill or knowledge, and (b) the conclusion determines the ultimate issues of fact in a case, the jury must make the journey from evidence to conclusion without the aid of expert testimony."[15]

When the matter to be decided is one which, by virtue of common experience, a jury can decide on its own, expert testimony will be excluded as being of no real assistance to the jury. For instance, whether a curb below a certain height was "inherently

---

State, 268 Ga. 196, 198, 486 S.E.2d 819, 822 (1997).

[9]Bishop v. State, 271 Ga. 291, 292, 519 S.E.2d 206 (1999).

[10]Smith v. State, 268 Ga. 196, 486 S.E.2d 819 (1997); Smith v. State, 247 Ga. 612, 277 S.E.2d 678 (1981).

[11]Allison v. State, 256 Ga. 851, 852, 353 S.E.2d 805, 807 (1987).

[12]Allison v. State, 256 Ga. 851, 852, 353 S.E.2d 805, 807 (1987).

[13]Allison v. State, 256 Ga. 851, 852, 353 S.E.2d 805, 807 (1987); Cooper v. State, 200 Ga. App. 560, 560–561, 408 S.E.2d 797, 798 (1991)

[14]Applebrook Country Dayschool, Inc. v. Thurman, 264 Ga. App. 591, 593, 591 S.E.2d 406, 409 (2003), cert. granted, (Apr. 27, 2004) and rev'd, 278 Ga. 784, 604 S.E.2d 832 (2004) and opinion vacated in part, 613 S.E.2d 192 (Ga. Ct. App. 2005); Sullivan v. Quisc, Inc., 207 Ga. App. 114, 115, 427 S.E.2d 86, 88 (1993); Jennette v. State, 197 Ga. App. 580, 582, 398 S.E.2d 734, 736 (1990).

[15]Carlock v. Kmart Corp., 227 Ga. App. 356, 361, 489 S.E.2d 99, 104 (1997); see also Moore v. State, 258 Ga. App. 293, 295, 574 S.E.2d 372, 375 (2002); Baxter v. Melton, 218 Ga. App. 731, 732, 463 S.E.2d 53, 55 (1995).

dangerous,"[16] whether the slope of a floor constituted a "dangerous condition,"[17] and whether a criminal assault in a grocery store parking lot was "foreseeable"[18] have been held to be conclusions within the ability of the jury to ascertain on its own, and thus, conclusions for which expert testimony is neither needed nor appropriate. Similarly, whether a driver exercised ordinary care so as to discover the presence of another vehicle and avoid a collision has been held to be a matter within the ken of the average juror and for which expert testimony is not needed.[19] The role of an expert is to assist the jury in arriving at a conclusion, not to act as a member of the jury by telling it what conclusion to reach.[20]

While expert testimony is available to aid the jury in understanding the evidence so as to reach its own conclusion, expert testimony which merely speaks in conclusory terms is typically excluded as offering a conclusion which is not beyond the ability of the jury to draw on its own from the evidence. For instance, in the context of motor vehicle accidents, expert testimony may very well be helpful in explaining the factors involved in, and the circumstances leading to, an accident.[21] However, when the jury has been presented with such information, it is capable of concluding on its own who was "at fault" in causing the accident, and expert testimony on this "next step" in the inferential process is unnecessary and merely operates to invade upon the function of the jury to determine such issues.[22] Similarly, while expert testimony may be of assistance in elucidating complex business transac-

---

[16]Warnke v. Pace Membership Warehouse, Inc., 215 Ga. App. 33, 449 S.E.2d 629 (1994).

[17]Sullivan v. Quisc, Inc., 207 Ga. App. 114, 427 S.E.2d 86 (1993).

[18]Carlock v. Kmart Corp., 227 Ga. App. 356, 489 S.E.2d 99 (1997).

[19]Rios v. Norsworthy, 266 Ga. App. 469, 473, 597 S.E.2d 421, 426 (2004).

[20]DeVooght v. Hobbs, 265 Ga. App. 329, 334, 593 S.E.2d 868, 873 (2004); Gage v. Tiffin Motor Homes, Inc., 153 Ga. App. 704, 707, 266 S.E.2d 345, 347 (1980); Travelers' Ins. Co. v. Thornton, 119 Ga. 455, 46 S.E. 678 (1904).

[21]See, e.g. Moore v. State, 258 Ga. App. 293, 574 S.E.2d 372 (2002) (computation of speed, distance, and human reaction times are beyond the ken of the average juror, and expert testimony on these matters may be admis-sible to assist the jury in determining whether a driver had time to avoid the collision).

[22]See, e.g. Deloach v. Deloach, 258 Ga. App. 187, 573 S.E.2d 444 (2002) (when evidence established that defendant was intoxicated at time of accident, and circumstances surrounding cause of accident were "relatively straightforward," jury was able to reach its own conclusions about cause of accident without police officer's testimony that defendant's intoxication was the cause); McMichen v. Moattar, 221 Ga. App. 230, 470 S.E.2d 800 (1996) (when police officer had testified as to what he observed at the accident scene and conclusions as to how the accident had occurred, error to allow the police officer to express an opinion as to which driver was at fault); Baxter v. Melton, 218 Ga. App. 731, 463 S.E.2d 53 (1995) (when police officer testified as to his estimate of vehicle speeds and the maximum safe

tions, an expert, having explained such transactions, may not go to the next step and opine that such transactions were "fraudulent."[23]

§ 2:6 Helpfulness of expert testimony—Legal conclusions

Closely related to the concept of the "ultimate issue" is that of the "legal conclusion." As a general rule, an expert may not provide testimony which amounts to a conclusion of law. "The expert may aid the jury, but the expert cannot act as a member of the jury; nor, while on the stand, can the expert transcend the functions of a witness, and under the guise of giving testimony state a legal conclusion."[1] For instance, an expert generally may not opine that certain conduct is "fraudulent,"[2] nor may an expert characterize a killing as either "justifiable"[3] or as a "homicide."[4] An expert generally may not offer an opinion as to the existence of a contractual relationship,[5] whether a party has a "contractual obligation,"[6] or whether one party may be held vicariously liable for the acts of another.[7] As a general rule, an expert is not permitted to testify that one party's conduct was "negligent,"[8] or that one party was "at fault."[9]

Nonetheless, not all expressions which sound of legal significance are deemed to be improper "legal conclusions." Due to the inherent limitations of language and the fact that terms of common usage overlap with those used in the law, it would be impractical to exclude all expert testimony merely because it hap-

---

speed for vehicles under the circumstances, the "jurors were fully capable of considering the evidence and drawing their own conclusions as to the ultimate fact of negligence, including whether or not [the defendant] was traveling too fast for conditions, without the aid of the expert opinion.")

[23]Adams v. State, 231 Ga. App. 279, 285, 499 S.E.2d 105, 111 (1998).

[Section 2:6]

[1]Travelers' Ins. Co. v. Thornton, 119 Ga. 455, 46 S.E. 678 (1904); see also DeVooght v. Hobbs, 265 Ga. App. 329, 334, 593 S.E.2d 868, 873 (2004); Gage v. Tiffin Motor Homes, Inc., 153 Ga. App. 704, 707, 266 S.E.2d 345, 347 (1980).

[2]Allen v. Columbus Bank & Trust Co., 244 Ga. App. 271, 277–278, 534 S.E.2d 917, 925 (2000); Adams v. State, 231 Ga. App. 279, 285, 499 S.E.2d 105, 111 (1998).

[3]Fordham v. State, 254 Ga. 59, 325 S.E.2d 755 (1985).

[4]Maxwell v. State, 263 Ga. 57, 428 S.E.2d 76 (1993).

[5]Clanton v. Von Haam, 177 Ga. App. 694, 696, 340 S.E.2d 627, 629–630 (1986).

[6]Gellis v. B. L. I. Const. Co., Inc., 148 Ga. App. 527, 540, 251 S.E.2d 800, 811 (1978).

[7]DeVooght v. Hobbs, 265 Ga. App. 329, 334, 593 S.E.2d 868, 873 (2004).

[8]Rios v. Norsworthy, 266 Ga. App. 469, 472, 597 S.E.2d 421, 425–426 (2004) (expert testimony that driver was "negligent" and had the "last clear chance" to avoid accident inadmissible); Jackson v. Ensley, 168 Ga. App. 822, 827, 310 S.E.2d 707, 711 (1983).

[9]McMichen v. Moattar, 221 Ga. App. 230, 470 S.E.2d 800 (1996).

pened to reference a term with legal ramifications. As has been noted by one court: "If we were to hold inadmissible questions which included a legal term in their body on the ground that it called for a legal conclusion, then questions could not be asked which included such common but legal words as: agent, arrest, assume, contract, deed, divorce, gift, license, marriage, mortgage, partner, etc."[10] Whether expert testimony constitutes an impermissible legal conclusion depends upon the nature of the inquiry. When the use of terminology with legal significance is merely incidental to the matter at issue, the fact that the terminology used is a legal conclusion does not render it inadmissible.[11] However, when the use of legal terminology touches directly upon the matter at issue, the use of such terminology constitutes an impermissible legal conclusion.[12]

Professional malpractice actions are an established exception to the general prohibition against the use of the legal conclusion that a party's conduct was or was not negligent. The court and jury, lacking the professional expertise in the given subject matter, must have a reliable basis to determine whether the professional's conduct constituted negligence.[13] Except in cases in which the alleged professional malpractice is so plain and clear that a jury would not need an expert to determine whether negligence

[10]Gage v. Tiffin Motor Homes, Inc., 153 Ga. App. 704, 708, 266 S.E.2d 345, 348 (1980).

[11]Medlock v. State, 263 Ga. 246, 248–249, 430 S.E.2d 754 (1993), 754, 756–757 (medical examiner's use of the term "homicide" not impermissible legal conclusion when it merely reinforced his prior testimony describing how child had died and was not directed toward addressing the issue as to whether the defendant's conduct was intentional or accidental); Gage v. Tiffin Motor Homes, Inc., 153 Ga. App. 704, 708, 266 S.E.2d 345, 348 (1980) (court found no impermissible legal conclusion when expert referenced contract as a "security agreement," but the existence of a security agreement was not at issue because the "contract had to be called something" to direct the witnesses' attention to it).

[12]Department of Transp. v. Franco's Pizza & Delicatessen, Inc., 200 Ga. App. 723, 409 S.E.2d 281 (1991) (on other grounds, White v. Fulton County, 264 Ga. 393, 444 S.E.2d 734 (1994)) (where "uniqueness" of land directly at issue for purposes of assessing property value in condemnation action, error to allow expert to testify that property was "unique"); (Hinson v. Department of Transp., 135 Ga. App. 258, 217 S.E.2d 606 (1975) (in condemnation action pertaining to "uniqueness" of property, expert's interpretation of zoning laws and testimony as to whether business could be relocated within certain zoning district called for impermissible legal conclusion).

[13]Savannah Valley Production Credit Ass'n v. Cheek, 248 Ga. 745, 747, 285 S.E.2d 689 (1982); Kapsch v. Stowers, 209 Ga. App. 767, 767, 434 S.E.2d 539 (1993); Austin v. Kaufman, 203 Ga. App. 704, 705, 417 S.E.2d 660, 663 (1992).

existed, expert testimony is required to establish this element of a plaintiff's case.[14]

Despite the general rule prohibiting expert testimony amounting to a legal conclusion, experts are nonetheless permitted to explain often complex and technical regulations and ordinances when such an explanation would assist the jury to understand the issues in the case.[15] For instance, in Stewart v. State, a criminal action involving alleged fraudulent acquisition of public assistance funds, a DFACS representative was permitted to testify as to the amount of public assistance to which the defendant was otherwise entitled under applicable rules and regulations in order to assist the jury in determining whether the defendant made false statements in applying for public assistance.[16] Such testimony on the application of various regulations and ordinances has been admitted to assist the jury in determining whether a defendant's conduct fell within or below the applicable standard of care.[17] When compliance with certain ordinances and regulations is expressly incorporated into a contract, or consti-

---

[14]In the context of medical malpractice actions, see, e.g.: Parker v. Knight, 245 Ga. 782, 267 S.E.2d 222 (1980); Crumbley v. Wyant, 188 Ga. App. 227, 372 S.E.2d 497 (1988); Killingsworth v. Poon, 167 Ga. App. 653, 307 S.E.2d 123 (1983); Phillips v. Cheek, 162 Ga. App. 728, 293 S.E.2d 22 (1982). In the context of legal malpractice actions, see e.g.: Howard v. Walker, 242 Ga. 406, 249 S.E.2d 45 (1978); Graves v. Jones, 184 Ga. App. 128, 361 S.E.2d 19 (1987).

[15]See, e.g. Hopkins v. Hudgins & Co., Inc., 218 Ga. App. 508, 462 S.E.2d 393 (1995) (permitting safety engineer to testify that defendant's loading procedure violated OSHA safety regulations); Ultima–Trimble, Ltd. v. Department of Transp., 214 Ga. App. 607, 448 S.E.2d 498 (1994) (in helping the jury to understand property value in condemnation proceeding, expert permitted to testify that setback requirement of ordinance would permit the plaintiff to build to easement taken by government);

[16]Stewart v. State, 246 Ga. 70, 74, 268 S.E.2d 906, 911 (1980).

[17]See, e.g. Hopkins v. Hudgins & Co., Inc., 218 Ga. App. 508, 462 S.E.2d 393 (1995) (permitting expert to testify

that employer's loading procedures were in violation of OSHA regulations); see also Allen v. Lefkoff, Duncan, Grimes & Dermer, P.C., 265 Ga. 374, 453 S.E.2d 719 (1995) (noting that expert testimony regarding ethical guidelines applicable to attorneys would be helpful in establishing standard of care violation in legal malpractice action); Donaldson v. Department of Transp., 236 Ga. App. 411, 511 S.E.2d 210 (1999) (finding that expert testimony on the Manual On Uniform Traffic Control Devices regulations was sufficient evidence upon which a jury could conclude ordinary negligence, but insufficient to establish negligence per se because no showing that Georgia had adopted such regulations as law); Spearman v. Georgia Bldg. Authority, 224 Ga. App. 801, 802, 482 S.E.2d 463, 464 (1997) (not error for trial court to refuse to give jury instruction that "[e]xpert testimony may incorporate reference to statutes, ordinances, regulations and privately set guidelines, and such may be considered as illustrative of ordinary negligence" where instruction did not indicate that violation of private standards did not establish negligence as a matter of law).

tutes a condition of fulfilling a contract, courts have permitted expert testimony regarding the requirements of such ordinances or regulations.[18]

§ 2:7 Helpfulness of expert testimony—Credibility

It is commonly held that expert testimony is never needed, and thus never admissible, on the credibility of another witness. "Credibility of a witness is not beyond the ken of the jurors but, to the contrary, is a matter solely within the province of the jury."[1] "In no circumstance may a witness' credibility be bolstered by the opinion of another, even an expert, as to whether the witness is telling the truth. . . . [A]n expert witness may not put his or her stamp of believability on [another witness'] story."[2] Testimony which amounts to little more than an opinion that another witness is or is not telling the truth has been routinely excluded as improper bolstering.[3]

However, expert testimony which is relevant to an issue in the case is not improper merely because it indirectly comments upon the truthfulness of a witness.[4] Important in this regard is whether the testimony has a legitimate purpose other than merely commenting on the credibility of another witness. For instance, in Rose v. Figgie International, Inc., a psychiatrist's testimony that the plaintiff suffered from psychological disorders causing her to

---

[18]See, e.g. Williamson v. Harvey Smith, Inc., 246 Ga. App. 745, 542 S.E.2d 151 (2000) (in contract dispute, expert permitted to testify that construction was completed in accordance with applicable ordinances and regulations when compliance with the same was a requirement of the contract); Wood v. Turner, 196 Ga. App. 815, 397 S.E.2d 161 (1990) (in contract dispute, inspector permitted to testify that certificate of occupancy not issued because sewer and water lines in contractor's development violated county ordinances).

[Section 2:7]

[1]State v. Oliver, 188 Ga. App. 47, 50, 372 S.E.2d 256, 260 (1988); see also Jennette v. State, 197 Ga. App. 580, 582, 398 S.E.2d 734, 736–737 (1990).

[2]State v. Oliver, 188 Ga. App. 47, 50–51, 372 S.E.2d 256, 260 (1988)

[3]Sinns v. State, 248 Ga. 385, 387, 283 S.E.2d 479, 481 (1981) (expert testimony on voluntariness of confession not admissible); Jennette v. State, 197 Ga. App. 580, 582, 398 S.E.2d 734, 736–737 (1990) (expert testimony regarding the "lying child syndrome" inadmissible); Gorski v. State, 201 Ga. App. 122, 123, 410 S.E.2d 338, 339 (1991) (expert testimony that victim is prone to lying or exaggeration inadmissible).

[4]Thomas v. State, 279 Ga. 363, 364, 613 S.E.2d 620, 620 (2005) (detective's opinion that two witnesses were not involved in crime relevant to explain criminal investigation and did not impermissibly convey that the detective believed the witnesses to be truthful); Parrish v. State, 237 Ga. App. 274, 277, 514 S.E.2d 458, 463 (1999) (expert's testimony on a victim's "learned helplessness" relevant to explain why victim did not evade attack despite opportunity to do so, and admissible despite the fact that such testimony tended to corroborate victim's story).

exaggerate physical ailments was relevant to issues of cause and extent of plaintiff's injuries, and was admissible despite the fact that it had the indirect effect of calling into question the credibility of plaintiff's claimed damages.[5] Expert testimony has been held to be admissible, in limited circumstances, on the reliability of an eyewitness' identification of a criminal defendant as the perpetrator of a crime when necessary to reveal weaknesses in the identification which would not be readily appreciated by the jury, despite the tendency such testimony has to call into question the credibility of the eyewitness.[6] Similarly, expert testimony on the proper interviewing techniques of child victims of abuse has occasionally been admitted to address how improperly suggestive or leading techniques may contaminate an interview, a matter not likely readily appreciated by the jury, despite the tendency such testimony has to call into question the credibility of a child's story.[7]

Expert testimony which offers an opinion that a witness' story is either consistent or inconsistent with the objective evidence in the case is not objectionable merely because it has the tendency to call into question the credibility of the witness' story.[8] For instance, expert testimony has been consistently admitted to explain that a child's behaviors are consistent with "child sexual abuse accommodation syndrome"—a syndrome used to explain the behaviors of children who have been sexually abused—when relevant to explain why a child did not immediately report the abuse, despite the tendency of such testimony to "vouch" for the child's allegations of abuse.[9] Expert medical testimony has been admitted to demonstrate that injuries suffered by a victim were

[5]Rose v. Figgie Intern., Inc., 229 Ga. App. 848, 495 S.E.2d 77 (1997).

[6]Johnson v. State, 272 Ga. 254, 256–257, 526 S.E.2d 549, 552 (2000).

[7]Barlow v. State, 270 Ga. 54, 55, 507 S.E.2d 416, 418 (1998); Pyron v. State, 237 Ga. App. 198, 200, 514 S.E.2d 51, 53 (1999) (while expert cannot opine that the child's allegations are false, an expert may offer testimony as to what are improperly leading and suggestive interviewing techniques so as to enable jury to better assess the credibility of the child's story).

[8]See, e.g. Rose v. Figgie Intern., Inc., 229 Ga. App. 848, 495 S.E.2d 77 (1997); Satterwhite v. State, 212 Ga. App. 543, 543, 442 S.E.2d 5 (1994) (detective permitted to testify that

physical evidence at crime scene conformed to victim's story); Holloway v. State, 137 Ga. App. 124, 126, 222 S.E.2d 898, 900 (1975) (expert permitted to testify that gun shot wounds suggested that defendant had shot victim at downward angle, and not from upward angle as contended by defendant).

[9]See, e.g. Morris v. State, 268 Ga. App. 325, 327–328, 601 S.E.2d 804, 807 (2004), cert. denied, (Oct. 25, 2004); Brownlow v. State, 248 Ga. App. 366, 368, 544 S.E.2d 472, 474–475 (2001); Odom v. State, 243 Ga. App. 227, 228, 531 S.E.2d 207, 209 (2000).

As discussed above, although expert testimony is admissible on the point that a child exhibits symptoms "consistent with" child victims of sexual abuse, expert testimony crosses

inconsistent with the defendant's explanation as to how the victim's injuries occurred.[10]

§ 2:8 Facts and data upon which an expert may rely as basis of opinion

O.C.G.A. § 24-9-67.1(a) provides, in part:

The opinion of a witness qualified as an expert under this Code section may be given on the facts as proved by other witnesses. The facts or data in the particular case upon which an expert bases an opinion or inference may be those perceived by or made known to the expert at or before the hearing or trial. If of a type reasonably relied upon by experts in the particular field in forming opinions or inferences on the subject, the facts or data need not be admissible in evidence in order for the opinion or inference to be admitted.[1]

This statute represents an amalgamation of what has historically been the law in Georgia and Rule 703 of the Federal Rules of Evidence. The first sentence carries forward what has, historically, been the law in Georgia. Indeed, the language of the first sentence—that an expert opinion "may be given on the facts as proved by other witnesses"—is identical to the language of the former O.C.G.A. § 24-9-67.[2] Essentially, this provision recognizes that the opinion of an expert need not be based on the

---

the line into impermissible bolstering when it does little more than vouch for the credibility of the child. See, e.g. Harper v. Patterson, 270 Ga. App. 437, 606 S.E.2d 887 (2004), cert. denied, (Mar. 28, 2005) (investigator's testimony which was not based on child sexual abuse accommodation syndrome, but merely narrated the allegations and concluded that allegations were consistent with sexual abuse inadmissible); Hilliard v. State, 226 Ga. App. 478, 481, 487 S.E.2d 81, 84 (1997) (school counselor's opinion that she "firmly believed" that child had been molested inadmissible); Roberson v. State, 214 Ga. App. 208, 210, 447 S.E.2d 640, 643 (1994) (social worker testimony that children at issue were capable of distinguishing between truth and fantasy amounted to commentary on credibility of children, and was not admissible); State v. Oliver, 188 Ga. App. 47, 50, 372 S.E.2d 256, 260 (1988) (while psychologist may testify generally about the ability of children of a certain age to distinguish between truth and falsity, psycholo-

gist may not testify that she determined the child in the particular case to be truthful).

[10]London v. State, 274 Ga. 91, 549 S.E.2d 394 (2001) (medical testimony used to establish that victim had been abused prior to fall down a stairway and that magnitude of injuries sustained during fall indicated that victim had been pushed prior to fall as opposed to falling accidentally as contended by defendant); Causey v. State, 215 Ga. App. 723, 452 S.E.2d 564 (1994) (forensic pathologist and neurosurgeon permitted to testify that injuries suffered by victim were inconsistent with seizure as alleged by defendant); Medlock v. State, 263 Ga. 246, 248–49, 430 S.E.2d 754, 756 (1993) (medical expert permitted to testify that injuries suffered by child resulted from the child being shaken and not from accidental fall as alleged by defendant).

[Section 2:8]

[1]O.C.G.A. § 24-9-67.1(a).

[2]The 2005 version of O.C.G.A. § 24-9-67, applicable to criminal cases,

expert's personal knowledge, but may be based on the evidence in record as proved by other witnesses and of which the expert has no independent, first-hand knowledge.[3] Historically, Georgia law has required that an expert's opinions be premised upon either: 1) facts within the expert's personal knowledge; or 2) facts which, although not within the expert's personal knowledge, are in evidence by the testimony of witnesses or by other legal means.[4]

The second two sentences of this statute adopt the language of Rule 703 of the Federal Rules of Evidence. Rule 703 is, essentially, a rule of convenience, and was designed to obviate the need for examining witnesses in order to authenticate the various sources of information upon which an expert may base an opinion, such as authoritative texts or medical records.[5] Before such authentication procedures may be dispensed with, however, the rule requires that the materials upon which the expert relies be "reasonably relied upon by experts in the particular field in forming opinions or inferences on the subject."

While the language of the statute is new, it is essentially similar to the law that has been developing under Georgia's common law prior to the 2005 enactment of the statute. Historically, Georgia courts had not been receptive to expert opinion testimony which was not based on the expert's own personal knowledge or upon facts in evidence, reasoning that to allow otherwise would be tantamount to allowing the proponent of the evidence to do indirectly that which he could not do directly, i.e. introduce otherwise inadmissible hearsay by virtue of the expert's reliance on it.[6] However, Georgia courts have increasingly recognized that an expert's reliance on hearsay evidence did not necessarily necessitate the exclusion of the expert's opinion when it was

---

also carries forward this same language.

[3]Peters v. State, 268 Ga. 414, 415, 490 S.E.2d 94, 96 (1997).

[4]Loper v. Drury, 211 Ga. App. 478, 481, 440 S.E.2d 32, 35 (1993); Brown v. State, 206 Ga. App. 800, 801, 427 S.E.2d 9, 9–10 (1992) ("Generally, an expert cannot state his opinion based upon facts not within his personal knowledge which are not otherwise admitted into evidence. [Cit.] In response to a hypothetical question, an expert may assume facts not within his personal knowledge, as long as the assumed facts are placed in evidence

by the testimony of other witnesses or by other legal means.").

[5]Advisory Committee Notes to Rule 703.

[6]See, e.g. Loper v. Drury, 211 Ga. App. 478, 482, 440 S.E.2d 32, 36 (1993) (noting that to allow an expert to base his testimony on a letter not in evidence "would permit the admission of hearsay, speculation and unsupported opinion, by the simple expedient of asking an expert to read the inadmissible matter into the record or testify to it while asserting that he relied upon it.").

based only partially upon hearsay.[7] These courts reasoned that the fact that an expert's testimony is based, in part, on hearsay is a matter for the jury to consider in determining the weight to be accorded the expert's opinions, and not a fact which will automatically disqualify the expert from giving the opinion.[8]

Such a rule conforms with common sense, as much of what qualifies a witness to offer "expert" opinions in the first instance will be that which is inherently "hearsay," such as the witness' study and review of materials in the course of the witness' education, training, and job-related experience.[9] Moreover, many experts frequently "reasonably rely" upon the documents prepared by others, and even the opinions of others, as a matter of course in their routine, day-to-day, professional activities.[10] By way of example, the Advisory Committee Notes to Rule 703 reference the fact that physicians frequently make "life-and-death" decisions based in part upon the reports and diagnoses of other health care providers, and that a physician's reliance on such reports should therefore suffice for evidentiary purposes in a judicial proceeding.[11]

By contrast, Georgia courts have consistently disallowed expert

[7]See, e.g. Roebuck v. State, 277 Ga. 200, 586 S.E.2d 651 (2003); Roberts v. Baker, 265 Ga. 902, 463 S.E.2d 694 (1995); King v. Browning, 246 Ga. 46, 268 S.E.2d 653 (1980); Williamson v. Harvey Smith, Inc., 246 Ga. App. 745, 749, 542 S.E.2d 151, 155 (2000); McEver v. Worrell Enterprises, 223 Ga. App. 627, 478 S.E.2d 445 (1996); Blackburn v. State, 180 Ga. App. 436, 437, 349 S.E.2d 286, 288 (1986).

[8]Leonard v. State, 269 Ga. 867, 870, 506 S.E.2d 853, 856 (1998); Williamson v. Harvey Smith, Inc., 246 Ga. App. 745, 749, 542 S.E.2d 151, 155 (2000); Beecher v. State, 240 Ga. App. 457, 523 S.E.2d 54 (1999); Blackburn v. State, 180 Ga. App. 436, 437, 349 S.E.2d 286, 288 (1986).

[9]Joiner v. Lane, 235 Ga. App. 121, 126, 508 S.E.2d 203, 209 (1998) ("[K]nowledge gained from hearsay by an expert, during the practice of his profession, may be used to express an opinion."); Austin v. Kaufman, 203 Ga. App. 704, 417 S.E.2d 660 (1992) (" 'An expert may testify as to his opinions derived from a book[.]' . . . However, medical articles are not themselves admissible as evidence."); Inman v.

State, 195 Ga. App. 805, 805–806, 395 S.E.2d 52, 53 (1990) ("While an expert witness may support his opinion by reference to books, statistical sources and other learned treatises, his testimony is inadmissible when it is merely a restatement of a textbook opinion rather than an independent expression of his own personal opinion."); see also Dayoub v. Yates–Astro Termite Pest Control Co., 239 Ga. App. 578, 521 S.E.2d 600 (1999) (recognizing that industry standards may form basis of expert's opinions).

[10]Stephens v. Howard, 221 Ga. App. 469, 471 S.E.2d 898 (1996) (testimony of physician admissible even though it was based in part on testing performed by a physical therapist whose testimony was not before the court); Doctors Hosp. of Augusta, Inc. v. Bonner, 195 Ga. App. 152, 392 S.E.2d 897 (1990) (testimony of physician admissible even though it was based in part on diagnosis of physician whose testimony not before the court).

[11]Advisory Committee Notes to Rule 703. By contrast, the Advisory Committee Notes state that this liber-

testimony which is premised primarily or solely upon hearsay.[12] The courts have reasoned that an expert's opinion which is based solely or primarily upon the out-of-court declarations of a third party not before the court would be little more than a vehicle for admitting otherwise inadmissible hearsay.[13] Similarly, courts have required that an expert's opinion be his or her own, and it has been consistently held that an expert may not operate as the mere "conduit" for the opinion of another.[14] This distinction between expert testimony which is based only in part upon hearsay, and expert testimony which is based solely or primarily upon hearsay, would appear to be carried forward by O.C.G.A. § 24–9–67.1(b), which requires that an expert's opinions be based upon "sufficient facts or data which are or will be admitted into evidence."

The last sentence of O.C.G.A. § 24–9–67.1(a) provides that "[f]acts or data that are otherwise inadmissible shall not be disclosed to the jury by the proponent of the opinion or inference unless the court determines that their probative value in assist-

---

alized rule "would not warrant admitting in evidence the opinion of an 'accidentologist' as to the point of impact in an automobile collision based on statements of bystanders since [the requirement of 'reasonable reliance'] is not satisfied."

[12]Leonard v. State, 269 Ga. 867, 870, 506 S.E.2d 853, 856 (1998) (expert testimony excluded when based solely on the hearsay reports of others and no independent evidence in the record); Green v. State, 266 Ga. 237, 466 S.E.2d 577 (1996) (opinion of expert in gang identification and deterrence inadmissible when based solely on private conversations with police officers not before the court); McEver v. Worrell Enterprises, 223 Ga. App. 627, 478 S.E.2d 445 (1996) (expert testimony inadmissible when based solely on phone conversations with other non-testifying witnesses).

[13]Leonard v. State, 269 Ga. 867, 870, 506 S.E.2d 853, 856 (1998). In Leornard, the court observed that:

[a]n opinion, based mainly on representations out of court, can be no more competent testimony than the representations. If the jury are not informed what the representations were, they do no know upon what hypothesis of facts the opinion rests. If

they are informed, they are still left with no evidence of the existence of the facts, except unsworn declarations of a third person out of court, which are not proof in courts of law.

Leonard v. State, 269 Ga. 867, 506 S.E.2d 853 (1998) (citing Moore v. State, 221 Ga. 636, 146 S.E.2d 895 (1966)).

[14]Leonard v. State, 269 Ga. 867, 871, 506 S.E.2d 853, 857 (1998); In Interest of A.S.M., 214 Ga. App. 668, 671, 448 S.E.2d 703, 706 (1994) ("An expert may have an opinion upon the facts testified to by other witnesses, but not their opinions. A witness' opinion must be his own and he cannot act as a mere conduit for the opinion of others."); Doctors Hosp. of Augusta, Inc. v. Bonner, 195 Ga. App. 152, 159, 392 S.E.2d 897, 903–904 (1990) ("A physician may not base his expert opinion solely on the hearsay opinion of another doctor, thereby acting as a mere conduit for the opinion of the first."); Mallard v. Colonial Life & Acc. Ins. Co., 173 Ga. App. 276, 276, 326 S.E.2d 6, 7 (1985) ("While an expert may base his opinion on facts provided to him by others, he may not simply restate the opinion of another expert.").

ing the jury to evaluate the expert's opinion substantially outweighs their prejudicial effect." This rule modifies an area in which there has been some inconsistency. On the one hand, several cases had held that while an expert may base his or her opinions in part upon hearsay, the expert should not be permitted to discuss the substance of this otherwise inadmissible hearsay.[15] This line of cases appears to have been motivated by the concern that to allow otherwise would simply create a vehicle for the admission of otherwise inadmissible hearsay by the simple expedient of having the expert purport to "rely" upon it.[16] On the other hand, other cases appeared to indicate that a jury should be permitted to consider such information so that a jury would be able to evaluate and weigh the credibility to be given to the expert's testimony.[17]

The language used in the statute is identical to the language of Rule 703, which, as explained by the Advisory Committee Notes to Rule 703, was designed to provide a presumption against the expert disclosing to the jury information which, although reasonably relied upon by the expert in forming the basis of the expert's opinion, is not itself admissible for any substantive purpose.[18] As also explained by the Advisory Committee Notes to Rule 703, when the information relied upon by the expert is not admissible for any substantive purpose, the trial court is to weigh the probative value of the information in assisting the jury to evaluate the expert's opinion against the prejudice that may result from the jury's potential misuse of the information for substantive purposes.[19]

The statute makes reference to this balancing test only when the evidence is presented by the proponent of the expert testimony, and not by the opposing party. As explained by the

---

[15]Coleman v. Fortner, 260 Ga. App. 373, 376, 579 S.E.2d 792, 795 (2003) (expert could properly testify about his use of tests performed by another expert in reaching his own opinion, but was restricted under hearsay rules from discussing the results or conclusions from such tests). This rule was often cited in the context of an expert basing his or her opinion on an authoritative text in the field. It was consistently held that while an expert may base his or her opinions on such texts, the expert could not simply recite the text for the jury in violation of the hearsay rules. See, e.g. Cantrell v. Northeast Georgia Medical Center, 235 Ga. App. 365, 508 S.E.2d 716

(1998); Austin v. Kaufman, 203 Ga. App. 704, 417 S.E.2d 660 (1992).

[16]See, e.g. Leonard v. State, 269 Ga. 867, 870, 506 S.E.2d 853, 856 (1998); Loper v. Drury, 211 Ga. App. 478, 482, 440 S.E.2d 32, 36 (1993).

[17]Roebuck v. State, 277 Ga. 200, 586 S.E.2d 651 (2003); Stewart v. State, 246 Ga. 70, 268 S.E.2d 906 (1980); King v. Browning, 246 Ga. 46, 268 S.E.2d 653 (1980); Blackburn v. State, 180 Ga. App. 436, 349 S.E.2d 286 (1986).

[18]Advisory Committee Notes to Rule 703.

[19]Advisory Committee Notes to Rule 703.

Advisory Committee Notes to Rule 703, the Rule does not prevent the presentation of the hearsay to the jury when offered by an adverse party, and otherwise inadmissible information may become admissible on rebuttal when the adversary has "opened the door" to the use of such information.[20] This new statute would thus be consistent with what has been the law in Georgia, which allowed an opposing party to cross-examine an expert regarding his or her reliance upon such hearsay so as to enable the jury to assess the credibility of the expert's opinions.[21]

§ 2:9   Reliability of expert opinion testimony

The 2000 amendments to Rule 702 of the Federal Rules of Evidence represent a codification of the general standards for assessing the "reliability" of expert testimony as enunciated in *Daubert* and its progeny.[1] The text of O.C.G.A. § 24–9–67.1(b) essentially traces the language of Rule 702.[2] As is discussed above, Georgia courts were hesitant, prior to 2005, to apply the factors enunciated by *Daubert* and its progeny in assessing the reliability, and hence admissibility, of expert testimony.[3] Indeed, several Court of Appeals decisions expressly declined the invitation to do so, reasoning that Georgia *Daubert* involved the application of Rule 702, which had not been adopted in Georgia.[4] Nonetheless, as is discussed below, even before the enactment of O.C.G.A. § 24–9–67.1(b), there was some similarity in analysis toward the end of ensuring expert testimony met certain minimum indicia of reliability so as to be admissible.

As the Georgia courts begin the process of applying O.C.G.A. § 24–9–67.1(b), this section will no doubt become significantly enriched with case law interpreting the requirements of this statute. However, until such time, the following subsections apply the law existing prior to the enactment of O.C.G.A. § 24–9–67.1(b) which represents an application of the principles set forth in the statute. A survey of the federal law in the Eleventh Circuit and the federal district courts in Georgia applying the principles enunciated in *Daubert* and Rule 702 is addressed in the following chapter.

---

[20]Advisory Committee Notes to Rule 703 of the Federal Rules of Evidence.

[21]Austin v. State, 275 Ga. 346, 566 S.E.2d 673 (2002).

[Section 2:9]

[1]See Chapter 1, § 1:7 for a discussion of Fed. R. Evid. 702 and its codification of Daubert and its progeny.

[2]See Chapter 1, § 1:7.

[3]See Chapter 1, § 1:8.

[4]See Chapter 1, § 1:8.

§ 2:10 Reliability of expert opinion testimony— Sufficiency of facts and data underlying opinions

O.C.G.A. § 24–9–67.1(b)(1) provides that expert testimony which is otherwise admissible must be "based upon sufficient facts or data which are or will be admitted into evidence at the hearing or trial[.]" In large measure, this requirement traces its federal counterpart of Rule 702 of the Federal Rules of Evidence. While this statute has been enacted only recently, the requirement that an expert's testimony be based upon sufficient facts or data is not necessarily novel to the Georgia courts. It has long been held that an expert's opinion must be based on something more than mere speculation or conjecture.[1] Where there is an insufficient factual basis underlying an expert's opinions, the opinion testimony amounts to little more than speculation and conjecture, and is thus without probative value and inadmissible.[2]

A good illustration of this analysis, as well as the difficulty in determining when the facts and data are "sufficient" enough so as to render an expert's opinion testimony admissible, may be found in Layfield v. Department of Transportation,[3] a case in which a motorist was injured after his vehicle ran off the road during a heavy rainstorm. On the issue of causation, an accident reconstructionist was offered to testify that the Department of Transportation's construction and maintenance of the roadway had allowed water to accumulate on the roadway, thus causing the motorist to lose control of his vehicle when it hydroplaned on the water. In upholding the exclusion of this opinion, the Court of Appeals observed that the accident reconstructionist had failed to

---

[Section 2:10]

[1]See, e.g. Allen v. Columbus Bank & Trust Co., 244 Ga. App. 271, 534 S.E.2d 917 (2000); Bankers Health & Life Ins. Co. v. Fryhofer, 114 Ga. App. 107, 111, 150 S.E.2d 365, 369 (1966) ("Speculation and conjecture by an expert is still speculation and conjecture[.]").

[2]Hobday v. Galardi, 266 Ga. App. 780, 598 S.E.2d 350 (2004), cert. denied, (Sept. 7, 2004) (when plaintiff's eye struck by debris at shooting range, expert testimony that targets improperly positioned due to risk of ricocheting bullets held inadmissible speculation because expert did not know what had hit plaintiff's eye or whether ricochet actually occurred); Georgia Transmission Corp. v. Barron, 255 Ga. App. 645, 566 S.E.2d 363 (2002) (expert's testimony on value of residential property, based on premise that property might be rezoned for commercial use sometime in the future, inadmissible speculation and conjecture); Allen v. Columbus Bank & Trust Co., 244 Ga. App. 271, 277–278, 534 S.E.2d 917, 924–925 (2000) (forensic accountant's conclusion that certain transactions may have been fraudulent and testimony regarding motives for the fraud not supported by any evidence in the record, and amounted "to nothing more than conjecture, which is not a sufficient basis for an expert's opinion.").

[3]Layfield v. Dept. of Transp., 271 Ga. App. 806, 611 S.E.2d 56 (2005), cert. granted, (Nov. 8, 2005) and judgment rev'd, 280 Ga. 848, 632 S.E.2d 135 (2006).

investigate any of the circumstances surrounding the accident, including how long and hard it had been raining, the point at which the motorist had lost control and the depth of the water on the roadway, and the effect of the water on the vehicle's tires.[4] The court also observed that the reconstructionist had failed to rule out alternative causes of the accident, such as the speed of the motorist's vehicle, the conduct of the motorist when he lost control of the vehicle, or the low tread on the vehicle's tires.[5] While the reconstructionist had placed heavy reliance on the fact that another driver had previously lost control of his vehicle on the same stretch of road during a rainstorm, the expert could not identify any similarities between the prior accident and the one at issue.[6] In upholding the exclusion of this testimony as "rank speculation," the court observed that the expert's conclusions hung from "tenuous threads," and that his testimony was nothing more than "a short-circuited analysis requiring quantum leaps of faith and logic[.]"[7]

Despite this harsh criticism from the Court of Appeals, Georgia's Supreme Court, in a split decision, reversed the lower appellate court, with the majority finding that the expert's opinion as to the cause of the crash was not speculative.[8] In so holding, the majority emphasized that some degree of speculation in an expert's opinion will not mandate exclusion of the expert's opinion, stating that "the appropriate standard for assessing the admissibility of the opinion of Ms. Layfield's expert is not whether it is speculative or conjectural to some degree, but whether it is wholly so."[9] The Court found that the issue as to whether the expert had "sufficient information from which to reach a probative opinion[]" did not go to the admissibility of his opinion, but

---

[4]Layfield v. Dept. of Transp., 271 Ga. App. 806, 807–808, 611 S.E.2d 56, 58 (2005), cert. granted, (Nov. 8, 2005) and judgment rev'd, 280 Ga. 848, 632 S.E.2d 135 (2006).

[5]Layfield v. Dept. of Transp., 271 Ga. App. 806, 808, 611 S.E.2d 56, 58 (2005), cert. granted, (Nov. 8, 2005) and judgment rev'd, 280 Ga. 848, 632 S.E.2d 135 (2006).

[6]Layfield v. Dept. of Transp., 271 Ga. App. 806, 808, 611 S.E.2d 56, 58–59 (2005), cert. granted, (Nov. 8, 2005) and judgment rev'd, 280 Ga. 848, 632 S.E.2d 135 (2006).

[7]Layfield v. Dept. of Transp., 271 Ga. App. 806, 808–809, 611 S.E.2d 56, 59 (2005), cert. granted, (Nov. 8, 2005) and judgment rev'd, 280 Ga. 848, 632 S.E.2d 135 (2006). See also Rios v.

Norsworthy, 266 Ga. App. 469, 597 S.E.2d 421 (2004) (in lawsuit arising out of motor vehicle accident, testimony of expert on commercial motor carrier industry standards that truck driver had failed to appropriately use mirrors to observe vehicles around him, was not attentive and alert, and that he was fatigued at time of accident either had "no factual basis or constitute[d] inadmissible speculation or conclusions without probative value.").

[8]Layfield v. Department of Transp., 280 Ga. 848, ___, 632 S.E.2d 135, 137 (2006).

[9]Layfield v. Department of Transp., 280 Ga. 848, ___, 632 S.E.2d 135, 137 (2006).

rather, presented a jury question as to the expert's credibility and the weight which should be assigned to his opinion.[10] The Court also found it significant that, in its procedural posture, the case had been before the trial court on summary judgment, and that the plaintiff was consequently entitled to have all evidence and inferences derived therefrom construed in her favor, even though a jury might not be persuaded by the presentation of her evidence.[11]

Notably, in arriving at its holding the Supreme Court did not address the admissibility standard of O.C.G.A. § 24–9–67.1 that expert opinion testimony be "based upon sufficient facts or data" in order to be admissible.[12] The three justice dissent strongly critiqued the majority's holding, stating flatly that "[u]nder the majority opinion, summary judgment will never be appropriate so long as a party can find an expert to make a statement supporting that party's case, even if that statement is nothing more than an unsupported conclusion."[13] The dissent agreed with the lower appellate court that the expert's conclusion as to the cause of the accident lacked a sufficient factual basis, and thus, had no probative value so as to create an issue of fact sufficient to survive summary judgment.[14]

In cases in which expert medical testimony is required to establish causation, such testimony must be based upon a reasonable probability, and expert testimony regarding only a *possible* link between conduct and an injury is insufficient to support a finding of causation.[15] Similarly, expert medical testimony regarding the need for future treatment must establish this need to be

---

[10]Layfield v. Department of Transp., 280 Ga. 848, ____, 632 S.E.2d 135, 138 (2006).

[11]Layfield v. Department of Transp., 280 Ga. 848, ____, 632 S.E.2d 135, 137 (2006); see also J.B. Hunt Transport, Inc. v. Brown, 236 Ga. App. 634, 512 S.E.2d 34 (1999) (testimony of an accident reconstructionist regarding how a motor vehicle accident occurred admitted over a challenge that the expert's opinion lacked a sufficient factual basis, where expert's testimony was based upon the deposition of the plaintiff, the investigating police officer's report, diagrams of the accident scene, photographs of damage to the plaintiff's vehicle, and data relating to vehicle speed obtained from a speed governor).

[12]See O.C.G.A. § 24–9–67.1(b)(1).

[13]Layfield v. Department of Transp., 280 Ga. 848, ____, 632 S.E.2d 135, 139 (2006) (Sears, J., dissenting).

[14]Layfield v. Department of Transp., 280 Ga. 848, ____, 632 S.E.2d 135, 139–140 (2006) (Sears, J., dissenting).

[15]Lewis v. Smith, 238 Ga. App. 6, 10, 517 S.E.2d 538, 542 (1999); Anthony v. Chambless, 231 Ga. App. 657, 500 S.E.2d 402 (1998) (physician's testimony that decedent may have survived aortic aneurysm had timely surgical procedure been performed speculation where physician did not take into account decedent's age, state of health, and possibility of post-operative complications).

beyond a mere possibility in order to support a claim for future medical expenses.[16]

§ 2:11   Reliability of expert opinion testimony— Reliability of principles and methods underlying methods

O.C.G.A. § 24–9–67.1(b)(2) provides that expert testimony must be "the product of reliable principles and methods[.]" This language traces the language of Rule 702 of the Federal Rules of Evidence. Given the statute's focus on the reliability of the methodology employed by the expert in arriving at his or her opinions, O.C.G.A. § 24–9–67.1(b)(2) also encapsulates the core holding of *Daubert*.[1] In enunciating a non-exhaustive list of factors courts may consider in assessing the reliability of an expert's methodology used to arrive at his or her conclusions, the *Daubert* Court cited the following factors: 1) whether the theory or technique has been, and can be, tested; 2) whether the theory or technique has been subjected to peer review and publication; 3) the known or potential error rate of the technique; 4) the existence and maintenance of standards controlling the technique's operation; and 5) whether the theory or technique has been generally accepted in the relevant scientific community.[2]

The concept that the methodology employed by an expert must be reliable is not novel to Georgia, and indeed, it has been expressly held by the Georgia Supreme Court that "[e]xpert testimony must be excluded if the testimony of the expert shows that the method used to reach the opinion is unreliable."[3] However, as discussed above, prior to the enactment of O.C.G.A.

---

[16]Womack v. Burgess, 200 Ga. App. 347, 408 S.E.2d 159 (1991) (expert testimony that likelihood of plaintiff's need for future surgical procedures was "50/50" insufficient to support claim for future medical expenses).

[Section 2:11]

[1]See Chapter 1, § 1:4 for a discussion of the *Daubert* decision.

[2]Daubert v. Merrell Dow Pharmaceuticals, Inc., 509 U.S. 579, 593–594, 113 S. Ct. 2786, 2796–2797, 125 L. Ed. 2d 469 (1993). In *Daubert*, the Court emphasized the fact that these factors are neither exclusive nor dispositive, and other factors may apply in making the admissibility determination. *Id. at 595.* In Kumho Tire

Co., Ltd. v. Carmichael, 526 U.S. 137, 150–151, 119 S. Ct. 1167, 1175, 143 L. Ed. 2d 238 (1999), the Supreme Court underscored the fact that the reliability assessment is a "flexible" inquiry, noting that the trial court has discretion in determining how to assess the reliability of the expert's testimony, and that the factors enunciated in *Daubert* may or may not be relevant to the inquiry depending upon the particular case. As is discussed in the next chapter, the federal courts have exercised this discretion in developing a wide variety of factors which may be helpful in assessing the reliability, and hence admissibility, of an expert's methodology.

[3]DuBois v. DuBois, 240 Ga. 314, 315, 240 S.E.2d 706, 707 (1977).

§ 24–9–67.1, several Georgia Court of Appeals decisions expressed an unwillingness to apply these specific factors toward the end of assessing the reliability of expert testimony.[4] Nonetheless, other decisions indicated a recognition of these factors in assessing the reliability of expert testimony.

Some courts have taken into account whether the expert's conclusions are supported by adequate testing. For instance, in Cromer v. Mulkey Enterprises, Inc.,[5] at issue was whether a physicist trained in biomechanics could offer testimony that a motor vehicle accident caused the plaintiff to suffer herniated disks and a torn rotator cuff. In upholding the exclusion of this testimony, the court found that there was "limited evidence in the record that the field of biomechanics includes a technique of determining if specific injuries result from specific accidents, let alone that that technique has reached a scientific stage of verifiable certainty."[6] Specifically, the court found it significant that there was no showing of any studies demonstrating the force and movement required to cause the specific types of injuries at issue.[7] Similarly, in Johnson v. Knebel,[8] at issue was whether a professional engineer trained in accident reconstruction could offer testimony that the forces involved in one of several motor vehicle accidents had caused the plaintiff's specific injuries. In reversing the Court of Appeals' allowing of such testimony, the Georgia Supreme Court relied, in part, upon the fact that the engineer had performed no tests or calculations in support of his conclusions.[9]

At other times, courts have considered whether the expert's conclusions are supported by relevant literature. For instance, the exclusion of the physicist's testimony in Cromer v. Mulkey Enterprises, Inc. was based also in part on the fact that there was no presentation of any authoritative publication supporting the physicist's proferred testimony.[10] By contrast, in Brown v. Hove, the court found that a neuroradiologist could offer testimony as to whether a motor vehicle accident had caused the plaintiff's injuries, relying in part upon the radiologist's identification of "tests and experiments, reported in radiological literature

---

[4]See Chapter 1, § 1:8.

[5]Cromer v. Mulkey Enterprises, Inc., 254 Ga. App. 388, 562 S.E.2d 783 (2002).

[6]Cromer v. Mulkey Enterprises, Inc., 254 Ga. App. 388, 393, 562 S.E.2d 783, 787 (2002).

[7]Cromer v. Mulkey Enterprises, Inc., 254 Ga. App. 388, 393, 562 S.E.2d

783, 787 (2002).

[8]Johnson v. Knebel, 267 Ga. 853, 485 S.E.2d 451 (1997).

[9]Johnson v. Knebel, 267 Ga. 853, 858–859, 485 S.E.2d 451, 455 (1997).

[10]Cromer v. Mulkey Enterprises, Inc., 254 Ga. App. 388, 393, 562 S.E.2d 783, 787 (2002).

with which he was required to be familiar," which provided support for his conclusions.[11]

The error rate of a technique or procedure, too, has informed the courts' decisions regarding the admissibility of expert testimony predicated on the same. For instance, in Evans v. State,[12] at issue was whether a physician could offer testimony as to what a defendant's blood alcohol content was based upon the application of a certain formula. In upholding the exclusion of such testimony, the court observed that the formula had a 20% margin of error, yielding an inherently inaccurate means by which to assess the subject's blood alcohol content.[13] In Viau v. State,[14] at issue was whether a physician could offer testimony that a machine designed to measure breath alcohol content may have produced an inaccurate reading, given the effect the subject's body temperature may have had on the test results. The court affirmed the exclusion of such testimony based in part on the fact that, with no margin of error having been provided, it was impossible to ascertain whether an elevated body temperature could have accounted for a test result exceeding twice the legal limit.[15]

§ 2:12   Reliability of expert opinion testimony—Reliable application of principles and methods to the facts of the case

O.C.G.A. § 24–9–67.1(b)(3) provides that, in order for an expert's testimony to be admissible, the expert must have "applied the principles and methods reliably to the facts of the case." Like subsection (b)(2), the language in this subsection is identical to that employed by Rule 702 of the Federal Rules of Evidence. Again, while, prior to the enactment of this statute, several Georgia Court of Appeals decisions refused to apply the language of Rule 702 because the rule had not been adopted by the Georgia legislature,[1] other decisions did apply the principle that not only must the expert's methodology and principles be reliable, but that the principles and methods must also be reliably applied to the facts of the case before the court.[2]

While the scientific or technical principles employed by an

---

[11]Brown v. Hove, 268 Ga. App. 732, 735, 603 S.E.2d 63, 65 (2004), cert. denied, (Jan. 10, 2005).

[12]Evans v. State, 253 Ga. App. 71, 558 S.E.2d 51 (2001).

[13]Evans v. State, 253 Ga. App. 71, 77–78, 558 S.E.2d 51, 56 (2001).

[14]Viau v. State, 260 Ga. App. 96, 579 S.E.2d 52 (2003).

[15]Viau v. State, 260 Ga. App. 96, 99, 579 S.E.2d 52, 56 (2003).

[Section 2:12]

[1]See Chapter 1, § 1:8.

[2]For instance, in Viau v. State, 260 Ga. App. 96, 579 S.E.2d 52 (2003), a physician was offered to testify that the results of an alcohol breath test can overestimate the subject's alcohol

expert may be reliable in and of themselves, such principles must be capable of being reliably applied to the facts of the case in order to be admissible. An extreme example may readily illustrate this point. While there is little doubt that the principles of Newtonian physics provide a reliable basis for determining the direction and velocity of moving objects, the application of Newtonian physics to determine the economic losses suffered by a party in a commercial dispute would be wholly without value.[3] Moreover, it is not enough for an expert to merely assert that certain principles or methods can be reliably applied to the facts of the case, the expert "must be able to relate the objective means used in applying the expert knowledge" to answer the question before the court.[4]

---

concentration when the subject's body temperature is elevated by virtue of the ambient temperature or physical exertion. In upholding the exclusion of this testimony, the court observed that there was no showing that the subject's temperature had remained elevated at the time she took the breath test. Viau v. State, 260 Ga. App. 96, 99, 579 S.E.2d 52 (2003) In Robinson v. State, 272 Ga. 131, 527 S.E.2d 845 (2000), a toxicologist was offered to testify that cocaine metabolites had been found in the victim's blood for the purpose of supporting the defendant's argument that the victim had acted aggressively towards the defendant, thus providing the defendant with a provocation defense to the charge of voluntary manslaughter. In upholding the exclusion of this testimony, the court observed that the expert could not say what, if any, effect the cocaine had on the victim. Robinson v. State, 272 Ga. 131, 133, 527 S.E.2d 845 (2000) In DuBois v. DuBois, 240 Ga. 314, 240 S.E.2d 706 (1977), an economist was offered to testify regarding the amount which would be spent for child support by hypothetical families for the purpose of determining a former spouse's entitlement to child support. In upholding the exclusion of this testimony, the court observed that the economist's figures were based on income and disposable income figures which were not "anywhere near" the amount of income earned by, or disposable in-

come enjoyed by, the other spouse. DuBois v. DuBois, 240 Ga. 314, 315, 240 S.E.2d 706 (1977)

[3]In Daubert v. Merrell Dow Pharmaceuticals, Inc., 509 U.S. 579, 113 S. Ct. 2786, 125 L. Ed. 2d 469 (1993), the Court used a similarly extreme example to illustrate the concept of the reliable application of a scientific principle to the facts of the case by observing:

> [t]he study of the phases of the moon, for example, may provide valid scientific "knowledge" about whether a certain night was dark, and if darkness is a fact in issue, the knowledge will assist the trier of fact. However (absent creditable grounds supporting such a link), evidence that the moon was full on a certain night will not assist the trier of fact in determining whether an individual was unusually likely to have behaved irrationally on that night.

Id. at 591.

[4]Johnson v. Knebel, 267 Ga. 853, 858, 485 S.E.2d 451, 455 (1997). This holding corresponds with the analysis of General Elec. Co. v. Joiner, 522 U.S. 136, 118 S. Ct. 512, 139 L. Ed. 2d 508 (1997), wherein the Court stated:

> Trained experts commonly extrapolate from existing data. But nothing in either Daubert or the Federal Rules of Evidence requires a district court to admit opinion evidence that is connected to existing data only by the ipse dixit of the expert. A court may conclude that there is simply too great an analytical gap between the data and the opinion proferred.

An example of the application of this principle may be found in JOHNSON V. KNEBEL,[5] where at issue was whether a professional engineer trained in accident reconstruction could offer testimony that the forces involved in one of several motor vehicle accidents had caused the plaintiff's specific injuries. In reversing the admission of this testimony, the court engaged in an analysis of the proper scope of the engineer's testimony, while at the same time, touching upon the issue of whether the expert could reliably apply the engineering principles in which he had been trained to the determination as to which of the several accidents had caused the plaintiff's specific injuries. The court observed that the engineer's expertise likely did enable him to reconstruct the vehicle's courses, rates of travel, and points of impact, from which the expert could likely infer the approximate speeds of the vehicles at the time of impact.[6] However, the court found that the question as to which of the several collisions caused the plaintiff's specific injuries could not be answered by simple engineering analysis, but required the application of principles, such as human physiology, anatomic structure, biomechanics, and osteology—principles about which the engineer had no knowledge.[7] Thus, while the engineering principles in which the expert was trained enabled him to provide reliable testimony on matters pertaining to accident reconstruction, there was no showing that these principles could be reliably applied so as to enable the expert to render conclusions about which of several collisions caused the plaintiff's specific injuries.

Whereas *Knebel* addressed, in a sense, the reliable application of *principles* to the facts of the case before the court, the case of Cromer v. Mulkey Enterprises, Inc.[8] addressed the reliable application of specific *methods* to the facts of the case. Following in the wake of *Knebel*, wherein the Georgia Supreme Court indicated that the application of principles of biomechanics was needed to address the issues of causation and injury, at issue in *Cromer* was whether a physicist with training in biomechanics could offer testimony that a motor vehicle accident had caused the plaintiff to suffer herniated disks and a torn rotator cuff. The physicist had based his testimony in part upon tests performed upon cadavers and volunteers in low-speed accidents. In upholding the exclusion of this testimony, the court, significantly, did not take issue with the reliability of these tests themselves. Rather, the court observed that there was no showing as to how

---

Id. at 146.

[5]Johnson v. Knebel, 267 Ga. 853, 485 S.E.2d 451 (1997).

[6]Johnson v. Knebel, 267 Ga. 853, 858, 485 S.E.2d 451, 455 (1997).

[7]Johnson v. Knebel, 267 Ga. 853, 858, 485 S.E.2d 451, 455 (1997).

[8]Cromer v. Mulkey Enterprises, Inc., 254 Ga. App. 388, 562 S.E.2d 783 (2002).

these tests would "answer the question" precisely before the court, namely, whether the plaintiff's injuries had been caused by a specific motor vehicle accident.[9]

---

[9]Cromer v. Mulkey Enterprises, Inc., 254 Ga. App. 388, 393, 562 S.E.2d 783, 787 (2002).

Chapter 3

Admissibility Determinations By The Federal Courts

> **KeyCite®:** Cases and other legal materials listed in KeyCite Scope can be researched through the KeyCite service on Westlaw®. Use KeyCite to check citations for form, parallel references, prior and later history, and comprehensive citator information, including citations to other decisions and secondary materials.

---

§ 3:1   General considerations

Rule 702 of the Federal Rules of Evidence provides the modern touchstone for assessing the admissibility of expert testimony. Incorporating several of the principles enunciated in *Daubert* and its progeny,[1] Rule 702 provides:

> [i]f scientific, technical, or other specialized knowledge will assist the trier of fact to understand the evidence or to determine a fact in issue, a witness qualified as an expert by knowledge, skill, experience, training, or education may testify thereto in the form of an opinion or otherwise, if (1) the testimony is based upon sufficient facts or data, (2) the testimony is the product of reliable principles and methods, and (3) the witness has applied the principles and methods reliably to the facts of the case.

As construed by the Eleventh Circuit, this Rule provides three overarching requirements to the admissibility of expert testimony: 1) qualification; 2) reliability; and 3) helpfulness. Indeed, the fol-

---

[Section 3:1]

[1]See Chapter 1, §§ 1:4 through 1:7 for a discussion of the Daubert "trilogy" and an overview of the status of modern federal law.

lowing tri-part test has been developed by the Eleventh Circuit as an outline for assessing the admissibility of expert testimony:

> 1) the expert is qualified to testify competently regarding the matters he intends to address; 2) the methodology by which the expert reaches his conclusions is sufficiently reliable as determined by the sort of inquiry mandated in Daubert; and 3) the testimony assists the trier of fact, through the application of scientific, technical, or specialized expertise, to understand the evidence or to determine a fact in issue.[2]

As established by Daubert, the trial court has a duty to assess expert testimony prior to its admission to the jury in order to ensure that the testimony is both relevant and reliable.[3] This "gatekeeping" role is founded in part upon the fact that "[e]xpert evidence can be both powerful and quite misleading because of the difficulty in evaluating it[,]"[4] and exists to ensure that the expert "employs in the courtroom the same level of intellectual rigor that characterizes the practice of an expert in the relevant

---

[2]City of Tuscaloosa v. Harcros Chemicals, Inc., 158 F.3d 548, 562 (11th Cir. 1998). See also Club Car, Inc. v. Club Car (Quebec) Import, Inc., 362 F.3d 775 (11th Cir. 2004), cert. denied, 543 U.S. 1002, 125 S. Ct. 618, 160 L. Ed. 2d 461 (2004); U.S. v. Frazier, 387 F.3d 1244 (11th Cir. 2004), cert. denied, 544 U.S. 1063, 125 S. Ct. 2516, 161 L. Ed. 2d 1114 (2005); Hudgens v. Bell Helicopters/Textron, 328 F.3d 1329 (11th Cir. 2003); Williamson Oil Co., Inc. v. Philip Morris USA, 346 F.3d 1287 (11th Cir. 2003); U.S. v. Hansen, 262 F.3d 1217 (11th Cir. 2001); Toole v. Baxter Healthcare Corp., 235 F.3d 1307 (11th Cir. 2000); Maiz v. Virani, 253 F.3d 641 (11th Cir. 2001); Allison v. McGhan Medical Corp., 184 F.3d 1300 (11th Cir. 1999).

[3]Daubert v. Merrell Dow Pharmaceuticals, Inc., 509 U.S. 579, 589, 113 S. Ct. 2786, 2795, 125 L. Ed. 2d 469 (1993).

[4]Daubert v. Merrell Dow Pharmaceuticals, Inc., 509 U.S. 579, 595, 113 S. Ct. 2786, 2798, 125 L. Ed. 2d 469 (1993); see also U.S. v. Frazier, 387 F.3d 1244, 1260 (11th Cir. 2004), cert. denied, 544 U.S. 1063, 125 S. Ct. 2516, 161 L. Ed. 2d 1114 (2005) (in observing that the importance of the trial court's gatekeeping role cannot be "overstated" due to the powerful,

and potentially misleading, nature of expert testimony, the court noted that "no other kind of witness is free to opine about a complicated matter without any firsthand knowledge of the facts in the case, and based upon otherwise inadmissible hearsay if the facts or data are 'of a type reasonably relied upon by experts in the particular field in forming opinions or inferences on the subject.' ").

On remand, the Ninth Circuit in Daubert v. Merrell Dow Pharmaceuticals, Inc., 43 F.3d 1311 (9th Cir. 1995), cautioned against those experts whose opinions are for hire, observing that a court should be mindful as to "whether the experts are proposing to testify about matters growing naturally and directly out of research they have conducted independent of the litigation, or whether they have developed their opinions expressly for purposes of testifying." In Allison v. McGhan Medical Corp., 184 F.3d 1300, 1319–1320 (11th Cir. 1999), this consideration informed the Eleventh Circuit's exclusion of an expert's causation testimony in a case where the expert had changed his opinion regarding the cause of a patient's illness only after meeting with the patient's attorney five years after he had last seen the patient.

field."[5] As stated by the Eleventh Circuit, a trial court's gatekeeping role serves the purpose of "insur[ing] that speculative and unreliable opinions do not reach the jury."[6] A trial court's gatekeeping role is not intended to supplant the role of the jury. Cross-examination, the presentation of contrary evidence, and instruction on burdens of proof remain the "traditional and appropriate means of attacking shaky but admissible evidence."[7] Rather, a trial court is to screen expert testimony which is both irrelevant and unreliable "because of its inability to assist in factual determinations, its potential to create confusion, and its lack of probative value."[8] "The courtroom is not the place for scientific guesswork, even of the inspired sort. Law lags science; it does not lead it."[9]

A trial court's determination as to the admissibility of an expert's testimony is subject to an abuse of discretion standard, and will not be reversed by the appellate court unless it was manifestly erroneous.[10] This deferential standard of review exists even when the trial court's determination as to the admissibility

---

[5]Kumho Tire Co., Ltd. v. Carmichael, 526 U.S. 137, 152, 119 S. Ct. 1167, 1176, 143 L. Ed. 2d 238 (1999); McClain v. Metabolife Intern., Inc., 401 F.3d 1233, 1237 (11th Cir. 2005).

[6]McClain v. Metabolife Intern., Inc., 401 F.3d 1233, 1237 (11th Cir. 2005)

[7]Daubert v. Merrell Dow Pharmaceuticals, Inc., 509 U.S. 579, 596, 113 S. Ct. 2786, 2798, 125 L. Ed. 2d 469 (1993); Allison v. McGhan Medical Corp., 184 F.3d 1300, 1311 (11th Cir. 1999).

[8]Allison v. McGhan Medical Corp., 184 F.3d 1300, 1311–1312 (11th Cir. 1999). In *Allison,* the court observed that "[w]hile meticulous Daubert inquiries may bring judges under criticism for donning white coats and making determinations that are outside their field of expertise, the Supreme Court has obviously deemed this less objectionable than dumping a barrage of questionable scientific evidence on a jury, who would likely be even less equipped than the judge to make reliability and relevance determinations and more likely than the judge to be awestruck by the expert's

mystique." *Id. at 1311.* See also Rider v. Sandoz Pharmaceuticals Corp., 295 F.3d 1194, 1197 (11th Cir. 2002) ("The *Daubert* trilogy, in shifting the focus to the kind of empirically supported, rationally explained reasoning required in science, has greatly improved the quality of the evidence upon which juries base their verdicts.").

[9]Rider v. Sandoz Pharmaceuticals Corp., 295 F.3d 1194, 1202 (11th Cir. 2002) (quoting Rosen v. Ciba–Geigy Corp., 78 F.3d 316, 319 (7th Cir. 1996)).

[10]General Elec. Co. v. Joiner, 522 U.S. 136, 141, 118 S. Ct. 512, 139 L. Ed. 2d 508 (1997); McClain v. Metabolife Intern., Inc., 401 F.3d 1233 (11th Cir. 2005); Club Car, Inc. v. Club Car (Quebec) Import, Inc., 362 F.3d 775, 780 (11th Cir. 2004), cert. denied, 543 U.S. 1002, 125 S. Ct. 618, 160 L. Ed. 2d 461 (2004); U.S. v. Frazier, 387 F.3d 1244, 1258 (11th Cir. 2004), cert. denied, 544 U.S. 1063, 125 S. Ct. 2516, 161 L. Ed. 2d 1114 (2005); McCorvey v. Baxter Healthcare Corp., 298 F.3d 1253, 1256 (11th Cir. 2002); Maiz v. Virani, 253 F.3d 641, 662 (11th Cir. 2001).

of the expert testimony is outcome determinative.[11] As recognized by the Eleventh Circuit, the trial court, by virtue of its first-hand familiarity with the factual and evidentiary issues in the case, is often in the best position to make the admissibility determination.[12] At the same time, the discretion afforded a trial court in determining *how* to assess the reliability of expert testimony does not permit a trial court the discretion of determining *whether* to assess the reliability of expert testimony.[13] The trial court's abdication of its gatekeeping duty itself constitutes an abuse of discretion,[14] and neither the difficulty of the task nor the court's lack of experience relieves the court of performing its gatekeeping function.[15] The Eleventh Circuit has consistently held that

---

[11]U.S. v. Brown, 415 F.3d 1257, 1266 (11th Cir. 2005), cert. denied, 126 S. Ct. 1570, 164 L. Ed. 2d 305 (U.S. 2006); Allison v. McGhan Medical Corp., 184 F.3d 1300, 1306 (11th Cir. 1999).

[12]U.S. v. Brown, 415 F.3d 1257, 1265–1266 (11th Cir. 2005), cert. denied, 126 S. Ct. 1570, 164 L. Ed. 2d 305 (U.S. 2006) (" 'Inherent in this abuse of discretion standard is the firm recognition that there are difficult evidentiary rulings that turn on matters uniquely within the purview of the district court, which has first-hand access to documentary evidence and is physically proximate to testifying witnesses and the jury.' . . . Being at the trial as the proceedings occur and the evidence unfolds, a trial court has an advantageous familiarity with the proceedings and 'may have insights not conveyed by the record' about the evidence and the issues relating to it.'"); Allison v. McGhan Medical Corp., 184 F.3d 1300, 1311 (11th Cir. 1999) ("Because of the painstaking analyses which district courts undertake in making these admissibility determinations, their efforts are well deserving of the deference that the Supreme Court has accorded through the abuse of discretion standard enunciated in *Joiner*.").

In addition to the trial court's unique familiarity with the factual and evidentiary issues, the courts have recognized that an additional reason for this deferential standard is that

"[e]videntiary issues often do not involve a 'generally recurring, purely legal matter' or a 'question readily resolved by reference to general legal principles and standards alone.' " U.S. v. Brown, 415 F.3d 1257, 1265 (11th Cir. 2005), cert. denied, 126 S. Ct. 1570, 164 L. Ed. 2d 305 (U.S. 2006). Thus, "[h]ow to apply evidentiary rules in all possible scenarios is not a matter amenable to close regulation, because the circumstances that arise during trial 'involve multifarious, fleeting, special, narrow facts that utterly resist generalization.' " *Id.*

[13]McClain v. Metabolife Intern., Inc., 401 F.3d 1233, 1238 (11th Cir. 2005).

[14]McClain v. Metabolife Intern., Inc., 401 F.3d 1233, 1238 (11th Cir. 2005).

[15]Allison v. McGhan Medical Corp., 184 F.3d 1300, 1310 (11th Cir. 1999); Kumho Tire Co., Ltd. v. Carmichael, 526 U.S. 137, 158–159, 119 S. Ct. 1167, 1179, 143 L. Ed. 2d 238 (1999) (Scalia, J., concurring) ("[T]rial court discretion in choosing the manner of testing expert reliability is not discretion to abandon the gatekeeping function. I think it worth adding that it is not discretion to perform the function inadequately. Rather, it is discretion to choose among reasonable means of excluding expertise that is fausse and science that is junky."); General Elec. Co. v. Joiner, 522 U.S. 136, 148, 118 S. Ct. 512, 520, 139 L. Ed. 2d 508 (1997) (Breyer, J., concur-

the trial court must take an active role in ensuring that speculative and unreliable opinions do not reach the jury.[16]

§ 3:2 Qualifications

Whether a witness is qualified as an expert in the field in which he or she is offering opinions is the "threshold" determination for the court under Rule 702.[1] Whether a witness is so qualified is an evidentiary determination to be made by the court, and is subject to the same abuse of discretion standard applicable to all determinations pertaining to the admissibility of expert testimony made by the court in the exercise of its gatekeeping role.[2] Irrespective of the content of his or her opinion, the expert must be shown to be competent to offer that opinion before the testimony is admissible.[3]

Rule 702 contemplates several ways in which a witness may be qualified to offer expert opinion testimony in a particular field by providing that a witness may be qualified by "knowledge, skill, experience, training, or education[.]"[4] For instance, an expert lacking in practical experience may nonetheless be sufficiently qualified by virtue of his or her educational background.[5] Conversely, a witness with little in the way of formal education on a topic may be qualified as an expert by virtue of his or her practical experience in the field.[6] One need not necessarily be a specialist in an area in order to provide expert testimony on the

---

ring) ("Of course, neither the difficulty of the task nor any comparative lack of expertise can excuse the judge from exercising the 'gatekeeper' duties that the Federal Rules of Evidence impose[.]").

[16]McClain v. Metabolife Intern., Inc., 401 F.3d 1233, 1238 (11th Cir. 2005); Rink v. Cheminova, Inc., 400 F.3d 1286, 1291 (11th Cir. 2005), cert. denied, 126 S. Ct. 419, 163 L. Ed. 2d 320 (U.S. 2005); McDowell v. Brown, 392 F.3d 1283 (11th Cir. 2004); Allison v. McGhan Medical Corp., 184 F.3d 1300, 1310 (11th Cir. 1999); McGee v. Evenflo Co., Inc., 2003 WL 23350439 (M.D. Ga. 2003), aff'd, 143 Fed. Appx. 299 (11th Cir. 2005).

[Section 3:2]

[1]Everett v. Georgia–Pacific Corp., 949 F. Supp. 856, 857 (S.D. Ga. 1996).

[2]U.S. v. Brown, 415 F.3d 1257, 1264–1266 (11th Cir. 2005), cert. denied, 126 S. Ct. 1570, 164 L. Ed. 2d

305 (U.S. 2006); Quiet Technology DC-8, Inc. v. Hurel–Dubois UK Ltd., 326 F.3d 1333, 1340–1341 (11th Cir. 2003); Wheat v. Sofamor, S.N.C., 46 F. Supp. 2d 1351, 1356 (N.D. Ga. 1999).

[3]Smith v. Ortho Pharmaceutical Corp., 770 F. Supp. 1561, 1566 (N.D. Ga. 1991).

[4]U.S. v. Frazier, 387 F.3d 1244, 1261 (11th Cir. 2004), cert. denied, 544 U.S. 1063, 125 S. Ct. 2516, 161 L. Ed. 2d 1114 (2005) (observing that an expert may be qualified in various ways).

[5]U.S. v. Bennett, 368 F.3d 1343 (11th Cir. 2004) (witness with educational background in chemistry qualified to provide analysis of methamphetamine and theoretical drug yield despite limited field experience in addressing such matters).

[6]U.S. v. Frazier, 387 F.3d 1244, 1261 (11th Cir. 2004), cert. denied, 544 U.S. 1063, 125 S. Ct. 2516, 161 L. Ed.

topic provided the witness is able to demonstrate sufficient familiarity with the topic such that the witness' testimony is of assistance to the jury.[7]

The point at which a non-specialist becomes sufficiently familiar with an area outside his or her area of specialization to offer expert testimony on the topic is not capable of ready definition, and this determination rests largely within the trial court's discretion. For instance, in Smith v. Ortho Pharmaceuticals, the court found a physician and a pharmacologist qualified to testify that an unborn infant's exposure to a spermicide had caused her birth defects, despite the fact that they had little or no formal education or experience in the fields of genetics, epidemiology, or teratology. The court found it significant, however, that in conjunction with the training which they did possess, the physician and pharmacologist had reviewed literature regarding the link between the spermicide and birth defects.[8] By contrast, in Everett v. Georgia–Pacific Corp., the court found that a physician with no specialized knowledge or training in toxicology was not qualified to testify that the plaintiff's exposure to a substance was the cause of his maladies.[9] Post-Daubert, courts have had a tendency to more closely scrutinize the expert's education, training, and experience in an effort to ensure that the expert is not testifying beyond the scope of his or her expertise.[10]

It is not sufficient for an expert to merely "rest upon his

2d 1114 (2005) (observing that experience alone may be sufficient to qualify a witness as an expert on a particular topic); Mullins v. Crowell, 228 F.3d 1305, 1316 n.20, (11th Cir. 2000) (foreman with experience in supervising craft-workers of all types qualified to provide expert testimony as to plaintiff's ability to perform job functions, despite the fact that he was not a medical, labor, or vocational expert).

[7]Smith v. Ortho Pharmaceutical Corp., 770 F. Supp. 1561, 1568 (N.D. Ga. 1991) ("a physician need not be a specialist in the area of his testimony to be considered an expert under Rule 702.").

[8]Smith v. Ortho Pharmaceutical Corp., 770 F. Supp. 1561, 1567 (N.D. Ga. 1991); see also Wheat v. Sofamor, S.N.C., 46 F. Supp. 2d 1351, 1356–1357 (N.D. Ga. 1999) (despite "serious concerns," court found anesthesiologist with no specialization in back ailments, their causes, or orthopedics

qualified to provide testimony that surgical device was cause of plaintiff's pain).

[9]Everett v. Georgia–Pacific Corp., 949 F. Supp. 856 (S.D. Ga. 1996) (observing that a physician "must, at a minimum, posses some specialized knowledge about the field in which he is to testify.").

[10]See, e.g. U.S. v. Brown, 415 F.3d 1257 (11th Cir. 2005), cert. denied, 126 S. Ct. 1570, 164 L. Ed. 2d 305 (U.S. 2006) (witness holding doctorate in plant pathology with some educational training in chemistry not qualified to provide testimony as to the similarity of chemical compounds to those regulated as controlled substances); Hall v. United Ins. Co. of America, 367 F.3d 1255 (11th Cir. 2004) (upholding trial court's determination that licensed professional counselor not qualified to opine on individual's mental capacity); U.S. v. Duque, 176 F.R.D. 691, 694–695 (N.D. Ga. 1998), aff'd, 199 F.3d 443

laurels."[11] An expert may not simply cite his or her "experience" as a basis for the opinion testimony; rather, the expert must be able to "explain how that experience leads to the conclusion reached, why that experience is a sufficient basis for the opinion, and how that experience is reliably applied to the facts."[12] Courts have cautioned against conflating the analysis between an expert's qualifications and the reliability or helpfulness of the expert's testimony, observing that while there is some "overlap" in these modes of analysis, they nonetheless remain conceptually distinct.[13] Thus, while an expert's impressive qualifications may bear upon the reliability of the expert's testimony, such qualifications are not a "guarantor" of the reliability of the methodology employed by the expert in arriving at his opinions.[14] A well-qualified expert may still offer testimony which is unreliable, thus necessitating a trial court's examination of the methodology employed by the expert, and the relevance of the expert's opinion, prior to making an admissibility determination.[15]

(11th Cir. 1999) (upholding trial court's finding that while polygraph examiner was qualified to testify about the administration of the polygraph examination at issue, he was not qualified to testify about the reliability of polygraph tests and their ability to accurately detect deception, as the appropriate field to comment upon such matters consists of "scientists engaged in psychological testing[.]"); McLendon v. Georgia Kaolin Co., Inc., 841 F. Supp. 415, 418 (M.D. Ga. 1994) (testimony of an "economic geologist" on value of kaolin in the subject tract of land excluded where, despite academic credentials, witness had minimal experience in evaluating the mineral for commercial use, the processes used to make the mineral commercially viable, or the market value of the mineral during the relevant time period).

[11]McDowell v. Brown, 392 F.3d 1283, 1298 (11th Cir. 2004) (citing Clark v. Takata Corp., 192 F.3d 750, 759 n.5, (7th Cir. 1999) (a " 'supremely qualified expert cannot waltz into the courtroom and render opinions unless those opinions are based on some recognized scientific method.' ").

[12]U.S. v. Frazier, 387 F.3d 1244, 1261 (11th Cir. 2004), cert. denied, 544 U.S. 1063, 125 S. Ct. 2516, 161 L. Ed. 2d 1114 (2005) (citing Advisory Committee Notes to Rule 702).

[13]U.S. v. Frazier, 387 F.3d 1244, 1260 (11th Cir. 2004), cert. denied, 544 U.S. 1063, 125 S. Ct. 2516, 161 L. Ed. 2d 1114 (2005); Quiet Technology DC-8, Inc. v. Hurel-Dubois UK Ltd., 326 F.3d 1333, 1341 (11th Cir. 2003).

[14]Quiet Technology DC-8, Inc. v. Hurel-Dubois UK Ltd., 326 F.3d 1333, 1341 (11th Cir. 2003).

[15]Quiet Technology DC-8, Inc. v. Hurel-Dubois UK Ltd., 326 F.3d 1333, 1341 (11th Cir. 2003); see also McDowell v. Brown, 392 F.3d 1283 (11th Cir. 2004). In McDowell, the court observed that a " 'supremely qualified expert cannot waltz into the courtroom and render opinions unless those opinions are based on some recognized scientific method.' " Id. at 1298 (citing Clark v. Takata Corp., 192 F.3d 750, 759 n.5, (7th Cir. 1999)). "Something doesn't become 'scientific knowledge' just because it's uttered by a scientist; nor can an expert's self-serving assertion that his conclusions were 'derived by the scientific method' be deemed conclusive." Id. at 1299 (citing Daubert v. Merrell Dow Pharmaceuticals, Inc., 43 F.3d 1311, 1315–1316 (9th Cir. 1995)). Similarly, in Allison v. McGhan Medical Corp., 184 F.3d 1300 (11th

§ 3:3   Reliable methodology

Daubert held that, in order to be admissible, expert testimony must not only be relevant, but reliable as well.[1] At the heart of this holding is the notion that an expert's opinion should be based on "more than subjective belief and unsupported speculation."[2] Prior to admitting an expert's testimony before a jury, *Daubert* charged the trial court with the task of examining the reasoning and methodology underlying an expert's conclusions to assess their reliability and determine whether they can be properly applied to the facts at issue.[3] Toward the end of ensuring that an expert's testimony rests on "good grounds," the *Daubert* Court articulated several factors which may be considered by the trial court. These factors include: 1) whether the expert's theory or technique has been, and can be, tested; 2) whether the theory or technique has been subject to peer review and publication; 3) the known or potential rate of error; 4) whether standards exist or are maintained to control the technique's operation; and 5) whether the theory or technique has been generally accepted in the relevant scientific community.[4]

The *Daubert* Court emphasized that the reliability inquiry is "a flexible one," and that other considerations may well apply.[5] In *Kumho Tire*, the Court again emphasized the flexible nature of this inquiry by pointing out that the factors articulated in *Daubert* did not constitute a "definitive checklist,"[6] and that, depending on the particular issues and facts involved in any given case, one or several of *Daubert's* factors may or may not apply.[7] These factors, then, may be properly viewed as indicia, or "badges," of reliability—helpful, but not necessarily dispositive, tools at the trial

---

Cir. 1999), the court observed that the gatekeeping role requires a trial court to " 'determine whether the evidence is genuinely scientific, as distinct from being unscientific speculation offered by a genuine scientist.' " *Id.* at 1316–1317 (citing Rosen v. Ciba–Geigy Corp., 78 F.3d 316, 319 (7th Cir. 1996)).

[Section 3:3]

[1] Daubert v. Merrell Dow Pharmaceuticals, Inc., 509 U.S. 579, 589, 113 S. Ct. 2786, 2795, 125 L. Ed. 2d 469 (1993).

[2] Daubert v. Merrell Dow Pharmaceuticals, Inc., 509 U.S. 579, 590, 113 S. Ct. 2786, 2795, 125 L. Ed. 2d 469 (1993).

[3] Daubert v. Merrell Dow Pharmaceuticals, Inc., 509 U.S. 579, 592–593, 113 S. Ct. 2786, 2796, 125 L. Ed. 2d 469 (1993).

[4] Daubert v. Merrell Dow Pharmaceuticals, Inc., 509 U.S. 579, 593–94, 113 S. Ct. 2786, 2796–2797, 125 L. Ed. 2d 469 (1993).

[5] Daubert v. Merrell Dow Pharmaceuticals, Inc., 509 U.S. 579, 594–595, 113 S. Ct. 2786, 2797–2798, 125 L. Ed. 2d 469 (1993).

[6] Kumho Tire Co., Ltd. v. Carmichael, 526 U.S. 137, 150, 119 S. Ct. 1167, 1175, 143 L. Ed. 2d 238 (1999).

[7] Kumho Tire Co., Ltd. v. Carmichael, 526 U.S. 137, 151, 119 S. Ct. 1167, 1175, 143 L. Ed. 2d 238 (1999).

court's disposal to assist it in assessing the reliability of the reasoning and methodology underlying an expert's conclusions. As noted by the Court in *Kumho Tire*, a trial court has considerable "leeway" in deciding *how* to determine whether particular expert testimony is reliable.[8] Indeed, as discussed below, the federal courts have employed several additional modes of analysis, dependent on the particular facts and circumstances of the case, in assessing the reliability of an expert's proffered testimony.

The burden of demonstrating the reliability of the principles and methodologies underlying an expert's opinions and conclusions rests on the proponent of the testimony.[9] The reliability of the expert's testimony must be established by a preponderance of the evidence.[10] The proponent may not simply ask the court to take "the expert's word for it," and an expert's mere assurances that he or she has employed a reliable methodology are insufficient to establish this burden.[11] A court should not admit an expert's opinion testimony that is "connected to existing data only by the *ipse dixit* of the expert."[12]

§ 3:4 Reliable methodology—Testing and error rate

The first factor proposed by *Daubert* for use in assessing the reliability of expert testimony is whether the theory or technique upon which the expert's conclusions are based has been, and can be, tested.[1] As noted by the Supreme Court: "Scientific methodology today is based on generating hypotheses and testing them to see if they can be falsified; indeed, this methodology is what dis-

---

[8]Kumho Tire Co., Ltd. v. Carmichael, 526 U.S. 137, 152, 119 S. Ct. 1167, 1176, 143 L. Ed. 2d 238 (1999); see also Quiet Technology DC-8, Inc. v. Hurel–Dubois UK Ltd., 326 F.3d 1333, 1341 (11th Cir. 2003) (Daubert "factors do not exhaust the universe of considerations that may bear on the reliability of a given expert opinion, and a federal court should consider any additional factors that may advance its Rule 702 analysis."); U.S. v. Brown, 415 F.3d 1257, 1267–1268 (11th Cir. 2005), cert. denied, 126 S. Ct. 1570, 164 L. Ed. 2d 305 (U.S. 2006).

[9]McClain v. Metabolife Intern., Inc., 401 F.3d 1233, 1238 (11th Cir. 2005); Siharath v. Sandoz Pharmaceuticals Corp., 131 F. Supp. 2d 1347, 1351 (N.D. Ga. 2001), aff'd, 295 F.3d 1194 (11th Cir. 2002).

[10]Allison v. McGhan Medical Corp., 184 F.3d 1300, 1306 (11th Cir. 1999).

[11]McClain v. Metabolife Intern., Inc., 401 F.3d 1233, 1239 (11th Cir. 2005) (citing Advisory Committee Notes to Rule 702); McGee v. Evenflo Co., Inc., 2003 WL 23350439 (M.D. Ga. 2003), aff'd, 143 Fed. Appx. 299 (11th Cir. 2005).

[12]General Elec. Co. v. Joiner, 522 U.S. 136, 146, 118 S. Ct. 512, 519, 139 L. Ed. 2d 508 (1997); McClain v. Metabolife Intern., Inc., 401 F.3d 1233, 1239 (11th Cir. 2005).

[Section 3:4]

[1]Daubert v. Merrell Dow Pharmaceuticals, Inc., 509 U.S. 579, 593, 113 S. Ct. 2786, 2796, 125 L. Ed. 2d 469 (1993).

tinguishes science from other fields of human inquiry."[2] Scientific testing is commonly employed to test and ascertain the validity and reliability of a particular theory or hypothesis. As explained by the Court in *Daubert*, validity addresses the issue as to whether a scientific principle supports what it purports to show, and reliability addresses the issue as to whether application of the principle produces consistent results.[3] Another relevant factor in assessing reliability, and one which commonly arises in the context of scientific testing, is the error rate of a particular test or technique.[4] Closely-related to this inquiry will be the existence and maintenance of standards controlling the test's or technique's operation.[5]

As observed in *Kumho Tire*, the *Daubert* factors, including testing, are not limited to those fields that are strictly "scientific," but apply to the "technical" fields, such as engineering, as well.[6] At the same time, it is recognized that, unlike those fields of laboratory science which customarily employ rigorous and replicable testing methods and protocols, fields such as engineering may often involve more "idiosyncratic" testing methods.[7] The fact that a specific test is not capable of replication is not necessarily indicative that the testing was not reliably performed, particularly where the performance of the testing is dependent upon case-specific facts.[8] Nonetheless, courts have rejected the argument that "experience alone" is sufficient so as to enable an engineer to arrive at a reliable conclusion, observing that "it is

---

[2]Daubert v. Merrell Dow Pharmaceuticals, Inc., 509 U.S. 579, 593, 113 S. Ct. 2786, 2796, 125 L. Ed. 2d 469 (1993).

[3]Daubert v. Merrell Dow Pharmaceuticals, Inc., 509 U.S. 579, 590 n.9, 113 S. Ct. 2786, 2795, 125 L. Ed. 2d 469 (1993).

[4]Daubert v. Merrell Dow Pharmaceuticals, Inc., 509 U.S. 579, 594, 113 S. Ct. 2786, 2797, 125 L. Ed. 2d 469 (1993).

[5]Daubert v. Merrell Dow Pharmaceuticals, Inc., 509 U.S. 579, 594, 113 S. Ct. 2786, 2797, 125 L. Ed. 2d 469 (1993).

[6]Kumho Tire Co., Ltd. v. Carmichael, 526 U.S. 137, 141, 147, 119 S. Ct. 1167, 143 L. Ed. 2d 238 (1999).

[7]McGee v. Evenflo Co., Inc., 2003 WL 23350439 (M.D. Ga. 2003), aff'd, 143 Fed. Appx. 299 (11th Cir. 2005).

[8]In addressing a statistician's methodology in a antitrust action, the Eleventh Circuit observed in City of Tuscaloosa v. Harcros Chemicals, Inc., 158 F.3d 548 (11th Cir. 1998), as follows:

Economic or statistical analysis of markets alleged to be collusive, for instance, cannot readily be repeatedly tested, because each such case is widely different from other such cases and because such cases cannot be made the subject of repeated experiments. The proper inquiry regarding the reliability of the methodologies implemented by economic and statistical experts in this context is not whether other experts, faced with similar facts, have repeatedly reached the same conclusions (because there will be few or no cases that have presented substantially similar facts). Instead, the proper inquiry is whether the techniques utilized by the experts are reliable in light of the factors (other than testing) identified in *Daubert* and in light of other factors

well known that engineers routinely rely upon established principles of physics, material sciences, and industrial design and often utilize technologically sophisticated and carefully calibrated testing methods and devices when arriving at their conclusions."[9]

It is not always required that an expert personally perform his or her own testing, and reliance on published tests performed by others may provide an expert with a sufficient foundation for his or her conclusions.[10] However, it is important that the testing which is performed approximate "real world" conditions, and testing which fails to do so is properly rejected as failing to set forth a "valid" connection between the testing and the matter before the court.[11] The existence of testing in support of an expert's conclusions is an important consideration in determining whether the expert's theories of causation are little more than speculation, and whether they can be established beyond a mere possibility and with the requisite degree of certainty.[12] For instance, expert testimony that a product's design was the cause of a

---

bearing on the reliability of the methodologies. *Id. at 566, n.25;* see also Webster v. Fulton County, Georgia, 85 F. Supp. 2d 1375, 1376 (N.D. Ga. 2000) (replicability of testing not the sine qua non of admissibility).

[9]McGee v. Evenflo Co., Inc., 2003 WL 23350439 (M.D. Ga. 2003), aff'd, 143 Fed. Appx. 299 (11th Cir. 2005) (citations and internal quotations omitted). Citing Milanowicz v. The Raymond Corp., 148 F. Supp. 2d 525, 532 (D.N.J. 2001), the court in *McGee* observed:

> It seems exactly backwards that experts who purport to rely on general engineering principles and practical experience might escape screening by the district court simply by stating that their conclusions were not reached by any particular method or technique. The moral of [this] approach would be, the less factual support for an expert's opinion, the better.

*Id. at *5.* See also U.S. v. Frazier, 387 F.3d 1244, 1262 (11th Cir. 2004), cert. denied, 544 U.S. 1063, 125 S. Ct. 2516, 161 L. Ed. 2d 1114 (2005) (citing Clark v. Takata Corp., 192 F.3d 750, 758 (7th Cir. 1999) ("In determining whether an expert's testimony is reliable, the Daubert factors are applicable in cases where an expert eschews

reliance on any rigorous methodology and instead purports to base his opinion merely on 'experience' or 'training.'").

[10]McGee v. Evenflo Co., Inc., 2003 WL 23350439 (M.D. Ga. 2003), aff'd, 143 Fed. Appx. 299 (11th Cir. 2005) ("Of course, hands-on testing or review of data gathered by others may sometimes serve as a reliable methodology and may serve as a substitute for actual testing[.]"); see also Siharath v. Sandoz Pharmaceuticals Corp., 131 F. Supp. 2d 1347, 1356–1359 (N.D. Ga. 2001), aff'd, 295 F.3d 1194 (11th Cir. 2002) (reviewing epidemiological studies relied upon by experts to ascertain whether such testing provided support for experts' theories of causation).

[11]Dale v. General Motors Corp., 109 F. Supp. 2d 1376, 1379–1381 (N.D. Ga. 1999) (expert's testing, purporting to demonstrate how seat belt defect caused belt to unlatch during motor vehicle accident, rejected as an unreliable "parlor trick," as testing did not approximate real world conditions).

[12]See, e.g. Siharath v. Sandoz Pharmaceuticals Corp., 131 F. Supp. 2d 1347, 1358 (N.D. Ga. 2001), aff'd, 295 F.3d 1194 (11th Cir. 2002) ("The absence of epidemiological support raises the question of whether the

patient's injuries has been excluded where no testing had been performed to rule out other potential causes of the patient's injuries.[13] Similarly, expert testimony regarding the feasibility of an alternative, and presumably safer, product design has been excluded where it was not supported by any testing demonstrating the viability of such a design.[14] In excluding this testimony, the court reasoned that "the history of engineering and science is filled with finely conceived ideas that are unworkable in practice."[15]

Expert testimony may be excluded where the testing or procedure upon which it is based is incapable of being tested so as to demonstrate that it is capable of yielding accurate results.[16] Expert testimony based upon a test or procedure may also be excluded where the rate of error for the test is demonstrably high,[17] or where there are insufficient controls on the testing so as to ensure that it produced accurate results.[18] Courts may consider "curious" or "skewed" testing results in determining

---

causation opinions of Plaintiffs' experts are merely speculative and not based on scientific knowledge.").

[13]McCorvey v. Baxter Healthcare Corp., 298 F.3d 1253, 1256 1257 (11th Cir. 2002) (upholding exclusion of engineer's testimony that catheter was defective, observing that the engineer "did not test alternative designs for the catheter; did not talk to medical personnel; was unable to cite scientific literature in support of his theories; and did not consider or test possibilities for failure that could have come from sources outside the product, such as the effect of improper storage conditions, contaminants, or human error."); see also Wheat v. Sofamor, S.N.C., 46 F. Supp. 2d 1351 (N.D. Ga. 1999); Lawson v. Smith and Nephew Richards, Inc., 1999 WL 1129677 (N.D. Ga. 1999); Baker v. Smith and Nephew Richards, Inc., 1999 WL 1129650 (N.D. Ga. 1999). These three latter cases all involved the same expert, an anesthesiologist, who opined that a certain surgical device used in back surgeries was the cause of the various plaintiffs' post-surgical complications and pain. While purporting to rely on a "differential diagnosis" in arriving at his conclusions, the court nevertheless excluded the testimony because the expert had failed to perform or obtain

any of the test results from radiological and neurological examinations essential in making such diagnoses and ruling out alternative causes of the plaintiffs' complications and pain.

[14]McGee v. Evenflo Co., Inc., 2003 WL 23350439 (M.D. Ga. 2003), aff'd, 143 Fed. Appx. 299 (11th Cir. 2005).

[15]McGee v. Evenflo Co., Inc., 2003 WL 23350439 (M.D. Ga. 2003), aff'd, 143 Fed. Appx. 299 (11th Cir. 2005) (citations omitted).

[16]U.S. v. Henderson, 409 F.3d 1293 (11th Cir. 2005), cert. denied, 126 S. Ct. 1331, 164 L. Ed. 2d 47 (U.S. 2006).

[17]U.S. v. Henderson, 409 F.3d 1293, 1303 (11th Cir. 2005), cert. denied, 126 S. Ct. 1331, 164 L. Ed. 2d 47 (U.S. 2006) (observing that the error rate for polygraph testing was "not much more reliable than random chance"); see also Hester v. City of Milledgeville, 598 F. Supp. 1456, 1463 (M.D. Ga. 1984) (discussing accuracy rates of various polygraph questioning techniques).

[18]U.S. v. Henderson, 409 F.3d 1293, 1303 (11th Cir. 2005), cert. denied, 126 S. Ct. 1331, 164 L. Ed. 2d 47 (U.S. 2006). In City of Tuscaloosa v. Harcros Chemicals, Inc., 158 F.3d 548 (11th Cir. 1998), the court par-

whether a testing procedure has been reliably applied.[19] These principles have frequently been applied in cases considering the admissibility of polygraph testing or expert testimony based on such testing. For instance, in United States v. Henderson,[20] the Eleventh Circuit upheld the exclusion of polygraph testing results based in part upon a magistrate court's finding that the theories underlying polygraphy were incapable of being adequately tested. Observing that a polygraph measures a subject's physiological responses to the posing of certain questions, with the examiner then interpreting this physiological data and opining on whether the subject was lying, the magistrate court found that there was no data showing that a subject's physiological responses were due to stress or anxiety associated with lying as opposed to some other cause.[21] Moreover, it was observed that the error rate for polygraph testing was "not much more reliable than random chance," and that the examiner's compliance with established testing protocols for administering polygraphs was self-imposed, with effective countermeasures existing so as to enable the subject of the testing to defeat accurate results.[22]

---

tially upheld the exclusion of a statistician's testimony in an action which alleged a price-fixing scheme in Alabama. Despite the geographic limitations of the allegations, the statistician included in his model sales data in Florida. The court upheld the exclusion of testimony based upon this model, observing that the inclusion of transactions which were not part of the alleged price-fixing conspiracy had "skewed" the calculations. *Id. at 566–567.*

[19]U.S. v. Gilliard, 133 F.3d 809 (11th Cir. 1998). In *Gilliard,* it was noted that polygraph results can yield "false positives," wherein innocent persons are determined to be lying about having committed an offense, and "false negatives," wherein guilty persons appear to be innocent. *Id. at 814.* The court observed that there are several questioning techniques employed in administering polygraph tests, some producing more accurate results than others. In upholding the exclusion of the polygraph evidence, the court relied in part upon the testimony of an expert that the polygraph

test in this case had combined two different questioning techniques, with the result that test results were "skewed" in favor of a finding that a criminal defendant was honest in denying the commission of an offense. *Id.*

See also U.S. v. Brown, 415 F.3d 1257 (11th Cir. 2005), cert. denied, 126 S. Ct. 1570, 164 L. Ed. 2d 305 (U.S. 2006) (upholding the exclusion of expert's testimony which produced "skewed" and "bizarre and curious" results entirely inconsistent with the results obtained by other experts).

[20]U.S. v. Henderson, 409 F.3d 1293 (11th Cir. 2005), cert. denied, 126 S. Ct. 1331, 164 L. Ed. 2d 47 (U.S. 2006).

[21]U.S. v. Henderson, 409 F.3d 1293, 1303 (11th Cir. 2005), cert. denied, 126 S. Ct. 1331, 164 L. Ed. 2d 47 (U.S. 2006).

[22]U.S. v. Henderson, 409 F.3d 1293, 1303 (11th Cir. 2005), cert. denied, 126 S. Ct. 1331, 164 L. Ed. 2d 47 (U.S. 2006).

§ 3:5   Reliable methodology—Peer review and publication

Whether a theory or technique has been subjected to peer review and publication is another factor bearing upon the reliability assessment.[1] The fact that a theory or technique has not been published is not dispositive.[2] *Daubert* recognized that some "well-grounded but innovative" theories very well may not be published, and others may be of too limited interest to have been published.[3] Nonetheless, publication, or lack thereof, is a relevant consideration, as "submission to the scrutiny of the scientific community is a component of 'good science,' in part because it increases the likelihood that substantive flaws in methodology will be detected."[4]

Courts have frequently looked to whether an expert's theories are supported by the relevant literature in the expert's particular field in making determinations as to the admissibility of the expert's testimony.[5] For instance, courts have frequently considered the findings of studies published in medical journals and texts in assessing the reliability of an expert's testimony that there is a causal connection between a plaintiff's ailments and exposure to a certain substance.[6] In making admissibility determinations, courts have found it significant that there is a

---

[Section 3:5]

[1]Daubert v. Merrell Dow Pharmaceuticals, Inc., 509 U.S. 579, 593, 113 S. Ct. 2786, 2797, 125 L. Ed. 2d 469 (1993).

[2]See, e.g. U.S. v. Brown, 415 F.3d 1257 (11th Cir. 2005), cert. denied, 126 S. Ct. 1570, 164 L. Ed. 2d 305 (U.S. 2006) (upholding admissibility of expert's testimony despite the fact that government produced no papers or studies in which the methodology or opinions of experts had been subjected to peer review).

[3]Daubert v. Merrell Dow Pharmaceuticals, Inc., 509 U.S. 579, 593, 113 S. Ct. 2786, 2797, 125 L. Ed. 2d 469 (1993).

[4]Daubert v. Merrell Dow Pharmaceuticals, Inc., 509 U.S. 579, 593–594, 113 S. Ct. 2786, 125 L. Ed. 2d 469 (1993).

[5]See, e.g. U.S. v. Great Lakes Dredge & Dock Co., 259 F.3d 1300 (11th Cir. 2001) (affirming admissibility of expert's testimony in part upon showing that methodology employed by expert in quantifying damages had been peer reviewed and accepted for publication).

[6]See, e.g. McClain v. Metabolife Intern., Inc., 401 F.3d 1233 (11th Cir. 2005) (considering epidemiological studies published in the New England Journal of Medicine and other publications for purpose of determining whether expert's theories of causal nexus between the plaintiffs' strokes and ingestion of weight-loss supplement are recognized); Allison v. McGhan Medical Corp., 184 F.3d 1300 (11th Cir. 1999) (considering published studies in assessing whether expert's theories of causal nexus between plaintiff's ailments and silicone breast implants are recognized); Siharath v. Sandoz Pharmaceuticals Corp., 131 F. Supp. 2d 1347 (N.D. Ga. 2001), aff'd, 295 F.3d 1194 (11th Cir. 2002) (considering epidemiological studies and medical treatises in determining whether expert's theories of causal nexus between the plaintiffs' strokes and ingestion of drug designed to suppress postpartum lactation are recognized).

lack of published studies supporting an expert's theories,[7] or that the weight of the published studies that do exist do not support an expert's theories.[8] An expert's failure to consider relevant publications in the field of industry can be an important factor in assessing the reliability of an expert's testimony.[9]

§ 3:6 Reliable methodology—General acceptance

Daubert overruled the requirement established in Frye v. United States[1] that, as a prerequisite to a scientific theory or technique being admitted as competent evidence, such theory or technique must have obtained the status of being generally accepted in the scientific community.[2] Nonetheless, while rejected as the "absolute prerequisite," the Court recognized that a theory or technique's general acceptance has a bearing on the reliability of an expert's methodology, and is one of several factors a trial court may consider in assessing the reliability of an expert's

---

[7]U.S. v. Gilliard, 133 F.3d 809, 815 (11th Cir. 1998) (upholding the exclusion of expert's testimony on defendant's polygraph test results in part because of the "paucity of tests and published studies addressing the validity" of the polygraph technique); Jack v. Glaxo Wellcome, Inc., 239 F. Supp. 2d 1308 (N.D. Ga. 2002) ("The court is also persuaded by the complete lack of any peer reviewed analysis purporting to establish a link between bupropion and panic attack or panic disorder. This factor is far from conclusive. Nevertheless, the complete silence on the subject from the medical community is persuasive.").

[8]Allison v. McGhan Medical Corp., 184 F.3d 1300, 1316 (11th Cir. 1999) (upholding exclusion of expert's opinion that silicone breast implants had caused the plaintiff's ailments in part because the expert's four studies cited in support of his theory "were in direct contrast to over twenty other epidemiological studies which found no statistical correlation between silicone breast implants and systemic disease"); Dale v. General Motors Corp., 109 F. Supp. 2d 1376 (N.D. Ga. 1999) (observing that published studies on the forces required to cause "inertial unlatching" of seatbelt did not support expert's theory that seatbelt unlatched during motor vehicle accident).

[9]McGee v. Evenflo Co., Inc., 2003 WL 23350439 (M.D. Ga. 2003), aff'd, 143 Fed. Appx. 299 (11th Cir. 2005) (expert, in concluding that child safety seat was defectively designed, did not research or incorporate into his opinions recognized federal motor vehicle safety standards, National Highway Traffic Safety Administration standards, or other industry standards, and could not state whether his opinions were consistent or inconsistent with such standards); Baker v. Smith and Nephew Richards, Inc., 1999 WL 1129650 (N.D. Ga. 1999) (rejecting expert's theories of causation in part because expert had relied on no learned treatises in reaching his conclusions, and expert's approach to determining causation had not itself been subjected to peer review).

[Section 3:6]

[1]Frye v. U.S., 293 F. 1013 (App. D.C. 1923).

[2]Daubert v. Merrell Dow Pharmaceuticals, Inc., 509 U.S. 579, 587–588, 113 S. Ct. 2786, 2793–2794, 125 L. Ed. 2d 469 (1993).

methodology.[3] As noted by *Daubert*, a known technique which has attracted only "minimal support" within the scientific community "may be properly viewed with skepticism."[4]

A theory or technique's general acceptance continues to be strong indicia of its reliability.[5] Indeed, where the reliability of a principle or method is generally recognized, a probing assessment into the reliability of the principle or method very well may not be indicated.[6] The general acceptance inquiry is not necessarily limited to the methodology underlying the expert's conclusions, but can extend to the expert's conclusions themselves.[7] Published studies in the pertinent field are commonly considered in a court's assessment of a theory or technique's general accep-

---

[3]Daubert v. Merrell Dow Pharmaceuticals, Inc., 509 U.S. 579, 594, 113 S. Ct. 2786, 2797, 125 L. Ed. 2d 469 (1993).

[4]Daubert v. Merrell Dow Pharmaceuticals, Inc., 509 U.S. 579, 594, 113 S. Ct. 2786, 2797, 125 L. Ed. 2d 469 (1993).

[5]See, e.g. U.S. v. Brown, 415 F.3d 1257, 1267 (11th Cir. 2005), cert. denied, 126 S. Ct. 1570, 164 L. Ed. 2d 305 (U.S. 2006) (upholding admissibility of expert's testimony where only Daubert factor satisfied was opinion and methodology's general acceptance); U.S. v. Abreu, 406 F.3d 1304, 1307 (11th Cir. 2005) (in upholding admissibility of fingerprint evidence, court noted the widespread acceptance of the reliability and admissibility of such evidence in other jurisdictions, noting that the trial court did not err "in giving greater weight to the general acceptance factor."); Quiet Technology DC-8, Inc. v. Hurel–Dubois UK Ltd., 326 F.3d 1333, 1343 (11th Cir. 2003) (in upholding admissibility of expert's opinions based on calculations input into a software program, the court observed that "the application and use of this kind of software is fairly widespread in the aviation industry."); Jack v. Glaxo Wellcome, Inc., 239 F. Supp. 2d 1308 (N.D. Ga. 2002) (upholding the exclusion of expert's testimony in part because no showing that medical community had accepted expert's effort to link use of drug with plaintiff's ailments).

[6]Kumho Tire Co., Ltd. v. Carmichael, 526 U.S. 137, 152, 119 S. Ct. 1167, 1176, 143 L. Ed. 2d 238 (1999) (recognizing that trial court has "discretionary authority needed to both avoid unnecessary 'reliability' proceedings in ordinary cases where the reliability of an expert's methods is properly taken for granted, and to require appropriate proceedings in the less usual or more complex cases where cause for questioning the expert's reliability arises."); McClain v. Metabolife Intern., Inc., 401 F.3d 1233, 1239 (11th Cir. 2005). In *McClain*, a case involving the issue of whether the plaintiffs' ingestion of a weight-loss supplement was the cause their strokes, the court observed that "[t]here is rarely a reason for a court to consider opinions that medical doctors routinely and widely recognize as true, like cigarette smoking causes lung cancer and heart disease, too much alcohol causes cirrhosis of the liver, and that the ingestion of sufficient amounts of arsenic causes death." *Id.* at 1239, n. 5. "The court need not undertake an extensive Daubert analysis on the general toxicity question when the medical community recognizes that the agent causes the type of harm a plaintiff alleges." *Id. at 1239.*

[7]General Elec. Co. v. Joiner, 522 U.S. 136, 146, 118 S. Ct. 512, 519, 139 L. Ed. 2d 508 (1997) (observing that "conclusions and methodology are not entirely distinct from one another."); Allison v. McGhan Medical Corp., 184

tance.[8] Indeed, the fact that a theory has been rejected in an "overwhelming majority" of studies mitigates against a finding that the theory enjoys general acceptance.[9]

As recognized by *Daubert,* an issue which arises in assessing a theory or technique's general acceptance is what constitutes the "relevant" scientific community to be considered.[10] This issue was considered in United States v. Duque,[11] a case involving the admissibility of polygraph evidence. The defendant's expert, a polygraph examiner who had administered the actual test, testified that the technique used was reliable. However, the government's expert, a psychologist, offered testimony that the technique was not generally accepted as capable of producing accurate results, and that there was general agreement that there is no unique physiological response to deception. In upholding the exclusion of the polygraph test results, the court found that the "relevant community consists of scientists engaged in psychological testing, not polygraph examiners."[12] In a similar vein, the fact that a theory or technique is generally accepted within a particular discipline is of little value where it has not been demonstrated that the discipline itself is reliable.[13]

Another issue which arises in assessing a theory or technique's general acceptance is the theory or technique's "particular degree of acceptance" within the relevant community."[14] In other words, how widely accepted must a theory be in order for it to be "gener-

---

F.3d 1300, 1315–1316 (11th Cir. 1999) (upholding the exclusion of expert opinion that was "out of sync with the conclusions in the overwhelming majority" of studies presented to the court); Wheat v. Sofamor, S.N.C., 46 F. Supp. 2d 1351, 1358 (N.D. Ga. 1999) (observing that, where an expert reaches a conclusion not shared by others in the field, a court is justified in being "wary that the methods have not been faithfully applied.").

[8]See, e.g. McClain v. Metabolife Intern., Inc., 401 F.3d 1233, 1245–1249 (11th Cir. 2005) (considering epidemiological studies published in the New England Journal of Medicine and other publications).

[9]Allison v. McGhan Medical Corp., 184 F.3d 1300, 1316 (11th Cir. 1999). In *Allison,* the court upheld the exclusion of an expert's opinion that silicone breast implants had caused the plaintiff's complained of symptoms, observing that the expert's "four stud-

ies were in direct contrast to over twenty other epidemiological studies which found no statistical correlation between silicone breast implants and systemic disease, strong evidence that a consensus exists in the general scientific community that no correlation exists.").

[10]Daubert v. Merrell Dow Pharmaceuticals, Inc., 509 U.S. 579, 594, 113 S. Ct. 2786, 2797, 125 L. Ed. 2d 469 (1993).

[11]U.S. v. Duque, 176 F.R.D. 691 (N.D. Ga. 1998), aff'd, 199 F.3d 443 (11th Cir. 1999).

[12]U.S. v. Duque, 176 F.R.D. 691, 694 (N.D. Ga. 1998), aff'd, 199 F.3d 443 (11th Cir. 1999).

[13]Kumho Tire Co., Ltd. v. Carmichael, 526 U.S. 137, 151, 119 S. Ct. 1167, 1175, 143 L. Ed. 2d 238 (1999) (citing astrology and necromancy as disciplines of "suspect" reliability).

[14]Daubert v. Merrell Dow

ally" accepted? It is perhaps impossible to formulate a precise line of demarcation as to when a theory or technique formulation moves into this realm. However, this consideration may be informed by the treatment of the theory or technique's admissibility in other jurisdictions,[15] or by "weighing the relative findings" of studies and other materials presented to the court.[16] Courts have cautioned against the admissibility of theories still in their "infancy."[17] "The courtroom is not the place for scientific guesswork, even of the inspired sort. Law lags science; it does not lead it."[18]

§ 3:7   Reliable methodology—Sufficiency of facts and data upon which opinions are based

In establishing the trial court's "gatekeeping" function of ensuring the methodology underlying an expert's conclusions are sufficiently reliable, the *Daubert* Court sought to preclude from a jury's consideration expert testimony which is based on little more than speculation.[1] In *Kumho Tire*, the Supreme Court refined this test by observing that an essential component of this inquiry is that the expert have a sufficient factual basis for his or her conclusions.[2] This admonition has been expressly incorporated

---

Pharmaceuticals, Inc., 509 U.S. 579, 594, 113 S. Ct. 2786, 2797, 125 L. Ed. 2d 469 (1993).

[15]U.S. v. Abreu, 406 F.3d 1304, 1307 (11th Cir. 2005) (observing the "widespread acceptance" of fingerprint evidence in other jurisdictions).

[16]Allison v. McGhan Medical Corp., 184 F.3d 1300, 1315 (11th Cir. 1999) ("While weighing the relative findings of the studies may seem to be a resurrection of the Frye standard (general acceptance in the scientific community), courts have noted that Daubert's suggested criteria to examine whether the theory has attained general acceptance within the scientific community . . . does just that.").

[17]Allison v. McGhan Medical Corp., 184 F.3d 1300, 1316 (11th Cir. 1999). In *Allison,* an expert attempting to establish a connection between silicone breast implants and the plaintiff's symptoms was questioned as to whether his theory was generally accepted. The expert testified in response that "the relevant community

is just now beginning to weigh in on the subject[,]" that the science on this topic was in its "dawning era," and that data establishing this connection "won't be around for ten to fifteen years." In upholding the exclusion of the expert's testimony, that court stated that while the expert's "theories may be proven in the future, and although he has strong beliefs regarding silicone related pathology, we find that his testimony is based more on personal opinion than on scientific knowledge." *Id. at 1319.*

[18]Rider   v.   Sandoz Pharmaceuticals Corp., 295 F.3d 1194, 1202 (11th Cir. 2002) (quoting Rosen v. Ciba–Geigy Corp., 78 F.3d 316, 319 (7th Cir. 1996)).

[Section 3:7]

[1]Daubert v. Merrell Dow Pharmaceuticals, Inc., 509 U.S. 579, 590, 113 S. Ct. 2786, 2795, 125 L. Ed. 2d 469 (1993).

[2]Kumho Tire Co., Ltd. v. Carmichael, 526 U.S. 137, 149, 119 S. Ct. 1167, 1175, 143 L. Ed. 2d 238

into Rule 702, which provides that, in order to be admissible, expert testimony must be based on "sufficient facts or data."

In a sense, this requirement imposes an obligation upon the expert to perform and show his or her "homework." "Conjecture by a qualified expert is of course worthy of careful attention, but the courtroom is 'not the place for guesswork, even of the inspired sort.' "[3] It is one thing for an expert to postulate theories regarding how something may have occurred; however, it is quite another for an expert to reliably testify as to how something did in fact occur in the matter before the court. The failure to perform indicated tests, run necessary calculations, or otherwise develop a concrete basis for one's opinions can leave such opinions without the requisite factual support.[4] The failure to show how an opinion as to likelihood has been, and can be, reliably quantified can render such evidence unreliable.[5] However plausible an expert's theory may be, it remains "subjective opinion and unsupported conjecture" absent a sufficient showing of how the facts of the case at hand lend support to the expert's theories.[6]

Application of these principles commonly occur in the context

---

(1999).

[3]McGee v. Evenflo Co., Inc., 2003 WL 23350439 (M.D. Ga. 2003), aff'd, 143 Fed. Appx. 299 (11th Cir. 2005) (quoting Rosen v. Ciba–Geigy Corp., 78 F.3d 316, 319 (7th Cir. 1996)) (internal punctuation omitted).

[4]See, e.g. Dale v. General Motors Corp., 109 F. Supp. 2d 1376, 1381 (N.D. Ga. 1999). In *Dale,* the trial court excluded an expert's testimony that a seatbelt had unlatched during the collision at issue, observing that the expert had "not demonstrated how his theory relates to the factual situation at hand[.]" *Id. at 1381.* Specifically, the court observed that, in support of his theory, the expert had not quantified the forces involved in the collision, analyzed their duration, determined the relative forces between the occupant and the seatbelt, or compared those forces involved in the subject matter collision to those in his experiments wherein the seatbelt did unlatch. *Id.*

[5]See, e.g. U.S. v. Frazier, 387 F.3d 1244, 1265 (11th Cir. 2004), cert. denied, 544 U.S. 1063, 125 S. Ct. 2516, 161 L. Ed. 2d 1114 (2005). In *Frazier,* the court upheld the exclusion of a forensic investigator's testimony that there was no forensic substantiation of the allegations of rape because no hair or seminal fluids were found at the crime scene as "expected." The court noted that the expert could not show offer any "hard" information regarding the rate of transfer of such items during sexual conduct, or explain how his experience or literature relied upon supported his "expectancy" opinion. *Id. at 1265.*

[6]McGee v. Evenflo Co., Inc., 2003 WL 23350439 (M.D. Ga. 2003), aff'd, 143 Fed. Appx. 299 (11th Cir. 2005). In *McGee,* a mechanical engineer was offered to opine that a child safety seat was defectively designed, and that such defect led to the child's injuries during a motor vehicle accident. Observing that the engineer's opinions were not supported by any testing or data, the court concluded that while the engineer's "conclusions may be altogether accurate, he has done nothing in this case to show that they are." *Id.*

See also Hall v. United Ins. Co. of America, 367 F.3d 1255 (11th Cir. 2004) (exclusion of opinion of licensed professional counselors retained as an expert to testify that individual not

of medical causation testimony. For instance, the testimony of a physician as to the cause of a plaintiff's ailments has been held unreliable where the opinion is not supported by the results of medical tests or procedures commonly obtained for the diagnosis of such conditions.[7] The failure of a physician to review a patient's medical history, or eliminate other causes of the patient's medical condition, can similarly result in a finding that the physician lacks sufficient data to make a reliable diagnosis.[8] It may not be enough for a physician to merely rely upon "medical logic" in support of his theories of causation; rather, these theories must be supported by empirical evidence.[9] Absent sufficient factual data supporting opinions of medical causation, a physician's theories amount to little more than assumptions or conclusory allegations.[10]

§ 3:8   Reliable methodology—Reliable application of methodologies to the case–specific facts

As a precondition for admissibility of an expert's testimony, Rule 702 of the Federal Rules of Evidence requires the expert to have "applied the principles and methods reliably to the facts of the case." In other words, it is not enough that the principles and methods employed by the expert are, as a general proposition, reliable or capable of reliable application. Rather, the expert must be able to demonstrate that, in arriving at his or her conclusions, otherwise reliable principles or methods were reliably ap-

---

competent to execute document upheld in part because counselor had not explained how he arrived at his opinion or how he came to an opinion contrary to that of the individual's own treating psychiatrist, who had concluded that individual was competent).

[7]Wheat v. Sofamor, S.N.C., 46 F. Supp. 2d 1351, 1359–139 (N.D. Ga. 1999) (physician's testimony that surgical instrumentation was the cause of patient's pain found unreliable where physician failed to obtain the results of neurological or radiological tests typically used to confirm such diagnoses).

[8]Everett v. Georgia–Pacific Corp., 949 F. Supp. 856, 858–859 (S.D. Ga. 1996) (physician's testimony that plaintiff's respiratory ailments caused by exposure to fumes excluded where physician could not state to what chemical plaintiff had been exposed, and did not review plaintiff's medical history in an effort to rule out other causes of plaintiff's ailments, such as smoking, allergies, or work in heavy industry).

[9]McDowell v. Brown, 392 F.3d 1283, 1330–1301 (11th Cir. 2004) (physicians' testimony that earlier surgery would have prevented patient's injuries found unreliable where theory lacked "empirical evidence or scientific support," and physicians could not "quantify" how patient's ultimate outcome would have been different had earlier surgery occurred).

[10]Baker v. Smith and Nephew Richards, Inc., 1999 WL 1129650 (N.D. Ga. 1999) ("Even more troubling is the lack of factual basis for his 'conclusions.' In the Eleventh Circuit, 'a party may not avoid summary judgment solely on the basis of an expert's opinion that fails to provide specific facts from the record to support its conclusory allegations.' ").

plied to the specific facts of the case.[1] As explained by the Supreme Court in *Kumho Tire*, this requirement is case-specific, and exists "to make certain that an expert, whether basing testimony upon professional studies or personal experience, employs in the courtroom the same level of intellectual rigor that characterizes the practice of an expert in the relevant field."[2]

Indeed, *Kumho Tire* presents a good demonstration of this concept. There, an expert in tire failure analysis offered the opinion that a tire's tread had separated from its carcass, causing the tire's "blowout" and ensuing injuries to the vehicle's passengers, due to a defect in the tire's design or manufacture. In arriving at this conclusion, the expert testified that he had engaged in a visual and tactile inspection of the tire to rule out tire misuse as a cause of the tread separation, explaining that because he was not able to find at least two of four signs indicating tire misuse as a cause for tread separation, the most likely explanation for the separation and ultimate blowout was a defect. In upholding the exclusion of the expert's opinion, the Court emphasized that it did not take issue with the general proposition that a visual and tactile inspection may be able to identify signs of tire misuse, or that an expert's experience may reliably inform his conclusions.[3] Rather, the court focused on the reasonableness of such an approach, along with the expert's particular method of analyzing the data gleaned from such an approach, in the context of the particular case.[4]

It is important to remember that it is the proponent of the expert's testimony who bears the burden of demonstrating that the methodology employed was reliable.[5] Accordingly, an expert must be able to rationally explain how the methodology employed led to the conclusion reached; otherwise, a court is justified in

---

[Section 3:8]

[1]Kumho Tire Co., Ltd. v. Carmichael, 526 U.S. 137, 153–157, 119 S. Ct. 1167, 1176–1179, 143 L. Ed. 2d 238 (1999).

[2]Kumho Tire Co., Ltd. v. Carmichael, 526 U.S. 137, 152, 119 S. Ct. 1167, 1176, 143 L. Ed. 2d 238 (1999).

[3]Kumho Tire Co., Ltd. v. Carmichael, 526 U.S. 137, 153, 156, 119 S. Ct. 1167, 1177–1178, 143 L. Ed. 2d 238 (1999).

[4]Kumho Tire Co., Ltd. v. Carmichael, 526 U.S. 137, 154–156, 119 S. Ct. 1167, 1177–1178, 143 L. Ed. 2d 238 (1999). The Court observed that, while the expert claimed to be able to reliably exclude tire misuse as a cause of the separation: 1) there was substantial evidence that the tire at issue had been used extensively, and had even received two puncture wounds; 2) the expert could not state with any specificity the usage the tire had received prior to the blowout; 3) the expert had not examined the tire until the day of his deposition; 4) the expert had not examined other similar tires for admittedly relevant data; and 5) much of the expert's conclusions were based on his "subjective" analysis. *Id. at 154–156.*

[5]McClain v. Metabolife Intern., Inc., 401 F.3d 1233, 1238 (11th Cir. 2005).

excluding the methodology.[6] A witness' proclaimed expertise does not, of course, render the witness' methodology reliable,[7] and "nothing in either *Daubert* or the Federal Rules of Evidence requires a district court to admit opinion evidence which is connected to existing data only by the *ipse dixit* of the expert."[8] Stated differently, a court's "gatekeeping function requires more than simply taking the expert's word for it."[9] Similarly, an expert's reliance on "experience" as a basis for his or her conclusions must be supported with an explanation of "how that experience leads to the conclusion reached, why that experience is a sufficient basis for the opinion, and how that experience is reliably applied to the facts."[10]

A trial court's inquiry is typically focused on the reliability of the methodology employed by the expert, not the conclusion the

---

[6]Michigan Millers Mut. Ins. Corp. v. Benfield, 140 F.3d 915, 921 (11th Cir. 1998). In *Benfield,* an expert in fire investigation testified that he had determined that a fire had been intentionally set by the placement of an oil lamp in a house, explaining that he had arrived at this determination by excluding all other possible causes of the fire. However, in upholding the exclusion of this testimony, the court observed that the expert could not explain the methodology he employed to rule out other possible causes of the fire, and could not rationally explain how he concluded that the fire had been intentionally set.

In McGee v. Evenflo Co., Inc., 2003 W.L. 2335049 (M.D. Ga. 2003), the district court excluded an engineer's testimony in part because it could find that the expert had "articulated a concrete, reliable basis for the challenged opinions or a clear method of arriving at his conclusions[,]" and instead, had merely "ambiguously explain[ed] that his opinions [were] based upon his review of the evidence and his general experience in the field[.]" *Id. at *7.* The court concluded by noting that while the expert's "conclusions may be altogether accurate, he has done nothing in this case to show that they are." *Id. at *14.*

[7]Rider   v.   Sandoz Pharmaceuticals Corp., 295 F.3d 1194,

1197 (11th Cir. 2002).

[8]General Elec. Co. v. Joiner, 522 U.S. 136, 146, 118 S. Ct. 512, 519, 139 L. Ed. 2d 508 (1997).

[9]McGee v. Evenflo Co., Inc., 2003 W.L. 2335049, *14 (M.D. Ga. 2003) (citing KW Plastics v. U.S. Can Co., 131 F. Supp. 2d 1289, 1292 (M.D. Ala. 2001)).

[10]McGee v. Evenflo Co., Inc., 2003 W.L. 2335049, *7 (M.D. Ga. 2003) (citing Advisory Committee Notes to Rule 702). See also U.S. v. Frazier, 387 F.3d 1244 (11th Cir. 2004), cert. denied, 544 U.S. 1063, 125 S. Ct. 2516, 161 L. Ed. 2d 1114 (2005). In *Frazier,* the district court permitted a forensic investigator to testify that no evidence of hair or seminal fluid was found at the scene of the alleged rape, and that such forensic evidence is commonly looked for in cases of alleged rape. The district court, however, excluded the expert's testimony that such evidence is "expected" in cases of actual rape, and that the absence of such evidence indicated that there had been no rape. In upholding the exclusion of this latter testimony, the Eleventh Circuit observed that the expert failed to explain how his own experience enabled him to quantify how often such evidence can be "expected" to be found in cases of actual rape. *Id. at 1265.*

expert has reached.[11] However, as noted in *Joiner*, the trial court is not foreclosed from considering the conclusions reached, as "conclusions and methodology are not entirely distinct from one another."[12] Where an expert claims to rely on a generally accepted methodology, and yet reaches a conclusion not shared by others in the field, a court is justified in being "wary that the methods have not been faithfully applied."[13] A court acts within its discretion in scrutinizing anomalous conclusions and rejecting an expert's testimony where the expert fails to "identify and defend the reasons why his scientific methodologies yielded novel results."[14]

These concepts have also been applied with respect to a physician's use of the commonly-employed "differential diagnosis" method to opine as to the cause of a patient's symptoms. For instance, in *Wheat v. Sofamor*,[15] an anesthesiologist was offered to testify that instrumentation manufactured by the defendant for use in spinal surgeries was the cause of the plaintiffs' back ailments. The anesthesiologist claimed that he was able to determine this based on a differential diagnosis, which the court recognized as a generally accepted methodology.[16] Nonetheless, in excluding the anesthesiologist's testimony as unreliable, the court observed that the anesthesiologist had failed to follow the standard procedures commonly employed in the differential diagnosis method.[17]

---

[11]Daubert v. Merrell Dow Pharmaceuticals, Inc., 509 U.S. 579, 595, 113 S. Ct. 2786, 2797, 125 L. Ed. 2d 469 (1993); Quiet Technology DC-8, Inc. v. Hurel–Dubois UK Ltd., 326 F.3d 1333, 1345 (11th Cir. 2003) (cross examination, not exclusion of evidence, is proper method of challenging accuracy of results where underlying methodology used in reaching results is sound).

[12]General Elec. Co. v. Joiner, 522 U.S. 136, 146, 118 S. Ct. 512, 519, 139 L. Ed. 2d 508 (1997).

[13]Wheat v. Sofamor, S.N.C., 46 F. Supp. 2d 1351, 1358 (N.D. Ga. 1999) (citing Lust By and Through Lust v. Merrell Dow Pharmaceuticals, Inc., 89 F.3d 594, 598 (9th Cir. 1996) (9TH Cir. 1999)).

[14]Allison v. McGhan Medical Corp., 184 F.3d 1300, 1315–1316 (11th Cir. 1999) (citing Lust By and Through Lust v. Merrell Dow Pharmaceuticals,

Inc., 89 F.3d 594, 598 (9th Cir. 1996) (9TH Cir. 1999)); cf. Quiet Technology DC-8, Inc. v. Hurel–Dubois UK Ltd., 326 F.3d 1333, 1345 (11th Cir. 2003) (finding that challenge to accuracy of results reached using valid methodology was a matter of weight for jury to consider, and did not present a situation where "jury was likely to be swayed by facially authoritative but substantively unsound, unassailable expert evidence.").

[15]Wheat v. Sofamor, S.N.C., 46 F. Supp. 2d 1351 (N.D. Ga. 1999).

[16]Wheat v. Sofamor, S.N.C., 46 F. Supp. 2d 1351, 1359 (N.D. Ga. 1999).

[17]Wheat v. Sofamor, S.N.C., 46 F. Supp. 2d 1351, 1359 (N.D. Ga. 1999). See also Lawson v. Smith and Nephew Richards, Inc., 1999 WL 1129677 (N.D. Ga. 1999), and Baker v. Smith and Nephew Richards, Inc., 1999 WL 1129650 (N.D. Ga. 1999), where the same anesthesiologist's testimony was

§ 3:9 Helpfulness

An interrelated, albeit distinct, requirement for the admissibility of expert testimony is that the expert's opinion or conclusion "assist the trier of fact to understand or determine a fact in issue."[1] In its simplest form, this test merely sets forth the well-recognized requirement that the expert's testimony concern matters beyond the comprehension of the average juror.[2] After all, expert testimony is of no real assistance "when it offers nothing more than what lawyers for the parties can argue in closing arguments."[3]

At the same time, the *Daubert* decision recognized that "helpfulness" issues are not always so "obvious," and may require a more sophisticated analysis. *Daubert* linked this "helpfulness" requirement to the concept of relevance, or "fit," by observing that the expert's proffered testimony must be "sufficiently tied to the facts of the case" if it is to be of assistance to the jury.[4] In other words, the proffered testimony must have "a valid scientific connection to the pertinent inquiry" as a precondition to admissibility.[5] The *Daubert* court noted that this may entail a subtle analysis, and that "scientific validity for one purpose is not necessarily scientific validity for other, unrelated purposes."[6]

In *Joiner*, the Supreme Court refined this concept in recognizing that experts commonly extrapolate from a set of given data or facts in arriving at their conclusions.[7] However, the Court also cautioned trial courts to be on guard for inferences or extrapolations which are unwarranted or which are simply taken too far by stating that a "court may conclude that there is simply too

---

excluded, partially because of his failure to obtain basic information important in arriving at a diagnosis by the differential diagnosis method.

[Section 3:9]

[1]Daubert v. Merrell Dow Pharmaceuticals, Inc., 509 U.S. 579, 592, 113 S. Ct. 2786, 2796, 125 L. Ed. 2d 469 (1993); Fed. R. Evid. 702.

[2]U.S. v. Frazier, 387 F.3d 1244, 1262 (11th Cir. 2004), cert. denied, 544 U.S. 1063, 125 S. Ct. 2516, 161 L. Ed. 2d 1114 (2005).

[3]U.S. v. Frazier, 387 F.3d 1244, 1262–1263 (11th Cir. 2004), cert. denied, 544 U.S. 1063, 125 S. Ct. 2516, 161 L. Ed. 2d 1114 (2005).

[4]Daubert v. Merrell Dow Pharmaceuticals, Inc., 509 U.S. 579, 591, 113 S. Ct. 2786, 2796, 125 L. Ed.

2d 469 (1993).

[5]Daubert v. Merrell Dow Pharmaceuticals, Inc., 509 U.S. 579, 591–592, 113 S. Ct. 2786, 2796, 125 L. Ed. 2d 469 (1993); see also Quiet Technology DC-8, Inc. v. Hurel-Dubois UK Ltd., 326 F.3d 1333, 1347–1348 (11th Cir. 2003); Siharath v. Sandoz Pharmaceuticals Corp., 131 F. Supp. 2d 1347, 1352 (N.D. Ga. 2001), aff'd, 295 F.3d 1194 (11th Cir. 2002).

[6]Daubert v. Merrell Dow Pharmaceuticals, Inc., 509 U.S. 579, 591, 113 S. Ct. 2786, 2796, 125 L. Ed. 2d 469 (1993); see also Rider v. Sandoz Pharmaceuticals Corp., 295 F.3d 1194, 1197 (11th Cir. 2002).

[7]General Elec. Co. v. Joiner, 522 U.S. 136, 146, 118 S. Ct. 512, 519, 139 L. Ed. 2d 508 (1997).

great an analytical gap between the data and the opinion proffered."[8] In doing so, the court observed that a court, in the
exercise of its gatekeeping function, may reject such extrapolations where there is an absence of support for the propriety of
making such an extrapolation under the circumstances, and
where the only support for such extrapolations is the "ipse dixit"
of the expert.[9]

Stated differently, courts should be wary of an expert "leaping
from an accepted scientific premise to an unsupported one."[10]
Courts should take care to ensure that each step of an expert's
analysis is sound, and not merely a "leap of faith" from one sound
premise to an unfounded one, as such leaps do not provide "good
grounds" for the opinion testimony and constitute little more
than "subjective speculation."[11] Similarly, courts should ensure
that the inferences or extrapolations drawn by an expert have a
sound empirical and scientific basis, rather than constituting
little more than a "guess."[12] Like the proverbial "house of cards,"
any step of an expert's analysis which is unreliable can render
the whole of the expert's opinion testimony unreliable.[13]

Application of this principle is often seen in "toxic tort" cases,
where expert testimony is used to establish both that a particu-

---

[8]General Elec. Co. v. Joiner, 522
U.S. 136, 146, 118 S. Ct. 512, 519, 139
L. Ed. 2d 508 (1997).

[9]General Elec. Co. v. Joiner, 522
U.S. 136, 146, 118 S. Ct. 512, 519, 139
L. Ed. 2d 508 (1997). On remand in
Daubert, the Ninth Circuit Court of
Appeals issued a similar admonition
that a court may not simply "take the
expert at his word" in determining
whether the expert's testimony is supported by sufficiently reliable science:
"[T]he expert's bald assurance of validity is not enough. Rather, the party
presenting the expert must show that
the expert's findings are based on
sound science, and this will require
some objective, independent validation
of the expert's methodology." Daubert
v. Merrell Dow Pharmaceuticals, Inc.,
43 F.3d 1311, 1316 (9th Cir. 1995).

[10]Allison v. McGhan Medical
Corp., 184 F.3d 1300, 1314 (11th Cir.
1999); see also Siharath v. Sandoz
Pharmaceuticals Corp., 131 F. Supp.
2d 1347, 1355 (N.D. Ga. 2001), aff'd,
295 F.3d 1194 (11th Cir. 2002).

[11]McClain v. Metabolife Intern.,
Inc., 401 F.3d 1233, 1245 (11th Cir.

2005).

[12]McDowell v. Brown, 392 F.3d
1283, 1300–1301 (11th Cir. 2004) (physicians' testimony that delay in surgery caused worsening of plaintiffs'
condition where alleged delay was between 4 and 24 hours, and only study
cited in support of theory addressed
consequences of 48 hour delay, properly excluded as a leap from a supported premise to an unsupported
one).

[13]McClain v. Metabolife Intern.,
Inc., 401 F.3d 1233, 1245 (11th Cir.
2005); Siharath v. Sandoz
Pharmaceuticals Corp., 131 F. Supp.
2d 1347, 1355 (N.D. Ga. 2001), aff'd,
295 F.3d 1194 (11th Cir. 2002) (quoting In re Paoli R.R. Yard PCB Litigation, 35 F.3d 717, 745 (3d Cir. 1994)
("Daubert's requirement that the expert testify to scientific knowledge—
conclusions supported for good
grounds for each step of the analysis—
means that any step that renders the
analysis unreliable under the Daubert
factors renders the expert's testimony
unreliable.") (emphasis in original).

lar substance is capable of producing a specific injury to humans, and that exposure to this substance in fact produced the plaintiff's complained-of injuries. For instance, courts have consistently questioned efforts to establish a substance's propensity to cause certain types of injuries in humans based on animal studies wherein animals are exposed to the substance in the course of laboratory testing. These courts have noted that biological differences between humans and animals, as well as differences in the level of exposure, can render the conclusion, based on such animal studies, that the substance caused the plaintiff's injuries, unreliable in the absence of credible explanation as to why such an extrapolation is warranted.[14] Similarly, recognizing that even minute differences in chemical structure can have profound effects on a substance's properties, courts have hesitated to accept testimony that the fact that a certain drug is recognized to have adverse effects in humans is indicative that a similar, albeit different, drug has similar effects.[15] Finally, case reports which may suggest a link between various patients' illnesses and exposure to a certain substance have been rejected as reliably establishing the fact that a plaintiff's exposure to the substance caused her complained-of maladies where the reports fail to demonstrate whether, and if so, how, a determination was made that the substance in fact caused the illness in the other patients.[16]

---

[14]Siharath v. Sandoz Pharmaceuticals Corp., 131 F. Supp. 2d 1347, 1366–1367 (N.D. Ga. 2001), aff'd, 295 F.3d 1194 (11th Cir. 2002); See also Rider v. Sandoz Pharmaceuticals Corp., 295 F.3d 1194, 1201 (11th Cir. 2002); Allison v. McGhan Medical Corp., 184 F.3d 1300, 1314 (11th Cir. 1999).

[15]McClain v. Metabolife Intern., Inc., 401 F.3d 1233, 1244–1246 (11th Cir. 2005); Siharath v. Sandoz Pharmaceuticals Corp., 131 F. Supp. 2d 1347, 1363–1365 (N.D. Ga. 2001), aff'd, 295 F.3d 1194 (11th Cir. 2002).

[16]McClain v. Metabolife Intern., Inc., 401 F.3d 1233, 1247–1248 (11th Cir. 2005); Siharath v. Sandoz Pharmaceuticals Corp., 131 F. Supp. 2d 1347, 1359–1363 (N.D. Ga. 2001), aff'd, 295 F.3d 1194 (11th Cir. 2002).

Chapter 4

Procedural Considerations

> **KeyCite**[R]: Cases and other legal materials listed in KeyCite Scope can be researched through the KeyCite service on Westlaw[R]. Use KeyCite to check citations for form, parallel references, prior and later history, and comprehensive citator information, including citations to other decisions and secondary materials.

---

§ 4:1 Pleading–stage expert affidavits in professional malpractice actions

In 1987, the Georgia legislature enacted O.C.G.A. § 9–11–9.1, which requires the submission of an expert's affidavit along with the complaint in most actions alleging professional malpractice.[1] The character of this special pleading requirement has not substantially changed since its initial legislative incarnation. The central command of O.C.G.A. § 9–11–9.1 has always required the plaintiff in a professional negligence action "to file with the complaint an affidavit of an expert competent to testify, which affidavit shall set forth specifically at least one negligent act or omission claimed to exist and the factual basis for each such claim."[2] As recognized by the Georgia courts, the purpose of this

---

[Section 4:1]

[1]For a detailed discussion of the legislative history of O.C.G.A. § 9–11–9.1, and its development through 1997, see Robert D. Brussack, Georgia's Professional Malpractice Affidavit Requirement, 31 Ga.L.Rev. 1031 (1997).

[2]O.C.G.A. § 9–11–9.1.

statute is to reduce the potential for frivolous malpractice suits.[3] It is a threshold pleading requirement which imposes a duty upon plaintiffs to provide some credible evidence of malpractice at the outset of a case so as to avoid unjustifiably exposing a professional to the expense and reputational harm associated with malpractice litigation.[4] As opposed to an expert affidavit upon summary judgment, a section 9.1 affidavit does not carry an evidentiary burden requiring a plaintiff to prove a prima facie case capable of withstanding a summary judgment motion before the defendant files its answer.[5]

§ 4:2   Pleading–stage expert affidavits in professional malpractice actions—Professional defendants to whom O.C.G.A § 9–11–9.1 applies

Though its substance has remained constant, the intervening years have brought various clarifications and procedural refinements to O.C.G.A. § 9–11–9.1. In 1997, spurred by continuing judicial debate over the professions to which the statute applied,[1] the statute was amended by adding an exhaustive list of 24

---

[3]Sood v. Smeigh, 259 Ga. App. 490, 492–493, 578 S.E.2d 158, 161 (2003).

[4]S K Hand Tool Corp. v. Lowman, 223 Ga. App. 712, 714, 479 S.E.2d 103, 105–106 (1996) (stating that O.C.G.A. § 9–11–9.1 "simply contemplates that parties allegedly damaged by malpractice show up front, by expert's affidavit, that they have some evidence of malpractice, which by its nature can be established only by professional or expert testimony.").

[5]Bowen v. Adams, 203 Ga. App. 123, 123–124, 416 S.E.2d 102, 102–103 (1992). For a discussion of expert affidavits upon summary judgment, see § 4:5 below.

[Section 4:2]

[1]Although O.C.G.A. § 9–11–9.1 was originally enacted as part of the Medical Malpractice Act of 1987, its language commanded the submission of an affidavit in "any action for damages alleging professional malpractice." Prior to 1997, the statute did not identify what "professions" fell within the ambit of the statute. Accordingly, Georgia courts did not limit the application of the statute to medical mal-

practice actions, but instead interpreted the statute to apply to a broad range of professionals other than those involved in health care. See e.g. Housing Authority of Savannah v. Greene, 259 Ga. 435, 437–438, 383 S.E.2d 867, 869 (1989) (in applying the statute to malpractice action against architect, the Georgia Supreme Court noted that while the preamble to the Medical Malpractice Act stated that O.C.G.A. § 9–11–9.1 "relate[s] to the requirement of an affidavit to accompany a complaint in an action for medical malpractice[,]" the statute had from its inception been interpreted as applying to professionals outside of the medical profession); see also Barr v. Johnson, 189 Ga. App. 136, 375 S.E.2d 51 (1988) (applying statute to malpractice action against attorney).

Seeking to create a bright line rule with respect to the professions to which the requirements of O.C.G.A. § 9–11–9.1 applied, the Georgia Supreme Court, in Gillis v. Goodgame, 262 Ga. 117, 414 S.E.2d 197 (1992), held that the expert affidavit requirement applied to the term "professional" as defined in O.C.G.A. §§ 14–7–2(2), 14–10–2(2), and 43–1–24. However, this rule was deemed over-

professions to which the expert affidavit requirement applied.[2] In 2005, the legislature added two more professions to the list of those covered by the statute.[3] With the creation of this list and corresponding strict interpretation by Georgia courts, it is now clear which professional malpractice defendants are entitled to a pleading-stage expert affidavit. In *Minnix v. Department of Transportation*, the Georgia Supreme Court held that the section 9.1 affidavit requirement applies to "professional malpractice suits against members of one of the [26] enumerated professions, and to one category of employer–a licensed health care facility–when that employer's liability is predicated upon the professional negligence of its agents or employees who are themselves among the licensed healthcare professionals listed. . .."[4]

---

inclusive and was modified by the Georgia Supreme Court two years later in Harrell v. Lusk, 263 Ga. 895, 896, 439 S.E.2d 896, 898–899 (1994), wherein the Court held that the affidavit requirement applied only to licensed professions regulated by state examining boards for which specialized training was necessary. This rule, too, was deemed over-inclusive, as it still required expert affidavits to be filed in cases such as those alleging negligence against a plumber. See Seely v. Loyd H. Johnson Const. Co., Inc., 220 Ga. App. 719, 724, 470 S.E.2d 283, 288 (1996).

Because of the abundant litigation attributed to deficiencies in O.C.G.A. § 9–11–9.1, "[a] number of unanswered judicial invitations were extended to the General Assembly to amend OCGA § 9–11–9.1 to clarify or limit its scope, or even to repeal it in its entirety." Minnix v. Department of Transp., 272 Ga. 566, 569, 533 S.E.2d 75, 78 (2000). For example, in 1993 the Georgia Supreme Court noted that the General Assembly had consistently rejected the opportunity to clarify the statute by restricting the affidavit requirement to the medical profession. Lutz v. Foran, 262 Ga. 819, 823, 427 S.E.2d 248, 252 (1993). One appellate court suggested that the statute be reconsidered "in view of its effect on the function of the courts, which is to dispense justice, and the unquestioned ineffectiveness of the statute in reduc-

ing litigation." Johnson v. Brueckner, 216 Ga. App. 52, 54, 453 S.E.2d 76, 78 (1994). Another appellate court stated that the statute was "fundamentally broken," had "largely failed to achieve its purpose," and instead "created an added layer of motions regarding the sufficiency of affidavits preceding the motions for summary judgment on the merits." Sisk v. Patel, 217 Ga. App. 156, 159–160, 456 S.E.2d 718, 720 (1995).

[2]The original list of enumerated professional included: architects; attorneys at law; certified public accountants; chiropractors; clinical social workers; dentists; dietitians; land surveyors; medical doctors; marriage and family therapists; nurses; occupational therapists; optometrists; osteopathic physicians; pharmacists; physical therapists; physicians' assistants; professional counselors; professional engineers; podiatrists; psychologists; radiological technicians; respiratory therapists; and veterinarians.

[3]The added professionals are audiologists and speech-language pathologists.

[4]Minnix v. Department of Transp., 272 Ga. 566, 570–571, 533 S.E.2d 75, 79 (2000). The Minnix court went on to state that had the General Assembly wanted the affidavit requirement to apply to the various professions and employers to which it had

Notably, the necessary implication of the *Minnix* holding is that O.C.G.A. § 9–11–9.1 does *not* apply to licensed professionals who are not included in that statute's list of 26 enumerated professions, nor to any employer of professionals other than a licensed health care facility even where that employer's liability arises out of the professional malpractice of its professional employee. Although it may be argued that this construction lessens the statute's effect in precluding frivolous malpractice actions, especially with respect to non-medical professionals against whom the complaint affidavit requirement can be avoided merely be suing only the professional's employer on a theory of *respondeat superior* liability, Georgia courts have dismissed that argument and given deference to the legislature. "[I]n enacting OCGA § 9–11–9.1, the General Assembly 'intended to enact a means by which the filing of frivolous malpractice actions would be curtailed,' but that it was authorized to limit 'the means of curtailment.' "[5]

§ 4:3   Pleading–stage expert affidavits in professional malpractice actions—Determining when a § 9–11–9.1 affidavit is required

While the amendments to O.C.G.A. § 9–11–9.1 have made clear which professionals come within the statute's ambit, a more basic determination in addressing compliance with O.C.G.A. § 9–11–9.1 is whether or not the plaintiff's claim is one for "professional negligence" in the first place. The filing of an expert affidavit is not always required simply because the allegedly negligent actor is a licensed health care facility or a member of one of the 26 covered professions. That is, where the allegedly negligent actor is a covered professional, but the allegedly negligent act or omission is one of "simple negligence," no expert testimony or complaint affidavit is required in order to establish liability.[1] As the court noted in *Lutz v. Foran*,[2] "If the professional's alleged negligence does not require the exercise of professional judgment and skill, the cause of action is based on a simple negligence

---

been previously applied by Georgia's appellate courts, it would have included exterminators, harbor pilots, landscape architects, real estate brokers, and plumbers, as well as the DOT and other employers. See also Sembler Atlanta Development I, LLC v. URS/Dames & Moore, Inc., 268 Ga. App. 7, 601 S.E.2d 397 (2004) (holding that complaint affidavit requirement did not apply to defendant civil engineering firm).

[5]Minnix v. Department of Transp., 272 Ga. 566, 571, 533 S.E.2d 75, 79–80 (2000).

[Section 4:3]

[1]See Creel v. Cotton States Mut. Ins. Co., 260 Ga. 499, 500, 397 S.E.2d 294, 295 (1990).

[2]Lutz v. Foran, 262 Ga. 819, 820, 427 S.E.2d 248, 250 (1993); superceded by statute as noted in, Minnix v. Department of Transp., 272 Ga. 566,

theory." A guideline for determining when an expert affidavit is required was articulated by the court in *Razete v. Preferred Research*.[3] The Razete court held that if the plaintiff can prove its case without evidence of a customary procedure and the defendant's violation of it, the case is not one for professional malpractice and no expert testimony is required.[4] However, if the Plaintiff was required to establish "the parameters of acceptable professional conduct" in order to prevail, then the action likely involved an allegation of professional malpractice.[5]

Examples of acts or omissions committed by professionals which constitute "simple negligence" include: failing to properly replace parts in a piece of medical equipment;[6] setting a heating pad switch to the wrong setting;[7] failing to assist a weakened patient out of a bed contrary to a procedure requiring that assistance be rendered;[8] negligently transmitting the wrong information to a client;[9] engaging in inappropriate sexual conduct with a client during the course of mental health treatment;[10] and physically assaulting a patient during treatment.[11] Likewise, intentional acts[12] or treatments for which consent has not been given[13] typically do not entail the exercise of professional judgment.[14] Conversely, acts that have been held to involve professional judgment and thus require a supporting affidavit include: failing to inform a patient of the need for follow-up care;[15] failing to require supervision of a patient suffering from a particular medical condi-

533 S.E.2d 75 (2000).

[3]Razete v. Preferred Research, Inc., 197 Ga. App. 69, 70, 397 S.E.2d 489, 490 (1990); See also, Peacock v. Beall, 223 Ga. App. 465, 465, 477 S.E.2d 883, 883 (1996).

[4]Razete v. Preferred Research, Inc., 197 Ga. App. 69, 70, 397 S.E.2d 489, 490 (1990).

[5]Razete v. Preferred Research, Inc., 197 Ga. App. 69, 70, 397 S.E.2d 489, 490 (1990).

[6]Lamb v. Candler General Hosp., Inc., 262 Ga. 70, 71, 413 S.E.2d 720, 722 (1992).

[7]Porter v. Patterson, 107 Ga. App. 64, 71, 129 S.E.2d 70, 75 (1962).

[8]Hillhaven Rehabilitation & Convalescent Center v. Patterson, 195 Ga. App. 70, 71, 392 S.E.2d 557, 558 (1990).

[9]Creel v. Cotton States Mut. Ins. Co., 260 Ga. 499, 500, 397 S.E.2d 294 (1990)

[10]Blier v. Greene, 263 Ga. App. 35, 38, 587 S.E.2d 190 (2003), cert. denied, (Jan. 20, 2004).

[11]MCG Health, Inc. v. Casey, 269 Ga. App. 125, 128, 603 S.E.2d 438, 442 (2004).

[12]See, e.g., Johnson v. Rodier, 242 Ga. App. 496, 529 S.E.2d 442 (2000); Smith v. Morris, Manning & Martin, LLP, 264 Ga. App. 24, 589 S.E.2d 840 (2003), cert. denied, (Mar. 1, 2004); Peacock v. Beall, 223 Ga. App. 465, 466, 477 S.E.2d 883, 884 (1996).

[13]See, e.g., Newton v. Porter, 206 Ga. App. 19, 424 S.E.2d 323 (1992).

[14]For further discussion on claims against professionals for acts which do not involve the exercise of professional judgment, see § 10.3.1.

[15]"Because determining and providing adequate care following a stent implant and shockwave lithotripsy involve 'decisions which normally require the evaluation of the medical condition of a particular patient and,

tion during the performance of certain activities of daily living;[16] failing to raise side rails on a patients bed;[17] failing to support a patient receiving stitches;[18] and using the wrong cleaning solution on a patient before surgery.[19]

As indicated above in § 4:2, while it is possible to have a simple negligence action against a defendant who is a professional listed in O.C.G.A. § 9–11–9.1(d), it is also possible to have a professional negligence action against a defendant professional not listed in O.C.G.A. § 9–11–9.1(d). Where an action calls into question the judgment of a defendant who is a member of a profession not covered by the statute, Georgia courts have held that no pleading-stage affidavit is required to support the action, though expert testimony will be necessary to support the action at the summary judgment stage.[20] Though it established that there are circumstances in which a professional negligence action may be brought without the need to file a supporting § 9.1 affidavit, the *Minnix* court made clear that the absence of a pleading-stage affidavit requirement does not relieve the plaintiff of its burden,

---

therefore, the application of professional knowledge, skill, and experience,' [plaintiff]'s claim is an action for medical malpractice. As [plaintiff] failed to oppose [defendant]'s affidavit by appropriate expert testimony, summary judgment was proper." Herndon v. Ajayi, 242 Ga. App. 193, 194–195, 532 S.E.2d 108, 110 (2000) (citations omitted).

[16]General Hospitals of Humana, Inc. v. Bentley, 184 Ga. App. 489, 491, 361 S.E.2d 718, 719 (1987) ("The evidence here clearly indicates that the medical condition of the patient was the determinative factor as to the degree of supervision the patient was accorded by the hospital staff. Thus, the alleged negligent act required the exercise of expert medical judgment by appellant's staff.").

[17]Robinson v. Medical Center of Cent. Georgia, 217 Ga. App. 8, 10, 456 S.E.2d 254, 256 (1995) (noting that the decision as to whether the side rails were in the appropriate position was a question of professional judgment, as opposed to simply failing to follow the instructions of another professional as to whether the rails should be up or down. See Smith v. North Fulton Medical Center, 200 Ga. App. 464, 408

S.E.2d 468 (1991)).

[18]Pomerantz v. Atlanta Dermatology & Surgery, P.A., 255 Ga. App. 698, 699, 566 S.E.2d 425, 426 (2002) ("Without any indication that [the patient] was going to lose consciousness or any warning by [the patient], the only possible negligence was the decision to seat [the patient] on the table during the procedure. Such a decision is a matter of professional judgment because a lay person is not expected to know when such a procedure could cause a patient to lose consciousness.").

[19]Shirley v. Hospital Authority of Valdosta/Lowndes County, 263 Ga. App. 408, 410, 587 S.E.2d 873, 875 (2003), cert. denied, (Mar. 1, 2004)(

"A jury would be incapable of determining without the help of expert testimony whether the hospital's employees exercised due care and correctly administered the surgical solution for medicating and/or cleaning [plaintiff]'s groin area.").

[20]Minnix v. Department of Transp., 272 Ga. 566, 533 S.E.2d 75 (2000); Sembler Atlanta Development I, LLC v. URS/Dames & Moore, Inc., 268 Ga. App. 7, 601 S.E.2d 397 (2004).

which is present in any professional negligence action, to produce expert testimony at trial establishing the parameters of acceptable professional conduct and the defendant's deviation therefrom.[21]

Where an affidavit must be filed with a complaint, the affidavit must be completed by an expert "competent to testify."[22] Prior to the 2005 adoption of O.C.G.A § 24–9–67.1, the admissibility of such expert evidence was often decided on competence grounds either at the pleading or the summary judgment stage.[23] An affiant whose professional expertise did not intersect with the expertise of the alleged negligent defendant could be ruled "per se" incompetent absent an affirmative showing of "common experience."[24] For example, in *Tye v. Wilson*[25] the court permitted a doctor to offer an affidavit alleging that a treating nurse negligently intubated a patient. Conversely, in *Piedmont Hosp., Inc. v. Milton*,[26] the court found a physician incompetent to comment upon a nurse's allegedly negligent post-operative care. Additionally, where professional licensing is involved, the affiant was required to be licensed to provide the relevant treatment in order to be competent.[27] As discussed more fully elsewhere in this treatise, the passing of O.C.G.A. § 24–9–67.1 has substantially solidified these issues and provided a statutory basis from which to challenge an expert's opinion based on his or her experience.[28] Specifically, O.C.G.A. § 24–9–67.1(d)(1) requires experts in all professional malpractice actions to be licensed in their profession in order to be permitted to testify, and O.C.G.A. §§ 24–9–67.1(c)

---

[21]Minnix v. Department of Transp., 272 Ga. 566, 572, 533 S.E.2d 75, 80 (2000).

[22]O.C.G.A. § 9–11–9.1

[23]See Hewett v. Kalish, 264 Ga. 183, 185, 442 S.E.2d 233, 235 (1994).

[24]Lee v. Visiting Nurse Health System of Metropolitan Atlanta, Inc., 223 Ga. App. 305, 308, 477 S.E.2d 445, 448 (1996) (noting an "expert from a different school [will] have to show that they share a common area of expertise, in order to be competent to give an opinion that the professional deviated from the standard of care required in that profession"). As noted by the Georgia Court of Appeals in HCA Health Services of Georgia, Inc. v. Hampshire, "in order for an affiant to be 'an expert competent to testify,' the expert either must be a member of the same professional school as the de-

fendant or, if from a different professional school, must state the particulars of how the methods of treatment are the same for the different schools in order to establish that the affiant possesses the expertise to be able to give an opinion regarding the applicable standard of care to which the defendant is held." HCA Health Services of Georgia, Inc. v. Hampshire, 206 Ga. App. 108, 111, 424 S.E.2d 293, 296 (1992).

[25]See Tye v. Wilson, 208 Ga. App. 253, 255, 430 S.E.2d 129, 131 (1993).

[26]Piedmont Hosp., Inc. v. Milton, 189 Ga. App. 563, 564, 377 S.E.2d 198, 199 (1988).

[27]Flowers v. Union Carbide Corp., 271 Ga. App. 438, 442, 610 S.E.2d 109, 113 (2005)

[28]See Chapter 1, §§ 1:13–1:14; Chapter 10, § 10:2.

and (d) require experts in medical malpractice actions to be members of the "same profession" as the defendant against whom they offer testimony and to be actively engaged in the practice or teaching of that profession. Importantly, O.C.G.A § 24–9–67.1(e) expressly states that an affiant must pass the requirements of that code section in order to be qualified to provide a O.C.G.A. § 9–11–1.1 affidavit.

Finally, Georgia's expert affidavit requirement does not apply to medical malpractice actions filed in federal court. The United States District Court for the Northern District of Georgia held in *Baird v. Celis*[29] that because the Georgia's expert affidavit statute directly contradicts the applicable Federal pleading requirements, it couldn't be applied in diversity actions. The United States District Court for the Southern District of Georgia similarly held in *Boone v. Knight.*[30]

§ 4:4   Pleading–stage expert affidavits in professional malpractice actions—Procedural concerns for affidavits filed with complaints

In addition to expanding the list of covered professionals, the 2005 amendments to O.C.G.A. § 9–11–9.1 eliminated a provision allowing for the belated filing of an expert affidavit, which previously permitted a plaintiff an additional 45 days to produce the affidavit upon a showing that the required affidavit could not be acquired due to the impending expiration of the relevant statute of limitations.[1] While belated filing is no longer possible, the requirements of the affidavit remain minimal. The Plaintiff is still only required to "set forth at least one claimed negligent act or omission by each defendant and its factual basis."[2] Additionally, the affiant need not rely upon established facts or their inde-

---

[29]Baird v. Celis, 41 F. Supp. 2d 1358, 1362 (N.D. Ga. 1999).

[30]Boone v. Knight, 131 F.R.D. 609, 611 (S.D. Ga. 1990).

[Section 4:4]

[1]Prior to the 2005 amendments, O.C.G.A. § 9–11–9.1(b) provided, in part, that "[t]he contemporaneous filing requirement of subsection (a) of this Code section shall not apply to any case in which the period of limitation will expire or there is a good faith basis to believe it will expire on any claim stated in the complaint within ten days of the date of filing and, because of such time constraints, the plaintiff has alleged that an affidavit

of an expert could not be prepared. In such cases, the plaintiff shall have 45 days after the filing of the complaint to supplement the pleadings with the affidavit." Significantly, a plaintiff was not required to show that the statute of limitations would in fact run within ten days of the filing of the complaint, only that a "good faith basis" existed to believe that the statute of limitations would run within ten days of the date of filing. Legum v. Crouch, 208 Ga. App. 185, 188, 430 S.E.2d 360, 363 (1993).

[2]Gadd v. Wilson & Co., Engineers & Architects, 262 Ga. 234, 235, 416 S.E.2d 285 (1992).

pendent knowledge[3] of these facts when drafting the required affidavit.[4] Furthermore, there is an announced and strong preference toward construing the substance of the affidavit in a manner most favorably to plaintiff with all doubts being resolved in the plaintiff's favor, even where unfavorable construction may be possible.[5] Finally, the Plaintiff is permitted thirty days and possibly longer, to amend the affidavit[6] in order to cure deficiencies identified in relevant motions.[7] Notwithstanding its apparent leniency, the failure to comply with the relevant affidavit requirements subjects a complaint to dismissal for failure to state a claim, which is a dismissal on the merits.[8] Insufficiency or absence

---

[3]Though an expert affidavit need not be based upon the affiant's personal knowledge of the relevant facts its must be sworn and properly notarized. See generally, Harvey v. Kidney Center of Cent. Georgia, Inc., 213 Ga. App. 319, 444 S.E.2d 590 (1994). Also, in the case of medical malpractice, it is not necessary for the affiant in a section 9.1 affidavit to attach medical records relied on as the factual basis for the testimony. See Williams v. Hajosy, 210 Ga. App. 637, 638, 436 S.E.2d 716, 718 (1993); § 10.7.1 infra. With the recent adoption of O.C.G.A. 24-9-67.1, the terms of which expressly apply to § 9.1 affidavits, experts may base their opinions on facts or data "perceived by or made known to the expert at or before the hearing or trial." O.C.G.A. § 24-9-67.1(a).

[4]See, e.g., St. Joseph Hosp., Augusta, Ga., Inc. v. Black, 225 Ga. App. 139, 483 S.E.2d 290 (1997) (overruled by, Threatt v. Forsyth County, 250 Ga. App. 838, 552 S.E.2d 123 (2001)) (holding that an expert affiant may base his opinion upon assumption that factual allegations of the complaint are true just as he could base his expert opinion at trial upon assumption of the truth of evidence adduced to support those allegations),

[5]See, e.g., Bala v. Powers Ferry Psychological Associates, 225 Ga. App. 843, 491 S.E.2d 380 (1997).

[6]A Plaintiff may not file an affidavit for the first time in response to the properly asserted affirmative defense of lack of required affidavit. Porquez v. Washington, 268 Ga. 649, 650, 492 S.E.2d 665, 667 (1997). Moreover, where an affidavit is present but insufficient to meet the requirements of O.C.G.A. § 9-11-9.1, courts are split on whether sufficiency may be supplied through amendment. Goodin v. Gwinnett Health System, Inc., 273 Ga. App. 461, 615 S.E.2d 129 (2005); Harvey v. Kidney Center of Cent. Georgia, Inc., 213 Ga. App. 319, 444 S.E.2d 590 (1994) (expert affidavit received by mail and lacking properly executed jurat was invalid and not amendable); But note, Phoebe Putney Memorial Hosp. v. Skipper, 235 Ga. App. 534, 535, 510 S.E.2d 101, 103 (1998) (holding that a affidavit that is not notarized may be amended at any time prior to a ruling of the Motion to Dismiss); See also, Bhansali v. Moncada, 275 Ga. App. 221, 620 S.E.2d 404 (2005), cert. denied, (Jan. 17, 2006) (citing *Putney Memorial* with approval.

[7]See O.C.G.A. 9-11-9.1(b) (. . .the plaintiff may cure the alleged defect by amendment pursuant to Code Section 9-11-15 within 30 days of service of the motion alleging that the affidavit is defective. The trial court may, in the exercise of its discretion, extend the time for filing said amendment or response to the motion, or both, as it shall determine justice requires).

[8]Lutz v. Foran, 262 Ga. 819, 427 S.E.2d 248 (1993); superceded by statute as noted in, Minnix v. Department

of an expert affidavit is an affirmative defense.[9] According to the 2005 amendments to the statute, the defense must be alleged by the defendant with specificity on or before the close of discovery.[10] If the defense is not properly raised, it is error for the court to enforce the affidavit requirement sua sponte.[11]

Where professional negligence is alleged against a professional listed in O.C.G.A. § 9–11–9.1(d) or a licensed health care facility, the need to file an expert affidavit is absolute. An affidavit must be filed even in cases of "clear and palpable" professional negligence[12] and cases in which the defendant admits negligence. The failure of plaintiffs to file an expert affidavit that is in compliance with section 9.1 has given rise to certain strategic pleading efforts whereby plaintiffs have sought to preserve their cause of action by amending the complaint pursuant to O.C.G.A. § 9–11–15 or by dismissing and re-filing the complaint pursuant to O.C.G.A. § 9–11–62. However, the Georgia courts and legislature have largely limited a plaintiff's ability to use these statutes to remedy a complaint not in compliance with section 9.1. For example, Georgia Courts of Appeal have held that if the original complaint asserts any allegations of professional negligence, the plaintiff cannot simply amend the complaint to add a proper affidavit.[13] Additionally, the legislature has removed a plaintiff's option to voluntarily dismiss the action and re-file it once the statute of limitations for the underlying professional malpractice claim has run. This occurred in *Moritz v. Orkin Exterminating Co., Inc.*,[14] where the Georgia Court of Appeals permitted a plaintiff to voluntarily dismiss an action when confronted by a Motion to Dismiss alleging failure to attach a required expert affidavit and re-file the suit with a compliant affidavit. O.C.G.A. § 9–11–9.1(c) now prohibits a plaintiff from taking advantage of this voluntary

---

of Transp., 272 Ga. 566, 533 S.E.2d 75 (2000).

[9]Frieson v. South Fulton Medical Center, 255 Ga. App. 217, 218, 564 S.E.2d 821, 822 (2002) (refusing to dismiss a claim filed without an expert affidavit against a hospital who did not file a responsive pleading, in spite of the fact that a motion to dismiss filed by the physician through whom liability flowed was granted); See also, Department of Transp. v. Mikell, 229 Ga. App. 54, 493 S.E.2d 219 (1997); But note, § 9–11–8(c) (failing to mention absence or insufficiency of an expert affidavit as one of the enumerated defenses).

[10]O.C.G.A. 9–11–9.1(b). Note that the previous version of the statute required the defendant to raise this defense "contemporaneously with its initial responsive pleading."

[11]Frieson v. South Fulton Medical Center, 255 Ga. App. 217, 218, 564 S.E.2d 821, 822–823 (2002).

[12]Mendoza v. Pennington, 239 Ga. App. 300, 301, 519 S.E.2d 715, 717 (1999).

[13]MCG Health, Inc. v. Casey, 269 Ga. App. 125, 128, 603 S.E.2d 438, 442 (2004); Epps v. Gwinnett County, 231 Ga. App. 664, 666, 499 S.E.2d 657, 660–661 (1998).

[14]Moritz v. Orkin Exterminating Co., Inc., 215 Ga. App. 255, 256, 450 S.E.2d 233, 234 (1994).

dismissal statute if the statute of limitations has run and the court finds that the affidavit was not within the plaintiff's possession and failure to file the same was not the product of mistake.[15] However, plaintiffs retain the ability to dismiss and re-file to save a claim rendered defective because of non-compliance with O.C.G.A. § 9–11–9.1 where the second action is re-filed within the applicable limitations period.[16] Also, a plaintiff who fails to satisfy section 9.1 may amend its complaint to add any non-professional negligence claim at any time prior to the entry of the pretrial order.[17]

§ 4:5 Expert affidavits at the summary judgment stage

In a professional negligence action, the summary judgment stage is where the specifics of an expert affiant's announced expertise may be challenged. Unlike the liberal pleading requirements of O.C.G.A. § 9–11–9.1, a plaintiff cannot meet the evidentiary burden of O.C.G.A. § 9–11–56 by merely presenting an expert's allegation of negligence.[1] This is because a conclusory opinion that a defendant was negligent or failed to adhere to a particular standard of care does not create an issue of *fact*.[2]

In a malpractice action, the defendant professional is competent to provide expert testimony on his or her own behalf.[3] As such, when a defendant professional files an affidavit based upon his or her personal knowledge of the facts alleging that he or she complied with the applicable standard of care, the defendant has pierced the plaintiff's pleading and is entitled to summary judgment unless the defendant's expert opinion is countered by

---

[15]See O.C.G.A. § 9–11–9.1(c) (stating that such complaints "shall not be subject to the renewal provisions of Section 9–2–61 . . . "). Note that O.C.G.A. 9–11–9.1(c) apparently only applies where a "motion to dismiss filed contemporaneously with the defendant's initial responsive pleading." Therefore, if voluntary dismissal is entered before a relevant motion to dismiss is filed relation back under O.C.G.A. § 9–2–61, may be still available to preserve a otherwise untimely claim.

[16]See Orkin Exterminating Co., Inc. v. Carder, 215 Ga. App. 257, 450 S.E.2d 217 (1994).

[17]Smith v. Morris, Manning & Martin, LLP, 264 Ga. App. 24, 25, 589 S.E.2d 840, 842 (2003), cert. denied, (Mar. 1, 2004).

[Section 4:5]

[1]Hailey v. Blalock, 209 Ga. App. 345, 346, 433 S.E.2d 337, 338 (1993). It should be noted that a § 9–11–9.1 affidavit is not in itself part of the pleadings, and therefore an amended or supplemental affidavit can contradict the initial affidavit without risking a dismissal of the action. See Thompson v. Ezor, 272 Ga. 849, 536 S.E.2d 749 (2000).

[2]Hillhaven Rehabilitation & Convalescent Center v. Patterson, 195 Ga. App. 70, 71, 392 S.E.2d 557, 558 (1990) (citing Loving v. Nash, 182 Ga. App. 253, 255, 355 S.E.2d 448, 450 (1987)).

[3]Williams v. Hajosy, 210 Ga. App. 637, 638, 436 S.E.2d 716, 718 (1993).

competent expert testimony provided by the plaintiff.[4] Thus, once a defendant professional gives his or her own expert opinion or the expert opinion of others that he or she complied with the standard of care, the burden shifts to the plaintiff to come forth with contrary expert testimony in order to create an issue of fact for trial.[5] To prevail, a plaintiff's expert must set forth the "particulars" of how the defendant was negligent, including an articulation of the applicable standard of care, and how and in what way the defendants conduct deviated therefrom.[6] Stated differently, an expert affidavit at the summary judgment stage must "establish the parameters of acceptable professional conduct" and "set forth specific facts as the basis for reaching the conclusion that the treatment did not meet the standard of care."[7] To do so, the expert's conclusions must be supported by record evidence or attached documentation.[8]

Even in ordinary negligence actions an expert affidavit opposing a Motion for Summary Judgment cannot stand upon unsupported conclusions of the defendant's negligence.[9] According to O.C.G.A. § 9–11–56(e), all supporting and opposing summary judgment affidavits must be based upon personal knowledge, set forth facts as would be admissible in evidence, demonstrate that the affiant is competent to the matters addressed within the affidavit, and attach sworn or certified copies of all papers referred to. These requirements apply regardless of whether the affidavit is provided by an expert or a lay witness.[10] For example, the

---

[4]Williams v. Hajosy, 210 Ga. App. 637, 638, 436 S.E.2d 716, 718 (1993).

[5]Loving v. Nash, 182 Ga. App. 253, 255, 355 S.E.2d 448 (1987) (citing Howard v. Walker, 242 Ga. 406, 249 S.E.2d 45 (1978)).

[6]Hillhaven Rehabilitation & Convalescent Center v. Patterson, 195 Ga. App. 70, 71, 392 S.E.2d 557, 558 (1990) (citing Loving v. Nash, 182 Ga. App. 253, 255, 355 S.E.2d 448 (1987)).

[7]Connell v. Lane, 183 Ga. App. 871, 872, 360 S.E.2d 433, 434 (1987).

[8]See Crawford v. Phillips, 173 Ga. App. 517, 518–519, 326 S.E.2d 593 (1985) (refusing to consider an expert affidavit offered in response to a Motion for Summary Judgment where cited relevant portions of the medical record were not cited or attached), See also, Estate of Patterson v. Fulton-

DeKalb Hosp. Authority, 233 Ga. App. 706, 505 S.E.2d 232 (1998).

[9]O.C.G.A. § 9–11–56(e) ("When a motion for summary judgment is made and supported as provided in this Code section, an adverse party may not rest upon the mere allegations or denials of his pleading, but his response, by affidavits or as otherwise provided in this Code section, must set forth specific facts showing that there is a genuine issue for trial. If he does not so respond, summary judgment, if appropriate, shall be entered against him.")

[10]See e.g. Denson Heating & Air Conditioning Co., Inc. v. Oglesby, 266 Ga. App. 147, 596 S.E.2d 685 (2004); Johnson v. Department of Transportation, 245 Ga. App. 839, 538 S.E.2d 879 (2001); Mansfield v. Colwell Construction Co., 242 Ga. App. 669, 530 S.E.2d 793 (2000) (in holding that the plain-

court in *Horney v. Panter*[11] found the affidavit of a plaintiff's expert insufficient to withstand a defendant's motion for summary judgment where the expert's opinion was based primarily on discussions with the plaintiff's attorney as to the factual nature of the case. The court held that the affidavit failed to create an issue of fact because the basis for the expert's opinion was hearsay and his testimony was not based upon his personal knowledge.[12] Similarly, the court in Gunnin v. Swat, Inc.,[13] found no material issue of fact where an expert affidavit opposing summary judgment was not based on personal knowledge but instead referred to records which were not in evidence. Because there was no valid basis for the expert's opinion, it was not probative to counter the defendant's affidavit.[14]

§ 4:6 Pretrial hearings on the admissibility of expert testimony and scheduling concerns

In federal court, it is common for the judge to determine the admissibility of proposed expert testimony at a pre-trial *"Daubert"* hearing pursuant to Federal Rule of Evidence 104(a).[12] O.C.G.A. § 24–9–67.1(d) contemplates the holding of similar hearings in Georgia state court actions.[3] That section reads, "Upon motion of a party, the court may hold a pretrial hearing to determine whether the witness qualifies as an expert and whether the expert's testimony satisfied the requirements of subsections (a) and (b) of this Code section [dealing with the reliability of testimony]. Such hearing and ruling shall be completed no later than the final pretrial conference contemplated under Code Sec-

tiff's expert failed to provide specific evidence of causation, the court noted that "[s]peculation and conjecture by an expert is still speculation and conjecture, and will not support a verdict.").

[11]Horney v. Panter, 204 Ga. App. 474, 420 S.E.2d 8 (1992).

[12]Horney v. Panter, 204 Ga. App. 474, 478, 420 S.E.2d 8, 11–12 (1992).

[13]Gunnin v. Swat, Inc., 195 Ga. App. 344, 393 S.E.2d 700 (1990).

[14]Gunnin v. Swat, Inc., 195 Ga. App. 344, 345, 393 S.E.2d 700, 701 (1990).

[Section 4:6]

[1]See Daubert v. Merrell Dow Pharmaceuticals, Inc., 509 U.S. 579, 592, 113 S. Ct. 2786, 2796, 125 L. Ed. 2d 469 (1993) ("Faced with a proffer of expert scientific testimony, then, the trial judge must determine at the outset, pursuant to Rule 104(a), whether the expert is proposing to testify to (1) scientific knowledge that (2) will assist the trier of fact to understand or determine a fact in issue.

[2]Rule 104(a) states that "[p]reliminary questions concerning the qualification of a person to be a witness, the existence of a privilege, or the admissibility of evidence shall be determined by the court. . ."

[3]O.C.G.A. § 24–9–67.1(d).

tion 9–11–16."[4] Motions to exclude expert testimony offered by an opposing party <u>during trial</u> will be denied as untimely under the new Georgia expert witness rules.[5]

In federal practice, such hearings generally take place following the request of a party for an in limine ruling excluding the opposition's proffered expert testimony. Depending upon the issues involved, the federal district court may or may not be required to conduct such a hearing.[6] For example, in *"Daubert II,"* the Ninth Circuit stated that "[w]here the opposing party thus raises a material dispute as to the admissibility of expert scientific evidence, the district court *must* hold an in limine hearing (a so-called *Daubert* hearing). . . .".[7] The Eleventh Circuit has held that *Daubert* hearings are not required, but "may be helpful in complicated cases involving multiple expert witnesses."[8] *Daubert* proceedings also provide a substantial preview as to how the party offering the expert testimony will attempt to establish its case at trial.[9]

Success in a *Daubert* hearing is of paramount importance to a litigant's case. Pursuant to the U. S. Supreme Court's ruling in *General Electric Co. v. Joiner*, a trial court's ruling on the admissibility of expert testimony will be reviewed only for an abuse of discretion even though such exclusion may be "outcome dispositive."[10] Thus, in cases where expert testimony is required to establish an element of a claim, parties often contemporaneously

---

[4]O.C.G.A. § 24–9–67.1(d).

[5]Bailey v. Edmundson, 280 Ga. 528, 630 S.E.2d 396 (2006) (Georgia Court of Appeals upholds trial court's ruling that Challenger to expert testimony during trial was not timely made).

[6]Compare Elcock v. Kmart Corp., 233 F.3d 734, 745 (3d Cir. 2000) (Daubert hearing was a "necessary predicate" to determination of particular expert testimony); U.S. v. Waters, 194 F.3d 926, 936 (8th Cir. 1999) (Daubert hearing generally required for admissibility of polygraph exams) with U.S. v. Lauder, 409 F.3d 1254, 1265 (10th Cir. 2005) (cases involving technological equipment do not necessarily require a Daubert hearing); U.S. v. Ambriz–Vasquez, 34 Fed. Appx. 356, 359 (9th Cir. 2002) (Daubert hearing not required upon objection to fingerprint evidence).

[7]Daubert v. Merrell Dow Pharmaceuticals, Inc., 43 F.3d 1311,

1319 n.10 (9th Cir. 1995) (emphasis added). Note that the Ninth Circuit Court of Appeals has found Daubert hearings not to be mandatory in other circumstances. See Hopkins v. Dow Corning Corp., 33 F.3d 1116, 1124 (9th Cir. 1994) ("the district court is not required to hold a Rule 104(a) hearing, but rather must merely make a determination as to the proposed expert's qualifications.").

[8]See Cook ex rel. Estate of Tessier v. Sheriff of Monroe County, Fla., 402 F.3d 1092, 1113 (11th Cir. 2005); U.S. v. Hansen, 262 F.3d 1217, 1234 (11th Cir. 2001).

[9]See Weisgram v. Marley Co., 528 U.S. 440, 455, 120 S. Ct. 1011, 1021, 145 L. Ed. 2d 958 (2000) ("It is implausible to suggest, post Daubert, that parties will initially present less than their best expert evidence . . . .")

[10]General Elec. Co. v. Joiner, 522 U.S. 136, 144, 118 S. Ct. 512, 517, 139 L. Ed. 2d 508 (1997).

file motions for summary judgment along with motions to exclude expert testimony such that if the testimony is excluded, judgment in the case-in-chief will simultaneously be granted as a matter of law. Such judgments are particularly advantageous to the party opposing the expert in that they are not subject to the *de novo* review afforded most summary judgment decisions[11] unless the appellate court first finds an abuse of discretion in excluding the expert testimony.

Another aim of filing a dispositive motion alongside a *Daubert* motion is an effort to preclude the opposing party from seeking to remedy the defects in its case by finding other evidence or experts or having the excluded expert change his or her testimony. Parties whose expert testimony is excluded often seek a continuance to find other testimony.

As with the decision to admit or exclude testimony, trial courts are granted broad discretion in ruling on such continuances, and "the denial of a continuance . . . will not be overturned unless arbitrary or unreasonable."[12] Nonetheless, the Eleventh Circuit has adopted a test for examining challenges to the denial of a motion for continuance.

First, we consider the extent of appellant's diligence in his [or her] efforts to ready his [or her] defense prior to the date set for hearing. Second, we consider how likely it is that the need for a continuance could have been met if the continuance had been granted. Third, we consider the extent to which granting the continuance would have inconvenienced the court and the opposing party, including its witnesses. Finally, we consider the extent to which the appellant might have suffered harm as a result of the district court's denial.[13]

Also relevant to the inquiry is whether or not a continuance has already been granted in the case.[14] Using this standard, the court has deferred to the decisions of trial courts to deny continuances both where sought in order to find a new expert[15] and where sought in order to mount a better *Daubert* challenge to an oppos-

---

[11]See Jones v. City of Columbus, Ga., 120 F.3d 248, 251 (11th Cir. 1997).

[12]Quiet Technology DC–8, Inc. v. Hurel-Dubois UK Ltd., 326 F.3d 1333, 1351 (11th Cir. 2003).

[13]Hashwani v. Barbar, 822 F.2d 1038, 1038 (11th Cir. 1987) (quoting U.S. v. 2.61 Acres of Land, More or Less, Situated in Mariposa County, State of Cal., 791 F.2d 666 (9th Cir. 1985); see also Quiet Technology DC–8, Inc. v. Hurel-Dubois UK Ltd., 326 F.3d 1333, 1351 (11th Cir. 2003).

[14]Quiet Technology DC–8, Inc. v. Hurel-Dubois UK Ltd., 326 F.3d 1333, 1351 (11th Cir. 2003); In re Kellogg, 197 F.3d 1116, 1119 (11th Cir. 1999).

[15]Rink v. Cheminova, Inc., 400 F.3d 1286, 1296 (11th Cir. 2005), cert. denied, 126 S. Ct. 419, 163 L. Ed. 2d 320 (U.S. 2005). "[A] litigant's failure to buttress its position because of confidence in the strength of that position is always indulged in at the litigant's own risk. Id. (quoting Lujan v. Nat'l Wildlife Fed'n, 497 U.S. 440, 456, 120 S.Ct. 1011, 1021, __ L.Ed.2d __, __(2000)).

ing expert.[16] Moreover, the U. S. Supreme Court had held that it is not error for an appellate court, in reversing the admission of expert testimony, to simultaneously direct a judgment in favor of the appellant where such testimony was the sole evidentiary basis for an element of the appellee's claim.[17]

The Eleventh Circuit case of *Rink v. Cheminova, Inc.* is a good example of how crucial the outcome of a *Daubert* hearing can be to a party's case.[18] *Rink* involved a putative class action against a pesticide manufacturer for injuries sustained due to pesticide exposure.[19] The plaintiffs' presented a chemical engineer who sought to give expert testimony as to the temperature conditions under which certain harmful chemicals were stored. Following a five day *Daubert* hearing, the trail court excluded the expert testimony, finding that there was too great an analytical gap between the data relied on and his opinions.[20] This single ruling triggered a domino effect that was catastrophic and ultimately fatal to the plaintiffs' case.

First, the court held that the testimony of all of the plaintiffs' other proffered experts, including toxicologists and the patients' treating physicians, had been rendered irrelevant because it all depended upon the findings of the chemical engineer.[21] Then, with all of the plaintiffs' experts having been excluded, the court found that they could not establish the essential element of causation and accordingly granted summary judgment in favor of the manufacturer.[22] Finally, the trial court also refused to grant the plaintiffs' request for a continuance in order to remedy their lacking causation evidence and find another expert.[23] Finding no abuse of discretion as to the exclusion of the engineer's testimony

---

[16]Quiet Technology DC–8, Inc. v. Hurel-Dubois UK Ltd., 326 F.3d 1333, 1350 (11th Cir. 2003).

[17]Weisgram v. Marley Co., 528 U.S. 440, 440, 120 S. Ct. 1011, 1013, 145 L. Ed. 2d 958 (2000) (affirming 8th Circuit Court of Appeals decision to direct judgment in favor of the defendant upon a finding that plaintiff's expert testimony, which was admitted at trial, was speculative and scientifically unsound, even though plaintiff won a jury verdict at trial and the Court of Appeals recognized that it had discretion to order a new trial).

[18]Rink v. Cheminova, Inc., 400 F.3d 1286 (11th Cir. 2005), cert. denied, 126 S. Ct. 419, 163 L. Ed. 2d 320 (U.S. 2005).

[19]Rink v. Cheminova, Inc., 400 F.3d 1286, 1289 (11th Cir. 2005), cert. denied, 126 S. Ct. 419, 163 L. Ed. 2d 320 (U.S. 2005).

[20]Rink v. Cheminova, Inc., 400 F.3d 1286, 1290 (11th Cir. 2005), cert. denied, 126 S. Ct. 419, 163 L. Ed. 2d 320 (U.S. 2005).

[21]Rink v. Cheminova, Inc., 400 F.3d 1286, 1290 (11th Cir. 2005), cert. denied, 126 S. Ct. 419, 163 L. Ed. 2d 320 (U.S. 2005).

[22]Rink v. Cheminova, Inc., 400 F.3d 1286, 1291 (11th Cir. 2005), cert. denied, 126 S. Ct. 419, 163 L. Ed. 2d 320 (U.S. 2005).

[23]Rink v. Cheminova, Inc., 400 F.3d 1286, 1291 (11th Cir. 2005), cert. denied, 126 S. Ct. 419, 163 L. Ed. 2d

or the refusal to grant a continuance, the Eleventh Circuit affirmed.[24]

Georgia law differs significantly from the federal rules regarding the timing of disclosure, and the required content for disclosure of expert opinions. Rule 26 of the Federal Rules of Civil Procedure contains a list of required disclosures for a party offering expert testimony and deadlines for the disclosure of such information.[25] By contrast, Georgia has no rule regarding mandatory expert disclosures and a party is entitled to discover an opposing party's expert's identity and the substance of the expert's opinions, only if discovery is propounded.[26] As such, until and unless Georgia adopts a practice rule that requires mandatory and specific expert disclosures such as those in Federal Rule 26(a)(2)(B), parties and trial courts may wish to consider adopting scheduling orders at the outset of a case which address expert disclosures and the timing of motions to exclude expert testimony. Even so, questions may be expected to arise as to a party's ability to add expert witnesses as late as mid-trial. Appellate courts in Georgia have traditionally held that a trial court commits reversible error in refusing to permit a party to present an expert's testimony, even if the expert was not identified during the discovery period.[27]

§ 4:7 Direct examination of experts at trial— Hypothetical questions

Hypothetical questions are often posed to experts who have no independent knowledge of facts established through other records

---

320 (U.S. 2005).

[24]Rink v. Cheminova, Inc., 400 F.3d 1286, 1296–1297 (11th Cir. 2005), cert. denied, 126 S. Ct. 419, 163 L. Ed. 2d 320 (U.S. 2005).

[25]Fed. R. Civ. Pro. 26(a)(2)(B)

Except as otherwise stipulated or directed by the court, this disclosure shall, with respect to a witness who is retained or specially employed to duties as an employee of the party regularly involve giving expert testimony, be accompanied by a written report prepared and signed by the witness. the report shall contain a complete statement of all opinions to be expressed and the basis and reasons therefore; the data or other information considered by the witness in forming the opinions; any exhibits to be used as a summary of or support for the opinions; the qualifications of the witness, including a list of all publications authored by the witness within the preceding ten years; the compensation to be paid for the study and testimony; and a listing of any other cases in which the witness has testified as an expert at trial or by deposition within the preceding four years.

[26]See O.C.G.A. § 9–11–26(b)(4)(A)(i), which permits parties to discover the identity of any expert witness that the adverse party expects to call at trial.

[27]See Hunter v. Nissan Motor Co., Ltd. of Japan, 229 Ga. App. 729, 752–753, 494 S.E.2d 751 (1997), accord Thakkar v. St. Ives Country Club, 250 Ga. App. 893, 553 S.E.2d 181 (2001).

or witnesses.[1] The facts of the hypothetical can be similar to the facts of the case before the jury.[2] In fact, the facts that form the hypothetical can be the same as the facts of the actual case.[3]

Generally, the facts forming the hypothetical must be facts placed in the record by either the testimony of witnesses or by other legal means.[4] The hypothetical may assume facts identical to testimony provided in the case.[5] Even if a fact not placed into evidence forms part of the hypothetical, the expert's opinion is not objectionable if, when answering the hypothetical, the expert is not predicated on that fact.[6] For example, in *Mutual Benefit Health & Accident Association of Omaha v. Hickman*, the plaintiff's counsel asked some hypothetical questions about whether a truck driver driving certain speeds who had one wheel fall into a hole would sustain injury.[7] Defendant's counsel objected because the speed of the truck had not been placed into evidence.[8] The court found the expert's testimony not objectionable because the speed of the truck was not a predicate to his answer of the question.[9] The expert had indicated that either a fast or slow speed could possibly cause injury.[10]

The expert's opinion is admissible if the facts stated in the hypothetical are circumstantial so long as there is some evidence to

[Section 4:7]

[1]Southern Bell Tel., Etc., Co. v. Jordan, 87 Ga. 69, 13 S.E. 202, 203 (1891); Kohl v. Tirado, 256 Ga. App. 681, 685, 569 S.E.2d 576, 579 (2002); Drawdy v. Department of Transp., 228 Ga. App. 338, 341, 491 S.E.2d 521, 525 (1997); Hill v. Yara Engineering Co., 157 Ga. App. 281, 282, 277 S.E.2d 256, 257 (1981).

[2]Evans v. DeKalb County Hospital Authority, 154 Ga. App. 17, 18, 267 S.E.2d 319, 321 (1980)

[3]Central of Georgia Ry. Co. v. McClifford, 120 Ga. 90, 47, 47 S.E. 590 (1904). See e.g., Seaboard Air Line Ry. v. Bradley, 125 Ga. 193, 54 S.E. 69, 71 (1906).

[4]Drawdy v. Department of Transp., 228 Ga. App. 338, 341, 491 S.E.2d 521, 525 (1997); Kines v. City of Rome, 220 Ga. App. 732, 733, 470 S.E.2d 311, 312 (1996); Mutual Ben. Health & Acc. Ass'n of Omaha v. Hickman, 100 Ga. App. 348, 361–62, 111 S.E.2d 380, 390 (1959).

[5]Adler v. Adler, 207 Ga. 394, 404, 61 S.E.2d 824, 831 (1950).

[6]Mutual Ben. Health & Acc. Ass'n of Omaha v. Hickman, 100 Ga. App. 348, 361–62, 111 S.E.2d 380, 390 (1959).

[7]Mutual Ben. Health & Acc. Ass'n of Omaha v. Hickman, 100 Ga. App. 348, 360–61, 111 S.E.2d 380, 389–90 (1959).

[8]Mutual Ben. Health & Acc. Ass'n of Omaha v. Hickman, 100 Ga. App. 348, 360–61, 111 S.E.2d 380, 389–90 (1959).

[9]Mutual Ben. Health & Acc. Ass'n of Omaha v. Hickman, 100 Ga. App. 348, 361–62, 111 S.E.2d 380, 390 (1959).

[10]Mutual Ben. Health & Acc. Ass'n of Omaha v. Hickman, 100 Ga. App. 348, 361–62, 111 S.E.2d 380, 390 (1959).

support those facts.[11] The trier of fact ultimately decides if the fact has been proven by circumstantial evidence.[12] However, the court decides if the expert's conclusion from the hypothetical is at least supported by circumstantial evidence before allowing the matter to go to the jury.[13] When the hypothetical is based on circumstantial evidence alone, then the jury must first determine if the fact assumed has been established by the evidence before considering the expert's opinion to the hypothetical.[14] Similarly, when a hypothetical is based on facts in dispute, it is allowed to be answered if there is some evidence to support the disputed fact.[15]

The rule that an expert may not testify to a hypothetical question based on facts not yet into evidence does not apply when the witness is also a defendant in the case. The defendant may be asked how he acted under different circumstances.[16] In the case *Cornelius v. Macon–Bibb County Hospital Authority*, the defendant physician in a medical malpractice case was asked "whether a patient who has pain out of proportion to the physical findings, nausea, vomiting, tachycardia and an unidentified mass on X-ray should be admitted to the hospital."[17] The lower court had excluded this question because there was no evidence that the decedent had suffered "pain out of proportion."[18] The Court reversed reasoning that the defendant may be thoroughly examined about his action and if he would have acted differently under different circumstances.[19]

The hypothetical need not contain a resume of every fact that has been entered into or been involved in the case.[20] However, a hypothetical question can not misstate or erroneously assume

---

[11]Cox v. Allen, 256 Ga. App. 53, 57–58, 567 S.E.2d 363, 367 (2002); Newman v. Thompson, 230 Ga. App. 671, 672, 497 S.E.2d 8, 9 (1998).

[12]Cox v. Allen, 256 Ga. App. 53, 57–58, 567 S.E.2d 363, 367 (2002); Newman v. Thompson, 230 Ga. App. 671, 672, 497 S.E.2d 8, 9 (1998); Shannon v. Kaylor, 133 Ga. App. 514, 517, 211 S.E.2d 368, 371 (1974).

[13]Newman v. Thompson, 230 Ga. App. 671, 672, 497 S.E.2d 8, 9 (1998).

[14]Cox v. Allen, 256 Ga. App. 53, 57–58, 567 S.E.2d 363, 367 (2002).

[15]Shannon v. Kaylor, 133 Ga. App. 514, 516, 211 S.E.2d 368, 371 (1974).

[16]Cornelius v. Macon–Bibb County Hosp. Authority, 243 Ga. App. 480, 483, 533 S.E.2d 420, 424 (2000).

[17]Cornelius v. Macon–Bibb County Hosp. Authority, 243 Ga. App. 480, 483, 533 S.E.2d 420, 424 (2000).

[18]Cornelius v. Macon–Bibb County Hosp. Authority, 243 Ga. App. 480, 483, 533 S.E.2d 420, 424 (2000).

[19]Cornelius v. Macon–Bibb County Hosp. Authority, 243 Ga. App. 480, 483, 533 S.E.2d 420, 424 (2000).

[20]Dimambro Northend Associates v. Williams, 169 Ga. App. 219, 221, 312 S.E.2d 386, 389 (1983).

facts not into evidence.[21] In *Kines v. City of Rome*, the court affirmed a trial court's holding reversing a worker's compensation award by an ALJ because certain hypothetical questions misstating facts should not have been admitted.[22] The ALJ had based his award largely from deposition testimony where an expert opined based on a hypothetical question, that job stress would be a significant factor to a heart attack assuming the person had little to no family history of heart disease.[23] The Court found this an erroneous assumption because the decedent's mother's side of the family indeed had a long history of heart disease.[24] However, if the expert's opinion did not rely on the misstated amount of question, it should nevertheless be admitted.[25]

Some cases seem to indicate a relaxation of the rule that the hypothetical must be based on facts placed into evidence.[26] For example, the case *In the Interest of M.C.J.* noted that an expert's opinion if based in part on facts not admitted into evidence goes to the evidence's weight and not its admissibility.[27]

§ 4:8   Appeal of issues pertaining to expert testimony

The U.S. Supreme Court has ruled that the standard of review for exclusion of expert testimony is abuse of the trial court's discretion.[1] This is true even when exclusion of the expert is outcome determinative.[2] Recent decisions by the Georgia Court of Appeals suggest that the Georgia courts will follow the federal rules in applying an abuse of discretion standard.[3]

---

[21]Kines v. City of Rome, 220 Ga. App. 732, 733, 470 S.E.2d 311, 312 (1996); Biggs v. McDougall, 175 Ga. App. 87, 88, 332 S.E.2d 381, 382 (1985).

[22]Kines v. City of Rome, 220 Ga. App. 732, 733, 470 S.E.2d 311, 312 (1996).

[23]Kines v. City of Rome, 220 Ga. App. 732, 733, 470 S.E.2d 311, 312 (1996).

[24]Kines v. City of Rome, 220 Ga. App. 732, 733, 470 S.E.2d 311, 312 (1996).

[25]Biggs v. McDougall, 175 Ga. App. 87, 89, 332 S.E.2d 381, 383 (1985).

[26]See e.g., Cox v. Allen, 256 Ga. App. 53, 58, 567 S.E.2d 363, 368 (2002); In re M.C.J., 242 Ga. App. 852, 857–58, 531 S.E.2d 404, 409 (2000).

[27]In re M.C.J., 242 Ga. App. 852, 857–58, 531 S.E.2d 404, 409 (2000). See also Cox v. Allen, 256 Ga. App. 53, 58, 567 S.E.2d 363, 368 (2002) (citing In the Interest of M.C.J. for this rule).

[Section 4:8]

[1]General Elec. Co. v. Joiner, 522 U.S. 136, 118 S. Ct. 512, 139 L. Ed. 2d 508 (1997).

[2]General Elec. Co. v. Joiner, 522 U.S. 136, 118 S. Ct. 512, 139 L. Ed. 2d 508 (1997).

[3]Cotten v. Phillips, 633 S.E.2d 655 (Ga. Ct. App. 2006).

Chapter 5

Product Liability

KeyCite[R]: Cases and other legal materials listed in KeyCite Scope can be researched through the KeyCite service on Westlaw[R]. Use KeyCite to check citations for form, parallel references, prior and later history, and comprehensive citator information, including citations to other decisions and secondary materials.

---

§ 5:1 Overview

Product liability[1] cases are generally prosecuted under three theories: strict liability, negligence, and breach of warranty.[2] By statute,[3] a product's manufacturer may be held strictly liable for

---

[Section 5:1]

[1]This chapter does not focus on product liability cases involving pharmaceuticals and other substances alleged to be hazardous. Those cases are addressed directly in the chapter dealing with toxic torts.

[2]See, e.g. Powell v. Harsco Corp., 209 Ga. App. 348, 349, 433 S.E.2d 608, 609 (1993).

[3]See O.C.G.A. § 51-1-11(b)(1). This statute provides:

The manufacturer of any personal property sold as new property directly or through a dealer or any other person shall be liable in tort, irrespective of privity, to any natural person who may use, consume, or reasonably be affected by the property and who suffers injury to his person or property because the property when sold by the manufacturer was not merchantable and reasonably suited to the use intended, and its condition when sold is the proximate cause of the injury sustained.

Other product liability statutes include those dealing with particular products such as food, O.C.G.A. § 51-1-23, or alcoholic beverages, O.C.G.A. § 51-1-24.

a defect in the manufacture[4] or design[5] of a product. When traveling under a theory of strict liability, the plaintiff need not prove that the defect was caused by the negligence of the manufacturer;[6] rather, the plaintiff need only prove that the product was "not merchantable and reasonably suited to the use intended," i.e., defective,[7] and that the defective condition was the proximate cause of the plaintiff's injury.[8] Because strict liability does not consider the propriety of the defendant's conduct, a plaintiff's expert need not prove *how* a defect was caused, just that a defect existed.[9] Thus, the same evidence which might be sufficient to support a strict liability claim against a product's manufacturer will not necessarily be sufficient for a claim based upon negligence against the manufacturer or another party alleged to be liable for a product's defect, such as a product seller.[10]

Though not always required to support a product liability action,[11] due to the complexities of proving a defect in a product's design or manufacture, as well as matters of causation, expert testimony will often be necessary to support a product liability

---

[4]Center Chemical Co. v. Parzini, 234 Ga. 868, 869, 218 S.E.2d 580, 582 (1975).

[5]Banks v. ICI Americas, Inc., 264 Ga. 732, 734, 450 S.E.2d 671, 673 (1994).

[6]S K Hand Tool Corp. v. Lowman, 223 Ga. App. 712, 716, 479 S.E.2d 103, 107 (1996).

[7]Jones v. NordicTrack, Inc., 274 Ga. 115, 117, 550 S.E.2d 101, 103 (2001) (the phrase " 'not merchantable and reasonably suited to the use intended' does not set forth a requirement of product use, for such language merely means that the plaintiff must show that the product is defective.").

[8]Williams v. American Medical Systems, 248 Ga. App. 682, 685, 548 S.E.2d 371, 373–374 (2001).

[9]See General Motors Corp. v. Blake, 237 Ga. App. 426, 429–430, 515 S.E.2d 166, 168–169 (1999); Firestone Tire & Rubber Co. v. King, 145 Ga. App. 840, 842, 244 S.E.2d 905, 908–909 (1978). In an action grounded in negligence, a plaintiff's burden is not met merely by proving that the product was defective, because the fact of defectiveness does not demonstrate any negligent action on the part of the

manufacturer. As such, where a plaintiff's expert fails to prove how an alleged defect occurred in a negligence action, summary judgment in favor of the defendant may be appropriate. Home Ins. Co. v. Caterpillar, Inc., 202 Ga. App. 522, 523–524, 414 S.E.2d 735, 736 (1992).

[10]U.S. Fidelity & Guar. Co. v. J. I. Case Co., 209 Ga. App. 61, 64, 432 S.E.2d 654, 657 (1993). However, more recent case law indicates that, for design defect cases, the plaintiff's burden of proof is the same regardless of whether the claim sounds in negligence or strict liability. See Ogletree v. Navistar Intern. Transp. Corp., 271 Ga. 644, 645, 522 S.E.2d 467, 469 (1999).

[11]Yaeger v. Canadair, Ltd., 189 Ga. App. 207, 207–208, 375 S.E.2d 469, 470 (1988) (a plaintiff "need not necessarily produce an expert's opinion" in order to prevail on summary judgment or at trial). The expert affidavit requirement of O.C.G.A. § 9–11–9.1 does not apply to product liability claims, even though it does apply to engineering malpractice. S K Hand Tool Corp. v. Lowman, 223 Ga. App. 712, 716, 479 S.E.2d 103, 107 (1996).

action.[12] In light of Georgia's historical mandate that expert testimony "always" be admissible, Georgia case law analyzing the reliability of expert testimony in product liability cases has been sparse. Generally, Georgia courts have permitted expert witnesses to provide their opinions on the basis of their qualifications and experience, and any flaws in the methodology employed were simply matters to be considered by the jury.[13] By contrast, federal courts in the post-*Daubert* era have meticulously evaluated the reliability of an expert's methodology in product liability cases prior to allowing the expert's testimony to reach the jury. Thus, the enactment of O.C.G.A. § 24–9–67.1, which adopts Rule 702 of the Federal Rules of Evidence and specifically encourages Georgia courts to draw from *Daubert* and its progeny, may be expected to significantly change the manner in which Georgia courts deal with expert testimony in product liability cases. Because of the wide divergence which exists in the manner in which Georgia and federal courts have dealt with expert testimony in product liability cases, as well as the prominence of product liability cases in the federal jurisprudence following in the wake of *Daubert*, this chapter addresses the treatment of product liability cases in both Georgia and federal courts.

§ 5:2 Manufacturing defects—Georgia law

A manufacturing defect occurs when a particular product departs from its design specifications.[1] In actions based solely upon an alleged manufacturing defect, it is assumed that the product's design was safe and that, had the product in question been manufactured in accordance with its design specifications,

---

[12]Carmical v. Bell Helicopter Textron, Inc., a Subsidiary of Textron, Inc., 117 F.3d 490, 495 (11th Cir. 1997) (applying Georgia law, summary judgment in favor of the defendant was affirmed where plaintiff's expert could not establish defect); Bunch v. Maytag Corp., 211 Ga. App. 546, 547–548, 439 S.E.2d 676, 677–678 (1993) (summary judgment granted in favor of defendant where plaintiff's experts could not establish causation).

[13]Yale & Towne, Inc. v. Sharpe, 118 Ga. App. 480, 489–490, 164 S.E.2d 318, 326–327 (1968) (noting that role of trial court was simply determining whether expert in product liability action had sufficient experience to be deemed a "prima facie expert"); see

also Cottrell, Inc. v. Williams, 266 Ga. App. 357, 363, 596 S.E.2d 789, 794 (2004) (engineer with some knowledge of electrical systems was permitted to testify that the origin of a truck fire was electrical); Firestone Tire & Rubber Co. v. Pinyan, 155 Ga. App. 343, 347, 270 S.E.2d 883, 887–888 (1980) (expert testimony that properly manufactured tires do not undergo spontaneous tread separation was admissible and presented sufficient jury question to support verdict in plaintiff's favor).

[Section 5:2]

[1]Thorpe, Venderbush, and Neal, Ga. Products Liability Law (3rd Ed. West 2002), § 6–1.

the product would have been safe for consumer use.[2] While manufacturing defects are often demonstrated by comparing the defective product to a properly manufactured unit from the same product line,[3] Georgia courts have historically been liberal in the method of proving that a product was in fact defective.

Though expert testimony as to a manufacturing defect must prove the existence of a defect, it has been held that such proof may be accomplished by way of circumstantial evidence.[4] Such a rule makes sense in light of the fact that products may be destroyed during the incident which forms the basis of the litigation, and under such circumstances, would not be available for inspection to determine the existence of a defect. For instance, expert testimony that a tire's blow out was caused by a manufacturing defect, as opposed to the tire's over-usage or some alternative cause, has been held admissible when based only upon an examination of a portion of the tire's tread recovered from the accident scene.[5] In that case, the court reasoned that to disallow such testimony by virtue of the fact that the expert did not have available for inspection the entire tire, which had been destroyed during the blow out and ensuing accident, would be tantamount to insulating manufacturers of defective products from liability.[6]

Similarly, Georgia courts have permitted proof of a defect by way of circumstantial evidence when, although the product has become unavailable for inspection in the state in which it existed at the time of the accident, this was not due to any fault on the part of the plaintiff.[7] For instance, in *Skil Corp. v. Lugsdin*,[8] a case involving the failure of a guard on a circular saw to close so as to prevent the blade's contact with the user's hand, the saw had been repaired as a matter of routine course following the accident. Despite the fact that the saw was not available in the state in which it existed at the time of the accident, evidence was presented that the saw was new, in good working condition, had not been tampered with, and had been used without incident for

---

[2]Banks v. ICI Americas, Inc., 264 Ga. 732, 733, 450 S.E.2d 671, 673 (1994).

[3]Banks v. ICI Americas, Inc., 264 Ga. 732, 733, 450 S.E.2d 671, 673 (1994).

[4]Folsom v. Sears, Roebuck & Co., Inc., 174 Ga. App. 46, 47, 329 S.E.2d 217, 218 (1985).

[5]Firestone Tire & Rubber Co. v. King, 145 Ga. App. 840, 840, 244 S.E.2d 905, 907 (1978).

[6]Firestone Tire & Rubber Co. v. King, 145 Ga. App. 840, 842, 244 S.E.2d 905, 908 (1978).

[7]However, where a product alleged to be defective is altered or destroyed by the affirmative conduct of the plaintiff after the accident, such conduct has been found to preclude the plaintiff's cause of action. See, e.g. Flury v. Daimler Chrysler Corp., 427 F.3d 939 (11th Cir. 2005), cert. denied, 126 S. Ct. 2967 (U.S. 2006) (informed by Georgia law).

[8]Skil Corp. v. Lugsdin, 168 Ga. App. 754, 309 S.E.2d 921 (1983).

the entire workday prior to the plaintiff's injury. Additionally, evidence of several prior complaints regarding similar failures with the same or similar model of saw was presented. Upon this evidence, the plaintiff's experts opined that there was no reasonable explanation for the saw's failure other than a defect with the spring which would have allowed the blade's guard to close.[9] Affirming the jury's verdict in favor of the plaintiff, the court held that the expert testimony, along with the other evidence, was sufficient to permit the jury to infer that the saw was defective when sold.[10]

It has routinely been held that it is not necessary for an expert, in testifying as to the existence of a manufacturing defect, to specify what about the product was defective; rather, it need only be shown that the product did not operate as intended and that this failure to operate was the proximate cause of the plaintiff's injury.[11] As is discussed below, this represents a more permissive approach than that taken by federal courts, which have placed greater significance on whether the expert is able to articulate what about the product was in fact defective.[12] The approach historically taken by Georgia courts in manufacturing defect actions has permitted experts to infer that a product was defective—or did not operate as intended—based upon the circumstances surrounding an accident. For instance, in an action against a car manufacturer alleging that a seatbelt had failed to operate as intended during a motor vehicle collision, expert testimony specifying the cause of the failure was found to be unnecessary to support a claim that the seatbelt was defective.[13] In an action alleging that an air bag had failed to operate as intended during a motor vehicle collision, expert testimony was deemed sufficient to support a claim of defect where the expert opined that the air bag had failed to work properly, but could not identify which component parts of the air bag had been defectively manufactured.[14] Similarly, in an action against the manufacturer of a penile implant, a physician's testimony that the plaintiff's injury was caused by a disconnection of the device's tubing was deemed sufficient to establish a defect despite the fact that the

---

[9]Skil Corp. v. Lugsdin, 168 Ga. App. 754, 757, 309 S.E.2d 921, 924 (1983).

[10]Skil Corp. v. Lugsdin, 168 Ga. App. 754, 757, 309 S.E.2d 921, 924 (1983).

[11]Williams v. American Med. Sys., 248 Ga. App. 683, 683, 548 S.E.2d 371, 373–374 (2001).

[12]See § 6:5, infra.

[13]General Motors Corp. v. Blake, 237 Ga. App. 426, 429, 515 S.E.2d 166, 168 (1999).

[14]Owens v. General Motors Corp., 272 Ga. App. 842, 846, 613 S.E.2d 651, 654–655 (2005). Though the expert, a repair technician, was not able to testify as to the engineering of the air bag sensor, the court found that he had studied the subject enough to testify as to how air bag sensors

physician could not state what had caused the tubing to discon-
nect.[15]

§ 5:3 Manufacturing defects—Federal law

In contrast to the traditional manner in which the Georgia
courts have handled expert testimony in product liability cases,
the federal courts have demonstrated a much greater willingness
to analyze the reliability of the expert's methodology underlying
his opinions prior to allowing the expert's opinions to be presented before a jury. These cases have tended to examine *how*
the expert arrived at the conclusion that a defect with the product, as opposed to some alternative cause, was in fact the cause
of the alleged failure of the product. In large measure, these
courts have focused on whether the expert has been able to reliably rule out obvious alternative explanations for the plaintiff's
injuries in arriving at his conclusion that a defect with the product must have been the cause of the plaintiff's injuries. In so doing, these cases stand in stark contrast to the manner in which
product liability cases have been dealt with by the Georgia courts,
which have heretofore not required evidence of a specific product
defect, only evidence that the product apparently did not perform
as intended.[1]

Kumho Tire Company, Ltd. v. Carmichael,[2] the third case of
the so-called "*Daubert* trilogy," arguably represents the starting
point for the modern analysis of expert testimony in federal product liability cases. *Kumho Tire* involved a deadly motor vehicle
accident resulting from the blowout of a tire on a minivan. In
claiming that the tire was defective in its manufacture or design,
the plaintiffs relied on the testimony of a tire failure analyst who
testified that the blowout was caused by a separation of the tire's
tread from its carcass. The expert testified that where tread
separation is not caused by "overdeflection" due to underinflation
of the tire, it is usually caused by a defect in the tire. The expert
conducted a two-factor test, involving visual and tactile inspection of the tire in question, and finding insufficient evidence of
overdeflection or some other less obvious cause of tread separation, concluded that a defect with the tire was therefore the cause
of the blowout.

In addressing the reliability of the expert's methodology, the

---

worked, and how the sensor in question failed when the weld attaching it
to the vehicle's frame broke. *Id.*

[15]Williams v. American Medical
Systems, 248 Ga. App. 682, 683, 548
S.E.2d 371, 374, (2001).

[Section 5:3]

[1]See § 6:2, *supra.*

[2]Kumho Tire Co., Ltd. v.
Carmichael, 526 U.S. 137, 119 S. Ct.
1167, 143 L. Ed. 2d 238 (1999).

Supreme Court held that while the expert's visual and tactile inspection may be a reasonable methodology for ascertaining the existence of a tire defect *in general*, the more pertinent inquiry was whether such methodology could be reliably applied to ascertain the existence of a tire defect given the particular facts of the case at hand.[3] In finding that the district court had acted within its discretion in excluding this testimony, the Supreme Court noted that the district court had observed that other factors, such as the age and overuse of the tire, could account for tread separation, but that the expert had not been able to provide any estimate as to how many miles the tire had traveled.[4] Additionally, the Court found it significant that there was no evidence that other experts in the industry employed the expert's two-factor test in making determinations as to the cause of tread separation.[5]

The Eleventh Circuit case of *McCorvey v. Baxter Healthcare Corp.*,[6] involved a patient who was injured when the balloon portion of a catheter placed in his bladder erupted. In support of his claim against the manufacturer of the catheter, the plaintiff offered the testimony of an engineer who claimed that the eruption was the result of a manufacturing or design defect.[7] In upholding the lower court's exclusion of the testimony, the Eleventh Circuit observed that the expert "did not test alternative designs for the catheter; did not talk to medical personnel; was unable to cite scientific literature in support of his theories; and did not consider or test possibilities for failure that could have come from sources

---

[3]Kumho Tire Co., Ltd. v. Carmichael, 526 U.S. 137, 157, 119 S. Ct. 1167, 1178, 143 L. Ed. 2d 238 (1999).

[4]Kumho Tire Co., Ltd. v. Carmichael, 526 U.S. 137, 154–155, 119 S. Ct. 1167, 1177, 143 L. Ed. 2d 238 (1999).

[5]Kumho Tire Co., Ltd. v. Carmichael, 526 U.S. 137, 157, 119 S. Ct. 1167, 1178, 143 L. Ed. 2d 238 (1999).

[6]McCorvey v. Baxter Healthcare Corp., 298 F.3d 1253 (11th Cir. 2002). It is worthy to note that the Supreme Court's decision in *Kumho* reversed the holding of the Eleventh Circuit, which, until then, had held that the Daubert gatekeeping analysis did not apply to non-scientific evidence. See Carmichael v. Samyang Tire, Inc., 131 F.3d 1433, 1435 (11th Cir. 1997),

judgment rev'd, 526 U.S. 137, 119 S. Ct. 1167, 143 L. Ed. 2d 238 (1999) (holding that Daubert applied only to expert testimony based upon the application of scientific principles, and not that founded on skill or experience based observations). Consequently, the Georgia federal court system did not apply the present analysis of Daubert and Federal Rule 702 in product liability cases until 1999. See Allison v. McGhan Medical Corp., 184 F.3d 1300, 1312 (11th Cir. 1999) ("[t]his Circuit has been twice overruled on Daubert decisions in precedent setting Supreme Court decisions in Joiner and Kumho Tire, both of which imposed stricter admissibility standards than the Eleventh Circuit had deemed appropriate".)

[7]McCorvey v. Baxter Healthcare Corp., 298 F.3d 1253, 1255–1256 (11th Cir. 2002).

outside the product, such as the effect of improper storage conditions, contaminants, or human error."[8] Responding to the contention that such deficits in the expert's methodology were matters for a jury's consideration, the court stated that this argument did not address the application of *Daubert*, but "instead seem[s] to implicitly reject the gatekeeper function of the trial courts[.]"[9]

§ 5:4   Design defects—Georgia law

The great majority of modern product liability cases involve allegations that a product's design was defective. A design defect occurs when a product is manufactured in accordance with its design specifications, but is nonetheless "not merchantable and reasonably suited to the use intended." Thus, a defective design renders every product in the line potentially defective. Because a design defect cannot be ascertained merely by comparing the allegedly defective product to another from the same product line, a standard must exist for ascertaining defectiveness.[1] In this regard, Georgia courts have employed a risk-utility balancing test, which weighs the risks inherent in the product's design against its benefit or utility.[2] The overlapping of the reasonableness inquiry involved in the risk-utility test with traditional negligence principles has led to the interpretation that the risk-utility test applies to all design defect claims, whether traveling under theories of negligence or strict liability.[3]

In proving that a product's design was defective, expert testimony has been admitted to show that, had the manufacturer conducted certain tests or taken certain measurements, the design defect would have been discovered before the product was marketed to the general public.[4] Questions posed to an expert regarding the adequacy of the manufacturer's internal testing

---

[8]McCorvey v. Baxter Healthcare Corp., 298 F.3d 1253, 1256–1257 (11th Cir. 2002).

[9]McCorvey v. Baxter Healthcare Corp., 298 F.3d 1253, 1257 (11th Cir. 2002).

[Section 5:4]

[1]Banks v. ICI Americas, Inc., 264 Ga. 732, 734, 450 S.E.2d 671, 673 (1994).

[2]Banks v. ICI Americas, Inc., 264 Ga. 732, 734, 450 S.E.2d 671, 673 (1994).

[3]Ogletree v. Navistar Intern. Transp. Corp., 271 Ga. 644, 645, 522 S.E.2d 467 (1999).

[4]See, e.g, Bryant v. Hoffmann–La Roche, Inc., 262 Ga. App. 401, 408, 585 S.E.2d 723, 729 (2003) (physician testified that, had pharmaceutical company conducted certain tests on drug, it would have detected flaws); see also Watkins v. Ford Motor Co., 190 F.3d 1213, 1217 (11th Cir. 1999) (design expert testified that, had Ford accepted an engineer's design proposal during its decision-making process, the vehicle would have been more stable).

standards are both permissible and relevant.[5] Experts have been held qualified to provide testimony as to the adequacy of testing procedures where they have been involved in, or have other relevant experience pertaining to, pre-market trials for the development of the type of product whose design is at issue in the case.[6]

Expert testimony that a manufacturer failed to act "reasonably" in its decision to design a product in a certain manner is not impermissible testimony as to the ultimate issue, and is admissible where the determination of negligence is beyond the ken of the jury.[7] For instance, in *Ford Motor Co. v. Stubblefield*, after a review of internal company reports and recommendations by company engineers pertaining to the design of the fuel system of the Ford vehicle at issue, various experts offered the opinion that the design of the fuel system was unreasonably dangerous, and that Ford had not acted reasonably in marketing the vehicle to the public with the existing fuel system.[8] In holding that the testimony of these experts did not constitute impermissible testimony as to an ultimate issue, the court reasoned that the decision-making process leading to the marketing of the vehicle with the existing fuel system was complicated,[9] and the opinions provided by the experts were "highly technical, sophisticated and peculiarly within the specialized science of [the] experts."[10]

---

[5]General Motors Corp. v. Moseley, 213 Ga. App. 875, 884, 447 S.E.2d 302, 311 (1994) (disapproved of on other grounds by Webster v. Boyett, 269 Ga. 191, 496 S.E.2d 459 (1998)).

[6]In Bryant v. Hoffmann–La Roche, Inc., 262 Ga. App. 401, 408, 585 S.E.2d 723, 729 (2003), a physician was qualified, by virtue of his involvement in several pre-market clinical trials in connection with drug development, to opine that flaws in pharmaceutical would have been discovered had certain tests been performed. However, in cases wherein it is alleged that a prescription drug is defective, expert testimony addressing whether the Federal Drug Administration (FDA) should have approved the marketing of the drug is inadmissible where the expert has no training or experience with regulatory requirements in obtaining FDA approval. *Id. at 407–408, 585 S.E.2d 723.*

[7]See Ford Motor Co. v. Stubblefield, 171 Ga. App. 331, 319 S.E.2d 470 (1984).

[8]Ford Motor Co. v. Stubblefield, 171 Ga. App. 331, 333, 319 S.E.2d 470, 475 (1984).

[9]The decision-making process was described as a "morass of conceptual, political, and practical issues." Ford Motor Co. v. Stubblefield, 171 Ga. App. 331, 334, 319 S.E.2d 470, 475 (1984).

[10]Ford Motor Co. v. Stubblefield, 171 Ga. App. 331, 334, 319 S.E.2d 470, 475 (1984).

§ 5:5   Design defects—Georgia law—Evidence of alternative designs

The factors to be considered in the risk-utility balancing test are not finite and will vary according to the facts of each case.[1] Nonetheless, certain factors predominate the majority of cases, and tend to be common battlegrounds for expert testimony. Perhaps the most important factor in determining whether a product was defectively designed is whether, at the time the product was manufactured, a viable alternative design existed that would have made the product safer.[2] It has been held that evidence of an alternative design is not required to support an action based upon design defect.[3] However, in 1994 the Georgia Supreme Court indicated a strong preference for proof of a feasible alternative design, noting that the availability of such a design is integral for purposes of determining whether a product can be said to be defective.[4] Even more recently, in 2001, the Georgia Supreme Court observed that evidence of a feasible alternative design is the "heart" of a case alleging a design defect, and that the appropriate analysis of such a case "necessarily" includes the consideration of viable alternative designs.[5] Because evidence as to the availability and utility of alternative product designs at a particular point in time will usually require specialized knowledge, expert testimony is the standard method by which parties introduce such evidence.[6]

Factors to consider in determining whether a viable alternative

---

[Section 5:5]

[1]Banks v. ICI Americas, Inc., 264 Ga. 732, 736, 450 S.E.2d 671, 675 (1994). Common factors include, but are not limited to: "the usefulness of the product; the gravity and severity of the danger posed by the design; the likelihood of that danger; the avoidability of the danger, i.e., the user's knowledge of the product, publicity surrounding the danger, or the efficacy of warnings, as well as common knowledge and the expectation of danger, and the user's ability to avoid danger; the state of the art at the time the product is manufactured; the manufacturer's ability to eliminate the danger without impairing the product's usefulness or making it too expensive; and the feasibility of spreading the loss in the price or by purchasing insurance."

[2]Thorpe, Venderbush, and Neal, Ga. Products Liability Law (3rd Ed. West 2002), § 7–2 ("There are several

reasons to think, however, that the Georgia Supreme Court would adopt a rule that in all but the most 'extreme' design defect cases, a prima facie case of design defect must include evidence of a feasible design alternative").

[3]Bodymasters Sports Industries, Inc. v. Wimberley, 232 Ga. App. 170, 173, 501 S.E.2d 556, 560 (1998).

[4]Banks v. ICI Americas, Inc., 264 Ga. 732, 736, 450 S.E.2d 671, 674 (1994).

[5]Jones v. NordicTrack, Inc., 274 Ga. 115, 118, 550 S.E.2d 101, 103 (2001).

[6]Expert testimony as to alternative designs has been employed in a variety of circumstances and across a wide array of products. Examples include: testimony that the manufacturer was aware of two reasonable, quick, and inexpensive alternative designs to an injury-causing circuit control defect in a mop assembly ma-

design exists include, but are not necessarily limited to: "the feasibility of an alternative design; the availability of an effective substitute for the product which meets the same need but is safer; the financial cost of the improved design; and the adverse effects from the alternative."[7] A good example of the application of these factors may be found in *Moore v. ECI Management*,[8] where the plaintiff's expert testified that the washer-dryer in question should have been pre-wired or equipped with a rejection feature so as to prevent miswiring and the risk of electrocution during installation. However, the evidence showed that no washer-dryer manufacturers employed such a rejection feature, and no studies had been done concerning the feasibility of such a design. Moreover, it was shown to be industry custom to intentionally leave the wiring unattached so as to accommodate different types of power outlets. In light of this, the court found the washer-dryer unit to be "state of the art" at the time it was sold, and affirmed summary judgment in favor of the manufacturer.[9]

Evidence demonstrating that a manufacturer was aware of safer alternative designs, but chose not to adopt such decisions due to cost considerations, may support a finding that a product's design was defective. For instance, in *Watkins v. Ford Motor Co.*,[10] a case involving the rollover of a sport utility vehicle, expert testimony was presented that Ford was aware of the stability problems with the vehicle, and that despite the fact that Ford engineers had submitted five proposals to improve the vehicle's stability, Ford had chosen the least expensive design option rather than one which would have made the vehicle more stable at an additional cost of only $83 per vehicle. Under these circum-

---

chine (Smith v. Ontario Sewing Machine Co., Ltd., 249 Ga. App. 364, 365, 548 S.E.2d 89 (2001), judgment vacated, 259 Ga. App. 30, 576 S.E.2d 38 (2002)); testimony that a drain cleaner consisting of 97% sulfuric acid should have been placed in a container with a handle, spill proof spout, and/or pre-measure dosages (Jones v. Amazing Products, Inc., 231 F. Supp. 2d 1228, 1243–1244 (N.D. Ga. 2002)); testimony that a car restraint system would have been more effective with an alternative shoulder strap placement and angle and with the addition of a lap belt (Volkswagen of America, Inc. v. Gentry, 254 Ga. App. 888, 890, 564 S.E.2d 733, 737 (2002)); and testi-

mony that a truck tractor should have been designed with a manual limiting valve to in order to reapportion braking forces between the front and rear axles to avoid jackknifing (Lindsey v. Navistar Intern. Transp. Corp., 150 F.3d 1307, 1312 (11th Cir. 1998)).

[7]Banks v. ICI Americas, Inc., 264 Ga. 732, 736 n.6, 450 S.E.2d 671, 675 (1994).

[8]Moore v. ECI Management, 246 Ga. App. 601, 542 S.E.2d 115 (2000).

[9]Moore v. ECI Management, 246 Ga. App. 601, 605, 542 S.E.2d 115, 120 (2000).

[10]Watkins v. Ford Motor Co., 190 F.3d 1213 (11th Cir. 1999).

stances, the court found that the evidence was sufficient to support the plaintiffs' design defect claim.[11]

§ 5:6   Design defects—Georgia law—Prior incident evidence

A common issue in design defect cases concerns the admissibility of evidence of other prior incidents involving the product in question for purposes of establishing that a manufacturer was on notice that the product was defective by virtue of similar product failures in the past. While evidence of similar acts or omissions on prior occasions is generally not admissible as proof of like acts or omissions on the occasion at issue,[1] an exception to this rule has evolved in product liability cases.[2] Such evidence of prior similar incidents is both relevant and admissible with respect to the issues of notice and punitive damages provided there is a showing of "substantial similarity" between the prior incidents and the incident at issue.[3] In order to meet this burden, the plaintiff must demonstrate substantial similarity in: 1) the product at issue and those involved in the prior incidents; 2) the nature of the defect in the product at issue and those involved in the prior incidents; or 3) the cause of the defect in the product at issue and those involved in the prior incidents.[4] For instance, in an action against a tire manufacturer, evidence of consumer claims previously honored by the tire manufacturer for tires manufactured at the same plant as the tire at issue was excluded where the plaintiff made no showing that the previous tires were of the same make and model as the tire at issue, that they suf-

---

[11]Watkins v. Ford Motor Co., 190 F.3d 1213, 1217 (11th Cir. 1999) (applying Georgia law); see also Mack Trucks, Inc. v. Conkle, 263 Ga. 539, 436 S.E.2d 635 (1993) (evidence that the manufacturer's engineers repeatedly informed the company of the need to replace a frame rail was sufficient to support a finding of conscious indifference).

[Section 5:6]

[1]Seaboard Coast Line R. Co. v. Clark, 122 Ga. App. 237, 239, 176 S.E.2d 596, 599 (1970).

[2]See General Motors Corp. v. Moseley, 213 Ga. App. 875, 877, 447 S.E.2d 302, 306 (1994) (disapproved of on other grounds by Webster v. Boyett, 269 Ga. 191, 496 S.E.2d 459 (1998)); Ray v. Ford Motor Co., 237 Ga. App. 316, 317, 514 S.E.2d 227, 230 (1999); Barger v. Garden Way, Inc., 231 Ga. App. 723, 729, 499 S.E.2d 737, 744 (1998).

[3]See Mack Trucks, Inc. v. Conkle, 263 Ga. 539, 544, 436 S.E.2d 635, 640 (1993); see also Carlton Co. v. Poss, 124 Ga. App. 154, 155, 183 S.E.2d 231, 233 (1971) ("Without a showing of substantial similarity, the evidence is irrelevant as a matter of law.").

[4]Cooper Tire & Rubber Co. v. Crosby, 273 Ga. 454, 455–456, 543 S.E.2d 21, 24 (2001) (citing Uniroyal Goodrich Tire Co. v. Ford, 218 Ga. App. 248, 260, 461 S.E.2d 877, 888 (1995)).

fered from the same defect as the tire at issue, or that the defects were caused by a similar problem as the tire at issue.[5]

A good example of the application of these principles may be found in *Ray v. Ford Motor Co.*,[6] a case wherein the plaintiff was injured when she was struck by her vehicle after she had parked it and removed the keys from the ignition. The plaintiff's expert sought to testify as to 546 prior incidents of inadvertent movement in other vehicles produced by the defendant manufacturer which allegedly suffered from the same defect,[7] citing four common factors in these prior incidents which were similar to the plaintiff's case. In response, the manufacturer's expert, who had compiled the databases from which the plaintiff's expert had gleaned his information, testified that the data upon which the plaintiff's expert based his testimony was unreliable in that the database information came from a variety of unverified hearsay sources, did not account for various underlying causes of inadvertent vehicle movement, and had been catalogued in a manner in which dissimilar incidents were grouped together. Finding that the trial court lacked a sufficient basis to determine if there was a substantial similarity between the 546 prior incidents and the incident underlying the plaintiff's claim, the appellate court affirmed the exclusion of the plaintiff's expert's testimony.[8]

Other cases have highlighted the importance of establishing similarity with respect to causation. For instance, in *Stovall v. DaimlerChrysler Motors Corp.*,[9] a case involving injuries arising out of an automobile's sudden and unexpected acceleration, expert testimony was offered as to thirteen prior incidents in which other vehicles had also suddenly and unexpectedly accelerated. While the expert identified the cause of the sudden acceleration in the plaintiff's case, the expert conceded that several different factors could have lead to the sudden acceleration in the prior

---

[5]Cooper Tire & Rubber Co. v. Crosby, 273 Ga. 454, 455–456, 543 S.E.2d 21, 24 (2001). Note that even where the products involved in the prior incidents were of the same make and model as the product that is the subject of the current litigation, evidence of prior incidents may not be admissible where the exemplar products have undergone modifications. See Karoly v. Kawasaki Motors Corp., U.S.A., 259 Ga. App. 225, 576 S.E.2d 625 (2003) (affirming admission of incidents involving similar, unmodified jet skis, but excluding incidents involving modified jet skis where showing of substantial similarity could not be made).

[6]Ray v. Ford Motor Co., 237 Ga. App. 316, 514 S.E.2d 227 (1999).

[7]The defect alleged by the plaintiffs was the lack of an ignition/transmission interlock device that would prevent removal of the ignition key unless the transmission was in "park." Ray v. Ford Motor Co., 237 Ga. App. 316, 316, 514 S.E.2d 227, 229 (1999).

[8]Ray v. Ford Motor Co., 237 Ga. App. 316, 319, 514 S.E.2d 227, 231 (1999).

[9]Stovall v. DaimlerChrysler Motors Corp., 270 Ga. App. 791, 793, 608 S.E.2d 245, 247 (2004).

incidents, and was unable to state which of these factors had lead to the sudden acceleration in the prior incidents. Under those circumstances, the court found that the expert had failed to provide the necessary correlation between the cause of the prior incidents and the cause of the plaintiff's incident, and held that evidence of the prior incidents was inadmissible.[10]

§ 5:7   Design defects—Georgia law—Evidence of compliance with standards or regulations

Expert testimony is commonly employed in actions alleging a design defect in order to show that the manufacturer either complied, or failed to comply, with industry standards,[1] internal company standards,[2] or federal regulations.[3] Commonly cited standards include those promulgated by the American National Standards Institute (ANSI);[4] the National Highway Traffic Safety Administration (NHTSA);[5] the Food and Drug Administration

---

[10]Stovall v. DaimlerChrysler Motors Corp., 270 Ga. App. 791, 793, 608 S.E.2d 245, 247–248 (2004).

[Section 5:7]

[1]See, e.g, Smith v. Ontario Sewing Machine Co., Ltd., 249 Ga. App. 364, 365, 548 S.E.2d 89, 93 (2001), judgment vacated, 259 Ga. App. 30, 576 S.E.2d 38 (2002) (expert testimony that design of sewing machine violated the American National Standards Institute standards); Dean v. Toyota Industrial Equipment Mfg., Inc., 246 Ga. App. 255, 260, 540 S.E.2d 233, 237 (2000) (expert testimony that equipping forklifts with backup alarms was industry standard);

[2]See, e.g, General Motors Corp. v. Moseley, 213 Ga. App. 875, 883–884, 447 S.E.2d 302, 310–11 (1994) disapproved of on other grounds by Webster v. Boyett, 269 Ga. 191, 496 S.E.2d 459 (1998)) (permitting party to pose questions to former CEO of GM about company's internal standards); Beamon v. Georgia Power Co., 199 Ga. App. 309, 313, 404 S.E.2d 463, 466 (1991) (expert testimony that "bucket truck" design violated power company standards).

[3]See, e.g, Volkswagen of America, Inc. v. Gentry, 254 Ga. App. 888, 891,

564 S.E.2d 733, 738 (2002) (jury entitled to consider expert testimony as to whether Volkswagen's passive restraint system complied with federal safety regulations pertaining to design of automobiles); General Motors Corp. v. Moseley, 213 Ga. App. 875, 883, 447 S.E.2d 302, 310 (1994) (expert testimony that GM tested trucks for side impact collisions at a speed greater than required under the Federal Motor Vehicle Safety Standards).

[4]Dupree v. Keller Industries, Inc., 199 Ga. App. 138, 141, 404 S.E.2d 291, 294 (1991) (expert relied on ANSI standards in claiming that hydraulic press was defective); Smith v. Ontario Sewing Machine Co., Ltd., 249 Ga. App. 364, 365, 548 S.E.2d 89, 93 (2001), judgment vacated, 259 Ga. App. 30, 576 S.E.2d 38 (2002) (expert testimony that machine design violated ANSI standards).

[5]Stovall v. DaimlerChrysler Motors Corp., 270 Ga. App. 791, 793, 608 S.E.2d 245, 248 (2004) (expert relied on NHTSA report in forming conclusion about vehicle defect); Volkswagen of America, Inc. v. Gentry, 254 Ga. App. 888, 891, 564, 564 S.E.2d 733 (2002) S.E.2d 733, 738 (2002) (expert testimony regarding Federal Motor Vehicle Safety Standards (FMVSS));

(FDA);[6] the Occupational Safety and Health Administration (OSHA);[7] and the United States Bureau of Standards.[8]

Compliance with industry or governmental standards does not necessarily relieve a defendant of liability,[9] but rather, is a factor to be weighed in the risk-utility balancing analysis for design defect cases.[10] In certain circumstances, it has been found that federal regulations merely constitute the minimal standard of care that must be exercised, and that state tort law may impose a higher standard of care.[11] Nonetheless, compliance with such standards is persuasive in refuting a claim of defect, and may establish federal preemption of the claim[12] or preclude a claim for

---

Chrysler Corp. v. Batten, 264 Ga. 723, 726, 450 S.E.2d 208, 212 (1994) (expert relied on NHTSA report regarding seat belts); Ford Motor Co. v. Sasser, 274 Ga. App. 459, 472, 618 S.E.2d 47, 58 (2005), cert. denied, (Nov. 18, 2005) (expert testimony regarding FMVSS pertaining to folding seats in vehicles).

[6]Bryant v. Hoffmann-La Roche, Inc., 262 Ga. App. 401, 407–408, 585 S.E.2d 723, 728–729 (2003) (expert testimony regarding FDA regulations).

[7]Dupree v. Keller Industries, Inc., 199 Ga. App. 138, 141, 404 S.E.2d 291, 294 (1991) (expert relied on OSHA standards in claiming that hydraulic press was defective).

[8]Atlanta Coca–Cola Bottling Co. v. Burke, 109 Ga. App. 53, 57–58, 134 S.E.2d 909, 913 (1964) (expert testimony that beverage bottles complied with the requirements of the U. S. Bureau of Standards).

[9]Banks v. ICI Americas, Inc., 264 Ga. 732, 736, 450 S.E.2d 671 (1994) ("a manufacturer's proof of compliance with industry-wide practices, state of the art, or federal regulations does not eliminate conclusively its liability for its design of allegedly defective products"); Volkswagen of America, Inc. v. Gentry, 254 Ga. App. 888, 894, 564 S.E.2d 733, 740 (2002) ("In Georgia, a plaintiff may pursue a claim against an automobile manufacturer even if the automobile is in compliance with U.S. safety standards"); Doyle v. Volkswagenwerk Aktiengesellschaft, 267 Ga. 574, 577, 481 S.E.2d 518, 521

(1997) (answering in the negative a certified question as to whether a product liability claim is precluded when an automobile is in compliance with the National Automobile Safety Act); Jackson v. International Harvester Co., 190 Ga. App. 765, 767, 380 S.E.2d 306, 308 (1989) (noting that compliance with industry standards or practice, although relevant to the issue of standard of care, is not a defense to negligence).

[10]See Dean v. Toyota Industrial Equipment Mfg., Inc., 246 Ga. App. 255, 259, 540 S.E.2d 233 (2000) (Proof of a manufacturer's compliance with federal regulations does not eliminate liability but is one factor that may be considered).

[11]Doyle v. Volkswagenwerk Aktiengesellschaft, 267 Ga. 574, 574–576, 481 S.E.2d 518, 519–521 (1997) (common law permits suit against automobile manufacturer despite its compliance with the National Automobile Safety Act); Bryant v. Hoffmann–La Roche, Inc., 262 Ga. App. 401, 408, 585 S.E.2d 723, 729 (2003) (FDA only imposes minimum standards and state law may impose a higher standard of care upon a drug manufacturer).

[12]Gentry v. Volkswagen of America, Inc., 238 Ga. App. 785, 788, 521 S.E.2d 13, 17 (1999) (in holding that a car's passive restraint system was not preempted by federal law, the court recognized the possibility of preemption by in dicta that a claim based solely on a car's failure to have

---

punitive damages.[13] Conversely, such evidence may be employed
to weigh in favor of a finding of defect.[14] Expert testimony pertaining to compliance or lack thereof with standards established by
federal regulations does not constitute impermissible testimony
as to the legal standard of care.[15] An expert's testimony as to his
or her understanding of the requirements of a federal regulation
is admissible provided the expert does not misstate the regulation at issue.[16]

§ 5:8 Design defects—Federal law

In a pair of opinions addressing allegations that bone screws
for use in back surgeries were defective, it was held that the
testimony of an orthopedist as to the existence of a defect, though
admissible, was not sufficient to create an issue of fact as to the
existence of a defect.[1] The orthopedist had testified that the
complication rate associated with the bone screw was as high as
63%, and that the product was not effective and unreasonably
dangerous.[2] Despite this testimony, the court found that the bone
screw's manufacturer was entitled to summary judgment, observing that "there is no liability for an 'unreasonably dangerous'
product absent some defect or defective condition[,]"[3] and that
there had been no evidence presented as to a particular characteristic of the bone screws which rendered them defective.[4]

Federal courts have cautioned that expert testimony which is
based upon little more than the expert's credentials and experience in the field, and which is not supported by adequate testing
or a showing of how the expert's experience enabled him to arrive
at the conclusion reached, is at risk of being found unreliable and

---

a lap belt would have been preempted).

[13]See Barger v. Garden Way, Inc.,
231 Ga. App. 723, 728, 499 S.E.2d 737,
742 (1998).

[14]See Luckie v. Piggly–Wiggly
Southern, Inc., 173 Ga. App. 177, 178,
325 S.E.2d 844 (1984) (citing
Chattanooga, R. & C.R. Co. v. White-
head, 90 Ga. 47, 15 S.E. 629 (1892))
(failure to comply with company rules
is illustrative of negligence).

[15]General Motors Corp. v.
Moseley, 213 Ga. App. 875, 883–84,
447 S.E.2d 302, 310–311 (1994) disapproved of on other grounds by Webster
v. Boyett, 269 Ga. 191, 496 S.E.2d 459
(1998).

[16]Volkswagen of America, Inc. v.
Gentry, 254 Ga. App. 888, 892, 564

S.E.2d 733, 738–739 (2002).

[Section 5:8]

[1]Wheat v. Sofamor, S.N.C., 46 F.
Supp. 2d 1351 (N.D. Ga. 1999); Jones
v. Sofamor S.N.C., 1999 WL 1062103
(N.D. Ga. 1999).

[2]Wheat v. Sofamor, S.N.C., 46 F.
Supp. 2d 1351, 1360 (N.D. Ga. 1999);
Jones v. Sofamor S.N.C., 1999 WL
1062103, *4 (N.D. Ga. 1999).

[3]Wheat v. Sofamor, S.N.C., 46 F.
Supp. 2d 1351, 1360 (N.D. Ga. 1999);
Jones v. Sofamor S.N.C., 1999 WL
1062103, *4 (N.D. Ga. 1999).

[4]Wheat v. Sofamor, S.N.C., 46 F.
Supp. 2d 1351, 1361 (N.D. Ga. 1999);
Jones v. Sofamor S.N.C., 1999 WL
1062103, *4 (N.D. Ga. 1999).

inadmissible. A detailed analysis of expert "design defect" testimony occurred in the district court decision of *McGee v. Evenflo Company, Inc.*,[5] a wrongful death case against the manufacturer of a child safety seat arising out of a child's death during a motor vehicle accident. The plaintiff's expert, a mechanical engineer, testified that the safety seat should have been equipped with a device to restrict its upward and rearward movement during a rear-impact accident, and that equipping the seat with such a device would have restricted the seat's movement during the accident and prevented the child's death.

In excluding this testimony, the court noted that the expert had not based his testimony regarding a viable alternative design on any testing, publication, or other recognized methodology,[6] and observed that "the history of engineering and science is filled with finely conceived ideas that are unworkable in practice."[7] "The requirement of testing is . . . necessary in most cases to 'ensure' that the focus of the jury's deliberation is on whether the manufacturer *could* have designed a safer product, not on whether an expert's proposed but untested hypothesis *might* bear fruit."[8] Rejecting the notion that the expert's experience itself provided a sufficiently reliable basis for his testimony,[9] the court noted that it would be "exactly backwards" to allow an expert to escape scrutiny simply by basing his opinion solely on his proclaimed experience, reasoning that "the moral of [such an] approach would be, the less factual support for an expert's opinion, the better."[10] Citing the Advisory Committee Notes to Rule 702, the court observed that where experience is claimed to form the basis of an expert's opinion, "the witness must explain how that experience leads to the conclusion reached, why that experience

---

[5]McGee v. Evenflo Co., Inc., 2003 WL 23350439 (M.D. Ga. 2003), aff'd, 143 Fed. Appx. 299 (11th Cir. 2005).

[6]Specifically, the expert had not: 1) considered relevant standards, practices, or publications in developing his theories; 2) subjected his theories to peer review; 3) tested his theories, or provided documentation or calculations in support of his theories; or 4) determined the feasibility of his suggested alternative designs, or their utility in relation to their risk. McGee v. Evenflo Co., Inc., 2003 WL 23350439 (M.D. Ga. 2003), aff'd, 143 Fed. Appx. 299 (11th Cir. 2005).

[7]McGee v. Evenflo Co., Inc., 2003 WL 23350439 (M.D. Ga. 2003), aff'd, 143 Fed. Appx. 299 (11th Cir. 2005)

(quoting Milanowicz v. The Raymond Corp., 148 F. Supp. 2d 525, 535 (D.N.J. 2001)).

[8]McGee v. Evenflo Co., Inc., 2003 WL 23350439 (M.D. Ga. 2003), aff'd, 143 Fed. Appx. 299 (11th Cir. 2005). The court further indicated that in addition to testing one's own theories, it may be necessary for an expert to test his opponent's theory or the effectiveness of his proposed alternative designs in order for his or her opinion to be admissible. *Id. at & 10–11.*

[9]McGee v. Evenflo Co., Inc., 2003 WL 23350439 (M.D. Ga. 2003), aff'd, 143 Fed. Appx. 299 (11th Cir. 2005).

[10]McGee v. Evenflo Co., Inc., 2003 WL 23350439 (M.D. Ga. 2003), aff'd, 143 Fed. Appx. 299 (11th Cir. 2005).

is a sufficient basis for the opinion, and how that experience is reliably applied to the facts."[11]

Similarly, in the Eleventh Circuit decision of *Dale v. General Motors Corp.*,[12] it was alleged that the plaintiff had sustained injuries because her seatbelt failed to restrain her during a motor vehicle accident. The plaintiff's mechanical engineer contended that the seatbelt's spring-loaded *side* release button had allowed the button to become depressed, and the belt to become unlatched, during the abrupt acceleration of the buckle during the accident. The engineer opined that the seatbelt should have been designed with an *end* release button, and that such a design would have prevented the unlatching of the seatbelt during the accident. In response, the manufacturer took issue with the contention that the seatbelt had in fact unlatched or otherwise failed during the accident, citing several studies showing that that the conditions necessary to create the unlatching effect simply did not occur in "real world" accidents. In excluding the plaintiff's expert's proffered testimony, the court noted that the expert's testimony failed to satisfy several of the reliability indicators of *Daubert*,[13] and that the expert offered no evidence establishing that a buckle with an end release button would be any safer or less subject to unlatching than one with a side release button.[14]

§ 5:9　Warning defects—Georgia law

A product's manufacturer has a duty to warn consumers of non-obvious and foreseeable dangers associated with the normal use of its product.[1] A product sold without an adequate warning

[11]McGee v. Evenflo Co., Inc., 2003 WL 23350439 (M.D. Ga. 2003), aff'd, 143 Fed. Appx. 299 (11th Cir. 2005) (citing Advisory Committee Notes to Rule 702).

[12]Dale v. General Motors Corp., 109 F. Supp. 2d 1376 (N.D. Ga. 1999).

[13]Dale v. General Motors Corp., 109 F. Supp. 2d 1376, 1382 (N.D. Ga. 1999). Specifically, the court observed that the expert's theory had been generally rejected by the scientific community, and that while the expert's unlatching theory had been empirically tested, these tests demonstrated that the belt did not unlatch as the expert had hypothesized. *Id.* at 1379–1382.

[14]Dale v. General Motors Corp., 109 F. Supp. 2d 1376, 1381 (N.D. Ga. 1999).

[Section 5:9]

[1]Moore v. ECI Management, 246 Ga. App. 601, 606, 542 S.E.2d 115, 120 (2000) (product manufacturer has duty to warn users of dangers of which it has actual or constructive knowledge); Wells v. Ortho Pharmaceutical Corp., 788 F.2d 741, 745 (11th Cir. 1986) (under Georgia law, manufacturer under duty to warn users of foreseeable, non-obvious dangers); see also Daniels v. Bucyrus–Erie Corp., 237 Ga. App. 828, 829, 516 S.E.2d 848, 849 (1999) (noting that an open and obvious danger may bar a 'failure to warn'

is considered to be in a "defective" condition.[2] Experts have occasionally been employed to opine that warnings are inadequate in that they do not sufficiently warn the consumer of the dangers posed by the manufacturer's product.[3] Expert testimony in this regard may pertain to the adequacy of the warning due to its content[4] or conspicuity,[5] and expert testimony will typically address alternative warnings that would have provided an adequate warning had they been placed on or with the product.[6] Georgia courts have historically engaged in little analysis with respect to the reliability of expert testimony on the adequacy of a warning.[7]

Because the duty to warn does not require a defendant to warn of obvious dangers,[8] proposed warnings that would not provide a user with any unknown or non-obvious information are insuf-

---

claim).

[2]Wabash Metal Products, Inc. v. AT Plastics Corp., 258 Ga. App. 884, 886, 575 S.E.2d 683, 685 (2002).

[3]Bryant v. Hoffmann–La Roche, Inc., 262 Ga. App. 401, 410, 585 S.E.2d 723, 730 (2003) (physician testified that package insert supplied with heart drug was inadequate to fully warn physicians of the dangers in prescribing the heart medication). In the case of prescription drugs, the learned intermediary doctrine requires that a manufacturer only warn physicians of the inherent risks of the drug, and need not warn the ultimate users. Presto v. Sandoz Pharmaceuticals Corp., 226 Ga. App. 547, 548–549, 487 S.E.2d 70, 73 (1997).

[4]See, e.g, Moore v. ECI Management, 246 Ga. App. 601, 604, 542 S.E.2d 115, 119 (2000)(expert opined that warnings were adequate); Continental Research Corp. v. Reeves, 204 Ga. App. 120, 126, 419 S.E.2d 48, 54 (1992) (expert testified that diamond symbol on defendant's warning that says "corrosive" and which has two pictures demonstrating the corrosive nature of the product "has been passed on by just about everybody as being the best message-giver of a corrosive material").

[5]See, e.g, Daniels v. Bucyrus-Erie Corp., 237 Ga. App. 828, 830, 516 S.E.2d 848, 850 (1999) (expert testi-

fied that warnings for forklift should have been placed in the cab or manual of the crane); Smoky Mountain Enterprises, Inc. v. Bennett, 183 Ga. App. 514, 515, 359 S.E.2d 366, 368 (1987) (expert opined that there should have been an external warning on the stove cautioning the consumer to read and adhere to the instructions contained in the manual).

[6]See, e.g, Daniels v. Bucyrus–Erie Corp., 237 Ga. App. 828, 829–830, 516 S.E.2d 848, 849–50 (1999) (testimony that crane should have contained warning to apprise bystanders tipping danger when crane was not appropriately "cribbed").

[7]But see Chrysler Corp. v. Batten, 264 Ga. 723, 728–29, 450 S.E.2d 208, 214 (1994) (Fletcher, J., dissenting) (expert did not have sufficient basis to testify as to defendant's knowledge of a defect where the testimony was in reference to an earlier design of the product at issue and for which only one accident had been reported).

[8]See, e.g, Moore v. ECI Management, 246 Ga. App. 601, 604, 542 S.E.2d 115, 119 (2000) (noting that injury from an open and obvious danger may bar a 'failure to warn' claim); Daniels v. Bucyrus–Erie Corp., 237 Ga. App. 828, 829, 516 S.E.2d 848, 849 (1999) (noting that an open and obvious danger may bar a 'failure to warn' claim).

ficient to show the warning's inadequacy.[9] Relevant to the issue of whether the duty to warn has been breached is whether the defendant had actual or constructive knowledge of the potential dangers posed by the product,[10] and expert testimony on this point has been found admissible. For instance, in *Bishop v. Farhat*, the court found that a product's distributor had constructive knowledge that latex gloves were capable of causing allergic reactions in light of an expert's testimony that allergic reactions to latex had been documented in medical literature and universally recognized as a risk for over ten years prior to the product's distribution.[11]

§ 5:10 Warning defects—Federal law

No reported decisions among the federal courts in Georgia address the reliability of expert testimony with regard to the adequacy of a product's warning, and this section therefore addresses the manner in which federal courts sitting outside Georgia have dealt with expert testimony on this topic. Expert testimony on the sufficiency of warnings generally addresses the adequacy of a warning's content, design, placement, and visibility to provide individuals coming into proximity with the product of its hazards,[1] and is often provided by persons with experience in the design of the type of product at issue or human factors analysis.[2] In assessing the reliability of such testimony, federal courts have placed a premium on whether the expert has tested the efficacy of a proposed alternative warning in both apprising individuals of the danger posed by the product *and* in modifying the behavior of individuals coming into contact with the product such that the danger is averted.[3] The failure to test the effectiveness of a proposed warning in modifying behavior has been found to render an expert's testimony that such a warning would have prevented

---

[9]See, e.g, Daniels v. Bucyrus–Erie Corp., 237 Ga. App. 828, 830, 516 S.E.2d 848, 850 (1999) (injured crane operator was "keenly aware of the very risk" about which the expert claimed he should have been warned).

[10]Moore v. ECI Management, 246 Ga. App. 601, 604, 542 S.E.2d 115, 119 (2000) (noting manufacturer has a duty to warn about dangers to which it has actual or constructive knowledge).

[11]Bishop v. Farhat, 227 Ga. App. 201, 206, 489 S.E.2d 323, 328 (1997).

[Section 5:10]

[1]See, e.g. Jaurequi v. Carter Mfg. Co., Inc., 173 F.3d 1076 (8th Cir. 1999).

[2]See, e.g. Williams v. Michelin North America, Inc., 381 F. Supp. 2d 1351, 1362 (M.D. Fla. 2005).

[3]See, e.g. Bourelle v. Crown Equipment Corp., 220 F.3d 532 (7th Cir. 2000); Jaurequi v. Carter Mfg. Co., Inc., 173 F.3d 1076 (8th Cir. 1999); Shepherd v. Michelin Tire Corp., 6 F. Supp. 2d 1307 (N.D. Ala. 1997).

the injury suffered by the plaintiff to be speculative and inadmissible.[4]

For instance, in *Shepherd v. Michelin Tire Corp.*,[5] an individual was killed after mounting and inflating a tire on the wrong-sized tire rim, causing the tire to explode. An expert was offered to testify that a "more elaborate and more eye-catching" warning than was then in use should have been placed on the tire so as to prevent the mounting of a tire to a wrong-sized rim. In excluding the expert's testimony as unreliable and inadmissible, the court observed that the expert had not tested the effectiveness of an alternative warning in preventing tires from being placed on the wrong-sized rim, and that the testing which had in fact been performed by others indicated that alternative warnings were in fact not effective behavior-modifiers in this regard.[6]

Similarly, in *Jaurequi v. Carter Manufacturing Co.*,[7] a farm worker's legs were amputated when he stepped in front of a combine collecting corn. Two experts were offered to testify that the warnings on the combine were insufficient in their content, design, and placement so as to adequately apprise worker's of the zone of danger immediately in front of the combine. In excluding such testimony, the court observed that neither expert had designed or tested the effectiveness of any proposed alternative warning, nor had they been able to point to the use of such alternative warnings by other manufacturers of the same or similar products.[8] In commenting on the effectiveness of any proposed warning, the court found it significant that the worker had been previously advised not to stand in front of the combine during its operation.[9]

Expert testimony on the adequacy of warnings has also been excluded where the expert had no experience in the design of the type of product at issue or other relevant experience,[10] or where

---

[4]Cummins v. Lyle Industries, 93 F.3d 362, 368–370 (7th Cir. 1996); Shepherd v. Michelin Tire Corp., 6 F. Supp. 2d 1307, 1311–1313 (N.D. Ala. 1997).

[5]Shepherd v. Michelin Tire Corp., 6 F. Supp. 2d 1307 (N.D. Ala. 1997).

[6]Shepherd v. Michelin Tire Corp., 6 F. Supp. 2d 1307, 1310–1313 (N.D. Ala. 1997); see also Cummins v. Lyle Industries, 93 F.3d 362, 370 (7th Cir. 1996) (expert testimony pertaining to alternative warnings that should have been placed on product inadmissible where expert had not tested the ef-

fectiveness of such warnings and conceded that he would not know the effectiveness of such warnings in modifying behavior in the absence of testing).

[7]Jaurequi v. Carter Mfg. Co., Inc., 173 F.3d 1076 (8th Cir. 1999).

[8]Jaurequi v. Carter Mfg. Co., Inc., 173 F.3d 1076, 1084 (8th Cir. 1999).

[9]Jaurequi v. Carter Mfg. Co., Inc., 173 F.3d 1076, 1083 (8th Cir. 1999).

[10]Williams v. Michelin North America, Inc., 381 F. Supp. 2d 1351,

the expert lacked familiarity with the operation of the product[11] or the setting in which it was used.[12]

§ 5:11   Causation testimony—Georgia law

Whatever theory a plaintiff travels under in prosecuting a product liability action, the plaintiff must prove that the alleged product defect was the proximate cause of his or her injury.[1] Expert testimony is employed both to establish and refute the contention that the plaintiff's injuries were the result of the alleged defect.[2] When attempting to establish causation, an expert should be prepared to rule out other possible causes in addition to explaining how the alleged defect would have caused the injury. For instance, in a case where a fire resulted from an allegedly defective gas oven, summary judgment was properly granted in favor of the defendant manufacturer where the plaintiff's expert could not rule out other possible causes of the fire that were unrelated to the product's design.[3]

However, even where an expert is unable to state that a product's defect was the cause of injury, causation may be established by the evidence as a whole.[4] Moreover, expert testimony has found not to be necessary where the jury can determine, based upon its own experience, whether a defect with the product caused the plaintiff's injuries. For instance, in *Owens v. General Motors Corporation*, the court found that expert

---

1362 (M.D. Fla. 2005).

[11]Jaurequi v. Carter Mfg. Co., Inc., 173 F.3d 1076 (8th Cir. 1999).

[12]Bourelle v. Crown Equipment Corp., 220 F.3d 532 (7th Cir. 2000).

[Section 5:11]

[1]Owens v. General Motors Corp., 272 Ga. App. 842, 613 S.E.2d 651 (2005); Hall v. Scott USA, Ltd., 198 Ga. App. 197, 200, 400 S.E.2d 700, 703 (1990).

[2]See, e.g. Cottrell, Inc. v. Williams, 266 Ga. App. 357, 360, 596 S.E.2d 789, 792 (2004) (engineer testified that fire leading to plaintiff's injury was caused by a faulty switch located on the floor of the plaintiff's truck); Volkswagen of America, Inc. v. Gentry, 254 Ga. App. 888, 890, 564 S.E.2d 733, 738 (2002) (engineer testified that, had car manufacturer implemented a number of design changes, decedent's life may have been spared); Crosby v. Cooper Tire & Rubber Co.,

240 Ga. App. 857, 858, 524 S.E.2d 313, 317 (1999), rev'd 273 Ga. 454, 543 S.E.2d 21 (2001) (expert opined that injuries suffered by plaintiff during vehicle's rollover caused by manufacturing defect with tire causing its tread to separate); Murphy v. Blue Bird Body Co., 207 Ga. App. 853, 858, 429 S.E.2d 530, 535 (1993) (human factors psychologist testified that appropriate warnings would have prevented accident); Smoky Mountain Enterprises, Inc. v. Bennett, 183 Ga. App. 514, 514, 359 S.E.2d 366, 367 (1987) (expert testified that most likely cause of fire was placement of stove in fireplace as opposed to design of the stove).

[3]Bunch v. Maytag Corp., 211 Ga. App. 546, 548, 439 S.E.2d 676, 678 (1993).

[4]Volkswagen of America, Inc. v. Gentry, 254 Ga. App. 888, 891, 564 S.E.2d 733, 738 (2002).

testimony was not required to establish that the alleged failure of a seatbelt and air bad during an automobile collision contributed to the plaintiff's injuries because the jury, based on its own experience, was capable of determining whether the failure of a seatbelt to restrain the plaintiff or the air bag to inflate caused the plaintiff to sustain more serious injuries than he would have had these items worker properly.[5]

A defense often asserted in the context of product liability actions is that of superceding cause.[6] This issue often arises where there has been a post-sale modification of a product, and expert testimony may be used to establish that such a modification, rather than the product's design or manufacture, was the cause of injury.[7] For instance, in *Omark Industries, Inc. v. Alewine*, a case involving a fire occasioned by a ruptured hydraulic line, the court found summary judgment in favor of the defendant appropriate where expert testimony established that the hydraulic fluid would not reach the temperature necessary to ignite during normal usage of the machine.[8] In light of such testimony, the court found that the cause of the fire could only be attributed to the manner in which the equipment had been installed and maintained, as opposed to any latent defect in the manufacture or design of the machine.[9] Similarly, in *Ogletree v. Navistar International Transp. Corp.*, a suit involving a manufacturer's failure to install an audible back-up alarm on a truck, the court found that summary judgment in favor of the manufacturer was appropriate where expert testimony established that the end user had modified the truck in such a way that a back-up alarm, even had one been installed, would have been disabled by the modification.[10]

§ 5:12 Causation testimony—Federal law

In assessing the admissibility of expert opinion testimony that a product defect was the cause of a plaintiff's injury, federal courts have placed considerable emphasis on whether an expert has been able to reliably rule out alternative factors as the cause

[5]Owens v. General Motors Corp., 272 Ga. App. 842, 847–848, 613 S.E.2d 651, 655–56 (2005).

[6]See, e.g. Union Carbide Corp. v. Holton, 136 Ga. App. 726, 729, 222 S.E.2d 105, 109 (1975).

[7]Such intervening acts insulate a defendant from liability where it was not foreseeable to the defendant, not triggered by any act by the defendant, and was sufficient in itself to cause the injury. Yaeger v. Canadair, Ltd., 189 Ga. App. 207, 208, 375 S.E.2d 469, 471 (1988).

[8]Omark Industries, Inc. v. Alewine, 171 Ga. App. 207, 208, 319 S.E.2d 24, 25 (1984).

[9]Omark Industries, Inc. v. Alewine, 171 Ga. App. 207, 208, 319 S.E.2d 24, 25 (1984).

[10]Ogletree v. Navistar Intern. Transp. Corp., 245 Ga. App. 1, 5, 535 S.E.2d 545, 549 (2000).

of the plaintiff's injury. For instance, in *Kumho Tire Co. v. Carmichael*,[1] a minivan rolled over after one of its tire's tread separated from its carcass, causing the tire to blow out. Expert testimony, based on a visual and tactile inspection of the tire in question, was offered to opine that a defect in the tire, as opposed to some other factor, had caused the tread separation. In finding that the district court had acted within its discretion in excluding this testimony, the Supreme Court noted that while other factors, such as the age and overuse of the tire, could also account for tread separation, the expert had not been able to provide any estimate as to how many miles the tire had traveled so as to exclude these possible alternate causes.[2]

The role of testing and providing empirical support for one's theories of causation has proven to be dispositive with respect to establishing the reliability, and admissibility, of expert causation testimony. For instance, in *McGee v. Evenflo Co.*,[3] a child was killed while the vehicle in which he was riding was rear-ended. The plaintiff's expert testified that the safety seat in which the child was riding should have been equipped with a device to restrict its upward and rearward movement during a rear-impact accident, and that equipping the seat with such a device would have in fact restricted the seat's movement during the accident so as to prevent the child's death. In excluding this testimony, the court first observed that the expert had failed to conduct any testing to support his conclusion that the design of the seat in fact caused the child's injuries and death.[4] Specifically, the expert failed to make any calculations on the various factors that would have bore upon the seat's performance during the accident, such as the speed of vehicles prior to the accident, the forces involved in the accident, or the position of the seat within the car.[5] The court then observed that the expert had failed to conduct any testing to support the conclusion that his proposed alternative design would have prevented the child's injuries and death.[6] Specifically, the expert failed to provide any testing or data showing that his proposed design could have been viably incorporated, how the proposed design would have affected the movement of

[Section 5:12]

[1]Kumho Tire Co., Ltd. v. Carmichael, 526 U.S. 137, 119 S. Ct. 1167, 143 L. Ed. 2d 238 (1999).

[2]Kumho Tire Co., Ltd. v. Carmichael, 526 U.S. 137, 154–155, 119 S. Ct. 1167, 1177, 143 L. Ed. 2d 238 (1999).

[3]McGee v. Evenflo Co., Inc., 2003 WL 23350439 (M.D. Ga. 2003), aff'd, 143 Fed. Appx. 299 (11th Cir. 2005).

[4]McGee v. Evenflo Co., Inc., 2003 WL 23350439 (M.D. Ga. 2003), aff'd, 143 Fed. Appx. 299 (11th Cir. 2005).

[5]McGee v. Evenflo Co., Inc., 2003 WL 23350439 (M.D. Ga. 2003), aff'd, 143 Fed. Appx. 299 (11th Cir. 2005).

[6]McGee v. Evenflo Co., Inc., 2003 WL 23350439 (M.D. Ga. 2003), aff'd, 143 Fed. Appx. 299 (11th Cir. 2005).

the seat during the accident and the forces acting upon the child, or how the proposed design would have in fact prevented injury to the child.[7]

In assessing the reliability of expert causation testimony, courts have also considered whether the expert's methodology is generally recognized and accepted in the relevant community. For instance, in *Kumho Tire*, the Court found it significant that there was no evidence that other experts in the industry employed the expert's visual and tactile inspection in making determinations as to the cause of tread separation.[8] The focus has not, however, been strictly limited to the expert's methodology, and courts have excluded expert testimony where, even though the expert has employed a commonly-recognized methodology, he has reached a conclusion which is "out of step" with others in the field. "When a scientist claims to rely on a method practiced by most scientists, yet presents conclusions that are shared by no other scientist, the district court should be wary that the method has not been faithfully applied."[9] For instance, in *Wheat v. Sofamor*, although an anesthesiologist used the commonly-employed method of differential diagnosis to conclude that bone screw devices were the cause of the plaintiff's pain, the court excluded the expert's testimony as unreliable, noting that no other experts had concluded that the bone screws at issue caused the type of pain about which the plaintiff had complained.[10]

---

[7]McGee v. Evenflo Co., Inc., 2003 WL 23350439 (M.D. Ga. 2003), aff'd, 143 Fed. Appx. 299 (11th Cir. 2005).

[8]Kumho Tire Co., Ltd. v. Carmichael, 526 U.S. 137, 157, 119 S. Ct. 1167, 1178, 143 L. Ed. 2d 238 (1999).

[9]Wheat v. Sofamor, S.N.C., 46 F. Supp.2d 1351, 1359 (N.D. Ga. 1999) (quoting Lust By and Through Lust v. Merrell Dow Pharmaceuticals, Inc., 89 F.3d 594, 598 (9th Cir. 1996)).

[10]Wheat v. Sofamor, S.N.C., 46 F. Supp.2d 1351, 1359 (N.D. Ga. 1999).

Chapter 6

Toxic Torts

> **KeyCite®**: Cases and other legal materials listed in KeyCite Scope can be researched through the KeyCite service on Westlaw®. Use KeyCite to check citations for form, parallel references, prior and later history, and comprehensive citator information, including citations to other decisions and secondary materials.

§ 6:1   Overview

The term "toxic tort" refers to a cause of action arising from a party's exposure to a substance alleged to be toxic, such as hazardous waste, asbestos, and increasingly, pharmaceuticals.[1] Expert testimony is often employed in these cases for purposes of showing that exposure to such a substance is the cause of the plaintiff's harm, as this entails a matter beyond the ability of the average juror to determine for himself.[2] Numerous federal cases have addressed the admissibility of expert testimony in the context of toxic tort cases, including the United States Supreme Court decisions of *Daubert*[3] and *Joiner*.[4] The primary issue in these cases has centered on matters of causation, with federal courts drawing a sharp distinction between the concepts of gen-

---

[Section 6:1]

[1]See BLACK'S LAW DICTIONARY (8th ed. 2004).

[2]See Magnan v. Miami Aircraft Support, Inc., 217 Ga. App. 855, 857, 459 S.E.2d 592, 595 (1995).

[3]Daubert v. Merrell Dow Pharmaceuticals, Inc., 509 U.S. 579, 113 S. Ct. 2786, 125 L. Ed. 2d 469 (1993).

[4]General Elec. Co. v. Joiner, 522 U.S. 136, 118 S. Ct. 512, 139 L. Ed. 2d 508 (1997).

eral and specific causation.[5] General causation focuses on whether the substance at issue is capable, as a general matter, of causing the type of injury alleged,[6] whereas specific causation focuses on whether the plaintiff's injuries were in fact caused by his or her exposure to this substance.[7] While not entirely absent from consideration in *Georgia's* reported decisions,[8] the Georgia courts have not appeared to focus as much as the federal courts have on this distinction.[9] Because of the divergence which exists in the manner in which Georgia and federal courts have dealt with expert testimony in toxic tort cases, as well as the prominence of toxic tort cases in the federal jurisprudence following in the wake of *Daubert*, this chapter addresses the treatment of toxic tort cases in both Georgia and federal courts.

§ 6:2   Georgia law

In Georgia, courts have historically considered the reliability of expert testimony in toxic tort cases by employing the "verifiable certainty" test enunciated in *Harper v. State,*[1] which considered whether the scientific procedures or techniques employed by the expert in arriving at his or her opinion had reached a "scientific stage of verifiable certainty."[2] In theory, this test was similar to the reliability test sanctioned by the United States Supreme Court in *Daubert*; however, until the enactment of O.C.G.A. § 24–9–67.1, Georgia courts had rejected the invitation to apply the *Daubert*, reasoning that it involved the application of Rule

---

[5]McClain v. Metabolife Intern., Inc., 401 F.3d 1233, 1237–1239 (11th Cir. 2005); Siharath v. Sandoz Pharmaceuticals Corp., 131 F. Supp. 2d 1347 (N.D. Ga. 2001), aff'd, 295 F.3d 1194 (11th Cir. 2002).

[6]McClain v. Metabolife Intern., Inc., 401 F.3d 1233, 1239 (11th Cir. 2005).

[7]McClain v. Metabolife Intern., Inc., 401 F.3d 1233, 1239 (11th Cir. 2005).

[8]See Fulmore v. CSX Transp., Inc., 252 Ga. App. 884, 891, 557 S.E.2d 64, 72 (2001) (recognizing distinction between general and specific causation, and necessity of showing both).

[9]Compare McClain v. Metabolife Intern., Inc., 401 F.3d 1233, 1237–1239 (11th Cir. 2005), and Siharath v. Sandoz Pharmaceuticals Corp., 131 F. Supp. 2d 1347 (N.D. Ga. 2001), aff'd,

295 F.3d 1194 (11th Cir. 2002), with Orkin Exterminating Co., Inc. v. Carder, 258 Ga. App. 796, 798, 575 S.E.2d 664, 668 (2002), and Jordan v. Georgia Power Co., 219 Ga. App. 690, 694, 466 S.E.2d 601, 606 (1995).

[Section 6:2]

[1]See, e.g. Orkin Exterminating Co., Inc. v. Carder, 258 Ga. App. 796, 799, 575 S.E.2d 664 (2002); Jordan v. Georgia Power Co., 219 Ga. App. 690, 693, 466 S.E.2d 601, 605 (1995); Orkin Exterminating Co., Inc. v. McIntosh, 215 Ga. App. 587, 593, 452 S.E.2d 159, 165 (1994).

[2]Orkin Exterminating Co., Inc. v. McIntosh, 215 Ga. App. 587, 593, 452 S.E.2d 159, 166 (1994); see also Harper v. State, 249 Ga. 519, 292 S.E.2d 389 (1982) (creating the verifiable certainty standard).

702 of the Federal Rules of Evidence, which had not been adopted in Georgia.[3]

§6:3 Georgia law—Qualifications

Georgia courts have recognized that expert testimony is generally required to establish whether an exposure to a certain substance was the cause of the plaintiff's maladies, reasoning that this inquiry entails the application of medical and scientific knowledge which lies outside the ability of the average lay person to ascertain on his own.[1] Experts who have testified with respect to such matters have included medical doctors,[2] toxicologists,[3] pharmacologists,[4] and epidemiologists.[5] Toxicology has been recognized by the Georgia courts to entail "the study of adverse actions of chemicals on the body."[6] Similarly, albeit somewhat more narrowly, pharmacology has been recognized by the courts as " 'the study of drugs as to their chemistry, source, physical properties, preparation and physiological effects on living tis-

---

[3]See Orkin Exterminating Co., Inc. v. Carder, 258 Ga. App. 796, 799, 575 S.E.2d 664, 668 (2002); Jordan v. Georgia Power Co., 219 Ga. App. 690, 693, 466 S.E.2d 601, 604 (1995); Orkin Exterminating Co., Inc. v. McIntosh, 215 Ga. App. 587, 592, 452 S.E.2d 159, 165 (1994).

[Section 6:3]

[1]See, e.g. Magnan v. Miami Aircraft Support, Inc., 217 Ga. App. 855, 857, 459 S.E.2d 592, 595 (1995) (expert testimony necessary to prove that eye problems were caused by exposure to pesticides); but see Great Atlantic & Pacific Tea Co. v. DuPee, 71 Ga. App. 148, 30 S.E.2d 365, 367–68 (1944) (testimony by several witnesses that they became sick shortly after consuming food held sufficient to establish cause even where expert testified that meat consumed contained no chemical poison).

[2]See e.g., Moresi v. Evans, 257 Ga. App. 670, 671–72, 572 S.E.2d 327, 330 (2002); Magnan v. Miami Aircraft Support, Inc., 217 Ga. App. 855, 856, 459 S.E.2d 592, 594–95 (1995); Jordan v. Santa Fe Engineering, Inc., 198 Ga. App. 600, 601, 402 S.E.2d 304, 305 (1991).

[3]See, e.g. Sinkfield v. Oh, 229 Ga. App. 883, 884, 495 S.E.2d 94, 95–96

(1997); Jordan v. Santa Fe Engineering, Inc., 198 Ga. App. 600, 601, 402 S.E.2d 304, 305 (1991); Moultrie Farm Center, Inc. v. Sparkman, 171 Ga. App. 736, 740, 320 S.E.2d 863, 867 (1984).

[4]See, e.g. Moresi v. Evans, 257 Ga. App. 670, 674–75, 572 S.E.2d 327, 332 (2002); Sinkfield v. Oh, 229 Ga. App. 883, 884, 495 S.E.2d 94, 95–96 (1997); Jordan v. Santa Fe Engineering, Inc., 198 Ga. App. 600, 601, 402 S.E.2d 304, 305 (1991).

[5]Flowers v. Union Carbide Corp., 271 Ga. App. 438, 610 S.E.2d 109 (2005).

[6]Jordan v. Santa Fe Engineering, Inc., 198 Ga. App. 600, 602, 402 S.E.2d 304, 306–07 (1991). See also Bernard D. Goldstein and Mary Sue Henifin, Reference Guide on Toxicology, in Reference Manual on Scientific Evidence 403 (Federal Judicial Center 2d ed. 2000) ("Toxicology classically is known as the science of poisons. A modern definition is 'the study of the adverse effects of chemicals on living organisms.' Although it is an age-old science, toxicology has only recently become a discipline distinct from pharmacology, biochemistry, cell biology, and related fields.").

sue.' "[7] Epidemiology has been defined as "the field of public health and medicine that studies the incidence, distribution, and etiology of disease in human populations."[8]

Toxicologists and pharmacologists have been found competent to testify as to the characteristics of chemicals or drugs, including the adverse effect such substances can have on the human body.[9] Courts have permitted these experts to testify over the objection that their testimony implicates medical issues requiring the testimony of a physician, noting that Georgia law "does not mandate that only medical doctors be permitted to testify regarding medical issues; others with certain training and experience may testify on issues within the parameters of their expertise."[10] Indeed, it has been recognized that pharmacologists are perhaps better suited than medical doctors to address the adverse effects drugs can have on the human body.[11] Nonetheless, the parameters of these experts' expertise is not without limits, and courts have generally limited the testimony of these experts to the effect certain substances can have on the human body, and excluded testimony from these experts as to whether the substance did in fact cause a plaintiff's specific illness or disease.[12] Similarly, such experts have been held not qualified to testify as to whether an

---

[7]Sinkfield v. Oh, 229 Ga. App. 883, 885, 495 S.E.2d 94, 96 (1997) (quoting Colusa Remedy Co. v. U.S., 176 F.2d 554, 558 (8th Cir. 1949)). See also Stedman's Medical Dictionary (26th ed. 1995) (defining pharmacology as "[t]he science concerned with drugs, their sources, appearance, chemistry, actions, and uses.").

[8]Michael D. Green, D. Michael Freedman, and Leon Gordis, Reference Guide on Epidemiology, in REFERENCE MANUAL ON SCIENTIFIC EVIDENCE 335 (Federal Judicial Center 2d ed. 2000). See also Stedman's Medical Dictionary (26th ed. 1995) (defining epidemiology as "[t]he study of the distribution and determinants of health-related states or events in specified populations, and the application of this study to control of health problems.").

[9]Moresi v. Evans, 257 Ga. App. 670, 675, 572 S.E.2d 327, 332 (2002) (pharmacologist qualified to testify regarding concept of adverse drug reaction and potential side effects of drug administered); Sinkfield v. Oh, 229 Ga. App. 883, 885, 495 S.E.2d 94,

96 (1997) (expert with doctorate in pharmacology and toxicology qualified to testify regarding effect various doses of drug would have on pregnant women and fetuses at various stages of pregnancy); Jordan v. Santa Fe Engineering, Inc., 198 Ga. App. 600, 602–03, 402 S.E.2d 304, 306–07 (1991) (toxicologist qualified to testify as to adverse effect of certain drug on body).

[10]Sinkfield v. Oh, 229 Ga. App. 883, 885, 495 S.E.2d 94, 96 (1997) (citing Goodman v. Lipman, 197 Ga. App. 631, 399 S.E.2d 255 (1990)).

[11]Sinkfield v. Oh, 229 Ga. App. 883, 885, 495 S.E.2d 94, 96 (1997) ("We question whether a medical doctor's pharmacological training is generally comparable to that of a doctor of pharmacology. Thus, it is difficult to see what medically trained professional could have been more qualified to testify about the effects of the particular drug at issue than Dr. Proctor, who had earned a Ph.D. with a double major of pharmacology and toxicology from a prominent university.").

[12]Moresi v. Evans, 257 Ga. App. 670, 675, 572 S.E.2d 327, 332 (2002)

individual's symptoms are consistent with causes other than the drug or substance at issue.[13]

§ 6:4 Georgia law—Causation

In order to prevail in a toxic tort case, a plaintiff must present proof of general and specific causation.[1] General causation refers to "whether exposure to a substance is capable of causing a particular injury or disease[,]" whereas specific causation refers to "whether exposure to a substance under the circumstances of the case caused a particular plaintiff's illness or disease."[2] While these elements of proof are somewhat related, there are important conceptual differences between them. For instance, while many chemicals contained in pesticides are known to be capable of having adverse effects on humans, a showing that an individual was exposed to such chemicals may not be enough to establish that the exposure was in fact the cause of the individual's illness where his or her symptoms are also consistent with an exposure to other substances or agents.[3]

A toxicological concept involving the interplay of general and specific causation is that of the "dose-response" relationship, which recognizes that the risk posed by a substance is a function of the quantity or concentration of the substance to which an in-

---

(while pharmacologist qualified to testify that the combined effect of two drugs ingested by plaintiff was capable of causing plaintiff's central nervous system depression, court found pharmacologist not qualified to testify how a depressed nervous system would affect the plaintiff's bladder, reasoning that such testimony concerned a medical question appropriately addressed by a medical doctor or pathologist); Jordan v. Santa Fe Engineering, Inc., 198 Ga. App. 600, 602–03, 402 S.E.2d 304, 306–07 (1991) (while toxicologist was qualified to testify concerning the adverse effect a substance consumed by decedent has on the body, not qualified to testify as to whether symptoms displayed by decedent prior to death were consistent with other known physical problems of decedent); see also Flowers v. Union Carbide Corp., 271 Ga. App. 438, 610 S.E.2d 109 (2005) (epidemiologist not qualified to offer opinion on medical histories of individuals exposed to asbestos).

[13]Jordan v. Santa Fe Engineering, Inc., 198 Ga. App. 600, 602–03, 402 S.E.2d 304, 306–07 (1991).

[Section 6:4]
[1]Fulmore v. CSX Transp., Inc., 252 Ga. App. 884, 891, 557 S.E.2d 64, 72 (2001).

[2]Fulmore v. CSX Transp., Inc., 252 Ga. App. 884, 891, 557 S.E.2d 64, 72 (2001).

[3]Boyd v. Orkin Exterminating Co., Inc., 191 Ga. App. 38, 40, 381 S.E.2d 295, 298 (1989) (upholding directed verdict in favor of pest control company, noting that "[a]lthough there was evidence that the children had suffered occasionally over the years from such symptoms as sore throat, runny nose, nausea, and rash, there was no showing that these symptoms, which were also consistent with common viral infections, had been caused by exposure to chlordane or heptachlor, [two of the chemicals used in the pest control company's pesticide].").

dividual has been exposed.[4] For instance, while it may be generally accepted that asbestos is capable of causing life-threatening illnesses, exposure to asbestos will only result in such consequences where the individual has been exposed to a quantity or concentration of the substance necessary to yield such adverse consequences.[5] Thus, it is not enough to merely show that the plaintiff was exposed to a substance which is generally capable of causing a particular illness or disease; it must also be shown that the plaintiff was exposed to a sufficient amount of the substance such that it was in fact capable of causing the plaintiff's illness or disease.[6] However, such a showing may not be necessary where the plaintiff's illness or disease can *only* be caused by overexposure to the substance at issue.[7]

In addressing the reliability of expert testimony in toxic tort cases, the Georgia courts have, at least indirectly, considered whether the expert's theories as to whether a substance or agent is capable of causing a particular harm have been generally accepted. For instance, in *Jordan v. Georgia Power Co.*,[8] at issue was whether electromagnetic radiation (EMF) emitted from near-by power lines had caused the plaintiff's non-Hodgkin's lymphoma. In holding that summary judgment in favor of Georgia Power was proper, the court found that, notwithstanding the testimony of the plaintiff's experts that electromagnetic radiation was capable of causing this type of lymphoma, "[t]he scientific ev-

---

[4]Fulmore v. CSX Transp., Inc., 252 Ga. App. 884, 886, 891–892, 557 S.E.2d 64, 68–69, (2001).

[5]See Fulmore v. CSX Transp., Inc., 252 Ga. App. 884, 886, 891–892, 557 S.E.2d 64, 68–69 (2001).

[6]Stewart v. CSX Transp., Inc., 268 Ga. App. 434, 602 S.E.2d 665 (2004); see also Chandler Exterminators, Inc. v. Morris, 262 Ga. 257, 257, 416 S.E.2d 277, 278 (1992) (upholding trial court's striking of expert testimony opining that plaintiff's damage was caused by exposure to chemical, where trial court, citing Hull v. Merck & Co., Inc., 758 F.2d 1474 (11th Cir. 1985), held that opinion evidence is insufficient to prove causation where "such evidence presumes exposure without showing evidence of significant toxicity levels.").

[7]Fulmore v. CSX Transp., Inc., 252 Ga. App. 884, 892, 557 S.E.2d 64, 72 (2001) (evidence that plaintiffs were exposed to asbestos over the "threshold level" at which exposure becomes harmful where it was undisputed that the plaintiffs suffered from asbestosis, which by definition "results only from an overexposure to asbestos"); see also John Crane, Inc. v. Jones, 262 Ga. App. 531, 535, 586 S.E.2d 26, 30 (2003), cert. granted, (Jan. 22, 2004) and aff'd, 278 Ga. 747, 604 S.E.2d 822 (2004) (noting "overwhelming evidence that exposure to asbestos caused the injury" where physician testified that "virtually all reported cases of mesothelioma appear in patients who have been occupationally exposed to asbestos").

[8]Jordan v. Georgia Power Co., 219 Ga. App. 690, 466 S.E.2d 601 (1995).

idence regarding whether EMFs cause harm of any kind is inconclusive[.]"[9]

Georgia courts have also considered whether an expert has been able to provide a reliable factual basis for his opinions on causation, and have held that expert testimony which merely provides a conclusory statement on causation is insufficient to create an issue of fact for the jury. For instance, in *Motorola, Inc. v. Ward*,[10] at issue was whether electromagnetic radiation emitted from a cellular phone was the cause of the plaintiff's malignant brain tumor. In finding that summary judgment in favor of the defendant was warranted, the court observed that the plaintiff's experts, despite testifying that the electromagnetic radiation was the cause of the plaintiff's cancer, had not "explained a mechanism by which an electromagnetic field can cause cancer, set out any statistical correlation between electromagnetic field exposure and cancer, or otherwise explained how the affiant reached his conclusion."[11]

The use of "challenge testing" has been found to be a reliable methodology for purposes of establishing that an exposure to a substance is the cause of the plaintiff's illness, at least under the *Harper v. State* test in effect prior to the enactment of O.C.G.A. § 24–9–67.1.[12] This methodology entails exposing an individual to the substance alleged to have caused his or her symptoms and observing the individual for the reappearance of those symptoms, and then discontinuing the individual's exposure to the substance and observing him or her for the disappearance of those same symptoms.[13]

---

[9]Jordan v. Georgia Power Co., 219 Ga. App. 690, 694, 466 S.E.2d 601, 606 (1995). Notwithstanding this finding, the Court of Appeals found that the trial court had erred in allowing the defendant's experts to testify before the jury that the "consensus in the scientific community" was that EMFs did not cause non-Hodgkin's lymphoma. *Id. at 693-694.* While the court itself apparently considered such testimony in determining whether the expert testimony that EMFs can cause non-Hodgkins lymphoma was sufficiently reliable so as to allow the plaintiff's claim to go to a jury, the court found that the presentation of such "consensus" testimony to the jury itself violated the rule against experts acting as a "mere conduit" for the opinions of other experts. *Id. at 693.*

[10]Motorola, Inc. v. Ward, 223 Ga. App. 678, 478 S.E.2d 465 (1996).

[11]Motorola, Inc. v. Ward, 223 Ga. App. 678, 679, 478 S.E.2d 465, 466 (1996).

[12]Orkin Exterminating Co., Inc. v. Carder, 258 Ga. App. 796, 800–01, 575 S.E.2d 664, 669 (2002) (finding challenge testing sufficiently reliable to warrant admission of test results, noting that the absence of controls or safeguards in the testing went to weight and not admissibility).

[13]Orkin Exterminating Co., Inc. v. Carder, 258 Ga. App. 796, 575 S.E.2d 664 (2002). In *Carder,* the plaintiff was exposed to various liquids, some of which contained the pesticides alleged to have caused the plaintiff's reaction. Other liquids to which the plaintiff

§ 6:5   Federal law

In federal court, toxic tort cases are "won or lost on the strength of the scientific evidence presented to prove causation."[1] In order to make out a successful toxic tort claim, a plaintiff must show both general causation and specific causation.[2] That is, a plaintiff must be able to show that the substance to which he or she was exposed is capable of causing the type of illness or disease from which the plaintiff is alleged to suffer, and that the plaintiff's exposure to the substance is in fact the cause of his or her illness or disease.[3] For purposes of the general causation element, cases may be categorized into one of two types: 1) those in which the toxicity of the substance at issue has been generally recognized; and 2) those in which the toxicity of the substance at issue has not been generally recognized.[4] In the first type of case, the court need not undertake an extensive *Daubert* analysis on the issue of whether the substance is capable of causing the harm alleged.[5] By way of illustration, included within this first category of cases are those involving asbestos, which is generally recognized to cause asbestosis, silica, which is generally recognized to cause silicosis, and cigarettes, which are generally recognized to cause lung cancer.[6] Rather, where general causation is "properly taken for granted," the focus of a *Daubert* inquiry will tend toward the issue of specific causation, i.e. "was plaintiff exposed to the toxin,

---

was exposed were "placebos" and did not contain the pesticides at issue.

[Section 6:5]

[1]Rider v. Sandoz Pharmaceuticals Corp., 295 F.3d 1194 (11th Cir. 2002).

[2]McClain v. Metabolife Intern., Inc., 401 F.3d 1233, 1237–1239 (11th Cir. 2005); Siharath v. Sandoz Pharmaceuticals Corp., 131 F. Supp.2d 1347, 1352 (N.D. Ga. 2001).

[3]McClain v. Metabolife Intern., Inc., 401 F.3d 1233, 1239 (11th Cir. 2005) ("General causation is concerned with whether an agent increases the incidence of disease in a group and not whether the agent caused any given individual's disease.") (quoting Michael D. Green, D. Michael Freedman, and Leon Gordis, Reference Guide on Epidemiology, in REFERENCE MANUAL ON SCIENTIFIC EVIDENCE 392 (Federal Judicial Center 2d ed. 2000)).

[4]McClain v. Metabolife Intern., Inc., 401 F.3d 1233, 1239 (11th Cir. 2005).

[5]McClain v. Metabolife Intern., Inc., 401 F.3d 1233, 1239 (11th Cir. 2005). The Eleventh Circuit has noted that this distinction is not a resurrection of the Frye "general acceptance" test, and is a pragmatic rule serving the interests of judicial economy. *Id.* at *1239, n.5.* "[T]he trial court does not need to waste time with a Daubert hearing 'where the reliability of an expert's methods is properly taken for granted, and to require appropriate proceedings in the less usual or more complex cases where cause for questioning the expert's reliability arises.'" *Id.* (quoting Kumho Tire Co., Ltd. v. Carmichael, 526 U.S. 137, 152, 119 S. Ct. 1167, 143 L. Ed. 2d 238 (1999)).

[6]McClain v. Metabolife Intern., Inc., 401 F.3d 1233, 1239 (11th Cir. 2005).

was plaintiff exposed to enough of the toxin to cause the alleged injury, and did the toxin in fact cause the injury?"[7]

In the second type of case, the plaintiff must affirmatively prove that the substance to which the plaintiff was exposed is capable of causing the type of harm from which the plaintiff suffers.[8] Toxicologists,[9] pharmacologists,[10] and medical doctors[11] are often employed toward this end, and the evidence proffered may include epidemiological studies,[12] specific case studies,[13] animal studies,[14] and chemical analogies.[15] As is discussed in detail below, issues with the admissibility of expert testimony arise where the data forming the basis of the expert's conclusions is incomplete or inconclusive, or where the expert has extrapolated from the data to reach a conclusion which is only tenuously supported by the data. Under such circumstances, courts have found too great an "analytical gap" to exist between the evidence relied on and the conclusion reached.[16] The remainder of this section addresses the types of evidence most often relied on by experts in this area, and how the courts addressed admissibility issues with respect to expert testimony relying on such evidence.

§ 6:6 Federal law—Epidemiological studies

Epidemiological studies are generally regarded as the "best evidence" for the purpose of establishing general causation in a toxic tort action.[1] Epidemiology is the medical science of determining the cause of disease in human beings by studying the pat-

---

[7]McClain v. Metabolife Intern., Inc., 401 F.3d 1233, 1239 (11th Cir. 2005).

[8]McClain v. Metabolife Intern., Inc., 401 F.3d 1233, 1239 (11th Cir. 2005).

[9]See, e.g. Siharath v. Sandoz Pharmaceuticals Corp., 131 F. Supp. 2d 1347 (N.D. Ga. 2001), aff'd, 295 F.3d 1194 (11th Cir. 2002).

[10]See, e.g. McClain v. Metabolife Intern., Inc., 401 F.3d 1233 (11th Cir. 2005); Siharath v. Sandoz Pharmaceuticals Corp., 131 F. Supp. 2d 1347 (N.D. Ga. 2001), aff'd, 295 F.3d 1194 (11th Cir. 2002).

[11]See, e.g. Allison v. McGhan Medical Corp., 184 F.3d 1300 (11th Cir. 1999); Bell v. Swift Adhesives, Inc., a div. of Reichhold Chemicals, Inc., 804 F. Supp. 1577 (S.D. Ga. 1992).

[12]See § 6:7, infra.

[13]See § 6:7, infra.

[14]See § 6:7, infra.

[15]See § 6:7, infra.

[16]See, e.g. General Elec. Co. v. Joiner, 522 U.S. 136, 146, 118 S. Ct. 512, 519, 139 L. Ed. 2d 508 (1997) ("Trained experts commonly extrapolate from existing data. But nothing in either Daubert or the Federal Rules of Evidence requires a district court to admit opinion evidence that is connected to existing data only by the ipse dixit of the expert. A court may conclude that there is simply too great an analytical gap between the data and the opinion proffered.").

[Section 6:6]

[1]Rider v. Sandoz Pharmaceuticals Corp., 295 F.3d 1194 (11th Cir. 2002); Siharath v. Sandoz

terns of disease in the human population.[2] Employing statistical studies, epidemiologists may conduct cohort studies, which compare the incidence of illness or disease between exposed and unexposed populations,[3] or case-control studies, which compare the incidence of exposure between persons with and without the illness or disease.[4] Epidemiological studies do not conclusively establish that a substance is capable of causing a particular malady, but rather, establish a certain likelihood that a malady would not have occurred absent exposure to the substance.[5] It has been recognized that practical limitations, including ethical and legal constraints on exposing persons to a possibly toxic substance for purposes of obtaining epidemiological data, may make epidemiological evidence for a particular substance difficult to come by.[6] Accordingly, the absence of epidemiological studies is not fatal to proof of a toxic tort claim.[7] However, at the same time, the absence of such studies creates "a high bar for [p]laintiffs to surmount" in reliably showing a substance is capable of causing the harm suffered by the plaintiff.[8]

Reliance on epidemiological studies does not, in itself, render

---

Pharmaceuticals Corp., 131 F. Supp. 2d 1347 (N.D. Ga. 2001), aff'd, 295 F.3d 1194 (11th Cir. 2002) ("The existence of relevant epidemiological studies can be a significant factor in proving general causation in toxic tort cases. . . . Indeed, epidemiological studies provide 'the primary generally accepted methodology for demonstrating a causal relation between a chemical compound and a set of symptoms or disease.'") (quoting Conde v. Velsicol Chemical Corp., 804 F. Supp. 972 (S.D. Ohio 1992)).

[2]Siharath v. Sandoz Pharmaceuticals Corp., 131 F. Supp. 2d 1347 (N.D. Ga. 2001), aff'd, 295 F.3d 1194 (11th Cir. 2002); Smith v. Ortho Pharmaceutical Corp., 770 F. Supp. 1561, 1573 (N.D. Ga. 1991); Michael D. Green, D. Michael Freedman, and Leon Gordis, Reference Guide on Epidemiology, in Reference Manual on Scientific Evidence 335 (Federal Judicial Center 2d ed. 2000).

[3]Smith v. Ortho Pharmaceutical Corp., 770 F. Supp. 1561, 1573–74 (N.D. Ga. 1991); Michael D. Green, D. Michael Freedman, and Leon Gordis, Reference Guide on Epidemiology, in REFERENCE MANUAL ON SCIENTIFIC EV-

IDENCE 340 (Federal Judicial Center 2d ed. 2000).

[4]Smith v. Ortho Pharmaceutical Corp., 770 F. Supp. 1561, 1573 (N.D. Ga. 1991); Michael D. Green, D. Michael Freedman, and Leon Gordis, Reference Guide on Epidemiology, in REFERENCE MANUAL ON SCIENTIFIC EVIDENCE 342 (Federal Judicial Center 2d ed. 2000).

[5]Smith v. Ortho Pharmaceutical Corp., 770 F. Supp. 1561, 1573 (N.D. Ga. 1991).

[6]Siharath v. Sandoz Pharmaceuticals Corp., 131 F. Supp. 2d 1347 (N.D. Ga. 2001), aff'd, 295 F.3d 1194 (11th Cir. 2002).

[7]Wells v. Ortho Pharmaceutical Corp., 788 F.2d 741, 745 (11th Cir. 1986); Siharath v. Sandoz Pharmaceuticals Corp., 131 F. Supp. 2d 1347 (N.D. Ga. 2001), aff'd, 295 F.3d 1194 (11th Cir. 2002).

[8]Siharath v. Sandoz Pharmaceuticals Corp., 131 F. Supp. 2d 1347 (N.D. Ga. 2001), aff'd, 295 F.3d 1194 (11th Cir. 2002); see also Rider v. Sandoz Pharmaceuticals Corp., 295 F.3d 1194 (11th Cir. 2002) (noting lack of epidemiological studies

an expert's testimony that a particular substance is capable of causing harm of the sort from which the plaintiff suffers reliable. Courts have cautioned against admitting testimony where too great an "analytical gap" exists between the epidemiological data upon which the expert has relied and the expert's ultimate conclusion.[9] In other words, where an expert makes a factually unsupported inference from existing studies to conclude that the particular substance at issue is capable of causing the harm suffered by the plaintiff, courts have found that such a "leap of faith" is little more than unreliable, and inadmissible, speculation.[10] It has been recognized that epidemiologists typically apply the following five criteria in determining whether a causal relationship exists between a particular substance and a particular malady: 1) the consistency of the association; 2) the specificity of the association; 3) the strength of the association; 4) the coherence of the association; and 5) the temporal relationship of the association.[11] In many instances, courts have found expert testimony unreliable where the studies relied upon lack one of these five criteria.[12]

Consistency of association considers whether the results of a study can be replicated in different studies on different populations.[13] This concept, of course, corresponds with the first factor of the *Daubert* reliability inquiry: whether a theory can be, and has

---

supporting expert's opinion is not necessarily fatal to the plaintiff's case).

[9]General Elec. Co. v. Joiner, 522 U.S. 136, 146, 118 S. Ct. 512, 519, 139 L. Ed. 2d 508 (1997).

[10]McClain v. Metabolife Intern., Inc., 401 F.3d 1233, 1248 (11th Cir. 2005).

[11]Smith v. Ortho Pharmaceutical Corp., 770 F. Supp. 1561, 1575 (N.D. Ga. 1991); see also Michael D. Green, D. Michael Freedman, and Leon Gordis, Reference Guide on Epidemiology, in REFERENCE MANUAL ON SCIENTIFIC EVIDENCE 375 (Federal Judicial Center 2d ed. 2000).

[12]The first three of these factors are discussed in detail below. The fourth factor, the temporal relationship, references the common-sense notion that, in order for a causal relation between exposure and disease to exist, the exposure must precede the disease. Smith v. Ortho Pharmaceutical Corp., 770 F. Supp. 1561, 1576 (N.D. Ga. 1991). " '[T]he chronological relationship between exposure and effect must

be biologically plausible.' . . . '[I]f a diseases or illness in an individual preceded the established period of exposure, then it cannot be concluded that the chemical caused the disease, although it may be possible to establish that the chemical aggravated a pre-existing condition or disease.' " McClain v. Metabolife Intern., Inc., 401 F.3d 1233, 1243 (11th Cir. 2005) (citing David L. Eaton, Scientific Judgment and Toxic Torts–A Primer In Toxicology For Judges and Lawyers, 12 J.L. & POL'Y 5, 39–40 (2003)). The final factor, the coherence of association, "considers whether it is biologically possible for the agent being studied to cause the disease or other effect at issue. This factor is usually explored through animal tests." Smith v. Ortho Pharmaceutical Corp., 770 F. Supp. 1561, 1576 (N.D. Ga. 1991). Animal testing is discussed in Section 7.4.2, *infra*.

[13]Smith v. Ortho Pharmaceutical Corp., 770 F. Supp. 1561, 1575 (N.D. Ga. 1991) ("The criterion rests on a basic principle of logic and science,

145

been, tested.[14] "The criterion of the scientific status of a theory is its falsifiability, or refutability, or testability[.]"[15] Expert testimony on causation has been found unreliable when based upon epidemiological studies allegedly demonstrating a correlation between exposure and disease where the majority of studies presented to the court found that no statistically significant correlation between exposure and the disease was found to exist.[16] This analysis also corresponds to the fourth factor of the Daubert reliability inquiry: whether the theory has been generally accepted.[17]

Specificity of association refers to the degree to which exposure to a substance causes the specific disease or syndrome.[18] Courts have found expert testimony on causation unreliable when based on studies demonstrating a correlation between exposure to the substance at issue and the incidence of a different disease or set of symptoms from which the plaintiff does not suffer.[19] Similarly, where studies examining the correlation between exposure and

---

namely, that if a causal relation exists, it will be repeated in later studies; if the relationship is not real or is a mere matter of chance, it will not be repeated. Because replication is important in ascertaining the reliability of data, almost all researchers agree the 'consistency' is one of the most important of the criteria."); see also Michael D. Green, D. Michael Freedman, and Leon Gordis, Reference Guide on Epidemiology, in REFERENCE MANUAL ON SCIENTIFIC EVIDENCE 376 (Federal Judicial Center 2d ed. 2000).

[14]Daubert v. Merrell Dow Pharmaceuticals, Inc., 509 U.S. 579, 593, 113 S. Ct. 2786, 2796, 125 L. Ed. 2d 469 (1993). Indeed, this concept is at the very heart of the scientific concept of "reliability," which inquires as to whether the "application of the principle produce[s] consistent results[.]" Id. at 590, n.9.

[15]Daubert v. Merrell Dow Pharmaceuticals, Inc., 509 U.S. 579, 593, 113 S. Ct. 2786, 2797, 125 L. Ed. 2d 469 (1993).

[16]Allison v. McGhan Medical Corp., 184 F.3d 1300, 1315 (11th Cir. 1999) (expert opinion unreliable where expert relied on four studies purporting to show correlation between silicone breast implants and systemic dis-

ease, which "were in direct contrast to over twenty other epidemiological studies which found no statistical correlation between silicone breast implants and systemic disease").

[17]Daubert v. Merrell Dow Pharmaceuticals, Inc., 509 U.S. 579, 594, 113 S. Ct. 2786, 2797, 125 L. Ed. 2d 469 (1993). See also Allison v. McGhan Medical Corp., 184 F.3d 1300, 1315–1316 (11th Cir. 1999) ("The [district] court found that Gershwin's proposed four studies were in direct contrast to over twenty other epidemiological studies which found no statistical correlation between silicone breast implants and systemic disease, strong evidence that a consensus exists in the general scientific community that no correlation exists. . . . We find that the district court did not abuse its discretion by considering that the proffered conclusions in studies with questionable methodologies were out of sync with the conclusions in the overwhelming majority of the epidemiological studies presented to the court.").

[18]Smith v. Ortho Pharmaceutical Corp., 770 F. Supp. 1561, 1576 (N.D. Ga. 1991).

[19]Allison v. McGhan Medical Corp., 184 F.3d 1300, 1315 (11th Cir.

disease reveal only an ill-defined syndrome or set of symptoms in the persons exposed, expert testimony purporting to establish a link between exposure and the plaintiff's specific disease has been found unreliable.[20] Conversely, where the subjects of the epidemiological studies upon which the expert bases his opinions of causation have been exposed to other agents which may also have contributed to the subjects' illnesses, or have been exposed to a different agent altogether, expert testimony purporting to establish a causal nexus between the agent at issue and the plaintiff's illness has been found unreliable.[21]

Strength of association refers to the risk posed to an exposed population, as compared to the unexposed population, of contracting the illness or disease.[22] This concept is commonly expressed in terms of whether there is a statistically significant correlation between incidence of exposure to a substance and the illness or disease. Reliance on epidemiological studies may prove unreliable where, although the studies show a correlation between exposure to a particular substance and a particular illness, the correlation is nonetheless statistically insignificant.[23] Where the "relative risk" is 4.0, the exposed population is said to be four times more likely to contract the disease than the unexposed population; where the relative risk is 10.0, the exposed population is ten times more likely to contract the disease, and so on.[24] A relative risk of 1.0 indicates that the substance has no effect on the

---

1999) (expert opinion that plaintiff's systemic disease caused by silicone breast implants unreliable when based upon epidemiological studies showing correlation between silicone exposure and certain illnesses, none of which plaintiff was alleged to have).

[20]Smith v. Ortho Pharmaceutical Corp., 770 F. Supp. 1561, 1576–79 (N.D. Ga. 1991).

[21]General Elec. Co. v. Joiner, 522 U.S. 136, 146, 118 S. Ct. 512, 519, 139 L. Ed. 2d 508 (1997) (expert opinion unreliable where expert relied on study where the study's subjects had been exposed to numerous other potential carcinogens); Siharath v. Sandoz Pharmaceuticals Corp., 131 F. Supp. 2d 1347 (N.D. Ga. 2001), aff'd, 295 F.3d 1194 (11th Cir. 2002) (expert opinion unreliable where the few subjects that had suffered the plaintiff's condition had also ingested a drug that had not also been ingested by the plaintiff).

[22]Smith v. Ortho Pharmaceutical Corp., 770 F. Supp. 1561, 1575 (N.D. Ga. 1991); see also Siharath v. Sandoz Pharmaceuticals Corp., 131 F. Supp. 2d 1347 (N.D. Ga. 2001), aff'd, 295 F.3d 1194 (11th Cir. 2002); Michael D. Green, D. Michael Freedman, and Leon Gordis, Reference Guide on Epidemiology, in REFERENCE MANUAL ON SCIENTIFIC EVIDENCE 376 (Federal Judicial Center 2d ed. 2000).

[23]Rider v. Sandoz Pharmaceuticals Corp., 295 F.3d 1194 (11th Cir. 2002); Siharath v. Sandoz Pharmaceuticals Corp., 131 F. Supp. 2d 1347 (N.D. Ga. 2001), aff'd, 295 F.3d 1194 (11th Cir. 2002); Allison v. McGhan Medical Corp., 184 F.3d 1300, 1315 (11th Cir. 1999).

[24]See Michael D. Green, D. Michael Freedman, and Leon Gordis, Reference Guide on Epidemiology, in REFERENCE MANUAL ON SCIENTIFIC EVIDENCE 349, 376 (Federal Judicial Center 2d ed. 2000).

incidence of disease, and a relative risk of 2.0 indicates a 50% greater likelihood that the exposed population will contract the disease than the unexposed population.[25] When the relative risk exceeds 2.0, it may be inferred that the substance more likely than not caused the individual's disease, and where the relative risk falls below 2.0, the association between exposure and incidence of disease is not statistically significant and it cannot be said that exposure to the substance more likely than not was the cause of a particular illness or disease.[26] Accordingly, expert testimony purporting to establish a causal link between exposure to a substance and disease has been found unreliable where epidemiological studies show the relative risk of exposure falls below 2.0.[27]

In all statistical studies, one has to account for systematic error, or "bias." In its epidemiological sense, the term bias does not necessarily connote prejudice or partisanship, as is often the case in the term's legal usage. Rather, bias may arise in the design of the study or method of data collection and analysis, and refers to anything in the study, other than random sampling error, which results in error in a study, thereby compromising the study's validity.[28] Forms of bias include selection bias, which refers to an error in observed association between exposure and incidence of disease arising out of the manner in which those selected to participate in a study are chosen,[29] and information bias, which occurs when inaccurate information is obtained regarding the study participants' disease or exposure status, often due to inaccuracies

---

[25]Siharath v. Sandoz Pharmaceuticals Corp., 131 F. Supp. 2d 1347 (N.D. Ga. 2001), aff'd, 295 F.3d 1194 (11th Cir. 2002); Smith v. Ortho Pharmaceutical Corp., 770 F. Supp. 1561, 1575 (N.D. Ga. 1991).

[26]Siharath v. Sandoz Pharmaceuticals Corp., 131 F. Supp. 2d 1347 (N.D. Ga. 2001), aff'd, 295 F.3d 1194 (11th Cir. 2002).

[27]Allison v. McGhan Medical Corp., 184 F.3d 1300, 1315 (11th Cir. 1999) (expert opinion unreliable where studies that the expert relied on showed a relative risk below 2.0); Siharath v. Sandoz Pharmaceuticals Corp., 131 F. Supp. 2d 1347 (N.D. Ga. 2001), aff'd, 295 F.3d 1194 (11th Cir. 2002) (expert opinion unreliable where two major studies showed no statistically significant association between the drug at issue and the type of illness suffered by the plaintiff).

[28]Michael D. Green, D. Michael Freedman, and Leon Gordis, Reference Guide on Epidemiology, in REFERENCE MANUAL ON SCIENTIFIC EVIDENCE 363 (Federal Judicial Center 2d ed. 2000); see also Smith v. Ortho Pharmaceutical Corp., 770 F. Supp. 1561, 1575 (N.D. Ga. 1991) ("Bias refers to the existence of factors in the design of a study or in the manner in which the study was carried out which might distort the result").

[29]See Michael D. Green, D. Michael Freedman, and Leon Gordis, Reference Guide on Epidemiology, in REFERENCE MANUAL ON SCIENTIFIC EVIDENCE 363–365 (Federal Judicial Center 2d ed. 2000). Hospital-based studies, where hospitalized patients are used as controls, serve to illustrate the problem. By way of example, a case-controlled study designed to assess the association between coronary heart disease and coffee may contain error if

in the information communicated by study participants to researchers.[30] In *Allison v. McGhan Medical Corporation*, the court found unreliable an expert's reliance on a study where its participants were aware of the hypothesis underlying the study, recognizing that this could have created a bias skewing the study's findings.[31]

Expert testimony has been found unreliable where the expert has attempted to reorganize or reclassify data in a study in order to reach a different conclusion proffered by the study's authors.[32] It has been recognized that such a process is in fundamental conflict with the notion of scientific methodology, and is tantamount to "looking for proof" in support of a pre-ordained conclusion, rather than the " 'scientific method, in which conclusions must be drawn from an accepted process.' "[33]

---

the control group (those without coronary heart disease) includes hospital patients who have been advised to avoid drinking coffee for unrelated reasons, such as avoiding aggravation of a stomach ulcer. Under such circumstances, the control group would understate the extent of coffee drinking expected in persons without coronary heart disease, thus exaggerating, or upwardly biasing, the observed association between coronary heart disease and coffee drinking. Similarly, a cohort study of cervical cancer which includes in the control group persons not at risk for the disease, such as men and women who have had their cervices removed, would result in error by overstating the association between exposure and the disease. *Id. at 364.*

[30]See Michael D. Green, D. Michael Freedman, and Leon Gordis, Reference Guide on Epidemiology, in REFERENCE MANUAL ON SCIENTIFIC EVIDENCE 365–369 (Federal Judicial Center 2d ed. 2000). By way of example, in a study designed to assess the association between birth defects and a mother's infection during pregnancy, mothers of malformed infants very may recall inconsequential symptoms, such as a fever or runny nose, occurring during their pregnancy that would likely be forgotten by mothers of healthy children. Even if the infection rates during pregnancy of moth-

ers of malformed children and mothers of healthy children were the same, the results of such a study would show an apparently higher rate of infection among mothers with malformed children due to differences in recall among the two groups. *Id. at 365;* see also Smith v. Ortho Pharmaceutical Corp., 770 F. Supp. 1561, 1575, (N.D. Ga. 1991) (discussing "maternal recall bias," "which refers to the assumption that women with malformed children will, when they think back, tend to recall what they were exposed to during pregnancy differently than women with non-malformed children.").

[31]Allison v. McGhan Medical Corp., 184 F.3d 1300, 1315 (11th Cir. 1999).

[32]See, e.g. Allison v. McGhan Medical Corp., 184 F.3d 1300, 1315 (11th Cir. 1999); Jack v. Glaxo Wellcome, Inc., 239 F. Supp. 2d 1308 (N.D. Ga. 2002).

[33]Jack v. Glaxo Wellcome, Inc., 239 F. Supp. 2d 1308, 1319 (N.D. Ga. 2002). In further critiquing the method of reclassifying or reorganizing data, the Jack court observed that such a method is "founded upon the premise that [the expert's] post hoc substituted judgment is superior to the classification made by the investigators who, [unlike the reclassifying expert] were in direct contact with the [study's subjects]." *Id. at 1316–1317.* Moreover,

§ 6:7 Federal law—Toxicological and pharmacological research

An individual's exposure to a certain substance alleged to be hazardous is, in itself, without much meaning for purposes of demonstrating that the exposure was the cause of the harm alleged absent a showing that the individual was exposed to the substance in a sufficient quantity, or over a sufficient time period, such that the exposure was capable of causing the toxic or adverse effect from which the individual suffers.[1] Simply put, there is a threshold of exposure to a harmful substance below which no adverse reaction can reasonably be expected to occur. A low dose exposure to a harmful substance will often have no consequence to an individual because the body is able to detoxify before any damage occurs.[2] For instance, whereas an individual of normal weight and tolerance, having consumed an entire bottle of wine in an hour, can reasonably be expected to become intoxicated, that same individual would not reasonably be expected to experience any intoxicating effects after consuming just a few sips of the wine over the course of the same time period.[3] Similarly, the risk of developing lung cancer from smoking one cigarette over a lifetime is perhaps so slight as to be insignificant when compared to the risk of developing lung cancer after smoking one pack of cigarettes per day over a period of decades.[4]

This concept is what toxicologists refer to as the "dose-response relationship," which describes the "relationship in which a change in amount, intensity, or duration of exposure to an agent is associated with a change—either an increase or decrease—in risk of disease."[5] It has been observed that the dose-response relation-

---

the court further noted that it would be difficult, if even possible, to test the validity of a reclassifying methodology or establish a rate of error. *Id.*

[Section 6:7]

[1]McClain v. Metabolife Intern., Inc., 401 F.3d 1233, 1241 (11th Cir. 2005) (citing Allen v. Pennsylvania Engineering Corp., 102 F.3d 194, 199 (5th Cir. 1996)) ("In toxic tort cases, '[s]cientific knowledge of the harmful level of exposure to a chemical plus knowledge that [the] plaintiff was exposed to such quantities are minimal facts necessary to sustain the plaintiff's burden.'").

[2]McClain v. Metabolife Intern., Inc., 401 F.3d 1233, 1242 (11th Cir. 2005).

[3]See, e.g. David L. Eaton, Scientific Judgment and Toxic Torts–A Primer In Toxicology For Judges and Lawyers, 12 J.L. & POL'Y 5, 6 (2003).

[4]See, e.g. David L. Eaton, Scientific Judgment and Toxic Torts–A Primer In Toxicology For Judges and Lawyers, 12 J.L. & POL'Y 5, 7 (2003).

[5]McClain v. Metabolife Intern., Inc., 401 F.3d 1233, 1241–42 (11th Cir. 2005) (quoting See Michael D. Green, D. Michael Freedman, and Leon Gordis, Reference Guide on Epidemiology,

ship is the "hallmark of the science of toxic torts[,]"[6] and that an expert's knowledge regarding the level of exposure sufficient to yield an adverse effect is a "key element" in assessing the reliability of the expert's testimony.[7] Expert testimony opining that exposure to a substance was the cause of an individual's harm has been found unreliable where the expert was unable to identify the level of exposure necessary to cause the type of harm suffered by the plaintiff.[8]

The testing of various substances on animals is commonly performed to study the effect such substances have on living tissue. Such studies typically involve exposing laboratory animals to various chemicals and drugs, monitoring their reaction to these substances, and comparing the outcome to a control group of animals who have not been exposed to the substance.[9] While such studies may be used to support a conclusion that the substance is capable of producing similar results in humans,[10] such a conclusion must be supported by a "credible scientific explanation of why such extrapolation is warranted."[11] Specifically, an expert should be able to demonstrate the similarities between humans and the animal species tested, and how these similarities warrant the conclusion that the substance would have a similar effect on humans.[12] Courts have demonstrated a notable reluctance to find such studies reliable for the purpose of showing that a

---

in REFERENCE MANUAL ON SCIENTIFIC EVIDENCE 390 (Federal Judicial Center 2d ed. 2000)).

[6]McClain v. Metabolife Intern., Inc., 401 F.3d 1233, 1240 (11th Cir. 2005).

[7]McClain v. Metabolife Intern., Inc., 401 F.3d 1233, 1241 (11th Cir. 2005).

[8]McClain v. Metabolife Intern., Inc., 401 F.3d 1233, 1242 (11th Cir. 2005) (expert testimony unreliable where expert was unable to provide an opinion as to general dose-response levels for Metabolife's toxicity).

[9]See Bernard D. Goldstein and Mary Sue Henifin, Reference Guide on Toxicology, in REFERENCE MANUAL ON SCIENTIFIC EVIDENCE 405 (Federal Judicial Center 2d ed. 2000).

[10]See, e.g., General Elec. Co. v. Joiner, 522 U.S. 136, 144, 118 S. Ct. 512, 139 L. Ed. 2d 508 (1997); Allison v. McGhan Medical Corp., 184 F.3d 1300, 1313–1314 (11th Cir. 1999).

[11]Siharath v. Sandoz Pharmaceuticals Corp., 131 F. Supp. 2d 1347 (N.D. Ga. 2001), aff'd, 295 F.3d 1194 (11th Cir. 2002); Bell v. Swift Adhesives, Inc., a div. of Reichhold Chemicals, Inc., 804 F. Supp. 1577, 1579–81 (S.D. Ga. 1992).

[12]Rider v. Sandoz Pharmaceuticals Corp., 295 F.3d 1194 (11th Cir. 2002) (in upholding the exclusion of expert causation testimony based on animal studies, the court noted that the plaintiff had failed to show how the vascular structure of humans and the animals tested were similar enough to warrant the conclusion that the substance's effect on a human's vascular system would be similar to the effect that it had on the vascular system of the animals tested). See also Bernard D. Goldstein and Mary Sue Henifin, Reference Guide on Toxicology, in REFERENCE MANUAL ON SCIENTIFIC EVIDENCE 419 (Federal Judicial Center 2d ed. 2000) ("The expert should review similarities and differences in the animal spe-

substance is capable of producing similar results in humans,[13] recognizing that interspecies differences in anatomical structure, metabolism, absorption, and other factors can result in variances in how humans and other animals react to various substances.[14] Moreover, the animals subjected to such testing are often exposed to significantly higher doses of the substances than the plaintiff in any given case.[15]

Courts have demonstrated a similar skepticism with respect to expert testimony inferring that because one drug has been shown to cause a certain type of malady, that another, arguably similar, drug is capable of causing the malady.[16] Courts have recognized that even though the two drugs may belong to the same class of pharmaceuticals, they nonetheless can have distinctive pharmacological properties, and that even minor dissimilarities in chemical structure can have a large difference in how persons will react to them.[17] The findings of the Food & Drug Administration (FDA) with respect to a drug may form the basis of an expert's

---

cies in which the compound has been tested and in humans. This analysis should form the basis of the expert's opinion as to whether extrapolation from animals to humans is warranted"); Siharath v. Sandoz Pharmaceuticals Corp., 131 F. Supp. 2d 1347 (N.D. Ga. 2001), aff'd, 295 F.3d 1194 (11th Cir. 2002) (quoting Cavallo v. Star Enterprise, 892 F. Supp. 756, 762 (E.D. Va. 1995)) ("To ensure that the expert's conclusion based on animal studies is reliable, there must exist 'a scientifically valid link between the sources or studies consulted and the conclusion reached.' ").

[13]See, e.g. Bell v. Swift Adhesives, Inc., a div. of Reichhold Chemicals, Inc., 804 F. Supp. 1577, 1579–81 (S.D. Ga. 1992) ("Although courts have recognized the relevance of animal studies in some toxic tort cases, they have tended to view such studies with suspicion, and several courts have specifically held that animal studies alone cannot prove causation in humans. '[Animal studies], singly or in combination, do not have the capability of proving causation in human beings in the absence of any confirmatory epidemiological data.' One court has gone so far as to hold that animal studies 'are of so little probative force and are

so potentially misleading as to be inadmissible.' ") (citations omitted).

[14]Siharath v. Sandoz Pharmaceuticals Corp., 131 F. Supp. 2d 1347 (N.D. Ga. 2001), aff'd, 295 F.3d 1194 (11th Cir. 2002).

[15]See, e.g. General Elec. Co. v. Joiner, 522 U.S. 136, 144, 118 S. Ct. 512, 139 L. Ed. 2d 508 (1997) (expert's methodology unreliable where expert relied on animal study in which mice in study were exposed to significantly higher amounts of substance than the plaintiff was exposed).

[16]See, e.g, McClain v. Metabolife Intern., Inc., 401 F.3d 1233, 1244–47 (11th Cir. 2005); Siharath v. Sandoz Pharmaceuticals Corp., 131 F. Supp. 2d 1347 (N.D. Ga. 2001), aff'd, 295 F.3d 1194 (11th Cir. 2002).

[17]See, e.g, McClain v. Metabolife Intern., Inc., 401 F.3d 1233, 1240, (11th Cir. 2005) (citing David L. Eaton, Scientific Judgment and Toxic Torts–A Primer In Toxicology For Judges and Lawyers, 12 J.L. & POL'Y 5, 10–11 (2003) ("[E]ven small differences in chemical structures can sometimes make very large differences in the type of toxic response that is produced."); Rider v. Sandoz Pharmaceuticals Corp., 295 F.3d 1194 (11th Cir. 2002) "[E]ven minor deviations in chemical

opinions; however, such findings must be treated with caution in light of the function of the FDA and the standards it employs in making regulatory decisions concerning the warnings to accompany drugs or restrictions in their sale. The FDA's standard for restricting a drug's approved usages, or entirely pulling a drug from the market, is based on a broad-ranging risk-benefit assessment of making drugs available to the public at large.[18] It has been recognized that the FDA's standards restricting or eliminating a drug's availability falls short of the "more likely than not" standard required in tort law to prove that a drug was the cause of a plaintiff's illness or disease.[19] Consequently, expert

---

structure can radically change a particular substance's properties and propensities."); Siharath v. Sandoz Pharmaceuticals Corp., 131 F. Supp. 2d 1347 (N.D. Ga. 2001), aff'd, 295 F.3d 1194 (11th Cir. 2002).

[18]See, e.g. McClain v. Metabolife Intern., Inc., 401 F.3d 1233, 1240, (11th Cir. 2005) (citing David L. Eaton, Scientific Judgment and Toxic Torts–A Primer In Toxicology For Judges and Lawyers, 12 J.L. & POL'Y 5, 34–35 (2003) ("Because a number of protective, often 'worst case' assumptions . . . are made in estimating allowable exposures for large populations, the criteria and the resulting regulatory levels . . . generally overestimate potential toxicity levels for nearly all individuals. Furthermore, because these guidelines are intended to be protective of all individuals in a population, including the very young, the very old, and other potentially 'sensitive' individuals, the theoretical risks from exposure at the guideline range level is likely to be substantially overestimated for the large majority of individuals in the population.").

[19]Rider v. Sandoz Pharmaceuticals Corp., 295 F.3d 1194 (11th Cir. 2002) (The FDA's "statement merely states that possible risks outweigh the limited benefits of the drug. This risk-utility analysis involves a much lower standard than that which is demanded by a court of law. A regulatory agency such as the FDA may choose to err on the side of caution. Courts, however, are required

by the Daubert trilogy to engage in objective review of evidence to determine whether it has sufficient basis to be considered reliable."); Siharath v. Sandoz Pharmaceuticals Corp., 131 F. Supp. 2d 1347 (N.D. Ga. 2001), aff'd, 295 F.3d 1194 (11th Cir. 2002) (citing Mitchell v. Gencorp Inc., 165 F.3d 778 (10th Cir. 1999) ("The methodology employed by a government agency 'results from the preventive perspective that the agencies adopt in order to reduce public exposure to harmful substances. The agencies' threshold of proof is reasonably lower than that appropriate in tort law, which traditionally makes more particularized inquires into cause and effect and requires a plaintiff to prove that it is more likely than not that another individual has caused him or her harm."); see also Margaret A. Berger, The Supreme Court's Trilogy on the Admissibility of Expert Testimony, in REFERENCE MANUAL ON SCIENTIFIC EVIDENCE 33 (Federal Judicial Center 2d ed. 2000) ("Proof of risk and proof of causation entail somewhat different questions because risk assessment frequently calls for a cost-benefit analysis. The agency assessing risk may decide to bar a substance or product if the potential benefits are outweighed by the possibility of risks that are largely unquantifiable because of presently unknown contingencies. Consequently, risk assessors may pay heed to any evidence that points to a need for caution, rather than assess the likelihood that a causal relationship in a specific case is more likely than

testimony which purports to base its opinion of causation on the FDA's actions has frequently been excluded as unreliable.[20]

§ 6:8   Federal law—Case reports

Medical literature which contains case reports that purport to establish an association between exposure and disease is often used to support a claim that a particular substance is capable of causing a particular illness or disease. However, courts have regarded such reports suspiciously, noting that such reports are merely anecdotal evidence which, in themselves, are ordinarily incapable of establishing causation[1] and which provide "one of the least reliable sources" of support for an expert opinion on general causation.[2] Unlike the case of epidemiological studies, case reports sometimes lack sufficient controls,[3] which exclude from a study variables which may contribute to a disease such that the association between the substance at issue and the disease can be reliably ascertained.[4] Case reports have been found not to be reliable scientific evidence for purposes of establishing general causation "because they simply describe reported phenomenon without comparison to the rate at which the phenomena occur in the general population or in a defined control group; do not isolate and exclude potentially alternative causes; and do not investigate or explain the mechanism of causation."[5]

Case reports often contain only very basic information, failing to provide little in the way of the patient's medical history or how other factors were excluded as causes of the patient's illness or

---

not.").

[20]See, e.g. McClain v. Metabolife Intern., Inc., 401 F.3d 1233 (11th Cir. 2005); Rider v. Sandoz Pharmaceuticals Corp., 295 F.3d 1194 (11th Cir. 2002); Siharath v. Sandoz Pharmaceuticals Corp., 131 F. Supp. 2d 1347 (N.D. Ga. 2001), aff'd, 295 F.3d 1194 (11th Cir. 2002).

[Section 6:8]

[1]Rider v. Sandoz Pharmaceuticals Corp., 295 F.3d 1194 (11th Cir. 2002).

[2]McClain v. Metabolife Intern., Inc., 401 F.3d 1233, 1250 (11th Cir. 2005).

[3]See McClain v. Metabolife Intern., Inc., 401 F.3d 1233, 1250–53 (11th Cir. 2005); Rider v. Sandoz Pharmaceuticals Corp., 295 F.3d 1194 (11th Cir. 2002); Siharath v. Sandoz Pharmaceuticals Corp., 131 F. Supp. 2d 1347 (N.D. Ga. 2001), aff'd, 295 F.3d 1194 (11th Cir. 2002).

[4]See, e.g. Michael D. Green, D. Michael Freedman, and Leon Gordis, Reference Guide on Epidemiology, in REFERENCE MANUAL ON SCIENTIFIC EVIDENCE 341 (Federal Judicial Center 2d ed. 2000).

[5]Siharath v. Sandoz Pharmaceuticals Corp., 131 F. Supp. 2d 1347 (N.D. Ga. 2001), aff'd, 295 F.3d 1194 (11th Cir. 2002); see also Rider v. Sandoz Pharmaceuticals Corp., 295 F.3d 1194 (11th Cir. 2002) (Case reports "reflect only reported data, not scientific methodology.").

disease.[6] Even where such reports purport to rule out other factors as potential causes of the patient's illness through the use of a method such as differential diagnosis, such reports may not take into account whether the observed association of the disease and exposure is, in reality, the result of an association of the disease and an independent, "confounding," factor.[7] Courts have recognized that controlled epidemiological studies are better able to isolate and exclude chance associations and confounding factors in determining an association between a certain substance and an illness or disease,[8] and have found anecdotal case studies particularly unreliable where controlled epidemiological studies demonstrate a lack of correlation between exposure to the substance and the illness or disease at issue.[9]

§ 6:9 Federal law—Differential diagnosis

Once general causation, i.e., that the substance at issue is capable of causing the type of harm suffered by the plaintiff, a showing still must be made of specific causation, i.e., that the

---

[6]Rider v. Sandoz Pharmaceuticals Corp., 295 F.3d 1194 (11th Cir. 2002).

[7]Rider v. Sandoz Pharmaceuticals Corp., 295 F.3d 1194 (11th Cir. 2002). To be sure, confounding factors can produce error in controlled epidemiological studies as well. By way of example, in a study showing an association between an increased rate of death and grey hair, the increased rate of death very well may be attributable to confounding factors, such as other morbidities associated with old age, as opposed to the grey hair itself. While older persons have a greater tendency to have grey hair, other morbidities associated with old age may be responsible for the observed association between grey hair and increased rate of death. Similarly, a study showing an association between pancreatic cancer and coffee drinking may lead one to infer a causal relationship between drinking coffee and pancreatic cancer. However, given the fact that smoking is a known risk factor for pancreatic cancer, and that many smokers happen to drink coffee, the observed association between pancreatic cancer and coffee drinking may, in reality, be an association between pancreatic cancer and smoking, a

"confounding" factor. See Michael D. Green, D. Michael Freedman, and Leon Gordis, Reference Guide on Epidemiology, in REFERENCE MANUAL ON SCIENTIFIC EVIDENCE 369–374 (Federal Judicial Center 2d ed. 2000).

[8]Siharath v. Sandoz Pharmaceuticals Corp., 131 F. Supp. 2d 1347 (N.D. Ga. 2001), aff'd, 295 F.3d 1194 (11th Cir. 2002).

[9]Allison v. McGhan Medical Corp., 184 F.3d 1300, 1316 (11th Cir. 1999); Siharath v. Sandoz Pharmaceuticals Corp., 131 F. Supp. 2d 1347 (N.D. Ga. 2001), aff'd, 295 F.3d 1194 (11th Cir. 2002). In *Siharath,* the court found an expert's reliance on case studies to show an association between a medication and stroke in postpartum women unreliable where the expert relied on several case reports wherein the women suffering strokes also had other risk factors for stroke. *Id. at 1359–1361.* Moreover, the court found it significant that, despite the fact that millions of women had taken the medication at issue for over a decade, only one case report existed which purported to establish an association between the medication and stroke. *Id. at 1359–1363.*

substance in fact was the cause of the plaintiff's harm. Medical doctors have commonly been offered towards this end, and perhaps the most commonly employed technique used by physicians is that of "differential diagnosis," a method which attempts to exclude all likely causes of a disease until, by process of elimination, only the most likely cause remains.[1] Courts have recognized that while the differential diagnosis methodology is useful for "ruling out" certain causes, it does little in the way of "ruling in" the substance at issue as the cause of the plaintiff's symptoms.[2] In other words, a differential diagnosis, having excluded other possible causes, assumes that the substance at issue is in fact capable of causing the plaintiff's illness or disease.[3] Thus, unless a differential diagnosis purporting to identify a particular substance as the cause of the plaintiff's malady is supported by a showing of general causation, the differential diagnosis methodology will generally be insufficient to establish that exposure to the substance is the cause of the plaintiff's harm.[4]

Federal courts have found that a temporal connection between exposure to a substance and the subsequent onset of an illness or disease to be, in itself, insufficient for purposes of showing that that the illness or disease was therefore caused by the exposure to the substance.[5] In *McClain v. Metabolife*, the Eleventh Circuit excluded expert testimony based on such *post hoc ergo propter hoc*, or "after this, because of this," reasoning, finding that it made the unjustified "assumption based on the false inference that a temporal relationship proves a causal connection."[6] However, federal courts have recognized that "challenge testing," a methodology which focuses on the temporal connection between exposure and illness by exposing an individual to a substance

---

[Section 6:9]

[1]See Siharath v. Sandoz Pharmaceuticals Corp., 131 F. Supp. 2d 1347 (N.D. Ga. 2001), aff'd, 295 F.3d 1194 (11th Cir. 2002); Baker v. Smith and Nephew Richards, Inc., 1999 WL 1129650, *5 (N.D. Ga. 1999); Stedman's Medical Dictionary (26TH Edition, 1995).

[2]McClain v. Metabolife Intern., Inc., 401 F.3d 1233, 1253 (11th Cir. 2005).

[3]Rider   v.   Sandoz Pharmaceuticals Corp., 295 F.3d 1194 (11th Cir. 2002); Siharath v. Sandoz Pharmaceuticals Corp., 131 F. Supp. 2d 1347 (N.D. Ga. 2001), aff'd, 295 F.3d 1194 (11th Cir. 2002).

[4]See McClain v. Metabolife Intern., Inc., 401 F.3d 1233, 1253 (11th Cir. 2005); Baker v. Smith and Nephew Richards, Inc., 1999 WL 1129650, *5 (N.D. Ga. 1999).

[5]See, e.g. McClain v. Metabolife Intern., Inc., 401 F.3d 1233, 1243 (11th Cir. 2005); Wheat v. Sofamor, S.N.C., 46 F. Supp. 2d 1351, 1358 (N.D. Ga. 1999). Of course, if an illness or disease precedes an individual's exposure to a substance, the exposure cannot be said to have caused the illness or disease. It may, however, be possible to prove that the exposure aggravated the preexisting illness or disease. *McClain, 401 F.3d at 1243*.

[6]McClain v. Metabolife Intern., Inc., 401 F.3d 1233, 1243 (11th Cir. 2005)

and monitoring for the appearance of symptoms, and then withdrawing the substance and monitoring for the dissipation of symptoms, can be particularly useful in demonstrating that exposure to a substance was the cause of the plaintiff's illness or disease.[7]

In considering the issue of causation, account needs to be taken of the background risk of developing a certain illness or disease, that is, the risk that all persons face with respect to developing a particular illness or disease even in the absence of having been exposed to the allegedly toxic substance at issue.[8] In many cases, there exist several known, and perhaps even unknown, causes of the illness or disease at issue, and expert testimony has been found unreliable where the expert could not explain and account for the risk that the plaintiff would have developed a particular illness or disease in the absence of exposure to an allegedly toxic substance.[9] In *McClain v. Metabolife*, the Eleventh Circuit noted that "the likelihood that the chemical caused the disease or illness in an individual should be considered in the context of other known causes."[10] There, the court found an expert's opinion unreliable because the expert could not show that the risk of suffering the plaintiff's malady from ingesting the substance at issue was beyond the usual incidence of suffering such malady.[11]

---

[7]Rider v. Sandoz Pharmaceuticals Corp., 295 F.3d 1194 (11th Cir. 2002).

[8]McClain v. Metabolife Intern., Inc., 401 F.3d 1233, 1243 (11th Cir. 2005) (expert opinion unreliable where expert failed to show evidence of an increased risk of heart attacks or strokes from taking substance at issue over the background risk of receiving such injuries); Bell v. Swift Adhesives, Inc., a div. of Reichhold Chemicals, Inc., 804 F. Supp. 1577, 1580 (S.D. Ga. 1992) (expert opinion unreliable where expert did not adequately discount other potential causes for the plaintiff's cancer).

[9]McClain v. Metabolife Intern., Inc., 401 F.3d 1233, 1243 (11th Cir. 2005) (finding expert opinion unreliable where expert failed to explain and account for the risk that the plaintiff would have a stroke or heart attack even had she not taken Metabolife).

[10]McClain v. Metabolife Intern., Inc., 401 F.3d 1233, 1243 (11th Cir. 2005) (quoting David L. Eaton, Scientific Judgment and Toxic Torts—A Primer In Toxicology For Judges and Lawyers, 12 J.L. & POL'Y 5, 40 (2003)).

[11]McClain v. Metabolife Intern., Inc., 401 F.3d 1233, 1244 (11th Cir. 2005).

Chapter 7

Actions Involving Real Property

> **KeyCite**[R]: Cases and other legal materials listed in KeyCite Scope can be researched through the KeyCite service on Westlaw[R]. Use KeyCite to check citations for form, parallel references, prior and later history, and comprehensive citator information, including citations to other decisions and secondary materials.

§ 7:1 Overview

This chapter examines the use of expert testimony in premises liability actions, wherein an individual is injured upon the premises of another, as well as actions involving damage to property itself. Premises liability actions often involve so-called "slip and fall" or "trip and fall" cases, wherein an individual is injured while on the property of another as a result of a temporary or permanent condition of the property. It has been frequently held that expert testimony is not necessary to support a claim that a condition on the premises is defective or poses an unreasonable risk of harm to an individual such that liability may attach to the property owner. Nonetheless, expert testimony is frequently employed to prove building or other industry standards toward the end of establishing or refuting liability. Cases involving damage to the property itself may involve claims of nuisance and trespass, negligent design and construction, and negligent inspection and repair. In contrast to premises liability actions, expert testimony in these latter types of cases is often essential for purposes of establishing applicable standards of care and the damages flowing from a deviation therefrom.[1]

§ 7:2   Premises liability actions

In Georgia, the owner or occupier of land may be subject to liability for a failure to exercise ordinary care so as to keep the premises reasonably safe.[1] "This duty of ordinary care requires the owner or occupier to protect the invitee from unreasonable risks of harm of which the owner has superior knowledge."[2] As such, often at issue in premises liability actions is whether the condition of the premises causing the plaintiff's injuries posed an unreasonable risk of harm. Traditionally, expert testimony has been rarely introduced in premises liability actions, as such actions are premised on theories of "simple negligence" and for which no expert testimony is required.[3] Nonetheless, expert testimony has been increasingly employed when the degree of danger a condition poses,[4] or the property owner's actual or constructive knowledge thereof,[5] is not readily apparent to a layperson.

Typical slip or trip and fall cases involve encounters with transient conditions on the premises, such as spilled liquids or other debris on the floor,[6] or static conditions on the premises,

---

[Section 7:1]

[1]Notably, Georgia courts have held that expert testimony regarding the applicable standard of care is a prerequisite to bringing an action for negligent construction. Howard v. McFarland, 237 Ga. App. 483, 487, 515 S.E.2d 629, 633 (1999) (citing Newberry v. D.R. Horton, Inc., 215 Ga. App. 858, 452 S.E.2d 560, 561 (1994)).

[Section 7:2]

[1]See O.C.G.A. § 51-3-1.

[2]Hamblin v. City Of Albany, 272 Ga. App. 246, 247–248, 612 S.E.2d 69, 71 (2005).

[3]Michael J. Gorby, Premises Liability in Georgia, § 2–8, 28 (Harrison 1998); see also Self v. Executive Committee of Georgia Baptist Convention of Georgia, Inc., 245 Ga. 548, 266 S.E.2d 168 (1980).

[4]See, e.g. Hagadorn v. Prudential Ins. Co., 267 Ga. App. 143, 145, 598 S.E.2d 865, 868 (2004) (expert testi-mony presented that plaintiff's fall in a parking lot was caused by the light-ing which created an "optical illusion" preventing the plaintiff "from appreci-ating the severity of the slope of the catch basin" upon which she tripped); cf. Pirkle v. Robson Crossing LLC, 272 Ga. App. 259, 261, 612 S.E.2d 83, 85 (2005) (upholding summary judgment over plaintiff's claim of an "optical il-lusion," noting that this assertion was not supported by expert testimony).

[5]See, e.g. Murray v. West Bldg. Materials of Georgia, 243 Ga. App. 834, 835, 534 S.E.2d 204, 205 (2000) (holding that evidence of continuous use of subject stairs "combined with expert testimony" was sufficient to demonstrate a hazardous condition and constructive knowledge); see also Flournoy v. Hospital Authority of Houston County, 232 Ga. App. 791, 792, 504 S.E.2d 198, 199 (1998).

[6]Michael J. Gorby, Premises Liability in Georgia, § 2–4 (Harrison 1998).

such as steps and ramps.[7] Given the fact that these conditions are frequently encountered by most persons, courts have often excluded expert testimony as to whether such conditions pose an unreasonable risk of harm as "unhelpful," reasoning that such a determination is within the ability of a jury to decide on its own.[8] For instance, in *Sullivan v. Quisc*,[9] an architect was offered to testify that the slope of a threshold to the restroom was constructed in such a way that a patron might slip. In upholding the exclusion of this testimony, the Court of Appeals found that this testimony was not needed because such a determination was within the common understanding of the jury, specifically noting that "[a] party may not bolster his opinion as to the ultimate issue with expert testimony when the jury could reach the same conclusion independently of the opinion of others. . . . In everyday life, persons are required to negotiate the floors, steps and doorways of buildings. It is within the experience and capacity of an average layman to determine whether a sloped threshold across the doorway in a restaurant is a hazardous condition."[10]

§ 7:3 Premises liability actions—Building codes and industry standards

Expert testimony as to the hazard posed by a condition on the

---

[7]Michael J. Gorby, Premises Liability in Georgia, § 2–3 (Harrison 1998).

[8]See, e.g. Sullivan v. Quisc, Inc., 207 Ga. App. 114, 115, 427 S.E.2d 86, 88 (1993).

Expert opinion testimony on issues to be decided by the jury, even the ultimate issue, is admissible where the conclusion of the expert is one which jurors would not ordinarily be able to draw for themselves; i.e., the conclusion is beyond the ken of the average layman. . . . However, it is equally clear that the scope of what is admissible as expert opinion testimony is not unlimited. It is the established rule in Georgia, that where (a) the path from evidence to conclusion is not shrouded in the mystery of professional skill or knowledge, and (b) the conclusion determines the ultimate issue of fact in a case, the jury must make the journey from evidence to conclusion without the aid of expert testimony.

Id. (citing Clanton v. Von Haam, 177 Ga. App. 694, 340 S.E.2d 627 (1986)); see also Steinberger v. Barwick Pharmacy, Inc., 213 Ga. App. 122, 124,

444 S.E.2d 341, 343–344 (1994) (upholding exclusion of expert testimony that a raised platform is "inherently dangerous"); Warnke v. Pace Membership Warehouse, Inc., 215 Ga. App. 33, 34, 449 S.E.2d 629, 630–631 (1994) (upholding exclusion of expert testimony stating that a curb was "inherently dangerous" because the height of the curb the plaintiff tripped over was "slightly below a normal curb height.").

[9]Sullivan v. Quisc, Inc., 207 Ga. App. 114, 427 S.E.2d 86 (1993).

[10]Sullivan v. Quisc, Inc., 207 Ga. App. 114, 115, 427 S.E.2d 86, 88 (1993); see also Warnke v. Pace Membership Warehouse, Inc., 215 Ga. App. 33, 449 S.E.2d 629, 630 (1994) (despite presentation of expert testimony indicating that the height of the curb upon which the plaintiff trip made the curb "inherently dangerous," court found that such a determination did not create an issue of fact because "the conclusion drawn by the expert [was] not one which is beyond the ken of the average layman.").

premises has been found admissible when the expert is able to offer testimony regarding a deviation from a specific standard which is beyond the common understanding of the average juror.[1] Accordingly, expert testimony has most often been admitted in slip and fall actions where the plaintiff has encountered a static condition on the premises, the construction of which is regulated by industry standards or building codes,[2] or where the plaintiff's injury was caused by machinery requiring specialized knowledge as to its operation.[3] Similarly, expert testimony has been admitted to show compliance with such specific standards or codes.[4]

In some instances, the failure to present expert testimony as to the deviation from industry standards or building codes has been

---

[Section 7:3]

[1]See e.g., Mac Intern.-Savannah Hotel, Inc. v. Hallman, 265 Ga. App. 727, 728–729, 595 S.E.2d 577, 579 (2004), cert. denied, (June 7, 2004); Wood v. Winn–Dixie Stores, Inc., 244 Ga. App. 187, 534 S.E.2d 556 (2000); Spearman v. Georgia Bldg. Authority, 224 Ga. App. 801, 482 S.E.2d 463 (1997).

[2]See e.g., Mac Intern.-Savannah Hotel, Inc. v. Hallman, 265 Ga. App. 727, 728–729, 595 S.E.2d 577, 579 (2004), cert. denied, (June 7, 2004) (expert testimony demonstrating that subject stairs were not in compliance with building code was sufficient to create an issue of fact for trial); Wood v. Winn–Dixie Stores, Inc., 244 Ga. App. 187, 534 S.E.2d 556 (2000) (expert testimony that ramp did not comply with code requirement of non-slip surface); Flournoy v. Hospital Authority of Houston County, 232 Ga. App. 791, 792, 504 S.E.2d 198, 199 (1998) (expert testimony stating that slope of ramp exceeded maximum allowable under building code); Hardeman v. Spires, 232 Ga. App. 694, 695, 503 S.E.2d 588, 590 (1998) (expert opinion that failure to supply handrail in violation of building code created a hazard of which homeowner was aware); but see Lynch v. Georgia Power Co., 185 Ga. App. 256, 258, 363 S.E.2d 777, 778–779 (1987) (opinion testimony based solely upon industry standards in effect after the incident occurred "had no probative value.").

[3]The most common examples of injury caused by machinery are cases in which the plaintiff is injured on an elevator or escalator. See e.g., Millar Elevator Service Co. v. O'Shields, 222 Ga. App. 456, 457, 475 S.E.2d 188, 190 (1996) (holding that expert testimony as to industry practice is admissible on the question of whether there has been compliance with a duty which the law imposes).

[4]See, e.g. Cole v. Cracker Barrel, Inc., 210 Ga. App. 488, 489, 436 S.E.2d 704, 706 (1993) (defendant's expert demonstrated that the subject floor in a slip and fall action was constructed " 'of a material commonly accepted in the building industry,' [and thus] the standard of ordinary care [had] been met."); Spearman v. Georgia Bldg. Authority, 224 Ga. App. 801, 803, 482 S.E.2d 463, 464–465 (1997) (plaintiff's expert testified that acceptable coefficient of friction of pavement, pursuant to industry standard, was the same whether the payment was wet or dry, whereas defendant's expert testified that the applicable standard applied only to dry pavement, and that a standard for wet pavement did not exist); see also Parker v. Hovers, 255 Ga. App. 184, 185, 564 S.E.2d 795, 797 (2002) (information contained in written materials proffered by plaintiff's expert, which conflicted with expert's opinion, construed against plaintiff such that the court presumed defendant's compliance with industry standards).

found to be fatal to a plaintiff's claim.[5] An expert should be able to demonstrate the applicability of the industry standard or building code to the condition at issue, and the inability to do so may result in the failure of the plaintiff's action.[6] The presentation of expert testimony regarding a violation of an applicable standard will not, in itself, create an issue of fact for the jury absent a showing that the violation also contributed to the plaintiff's injury.[7]

Expert testimony regarding industry standards has been found admissible not only for purposes of demonstrating that a condition on the premises was unreasonably dangerous, but also for purposes of demonstrating knowledge of the hazard.[8] For instance, in *Val D'Aosta Co. v. Cross*,[9] where an expert testified that the beveling of the edge of a handicap access ramp was inconsistent with the requirements of the Americans with Dis-

---

[5]See, e.g. Garrett v. Hanes, 273 Ga. App. 894, 895, 616 S.E.2d 202, 204–205 (2005) (summary judgment affirmed where plaintiff presented "no expert testimony that the step was negligently designed, constructed, or maintained."); accord Poythress v. Savannah Airport Com'n, 229 Ga. App. 303, 305–306, 494 S.E.2d 76, 78 (1997).

[6]Porter v. Omni Hotels, Inc., 260 Ga. App. 24, 27, 579 S.E.2d 68, 71 (2003) (affirming summary judgment where, despite plaintiff's assertion that lack of handrails on the stairs upon which he fell violated ANSI standards, plaintiff "failed to show, through expert testimony or otherwise, that it applied to the staircases in question."); see also Rather v. Worrell, 260 Ga. App. 174, 581 S.E.2d 568 (2003) (noting that the plaintiff "has not pointed to any evidence that the lack of a handrail constituted a hazard. No expert testified that one was required, and we are essentially asked to recognize that a single step required a handrail as a matter of law. This, we cannot do.").

[7]Mitchell v. Austin, 261 Ga. App. 585, 587, 583 S.E.2d 249, 251 (2003) (affirming summary judgment where, although plaintiff presented expert testimony as to deviation from building code in the construction of the stairs upon which plaintiff fell, no

testimony was provided to demonstrate that these deviations caused or contributed to the injury); Yasinsac v. Colonial Oil Properties, Inc., 246 Ga. App. 484, 486, 541 S.E.2d 109, 111 (2000) (noting that expert testimony as to the presence of a building code violation alone is not necessarily enough to survive summary judgment because "[n]egligence per se is not liability per se"); see also Herrin v. Peeches Neighborhood Grill & Bar, Inc., 235 Ga. App. 528, 533, 509 S.E.2d 103, 107–108 (1998) (upholding summary judgment because plaintiff presented no evidence that defendant was aware of violation of industry standards).

[8]See e.g., Val D'Aosta Co. v. Cross, 241 Ga. App. 583, 584, 526 S.E.2d 580, 581–582 (1999) (expert testimony regarding defendant's failure to comply with American National Standards Institute ("ANSI") standards created hazardous condition); see also Davis v. GBR Properties, Inc., 233 Ga. App. 550, 551, 504 S.E.2d 204, 206 (1998) (holding that "[e]vidence that the ramp failed to comply with such standards constitutes some evidence from which the jury could find that the ramp constituted a hazardous condition.").

[9]Val D'Aosta Co. v. Cross, 241 Ga. App. 583, 584, 526 S.E.2d 580, 581 (1999)

abilities Act and standards promulgated by the American National Standards Institute (ANSI), the court found that this testimony was sufficient not only to establish the existence of a hazard, but also to demonstrate superior knowledge of the hazard on the part of the premises owner, who was required to maintain a compliant ramp by statute.[10]

§ 7:4   Premises liability actions—Liability for third–party criminal acts

Ordinarily, the criminal act of a third party severs the chain of causation between the original tortfeasor's conduct and a plaintiff's injury. However, where criminal conduct on a land owner or occupier's premises is foreseeable, the owner or occupier may be held liable for an invitee's injuries occasioned by such conduct which occur on his premises.[1] In *Sturbridge Partners v. Walker*,[2] the Georgia Supreme Court held that a crime is foreseeable, so as to render a property owner or occupier potentially liable for injuries arising out of the crime occurring on the premises, where it is substantially similar to prior crimes occurring on or near the property such that a reasonable person would have taken ordinary precautions to protect invitees from that risk.[3]

Expert testimony has been offered to demonstrate that the crime which occurred on the defendant's premises was reasonably foreseeable such that the defendant should have exercised diligence to guard against the threat.[4] However, as noted by the Georgia Court of Appeals in *Carlock v. Kmart Corp.*, a trial court does not abuse its discretion in excluding expert testimony as to the foreseeability of criminal conduct on a land owner's premises where the jury is competent to make this determination on its

---

[10]Val D'Aosta Co. v. Cross, 241 Ga. App. 583, 584, 526 S.E.2d 580, 581 (1999) (citing O.C.G.A. §§ 30–3–1, 30–3–8); see also Hicks v. Walker, 262 Ga. App. 216, 218, 585 S.E.2d 83, 86 (2003) (holding that "evidence of nonconformity with code standards may be proof of a landowner's superior knowledge.")

[Section 7:4]

[1]Days Inns of America, Inc. v. Matt, 265 Ga. 235, 236, 454 S.E.2d 507, 508 (1995).

[2]Sturbridge Partners, Ltd. v. Walker, 267 Ga. 785, 482 S.E.2d 339 (1997).

[3]Sturbridge Partners, Ltd. v. Walker, 267 Ga. 785, 786, 482 S.E.2d 339, 341 (1997) (noting that the prior crime does not need to be identical to the crime at issue to establish foreseeability, and that crimes against property may be used to determine the foreseeability of crimes against the person if the "location, nature and extent of the prior criminal activities and their likeness, proximity or other relationship" is similar to the crime in question).

[4]See e.g., McNeal v. Days Inn of America, Inc., 230 Ga. App. 786, 498 S.E.2d 294 (1998).

own.[5] In affirming the trial court's exclusion of such testimony, the *Carlock* court noted that "[i]t is the established rule in Georgia, that where (a) the path from evidence to conclusion is not shrouded in the mystery of professional skill or knowledge, and (b) the conclusion determines the ultimate issues of fact in a case, the jury must make the journey from evidence to conclusion without the aid of expert testimony. A party may not bolster his [case] as to the ultimate issue with expert testimony when the jury could reach the same conclusion independently of the opinion of others."[6]

Evidence tending to establish the foreseeability of a criminal act does not obviate a plaintiff's obligation to demonstrate that an act of negligence on the part of the premises owner or occupier was the proximate cause of the plaintiff's injury.[7] Toward that end, an expert's testimony must demonstrate that the criminal act was the "natural and probable consequence" of the premises owner or occupier's negligence."[8] For instance, in *McNeal v. Days Inn of America*,[9] the Court of Appeals, in reversing the trial court's grant of summary judgment to the defendant, noted that expert testimony indicating that the security measures on the premises were inadequate given the prior crimes on the property was sufficient to establish an issue of fact for the jury.[10]

§ 7:5 Environmental contamination of property

In addition to actions arising out of injuries occurring to individuals on the premises of a landowner, actions also arise out of damage to the property itself. These actions may involve the underground intrusion of contaminants from one parcel of land to another, such as petroleum products leaking from an underground pipeline[1] or methane migrating from a landfill onto lots in an

---

[5]Carlock v. Kmart Corp., 227 Ga. App. 356, 489 S.E.2d 99 (1997).

[6]Carlock v. Kmart Corp., 227 Ga. App. 356, 361, 489 S.E.2d 99, 104 (1997) (citing Baxter v. Melton, 218 Ga. App. 731, 732, 463 S.E.2d 53, 55 (1995)).

[7]See, e.g. FPI Atlanta, L.P. v. Seaton, 240 Ga. App. 880, 884, 524 S.E.2d 524, 529 (1999) ("[i]nherent in every case of liability for third party criminal conduct is the existence of concurrent proximate cause of the landlord's prior negligent act or omission.") (citing Sutter v. Hutchings, 254 Ga. 194, 197(1), 327 S.E.2d 716, 719 (1985)).

[8]Southern Ry. Co. v. Webb, 116 Ga. 152, 155–156(1), 42 S.E. 395 (1902).

[9]McNeal v. Days Inn of America, Inc., 230 Ga. App. 786, 498 S.E.2d 294 (1998).

[10]McNeal v. Days Inn of America, Inc., 230 Ga. App. 786, 787, 498 S.E.2d 294, 296 (1998).

[Section 7:5]

[1]See, e.g. Hoffman v. Atlanta Gas Light Co., 206 Ga. App. 727, 426 S.E.2d 387 (1992).

adjoining subdivision.[2] These actions may also involve the intrusion of contaminants from one parcel of land to another by way of water[3] or air.[4] Such actions often sound in the common law theories of nuisance and trespass,[5] with claims that the contamination has resulted in actual physical damage to the property,[6] reduced or entirely destroyed the marketability of the property,[7] or hampered the owner's use and enjoyment the property.[8] Additionally, such actions may involve allegations that the intrusion of contaminants has resulted in personal injuries, such as an illness or disease.[9] In addition to common law causes of action,

---

[2]See, e.g. Hammond v. City of Warner Robins, 224 Ga. App. 684, 482 S.E.2d 422 (1997); City of Warner Robins v. Holt, 220 Ga. App. 794, 470 S.E.2d 238 (1996).

[3]See, e.g. Tyler v. Lincoln, 236 Ga. App. 850, 513 S.E.2d 6 (1999), rev'd on other grounds, 272 Ga. 118, 527 S.E.2d 180 (2000) (discharge of contaminants into pond by storm water run-off from nearby subdivision under development).

[4]See, e.g. Payne v. Terrell, 269 Ga. App. 540, 604 S.E.2d 551 (2004), rev'd on other grounds, 280 Ga. 51, 622 S.E.2d 330 (2005) (ammonia emissions from manure generated on poultry farm traveling to nearby residence).

[5]See, e.g. City of Warner Robins v. Holt, 220 Ga. App. 794, 470 S.E.2d 238 (1996); Hoffman v. Atlanta Gas Light Co., 206 Ga. App. 727, 426 S.E.2d 387 (1992).

[6]See, e.g. McElmurray v. Augusta–Richmond County, 274 Ga. App. 605, 618 S.E.2d 59 (2005), cert. denied, (Apr. 25, 2006) (allegation that sewage sludge which owner permitted county to deposit on farmland for fertilizing qualities contained high heavy metal content which destroyed farm's crops and cattle).

[7]See, e.g. Hammond v. City of Warner Robins, 224 Ga. App. 684, 482 S.E.2d 422 (1997) (allegation that methane migrating from city landfill onto subdivision lot resulted in diminution of market value); Hoffman v. Atlanta Gas Light Co., 206 Ga. App.

727, 426 S.E.2d 387 (1992) (allegation that petroleum migrating from leaking underground pipeline onto adjoining lot rendered property entirely unmarketable).

[8]See, e.g. Payne v. Terrell, 269 Ga. App. 540, 604 S.E.2d 551 (2004), cert. denied, (Apr. 26, 2005) and cert. granted, (May 23, 2005) and judgment rev'd, 280 Ga. 51, 622 S.E.2d 330 (2005) and opinion vacated, 278 Ga. App. 676, 629 S.E.2d 839 (2006) (allegation that ammonia emissions from poultry farm would result in unpleasant and irritating odor on landowner's premises); Tyler v. Lincoln, 236 Ga. App. 850, 513 S.E.2d 6 (1999), rev'd, 272 Ga. 118, 527 S.E.2d 180 (2000) and opinion vacated in part, 243 Ga. App. 785, 534 S.E.2d 479 (2000) (allegation that discharge of contaminants into pond by storm water run-off destroyed pond's recreational and aesthetic value).

[9]See, e.g. Payne v. Terrell, 269 Ga. App. 540, 604 S.E.2d 551 (2004), rev'd on other grounds, 280 Ga. 51, 622 S.E.2d 330 (2005) (expert testimony that ammonia emissions from poultry farm would have adverse health consequences on nearby persons); Jordan v. Georgia Power Co., 219 Ga. App. 690, 466 S.E.2d 601 (1995) (allegation that electromagnetic radiation emitted from nearby power lines caused plaintiff's non-Hodgkin's lymphoma).

This chapter does not focus on expert testimony pertaining to whether a substance is "hazardous" and capable of causing harm of the

federal statutes such as the Comprehensive Environmental Response, Compensation, and Liability Act (CERCLA),[10] or Georgia's counterpart, the Hazardous Site Response Act (HSRA),[11] may provide a cause of action for contribution or indemnification against certain responsible parties for expenses incurred in the clean-up of such contamination.[12]

In cases involving the contamination of property, expert testimony will often be necessary for purposes of establishing the source of the contamination. Expert testimony in this regard may focus on the ruling in or ruling out of alternative sources of the contamination found on the property.[13] For instance, in *McElmurray v. Augusta–Richmond County,*[14] several of the plaintiff's dairy cows unexpectedly died after the plaintiff entered into an agreement with a city, wherein the city was permitted to deposit sewage sludge on the plaintiff's farmland as fertilizer. The plaintiff alleged that the livestock died of heavy metal poisoning, and contended, among other things, the heavy metals had come from the sewage sludge. The defendant contended the deaths were attributable to some other source, such as commercial fertilizers. In finding that the trial court had improvidently granted summary judgment in favor of the city, the court found it significant that the plaintiff's expert was able to rule out commercial fertilizers as a source of this contamination by virtue of the fact that commercial fertilizers historically did not contain high levels of heavy metals and the fact that no other farms in the area, which purchased commercial fertilizer from same source as plaintiff, had experienced similar blights.[15]

Often at issue in cases involving the underground migration of contaminants from one property to another is whether it was

---

sort from which a plaintiff suffers (general causation), or whether the substance to which the plaintiff was exposed in fact caused the illness or disease from which the plaintiff suffers (specific causation). For a discussion of expert testimony on these issues, see toxic torts *infra.*

[10]42 U.S.C.A. § 9201 et seq.

[11]O.C.G.A. § 12–8–90 et. seq.

[12]See, e.g. Redwing Carriers, Inc. v. Saraland Apartments, 94 F.3d 1489 (11th Cir. 1996); Canadyne–Georgia Corp. v. Bank of America, 174 F. Supp. 2d 1360 (M.D. Ga. 2001); Chem–Nuclear Systems, Inc. v. Arivec Chemicals, Inc., 978 F. Supp. 1105 (N.D. Ga. 1997).

[13]See, e.g. Hammond v. City of Warner Robins, 224 Ga. App. 684, 687, 482 S.E.2d 422, 426 (1997) (whereas plaintiff's expert opined that methane found in soil on plaintiff's property originated from decaying organic material in nearby city landfill, defendant's expert opined that methane originated from decaying construction debris in developing subdivision).

[14]McElmurray v. Augusta–Richmond County, 274 Ga. App. 605, 618 S.E.2d 59 (2005), cert. denied, (Apr. 25, 2006).

[15]McElmurray v. Augusta–Richmond County, 274 Ga. App. 605, 617, 618 S.E.2d 59, 69 (2005), cert. denied, (Apr. 25, 2006).

possible for the contaminants to migrate from the defendant's property onto the plaintiff's property.[16] Proof of adequate testing can play a crucial role in ascertaining the source of the contamination. For instance, in *Hammond v. City of Warner Robins*,[17] a case involving the diminution of a property's market value by virtue of the presence of methane gas in the property's soil, the plaintiff alleged that this methane had been produced by the decay of organic matter in a nearby city landfill, and had migrated through the porous soil onto the plaintiff's property. The city moved for summary judgment on the plaintiff's claim, offering expert testimony that the erection of a nonporous clay barrier between the landfill and the plaintiff's property made it "highly improbable" that the methane in the landfill could have migrated onto the plaintiff's property. In reversing the trial court's grant of summary judgment to the city, the court focused on the testing employed by both the city and the plaintiff's expert. While the "test holes" created by the city's expert did not show the presence of methane on the plaintiff's property, they had only been dug to a depth of two and one-half feet; by contrast, the test holes dug by the plaintiff's expert were dug to a depth of 30 feet, and showed the presence of methane on the plaintiff's property.[18]

At times, the central focus of an environmental case is not contamination which has already taken place, but rather, contamination which may take place in the future.[19] This is particularly true in actions for injunctive relief.[20] These cases often turn on an expert's ability to reliably construct a model projecting the future migration and dispersal of a pollutant. For instance, in *Payne v. Terrell*,[21] at issue was the nuisance which would be created if the defendant were permitted to construct a

---

[16]See, e.g. Tyler v. Lincoln, 236 Ga. App. 850, 513 S.E.2d 6 (1999), rev'd, 272 Ga. 118, 527 S.E.2d 180 (2000) and opinion vacated in part, 243 Ga. App. 785, 534 S.E.2d 479 (2000) (discussing competing expert testimony on whether storm water run-off from nearby subdivision under development contaminated plaintiff's property).

[17]Hammond v. City of Warner Robins, 224 Ga. App. 684, 482 S.E.2d 422 (1997).

[18]Hammond v. City of Warner Robins, 224 Ga. App. 684, 688, 482 S.E.2d 422, 426–427 (1997).

[19]See, e.g. Hammond v. City of Warner Robins, 224 Ga. App. 684, 688, 482 S.E.2d 422, 426 (1997) (where

plaintiff's application for refinancing of property loan denied because of risk posed by methane gas from nearby landfill, plaintiff's expert testified that methane detected on nearby property would continue to migrate so as to contaminate plaintiff's property).

[20]See, e.g. Superior Farm Management, L.L.C. v. Montgomery, 270 Ga. 615, 617, 513 S.E.2d 215, 218 (1999) (expert testimony indicated that proposed hog farm would produce solid waste that could contaminate the groundwater); Hoffman v. Atlanta Gas Light Co., 206 Ga. App. 727, 426 S.E.2d 387 (1992) (spreading contamination of soil from leaking petroleum pipeline).

[21]Payne v. Terrell, 269 Ga. App. 540, 604 S.E.2d 551 (2004), rev'd on

poultry farm near the plaintiff's residence. The plaintiff alleged that the ammonia emissions produced by the farm's manure would reach the plaintiff's property in sufficient quantities and concentrations so as to not only interfere with the plaintiff's use and enjoyment of his land, but also cause adverse health effects. Both the plaintiff's and the defendant's experts created "air models" in an effort to assess the impact of the ammonia emissions on the plaintiff's property. In critiquing the methodology employed by the defendant's expert, the court observed that the expert had underestimated the expected *quantity* of ammonia emissions by basing his model on a farm containing smaller, and a fewer number of, poultry houses than the defendant's proposed farm.[22] Further, the court noted that the defendant's expert had arrived at a questionable estimate of the *concentration* of ammonia emissions expected to reach the plaintiff's property by failing to comply with state regulatory guidelines for assessing the impact of air pollutant emissions, and by calculating the dispersal of such emissions with dated geographic and weather patterns that did not reflect the terrain or wind speed and direction in the area.[23]

In *Jordan v. Georgia Power Co.*,[24] at issue was whether electromagnetic radiation emitted from nearby power lines onto the plaintiff's property had caused the plaintiff's non-Hodgkin's lymphoma. In rejecting the plaintiff's claim, the court found that no actionable claim for trespass arose out of the emissions because of the inconclusive evidence that such radiation caused the type of harm from which the plaintiff suffered.[25]

§ 7:6 Negligent design and construction

Litigation surrounding the construction of homes and other structures abounds. Such claims are as varied as the types of problems which may arise with a home or other structure, and may allege negligence in the design of the structure itself[1] or the

---

other grounds, 280 Ga. 51, 622 S.E.2d 330 (2005).

[22]Payne v. Terrell, 269 Ga. App. 540, 541–542, 604 S.E.2d 551, 554 (2004), rev'd on other grounds, 280 Ga. 51, 622 S.E.2d 330 (2005).

[23]Payne v. Terrell, 269 Ga. App. 540, 541–542, 604 S.E.2d 551, 554 (2004), rev'd on other grounds, 280 Ga. 51, 622 S.E.2d 330 (2005).

[24]Jordan v. Georgia Power Co., 219 Ga. App. 690, 466 S.E.2d 601 (1995).

[25]Jordan v. Georgia Power Co., 219 Ga. App. 690, 694–695, 466 S.E.2d 601, 606 (1995).

[Section 7:6]

[1]See, e.g. Housing Authority of Savannah v. Gilpin & Bazemore/ Architects & Planners, Inc., 191 Ga.

surrounding premises.[2] Such claims may also allege negligence in the construction of the structure, such as the use of improper methods in constructing a structure,[3] the use of improper materials in the building of a structure,[4] or inadequacies with the structure's foundation.[5] Such actions are typically brought against the building contractors who constructed the structure, or the architects and engineers involved in the design of the structure.

§ 7:7   Negligent design and construction—Negligent design

"[P]ersons performing architectural and engineering services are performing professional services, and the law imposes upon such persons the duty to exercise a reasonable degree of skill and care, as determined by the degree of skill and care ordinarily employed by their respective professions under similar conditions and like circumstances."[1] As is the case in any negligence action against a professional, a jury should not be permitted to speculate as to the standard of conduct as to which members of these professions are held in determining whether the professional complied with that standard.[2] Accordingly, expert testimony is generally required in an action alleging professional malfeasance

---

App. 400, 381 S.E.2d 550 (1989) (alleging faulty design in heating system led to carbon monoxide poisoning of apartment tenant).

[2]See, e.g. Ponce de Leon Condominiums v. DiGirolamo, 238 Ga. 188, 232 S.E.2d 62 (1977) (alleging negligent design of grading and paving system of land under development, allowing surface water runoff to drain onto plaintiff's property).

[3]See, e.g. Hall v. Harris, 239 Ga. App. 812, 521 S.E.2d 638 (1999) (alleging improper installation of synthetic stucco, resulting in moisture penetration behind the stucco and consequent structural damage); Hudson v. Santangelo, 228 Ga. App. 768, 492 S.E.2d 673 (1997) (alleging improper use of nails instead of screws to secure porch railing to posts, resulting in insecure attachment of railing to posts).

[4]See, e.g. Hall v. Harris, 239 Ga. App. 812, 521 S.E.2d 638 (1999) (alleging use of synthetic stucco was improper in residential construction due to greater opportunity for mois-

ture to penetrate behind stucco); Williams v. Runion, 173 Ga. App. 54, 325 S.E.2d 441 (1984) (alleging that builder's use moisture-filled wood to construct ceiling trusses allowed wood to warp and nails attaching ceiling to trusses to rust, eventually causing ceiling to fall).

[5]See, e.g. Jennings v. Smith, 226 Ga. App. 765, 487 S.E.2d 362 (1997) (alleging failure to properly compact soil prior to laying of foundation, resulting in uneven settlement and resulting cracks in the structure's veneer); Cherry v. Ward, 204 Ga. App. 833, 420 S.E.2d 763 (1992) (alleging failure to properly pour foundation walls allowed water leakage in basement).

[Section 7:7]

[1]Housing Authority of Savannah v. Greene, 259 Ga. 435, 436, 383 S.E.2d 867, 868 (1989); see also R.H. Chastain v. Atlanta Gas Light Co., 122 Ga. App. 90, 93, 176 S.E.2d 487, 491 (1970).

[2]H. Elton Thompson & Associates, P.C. v. Williams, 164 Ga. App. 571, 572, 298 S.E.2d 539, 540 (1982).

against architects and engineers in order to establish the applicable standard of care and whether there was a deviation therefrom.[3] A rare exception exists to this general requirement when the negligence of the architect or engineer is so "clear and palpable" that the jury can ascertain negligence without the assistance of expert testimony.[4]

Both architects and engineers are listed among the professions against whom an expert affidavit must be filed with a complaint sounding in professional negligence.[5] O.C.G.A. § 24-9-67.1 requires such an expert opining as to the standard of care of the defendant professional to have been licensed to practice in his or her profession at the time the negligence is alleged to have occurred.[6] However, because the affidavit requirement of O.C.G.A. § 9-11-9.1 applies, with the one exception of licensed healthcare facilities, only to the negligence of individuals, an action brought against an architectural or engineering firm based on the negligence of one of its employed professionals need not be supported by an expert affidavit at the pleadings stage.[7]

A deviation from the applicable standard of care may be shown by expert testimony as to generally accepted design practices or applicable ordinances establishing design standards.[8] However, it is insufficient for an expert to offer alternative designs which allegedly would have prevented the damage which forms the basis of the litigation without a showing that the applicable standard of care required the institution of such designs.[9] Additionally, expert testimony as to negligence will not create an issue of fact for a jury's determination where the alleged breach of duty does not directly relate to the task which the architect or engineer was

---

[3]Housing Authority of Savannah v. Greene, 259 Ga. 435, 436, 383 S.E.2d 867 (1989); Ponce de Leon Condominiums v. DiGirolamo, 238 Ga. 188, 191-192, 232 S.E.2d 62, 65 (1977); H. Elton Thompson & Associates, P.C. v. Williams, 164 Ga. App. 571, 572, 298 S.E.2d 539, 540 (1982); R.H. Chastain v. Atlanta Gas Light Co., 122 Ga. 90, 93, 176 S.E.2d 487, 491 (1970).

[4]Housing Authority of Savannah v. Greene, 259 Ga. 435, 436, 383 S.E.2d 867 (1989); H. Elton Thompson & Associates, P.C. v. Williams, 164 Ga. App. 571, 572, 298 S.E.2d 539, 540 (1982).

[5]O.C.G.A. § 9-11-9.1(d); see also Jordan, Jones & Goulding, Inc. v. Wilson, 197 Ga. App. 354, 398 S.E.2d 385 (1990); Housing Authority of Savannah v. Gilpin & Bazemore/ Architects & Planners, Inc., 191 Ga. App. 400, 381 S.E.2d 550 (1989).

[6]O.C.G.A. § 24-9-67.1(c)(1).

[7]Sembler Atlanta Development I, LLC v. URS/Dames & Moore, Inc., 268 Ga. App. 7, 8-9, 601 S.E.2d 397, 399 (2004); see also Minnix v. Department of Transp., 272 Ga. 566, 570-571, 533 S.E.2d 75, 79 (2000).

[8]Samuelson v. Lord, Aeck & Sergeant, Inc., 205 Ga. App. 568, 573, 423 S.E.2d 268, 272 (1992).

[9]H. Elton Thompson & Associates, P.C. v. Williams, 164 Ga. App. 571, 573, 298 S.E.2d 539, 540-541 (1982).

employed to perform.[10] For instance, in a suit involving a construction worker's fall from a walkway on a bridge under construction, expert testimony that the engineering firm designing the walkway was negligent in designing it without guardrails or barriers so as to prevent such falls was found insufficient to create an issue of fact for the jury where the court found, as a matter of law, that it was the duty of the contractor, not the engineering firm, to provide for the safety of workers under its employment.[11]

§ 7:8 Negligent design and construction—Negligent construction

Independent of any contract which may exist as between a building contractor and a homeowner, the law deems the contractor to have implicitly warranted that he has built a home in a "fit and workmanlike manner."[1] Accordingly, "the law imposes upon building contractors and others performing skilled services the obligation to exercise a reasonable degree of care and skill as, under similar conditions and like circumstances, is ordinarily employed by others of the same profession."[2] Thus, in proving negligence in the construction of a home or other structure, it is necessary to present competent evidence demonstrating that the

---

[10]National Foundation Co. v. Post, Buckley, Schuh & Jernigan, Inc., 219 Ga. App. 431, 433, 465 S.E.2d 726, 729 (1995).

[11]National Foundation Co. v. Post, Buckley, Schuh & Jernigan, Inc., 219 Ga. App. 431, 434, 465 S.E.2d 726, 730 (1995). The *National Foundation* case represents an interesting conflict between the role of an expert in establishing the applicable standards of professional conduct and the court's role in determining the legal duty applicable to the defendant as an issue of law. There, an expert opined that the failure of the defendant engineers designing the walkway to provide for safety barriers and handrails on the walkway fell below the generally accepted standard of care. Notwithstanding this testimony, the court determined as a matter of law that the engineers had no duty to provide for safety apparatuses on the walkway,

and observed that to accept the expert's testimony as establishing such a duty "in effect would remove the issue of legal duty from the breast of the court and vest it within the waiting grasp of the retained expert. Though appellant's arguments in this regard are enticing, '[w]e cannot succumb to this siren's call.'" National Foundation Co. v. Post, Buckley, Schuh & Jernigan, Inc., 219 Ga. App. 431, 435, 465 S.E.2d 726, 730 (1995)

[Section 7:8]

[1]Williams v. Runion, 173 Ga. App. 54, 57, 325 S.E.2d 441, 446 (1984).

[2]Howell v. Ayers, 129 Ga. App. 899, 900, 202 S.E.2d 189, 190–191 (1973); see also Wilson v. Brighton Homes, Inc., 204 Ga. App. 677, 679, 420 S.E.2d 360, 361 (1992); Williams v. Runion, 173 Ga. App. 54, 325 S.E.2d 441 (1984).

building contractor did not comply with the standard of care required of him by the profession.[3]

An action alleging negligence against a building contractor is not required, at the pleadings stage, to be supported with an expert affidavit pursuant to O.C.G.A. § 9–11–9.1.[4] Nonetheless, in order for such an action to ultimately prevail, competent expert testimony is generally required to demonstrate negligence on the contractor's part.[5] This requirement exists because building contractors provide skilled services beyond the ken of the average juror, and the jury is "not permitted to speculate as to the standard against which to measure the acts of the professional in determining whether he exercised a reasonable degree of care."[6]

Expert testimony is not, however, required in all cases of negligent construction, and where the evidence of negligence is "clear and palpable," expert testimony will not be required to support a claim.[7] For instance, a contractor's failure to install a product in accordance with manufacture specifications has been held to constitute sufficient evidence of a deviation from the applicable standard of care such that expert testimony is not

[3]Hudgins v. Bacon, 171 Ga. App. 856, 860, 321 S.E.2d 359, 364 (1984) (In an action against a builder, "it is essential to present competent evidence as to the acceptability of specific professional conduct."); Coursey Bldg. Associates v. Baker, 165 Ga. App. 521, 301 S.E.2d 688 (1983).

[4]O.C.G.A. § 9–11–9.1(d); Minnix v. Department of Transp., 272 Ga. 566, 570–571, 533 S.E.2d 75, 79 (2000) (holding that, pursuant to 1997 amendments to O.C.G.A. § 9–11–9.1, the requirement of an expert affidavit at the pleading stage of litigation applies only to those professions explicitly listed in the statute).

[5]Howard v. McFarland, 237 Ga. App. 483, 487, 515 S.E.2d 629, 633 (1999) ("It is well established that plaintiffs in a negligent construction case must establish the standard of care applicable to the defendant builder by the introduction of expert testimony.") (citing Newberry v. D.R. Horton, Inc., 215 Ga. App. 858, 452 S.E.2d 560 (1994)); Rentz v. Brown, 219 Ga. App. 187, 188, 464 S.E.2d 617,

619 (1995) (" 'In an action against a builder, it is essential to present competent evidence as to the acceptability of specific professional conduct.' . . . [T]he standard of care must be established through expert testimony.") (citing Hudgins v. Bacon, 171 Ga. App. 856, 321 S.E.2d 359 (1984)).

[6]Marquis Towers, Inc. v. Highland Group, 265 Ga. App. 343, 346, 593 S.E.2d 903, 906 (2004) (citing Department of Transp. v. Mikell, 229 Ga. App. 54, 58, 493 S.E.2d 219, 222 (1997)); Bilt Rite of Augusta, Inc. v. Gardner, 221 Ga. App. 817, 817, 472 S.E.2d 709, 710 (1996); H. Elton Thompson & Associates, P.C. v. Williams, 164 Ga. App. 571, 298 S.E.2d 539 (1982).

[7]See, e.g. Khoury Const. Co., Inc. v. Earhart, 191 Ga. App. 562, 382 S.E.2d 392 (1989) (where evidence was presented that hardwood floors creaked loudly and moved up and down when walked on, expert testimony was not required to establish that floor had been negligently installed).

required to support a claim.[8] Where a defendant building contractor testifies that he should have performed an act, and the evidence shows that the act was not performed, the contractor's negligence may become a clear and palpable case of negligence such that expert testimony is not required.[9]

Expert testimony offered by a plaintiff must establish both the standard of care applicable to the builder and why the structure, as constructed, failed to comply with this standard.[10] It is insufficient for an expert to merely state that he would have performed the work in a different way; rather, the standard to which a builder is held is the standard of care generally employed by the industry.[11] The applicable standard of care may be established by way of testimony as to general industry practices[12] or local building codes.[13] However, the building codes must be shown to be those applicable at the time the construction was performed[14] and for the type of structure at issue.[15] Manufacturer's specifications for the installation of building materials also provides evidence of the applicable standard of care for the installation of the material.[16]

---

[8]Bilt Rite of Augusta, Inc. v. Gardner, 221 Ga. App. 817, 818-819, 472 S.E.2d 709, 711 (1996).

[9]Crosby v. DeMeyer, 229 Ga. App. 672, 673–674, 494 S.E.2d 568, 569–570 (1997); Hudgins v. Bacon, 171 Ga. App. 856, 859–861, 321 S.E.2d 359, 364–365 (1984).

[10]Hudson v. Santangelo, 228 Ga. App. 768, 773, 492 S.E.2d 673, 677 (1997).

[11]Hudson v. Santangelo, 228 Ga. App. 768, 773, 492 S.E.2d 673, 677 (1997); Rentz v. Brown, 219 Ga. App. 187, 188–189, 464 S.E.2d 617, 619 (1995) ("The only evidence presented on [the standard of construction] concerned what the witnesses would have done if they had constructed the house or what recommended practice might have been, but no evidence was presented establishing the applicable standard of care in the industry. . . . Mere custom or practice, standing alone, is not sufficient. There must be evidence of a universal custom or practice."); cf. Hudgins v. Bacon, 171 Ga. App. 856, 859–860, 321 S.E.2d 359, 364–365 (1984) (finding that where defendant contractor testified

that he should have and did perform an act which the evidence showed was not in fact done, plaintiff had met his burden in presenting "competent evidence as to the acceptability of the specific professional conduct[,]" even though no evidence of the "standard of care in the profession generally" was shown).

[12]Wilson v. Brighton Homes, Inc., 204 Ga. App. 677, 679, 420 S.E.2d 360, 361 (1992).

[13]Cherry v. Ward, 204 Ga. App. 833, 833, 420 S.E.2d 763, 765 (1992); Williams v. Runion, 173 Ga. App. 54, 58, 325 S.E.2d 441, 447 (1984).

[14]Rentz v. Brown, 219 Ga. App. 187, 188, 464 S.E.2d 617, 619 (1995); see also Williams v. Runion, 173 Ga. App. 54, 58, 325 S.E.2d 441, 447 (1984).

[15]Wise v. Tidal Const. Co., 270 Ga. App. 725, 728–729, 608 S.E.2d 11, 14 (2004), cert. denied, (Mar. 28, 2005).

[16]Bilt Rite of Augusta, Inc. v. Gardner, 221 Ga. App. 817, 818-819, 472 S.E.2d 709, 711 (1996). However, manufacturer's specifications do not necessarily define the standard of care, as they may establish standards which

An expert need not be a member of the precise field in which the defendant contractor practices in order to provide standard of care testimony where the expert has experience enabling him to provide competent testimony.[17] However, the testimony of a witness in a somewhat related, albeit different, field of expertise may prove insufficient to support a claim. For instance, the testimony of a civil engineer with expertise in "soil mechanics and the use of soils to support structures," offered in support of a claim that the builder's failure to remove organic matter from the soil prior to laying a house's foundation was negligent, was found insufficient to support a claim against the builder because the engineer could not establish the standard of care required of contractors in preparing land for the laying of a foundation.[18] Similarly, the testimony of an engineer regarding the standard practices of plumbers was found insufficient where there was no showing of "overlapping expertise" between the engineer and the defendant plumbers with respect to the aspect of construction at issue.[19]

As is true in any negligence case, there must be a showing that negligence in the construction of a structure was the proximate cause of the damage alleged.[20] Expert testimony is thus often essential in establishing causation in cases where the cause of damage is not readily apparent. For instance, expert testimony is often presented as to whether the installation or use of certain building materials was the cause of moisture[21] or termite damage

---

either fall below, or which exceed, the standard in the profession. *Id.*

[17]Coursey Bldg. Associates v. Baker, 165 Ga. App. 521, 301 S.E.2d 688 (1983) (expert with degree in civil engineering who had been engaged as "structural engineer" for 25 years in the structural design of buildings competent to testify as to standard of care applicable to a contractor regarding construction of basement wall).

[18]Wise v. Tidal Const. Co., 270 Ga. App. 725, 727, 608 S.E.2d 11, 14 (2004), cert. denied, (Mar. 28, 2005). The court also observed that the engineer lacked any knowledge as to how the builder had prepared the land prior to laying the foundation. *Id.*

[19]Seely v. Loyd H. Johnson Const. Co., Inc., 220 Ga. App. 719, 722, 470 S.E.2d 283, 287 (1996).

[20]See, e.g. Seely v. Loyd H. Johnson Const. Co., Inc., 220 Ga. App. 719, 723, 470 S.E.2d 283, 288 (1996) (subsequent, intervening act of independent contractor in repairing leaking pipe found to be cause of injury); Florence v. Knight, 217 Ga. App. 799, 800, 459 S.E.2d 436, 438 (1995) (evidence of building code violation does not create issue of fact for trial in absence of a showing that the violation was the proximate cause of injury); McCurley v. Ludwig, 215 Ga. App. 798, 452 S.E.2d 554 (1994) (no evidence presented that negligence in construction of roof caused uncompleted roof to collapse during storm).

[21]See, e.g. Clearwater Const. Co. v. McClung, 261 Ga. App. 789, 584 S.E.2d 61 (2003) (expert testimony as to whether installation of synthetic stucco was cause of moisture damage

to the structure.[22] Similarly, expert testimony may be presented to demonstrate that the inadequate compaction of the soil prior to laying a foundation caused settlement of, and consequential damage to, the structure,[23] or that the inadequate construction of a foundation was the cause of water leaking inside of the structure.[24]

§ 7:9 Termite inspections

Actions are commonly brought for structural damage to a home occasioned by wood-destroying agents. Such actions typically involve termite infestation, but may involve moisture damage occasioned by the allegedly negligent use or installation of building materials such as synthetic stucco.[1] The law is somewhat unsettled as to whether a claim brought against one inspecting or treating a home for termites is in the nature of a professional negligence action for which expert testimony is required to establish liability. Because home inspectors and exterminators are not among the professionals identified in O.C.G.A. § 9–11–9.1(d), an expert's affidavit is not required to be filed along with a complaint alleging negligent treatment and inspection.[2] Even if an affidavit is not required to be filed with the Complaint, expert testimony may be required regarding standard of care at trial. Rather than purporting to define what is and what is not a professional malpractice action, O.C.G.A. § 9–11–9.1 merely establishes an initial pleading requirement for certain enumerated professions.[3] Pest control operators are subject to extensive regu-

---

to structure).

[22]See, e.g. Hall v. Harris, 239 Ga. App. 812, 521 S.E.2d 638 (1999) (expert testimony as to whether installation of synthetic stucco allowed water intrusion into structure and consequent termite damage).

[23]See, e.g. Jennings v. Smith, 226 Ga. App. 765, 487 S.E.2d 362 (1997); see also General Pipeline Co. v. Hardin, 267 Ga. App. 495, 600 S.E.2d 427 (2004).

[24]See, e.g. Wilson v. Brighton Homes, Inc., 204 Ga. App. 677, 420 S.E.2d 360 (1992); Cherry v. Ward, 204 Ga. App. 833, 420 S.E.2d 763 (1992).

[Section 7:9]

[1]See, e.g. Colormatch Exteriors, Inc. v. Hickey, 275 Ga. 249, 249–250,

569 S.E.2d 495, 496 (2002) (synthetic stucco); Hall v. Harris, 239 Ga. App. 812, 815, 521 S.E.2d 638, 641 (1999) (synthetic stucco).

[2]Vester v. Mug A Bug Pest Control, Inc., 231 Ga. App. 644, 648, 500 S.E.2d 406, 410 (1998) (overruled on other grounds by, Harris v. Murray, 233 Ga. App. 661, 504 S.E.2d 736 (1998)) and, rev'd on other grounds by Mug A Bug Pest Control v. Vester, 270 Ga. 407, 509 S.E.2d 925 (1999) (recognizing that the 1997 amendments to O.C.G.A. § 9–11–9.1, which for the first time expressly defined the professionals to whom the affidavit requirement applied, did not list termite exterminators among the named professionals).

[3]Minnix v. Department of Transp., 272 Ga. 566, 571–572, 533

lations[4] and must be licensed to practice within the state.[5] Perhaps out of an abundance of caution, expert testimony has often been used in such actions, particularly with respect to matters of causation.[6] It has been held that an expert in such an action need not hold a pest control operator's license in order to testify as to the standard of care in the industry.[7] However, if an action against a pest control operator may be considered to sound in professional malpractice, the recent enactment of O.C.G.A. § 24–9–67.1(c)(1) may require licensure as a prerequisite to expert witness qualification in such cases.[8]

Actions against pest control operators often arise in the context of a termite inspection performed in conjunction with the sale of a home.[9] Where the negligence alleged is a failure to discover evidence of an active infestation, a pest control operator can, of course, only be held liable for failing to discover the infestation if

---

S.E.2d 75, 80 (2000) ("The inclusion or exclusion of a profession or employer from the statute's ambit does not change a plaintiff's burden in a professional malpractice case to produce at trial expert testimony 'to establish the parameters of acceptable professional conduct, a significant deviation from which would constitute malpractice.' "). Case law prior to Minnix had indicated that the affidavit requirement of O.C.G.A. § 9–11–9.1 applied to all professional malpractice actions. See, e.g. Raley v. Terminix Intern. Co., L.P., 215 Ga. App. 324, 325, 450 S.E.2d 343, 344 (1994) (O.C.G.A. § 9–11–9.1 applies to any action, whether sounding in tort or contract, for professional malpractice); Hopkinson v. Labovitz, 231 Ga. App. 557, 560, 499 S.E.2d 338, 340 (1998), aff'd, 271 Ga. 330, 519 S.E.2d 672 (1999) (Beasley, J. concurring) ("O.C.G.A § 9–11–9.1 requires an affidavit of an expert in every case alleging professional malpractice"). However, case law following Minnix has made it clear that professional malpractice actions may exist against persons or entities not listed in O.C.G.A. § 9–11–9.1, and that even though such actions need not be supported by an expert affidavit at the pleading stage, expert testimony must nonetheless be presented in order to carry the plaintiff's burden of proof at

trial. See Sembler Atlanta Development I, LLC v. URS/Dames & Moore, Inc., 268 Ga. App. 7, 601 S.E.2d 397 (2004).

[4]See, e.g. The Structural Pest Control Act, codified at O.C.G.A. § 43–45–1 et seq.

[5]O.C.G.A. § 43–45–24.

[6]See, e.g. American Pest Control, Inc. v. Pritchett, 201 Ga. App. 808, 809, 412 S.E.2d 590, 592 (1991); Getz Services, Inc. v. Perloe, 173 Ga. App. 532, 534, 327 S.E.2d 761, 764 (1985).

[7]Dayoub v. Yates–Astro Termite Pest Control Co., 239 Ga. App. 578, 580, 521 S.E.2d 600, 602 (1999) (reversing trial court's exclusion of expert's testimony on the basis that he was not a licensed pest control operator where the witness had a doctorate in entomology, had experience and training in pest control, and acted as a consultant to pest control companies).

[8]See O.C.G.A. § 24–9–67.1(c)(1).

[9]See e.g., Power v. Georgia Exterminators, Inc., 243 Ga. App. 355, 532 S.E.2d 475 (2000); American Pest Control, Inc. v. Pritchett, 201 Ga. App. 808, 412 S.E.2d 590 (1991); Getz Exterminators of Georgia, Inc. v. Towe, 193 Ga. App. 268, 387 S.E.2d 338 (1989).

it was present at the time of the inspection.[10] Moreover, a defendant pest control operator can only be held liable for those damages occasioned by his failure to discover the infestation, and not those which existed prior to the time of the inspection.[11] Accordingly, expert testimony in such cases is typically geared toward establishing whether the infestation was present at the time of the inspection and whether a reasonable inspection would have discovered the evidence of the infestation.[12]

§ 7:10   Eminent Domain Cases

The Georgia Legislative has recently amended Georgia's eminent domain statutes to specifically exclude from the Daubert Standard expert testimony regard issues of just and adequate compensation for property owners.[1]

---

[10]Power v. Georgia Exterminators, Inc., 243 Ga. App. 355, 360, 532 S.E.2d 475, 480 (2000) ("Discovery of damage without proof it had been present at the time of an earlier inspection does not give rise to an action for negligent inspection."). By contrast, where the pest control operator was hired not only to inspect the premises, but also to treat the premises for termites, the operator can be held liable under a theory of negligent treatment for termite damage not in existence at the time of the initial inspection and treatment. Power v. Georgia Exterminators, Inc., 243 Ga. App. 355, 360, 532 S.E.2d 475, 479–480 (2000).

[11]Orkin Exterminating Co., Inc. v. Durden, 189 Ga. App. 479, 482, 376 S.E.2d 376, 378 (1988) (because "there was no evidence concerning the cost to repair only that damage that occurred after the 1973 inspection, the jury verdict was without its necessary foundation and must fail.").

[12]Power v. Georgia Exterminators, Inc., 243 Ga. App. 355, 360, 532 S.E.2d 475, 480 (2000); see also Artzner v. A & A Exterminators, Inc., 242 Ga. App. 766, 768, 531 S.E.2d 200, 203 (2000) (defendant's expert testified that termite damage can occur rapidly, and that damage seen at time of discovery did not mean that infestation existed at the time of the inspection); American Pest Control, Inc. v. Pritchett, 201 Ga. App. 808, 809, 412 S.E.2d 590, 592 (1991) (plaintiff's expert testified that termite damage had been present for at least five years prior to inspection).

[Section 7:10]

[1]See O.C.G.A. § 22–1–14.

Chapter 8

Psychological Testimony And Related Matters

> **KeyCite®:** Cases and other legal materials listed in KeyCite Scope can be researched through the KeyCite service on Westlaw®. Use KeyCite to check citations for form, parallel references, prior and later history, and comprehensive citator information, including citations to other decisions and secondary materials.

§ 8:1   Psychological syndromes and profiles

Expert testimony is sometimes used to demonstrate that a person exhibits symptoms or behaviors consistent with others known to fall within a psychological classification to explain conduct. Such testimony regarding psychological syndromes or profiles has met with mixed results and a good measure of skepticism by Georgia courts.

§ 8:2   Psychological syndromes and profiles—Battered person syndrome

Battered person syndrome "describes a series of common characteristics that appear in individuals who are physically and psychologically abused for a long time by a dominating and controlling person in their lives."[1] Expert testimony regarding this syndrome is often used to explain why a person in an abusive re-

---

[Section 8:2]

[1]Mobley v. State, 269 Ga. 738, 739, 505 S.E.2d 722, 723 (1998);

Johnson v. State, 266 Ga. 624, 626, 469 S.E.2d 152, 154 (1996).

lationship may act in a way which is seemingly counter-intuitive, such as failing to leave an abusive spouse or significant other or failing to report the abuse to the police or friends.[2] Expert testimony regarding this syndrome is perhaps most often used in conjunction with a criminal defendant's defense that her slaying of the abuser was justifiable or performed in self-defense. In this context, such testimony is used to explain why the defendant may have perceived that she was acting in self-defense at the time the homicide was committed.[3] Specifically, expert testimony regarding this syndrome is used to demonstrate the *reasonableness* of the defendant's subjective belief in the imminence of physical abuse at the hands of the victim, even though, objectively, the victim may not have been threatening the defendant with imminent physical harm at the time the homicide was committed.[4]

It has been held that the battered woman syndrome is a "scientifically established theory."[5] Georgia courts have recognized that this syndrome involves a "complex area of human response and behavior."[6] Consequently, expert testimony as to "why a person suffering from battered woman's syndrome would not leave her mate, would not inform police or friends, and would fear increased aggression against herself" has been held admissible because these are "conclusions that jurors could not ordinarily draw for themselves."[7] In other words, expert testimony on the syndrome assists the jury to understand the evidence by providing an "interpretation of the facts which differs from the ordinary lay perception."[8] Expert testimony on the syndrome authorizes a jury to find that, notwithstanding any lapse in time since the victim's last assault upon the defendant, the defendant honestly was trying to defend herself even though she was not

[2]Smith v. State, 268 Ga. 196, 486 S.E.2d 819 (1997); Smith v. State, 247 Ga. 612, 277 S.E.2d 678 (1981).

[3]See, e.g. Mobley v. State, 269 Ga. 738, 505 S.E.2d 722 (1998); Smith v. State, 268 Ga. 196, 486 S.E.2d 819 (1997).

[4]Mobley v. State, 269 Ga. 738, 739–740, 505 S.E.2d 722, 723 (1998); Smith v. State, 268 Ga. 196, 199, 486 S.E.2d 819, 822 (1997)(noting that the issue "is not whether the danger was in fact imminent, but whether, given the circumstances as the defendant perceived them, the defendant's belief was reasonable that the danger was imminent."); Smith v. State, 247 Ga. 612, 277 S.E.2d 678 (1981).

[5]Smith v. State, 268 Ga. 196,

198, 486 S.E.2d 819, 821–822 (1997).

[6]Bishop v. State, 271 Ga. 291, 292, 519 S.E.2d 206 (1999); Johnson v. State, 266 Ga. 624, 627, 469 S.E.2d 152, 154 (1996); see also Smith v. State, 268 Ga. 196, 198, 486 S.E.2d 819, 822 (1997)(referring to the syndrome as a "unique and almost mysterious area of human response and behavior").

[7]Smith v. State, 268 Ga. 196, 486 S.E.2d 819 (1997); Smith v. State, 247 Ga. 612, 277 S.E.2d 678 (1981).

[8]Bishop v. State, 271 Ga. 291, 292, 519 S.E.2d 206 (1999); Smith v. State, 268 Ga. 196, 198, 486 S.E.2d 819, 822 (1997); Johnson v. State, 266 Ga. 624, 626, 469 S.E.2d 152, 153–154 (1996).

being assaulted at the time she attacked the victim.[9] At the same time, while an expert may explain the syndrome and opine that the defendant was in fact suffering from the syndrome, an expert may not go so far as to offer an opinion that the defendant in fact had a reasonable fear for her own life, as this is an inference which the jury can draw on its own.[10]

The first permutation of battered person syndrome appeared as "battered woman syndrome" in *Smith v. State*,[11] as a case wherein the defendant was charged with murdering her live-in boyfriend. However, as the syndrome's contemporary moniker suggests, the syndrome has not been limited to situations in which a female is the victim of violence at the hands of a male, but has been applied in the context of a husband's slaying of an estranged wife.[12] Similarly, while the syndrome is typically addressed in the context of a marital or long-term dating relationship, it has been applied in the context of other close relationships, such as where a son slayed his stepfather.[13]

Courts have placed limitations on just how far a criminal defendant may go in employing this syndrome in support of a claim of self-defense, and the mere fact that a defendant asserts this syndrome in support of a claim of justification will not necessarily result in the admission of expert testimony on this syndrome. Expert testimony that a person suffered from the syndrome is not, standing alone, enough to render such testimony admissible for purposes of proving self-defense or justification.[14] Rather, the expert testimony must be supported by facts in evidence. An expert must not only be able to describe the battered person syndrome and offer an opinion that the defendant falls within the profile, but must also be able to apply the model to the facts as shown by the evidence.[15] Absent evidence of abuse so as to engender a reasonable belief in the imminence of the victim's use of unlawful force, expert testimony on battered person syndrome is simply not relevant.[16] Evidence which supports a finding of battered person syndrome includes evidence of a close personal relationship between the defendant and the victim, a pattern of

---

[9]Chapman v. State, 258 Ga. 214, 216, 367 S.E.2d 541, 543 (1988).

[10]Jenkins v. State, 219 Ga. App. 339, 342, 465 S.E.2d 296, 299 (1995).

[11]Smith v. State, 247 Ga. 612, 277 S.E.2d 678 (1981).

[12]Hufstetler v. State, 274 Ga. 343, 344–345, 553 S.E.2d 801, 802 (2001) (expert testified that "battered woman syndrome," "battered person syndrome," and "battered spouse syndrome" were not separate syndromes, but "all under the same canopy.").

[13]Freeman v. State, 269 Ga. 337, 338, 496 S.E.2d 716, 718 (1998).

[14]Mobley v. State, 269 Ga. 738, 740, 505 S.E.2d 722, 723 (1998).

[15]Bishop v. State, 271 Ga. 291, 293, 519 S.E.2d 206, 208 (1999).

[16]Adame v. State, 244 Ga. App. 257, 259, 534 S.E.2d 817, 821 (2000).

physical, sexual, or psychological abuse, and the defendant's reasonable apprehension of harm.[17]

Courts have consistently rejected efforts to introduce expert testimony on the syndrome absent a sufficient factual predicate to demonstrate that the syndrome is applicable. For instance, in *Johnson v. State*, the court excluded as irrelevant expert testimony that the defendant was suffering from a psychological condition "activated and driven by the same psychological dynamics" as battered person syndrome when the defendant had killed an unrelated third party.[18] The court refused to acknowledge the applicability of the syndrome under the facts of the case, noting that the admissibility of expert testimony on the syndrome is limited to those "unique" situations in which expert testimony is needed to address "a complex area of human response and behavior" in order to show that the defendant had the mental state necessary to support a defense of justification.[19] Similarly, in *Weems v. State*, expert testimony that the defendant had suffered from a "catastrophic reaction" similar to battered person syndrome was ruled inadmissible in support of a self-defense claim where the defendant had fired a gun into a crowd after being beaten by drug dealers believed to be in the crowd.[20] The court reasoned that the reasonableness of the defendant's claimed belief that his conduct was necessary to avoid imminent death or bodily harm was not a matter which was "beyond the ken of the average juror."[21]

Conversely, because battered person syndrome is a complex area of human behavior beyond the understanding of an ordinary lay person, facts tending to suggest a diagnosis of battered person syndrome are not enough to admit the syndrome into evidence; rather, the fact that one suffers from this syndrome must be supported by expert testimony.[22] While the syndrome is most often used in support of a criminal defendant's defense of justification,

---

[17]Mobley v. State, 269 Ga. 738, 740, 505 S.E.2d 722, 723–724 (1998) (expert testimony on battered person syndrome inadmissible in support of a self-defense claim where defendant and victim were foster children who had lived in the same household for only six months, there was no history of sexual abuse between them, the only evidence of physical abuse was a shoving match between them months prior to defendant's shooting of victim, and there was scant evidence of psychological abuse); see also Chester v. State, 267 Ga. 9, 11–12, 471 S.E.2d 836, 837–838 (1996)(expert testimony on battered person syndrome irrelevant where no evidence of physical abuse, but only issuance of verbal threats by the victim).

[18]Johnson v. State, 266 Ga. 624, 469 S.E.2d 152 (1996).

[19]Johnson v. State, 266 Ga. 624, 627, 469 S.E.2d 152 (1996).

[20]Weems v. State, 268 Ga. 142, 144, 485 S.E.2d 767, 771 (1997).

[21]Weems v. State, 268 Ga. 142, 144, 485 S.E.2d 767, 771 (1997).

[22]Bishop v. State, 271 Ga. 291, 293, 519 S.E.2d 206, 208 (1999).

its use has not been limited to this context. Expert testimony on the syndrome has been used *against* a criminal defendant to explain why the victim had not previously reported abuse after the defendant had sought to question the credibility of the victim's claim of abuse.[23]

§ 8:3 Psychological syndromes and profiles—Child sexual abuse accommodation syndrome

Child sexual abuse accommodation syndrome ("CSAAS"), describes various emotional stages commonly experienced by children following abuse.[1] These stages have been identified as follows:

> 1) secrecy (children are usually reluctant to disclose the assault); 2) helplessness (the children feel they can do nothing to prevent the abuse); 3) accommodation (children attempt to rationalize or accommodate the abuse by pretending to be asleep, for instance); 4) delayed, conflicting and unconvincing disclosure; and 5) recantation.[2]

In addition, victims of child sexual abuse may display a variety of common behaviors and symptoms, including bedwetting, nightmares, adoption of adult behaviors, such as sexually precocious mannerisms, regressive behaviors, and poor performance in school.[3]

In *Allison v. State*, the first Georgia Supreme Court case to address this syndrome, the Court held that expert testimony regarding this syndrome, and the fact that a child exhibits symptoms consistent with this syndrome, is admissible because "[l]aymen would not understand this syndrome without expert testimony, nor would they be likely to believe that a child who denied a sexual assault, or who was reluctant to discuss an assault, in fact had been assaulted."[4] The Court, however, excluded expert testimony that the child had in fact been sexually abused, as the jury was capable, given evidence of the syndrome and the fact

---

[23]Parrish v. State, 237 Ga. App. 274, 514 S.E.2d 458 (1999); see also Watson v. State, 278 Ga. 763, 604 S.E.2d 804 (2004); Paz v. State, 239 Ga. App. 278, 521 S.E.2d 362 (1999).

[Section 8:3]

[1]Allison v. State, 256 Ga. 851, 852, 353 S.E.2d 805, 807 (1987).

[2]Allison v. State, 256 Ga. 851, 852, 353 S.E.2d 805, 807 (1987).

[3]Allison v. State, 256 Ga. 851, 852, 353 S.E.2d 805, 807 (1987); see

also Hall v. State, 196 Ga. App. 523, 524, 396 S.E.2d 271, 272 (1990).

[4]Allison v. State, 256 Ga. 851, 852, 353 S.E.2d 805, 807 (1987); Lee v. State, 250 Ga. App. 110, 111, 550 S.E.2d 696 (2001)(expert testified that reasons for recantation may include the child's realization that her family will break up, that the perpetrator may go to jail, or that family members will not believe her disclosure).

that the child exhibited symptoms consistent with the syndrome, to draw this inference on their own.[5]

Courts subsequently considering the admissibility of expert testimony on this syndrome have consistently drawn a line of demarcation between, on the one hand: a) expert testimony discussing the syndrome, and the fact that a child demonstrates symptoms consistent with the syndrome, which is admissible; and, on the other b) expert testimony to the effect that the child is truthful in his or her disclosure of sexual abuse or that the child was in fact sexually abused.[6] Courts have reasoned that, in the first case, the ultimate issue, i.e. whether the child was sexually abused, is left for the jury, and in the second instance, the expert has invaded the province of the jury by answering the question ultimately to be decided by it.[7] Expert testimony to the effect that the child was telling the truth regarding the allegations of sexual abuse or that the child was in fact sexually abused has been held to constitute an inadmissible bolstering of the credibility of the child, and constituting neither "scientific [n]or psychological matters the jury would need expert assistance to understand."[8] Similarly, expert testimony that the defendant was the perpetrator of sexual abuse is inadmissible as invading the province of the jury.[9]

While psychologists are often employed to provide testimony regarding this syndrome, others with sufficient experience have been accepted by the courts as competent to provide testimony pertaining to the syndrome. Testimony from social workers,[10] pediatricians,[11] pediatric nurses,[12] and police officers,[13] have been

---

[5]Allison v. State, 256 Ga. 851, 853, 353 S.E.2d 805, 808 (1987).

[6]See, e.g. Morris v. State, 268 Ga. App. 325, 601 S.E.2d 804 (2004), cert. denied, (Oct. 25, 2004); Brownlow v. State, 248 Ga. App. 366, 544 S.E.2d 472 (2001); Odom v. State, 243 Ga. App. 227, 531 S.E.2d 207 (2000).

[7]Morris v. State, 268 Ga. App. 325, 327–328, 601 S.E.2d 804, 807 (2004), cert. denied, (Oct. 25, 2004); Brownlow v. State, 248 Ga. App. 366, 368, 544 S.E.2d 472, 474–475 (2001); Odom v. State, 243 Ga. App. 227, 228, 531 S.E.2d 207, 209 (2000).

[8]Putnam v. State, 231 Ga. App. 190, 192, 498 S.E.2d 340, 343 (1998); Thompson v. State, 233 Ga. App. 364, 365, 504 S.E.2d 234, 235 (1998); see also Castro v. State, 241 Ga. App. 546,

527 S.E.2d 12 (1999); but see Hall v. State, 255 Ga. App. 631, 566 S.E.2d 374 (2002)(expert testimony that child was "telling the truth" in making allegations of molestation not objectionable where defendant elicited such testimony on cross-examination).

[9]Putnam v. State, 231 Ga. App. 190, 192, 498 S.E.2d 340, 343 (1998).

[10]Siharath v. State, 246 Ga. App. 736, 541 S.E.2d 71 (2000).

[11]Braggs v. State, 189 Ga. App. 275, 375 S.E.2d 464 (1988).

[12]Morris v. State, 268 Ga. App. 325, 601 S.E.2d 804 (2004), cert. denied, (Oct. 25, 2004).

[13]Weeks v. State, 270 Ga. App. 889, 608 S.E.2d 259 (2004), cert. denied, (Apr. 26, 2005); McCrickard v. State, 249 Ga. App. 715, 549 S.E.2d 505

accepted in this regard upon a showing of sufficient experience in addressing the syndrome.

Georgia courts have recognized that children "are often immature, inarticulate, frightened, and confused about the abuse they have received."[14] Often at issue in cases involving allegations of child sexual abuse is not only the substantive content of the child's disclosure, but *how* the child came to make the allegations in the first instance.[15] Courts have allowed a defendant to introduce expert testimony regarding the proper techniques for interviewing children alleged to have been sexually abused, and whether those interviewing the child at issue employed proper interviewing techniques, or improper techniques such as the use of leading or suggestive questioning which may have influenced the child's disclosure.[16] Courts have reasoned that such matters are within the knowledge of the average juror, and that such testimony is necessary to "level [the] playing field" for those accused of such crimes, particularly in light of the "liberal approach" to the introduction of evidence in cases of child abuse.[17] While such a rebuttal expert may not comment directly on the credibility of a child's disclosure, the fact that such testimony may indirectly call into question the credibility of the child's disclosure does not render the testimony inadmissible.[18] Moreover, where expert testimony on CSAAS is offered, the defendant may, despite the general inadmissibility of a child victim's sexual history, offer evidence about other causes of the child's exhibition of symptoms consistent with CSAAS, including evidence of prior molestation of the child by a person other than the defendant.[19]

§ 8:4 Psychological syndromes and profiles—Abuser profiles and syndromes

On the flip side of cases wherein abuse is at issue, expert

(2001); but see Harper v. Patterson, 270 Ga. App. 437, 606 S.E.2d 887 (2004), cert. denied, (Mar. 28, 2005) (police officer's testimony that child's symptoms were consistent with those of a sexually abused child, based only on results of police investigation, not admissible, as the conclusion was not beyond ken of average juror).

[14]Barlow v. State, 270 Ga. 54, 54, 507 S.E.2d 416, 417 (1998).

[15]Barlow v. State, 270 Ga. 54, 55, 507 S.E.2d 416, 417 (1998).

[16]Barlow v. State, 270 Ga. 54, 55, 507 S.E.2d 416, 417 (1998); Pyron v. State, 237 Ga. App. 198, 198–199, 514

S.E.2d 51, 52 (1999); see also Beck v. State, 250 Ga. App. 654, 551 S.E.2d 68 (2001).

[17]Pyron v. State, 237 Ga. App. 198, 199, 514 S.E.2d 51, 52–53 (1999).

[18]Barlow v. State, 270 Ga. 54, 55, 507 S.E.2d 416, 418 (1998); Pyron v. State, 237 Ga. App. 198, 200–201, 514 S.E.2d 51, 53 (1999).

[19]Duck v. State, 210 Ga. App. 205, 435 S.E.2d 725 (1993) (overruled on other grounds by, Strickland v. State, 223 Ga. App. 772, 479 S.E.2d 125 (1996)); Marion v. State, 206 Ga. App. 159, 424 S.E.2d 838 (1992).

testimony as to whether the accused fits the "profile" of an abuser is often sought to be admitted. Such testimony may either be proffered by the State in an effort to show that the defendant shares characteristics typical of known abusers, or proffered by the defendant in an effort to show that he or she does not share these characteristics. Interestingly, while expert testimony that a spouse or child exhibits behaviors "consistent with" a battered spouse or abused child is routinely admitted by the courts, Georgia courts have been decidedly less receptive to expert testimony that the accused does or does not share characteristics "consistent with" abusers or pedophiles. This seeming incongruity has led one concurring opinion to decry "the appearance of an unlevel playing field, with the state being allowed to present such 'soft science' but the defendant from being prohibited from doing likewise."[1]

While expert testimony regarding whether a defendant fits a certain "profile" is routinely excluded, the rationale varies depending on whether the evidence is offered by the defense or prosecution. When offered by a defendant, the courts most often reason that such testimony is offered for the improper purpose of bolstering the defendant's credibility, and that a jury is not in need of expert assistance in making its determination as to the credibility of the defendant. For instance, in the seminal case of *Jennette v. State*,[2] a defendant accused of sexually assaulting teenage girls sought to present expert testimony that, based upon a battery of psychological tests administered to him, he did not fit the profile of a child sex abuser. In excluding such testimony, the

---

[Section 8:4]

[1]Gilstrap v. State, 215 Ga. App. 180, 183, 450 S.E.2d 436, 439 (1994) (Andrews, J., concurring). In this concurrence, Judge Andrews expressed an incisive commentary on the proliferation of "syndrome" evidence in Georgia, commenting as follows:

Evidence of "syndromes" should be greeted with caution, if not suspicion. In this age earmarked by the denial of personal responsibility, it sometimes appears that the defense strategy of choice is to formulate a new syndrome as the situation dictates. Our current legal lexicon includes such phenomena as the battered wife syndrome, the abused child syndrome, and the post-traumatic stress syndrome, and the catalogue is expanding. . . . [I]n Georgia an expert is permitted to describe the abused child syndrome but may not conclude that the child was abused. This often results in the admissibility of such evidence depending on a semantical distinction, in that experts are permitted to describe the syndrome and then state that the victim's behavior was consistent with that syndrome.

It is difficult to explain why we should put stock in psychological evaluation and opinion with regard to syndromes pertaining to victims, yet extend no credence to syndromes or profiles relating to offenders. Perhaps the better solution would be to exclude all syndrome evidence.

Id.

[2]Jennette v. State, 197 Ga. App. 580, 398 S.E.2d 734 (1990).

court cited to *Smith v. State*,[3] a case wherein expert testimony on battered woman syndrome was admitted, for the proposition that an expert may offer opinions, even on the ultimate issue to be decided by the jury, where the conclusion the expert has drawn would not be one which the jury would ordinarily be able to draw for itself.[4] The court further noted that expert testimony on the ultimate issue is not, however, permitted where the expert's conclusion is not "shrouded in the mystery of professional skill or knowledge," and the jury is therefore able to reach the same conclusion without the aid of expert testimony.[5] Observing that the expert's proffered testimony merely went to the credibility and believability of the defendant's own testimony that he did not commit the acts of sexual assault, and further, spoke to the "ultimate fact" of whether he had committed these acts, the court excluded the expert's testimony by noting that the proffered testimony did not involve " 'unique and mysterious areas of human response' necessitating expert testimony[,]' and that the jury could, without the help of expert testimony, determine the credibility of the defendant's denial of having committed the alleged acts of molestation and his capability of performing these alleged acts.[6] Georgia courts considering the admissibility of such testimony when offered by a defendant have consistently ruled in accordance with this decision.[7]

When such profile evidence is offered against a defendant by the prosecution, courts have held that, unless the defendant has placed his character in issue or raised a defense for which profile evidence is relevant to rebut, expert testimony that a defendant fits the profile of a typical abuser impermissibly places the defendant's character at issue.[8] For instance, in *Sanders v. State*,[9] the prosecution offered the testimony of a psychologist to provide testimony about the characteristics of a typical child abuser in conjunction with testimony elicited from other witnesses tending to establish that the defendant, accused of child abuse, shared a similar personal history with and characteristics of the typical

---

[3]Smith v. State, 247 Ga. 612, 277 S.E.2d 678 (1981).

[4]Jennette v. State, 197 Ga. App. 580, 582, 398 S.E.2d 734, 736 (1990).

[5]Jennette v. State, 197 Ga. App. 580, 582, 398 S.E.2d 734, 736 (1990).

[6]Jennette v. State, 197 Ga. App. 580, 582–583, 398 S.E.2d 734, 736–737 (1990).

[7]Hudson v. State, 218 Ga. App. 671, 462 S.E.2d 775 (1995); Gilstrap v. State, 215 Ga. App. 180, 450 S.E.2d 436 (1994); Lewis v. State, 212 Ga. App. 310, 441 S.E.2d 851 (1994); Knight v. State, 206 Ga. App. 529, 426 S.E.2d 1 (1992).

[8]This rationale has not been limited to the context of claims of abuse, but has also been applied where the prosecution sought to demonstrate that a defendant fit the profile of a serial arsonist. See Penson v. State, 222 Ga. App. 253, 474 S.E.2d 104 (1996).

[9]Sanders v. State, 251 Ga. 70, 303 S.E.2d 13 (1983).

abuser. The court excluded the expert's testimony, finding that, in conjunction with the evidence of the defendant's personal history and characteristics, such testimony "clearly" implicated the defendant's character, leading the jury to the necessary inference that the defendant fit the profile of a child abuser and had in fact committed the crime for which he was charged.[10] The court held that unless a defendant has placed his or her character in issue, or has raised a defense in which the profile evidence is relevant to rebut, neither expert testimony regarding the profile, nor evidence showing a defendant's personality traits or personal history are consistent with such a profile, are admissible.[11]

Efforts to introduce "syndrome" or "profile" testimony as to why a child may make a false allegation of abuse have been squarely rejected by the courts as efforts to employ expert testimony to improperly comment upon the credibility of a witness, and not beyond the ability of the jury to understand on its own. Expert testimony on the "lying child syndrome,"[12] the "sexual abuse allegation in divorce syndrome,"[13] and the propensity of children to make false allegations in retribution,[14] have all been rejected as improper efforts to have an expert comment upon the credibility of an accuser.

§ 8:5 Psychological syndromes and profiles—Post Traumatic Stress Disorder (syndrome) and other syndromes

Post-traumatic stress disorder (PTSD) is defined in the Diagnostic & Statistical Manual of Mental Disorders (4th ed. 1994) (DSM–IV) as "the development of characteristic symptoms following exposure to an extreme traumatic stressor involving direct personal experience of an event that involves actual or threatened death or serious injury[.]"[1] It is manifested by "persistent symptoms of anxiety . . . that were not present before the

---

[10]Sanders v. State, 251 Ga. 70, 76, 303 S.E.2d 13, 18 (1983).

[11]Sanders v. State, 251 Ga. 70, 76, 303 S.E.2d 13, 18 (1983); see also Parrish v. State, 237 Ga. App. 274, 277, 514 S.E.2d 458, 463 (1999)("Such a 'profile' suggests to the jurors that the defendant shares the characteristics of the typical abuser and, as such, places the character of the defendant in issue."); but see Exley v. State, 198 Ga. App. 748, 749, 402 S.E.2d 798, 899 (1991)(psychiatrist's testimony which defined the term pedophile, with no discussion of defendant's personal history or traits, properly admitted, as such testimony did not place defendant's character in issue).

[12]Jennette v. State, 197 Ga. App. 580, 398 S.E.2d 734 (1990).

[13]Stewart v. State, 210 Ga. App. 474, 436 S.E.2d 679 (1993).

[14]Duncan v. State, 232 Ga. App. 157, 500 S.E.2d 603 (1998).

[Section 8:5]

[1]See Carter v. Glenn, 243 Ga. App. 544, 549 n.2, 533 S.E.2d 109, 115 (2000); Southwire Co. v. George, 266 Ga. 739, 740 n.1, 470 S.E.2d 865, 866

trauma."[2] To date, no Georgia court has determined whether PTSD is a scientifically valid condition such that expert testimony regarding PTSD is admissible.[3] Indeed, the Georgia Supreme Court has specifically declined to offer an opinion as to whether this disorder is scientifically valid so as to be admissible.[4]

Notwithstanding this, expert testimony regarding a plaintiff's suffering from PTSD has routinely been admitted in a variety of civil actions,[5] including actions for emotional distress[6] or for workers' compensation benefits.[7] Courts, however, appear to be more skeptical in admitting expert testimony regarding this disorder in criminal cases, particularly where it is offered for the purpose of establishing a justification defense to the commission of a crime.[8] While expert testimony regarding PTSD has been admitted in some criminal cases in conjunction with this defense,[9] courts have often rejected expert testimony regarding a defendant's PTSD as irrelevant to a justification defense or not beyond the ken of the jury. For instance, in *Bryant v. State*, the court held it was not error to exclude expert testimony that a defendant in a murder case suffered from PTSD as a result of early childhood abuse, noting that while specific acts of violence by the

---

(1996).

[2]Carter v. Glenn, 243 Ga. App. 544, 549 n.2, 533 S.E.2d 109. 115 (2000); Southwire Co. v. George, 266 Ga. 739, 740 n.1, 470 S.E.2d 865, 866 (1996).

[3]Kennedy v. State, 274 Ga. 396, 399 n.16, 554 S.E.2d 178, 181 (2001); Carter v. Glenn, 243 Ga. App. 544, 549 n.2, 533 S.E.2d 109, 115 (2000); Prickett v. State, 220 Ga. App. 244, 247, 469 S.E.2d 371, 374–375 (1996) (overruled on other grounds by, State v. Belt, 269 Ga. 763, 505 S.E.2d 1 (1998)).

[4]Yeager v. State, 274 Ga. 216, 218, 552 S.E.2d 809, 811 (2001); Johnson v. State, 266 Ga. 624, 625 n.3, 469 S.E.2d 152, 153 (1996).

[5]For a more complete discussion of expert testimony as it is used to prove personal damages in civil actions, see Chapter on Personal Injury Testing *Supra*.

[6]See, e.g. City of Gainesville v. Waters, 258 Ga. App. 555, 574 S.E.2d 638 (2002); Cook v. Partain, 224 Ga. App. 251, 480 S.E.2d 279 (1997).

[7]See, e.g. Southwire Co. v. George, 266 Ga. 739, 470 S.E.2d 865 (1996); Howard v. Superior Contractors, 180 Ga. App. 68, 348 S.E.2d 563 (1986); see also Trammel v. Bradberry, 256 Ga. App. 412, 568 S.E.2d 715 (2002).

[8]Yeager v. State, 274 Ga. 216, 218, 552 S.E.2d 809, 811 (2001).

[9]Porter v. State, 243 Ga. App. 498, 532 S.E.2d 407 (2000)(trial court erred in excluding evidence that defendant in child abuse case suffered from a psychological condition which caused her to "block out" and deny child abuse perpetrated by her husband); cf. Kennedy v. State, 274 Ga. 396, 554 S.E.2d 178 (2001) (even if court erred in excluding expert testimony that defendant in murder case suffered from PTSD so as to cause her not to remember killing of husband due to psychotropic amnesia, error was harmless in that court had permitted expert testimony on battered woman syndrome); see also Paul v. State, 272 Ga. 845, 537 S.E.2d 58 (2000)(trial court erred in making disparaging remarks regarding expert's opinions that defendant suffered from PTSD when offered as defense to crime).

victim may have been relevant to the defendant's claim of self-defense, acts of violence against the defendant by persons other than the victim was not.[10] Similarly, in *Johnson v. State*, expert testimony that a defendant in a murder case suffered from a psychological syndrome "similar" to PTSD was held not to be admissible because there was no evidence that defendant's conduct in killing an unrelated person was rooted in a "complex area of human response."[11] An apparent undercurrent of these holdings is a sense that syndrome evidence had been "stretched too far."

As in the case of battered person syndrome or child sexual abuse accommodation syndrome, expert testimony regarding rape trauma syndrome may be offered to explain various seemingly incongruous behaviors of a rape victim, such as a delay in disclosure, are consistent with the behaviors of rape victims.[12] It has been observed that rape trauma syndrome has not been shown to be a reliable scientific principle in Georgia.[13] Nonetheless, Georgia courts have appeared willing to admit such testimony. For instance, in one case, the witness' testimony that the victim exhibited behaviors consistent with those of rape victims was found to be based on her personal observations of the victim, and thus did not amount to "expert" testimony.[14] In another opinion, the expert's testimony that rape victims often delay disclosing the crime, as the victim did here, was found non-

---

[10]Bryant v. State, 271 Ga. 99, 515 S.E.2d 836 (1999).

[11]Johnson v. State, 266 Ga. 624, 469 S.E.2d 152 (1996) (court held that expert testimony that criminal defendant in murder case suffered from a psychological syndrome "similar" to PTSD not admissible because there was no evidence that defendant's conduct in killing an unrelated person was rooted in a complex area of human response, and the defense of justification is based on fears of a reasonable person, not those of a particular defendant); see also Yeager v. State, 274 Ga. 216, 218, 552 S.E.2d 809, 811 (2001)(defendant not entitled to charge that jury could consider defendant's PTSD in connection with claim that he killed wife in self-defense because, despite expert testimony that defendant suffered from PTSD, no evidence in record that defendant be-

lieved that deadly force was necessary to protect himself from his wife).

[12]See, e.g. Stevenson v. State, 272 Ga. App. 335, 612 S.E.2d 521 (2005); Edmonson v. State, 212 Ga. App. 449, 442 S.E.2d 300 (1994) (overruled on other grounds by, Curtis v. State, 275 Ga. 576, 571 S.E.2d 376 (2002)).

[13]Prickett v. State, 220 Ga. App. 244, 247, 469 S.E.2d 371, 375 (1996) (overruled on other grounds by, State v. Belt, 269 Ga. 763, 505 S.E.2d 1 (1998)); Edmonson v. State, 212 Ga. App. 449, 451 n.1, 442 S.E.2d 300, 302 (1994) (overruled on other grounds by, Curtis v. State, 275 Ga. 576, 571 S.E.2d 376 (2002)).

[14]Edmonson v. State, 212 Ga. App. 449, 442 S.E.2d 300 (1994) (overruled on other grounds by, Curtis v. State, 275 Ga. 576, 571 S.E.2d 376 (2002)).

objectionable where the expert qualified her testimony by explaining that that there are no typical behaviors of rape victims.[15]

§ 8:6 Reliability of eyewitness identification

Expert testimony on the reliability of eyewitness identifications seeks to explain why a witness' identification of an individual as the perpetrator may not be accurate. Such testimony may cite several reasons for the unreliability of identifications, including: 1) the fading of memory over time;[1] 2) the adverse impact stress inherent in a criminal encounter may have on the ability to accurately recall details of the encounter, including the perpetrator's face;[2] 3) the effect environmental conditions, such as lighting or weather, can have on the accuracy of identification;[3] 4) inaccuracies in cross-racial identifications;[4] 5) the impact arguably suggestive investigative techniques may have on identification, such as showing a photograph of a defendant to the witness prior to having the witness attend an in-person line-up;[5] and 6) the correlation between a witness' confidence that he or she has made a correct identification with the accuracy of such an identification.[6]

Historically, such expert testimony, most often provided by psychologists or psychiatrists, has been inadmissible in Georgia. In *Jones v. State*, the Georgia Supreme Court held that "[t]he determination of the credibility of a witness, including the accuracy of an eyewitness' identification, is a matter exclusively within the jury's province. . . . The memory of a witness may not be disparaged by other witnesses in order to impeach that testimony; it must be done by cross examination of the witness whose recollection is attacked."[7] While the *Jones* court indicated that a limited exception to this rule of exclusion exists where the eyewitness suffers from "organic or mental disorders" which impair the wit-

---

[15]Stevenson v. State, 272 Ga. App. 335, 612 S.E.2d 521 (2005).

[Section 8:6]

[1]See, e.g. Johnson v. State, 272 Ga. 254, 526 S.E.2d 549 (2000); Cox v. State, 197 Ga. App. 240, 398 S.E.2d 262 (1990).

[2]See, e.g. Johnson v. State, 272 Ga. 254, 526 S.E.2d 549 (2000); Norris v. State, 258 Ga. 889, 890, 376 S.E.2d 653, 654 (1989); Cox v. State, 197 Ga. App. 240, 398 S.E.2d 262 (1990).

[3]Johnson v. State, 272 Ga. 254, 526 S.E.2d 549 (2000).

[4]See, e.g. Johnson v. State, 272 Ga. 254, 526 S.E.2d 549 (2000); Norris

v. State, 258 Ga. 889, 890, 376 S.E.2d 653, 654 (1989); Cox v. State, 197 Ga. App. 240, 398 S.E.2d 262 (1990).

[5]See, e.g. Johnson v. State, 272 Ga. 254, 257, 526 S.E.2d 549 (2000); Norris v. State, 258 Ga. 889, 890, 376 S.E.2d 653, 654 (1989).

[6]See, e.g. Johnson v. State, 272 Ga. 254, 526 S.E.2d 549 (2000); Norris v. State, 258 Ga. 889, 890, 376 S.E.2d 653, 654 (1989); Cox v. State, 197 Ga. App. 240, 398 S.E.2d 262 (1990).

[7]Jones v. State, 232 Ga. 762, 764–765, 208 S.E.2d 850, 853 (1974) (overruled by, Johnson v. State, 272 Ga. 254, 526 S.E.2d 549 (2000)).

ness' mental or physical faculties, where such conditions are not present, factors affecting the reliability of an eyewitness' identification are not matters beyond the understanding of an ordinary juror, and such factors may be adequately brought to the jury's attention through cross-examination.[8]

For several years following the *Jones* case, Georgia courts routinely excluded such expert testimony.[9] Direct and cross-examination of eye-witnesses as to the reliability of their identification, along with specific instructions as to how the jury may evaluate the reliability of eye-witness identifications, have been the preferred methods for attacking the reliability of eye-witness identifications. Pertinent factors in considering the reliability of eye-witness identification include: 1) the opportunity of the witness to view the alleged perpetrator; 2) the degree of attention the witness displayed at the time of the viewing; 3) the possibility of mistaken identity; 4) the influence other sources might have on the identification; 5) prior misidentifications by the witness; and 6) the level of certainty shown by the witness of his or her identification.[10]

However, in 2000, the Georgia Supreme Court disapproved of

---

[8]Jones v. State, 232 Ga. 762, 765, 208 S.E.2d 850, 853 (1974) (overruled by, Johnson v. State, 272 Ga. 254, 526 S.E.2d 549 (2000)). In addition to disallowing such testimony on the basis that it impermissibly sought to comment on the credibility of a witness, the Court also found it significant that, notwithstanding the expert's professional experience, the expert had not interviewed and had no knowledge of the eyewitnesses whose identification was to be discredited. As additional grounds for excluding the expert's testimony, the Court stated that "[e]xpert testimony concerning a witness' credibility is also excluded where there is a total lack of or insufficient observation of the assailed witness by the expert." *Id. at 765, 208 S.E.2d 850.*

[9]See, e.g. Johnson v. State, 271 Ga. 375, 382, 519 S.E.2d 221, 229 (1999) Gardiner v. State, 264 Ga. 329, 333, 444 S.E.2d 300, 304 (1994) (factors bearing on reliability of eyewitness identification are "within knowledge of the jury and [are] not a proper subject for expert opinion testimony."); Norris v. State, 258 Ga. 889, 890, 376 S.E.2d

653, 654 (1989) ("The memory of a witness may not be disparaged by another witness in order to impeach that testimony; it must be done by cross-examination."); Johnson v. State, 236 Ga. App. 252, 257, 511 S.E.2d 603, 608 (1999); Sawyers v. State, 211 Ga. App. 668, 669, 440 S.E.2d 256, 258 (1994) ("The law generally disallows expert testimony regarding inaccuracies in eyewitness identification. . . . The determination of a witness' credibility, including the accuracy of eyewitness identification, is within the exclusive province of the jury.") (citations omitted); Cox v. State, 197 Ga. App. 240, 241, 398 S.E.2d 262, 264 (1990).

[10]See, e.g. Johnson v. State, 272 Ga. 254, 260 n.6, 526 S.E.2d 549, 555 (2000); Allen v. State, 268 Ga. App. 519, 602 S.E.2d 250 (2004), cert. denied, (Oct. 12, 2004). Recently, mounting attacks have been made on the propriety of including the "level of certainty" factor within the jury instructions in light of studies demonstrating a poor correlation between a witness' confidence in the accuracy of his or her identification and the actual accuracy of such an identification. See, e.g. Jones v. State, 273 Ga. 213, 218–219, 539 S.E.2d

case law suggesting that such testimony was to be excluded as a matter of law, and held that the admissibility of expert testimony regarding the reliability of eyewitness identification fell squarely within the discretion of the trial court, noting that this was consistent with the "modern trend" in dealing with such testimony.[11] In *Johnson v. State,* the Court held that where eyewitness identification of the accused is a "key element" of the prosecution's case, and there is no "substantial corroboration" of the identification by other evidence, a trial court may not exclude an expert's testimony regarding the reliability of eyewitness identification "without carefully weighing whether the evidence would assist the jury in assessing the reliability of eyewitness testimony and whether expert testimony is the only effective way to reveal any weakness in an eyewitness identification."[12] The *Johnson* Court noted that expert testimony on the reliability of eyewitness testimony may be especially appropriate where it involves issues which are "counterintuitive" or "contrary to common wisdom," such as the absence of a correlation between witness confidence in his or her identification and the accuracy of such identification, or the adverse effect the stress of a criminal encounter can have on the accuracy of the identification of the perpetrator of the crime.[13]

The *Johnson* case does not represent a wholesale change in

143, 148–149 (2000); Smith v. State, 273 Ga. App. 220, 614 S.E.2d 855 (2005). In Brodes v. State, 279 Ga. 435, 614 S.E.2d 766 (2005), relying in part on the testimony of an expert whose testimony had been previously excluded in several of the cases cited above, the Georgia Supreme Court disapproved of the continued use of the "level of certainty" factor in jury instructions "[i]n light of the scientifically-documented lack of correlation" between the confidence a witness expresses in his or her identification and the accuracy of the identification, and the "critical importance" jury instructions play as a "lamp to guide the jury's feet in journeying through the testimony in search of a legal verdict." *Id.* at 769. As noted by the dissent in *Brodes,* the Court did not hold, however, that evidence by way of lay or expert testimony regarding the certainty of a witness' identification is inadmissible. *Id. at 444, 614 S.E.2d 766* (Carley, J., dissenting).

[11]Johnson v. State, 272 Ga. 254, 256–257, 526 S.E.2d 549, 552 (2000).

[12]Johnson v. State, 272 Ga. 254, 257, 526 S.E.2d 549, 552–553 (2000).

[13]Johnson v. State, 272 Ga. 254, 256 n.2, 526 S.E.2d 549, 552 (2000). In *Johnson,* the Court found that much of the expert's proffered testimony regarding factors affecting the ability to identify another were well within the knowledge of the average juror, including the lighting and weather at the time the individual was seen, the fading of memory with time, and the influence other sources such as photos may have on the identification. However, the expert's proffered testimony also discussed factors less likely to be understood by the average juror, including the adverse impact stress can have on identification, difficulties in cross-racial identification, the likelihood that a victim of a violent crime would be focused on the weapon employed as opposed to the perpetrator's face, and studies indicating a poor correlation between the confidence a wit-

direction regarding the admissibility of expert testimony regarding the reliability of eyewitness identifications. Indeed, the Court upheld the exclusion of the expert's testimony as not applied to the facts, noting that such testimony should be "sufficiently tied to the facts of the case," and that where such testimony "addresses solely generalized concepts" of psychology it is properly excluded.[14] Moreover, the Johnson Court noted that while an expert may provide testimony regarding scientific research addressing the accuracy (or lack thereof) of eyewitness identifications, an expert may not testify as to the credibility of an individual witness, and a particular eyewitness' personal ability to identify another person is a matter to be explored exclusively on direct and cross-examination of the witness.[15] Courts since *Johnson* have continued to grant broad discretion to a trial court's determination as to whether to admit expert testimony on this subject.[16]

---

ness expresses in his or her identification and the actual accuracy of the identification. *Id. at 259–260, 526 S.E.2d 549.*

[14]Johnson v. State, 272 Ga. 254, 255 n.1, 526 S.E.2d 549, 551 (2000). Despite the expert's proffered testimony on factors affecting the reliability of eyewitness identification which were not common knowledge, many of these factors were not applicable to the facts of the case. The witness, who was not the victim of the crime, was not under stress when she saw the defendant prior to the crime's commission, and was not faced with a deadly weapon when she viewed the defendant. While the witness was of a different race than the defendant, she had not described the defendant to the police through generalized racial characteristics, but provided a detailed description of his facial characteristics. Moreover, a composite drawing based on the witness' description of the defendant, created less than 24 hours after the crime's commission, was available for the jury to see. *Id. at 259–260, 526 S.E.2d 549.* See also Norris v. State, 258 Ga. 889, 890, 376 S.E.2d 653, 654 (1989) (expert's testimony excluded, in part, because expert had not examined the eyewitness and expert's testimony that stress can have

an adverse impact on witness' ability to make an accurate identification was not supported by evidence that eyewitness was under stress when he observed the defendant); Jones v. State, 232 Ga. 762, 764–765, 208 S.E.2d 850, 853 (1974) (overruled by, Johnson v. State, 272 Ga. 254, 526 S.E.2d 549 (2000))(expert testimony excluded, in part, where testimony "would have been based exclusively on hypothetical questions and the witness would have been testifying with no knowledge or interview of the eyewitnesses whose testimony was sought to be discredited.").

[15]Johnson v. State, 272 Ga. 254, 257 n.3, 526 S.E.2d 549, 552 (2000).

[16]Allen v. State, 268 Ga. App. 519, 602 S.E.2d 250 (2004), cert. denied, (Oct. 12, 2004)(while expert testimony "may have been 'helpful in some degree to the jury[,]'" trial court did not abuse discretion in excluding expert testimony where eyewitness identification was not the sole evidence linking defendant to crime, and independent corroborating evidence linked defendant to the crime); Evans v. State, 261 Ga. App. 22, 24, 581 S.E.2d 676, 678 (2003); Armstead v. State, 255 Ga. App. 385, 387, 565 S.E.2d 579, 581 (2002).

§ 8:7   Polygraphs and other "truth" tests

Polygraphs have long been regarded skeptically by the law. Indeed, the famed case of *Frye v. United States*, which established the long-employed "general acceptance" test as the standard for the admissibility of scientific evidence in federal court until *Daubert*, concerned the admissibility of a rudimentary form of the polygraph.[1] Today's polygraphs operate by using instruments to record various physiological information, including blood pressure, pulse, respiration rate, and galvanic skin resistance, the subject of the exam exhibits in response to various questions.[2] While polygraphs are not "lie detectors," the underlying principle behind the polygraph is that an individual who is not telling the entire truth in response to a question will exhibit different physiological responses, presumably occasioned by the psychological stress of lying or being caught lying, than one who is telling the truth.[3] While several questioning techniques exist, perhaps the most common is the control question technique, wherein "control" questions designed to elicit a lie are posed to the subject, and the subject's physiological responses to these control questions are compared to the subject's physiological responses to questions relevant to the incident at issue. In theory, a truthful subject will have a greater physiological response to the control questions than the relevant questions, and a deceptive subject will have a greater physiological response to the relevant questions than the control questions.[4]

Until 1977, the results of polygraph tests were flatly held to be inadmissible in Georgia due to the fact that they had not gained "scientific acceptance as an accurate means of detecting decep-

---

[Section 8:7]

[1]Frye v. U.S., 293 F. 1013 (App. D.C. 1923). In *Frye,* the "deception test" at issue measured changes in a subject's systolic blood pressure. The underlying premise of the test was that "conscious deception or falsehood, concealment of facts, or guilt of crime, accompanied by fear of detection when the person is under examination" would result in qualitatively and quantitatively different measurements in the subject's systolic blood pressure than if the subject, notwithstanding fear of detection, was telling the truth. *Id. at 1013–1014.* The court refused to admit the defendant's expert's testimony regarding the results of the defendant's test, stating that it had "not yet gained such standing and sci-

entific recognition among physiological and psychological authorities as would justify the courts in admitting expert testimony deduced from the discovery, development, and experiments thus far made." *Id. at 1014.*

[2]See Ligons, Polygraph Evidence: Where Are We Now?, 65 Mo. L.Rev. 209 (2000).

[3]See Ligons, Polygraph Evidence: Where Are We Now?, 65 Mo. L.Rev. 209 (2000).

[4]See Ligons, Polygraph Evidence: Where Are We Now?, 65 Mo. L.Rev. 209 (2000); see also Bessent, Admissibility of Polygraph Evidence and Repressed Memory Evidence when Offered By The Accused, 55 U. Miami L.Rev. 975 (2001).

tion[.]"[5] However, in 1977, the Georgia Supreme Court held that the results of a polygraph are admissible, provided the admissibility is stipulated to by the parties.[6] This rule holds to this day,[7] and is applicable, not only in criminal cases, but in civil cases as well.[8] The scientific unreliability of polygraphs as a means of detecting deception in a subject's responses continues to be cited as the rationale for this rule of excluding polygraph results absent stipulation of the parties.[9]

The "results" of a polygraph include not only the actual charts from the graphing of the subject's responses to the questions posed during the polygraph examination, but the opinions of an expert as to the truthfulness or falsity of the subject's responses to the questions posed.[10] The fact that the parties have stipulated to the admissibility of polygraph results does not, in itself, prevent a party from then challenging the accuracy of the results or the polygraph operator's conclusions as to whether the responses are indicative of deception.[11] Indeed, in *Sisson v. State*, the trial court's exclusion of such rebuttal testimony from a defendant's expert was held to be reversible error given the "critical" nature of such evidence to the defense.[12] It has also been held to be error to admit only polygraph results indicating deception

---

[5]See, e.g. Salisbury v. State, 221 Ga. 718, 719, 146 S.E.2d 776, 777 (1966); Chambers v. State, 141 Ga. App. 438, 442–443, 233 S.E.2d 818, 822 (1977), rev'd, 240 Ga. 76, 239 S.E.2d 324 (1977). In *Chambers,* the court also expressed the concern that the admission of the results of a polygraph, purporting to be a test designed to ascertain the truth or falsity of a statement, would impede upon the jury's traditional role of determining the credibility of witnesses, and create the risk that the jury would abandon this role and simply defer to the test's results. *Id. at 443, 233 S.E.2d 818.*

[6]State v. Chambers, 240 Ga. 76, 76–77, 239 S.E.2d 324, 325 (1977).

[7]See, e.g. Bantz v. Allstate Ins. Co., 263 Ga. App. 855, 855, 589 S.E.2d 621, 622 (2003), cert. denied, (Feb. 16, 2004); Lockett v. State, 258 Ga. App. 178, 573 S.E.2d 437 (2002).

[8]Bantz v. Allstate Ins. Co., 263 Ga. App. 855, 855, 589 S.E.2d 621, 622 (2003), cert. denied, (Feb. 16, 2004); Munford, Inc. v. Anglin, 174 Ga. App. 290, 294, 329 S.E.2d 526, 530 (1985).

[9]Lockett v. State, 258 Ga. App. 178, 180, 573 S.E.2d 437, 440 (2002); Munford, Inc. v. Anglin, 174 Ga. App. 290, 294, 329 S.E.2d 526, 530 (1985).

[10]Thompson v. State, 257 Ga. App. 426, 428, 571 S.E.2d 158, 160 (2002); Sisson v. State, 181 Ga. App. 784, 786, 353 S.E.2d 836, 838 (1987).

[11]Sisson v. State, 181 Ga. App. 784, 788–789, 353 S.E.2d 836, 839–840 (1987). The parties may, however, include in their stipulation that the defendant will not have the right to present rebuttal testimony regarding the operator's conclusions. *Id. at 789, 353 S.E.2d 836.*

[12]Sisson v. State, 181 Ga. App. 784, 787, 353 S.E.2d 836, 839 (1987). In *Sisson,* the parties had stipulated as to the admissibility of the results of the defendant's polygraph test. The polygraph operator testified that it was his opinion that the defendant had not been truthful in responding to certain questions posed during the examination. The proffered testimony of the defendant's expert, a psychologist with extensive experience with poly-

while excluding "inconclusive" polygraph results; otherwise, only evidence of guilt would be admitted while evidence tending to call into question the reliability of the results or tending to exculpate the defendant would be excluded.[13]

As a general matter, absent stipulation, it is impermissible for the State to reference the fact that a polygraph examination was administered for the purpose of either bolstering the credibility of one of its witnesses or impugning the credibility of the defendant.[14] Such evidence may, however, be admitted where necessary to explain an actor's conduct, but only when the conduct and motives of the actor are matters relevant to an issue at trial.[15] It has been noted that it is rare that the conduct and motives of the police in conducting a criminal investigation will be relevant to any issue at trial.[16] However, reference to the fact that a witness has taken a polygraph has been held admissible to rebut a suggestion of impropriety in police conduct by the defense.[17] Moreover, reference to the fact a witness has taken a polygraph has been admitted to explain why the witness has changed his or her story for the purpose of aiding a jury to resolve conflicts in the stories.[18]

---

graphs, included the lack of diagnostic sensitivity and accuracy of polygraphs in general and the type of polygraph used to test the defendant in particular. The expert testified as to the high error rate of polygraph tests, and the fact that a high percentage of polygraph tests resulted in "false positives," i.e. identifying innocent persons as being guilty. The expert explained that polygraphs are not "lie detectors," and can only assess the degree of emotional arousal (but not the type of emotion aroused) following the posing of a question, and concluded that it was impossible to ascertain, based upon the results of the polygraph administered, whether the defendant was being deceptive in his responses. Sisson v. State, 181 Ga. App. 784, 353 S.E.2d 836 (1987)

[13]Lawson v. State, 162 Ga. App. 579, 580, 292 S.E.2d 421, 422 (1982).

[14]Wilson v. State, 254 Ga. 473, 476, 330 S.E.2d 364, 366 (1985); Cromer v. State, 253 Ga. 352, 356, 320 S.E.2d 751, 755 (1984).

[15]Morris v. State, 264 Ga. 823, 824–825, 452 S.E.2d 100, 102 (1995);

Cromer v. State, 253 Ga. 352, 356, 320 S.E.2d 751, 755 (1984).

[16]Morris v. State, 264 Ga. 823, 824–825, 452 S.E.2d 100, 102 (1995); Wilson v. State, 254 Ga. 473, 476 S.E.2d 364, 366 (1985). In *Morris,* the prosecutor had elicited testimony from a police office that an individual had "checked out" on a polygraph examination for the ostensible purpose of explaining why the individual was ruled out as a suspect in a police investigation. Finding that the issue of why the police ruled out this individual as a suspect was not relevant to any issue in the case, the court held that the admission of such testimony was reversible error in light of the fact that the defendant had implicated the individual as the perpetrator of the crime, and reference to the fact that the individual "checked out" on the polygraph improperly bolstered the individual's credibility. *Id.* at 824–825, 601 S.E.2d 804.

[17]Carr v. State, 259 Ga. 318, 380 S.E.2d 700 (1989); Cromer v. State, 253 Ga. 352, 320 S.E.2d 751 (1984).

[18]Bantz v. Allstate Ins. Co., 263

Upon request, a party has the right, where polygraph results are admitted at trial, to a jury instruction that the examiner's opinions may be used only to indicate whether, at the time of the examination, the person examined believed that he was telling the whole truth.[19] Courts have cited the concern that, without such a limiting instruction, the jury will be left to erroneously conclude that a polygraph is infallible, conclusive on the issue of "truth," and that only the polygraph operator can be relied upon as to the issue of "truth."[20] Unlike other documentary evidence, polygraph results cannot "go out" with the jury. Polygraph results are not direct evidence, but "opinion" evidence, and allowing such evidence to go out with the jury would unfairly emphasize the testimony of the polygraph examiner while denying the jury the opportunity to rehear the oral testimony of other witnesses.[21]

Other techniques or procedures designed to detect or elicit the truth have not fared well under Georgia law. In *Harper v. State*, it was held that neither a witness' statements while under the influence of sodium amytal, a so-called "truth serum," nor an expert's opinions based upon these statements, are admissible, as it has not been established with "verifiable certainty" that "truth serum compels a person to tell the truth."[22] Similarly, the use of a "voice stress analysis" to demonstrate that a person was deceptive in responding to questions has been held inadmissible as not having been shown to have reached a "scientific stage of verifiable certainty."[23]

Hypnosis may sometimes be employed in an effort to "refresh" the memory of a witness. Georgia courts have recognized dangers inherent in an effort to refresh or uncover a witness' memories through hypnosis. One danger is referred to as "cementing," which occurs when the subject of hypnosis recounts a version of a certain memory while having suspended his or her critical judgment, a natural incident of hypnosis. The memory then may become "cemented" in the witness' mind as an accurate depiction of events, whatever the actual accuracy of the memory may in

---

Ga. App. 855, 589 S.E.2d 621 (2003), cert. denied, (Feb. 16, 2004); Jackson v. State, 268 Ga. 391, 490 S.E.2d 84 (1997); Newberry v. State, 260 Ga. 416, 395 S.E.2d 813 (1990).

[19]Lockett v. State, 258 Ga. App. 178, 181, 573 S.E.2d 437, 441 (2002). Included in this charge is a direction that the jury is not bound by the examiner's opinions, and may even disregard them in their entirety. *Id.* at 181, 573 S.E.2d 437.

[20]Harris v. State, 168 Ga. App. 458, 461, 309 S.E.2d 431, 434–435 (1983).

[21]Harris v. State, 168 Ga. App. 458, 461, 309 S.E.2d 431, 434 (1983).

[22]Harper v. State, 249 Ga. 519, 526, 292 S.E.2d 389, 396 (1982).

[23]Price v. State, 269 Ga. 373, 375, 497 S.E.2d 797, 799 (1998).

fact be.[24] A second danger is referred to as "confabulation," which occurs when the subject of hypnosis responds to suggestion or expectation while in a hypnotic state, filling in the "gaps" of his or her memory in an effort to compensate for the lack of actual recall. This filling in of gaps can be due to an unconscious attempt by the subject to be a "good" witness, or can be the result of leading or suggestive questioning techniques by the examiner.[25]

It has long been held that the reliability of hypnosis has not been established, and thus, statements made by a person while under a hypnotic trance are inadmissible.[26] Similarly, an expert's testimony about what the witness said while under a hypnotic trance is not admissible.[27] Given the dangers of "implanted" or "tainted" memories, where the party subjecting the witness to hypnosis calls the witness to testify, the witness may only testify as to the specific content of statements, which have been recorded, which he or she made prior to hypnosis.[28]

§ 8:8 Sanity and competency

Historically, one of the most prominent uses of expert psychological testimony has been in the area of a criminal defendant's assertion of insanity as an affirmative defense to a crime with which the defendant has been charged. When insanity is used as an affirmative defense to a crime, the defendant has the burden of proving that, at the time of the crime's commission, he either: 1) did not have the mental capacity to distinguish between right and wrong; or 2) suffered from a "delusional compulsion" which overpowered his will to resist the commission of the offense.[1] The defendant's evidence must be sufficient to overcome a presumption that the defendant was sane at the time of the crime's commission.[2] Typically, either psychiatrists[3] or psychologists[4] will be offered to provide expert testimony in support of or in opposition

[24]Walraven v. State, 255 Ga. 276, 281, 336 S.E.2d 798, 802 (1985).

[25]Walraven v. State, 255 Ga. 276, 281, 336 S.E.2d 798, 802 (1985).

[26]Tucker v. State, 249 Ga. 323, 326, 290 S.E.2d 97, 100 (1982); Collier v. State, 244 Ga. 553, 557, 261 S.E.2d 364, 370 (1979) (overruled on other grounds by, Thompson v. State, 263 Ga. 23, 426 S.E.2d 895 (1993)); Alderman v. State, 241 Ga. 496, 510, 246 S.E.2d 642, 651 (1978); Emmett v. State, 232 Ga. 110, 115, 205 S.E.2d 231, 235 (1974).

[27]Alderman v. State, 241 Ga. 496, 510, 246 S.E.2d 642, 651 (1978).

[28]Walraven v. State, 255 Ga. 276, 282, 336 S.E.2d 798, 803 (1985).

[Section 8:8]

[1]O.C.G.A. §§ 16-3-2; 16-3-3. See also Boswell v. State, 275 Ga. 689, 690, 572 S.E.2d 565, 567 (2002); Freeman v. State, 132 Ga. App. 742, 743–44, 209 S.E.2d 127, 129 (1974).

[2]Historically, courts routinely held that a court could simply disregard the defendant's expert testimony and rely solely on this presumption of sanity. See, e.g. Kirk v. State, 252 Ga. 133, 133, 311 S.E.2d 821, 822 (1984); Peek v. State, 250 Ga. 50, 51, 295 S.E.2d 834, 835 (1982); Moses v. State,

to the insanity defense. However, courts have not required experts to hold these qualifications in order to be deemed competent to offer such testimony, and licensed clinical social workers[5] and medical doctors[6] have also been held qualified to provide testimony regarding the insanity defense.

By statute, a defendant is required to provide notice of his intent to raise the defense of insanity as a prerequisite to the admissibility of expert testimony on this issue.[7] Following such notice, the trial court appoints a psychiatrist or licensed psychologist to examine the defendant and testify at trial after the defense and prosecution have presented their evidence.[8] A defendant's failure to make himself available for evaluation by the court-appointed expert will result in the inability of the defendant to provide the testimony of his own retained-expert.[9] While the State may introduce its own expert testimony regarding the

---

245 Ga. 180, 181, 263 S.E.2d 916, 919 (1980) (overruled by, Nagel v. State, 262 Ga. 888, 427 S.E.2d 490 (1993)). However, more recent cases have held that the expert testimony should be carefully considered and not arbitrarily discounted in favor of this presumption. See, e.g. Nagel v. State, 262 Ga. 888, 891, 427 S.E.2d 490, 492 (1993).

[3]See e.g., Brown v. State, 262 Ga. 833, 834, 426 S.E.2d 559, 561 (1993); Harris v. State, 256 Ga. 350, 349 S.E.2d 374 (1986).

[4]See, e.g. Frazier v. State, 216 Ga. App. 111, 112, 452 S.E.2d 803, 804 (1995); Butler v. State, 252 Ga. 135, 137, 311 S.E.2d 473, 475 (1984); Peek v. State, 250 Ga. 50, 50, 295 S.E.2d 834, 835 (1982); cf. Smith v. State, 141 Ga. App. 720, 721–22, 234 S.E.2d 385, 387 (1977) (trial court did not err in excluding as an expert a witness who had only a bachelor's degree in psychology, and had only worked as a technician for eleven months).

[5]O.C.G.A. § 43–10A–12(c) ("[l]licensed clinical social workers may . . . provide psychosocial evaluation . . . to determine the nature of an individual's mental, cognitive, emotional, behavioral, and interpersonal problems or conditions"); Adams v. State, 275 Ga.

867, 868, 572 S.E.2d 545, 547 (2002) (admitting licensed social worker's testimony because she had education and experience in evaluating mental conditions of patients).

[6]Ellis v. State, 168 Ga. App. 757, 759, 309 S.E.2d 924, 926 (1983); see also Petty v. Folsom, 229 Ga. 477, 192 S.E.2d 246 (1972) (physician who did not practice as psychiatrist competent to provide expert testimony on sanity).

[7]O.C.G.A. § 17–7–130.1; Abernathy v. State, 265 Ga. 754, 754, 462 S.E.2d 615, 615 (1995); Cox v. State, 216 Ga. App. 86, 453 S.E.2d 471 (1995) (no error in excluding expert testimony on insanity where defendant failed to comply with notice provisions). While O.C.G.A. § 17–7–130.1 addresses "psychiatrists" and 'licensed psychologists," a licensed mental health counselor has also been found competent to testify as the court-appointed expert. Payne v. State, 273 Ga. 317, 319, 540 S.E.2d 191, 193 (2001).

[8]O.C.G.A. § 17–7–130.1. Both sides are permitted to cross-examine the court-appointed witness and introduce rebuttal evidence. Id.

[9]Moses v. State, 256 Ga. 831, 832, 353 S.E.2d 348, 349 (1987); Strickland v. State, 257 Ga. 230, 233, 357 S.E.2d 85, 88 (1987).

defendant's insanity defense, it may not do so where the defendant produced no expert testimony in support of his defense.[10]

Courts have consistently rejected challenges to an expert's opinion regarding the defendant's sanity as invading the province of the jury by commenting upon an "ultimate issue," reasoning that opinion testimony regarding an individual's sanity is a proper matter for expert testimony because it is beyond the ken of the jury.[11] Typically, such testimony will address the defendant's psychological diagnosis, and how the diagnosed condition impacted upon the defendant's mental state during the crime's commission.[12] Courts have typically permitted such experts to track the language of the affirmative defense of insanity, allowing experts to conclude that either the defendant was or was not able to distinguish between right and wrong at the time of the offense,[13] or the defendant was or was not under the influence of a "delusional compulsion" at the time of the offense,[14] or both. An expert may not, however, testify as to how the defendant's mental

---

[10]Abernathy v. State, 265 Ga. 754, 754, 462 S.E.2d 615, 615 (1995).

[11]Brown v. State, 262 Ga. 833, 834, 426 S.E.2d 559, 561 (1993) (psychologist's testimony on sanity admissible over objection that such evidence constituted an opinion on the ultimate issue); Smith v. State, 247 Ga. 612, 616–17, 277 S.E.2d 678, 681–82 (1981) (citing expert testimony on sanity as an example of rule that expert may testify on an ultimate issue when it is a matter beyond comprehension of the jury); Espy v. Preston, 199 Ga. 608, 608, 34 S.E.2d 705, 715 (1945) ("[s]anity or insanity is a proper subject for opinion evidence"); Pyron v. State, 237 Ga. App. 198, 199, 514 S.E.2d 51, 52 (1999) (noting expert testimony on insanity is admissible testimony on ultimate issue because jury would not be able to draw such a conclusion on its own); Argonaut Ins. Co. v. Allen, 123 Ga. App. 741, 744, 182 S.E.2d 508, 511 (1971) (citing expert testimony on insanity as example of conclusion beyond comprehension of average person).

[12]See e.g., Fuss v. State, 271 Ga. 319, 321, 519 S.E.2d 446, 449 (1999) (expert testified that defendant could act rationally in his psychotic state); Butler v. State, 252 Ga. 135, 137, 311 S.E.2d 473, 475 (1984) (forensic psychiatrist testified that he diagnosed appellant with paranoid schizophrenia and the condition caused the appellant to be unable to distinguish between right and wrong at the time of the offense); Peek v. State, 250 Ga. 50, 50, 295 S.E.2d 834, 835 (1982) (psychiatrist testified that defendant suffered from bouts of the schizophrenia, paranoid type, which caused him to suffer a delusion at the time of the offense); Jones v. State, 191 Ga. App. 561, 561, 382 S.E.2d 612, 613 (1989) (experts at trial testified that appellant suffered from an explosive disorder, a type of personality disorder which manifests itself from an anti-social act).

[13]Hancock v. State, 277 Ga. 835, 836–37, 596 S.E.2d 127, 129–30 (2004); Boswell v. State, 275 Ga. 689, 691, 572 S.E.2d 565, 568 (2002); Freeman v. State, 132 Ga. App. 742, 743, 209 S.E.2d 127, 129 (1974) (psychiatrist testified that he thought defendant was not capable of making a judgment in terms of right or wrong).

[14]Hancock v. State, 277 Ga. 835, 836–37, 596 S.E.2d 127, 129–30 (2004); Boswell v. State, 275 Ga. 689, 691, 572 S.E.2d 565, 568 (2002); Harris v. State, 256 Ga. 350, 354, 349 S.E.2d 374, 377 (1986).

state at the time of the offense should impact his legal account-ability, as such an opinion would constitute an impermissible legal conclusion.[15] Expert testimony on the defense of insanity is relevant only where it bears upon the defendant's mental state at the time of the offense.[16] Thus, expert testimony that a defendant is not, at the time of trial, competent to stand trial is, in itself, ir-relevant to the insanity defense.[17]

Expert testimony on an individual's sanity, or competency, is also prominent at civil commitment hearings. Such a hearing may occur upon a criminal defendant's acquittal of a crime by reason of insanity.[18] It may also occur independently of any crim-inal trial upon the filing of a petition with the court for the invol-untary hospitalization of an individual,[19] or the filing of a petition for release by one who has previously been involuntarily hospital-ized.[20] The standard for civil commitment requires a showing that the individual sought to be involuntarily committed suffers from a mental illness, and that this person either presents a substantial risk of harm to himself or others as made apparent

---

[15]Bryant v. State, 191 Ga. 686, 717–18, 13 S.E.2d 820, 840–41 (1941) (noting that while expert opinion as to whether the defendant knew right from wrong is proper, expert opinion as to the defendant's criminal respon-sibility is improper); Kirkland v. State, 166 Ga. App. 478, 481–82, 304 S.E.2d 561, 565 (1983) (finding that while an expert may be competent to testify as to a party's mental state, such an expert is not competent to testify as to how that mental state affects legal ac-countability); Kirk v. State, 168 Ga. App. 226, 229, 308 S.E.2d 592, 597 (1983) (finding expert testimony that defendant fit the legal definition of insanity objectionable because the testimony constituted a legal conclu-sion and thereby invaded the province of the jury).

[16]Kirk v. State, 168 Ga. App. 226, 229, 308 S.E.2d 592, 596–97 (1983) (psychiatrist's testimony that defen-dant was in need of hospitalization ir-relevant where it did not concern defendant's mental state on the eve-ning of the offense).

[17]Where a defendant asserts that he is not competent to stand trial, a defendant must show he does not understand the nature or the object of

the proceedings against him, and that he would be incapable of assisting his attorney in his defense. See, e.g, Adams v. State, 275 Ga. 867, 867–88, 572 S.E.2d 545, 547 (2002); Smalls v. State, 153 Ga. App. 254, 255, 265 S.E.2d 83, 84 (1980); Echols v. State, 149 Ga. App. 620, 620–21, 255 S.E.2d 92, 95 (1979); Currelley v. State, 145 Ga. App. 29, 29, 243 S.E.2d 307, 308 (1978). This issue is separate and distinct from the issue as to whether the defendant was sane at the time of the offense for which he is charged, and evidence on the former is irrele-vant on the latter. Hudson v. State, 273 Ga. 124, 127, 538 S.E.2d 751, 754 (2000).

[18]Gross v. State, 210 Ga. App. 125, 126, 435 S.E.2d 496, 498 (1993).

[19]See O.C.G.A. §§ 37–3–61 and 37–3–62. At such release hearings, the patient must overcome a presumption of insanity. O.C.G.A. § 24–4–2; Butler v. State, 258 Ga. 344, 369 S.E.2d 252 (1988); Gross v. State, 210 Ga. App. 125, 126, 435 S.E.2d 496, 498 (1993).

[20]See, e.g. Clark v. State, 245 Ga. 629, 635, 266 S.E.2d 466, 472 (1980); Gross v. State, 262 Ga. App. 328, 329, 585 S.E.2d 671, 672 (2003).

by recent threats of violence or overt acts, or the person is unable to care for his or her own "physical health and safety as to create an imminently life-endangering crisis."[21]

The testimony presented at such hearings concerns an individual's mental health diagnosis, how this diagnosis affects the individual's ability to function in society, and whether the individual is in need of involuntary hospitalization as a result of his or her condition.[22] Such hearings are before a judge, not a jury.[23] In cases where an involuntarily committed patient is seeking release, courts have historically held that the court, as the trier of fact, is at liberty to disregard expert testimony regarding the defendant's sanity and rely solely on the presumption of insanity.[24] However, more recent cases have held that the courts must carefully consider the expert testimony presented, and may not arbitrarily disregard the testimony in favor of this presumption.[25]

---

[21]O.C.G.A. § 37–3–1(9.1); Clark v. State, 245 Ga. 629, 638, 266 S.E.2d 466, 473 (1980).

[22]See e.g., Clark v. State, 245 Ga. 629, 632, 266 S.E.2d 466, 470 (1980) (treating physician's testimony that patient's schizophrenia was in remission and that he presented no risk of harm to himself or others); Gross v. State, 262 Ga. App. 328, 329, 585 S.E.2d 671, 672 (2003) (treating psychiatrist's testimony that patient's schizophrenia required continued supervision, and that, if released, the patient posed a risk of danger to himself and others); Butler v. State, 225 Ga. App. 288, 290, 483 S.E.2d 385, 387 (1997) (testimony that patient, with medication, no longer posed a danger to herself or others, and that patient would likely continue taking her medication); Gross v. State, 210 Ga. App. 125, 435 S.E.2d 496 (1993) (psychologist's testimony that patient was unable to care for himself, and that, if released, medication compliance could

not be effectively monitored with the result that patient was at risk of acting on delusional beliefs); Cox v. State, 171 Ga. App. 550, 550–51, 320 S.E.2d 611, 611–12 (1984) (expert testimony that individual suffered from paranoid schizophrenia, but that such condition could be managed through medication).

[23]Bell v. State, 244 Ga. 211, 211, 259 S.E.2d 465, 465 (1979).

[24]See, e.g. Butler v. State, 258 Ga. 344, 369 S.E.2d 252 (1988); Gross v. State, 210 Ga. App. 125, 126, 435 S.E.2d 496, 498 (1993); Cox v. State, 171 Ga. App. 550, 551, 320 S.E.2d 611, 612 (1984); Moses v. State, 167 Ga. App. 556, 558, 307 S.E.2d 35, 38 (1983) (overruled by, Nagel v. State, 262 Ga. 888, 427 S.E.2d 490 (1993)).

[25]See, e.g. Gross v. State, 262 Ga. App. 328, 329, 585 S.E.2d 671, 672 (2003); Nagel v. State, 262 Ga. 888, 891, 427 S.E.2d 490, 492 (1993).

Chapter 9

Medical Malpractice

> **KeyCite**[®]: Cases and other legal materials listed in KeyCite Scope can be researched through the KeyCite service on Westlaw[®]. Use KeyCite to check citations for form, parallel references, prior and later history, and comprehensive citator information, including citations to other decisions and secondary materials.

§ 9:1   Overview

The term "medical malpractice" does not necessarily signify an action brought against a physician, and the term has been applied to a wide range of professionals in the health care industry, including, but not limited to, nurses,[1] physical therapists,[2] den-

---

[Section 9:1]

[1]Deese v. Carroll City County Hosp., 203 Ga. App. 148, 416 S.E.2d 127 (1992).

[2]Augustine v. Frame, 206 Ga. App. 348, 349, 425 S.E.2d 296, 296 (1992).

tists,[3] optometrists,[4] and dieticians.[5] Perhaps in no other area of law is expert testimony more abundant in cases involving allegations of medical malpractice. This is so because the issue as to whether a medical provider's acts or omissions constituted negligence, i.e., departed from the standard of care applicable to such providers, is not an issue which a layperson is deemed competent to decide without the assistance of an expert who can define the applicable standard of care. Similarly, whether a medical provider's acts or omissions had a causal effect on the patient's claimed injuries is an issue which is not ordinarily susceptible to a lay person's determination absent the assistance of one with medical knowledge.[6] The law presumes a medical professional's conduct complied with the applicable standard of care,[7] and expert medical testimony is ordinarily required to overcome this presumption.[8] The fact that a course of treatment is not successful in curing the patient of his or her malady is insufficient to raise a presumption that the care provided was not in accordance with the standard of care.[9]

§ 9:2   Qualifications

In addition to adopting the federal standards for the admissibility of expert testimony, O.C.G.A. § 24-9-67.1 provides for additional requirements with respect to the qualifications of those experts testifying in professional malpractice actions in general, and medical malpractice actions in particular.[1] Globally, in order for an expert's testimony regarding the applicable standard of care to be admissible in any professional malpractice action, including a medical malpractice action, the expert must have been licensed by an appropriate regulatory agency to practice or teach his or her profession at the time the allegedly negligent act

---

[3]See e.g. Francis v. Reynolds, 215 Ga. App. 418, 418, 450 S.E.2d 876, 876 (1994).

[4]Zechmann v. Thigpen, 210 Ga. App. 726, 727, 437 S.E.2d 475, 477 (1993).

[5]Charter Peachford Behavioral Health System v. Kohout, 233 Ga. App. 452, 454, 504 S.E.2d 514, 519–20 (1998).

[6]Zwiren v. Thompson, 276 Ga. 498, 500, 578 S.E.2d 862, 865 (2003); Pilzer v. Jones, 242 Ga. App. 198, 201, 529 S.E.2d 205, 208 (2000); Wilson v. Kornegay, 108 Ga. App. 318, 320, 132 S.E.2d 791, 793 (1963).

[7]Shea v. Phillips, 213 Ga. App. 269, 271, 98 S.E.2d 552 (1957).

[8]Beach v. Lipham, 276 Ga. 302, 303, 578 S.E.2d 402 (2003).

[9]Brooks v. Coliseum Park Hosp., Inc., 187 Ga. App. 29, 33, 369 S.E.2d 319, 322 (1988); Sullivan v. Henry, 160 Ga. App. 791, 800, 287 S.E.2d 652, 659 (1982); Blount v. Moore, 159 Ga. App. 80, 81, 282 S.E.2d 720, 722 (1981); Hayes v. Brown, 108 Ga. App. 360, 363, 133 S.E.2d 102, 105 (1963).

[Section 9:2]

[1]O.C.G.A. § 24-9-67.1(c).

or omission which is at issue occurred.[2] In medical malpractice actions, two additional requirements apply in order for the expert's standard of care testimony to be admissible. First, such an expert must have had, at the time the allegedly negligent act or omission occurred, "actual professional knowledge and experience in the area of practice or specialty" in which the expert's opinion is to be given.[3] Such knowledge and experience must be demonstrated either by: 1) the expert's active practice in the specialty regarding which the opinion is to be given for at least three of the last five years;[4] or 2) by the expert's teaching of his or her profession for at least three of the last five years.[5] Second, such an expert must, as a general rule, be a member of the same "profession" as the individual whose allegedly negligent conduct or omission is at issue.[6]

§ 9:3 Qualifications—The licensure requirement in professional malpractice actions other than medical malpractice

Historically, courts have generally held that an expert's licensure in the area in which he or she is providing expert testimony is not a prerequisite to the admissibility of such testimony, but rather, a matter for the jury to consider in assigning the weight to be given the expert's testimony.[1] Courts noted that a licensure requirement was not required, on its face, by the former version of O.C.G.A. § 24–9–67, and reasoned that such a requirement could have the effect of excluding the testimony of an otherwise well-qualified expert who happened not to hold a license.[2] Similarly, courts rejected the notion that the expert should have been licensed in the pertinent profession at the time the professional's conduct, which is the subject matter of the ac-

---

[2]O.C.G.A. § 24–9–67.1(c)(1).

[3]O.C.G.A. § 24–9–67.1(c)(2).

[4]O.C.G.A. § 24–9–67.1(c)(2)(A).

[5]O.C.G.A. § 24–9–67.1(c)(2)(B).

[6]O.C.G.A. § 24–9–67.1(c)(2)(C).

[Section 9:3]

[1]See, e.g. Williamson v. Harvey Smith, Inc., 246 Ga. App. 745, 748, 542 S.E.2d 151, 155 (2000); In Interest of C.W.D., 232 Ga. App. 200, 206–07, 501 S.E.2d 232, 239 (1998).

[2]Dayoub v. Yates–Astro Termite Pest Control Co., 239 Ga. App. 578, 580, 521 S.E.2d 600, 602 (1999). In *Dayoub,* the plaintiff presented an expert who held a doctorate in entomology and had experience in consulting with pest control companies and the Georgia Department of Agriculture in a case alleging the negligent application of pesticides. In reversing the trial court's exclusion of the expert's testimony because the expert did not hold a pest control operator's license, the court stated, citing the former version of O.C.G.A. § 24–9–67, that the trial court's imposition of such a requirement was "arbitrary and capricious and imposed a standard of qualification greater than that imposed by law." Dayoub v. Yates-Astro Termite Pest Control Co., 239 Ga. App. 578, 580, 521 S.E.2d 600 (1999)

tion, occurred. These courts reasoned that the fact that the expert was not licensed at such time did not mean that the expert could not become familiar with the standards of conduct applicable at the time of the conduct at issue.[3]

Courts have struggled with the boundaries regarding whether and when a witness has obtained a sufficient quantum of knowledge absent a license or professional certification. For instance, in *Murray v. Department of Transportation*,[4] a case decided by the Court of Appeals in 1999, an expert was found competent to testify as to "generally accepted engineering standards in effect on March 11, 1940" based solely on his averment that he had "personal knowledge" of the standards in effect some half-century ago.[5] In highly technical and specialized fields where technological innovations render the prior way of doing things quickly obsolete, and knowledge is constantly evolving, parties may argue for requiring an expert, who is presented to testify on standards since rendered obsolete, to have had actual, working knowledge of such historical standards, as demonstrated by having been licensed in the field at the time the allegedly negligent professional conduct occurred. While it may be possible to become familiar with historical standards and practices no longer in existence, "[c]ompetency as an expert is not demonstrated by mere familiarity."[6]

O.C.G.A. § 24–9–67.1 directly addresses this concern by providing that, as a prerequisite to the admissibility of an expert's testimony regarding "the acceptable standard of conduct of the professional whose conduct is at issue," the expert providing such testimony must have been licensed to practice his or her profession at the time of the allegedly negligent professional conduct at issue.[7] The expert must have been licensed by "an appropriate regulatory agency" in the state in which the expert was either practicing or teaching.[8] The statute's focus is on licensure at the time of the allegedly negligent professional conduct which is the subject matter of the expert's testimony, and the statute does not appear to require licensure at the time the expert's testimony is given.

---

[3]Goodman v. Lipman, 197 Ga. App. 631, 399 S.E.2d 255 (1990). Citing Grindstaff v. Coleman, 681 F.2d 740, 743 (11th Cir. 1982), the court observed that a "rule which would require an expert witness to have been an expert at the time of the questioned event would prevent proof based upon knowledge of historical events. Application of standards to conduct which predates the oldest living expert would be excluded by such a ruling[.]" *Id. at*

632.

[4]Murray v. Department of Transp., 240 Ga. App. 285, 523 S.E.2d 367 (1999).

[5]Murray v. Department of Transp., 240 Ga. App. 285, 296–287, 523 S.E.2d 367, 368–369 (1999).

[6]Bethea v. Smith, 176 Ga. App. 467, 469, 336 S.E.2d 295, 297 (1985).

[7]O.C.G.A. § 24–9–67.1(c)(1).

[8]O.C.G.A. § 24–9–67.1(c)(1).

§ 9:4 Qualifications—The active practice or teaching requirement in medical malpractice actions

In addition to the licensure requirement applicable in professional malpractice actions as discussed immediately above,[1] O.C.G.A. § 24–9–67.1 imposes an additional requirement in medical malpractice actions. In order for the expert to be deemed qualified to render an opinion, the statute requires the expert to have "had actual professional knowledge and experience in the area of practice or specialty in which the opinion is to be given[.]"[2] This professional knowledge and experience may be demonstrated in two alternate ways under the statute: by a showing of either: a) sufficient practice; or b) teaching in the area in which the testimony is to be provided. With respect to the practice requirement, the expert must have been "regularly engaged" in the "active practice specialty of his or her profession" for at least three of the last five years.[3] This practice must have been performed with "sufficient frequency" so as to establish an "appropriate level of knowledge" in performing the procedure, diagnosing the condition, or rendering the treatment which is alleged to have been performed negligently.[4] The question as to whether the expert has engaged in active practice with sufficient frequency so as to establish an "appropriate level of knowledge" is a determination to be made by the court.[5]

With respect to the teaching requirement, the expert must have been "regularly engaged" in the "teaching of his or her profession" as an employed member of the faculty of an educational institution accredited in the teaching of the profession for at least three of the last five years.[6] As with the practice requirement, this teaching must have been performed with "sufficient frequency" so as to establish an "appropriate level of knowledge" in teaching others how to perform the procedure, diagnose the condition, or render the treatment which is alleged to have been performed negligently.[7] Again, the question as to whether the expert has engaged in the teaching of these matters with sufficient frequency so as to establish an "appropriate level of knowledge" is a determination to be made by the court.[8]

In one of the earliest decisions interpreting the new expert testimony statute, the Court of Appeals held that the statute did not apply to preclude the testimony of a medical expert who treated patients for similar complaints merely because the expert

---

[Section 9:4]

[1]See § 1:2.

[2]O.C.G.A. § 24–9–67.1(c)(2).

[3]O.C.G.A. § 24–9–67.1(c)(2)(A).

[4]O.C.G.A. § 24–9–67.1(c)(2)(A).
[5]O.C.G.A. § 24–9–67.1(c)(2)(A).
[6]O.C.G.A. § 24–9–67.1(c)(2)(B).
[7]O.C.G.A. § 24–9–67.1(c)(2)(B).
[8]O.C.G.A. § 24–9–67.1(c)(2)(A).

and the defendants had different medical specialties.[9] This requirement reverses prior Georgia law, which did not require an expert physician to practice in the same specialty as the defendant physician, provided the expert and defendant belonged to the "same school of medicine."[10]

The statute is somewhat unclear as to when the practice or teaching was to have occurred. On one hand, the language "for at least three of the *last* five years" indicates that relevant time period is the five years prior to the time of the expert's giving of the testimony. Under this construction, the practice and teaching requirement would operate to ensure that the expert's knowledge is not too "stale" or "dated" at the time the testimony is given. On the other hand, this requirement appears to be modified by the same clause which requires the expert to have been licensed at the time of the allegedly negligent professional conduct.[11] Under such a construction, the practice and teaching requirement would bolster the purpose behind the licensure requirement by requiring the expert to not only have been licensed, but also to have had a certain minimum of practical knowledge and experience in the pertinent area, at the time of the allegedly negligent conduct.

§ 9:5   Qualifications—The same profession requirement in medical malpractice actions

O.C.G.A. § 24–9–67.1, subject to two exceptions, requires that an expert providing standard of care testimony in a medical malpractice action be of the "same profession" as the defendant whose conduct is at issue.[1] The first exception is that a doctor of medicine (an allopath, or "M.D.") may testify as to the standard of care applicable to a doctor of osteopathy (an osteopath, or "D.O"),[2] and vice-versa.[3] The second exception is that a physician may testify as to the standard of care applicable to certain other

---

[9]Cotten v. Phillips, 633 S.E.2d 655 (Ga. Ct. App. 2006) (Court of Appeals upheld trial court's decision to admit testimony of vascular surgeon in action against orthopedic surgeon).

[10]See, e.g. Beatty v. Morgan, 170 Ga. App. 661, 662, 317 S.E.2d 662, 664 (1984) ("The law of this state has not reached the point at which a physician testifying as an expert witness on the standard of care exercised by another physician is required to be a specialist in the area of medicine practiced by the either physician.").

[11]O.C.G.A. § 24–9–67.1(c). Both the "licensure" requirement of O.C.G.A. § 24–9–67.1(c)(1), and the "practice" and "teaching" requirements of O.C.G.A. § 24–9–67.1(c)(2), are subject to the clause "at the time the act or omission is alleged to have occurred[.]"

[Section 9:5]

[1]O.C.G.A. § 24–9–67.1(c)(2)(C)(i).

[2]O.C.G.A. § 24–9–67.1(c)(2)(C)(ii).

[3]O.C.G.A. § 24–9–67.1(c)(2)(C)(iii).

specifically-enumerated health care providers, such as a nurse,[4] provided that the physician has knowledge of the standard of care applicable to the other health care provider.[5] This knowledge must have been derived from having, during at least three of the last five years immediately preceding the time the act or omission is alleged to have occurred, "supervised, taught, or instructed" such health care providers.[6] At the same time, these other types of health care providers are not deemed competent to testify as to the standard of care applicable to a physician.[7]

Prior to the statute's enactment, the general rule was that "a member of a school of practice other than that to which the defendant belongs is not competent to testify as an expert in a malpractice case."[8] This rule was, however, subject to exception where there was "proof by competent evidence that the methods of treatment are the same despite the difference in the nomenclature of the schools involved[.]"[9] This determination hinged upon a showing that there is a sufficient "overlap" in the different schools such that the expert was competent to opine upon the standard of care applicable to the defendant.[10] Under this test, osteopathic doctors were permitted to testify as to the standard of care ap-

---

[4]O.C.G.A. § 24–9–67.1(c)(2)(D). The other health care providers specifically identified in the statute include nurses, nurse practitioners, certified registered nurse anesthetists, nurse midwives, physician's assistants, physical therapists, occupational therapists, and "medical support staff."

[5]O.C.G.A. § 24–9–67.1(c)(2)(D).

[6]O.C.G.A. § 24–9–67.1(c)(2)(D).

[7]O.C.G.A. § 24–9–67.1(c)(2)(D).

[8]Sandford v. Howard, 161 Ga. App. 495, 497, 288 S.E.2d 739, 740 (1982).

[9]Sandford v. Howard, 161 Ga. App. 495, 497, 288 S.E.2d 739, 741 (1982). In Chandler v. Koenig, 203 Ga. App. 684, 417 S.E.2d 715 (1992), the court found that despite a pharmacologist's impressive credentials and the fact that he likely had knowledge of the properties and interactions of medications that far exceeded that of the average doctor, there was no showing of how this undisputed expertise "provided him with expert knowledge of the standard of care in prescribing drugs ordinarily employed throughout

the general medical profession by physicians who are years removed from the intensive pharmacological training they received in medical school and for whom the prescribing of drugs is but one facet of their practice." Chandler v. Koenig, 203 Ga. App. 684, 687, 417 S.E.2d 715 (1992) Similarly, in Riggins v. Wyatt, 215 Ga. App. 854, 452 S.E.2d 577 (1994), the court disallowed the testimony of professor of applied biomechanics from testifying that a physician deviated from the standard of care in using a biomechanical device to treat a patient's fracture, finding that a "person cannot be qualified as an expert in an area where he or she would not be lawfully qualified (by holding a valid state license) to perform the treatment which is the subject of the expert opinion." Riggins v. Wyatt, 215 Ga. App. 854, 855, 452 S.E.2d 577 (1994)

[10]Sandford v. Howard, 161 Ga. App. 495, 497–498, 288 S.E.2d 739, 741 (1982) (in finding that an orthopedist was competent to testify as to the standard of care applicable to a podiatrist, the court observed that "the barriers between schools of practice are not insurmountable in this state.").

plicable to medical doctors, provided that a sufficient showing of "overlap" in the methods of diagnosis and treatment between the two schools had been made.[11] Similarly, medical doctors were permitted to testify as to the standard of care applicable to podiatrists, provided that a sufficient showing of "overlap" in the methods of diagnosis and treatment existed between the two schools.[12] Indeed, nurses were permitted to testify as to the standard of care applicable to physicians upon a sufficient showing of "overlap" in the methods of performing a procedure.[13]

This "same profession" requirement places more definitive rules for determining the competency of an expert to testify on a particular subject matter than had existed previously under Georgia law. Globally, it codifies the general rule under common law that an expert must be a member of the same "professional school of practice" as the defendant in order to provide competent testimony as to the standard of care applicable to the defendant.[14] It acknowledges the essential similarity of practice be-

---

However, in Bethea v. Smith, 176 Ga. App. 467, 336 S.E.2d 295 (1985), the court emphasized that the holding in *Sandford* did not mean "that such 'barriers' are non-existent[,]" and found that a podiatrist was not qualified to testify as to the standard of care applicable to an orthopedic surgeon where there had been an insufficient showing that the methods of diagnosis and treatment for the condition at issue were the same for podiatrists and orthopedists. Bethea v. Smith, 176 Ga. App. 467, 468, 336 S.E.2d 295 (1985) The court observed that while it was possible for a podiatrist to gain familiarity with the standard of care employed by orthopedists, mere familiarity alone does not qualify one as an expert. Bethea v. Smith, 176 Ga. App. 467, 469, 336 S.E.2d 295 (1985)

[11]Hicks v. Mauldin, 190 Ga. App. 660, 379 S.E.2d 806 (1989) (osteopath found qualified to testify against an allopath, or medical doctor); cf Milligan v. Manno, 197 Ga. App. 171, 397 S.E.2d 713 (1990) (osteopath found not qualified to testify against medical doctor where no showing that methods of treating plaintiff's condition were the same among the different schools of medicine).

[12]Bennett v. Butlin, 236 Ga. App. 691, 512 S.E.2d 13 (1999) (orthopedist found qualified to testify as to standard of care applicable to podiatrist); cf. Hewett v. Kalish, 210 Ga. App. 584, 436 S.E.2d 710 (1993), rev'd on other grounds, 264 Ga. 183, 442 S.E.2d 233 (1994) (medical doctor not permitted to testify as to standard of care applicable to podiatrist where lack of evidence that methods of treatment for patient's condition were the same).

[13]Avret v. McCormick, 246 Ga. 401, 271 S.E.2d 832 (1980) (nurse competent to testify that physician negligently failed to keep needle sterilized); Nowak v. High, 209 Ga. App. 536, 433 S.E.2d 602 (1993) (nurse competent to testify that physician negligently administered injection).

[14]See, e.g. Sandford v. Howard, 161 Ga. App. 495, 497, 288 S.E.2d 739, 740 (1982) ("The general rule is that a member of a school of practice other than that to which the defendant belongs is not competent to testify as an expert in a malpractice case."); Hewett v. Kalish, 210 Ga. App. 584, 586, 436 S.E.2d 710, 712–713 (1993), rev'd on other grounds, 264 Ga. 183, 442 S.E.2d 233 (1994) (" 'In order for an affiant to be an 'expert competent

tween doctors of osteopathy and doctors of medicine,[15] and dispenses with the need of showing that the methods of diagnosing and treating a particular condition are the same for the two schools of medicine.[16] The statute abolishes the narrow exception in which nurses, upon a showing that a medical procedure falls within the competency of a nurse to perform, have been found qualified to testify as to the standard of care applicable to a physician in performing that same procedure.[17] Finally, the statute delineates the circumstances under which a physician may be found competent to testify as to the standard of care applicable to various "medical support staff."[18]

§ 9:6 Qualifications—Table

Requirements for Expert Witness Qualification Under O.C.G.A. § 24–9–67.1

	All Civil Cases	Professional Malpractice	Medical Malpractice
Compliance with FRE 702 and *Daubert*	✓	✓	✓
Licensure in the witness's profession at the time of the alleged act/omission		✓	✓
Active practice or teaching for at least three of the previous five years			✓
Membership in the same profession as the person whose conduct is at issue			✓

to testify,' the expert must be a member of the same professional school as the defendant or, if from a different professional school, must state the particulars how the methods of treatment are the same for the different schools in order to establish that the affiant possesses the expertise to be able to give an opinion regarding the applicable standard of care to which the defendant is held.' ").

[15]Hicks v. Mauldin, 190 Ga. App. 660, 379 S.E.2d 806 (1989) (osteopathic doctor qualified to testify as to standard of care of medical doctor).

[16]See, e.g. Milligan v. Manno, 197 Ga. App. 171, 397 S.E.2d 713 (1990).

[17]See, e.g. Avret v. McCormick, 246 Ga. 401, 271 S.E.2d 832 (1980); Nowak v. High, 209 Ga. App. 536, 433 S.E.2d 602 (1993).

[18]See, e.g. Goring v. Martinez, 224 Ga. App. 137, 479 S.E.2d 432 (1996) (orthopedist's mere familiarity with occupational and physical therapy did not qualify him to testify as to standard of care applicable to occupational therapist).

§ 9:7   Standard of care—Necessity of expert testimony

As a general rule, expert medical testimony is required to establish negligence in all cases alleging medical malpractice.[1] Such a requirement exists because the jury, lacking a medical care provider's specialized knowledge in matters of medicine, is not competent to ascertain the standards of conduct applicable to such providers, or whether a providers' conduct fell below such standards of conduct, absent expert testimony on this subject.[2]

> The court and jury must have a standard measure which they are to use in measuring the acts of a doctor to determine whether he exercised a reasonable degree of care and skill; they are not permitted to set up and use any arbitrary or artificial standard of measurement that the jury may wish to apply. The proper standard of measurement is to be established by testimony of physicians, for it is a medical question.[3]

Indeed, absent such testimony, any judgment against a defendant provider would be arbitrary and lacking foundation.[4] Where no expert testimony has been presented that an act or omission

---

[Section 9:7]

[1]Beach v. Lipham, 276 Ga. 302, 303–304, 578 S.E.2d 402, 405 (2003)) "[U]nder Georgia law, the presumption is that, in the absence of evidence to the contrary, medical services were performed in an ordinary, skillful manner. The proof required to rebut that presumption must come from expert medical witnesses."); Parker v. Knight, 245 Ga. 782, 782, 267 S.E.2d 222, 223 (1980); Bowling v. Foster, 254 Ga. App. 374, 562 S.E.2d 776 (2002); Ketchup v. Howard, 247 Ga. App. 54, 543 S.E.2d 371 (2000); Packer v. Gill, 193 Ga. App. 388, 388 S.E.2d 338 (1989); Crumbley v. Wyant, 188 Ga. App. 227, 229, 372 S.E.2d 497, 499 (1988); Killingsworth v. Poon, 167 Ga. App. 653, 654, 307 S.E.2d 123, 124 (1983); Phillips v. Cheek, 162 Ga. App. 728, 729, 293 S.E.2d 22, 23 (1982); Self v. Executive Committee of Georgia Baptist Convention of Georgia, Inc., 245 Ga. 548, 266 S.E.2d 168 (1980); Slack v. Moorhead, 152 Ga. App. 68, 262 S.E.2d 186 (1979); Shea v. Phillips, 213 Ga. 269, 271, 98 S.E.2d 552, 555 (1957).

[2]Savannah Valley Production Credit Ass'n v. Cheek, 248 Ga. 745, 747, 285 S.E.2d 689, 691 (1982); Kapsch v. Stowers, 209 Ga. App. 767, 767, 434 S.E.2d 539, 540 (1993); Wagner v. Timms, 158 Ga. App. 538, 539, 281 S.E.2d 295, 297 (1981); Wilson v. Kornegay, 108 Ga. App. 318, 320, 132 S.E.2d 791, 793 (1963).

[3]Killingsworth v. Poon, 167 Ga. App. 653, 655, 307 S.E.2d 123, 125 (1983) (citing Hayes v. Brown, 108 Ga. App. 360, 133 S.E.2d 102 (1963)); see also Austin v. Kaufman, 203 Ga. App. 704, 417 S.E.2d 660 (1992) (citing Horney v. Lawrence, 189 Ga. App. 376, 375 S.E.2d 629 (1988) ("In a medical malpractice case, the general rule is that medical testimony must be introduced to inform the jurors what is a proper method of treating a particular case. The jury must have a standard measure which they are to use in measuring the acts of the doctor in determining whether he exercised a reasonable degree of care and skill.") (internal quotations and punctuation omitted).

[4]Killingsworth v. Poon, 167 Ga. App. 653, 655, 307 S.E.2d 123, 125 (1983); Wagner v. Timms, 158 Ga. App. 538, 539, 281 S.E.2d 295, 297 (1981); see also Wilson v. Kornegay, 108 Ga. App. 318, 320, 132 S.E.2d 791, 793 (1963) ("More than twenty-three

on the part of a health care provider fell below the applicable standard of care, there is no issue of fact to present to the jury for its determination.[5]

§ 9:8 Standard of care—Necessity of expert testimony— Cases not involving the exercise of professional judgment

Of course, the mere fact that an injury occurs in a medical or hospital setting does not necessarily convert an action to recover for that injury a "medical malpractice" action for which expert testimony is required.[1] For instance, a patient's action against a hospital for injuries arising out of the patient's slipping on a puddle of water on a bathroom floor caused by a leaking faucet is not an action sounding in "medical malpractice."[2] Similarly, the mere fact that a suit calls into question the conduct of one who happens to be a medical professional does not necessarily make the action one for "medical malpractice" for which expert testimony is required to establish the professional's negligence.[3] Rather, the determinative issue as to whether expert testimony is required to establish a medical professional's negligence is whether the action calls into question the conduct of the medical professional in his or her area of expertise.[4]

By way of example, expert testimony is not required to establish a medical professional's negligence when a hospital employee drops a patient during transport[5] or during a medical procedure.[6] Similarly, a hospital employee's failure to use instrumentation in

---

hundred years ago Aristotle, in his work on Politics, wrote: 'As the physician ought to be judged by the physician, so ought men to be judged by their peers.' And for centuries the courts of this and other countries have, almost without exception, held that expert medical evidence is required to establish negligence respecting the service a physician or surgeon renders his patient.").

[5]Shea v. Phillips, 213 Ga. 269, 271, 98 S.E.2d 552, 555 (1957).

[Section 9:8]

[1]Jones v. Bates, 261 Ga. 240, 242, 403 S.E.2d 804, 806 (1991).

[2]Self v. Executive Committee of Georgia Baptist Convention of Georgia, Inc., 245 Ga. 548, 266 S.E.2d 168 (1980).

[3]Dent v. Memorial Hosp. of Adel, 270 Ga. 316, 318, 509 S.E.2d 908, 910 (1998); Jones v. Bates, 261 Ga. 240, 403 S.E.2d 804, 806 (1991).

[4]Jones v. Bates, 261 Ga. 240, 403 S.E.2d 804, 806 (1991); Chafin v. Wesley Homes, Inc., 186 Ga. App. 403, 403, 367 S.E.2d 236, 237 (1988); Candler General Hosp., Inc. v. McNorrill, 182 Ga. App. 107, 110, 354 S.E.2d 872, 876 (1987) ("If the alleged negligent act or omission of a hospital employee does not require the exercise of expert medical judgment, the fact that the employee also has expert medical credentials does not make the case one of 'medical malpractice.' ").

[5]Candler General Hosp., Inc. v. McNorrill, 182 Ga. App. 107, 110, 354 S.E.2d 872, 876 (1987) (nurse's misjudgment in assessing his ability to

accordance with manufacturer guidelines[7] or a physician's orders[8] is not a medical decision for which expert testimony is required to establish negligence. By contrast, the level of supervision a patient requires, when based upon a determination as to the patient's medical condition, is a matter involving medical judg-

---

support a patient's weight during transfer of patient to wheelchair, causing patient to fall and sustain injuries, was not a judgment requiring expert medical judgment); see also Strickland v. Hospital Authority of Albany/Dougherty County, 241 Ga. App. 1, 525 S.E.2d 724 (1999) (decision of hospital employees to transfer patient to wheelchair in certain matter, causing the patient injuries, was not a medical decision for which expert testimony was required to show negligence where patient's husband had successfully transferred patient on two previous occasions and decision to transfer patient in manner chosen was done not out of medical necessity, but "convenience").

[6]Lane v. Tift County Hosp. Authority, 228 Ga. App. 554, 492 S.E.2d 317 (1997) (citing Johnson v. Wills Memorial Hosp. & Nursing Home, 178 Ga. App. 459, 343 S.E.2d 700 (1986) (in finding that no expert testimony was required to establish negligence of hospital employees who dropped patient during x-ray procedure, the court stated that " 'the protection of patients is not a medical function of a hospital; rather, it is a service provided by the hospital to its patients.' ").

[7]Lamb v. Candler General Hosp., Inc., 262 Ga. 70, 71, 413 S.E.2d 720, 721 (1992) ("It is well recognized that a hospital may be liable in ordinary negligence for furnishing defective equipment for use by physicians and surgeons in treating patients."). By way of comparison, in Jones v. Bates, 261 Ga. 240, 403 S.E.2d 804 (1991), at issue was whether a complaint should have been dismissed for failure to file the affidavit of an expert pursuant to O.C.G.A. § 9–11–9.1 where the alleged negligence was a physician's removal of a heat shield from a lamp, causing

burns to patient under anesthesia, in order to get more light for a procedure. The court found that it was error to dismiss the case for failure to file an expert affidavit averring professional negligence because the decision to obtain more light by way of removing the heat shield, in lieu of utilizing other sources of light for the procedure, did not necessarily state a claim involving medical judgment. Jones v. Bates, 261 Ga. 240, 242, 403 S.E.2d 804 (1991) However, the court did note that decision to obtain more light in the first instance very well may have been a decision involving medical judgment, for which the presentation of expert testimony might be required. Id.

[8]Dent v. Memorial Hosp. of Adel, 270 Ga. 316, 509 S.E.2d 908 (1998). In finding that the plaintiff's allegations that a nurse had failed to activate an alarm on apnea monitor as ordered by a physician and had failed to ensure a "crash cart" was equipped for pediatric patients sounded in ordinary, not professional, negligence, the court observed:

> Whether to use certain equipment at all, what type of equipment to use, and whether certain equipment should be available in a specific case certainly are decisions which normally require the evaluation of the medical condition of a particular patient and, therefore, the application of professional knowledge, skill, and experience. However, the failure to operate equipment correctly or in accordance with a doctor's instructions or to keep certain equipment on hand is only ordinary, not professional negligence. . . . An administrative act not involving professional knowledge, skill or experience is not required to be the subject of an expert opinion.

Dent v. Memorial Hosp. of Adel, 270 Ga. 316, 318, 509 S.E.2d 908 (1998)

ment for which expert testimony is required to establish negligence.[9] Thus, a medical professional's determination not to supervise a patient's bathing,[10] or a decision to use a certain form of transport over another,[11] requires the presentation of expert testimony to establish negligence where the determination is based on an assessment of the patient's medical condition.

Expert medical testimony is not required to establish the existence of the physician-patient relationship, as this is a matter invoking principles which are contractual, and not medical, in nature.[12] Similarly, a hospital's failure to supervise its own employees so as to safeguard patients from the risk of a criminal assault is not a matter invoking professional medical judgment so as to require expert medical testimony to establish negligence.[13]

§ 9:9   Standard of care—Necessity of expert testimony— "Pronounced results" and obvious medical negligence

An exception to the general rule that expert medical testimony is required to establish that a medical professional's conduct fell below the applicable standard is what has been referred to as cases of "pronounced results." Where the medical treatment "is so obviously negligent that jurors would recognize the negligence by reason of common knowledge and experience," expert medical testimony is not necessary to establish the medical professional's

---

[9]General Hospitals of Humana, Inc. v. Bentley, 184 Ga. App. 489, 361 S.E.2d 718 (1987) (where elderly patient slipped and fell while exiting hospital bath without assistance, expert testimony required to establish hospital's failure to supervise patient's bath or provide assistance, as the level of supervision patient required was based on physician's determination as to patient's medical condition and ability to care for herself).

[10]See, e.g. Holloway v. Northside Hosp., 230 Ga. App. 371, 496 S.E.2d 510 (1998) (where patient fell at hospital, alleged negligence of hospital nurses in failing to exercise proper care to prevent patient from falling called into question nurses' professional judgment in assessing degree of support patient required); Bulloch County Hosp. Authority v. Parker, 196 Ga. App. 438, 439, 396 S.E.2d 37, 38 (1990) ("Expert testimony would be required to establish whether permit-

ting plaintiff to shower without continuous assistance was negligence.").

[11]Sparks v. Southwest Community Hosp. & Medical Center, Inc., 195 Ga. App. 858, 395 S.E.2d 68 (1990) (Hospital employee's decision to transport patient by one type of wheelchair over another required assessment of patient's medical condition, and hence, expert testimony was required to establish negligence).

[12]Minster v. Pohl, 206 Ga. App. 617, 619, 426 S.E.2d 204, 206 (1992) (expert's opinion that no physician-patient relationship existed was "no more than a non-medical opinion from a witness who happened to be a physician[,]" and opinion "was neither probative nor admissible as expert medical testimony.").

[13]Bunn-Penn v. Southern Regional Medical Corp., 227 Ga. App. 291, 488 S.E.2d 747 (1997).

negligence.[1] This exception was first addressed by the Georgia Supreme Court in *Shea v. Phillips*,[2] wherein the Court stated:

> Where the result of the medical treatment is so pronounced as to become apparent, as where a leg or limb which has been broken is shorter than the other after such treatment, or where a doctor undertakes to stitch a wound on his patient's cheek, and, by an awkward move, thrusts his needle in the patient's eye, this fact may be testified to by anyone competent to testify[.][3]

The exception has been applied in a case where, following a subcutaneous injection given for the relief of muscular pain, the patient suffered a punctured lung, for the stated reason that it "is widely known and generally understood by laymen that subcutaneous injections ostensibly given only for the relief of muscular pain should not, if administered correctly, result in the puncture of internal organs."[4] It has also been applied in a case where a patient suffered debilitating back pain not previously present after being left unattended by chiropractor for fifteen minutes while strapped to a machine designed to stretch the patient's spinal column.[5]

It has been observed, however, that this is a "very narrow" exception to the general requirement of expert testimony,[6] and that application of this exception is "exceedingly rare."[7] The exception was found inapplicable in a case where a patient's leg ultimately required amputation due to a catheter breaking off, and eventually lodging, inside the patient's arterial system during surgery.[8] Similarly, expert testimony has been held to be required to establish professional negligence in cases where an artery is unintentionally punctured during surgery,[9] or where a post-operative infection develops at the site of the surgery.[10] The rationale underlying these cases is that, as a general matter,

---

[Section 9:9]

[1]Johnson v. Jones, 178 Ga. App. 346, 350, 343 S.E.2d 403, 407 (1986); Landers v. Georgia Baptist Medical Center, 175 Ga. App. 500, 501–502, 333 S.E.2d 884, 887 (1985).

[2]Shea v. Phillips, 213 Ga. 269, 98 S.E.2d 552 (1957).

[3]Shea v. Phillips, 213 Ga. 269, 271–272, 98 S.E.2d 552, 555 (1957).

[4]Killingsworth v. Poon, 167 Ga. App. 653, 656, 307 S.E.2d 123, 126 (1983) (further stating that one "does not need scientific knowledge or training to understand that, ordinarily speaking, such results are unnecessary, and are not to be anticipated if reasonable care can be exercised by the operator.").

[5]Caldwell v. Knight, 92 Ga. App. 747, 89 S.E.2d 900 (1955).

[6]Cherokee County Hosp. Authority v. Beaver, 179 Ga. App. 200, 201, 345 S.E.2d 904, 905 (1986).

[7]Killingsworth v. Poon, 167 Ga. App. 653, 656, 307 S.E.2d 123, 126 (1983).

[8]Shea v. Phillips, 213 Ga. 269, 98 S.E.2d 552 (1957).

[9]Morrison v. Koornick, 201 Ga. App. 367, 411 S.E.2d 105 (1991).

[10]Landers v. Georgia Baptist Medical Center, 175 Ga. App. 500, 333 S.E.2d 884 (1985); see also Johnson v.

what the applicable standard of care is and whether the medical provider complied with that standard are not matters within the understanding of the average layperson.[11]

§ 9:10 Standard of care—Necessity of expert testimony— "Informed consent" cases

The role of expert testimony in cases addressing a medical professional's liability for an "unauthorized touching" of a patient is unclear due to the somewhat unique history of Georgia's "informed consent" doctrine.[1] "The doctrine of informed consent requires doctors to disclose enough information regarding a proposed medical treatment in order for patients to make fully informed decisions about whether to undergo the proposed treatment."[2] Prior to 1988, however, Georgia law did not impose this duty upon physicians, and only required that a doctor "disclose in general terms the treatment or course of treatment in connection with which the consent is given."[3] In 1988, the legislature enacted O.C.G.A. § 31–9–6.1, a limited adoption of the informed consent doctrine. This statute requires that, for only certain specified types of procedures,[4] a patient be given the following specified information: 1) the condition requiring the proposed treatment; 2) the nature and purpose of the proposed treatment; 3) the likelihood of the treatment's success; 4) practical alternatives to the

Jones, 178 Ga. App. 346, 343 S.E.2d 403 (1986) (physician's treatment of patient's psychiatric disorder, insect bites, ear problems, and head cold not matters which a jury can ascertain negligence by virtue of common knowledge, and expert medical testimony required to establish negligence); Cherokee County Hosp. Authority v. Beaver, 179 Ga. App. 200, 345 S.E.2d 904 (1986) (where plaintiff suffered weakness in leg following injection, expert testimony required to establish negligence in administration of injection); Dobbs v. Cobb E.N.T. Associates, P.C., 165 Ga. App. 238, 299 S.E.2d 141 (1983) (where plaintiff suffered partial blindness following surgery on fractured nose, "pronounced results" exception did not apply and expert testimony required to establish negligence).

[11]See, e.g. Shea v. Phillips, 213 Ga. 269, 271, 98 S.E.2d 552, 555 (1957); Killingsworth v. Poon, 167 Ga. App. 653, 655, 307 S.E.2d 123, 125 (1983).

[Section 9:10]

[1]For a discussion of this history, see J. Harold Richards, Informed Confusion: The Doctrine of Informed Consent in Georgia, 37 Ga. L.Rev. 1129 (2003).

[2]J. Harold Richards, Informed Confusion: The Doctrine of Informed Consent in Georgia, 37 Ga. L.Rev. 1129, 1135 (2003).

[3]O.C.G.A. § 31–9–6; Young v. Yarn, 136 Ga. App. 737, 222 S.E.2d 113 (1975) (overruled by, Ketchup v. Howard, 247 Ga. App. 54, 543 S.E.2d 371 (2000)).

[4]These procedures include: 1) a surgical procedure under general anesthesia, spinal anesthesia, or major regional anesthesia; 2) an amniocentesis diagnostic procedure; and 3) a diagnostic procedure involving the intravenous or intraductal injection of contrast materials. O.C.G.A. § 31–9–6.1(a).

propose treatment; and 5) the prognosis if the treatment is rejected.[5] Moreover, for such procedures, a patient must be informed of the "material risks" of the treatment which, "if disclosed to a reasonably prudent person in the patient's position, could reasonably be expected to cause such prudent person to decline such proposed surgical or diagnostic procedure[.]"[6] The statute goes on to provide that the failure to comply with the requirements of the Code section "shall not constitute a separate cause of action but may give rise to an action for medical malpractice[,]" and an expert affidavit as required by O.C.G.A. § 9–11–9.1 shall be filed with a complaint alleging "negligence" for failure to comply with the requirements of the Code section.[7]

In 2000, the Georgia Supreme Court in *Albany Urology Clinic v. Cleveland*, considered the scope of the informed consent doctrine in light of O.C.G.A. § 31–9–6.1, holding that because the statute was in derogation of common law, it must be strictly construed so as to require disclosure of only the information set forth in the statute and only for those procedures specifically identified in the statute.[8] However, a few months later, a divided Court of Appeals in *Ketchup v. Howard* overruled the common law principle that the material risks of a procedure need not be disclosed to the patient, and held that O.C.G.A. § 31–9–6.1 had no "limiting effect" on the court's adoption of a new common law

---

[5]O.C.G.A. § 31–9–6.1(a).

[6]O.C.G.A. § 31–9–6.1(a)(3).

[7]O.C.G.A. § 31–9–6.1(d). A written consent disclosing in general terms the information set forth in subsection (a) is "rebuttably presumed" to be a valid consent, whereas a consent not reduced to writing receives no such presumption. O.C.G.A. § 31–9–6.1(b) Subsection (c) of the statute imposes the duty to obtain the consent upon the physician. O.C.G.A. § 31–9–6.1(c). Disclosure of the information set forth in subsection (a) is not required where: 1) an emergency exists; 2) the treatment is "generally recognized by reasonably prudent physicians" as not involving a "material risk"; 3) the patient or other person authorized to consent on the patient's behalf makes a written request that the information not be disclosed; 4) a prior consent disclosing the information set forth in subsection (a) was previously given within 30 days of the procedure; or 5) the treatment was unforeseen at the time the consent was obtained, and

the patient has consented to allow the responsible physician to make decisions concerning such treatment. O.C.G.A. § 31–9–6.1(e).

[8]Albany Urology Clinic, P.C. v. Cleveland, 272 Ga. 296, 298-299, 528 S.E.2d 777, 779-780 (2000).

(The Court held that § 31–9–6.1 set forth six specified categories of information that must be disclosed by medical care providers to their patients before they undergo certain specified surgical or diagnostic procedures and the Georgia informed consent statute did not impose a general requirement of disclosure upon physicians; rather, it required physicians to disclose only those factors listed in O.C.G.A. § 31–9–6.1.

The Court further held that because O.C.G.A. § 31–9–6.1 was in derogation of the common law rule against requiring physicians to disclose medical risks to their patients, it must be strictly construed and could not be extended beyond its plain an explicit terms.)

Id.

informed consent doctrine.[9] In setting forth a new common law principle applicable in cases not falling within the ambit of O.C.G.A. § 31–9–6.1, the court adopted a "lay standard," as contrasted to a "professional standard,"[10] as to when a physician has a duty to disclose risks inherent in a proposed treatment.[11] In discussing the role of expert testimony in proving this lay standard for disclosure, the court stated:

> [T]he physician's disclosure duty is measured by the patient's need for information rather than by the standards of the medical profession. While expert testimony would be required to establish that the risk which allegedly caused the injury is one which is known or should be known, the lay standard would not ordinarily require expert testimony regarding medical standards to establish the physician's duty to disclose; rather, it is for the jury to determine whether a reasonable person in the patient's position would have considered the risk significant in making the decision to have or reject the proposed treatment.[12]

The court also adopted this same standard for the need for expert testimony with respect to procedures falling within the ambit of O.C.G.A. § 31–9–6.1.[13]

Adding a layer of complexity to the law in this regard, courts have distinguished between two types of consent in the context of the provision of medical care: 1) "basic" consent and 2) "informed" consent. "Basic" consent is "that consent which avoids a battery,"[14] and "a medical 'touching' without consent is like any other touching without consent: it constitutes the intentional tort of

---

[9]Ketchup v. Howard, 247 Ga. App. 54, 61–62, 543 S.E.2d 371, 377–378 (2000). Two special concurrences, while concurring in the result reached in the case before the court, criticized the majority's opinion as contrary to the Supreme Court's statement in *Cleveland* that there is no common law duty to disclose the material risks of a procedure, and as contrary to the legislature's expression that such a duty arises only in those limited circumstances delineated by O.C.G.A. § 31–9–6.1. Ketchup v. Howard, 247 Ga. App. 54, 74-75, 543 S.E.2d 371 (2000) (J. Andrews, concurring), and 75–77 (J. Ruffin, concurring).

[10]Ketchup v. Howard, 247 Ga. App. 54, 62, 543 S.E.2d 371, 378 (2000). Under the "professional standard," which the court recognized is the standard employed by the slight

majority of states, the physician is required to disclose those risks which a reasonably prudent physician would disclose under similar circumstances. Ketchup v. Howard, 247 Ga. App. 54, 62, 543 S.E.2d 371 (2000) In most cases, the court observed, expert medical testimony is required to establish whether and to what extent a physician has a duty to disclose. *Id.*

[11]Ketchup v. Howard, 247 Ga. App. 54, 62, 543 S.E.2d 371, 378 (2000).

[12]Ketchup v. Howard, 247 Ga. App. 54, 62, 543 S.E.2d 371, 378 (2000).

[13]Ketchup v. Howard, 247 Ga. App. 54, 63, 543 S.E.2d 371, 378 (2000).

[14]Ketchup v. Howard, 247 Ga. App. 54, 55–56, 543 S.E.2d 371, 374 (2000); Pope v. Davis, 261 Ga. App.

battery for which any action will lie."[15] "Informed" consent, by contrast, "involves a medical professional fully informing a patient of the risks and alternatives to the proposed treatment so that the patient's right to decide is not diminished by lack of relevant information."[16] Presumably, in cases in which the issue is the lack of "basic" consent, no expert testimony would be required to establish that the medical professional's conduct amounted to the intentional tort of battery.[17] However, this matter is not so clear, and it has been held that whether the provision of medical treatment without a patient's "basic" consent requires expert medical testimony to prove a deviation from the standard of care hinges upon the determination as to whether the professional's conduct entailed the exercise of professional judgment.[18]

Perhaps notably, decisions after 2000 have either failed to reference the principles enunciated in *Ketchup*,[19] or have declined to apply *Ketchup*, holding that its application is prospective only,

---

308, 309, 582 S.E.2d 460, 461 (2003).

[15]Ketchup v. Howard, 247 Ga. App. 54, 55–56, 543 S.E.2d 371, 374 (2000); see also Harris v. Leader, 231 Ga. App. 709, 710, 499 S.E.2d 374, 376 (1998).

[16]Ketchup v. Howard, 247 Ga. App. 54, 56, 543 S.E.2d 371, 374 (2000); Pope v. Davis, 261 Ga. App. 308, 309, 582 S.E.2d 460, 461–462 (2003).

[17]See, e.g. Bowling v. Foster, 254 Ga. App. 374, 562 S.E.2d 776 (2002) (observing that patient had a right to pursue battery claim independent of medical malpractice claim, but claim for battery nonetheless waived where patient signed consent form to procedure at issue); MCG Health, Inc. v. Casey, 269 Ga. App. 125, 127–128, 603 S.E.2d 438, 441 (2004) ("Claims based on ordinary negligence or an intentional tort such as battery fall outside the [expert affidavit] requirements of O.C.G.A. § 9–11–91."); Williams v. Knight, 211 Ga. App. 420, 420, 439 S.E.2d 507, 508 (1993) ("failure to avoid consequences by the exercise of ordinary care" not a valid defense to battery claim).

[18]King v. Dodge County Hosp. Authority, 274 Ga. App. 44, 616 S.E.2d 835 (2005). In *King*, at issue was whether an expert affidavit as required

by O.C.G.A. § 9–11–9.1 was needed to support a complaint for battery arising out of a nurse's repeated attempts to administer an intravenous antibiotic despite the patient's insistence that the nurse desist. Observing that whether expert testimony was required to support the patient's claim of battery was an "extremely close" issue, the court found that expert testimony was required, observing:

[T]he issue is whether in making that decision, she was required to weigh alternatives and to apply her specialized knowledge and skill. While she may have known that King fervently wanted her to stop, she still had orders from King's physician requiring intravenous administration of the antibiotics. She had to assess her capability of accomplishing what the doctor ordered in light of her difficulty in finding a vein in *King's* arm. She was required to decide whether King's illness absolutely required this mode of treatment or whether it could be safely abandoned. These questions all required professional decision-making . . . . Lacking medical expertise, the factfinder could not resolve this issue without the assistance of expert medical opinion[.]

King v. Dodge County Hosp. Authority, 274 Ga. App. 44, 47, 616 S.E.2d 835 (2005)

[19]See, e.g. Bowling v. Foster, 254 Ga. App. 374, 562 S.E.2d 776 (2002);

and the conduct at issue occurred prior to the *Ketchup* decision.[20] It appears that, where O.C.G.A. § 31–9–6.1 is applicable, a physician's failure to make the disclosures required does not create a cause of action, i.e., battery, independent of one for medical malpractice, and expert testimony is required to establish the duty owed by the physician to the patient.[21] However, a claim that a physician has fraudulently failed to make the disclosures required of O.C.G.A. § 31–9–6.1 does not constitute a "medical malpractice" action for which expert testimony must be used to support.[22] Moreover, "where a physician knowingly misrepresents a patient's condition or the proper treatment, or fails to truthfully respond to a patient's queries about a diagnosis or treatment, or performs procedures outside the scope of consent, a patient's consent may be vitiated, and the physician may be liable for having committed a battery."[23]

§ 9:11 Defining the applicable standard of care

The standard of conduct, or "standard of care," is defined as "that which, under similar conditions and like circumstances, is ordinarily employed by the medical profession generally."[1] By contrast, the standard is not defined by what an expert or individual doctor "thought advisable and would have done under the circumstances."[2] Accordingly, questions seeking to determine how an expert witness would have acted are properly excluded as ir-

Bethea v. Coralli, 248 Ga. App. 853, 546 S.E.2d 542 (2001) (citing *Albany,* but not *Ketchup,* for prevailing state of law).

[20]See, e.g. Murphy v. Berger, 273 Ga. App. 798, 616 S.E.2d 132 (2005); Pope v. Davis, 261 Ga. App. 308, 582 S.E.2d 460 (2003).

[21]Bowling v. Foster, 254 Ga. App. 374, 562 S.E.2d 776 (2002) (alleged failure to advise patient of steroid injections in lieu of surgery performed); Bethea v. Coralli, 248 Ga. App. 853, 546 S.E.2d 542 (2001) (alleged failure to advise patient of less invasive procedure than catheterization given).

[22]Bowling v. Foster, 254 Ga. App. 374, 381, 562 S.E.2d 776, 782 (2002) (no expert testimony required to establish alleged fraud in a physician's failure to disclose, as such "claims do

not require proof of a professional standard of care.").

[23]Albany Urology Clinic, P.C. v. Cleveland, 272 Ga. 296, 301, 528 S.E.2d 777, 781 (2000); see also Blackwell v. Goodwin, 236 Ga. App. 861, 513 S.E.2d 542 (1999).

[Section 9:11]

[1]Johnson v. Riverdale Anesthesia Associates, P.C., 275 Ga. 240, 241–242, 563 S.E.2d 431, 433 (2002); Kenney v. Piedmont Hospital, 136 Ga. App. 660, 664, 222 S.E.2d 162 (1975).

[2]Johnson v. Riverdale Anesthesia Associates, P.C., 275 Ga. 240, 241–242, 563 S.E.2d 431, 433 (2002); McNabb v. Landis, 223 Ga. App. 894, 896, 479 S.E.2d 194, 196 (1996); Slack v. Moorhead, 152 Ga. App. 68, 71, 262 S.E.2d 186, 188 (1979); Mayo v. McClung, 83 Ga. App. 548, 556, 64 S.E.2d 330, 335 (1951).

relevant.[3] Thus, an expert's testimony as to how he or she would have elected to treat a patient, without a showing of what the standard applicable to medical community in general required under the circumstances, is insufficient to establish that the treatment provided fell below the standard of care.[4] This distinction is premised on the sound principle that physicians, in the exercise of their medical judgment, can choose different courses of treatment for a patient, and this fact does not necessarily mean that one approach fell below the standard of care. As stated by the Supreme Court:

> When confronted with the same or similar situation, different physicians will, quite naturally, often elect to administer differing treatments, and will exercise their judgments regarding a patient's care differently. However, merely because these procedures and treatments differ, it does not automatically follow that one of them fails to comply with the applicable standard of care.[5]

Similarly, the applicable standard of care is measured by the medical profession generally, as opposed to the medical profession of the particular locality in which the defendant practiced.[6] This rule represents a recognition that there is relatively equal access to information within the medical community, and that modern educational regimens and information accessibility do not justify the imposition of lower standards for those practicing in more remote, rural localities than for those practicing in larger urban areas.[7] Hence, an expert need not be familiar with standards of the particular community in which the defendant prac-

---

[3]Johnson v. Riverdale Anesthesia Associates, P.C., 275 Ga. 240, 242, 563 S.E.2d 431, 433 (2002); McNabb v. Landis, 223 Ga. App. 894, 896, 479 S.E.2d 194, 196 (1996).

[4]Bowling v. Foster, 254 Ga. App. 374, 377, 562 S.E.2d 776, 779–780 (2002); Wagner v. Timms, 158 Ga. App. 538, 539, 281 S.E.2d 295, 296 (1981); Slack v. Moorhead, 152 Ga. App. 68, 71, 262 S.E.2d 186, 188 (1979).

[5]Johnson v. Riverdale Anesthesia Associates, P.C., 275 Ga. 240, 242–243, 563 S.E.2d 431, 433 (2002); see also Brannen v. Prince, 204 Ga. App. 866, 421 S.E.2d 76 (1992) (overruled on other grounds by, Gillis v. City of Waycross, 247 Ga. App. 119, 543 S.E.2d 423 (2000)).

[6]Candler General Hosp., Inc. v. McNorrill, 182 Ga. App. 107, 354 S.E.2d

872 (1987); Hodges v. Effingham County Hosp. Authority, 182 Ga. App. 173, 355 S.E.2d 104 (1987); Richmond County Hosp. Authority Operating University Hosp. v. Dickerson, 182 Ga. App. 601, 356 S.E.2d 548 (1987); Candler General Hosp. v. Joiner, 180 Ga. App. 455, 349 S.E.2d 756 (1986).

[7]Ross v. Chatham County Hosp. Authority, 200 Ga. App. 448, 408 S.E.2d 490 (1991); Murphy v. Little, 112 Ga. App. 517, 522, 145 S.E.2d 760, 764 (1965) ("Reasons for [imposing the 'locality rule'] which might have obtained in times past, where transportation was difficult, medical schools and hospitals often inaccessible, and doctors licensed to practice with little or no formal training, no longer have any validity. Medical practitioners frequently receive a part or all of their education in States other than the one in which they settle to practice[.]"). In

tices in order to provide competent testimony as to the standards applicable to the defendant.[8] An expert's opinion testimony which applies local standards in lieu of general standards is not probative and inadmissible.[9]

By contrast, where at issue is not the professional judgment of a medical care provider, but rather, the sufficiency of the facilities and services furnished by a hospital, the standard of care is "localized," and measured by reference to those facilities and services furnished by other hospitals in the area.[10] The rationale for this "locality rule" is based on a recognition that the facilities and

---

Wade v. John D. Archbold Memorial Hosp., 252 Ga. 118, 311 S.E.2d 836 (1984), the Georgia Supreme Court, in finding that a physical therapist should be judged by standards applicable generally, as opposed to locally, observed:

[W]e find that the "locality rule" should not be applied to physical therapists employed by a hospital, for, although the ability of a small rural hospital to provide certain facilities and services is unquestionably limited by its location and resources, the judgment of a hospital's physical therapist is not so limited. Any person now desiring to become a physical therapist in this state must meet certain requirements to receive a license to practice their profession. . . . One of these requirements is that the applicant must be 'a graduate of an educational program that prepares physical therapists and which is accredited by a recognized accrediting agency and approved by the board [State Board of Physical Therapy]. . . . Thus, since hospitals across the state must employ physical therapists who have received essentially the same level of training, given the same or similar circumstances (i.e. given the same facilities, working conditions, etc.) the judgment of a physical therapist should not vary depending upon the location of his or her hospital.

Wade v. John D. Archbold Memorial Hosp., 252 Ga. 118, 119, 311 S.E.2d 836 (1984)

[8]Murphy v. Little, 112 Ga. App. 517, 522, 145 S.E.2d 760, 764 (1965) (fact that expert physician never practiced in Valdosta, Georgia and was unfamiliar with particular standards of

medical community in Valdosta did not preclude expert from opining that defendant's conduct fell below standard of care where expert was familiar with standards applicable to the medical community in general).

[9]Landers v. Georgia Baptist Medical Center, 175 Ga. App. 500, 333 S.E.2d 884 (1985) (expert affidavit which stated that physician failed to comply with standard of care employed in Fulton County, Georgia insufficient); Wagner v. Timms, 158 Ga. App. 538, 539, 281 S.E.2d 295, 296–297 (1981) (expert's testimony that surgeon in "sophisticated medical community" should not have attempted to treat patient in manner as surgeon had "was of no evidentiary value as it was obviously predicated on the standard of care and skill exercised by the profession locally rather than the profession generally."); cf. McDaniel v. Hendrix, 260 Ga. 857, 401 S.E.2d 260 (1991) (expert affidavit which stated that defendant deviated from standard of care in *Atlanta,* Georgia, as well as the "acceptable" standard of care, not defective).

[10]Candler Gen. Hosp., Inc. v. McNorrill, 182 Ga. App. 108–109, 354 S.E.2d 872, 875 (1987) (" 'A hospital owes its patients only the duty of exercising ordinary care to furnish equipment and facilities reasonably suited to the uses intended and such as are in general use under the same, or similar, circumstances in the area.' "); Johnson v. Wills Memorial Hosp. & Nursing Home, 178 Ga. App. 459, 343 S.E.2d 700 (1986).

services capable of being provided by a hospital are limited by re-sources and location,[11] and the facilities and services available in a small, rural hospital should not be measured by those available in a larger, urban hospital.[12] Accordingly, expert testimony pertaining to a hospital's failure to provide adequate equipment and facilities has been excluded where the expert was not famil-iar with working in a hospital the size of the defendant hospital, or working in a community of the size in which the defendant hospital was located.[13]

§ 9:12   Standard of care—Sufficiency of expert testimony

Courts have rejected an overly-formalistic approach in assess-ing the adequacy of an expert's testimony addressing whether there has been a deviation from the applicable standard of care. An expert need not recite "magic words" to the effect that a health care provider's conduct fell below the standard of care provided it is clear from the substance of the expert's testimony that this is the opinion held by the expert.[1] "Magic words alone, no matter how often repeated, do not make a fact. Rather the facts in the record must be sufficient to meet the legal standard embodied in the magic words."[2]

Similarly, an expert's mere incantation of "magic words" to the effect that a physician's conduct fell below the "standard of care"

---

[11]Wade v. John D. Archbold Memorial Hosp., 252 Ga. 118, 119, 311 S.E.2d 836, 837 (1984).

[12]Candler Gen. Hosp., Inc. v. McNorrill, 182 Ga. App. 109, 354 S.E.2d 872, 875 (1987).

[13]Smith v. Hospital Authority of Terrell County, 161 Ga. App. 657, 288 S.E.2d 715 (1982); cf. Gusky v. Candler General Hosp., Inc., 192 Ga. App. 521, 385 S.E.2d 698 (1989) (where com-plaint alleged that hospital failed to notify referring physician that its CAT scan machine was inoperable, result-ing in a delay of the diagnosis of pa-tient's condition, plaintiff's complaint did not call into question the hospital's lack of resources, but rather, the judg-ment of those charged with the sched-uling of patients for the CAT scan in failing to advise physician of machines unavailability so that alternate ar-

rangements could be made).

[Section 9:12]

[1]Tysinger v. Smisson, 176 Ga. App. 604, 605, 337 S.E.2d 49, 51 (1985) ("The failure of a medical expert to use 'magic words' in accusing a colleague of negligence in a medical malpractice case will not deprive his opinion of all efficacy where it is clear that the wit-ness is of the opinion that the col-league failed to exercise due care in treating the patient."); see also Sanders v. Ramo, 203 Ga. App. 43, 45, 416 S.E.2d 333, 335 (1992); Dent v. Memorial Hosp. of Adel, Inc., 200 Ga. App. 499, 503, 408 S.E.2d 473, 476 (1991); Hively v. Davis, 181 Ga. App. 733, 734, 353 S.E.2d 622, 624 (1987).

[2]Jackson v. Gershon, 251 Ga. 577, 579, 308 S.E.2d 164, 166–167 (1983).

is not in itself sufficient to establish negligence.[3] Such an opinion is little more than a legal conclusion devoid of any factual basis.[4] Rather, an expert must be able to provide the "particulars," including "an articulation of the minimum standard of acceptable professional conduct, and how and in what way [the physician] deviated therefrom."[5] In other words, expert testimony must set forth the "parameters" of acceptable professional conduct, as well as the specific facts providing the basis for the conclusion that the treatment fell below the standard of care.[6] Without a showing of what the standard of care required and in what way the defendant physician's conduct fell below this standard, an expert's testimony is insufficient to create an issue of fact for the jury's consideration.[7]

§9:13 Expert testimony on causation

As is the case with any action sounding in tort, mere proof of a medical provider's negligence is insufficient to sustain a recovery; rather, there must be proof that the medical negligence alleged

---

[3]Bushey v. Atlanta Emergency Group, 179 Ga. App. 827, 829, 348 S.E.2d 98, 100 (1986) ("[T]he problem is not the absence of 'magic words'; they are there, and that is all that is there. There are no facts to back them up. Plaintiff's experts looked at the evidence and simply drew legal conclusions.").

[4]Hillhaven Rehabilitation & Convalescent Center v. Patterson, 195 Ga. App. 70, 71, 392 S.E.2d 557, 558 (1990); Bushey v. Atlanta Emergency Group, 179 Ga. App. 827, 829, 348 S.E.2d 98, 101 (1986) ("To allow the conclusory affidavit here would completely avoid the necessity of counter evidence. Omitting any factual basis, or explicit comparison between what was done and what should have been done, or particulars describing in what manner medical standards were deviated from, a mere naked conclusion of violation would suffice. But meeting factual evidence with a bare conclusion does not create an issue of fact.").

[5]Loving v. Nash, 182 Ga. App. 253, 355 S.E.2d 448 (1987); see also Austin v. Kaufman, 203 Ga. App. 704, 705, 417 S.E.2d 660, 662 (1992); Horney v. Lawrence, 189 Ga. App. 376, 377, 375 S.E.2d 629, 630 (1988); Wagner v. Timms, 158 Ga. App. 538, 539, 281 S.E.2d 295, 297 (1981).

[6]Kirk v. Ashley, 199 Ga. App. 805, 807, 406 S.E.2d 82, 84 (1991); Connell v. Lane, 183 Ga. App. 871, 872, 360 S.E.2d 433, 434 (1987); see also Sparks v. Hoff, 186 Ga. App. 907, 908, 368 S.E.2d 830, 831 (1988) (citing Beauchamp v. Wallace, 180 Ga. App. 554, 555, 349 S.E.2d 791 (1986)) (in prosecuting medical malpractice claim, plaintiff must provide "medical testimony to inform the jury of the proper method for treating a case such as [the plaintiff's], i.e. what should have been done, and comparing that to what was actually done, so as to illustrate the professional malfeasance involved.").

[7]Chafin v. Wesley Homes, Inc., 186 Ga. App. 403, 404, 367 S.E.2d 236, 238 (1988); Minchey v. Zane, 188 Ga. App. 733, 734, 374 S.E.2d 225, 226 (1988); Majeed v. McBryar, 184 Ga. App. 807, 809, 363 S.E.2d 59, 61 (1987).

was the proximate cause of the patient's injuries.[1] Generally, whether a medical provider's negligence was in fact the cause of the patient's injuries is a "medical question" beyond the ability of the average lay person to ascertain on his or her own, and thus, expert medical testimony is required to establish this element of a plaintiff's claim.[2]

The role of the expert witness in a medical malpractice action is to provide the jury with a realistic assessment of the likelihood that a medical care provider's alleged negligence caused the patient's injuries.[3] In doing so, the expert must provide a basis for both the confidence with which the expert's conclusion is formed as well as the probability that the conclusion is accurate.[4] Expert testimony that merely establishes that there is a possibility that a medical provider's negligence resulted in injuries to the patient is insufficient;[5] rather, "the expert's testimony must show as an evidentiary threshold that the expert's opinion regarding causation is based, at the least, on the determination that 'there

---

[Section 9:13]

[1]Bowling v. Foster, 254 Ga. App. 374, 378, 562 S.E.2d 776, 780 (2002); Grantham v. Amin, 221 Ga. App. 458, 459, 471 S.E.2d 525, 527 (1996).

[2]Zwiren v. Thompson, 276 Ga. 498, 500, 578 S.E.2d 862, 865 (2003); Pilzer v. Jones, 242 Ga. App. 198, 201, 529 S.E.2d 205, 208–209 (2000).

[3]Zwiren v. Thompson, 276 Ga. 498, 500–501, 578 S.E.2d 862, 865 (2003); Jones v. Orris, 274 Ga. App. 52, 57, 616 S.E.2d 820, 824 (2005), cert. denied, (Oct. 24, 2005).

[4]Zwiren v. Thompson, 276 Ga. 498, 501, 578 S.E.2d 862, 865 (2003).

[5]Pilzer v. Jones, 242 Ga. App. 198, 201, 529 S.E.2d 205, 209 (2000) ("Testimony showing merely a possibility that the negligence caused the injury is not sufficient to establish the necessary causal connection."); Anthony v. Chambless, 231 Ga. App. 657, 659, 500 S.E.2d 402, 404 (1998) ("Although it is not necessary for the plaintiff's experts to use the magic words 'reasonable degree of medical certainty' in describing the decedent's prospect for survival with appropriate treatment, such prospect must be more than a mere chance or speculation."); Abdul–Majeed v. Emory University Hosp., 225 Ga. App. 608, 608, 484 S.E.2d 257, 258–259 (1997) (overruled on other grounds by, Ezor v. Thompson, 241 Ga. App. 275, 526 S.E.2d 609 (1999)) (expert testimony that "it would be more likely that there was a possibility" that patient's life would have been saved had physician provided adequate care insufficient to establish that the alleged negligence was a cause of the patient's death); Grantham v. Amin, 221 Ga. App. 458, 459, 471 S.E.2d 525, 527 (1996) ("Negligence alone is insufficient to sustain recovery for wrongful death in a medical malpractice action. It must be proven that the death of a patient proximately resulted from such want of care or skill. A bare possibility of such result is not sufficient."); R.J. Taylor Memorial Hosp., Inc. v. Gilbert, 213 Ga. App. 104, 106, 443 S.E.2d 656, 658 (1994), rev'd on other grounds, 265 Ga. 580, 458 S.E.2d 341 (1995); Maddox v. Houston County Hospital Authority, 158 Ga. App. 283, 284, 279 S.E.2d 732 (1981).

was a reasonable probability that the negligence caused the injury.' "[6]

Courts have been quick to note that a patient is undergoing treatment for a reason, and the fact that a course of treatment is not successful in effecting a cure does not raise a presumption that the unfortunate result was occasioned by negligence on the part of the health care provider.[7] Consequently, it is essential that expert testimony be able to reliably state how the allegedly negligent treatment—as distinct from the condition for which treatment has been sought, or any other preexisting medical condition—contributed to or caused the patient's unfavorable result.[8] "[T]here can be no recovery for medical negligence involving an injury to the patient where there is no showing to any reasonable degree of medical certainty that the injury could have

---

[6]Zwiren v. Thompson, 276 Ga. 498, 501, 578 S.E.2d 862, 865 (2003); Abdul–Majeed v. Emory University Hosp., 225 Ga. App. 608, 608, 484 S.E.2d 257, 258–259 (1997) (overruled on other grounds, Ezor v. Thompson, 241 Ga. App. 275, 526 S.E.2d 609 (1999)) ("Certainty is not required, but the plaintiff must show a probability rather than merely a possibility that the alleged negligence caused the injury or death.") (emphasis in original).

However, where other evidence, medical or non-medical in nature, establishes causation, expert testimony establishing only a possibility of a causal connection between the alleged negligence and the result may be sufficient. See Cannon v. Jeffries, 250 Ga. App. 371, 551 S.E.2d 777 (2001).

[7]Cherokee County Hosp. Authority v. Beaver, 179 Ga. App. 200, 202, 345 S.E.2d 904, 906 (1986); Bushey v. Atlanta Emergency Group, 179 Ga. App. 827, 828, 348 S.E.2d 98, 99–100 (1986); Sullivan v. Henry, 160 Ga. App. 791, 800, 287 S.E.2d 652, 659 (1982); Blount v. Moore, 159 Ga. App. 80, 81, 282 S.E.2d 720, 722 (1981).

[8]See, e.g. Pilzer v. Jones, 242 Ga. App. 198, 529 S.E.2d 205 (2000). In *Pilzer,* at issue was whether a physician's perforation of the patient's

bowel during a diagnostic procedure caused the patient to require a permanent colostomy, or whether this was a function of the patient's underlying bowel disease for which he was seeing the physician in the first place. In finding that the patient had failed to establish that any negligence on the part of the physician had caused the patient's need for a permanent colostomy, the court noted that expert testimony presented by the physician established to a reasonable degree of probability that the need for the permanent colostomy was due to the patient's underlying medical condition, and that the patient's expert had established only that there was a possibility that any negligence on the part of the physician was a cause of the patient's need for a permanent colostomy. Pilzer v. Jones, 242 Ga. App. 198, 201, 529 S.E.2d 205 (2000)

See also Parrott v. Chatham County Hospital Authority, 145 Ga. App. 113, 243 S.E.2d 269 (1978) (where physician was allegedly negligent in failing to timely diagnose and treat patient's fractured skull, resulting in a six day delay in treatment, directed verdict in favor of defendants proper where no medical evidence presented that patient's pain would have been any less during six day period had condition been timely diagnosed and treated).

been avoided."[9] Similarly, expert testimony that a provider was negligent in failing to timely diagnose a condition must also show how such a failure or delay in diagnosis worsened the patient's condition.[10] The temporal proximity of the treatment rendered by a health care provider and the injury complained of is not, standing alone, sufficient to establish a causal connection between any negligence on the part of the provider and the complained-of injury.[11]

A good example of the application of these principles may be

---

[9]Goggin v. Goldman, 209 Ga. App. 251, 253, 433, 433 S.E.2d 85 (1993) S.E.2d 85, 87 (1993).

[10]See, e.g. Cannon v. Jeffries, 250 Ga. App. 371, 551 S.E.2d 777 (2001). In *Jeffries,* a medical expert alleged by affidavit that a physician had been negligent in failing to test a mother for a chlamydia infection, and that this infection caused a premature rupture of membranes leading to the death of the infant. At deposition, the expert conceded that the premature labor could have been triggered by causes unrelated to the infection, and could not identify how much more likely it was that the infection, as opposed to the other potential causes, led to the premature membrane rupture. Under such circumstances, the court found that the expert's testimony was insufficient to establish causation. Cannon v. Jeffries, 250 Ga. App. 371, 372-373, 551 S.E.2d 777 (2001)

　　See also Jones v. Orris, 274 Ga. App. 52, 616 S.E.2d 820 (2005), cert. denied, (Oct. 24, 2005) (expert testimony that physician negligent in failing to timely diagnose appendicitis insufficient to support plaintiff's claim that post-surgical adhesions following appendectomy were causing fertility problems where testimony could not establish to what extent delay in diagnosis caused plaintiff's post-surgical adhesions); Dowling v. Lopez, 211 Ga. App. 578, 440 S.E.2d 205 (1993) (expert testimony that physician negligent in failing to timely diagnose cancer insufficient survive summary judgment where no proof that decedent did not have terminal cancer at time physician saw patient); Watson v.

U.S., 346 F.2d 52 (5th Cir. 1965) (in case decided under Georgia law, physician's failure to timely diagnose arteriosclerotic condition of patient's leg not actionable where no showing that loss of leg could have been avoided had timely diagnosis been made).

[11]See, e.g. Cherokee County Hosp. Authority v. Beaver, 179 Ga. App. 200, 345 S.E.2d 904 (1986). Following an injection of pain medicine, a patient experienced immediate pain radiating down her right leg, followed by a continued limpness in her right leg. In observing that the patient had not presented expert testimony establishing that the continued limpness was caused by the allegedly negligent administration of the injection, the court observed:

[T]here is no probative evidence whatsoever which would authorize a finding that Mrs. Beaver suffered a "result," pronounced or otherwise, attributable to her injection. The evidence is only that the injection was closely followed in time by the occurrence of pain and weakness in Mrs. Beaver's leg, which weakness continues. This evidence, standing alone, would not only be insufficient to authorize a finding that the injection was negligently administered, it would not even be sufficient to authorize an inference that the injection is a proximate cause of the weakness in Mrs. Beaver's leg. . . . Under the record before us, the unexplained weakness in Mrs. Beaver's leg is merely a physical symptom which may in fact be a manifestation of the pre-existing condition which forced her to seek emergency treatment in the first instance, rather than an indication of an unexpected result of the medical treatment that she received at the Hospital.

found in *Anthony v. Chambless*,[12] where at issue was whether any treatment a health care professional could have provided the patient would have changed the patient's outcome. There, a patient was evaluated by a physician at a local hospital following the patient's fall from a bridge onto the interstate. Due to lack of surgical capabilities at the hospital, the physician made the decision to transfer the patient to another hospital 40 minutes away for surgery, as opposed to a hospital which was located only 20 minutes away. Following the patient's arrival at this other hospital, the patient died of a ruptured thoracic aorta occasioned by his fall. Expert testimony was presented that the physician was negligent in sending the patient to the more remote hospital in lieu of the closer one, and that the patient would have had an 80% chance of survival had the ruptured aorta been repaired within one hour after the patient's fall. In finding such testimony too speculative to support the plaintiff's claim, the court observed that, even had the decision been made to transfer the patient to the nearby hospital, the evidence was such that the patient still would not have received treatment within the first hour of the rupture, and that life-saving treatment was factually impossible under the circumstances of the case.[13]

Where a health care provider's alleged negligence subjects a patient to unnecessary medical procedures, expert testimony must establish that, to a reasonable degree of medical probability, the additional medical procedures would have been unnecessary but for the alleged negligence. For instance, in *Bowling v. Foster*,[14] a physician was alleged to have negligently failed to employ more conservative modes of therapy prior to proceeding with surgery, thus subjecting the patient to unnecessary surgery. Such alleged negligence was not found to be actionable where there was no expert testimony establishing that the proposed conservative therapy would have been effective so as to obviate the need for surgery in the first instance.[15] Similarly, in *R.J. Taylor Memorial Hospital v. Gilbert*,[16] a patient underwent a course of treatment for breast cancer after a hospital negligently lost her biopsy sample, rendering impossible a definitive determination as to whether the patient in fact suffered from breast cancer. Expert testimony presented by the patient stated that, in light of the

---

Cherokee County Hosp. Authority v. Beaver, 179 Ga. App. 200, 201-202, 345 S.E.2d 904 (1986)

[12]Anthony v. Chambless, 231 Ga. App. 657, 500 S.E.2d 402 (1998).

[13]Anthony v. Chambless, 231 Ga. App. 657, 660–661, 500 S.E.2d 402, 405–406 (1998).

[14]Bowling v. Foster, 254 Ga. App. 374, 562 S.E.2d 776 (2002).

[15]Bowling v. Foster, 254 Ga. App. 374, 378, 562 S.E.2d 776, 780 (2002).

[16]R.J. Taylor Memorial Hosp., Inc. v. Gilbert, 213 Ga. App. 104, 443 S.E.2d 656 (1994), rev'd on other grounds, 265 Ga. 580, 458 S.E.2d 341 (1995).

loss of the biopsy sample, it was not possible to ascertain whether the patient had breast cancer. Expert testimony presented by the hospital, on the other hand, stated that, despite the loss of the biopsy sample, other medical evidence indicated, to a reasonable degree of medical certainty, the patient had breast cancer. In finding that the patient's expert testimony was insufficient to support her claim, the court observed that such testimony established only a possibility that the patient had not suffered from breast cancer and, thus, only a possibility that the additional treatment was unnecessary.[17]

§ 9:14 Procedural requirements—Professional's affidavit to be filed with complaint

O.C.G.A. § 9–11–9.1 provides that, in civil actions alleging professional malpractice against certain professionals enumerated by statute, the plaintiff is required to file with the complaint an expert's affidavit in support of the claim of professional malpractice.[1] Such an expert must be "competent" to testify as to the alleged professional negligence.[2] The affidavit must "set forth specifically at least one negligent act or omission claimed to exist and the factual basis for each such claim."[3] The purpose of the affidavit requirement is to ensure that, before a claim for malpractice may go forward, a qualified medical expert can aver under oath that there is at least one act of medical negligence.[4]

O.C.G.A. § 9–11–9.1(d) provides a list of 26 professionals as to whom an expert affidavit alleging professional negligence must be filed with the complaint. Among the professionals listed are several "medical" professionals, including: medical doctors, osteopathic physicians, podiatrists, physician's assistants, occupational therapists, physical therapists, nurses, dentists,

---

[17]R.J. Taylor Memorial Hosp., Inc. v. Gilbert, 213 Ga. App. 104, 105–106, 443 S.E.2d 656, 657–658 (1994), rev'd on other grounds, 265 Ga. 580, 458 S.E.2d 341 (1995).

[Section 9:14]

[1]O.C.G.A. § 9–11–9.1(a).

[2]O.C.G.A. § 9–11–9.1(a). O.C.G.A. § 24–9–67.1(e) specifically provides that "[a]n affiant must meet the requirements of this Code section in order to be deemed qualified to testify as an expert by means of the affidavit required under Code § 9–11–

9.1[,]" and O.C.G.A. § 24–9–67.1(c) provides for the qualifications a witness must possess in order to provide competent expert testimony in professional malpractice, including medical malpractice, actions. For a discussion of the minimum qualifications required of experts testifying in medical malpractice actions, see Section 10.2 supra.

[3]O.C.G.A. § 9–11–9.1(a).

[4]Sood v. Smeigh, 259 Ga. App. 490, 493, 578 S.E.2d 158, 161 (2003).

chiropractors, dietitians, optometrists, podiatrists, radiological technicians, and respiratory therapists.[5]

Not every action against one who happens to be a medical professional asserts a claim for medical negligence,[6] and an action sounding in ordinary negligence as to a medical professional need not be supported by an expert's affidavit.[7] In cases where an affidavit is required to be filed with the complaint, it is well-settled that such an affidavit is subject to a lower evidentiary standard than that which must be met in order to overcome a motion for summary judgment.[8] Provided the affidavit meets the minimal requirements of O.C.G.A. § 9–11–9.1, courts have construed the sufficiency of such affidavits in light of the liberal "notice pleading" requirements of the Civil Practice Act.[9] For instance, it has been held that it is not necessary for a 9.1 affidavit to define the applicable standard of care[10] or attach the medical records relied upon as the factual basis of the affidavit.[11]

By contrast, an affidavit which satisfies the pleading requirements of O.C.G.A. § 9–11–9.1 will not necessarily be sufficient to meet the evidentiary burden required to overcome a motion for

---

[5]O.C.G.A. § 9–11–9.1(d). In addition, other arguably "non-medical," albeit "health care," professionals as to whom an expert affidavit is required to be filed with the complaint include: psychologists, professional counselors, marriage and family therapists, clinical social workers, pharmacists, audiologists, speech-language therapists, and veterinarians. Of the 26 listed professions, only five—architects, attorneys, certified public accountants, land surveyors, and professional engineers—do not fall within the "health care" industry.

[6]See Section 10.3.1 above for a discussion as to when an action against a healthcare professional sounds in ordinary negligence as opposed to professional negligence.

[7]See, e.g. Upson County Hosp., Inc. v. Head, 246 Ga. App. 386, 389, 540 S.E.2d 626, 630 (2000); Herndon v. Ajayi, 242 Ga. App. 193, 194, 532 S.E.2d 108, 110 (2000) ("Whether or not an act or omission sounds in simple negligence or medical malpractice depends on whether the conduct, even if supervisory or administrative, involved a medical judgment.").

[8]See, e.g. Dozier v. Clayton County Hosp. Authority, 206 Ga. App. 62, 66, 424 S.E.2d 632, 636 (1992); Sanders v. Ramo, 203 Ga. App. 43, 44, 416 S.E.2d 333, 334 (1992); Bowen v. Adams, 203 Ga. App. 123, 123, 416 S.E.2d 102, 102 (1992).

[9]Porquez v. Washington, 268 Ga. 649, 652, 492 S.E.2d 665, 668 (1997); Dozier v. Clayton County Hosp. Authority, 206 Ga. App. 62, 66, 424 S.E.2d 632, 636 (1992); 0–1 Doctors Memorial Holding Co. v. Moore, 190 Ga. App. 286, 288, 378 S.E.2d 708, 710 (1989) (observing that the affidavit requirement of O.C.G.A. § 9–11–9.1 is more akin to the requirement that fraud be pled with particularity, as set forth in O.C.G.A. § 9–11–9(b), than to the evidentiary standards applicable in the context of motions for summary judgment under O.C.G.A. § 9–11–56).

[10]Bowen v. Adams, 203 Ga. App. 123, 124, 416 S.E.2d 102, 103 (1992); 0–1 Doctors Memorial Holding Co. v. Moore, 190 Ga. App. 286, 287, 378 S.E.2d 708, 710 (1989).

[11]Williams v. Hajosy, 210 Ga. App. 637, 638, 436 S.E.2d 716, 718 (1993).

summary judgment under O.C.G.A. § 9–11–56.[12] An expert's affidavit on summary judgment may not simply offer a conclusory pronouncement that the defendant was negligent; rather, the affidavit must define the "particulars" as to what is required by the standard of care and the "particulars" as to how the defendant's conduct or omissions fell below the applicable standard.[13] Moreover, certified copies of the medical records upon which the expert's opinion is based must accompany the affidavit or otherwise be in evidence in the record before the court.[14]

§ 9:15 Procedural requirements—Reliance on medical records and opinions of others not in evidence

O.C.G.A. § 24–9–67.1(a) provides that the facts or data upon which an expert bases his opinion need not be in evidence provided the facts or data are of a type "reasonably relied upon" by experts in the field. This statute, codified in 2005, adopts the language of Rule 703 of the Federal Rules of Evidence but may not represent a wholesale shift in Georgia law as it has developed over the years.[1]

Historically, in order to be admissible, an expert's opinion testimony was required to be based either on the expert's own personal knowledge, or upon facts which had been testified to by other witnesses or had otherwise been admitted into evidence.[2] Under this rule, a medical provider's diagnosis of a patient could, of course, be based upon the provider's own examination of the

---

[12]See Hailey v. Blalock, 209 Ga. App. 345, 346, 433 S.E.2d 337, 338 (1993); Williams v. Hajosy, 210 Ga. App. 637, 638, 436 S.E.2d 716, 718 (1993); Dozier v. Clayton County Hosp. Authority, 206 Ga. App. 62, 66, 424 S.E.2d 632, 636 (1992).

[13]Hillhaven Rehabilitation & Convalescent Center v. Patterson, 195 Ga. App. 70, 71, 392 S.E.2d 557, 558 (1990); Loving v. Nash, 182 Ga. App. 253, 255, 355 S.E.2d 448, 450 (1987); see also Sparks v. Hoff, 186 Ga. App. 907, 908, 368 S.E.2d 830, 831 (1988) (citing Beauchamp v. Wallace, 180 Ga. App. 554, 555, 349 S.E.2d 791, 792 (1986)) (expert affidavit must provide "medical testimony to inform the jury of the proper method for treating a case such as [the plaintiff's], i.e. what should have been done, and comparing that to what was actually done, so as to illustrate the professional malfeasance involved."); Connell v. Lane,

183 Ga. App. 871, 872, 360 S.E.2d 433, 434 (1987) (expert affidavit must "establish 'the parameters of acceptable professional conduct'" and "set forth specific facts as the basis for reaching the conclusion that treatment did not meet the standard of care.").

[14]Hailey v. Blalock, 209 Ga. App. 345, 347, 433 S.E.2d 337, 338–39 (1993); Johnson v. Srivastava, 199 Ga. App. 696, 697, 405 S.E.2d 725, 726 (1991); Lance v. Elliott, 202 Ga. App. 164, 167, 413 S.E.2d 486, 488-489 (1991); Loving v. Nash, 182 Ga. App. 253, 255, 355 S.E.2d 448, 450 (1987).

[Section 9:15]

[1]See Chapter 2, Section 2.5.

[2]See, e.g. Loper v. Drury, 211 Ga. App. 478, 481–482, 440 S.E.2d 32, 35–36 (1993); Brown v. State, 206 Ga. App. 800, 801, 427 S.E.2d 9, 9–10 (1992).

patient.[3] However, under this rule, it has also been held that a medical provider's diagnosis based in part upon, for example, a radiologist's report is inadmissible unless the report itself has been admitted into evidence under a hearsay exception,[4] or the radiologist himself has testified at trial about his findings as set forth in the report.[5]

This rule is based on the premise that an expert should not be the mere "conduit" for the opinion of another, and that an expert's opinions should be his or her own.[6] However, at the same time, much of what qualifies a witness as an expert is his or her knowledge developed from study of the writings of others.[7] Moreover, medical providers, and particularly physicians, often base the diagnoses and opinions developed in everyday practice upon the data collected, and the diagnoses and opinions developed, by other providers.[8] Perhaps in light of these realities, Georgia courts have increasingly demonstrated a leniency with respect to the application of the traditional rule. For instance, courts have held that, provided an expert is not basing his or her opinion entirely on hearsay evidence, the fact that the expert's opinion is based in part on hearsay is a matter of weight for the jury to consider, and does not result in the wholesale exclusion of the expert's opinion.[9] Some courts have focused on the qualitative nature of the information relied upon, observing that it is permissible for an expert to base his or her opinion upon facts and data collected by others, but not on the opinions developed by others.[10] However, even this distinction has at times given way to the rule that, provided the

---

[3]See, e.g. In Interest of A.S.M., 214 Ga. App. 668, 671, 448 S.E.2d 703, 706 (1994).

[4]Stouffer Corp. v. Henkel, 170 Ga. App. 383, 386, 317 S.E.2d 222, 226–227 (1984).

[5]Hyles v. Cockrill, 169 Ga. App. 132, 134–135, 312 S.E.2d 124 (1983) (overruled on other grounds by, Ketchup v. Howard, 247 Ga. App. 54, 543 S.E.2d 371 (2000)).

[6]In Interest of A.S.M., 214 Ga. App. 668, 671, 448 S.E.2d 703, 706 (1994); Mallard v. Colonial Life & Acc. Ins. Co., 173 Ga. App. 276, 276, 326 S.E.2d 6, 6–7 (1985).

[7]See, e.g. Cantrell v. Northeast Georgia Medical Center, 235 Ga. App. 365, 508 S.E.2d 716 (1998); Austin v. Kaufman, 203 Ga. App. 704, 417 S.E.2d 660 (1992) (recognizing that a physician may base his or her opinion on

medical textbooks or treatises, but may not merely recite the text of the book or treatise into evidence).

[8]See Advisory Committee Notes to Rule 703.

[9]See, e.g. Stephens v. Howard, 221 Ga. App. 469, 470, 471 S.E.2d 898, 899–900 (1996); Doctors Hosp. of Augusta, Inc. v. Bonner, 195 Ga. App. 152, 159–160, 392 S.E.2d 897, 903–904 (1990).

[10]See, e.g. Byrd v. State, 261 Ga. App. 483, 484, 583 S.E.2d 170, 171 (2003) (chemist's opinion, based not on the opinion of another, but on the data collected by another, admissible); Coleman v. Fortner, 260 Ga. App. 373, 579 S.E.2d 792 (2003) (accident reconstructionist's opinion, based on tests performed by another, not the other's conclusions drawn from the testing, admissible); In Interest of A.S.M., 214 Ga. App. 668, 671–672, 448 S.E.2d

expert is not merely restating the opinion of another, the fact that the expert's opinion is based in part on the opinion of another does not render the expert's opinion inadmissible.[11]

Georgia's adoption of Rule 703 provides some clarity in this area. As explained by the Advisory Committee Notes, Rule 703 operates as an exception to the general rule proscribing an expert's reliance on hearsay, and is driven by practical concerns of convenience.

> [A] physician in his own practice bases his diagnosis on information from numerous sources and of considerable variety, including statements by patients and relatives, reports and opinions from nurses, technicians and other doctors, hospital records, and X rays. Most of them are admissible in evidence, but only with the expenditure of substantial time in producing and examining various authenticating witnesses. The physician makes life-and-death decisions in reliance upon them. His validation, expertly performed and subject to cross-examination, ought to suffice for judicial purposes.[12]

Thus, O.C.G.A. § 24–9–67.1(a) represents a codification of the rule that has been developing in Georgia, wherein an expert's reliance on what would otherwise be considered hearsay does not in itself render the expert's opinion testimony inadmissible, provided such hearsay is of the sort "reasonably relied upon" by experts in the field.

703, 706 (1994) (social worker's opinion, based not on the raw data collected by another, but on the interpretation of data by another, inadmissible).

[11]Doctors Hosp. of Augusta, Inc. v. Bonner, 195 Ga. App. 152, 159–160, 392 S.E.2d 897, 903–904 (1990); Life Ins. Co. of Georgia v. Dodgen, 148 Ga. App. 725, 729–730, 252 S.E.2d 629, 633 (1979) (opinion of physician performing autopsy as to cause of death not inadmissible because physician relied in part on opinion of another performing microscopic examination of decedent's aorta).

[12]Advisory Committee Notes to Rule 703.

Chapter 10

Motor Vehicle Accidents

KeyCite®: Cases and other legal materials listed in KeyCite Scope can be researched through the KeyCite service on Westlaw®. Use KeyCite to check citations for form, parallel references, prior and later history, and comprehensive citator information, including citations to other decisions and secondary materials.

---

§ 10:1   Overview

Experts are often called upon in Georgia to explain both the cause of a motor vehicle collision and the damages flowing therefrom. Typically, experts will be required to prove an accident was caused by poor road design, but not all road maintenance or repair cases will require expert testimony. Police officers are frequently called to testify about how a collision occurred, but some courts restrict testimony from investigating officers that assigns "fault." Plaintiffs are frequently permitted to testify, without the use of expert testimony, on topics such as property damage and to personal injuries that are easily explained and immediately apparent.

§ 10:2   Establishing roadway design and maintenance standards

The planning and design of a roadway entails the employment of professional engineering services, and hence, an action premised upon the negligent planning or design of a roadway generally must be supported by competent expert testimony.[1] Matters involving professional engineering and design judgment are broad and varied, and may include such matters as the design of bridges and guardrails,[2] the establishment of the width and slope of a roadway,[3] the design of interstate access ramps[4] and merging lanes,[5] the design of a roadway's curves,[6] and the design and layout of intersections and approaching areas.[7] Professional engineering and design may also include the establishment of speed limits,[8] and the determination as to whether and where to place traffic control devices such as stop signs,[9] traffic signals,[10] or

[Section 10:2]

[1]Murray v. Department of Transp., 240 Ga. App. 285, 523 S.E.2d 367 (1999); Department of Transp. v. Gilmore, 209 Ga. App. 656, 434 S.E.2d 114 (1993); Jackson v. Department of Transp., 201 Ga. App. 863, 412 S.E.2d 847 (1991).

Such actions are often brought against the Georgia Department of Transportation. In Minnix v. Department of Transp., 272 Ga. 566, 533 S.E.2d 75 (2000), the Georgia Supreme Court considered the issue as to whether a complaint filed against the DOT, predicated upon the professional negligence of DOT agents or employees, must be supported by an expert affidavit pursuant to O.C.G.A. § 9–11–9.1. Amendments to this statute in 1997 specifically identify the categories of defendants against whom an affidavit under this statute is required: 1) the licensed professionals identified in the statute; and 2) licensed health care facilities alleged to be liable by virtue of the negligence of those licensed health care professionals identified in the statute. Thus, because the DOT was omitted from the statute, an expert affidavit need not be filed along with a complaint alleging that the DOT is liable by virtue of the professional negligence of its agents or employees. Minnix v. Department of Transp., 272 Ga. 566, at 571, 533 S.E.2d 75 (2000) Nonetheless, the Court observed that the fact that O.C.G.A. § 9–11–9.1 does not require an expert affidavit to be filed with a

complaint against the DOT does not alter the requirement that, where the action is one asserting professional negligence, such a claim must be supported by competent expert testimony at trial. Minnix v. Department of Transp., 272 Ga. 566, at 571–572, 533 S.E.2d 75 (2000)

[2]See, e.g. Adams v. Coweta County, 208 Ga. App. 334, 430 S.E.2d 599 (1993).

[3]See, e.g. Steele v. Georgia Dept. of Transp., 271 Ga. App. 374, 609 S.E.2d 715 (2005).

[4]See, e.g. Hubbard v. Department of Transp., 256 Ga. App. 342, 568 S.E.2d 559 (2002).

[5]See, e.g. Fraker v. C.W. Matthews Contracting Co., Inc., 272 Ga. App. 807, 614 S.E.2d 94 (2005), cert. denied, (Sept. 19, 2005).

[6]See, e.g. Steele v. Georgia Dept. of Transp., 271 Ga. App. 374, 609 S.E.2d 715 (2005).

[7]See, e.g. Department of Transp. v. Dupree, 256 Ga. App. 668, 570 S.E.2d 1 (2002).

[8]See, e.g. Department of Transp. v. Mikell, 229 Ga. App. 54, 493 S.E.2d 219 (1997).

[9]See, e.g. Department of Transp. v. Mikell, 229 Ga. App. 54, 493 S.E.2d 219 (1997).

[10]See, e.g. Department of Transp. v. Dupree, 256 Ga. App. 668, 570 S.E.2d 1 (2002); Whitley v. Gwinnett County, 221 Ga. App. 18, 470 S.E.2d 724 (1996).

traffic regulation devices in construction areas.[11] The engineering
and design involved in such matters take into account safety
considerations which are often overlooked by the motoring public,
such as appropriate sight distances, perception and reaction
times, and braking distances.[12]

On the other hand, an action premised upon the negligent
maintenance or repair of a roadway does not necessarily call into
question professional judgment, and, when professional judgment
is not called into question, the plaintiff need not offer expert
testimony.[13] Thus, the failure to maintain bushes or shrubs at an
intersection so as to provide a motorist with a clear view of
oncoming traffic is not a matter requiring expert testimony.[14] The
installation, repair, and maintenance of roadway appurtenances,
such as guardrails, have also been held to be matters not necessarily requiring expert testimony.[15] By contrast, it has been
recognized that the presence of wear and tear on a roadway will
inevitably exist, and that expert testimony, or the presentation of
engineering standards, is required to demonstrate whether ruts
in the roadway were sufficiently hazardous to require repaving of
the roadway's surface.[16]

Actions against the Georgia Department of Transportation for
the negligent design of a highway are subject to the Georgia Tort
Claims Act. A provision of this Act provides that the State shall
not be held liable for losses resulting from the "plan or design for
the construction of or improvement to highways, roads, streets,
bridges, or other public works where such plan or design is prepared in substantial compliance with generally accepted engineering or design standards in effect at the time of preparation of the
plan or design."[17] Under this statute, the relevant inquiry is
focused on the generally accepted standards in existence *at the*

[11]See, e.g. Department of Transp. v. Cushway, 240 Ga. App. 464, 464–465, 523 S.E.2d 340, 341 (1999) ("Since the average layman is not familiar with the design and function of traffic control devices, when a plaintiff claims that the choice and placement of traffic control devices were negligent, the claim usually asserts negligent engineering design decisions which sound in professional negligence[.]").

[12]See, e.g. Department of Transp. v. Dupree, 256 Ga. App. 668, 678, 570 S.E.2d 1, 9–10 (2002), for a discussion of expert testimony on the myriad considerations involved in the widening of an a crossroad at an intersec-

tion so as to enable crossing motorists and pedestrians to cross the increased distance in safety.

[13]Drawdy v. Department of Transp., 228 Ga. App. 338, 339, 491 S.E.2d 521, 523–524 (1997); Adams v. Coweta County, 208 Ga. App. 334, 336, 430 S.E.2d 599, 601 (1993).

[14]Department of Transp. v. Mikell, 229 Ga. App. 54, 493 S.E.2d 219 (1997).

[15]Adams v. Coweta County, 208 Ga. App. 334, 430 S.E.2d 599 (1993).

[16]Johnson v. Department of Transp., 245 Ga. App. 839, 538 S.E.2d 879 (2000).

[17]O.C.G.A. § 50-21-24(10).

time of the roadway's design, not on those standards in existence at the time of the accident.[18] It has been held that the Georgia Department of Transportation may not be liable for failing to upgrade a roadway's design to conform to existing engineering or design standards.[19] Thus, absent expert testimony as to the generally accepted standards at the time of the roadway's design, as well as expert testimony as to how the design deviated from the then-applicable standards, no action against the Department of Transportation sounding in negligent planning or design can lie.[20] However, when there is a modification in the design of the roadway which is alleged to have been negligently performed, the engineering and standards in existence at the time of the modification will be the pertinent standards, as opposed to those standards in effect at the time of the roadway's initial design.[21]

Georgia courts have recognized that certain publications, such as the Manual of Uniform Traffic Control Devices, set forth generally accepted engineering design standards for matters within their purview.[22] However, it is not required that expert testimony regarding design standards be based upon any particular publi-

---

[18]Department of Transp. v. Cox, 246 Ga. App. 221, 223, 540 S.E.2d 218, 220 (2000); Daniels v. Department of Transp., 222 Ga. App. 237, 238–239, 474 S.E.2d 26, 27–28 (1996).

[19]Department of Transp. v. Cox, 246 Ga. App. 221, 223, 540 S.E.2d 218, 220 (2000); Daniels v. Department of Transp., 222 Ga. App. 237, 239, 474 S.E.2d 26, 27–28 (1996).

[20]Department of Transp. v. Cox, 246 Ga. App. 221, 223, 540 S.E.2d 218, 220 (2000); Lennen v. Department of Transp., 239 Ga. App. 729, 730–731, 521 S.E.2d 885, 887 (1999); Daniels v. Department of Transp., 222 Ga. App. 237, 239, 474 S.E.2d 26, 27–28 (1996).

[21]Steele v. Georgia Dept. of Transp., 271 Ga. App. 374, 609 S.E.2d 715 (2005) (relevant engineering and design standards were those in effect at time of DOT's improvements to road in 1970s and 1980s, as opposed to those engineering standards in effect at the time the road was original construction in the 1930s); cf. Department of Transp. v. Cox, 246 Ga. App. 221, 540 S.E.2d 218 (2000) (resurfacing of roadway in 1990s, which did not alter the geometric layout of roadway, did not change standards applicable to

the design of roadway from being those in effect when the roadway was designed in the 1960s).

[22]Department of Transp. v. Brown, 267 Ga. 6, 8, 471 S.E.2d 849, 851 (1996); Department of Transp. v. Cushway, 240 Ga. App. 464, 465, 523 S.E.2d 340, 341 (1999). The Manual of Uniform Traffic Control Devices (MUTCD) is a publication providing standards for the design and application of traffic control devices, and contains standards that fall into three distinct categories: 1) mandatory; 2) advisory; and 3) permissive. Hubbard v. Department of Transp., 256 Ga. App. 342, 351, 568 S.E.2d 559, 567–568 (2002). Whether and how to implement the advisory or permissive standards is a matter calling into question professional judgment, and thus, a claim that there has been a negligent deviation from such standards is matter requiring expert testimony. Department of Transp. v. Mikell, 229 Ga. App. 54, 58, 493 S.E.2d 219, 223 (1997). By contrast, it has been held that expert testimony is not necessary to support a claim that there has been a deviation from the mandatory standards, as compliance with the mandatory standards is not a matter of pro-

cation, such as the MUTCD.[23] At the same time, an expert's opinion which is based exclusively upon published standards which were not in effect at the time of the highway's design provides insufficient evidence as to the generally accepted standards applicable to the highway's design.[24]

§ 10:3   Accident reconstruction

The reconstruction of a motor vehicle collision is often a critical component of a lawsuit involving such accidents. Indeed, in cases where the cause of the accident is not readily apparent to a lay observer, the failure to produce the expert testimony of a witness with expertise in accident reconstruction can be fatal to a claim.[1] Accident reconstructionists generally offer testimony regarding

---

fessional judgment. Department of Transp. v. Cushway, 240 Ga. App. 464, 465, 523 S.E.2d 340, 341 (1999). While the MUTCD is recognized as a source for design standards, it is not the exclusive source for ascertaining generally accepted design standards for traffic control devices. Department of Transp. v. Cushway, 240 Ga. App. 464, 465, 523 S.E.2d 340, 341 (1999).

[23]Georgia Dept. of Transp. v. Brown, 218 Ga. App. 178, 460 S.E.2d 812 (1995), aff'd, 267 Ga. 6, 471 S.E.2d 849 (1996) (despite the fact that no standards for transitioning all-way stop intersection to two-way intersection were set forth in MUTCD, other evidence existed as to these standards); see also Murray v. Department of Transp., 240 Ga. App. 285, 523 S.E.2d 367 (1999). In *Murray,* an expert was found competent to offer testimony on the general engineering design standards applicable to a highway completed in 1940, despite a challenge that the applicable standards were not published until seven months after the design of the highway. The court found this testimony to be competent based on the expert's testimony that, despite the nonexistence of published standards, he nonetheless had obtained personal knowledge of the generally accepted standards in effect in 1940. Murray v. Department of Transp., 240 Ga. App. 285, at 287, 523 S.E.2d 367 (1999) While this holding was premised on the sound principle

that standards need not be published in order for an expert to testify as to what the standards are, the result in *Murray* may be different under O.C.G.A. § 24-9-67.1(c)(1), which provides that, in an action alleging professional malpractice, an expert must have been licensed in his profession at the time of the alleged malpractice in order to provide competent testimony as to the acceptable standard of conduct at issue.

[24]Daniels v. Department of Transp., 222 Ga. App. 237, 238, 474 S.E.2d 26, 27 (1996).

[Section 10:3]

[1]See, e.g. Johnson v. Department of Transp., 245 Ga. App. 839, 538 S.E.2d 879 (2000). In *Johnson,* the plaintiff claimed that the DOT's negligence in allowing ruts to remain in the roadway had allowed water to accumulate thereon, thus causing the plaintiff's vehicle to hydroplane and crash when encountering this water. Unimpressed with the mere presence of ruts on the roadway, the presence of which was "guarantee[d] . . . to some degree on any roadway", the court observed that the dispositive question was whether there ruts in the road at the point where the plaintiff had lost control of his vehicle caused the collision. Johnson v. Department of Transp., 245 Ga. App. 839, at 840, 538 S.E.2d 879 (2000). In granting summary judgment in favor of the DOT because there had been no show-

the sequence of events leading up to a motor vehicle accident so as to enable a jury to make a determination as to how the accident occurred.[2] Such experts often offer testimony regarding the speeds of the vehicles involved in an accident, as deduced from physical evidence at the accident scene, such as skid marks, the distances traveled following impact, and physical damage to the vehicles involved.[3] Particularly in light of the fact that those involved in the accident will often have a different interpretation of the events leading up to the accident, such testimony can be helpful in conveying, based on the objective evidence left behind at the accident scene, matters such as the positions and directions of travel of the vehicles prior to and at the time of impact.[4]

---

ing that the ruts had placed a causative role in the accident, the court observed that there had been "no expert testimony as to how and why the incident occurred[.]" Johnson v. Department of Transp., 245 Ga. App. 839, at 841, 538 S.E.2d 879 (2000). See also Mansfield v. Colwell Const. Co., 242 Ga. App. 669, 673, 530 S.E.2d 793, 797 (2000) (in case where plaintiff's decedent was killed after vehicle plunged from hill into rock quarry, court granted summary judgment in favor of rock quarry, observing that "[n]o accident reconstruction evidence or expert testimony was offered to prove the actual cause of the van's precipitous plunge off the bluff.").

[2]See, e.g. Massee v. State Farm Mut. Auto. Ins. Co., 128 Ga. App. 439, 197 S.E.2d 459 (1973). In *Massee*, the court overruled an objection to expert opinion testimony as to how an accident occurred as invading the province of the jury, observing that the expert had not offered an opinion on the ultimate question of negligence. Rather, the expert "gave his opinion, based on certain facts, as to the sequence of events. This is the purpose of having an expert witness testify. Use of expert witnesses to reconstruct the sequence of events in automobile collisions has now become commonplace."). Massee v. State Farm Mut. Auto. Ins. Co., 128 Ga. App. 439, at 444, 197 S.E.2d 459 (1973).

[3]See, e.g. Edge v. Fugatt, 264 Ga. App. 28, 589 S.E.2d 845 (2003) (expert testimony regarding speed of vehicle involved in accident based on calculated rendered from length of skid marks); Gilpatrick v. State, 226 Ga. App. 692, 487 S.E.2d 461 (1997) (expert testimony regarding speed of vehicle based upon skid marks and impact damage to vehicles); Massee v. State Farm Mut. Auto. Ins. Co., 128 Ga. App. 439, 445, 197 S.E.2d 459, 463 (1973) ("A qualified witness may give opinion evidence as to speed based on data observed immediately after a collision, such as skid marks, distances, and positions of and damage to the vehicles."); Reeves v. Morgan, 121 Ga. App. 481, 174 S.E.2d 460 (1970), rev'd on other grounds, 226 Ga. 697, 177 S.E.2d 68 (1970) (expert testimony as to fact that that skid marks and physical evidence at accident scene provided no indication as to speed of vehicle).

[4]See, e.g. Johnson v. Knebel, 267 Ga. 853, 485 S.E.2d 451 (1997) (professional engineer's expertise "probably enabled him to reconstruct the course and rate of travel, and points of impact of the cars involved in the collisions. From that reconstruction, expert opinions likely could be drawn as to matters such as the approximate distance between cars at the time brakes were applied, and the approximate speeds of travel at the points of impact."); Cleveland v. Bryant, 236 Ga. App. 459, 512 S.E.2d 360 (1999) (where plaintiff claimed that accident caused by tractor-trailer pulling into her lane of travel, accident reconstructionist testi-

At times, experts may be called to comment upon issues touching upon the avoidability of an accident. For instance, the issue as to whether a driver, while driving at a certain speed, had sufficient time to perceive and react to a roadway hazard so as to be able to avoid the hazard has been the subject of expert testimony.[5] Indeed, it has been observed that "computations of speed, distance, and human reaction times [are] beyond the ken of the average juror[,]" and therefore, appropriate matters for expert testimony.[6] At other times, such experts may be called upon to testify as to how various deficiencies in the design[7] or maintenance[8] of a roadway or intersection contributed to an accident.

§ 10:4 Accident reconstruction—Qualifications

The term "accident reconstructionist" is, of course, an amorphous term, and there are no definitive qualifications to which courts have looked in determining whether a witness is qualified to offer such testimony.[1] Rather courts have examined the proffered testimony in an effort to ensure that it falls within the wit-

---

mony used to demonstrate that damage to plaintiff's vehicle and other accident scene evidence inconsistent with plaintiff's version of events); Massee v. State Farm Mut. Auto. Ins. Co., 128 Ga. App. 439, 197 S.E.2d 459 (1973) (expert testimony helpful in enabling the jury to understand how an accident occurred based on such particulars as the point of collision, the direction in which vehicles were heading, the damage to the vehicles, and the final resting places of vehicles).

[5]Department of Transp. v. Dupree, 256 Ga. App. 668, 570 S.E.2d 1 (2002) (expert testimony discussing distance needed for drivers traveling at speed limit to perceive and react to pedestrians in intersection so as to avoid collision); High v. Parker, 234 Ga. App. 675, 507 S.E.2d 530 (1998) (police officer testimony that, due to distance required to evade vehicle pulling into motorist's lane of travel, accident would have occurred irrespective of whether motorist was traveling at the speed limit or in excess of speed limit).

[6]Moore v. State, 258 Ga. App. 293, 296, 574 S.E.2d 372, 376 (2002).

[7]See, e.g. Steele v. Georgia Dept. of Transp., 271 Ga. App. 374, 609

S.E.2d 715 (2005) (expert testimony that DOT's failure to modify speed limit and provide for adequate sight distance at intersection was cause of accident); Lennen v. Department of Transp., 239 Ga. App. 729, 521 S.E.2d 885 (1999) (expert testimony that DOT's failure to install traffic control device at intersection was cause of accident); Department of Transp. v. Mikell, 229 Ga. App. 54, 493 S.E.2d 219 (1997) (expert testimony that positioning of stop sign at intersection was cause of accident).

[8]See, e.g. Johnson v. Department of Transp., 245 Ga. App. 839, 538 S.E.2d 879 (2000) (expert testimony that ruts on roadway allowed water to accumulate on roadway, thus causing plaintiff to lose control of vehicle when it hydroplaned); Drawdy v. Department of Transp., 228 Ga. App. 338, 491 S.E.2d 521 (1997) (expert testimony that depression in roadway allowed water to accumulate, thus causing plaintiff's vehicle to hydroplane).

[Section 10:4]

[1]Massee v. State Farm Mut. Auto. Ins. Co., 128 Ga. App. 439, 197 S.E.2d 459 (1973) (observing that experienced auto-wrecker driver has been found competent to offer opinions, based on

ness' demonstrated qualifications. As a general rule, courts have found that police officers with appropriate experience and training in accident investigation are qualified to testify as to the cause of a motor vehicle accident.[2] For instance, police officers with sufficient training and experience have been permitted to offer testimony as to the speed of a vehicle as deduced from the skid marks at the accident scene.[3] Similarly, sufficiently qualified police officers have been permitted to reconstruct the sequence of events leading up to the collision based upon physical evidence at the accident scene, such as the position of and damage to the vehicles involved.[4]

Professional engineers are often called upon to reconstruct how an accident occurred, including the calculation of vehicle speeds, courses of travel, and positions prior to and at the time of collision.[5] Professional engineers have also offered testimony as to how various aspects of a roadway's design contributed to an accident.[6] The courts have indicated that those with qualifications in accident reconstruction and biomechanics may be able to offer

---

observation of accident scene, as to the pints of impact between the vehicles involved in a collision).

[2]Jefferson Pilot Life Ins. Co. v. Clark, 202 Ga. App. 385, 414 S.E.2d 521 (1991) (observing that, where officer had 20 years of experience as a patrolman, had attended numerous courses on traffic accident investigation, and had investigated hundreds of accidents over the course of his career, "[t]here can be no doubt that a police officer with investigative experience on automobile collisions is an expert."); Massee v. State Farm Mut. Auto. Ins. Co., 128 Ga. App. 439, 443, 197 S.E.2d 459, 462 (1973) ("there should not be any doubt that a police officer with investigative training and experience on automobile collisions is an expert."); cf. Avant Trucking Co., Inc. v. Stallion, 159 Ga. App. 198, 283 S.E.2d 7 (1981) (not error to disallow police officer from offering opinion as to cause of accident where officer found not to be an expert in accident reconstruction).

[3]Reeves v. Morgan, 121 Ga. App. 481, 174 S.E.2d 460 (1970), rev'd on other grounds, 226 Ga. 697, 177 S.E.2d 68 (1970) (police officer with three years of experience and training in investigating motor vehicle accidents

permitted to offer opinion on speed of vehicle as deduced from skid marks and other physical evidence at accident scene); Rouse v. Fussell, 106 Ga. App. 259, 126 S.E.2d 830 (1962).

[4]Furlong v. Dyal, 246 Ga. App. 122, 539 S.E.2d 836 (2000); Felton v. White, 197 Ga. App. 367, 398 S.E.2d 425 (1990) (officer permitted to testify that, based observations of physical evidence at accident scene, position of the vehicles, damage to vehicles, and interviews with witnesses, it was his conclusion that drivers involved in accident had lost control of their vehicles); Massee v. State Farm Mut. Auto. Ins. Co., 128 Ga. App. 439, 197 S.E.2d 459 (1973) (officer permitted to testify about particulars of accident, including point of collision, direction in which vehicles were heading, the drivers of the vehicles, damage to the vehicles, and final resting places of vehicles).

[5]See, e.g. Johnson v. Knebel, 267 Ga. 853, 485 S.E.2d 451 (1997).

[6]See, e.g. Department of Transp. v. Dupree, 256 Ga. App. 668, 570 S.E.2d 1 (2002) (excessive speed limit and insufficient traffic control devices at intersection); Lennen v. Department of Transp., 239 Ga. App. 729,

testimony not only as to how the motor vehicle collision occurred, but also as to the "secondary impacts" suffered by those inside the passenger compartments of the vehicles;[7] however, some courts have stopped short of allowing such experts to opine as to whether a specific collision was the cause of a motorist's specific injuries absent training in medicine.[8]

§ 10:5 Accident reconstruction—Sufficiency of factual basis

Courts have excluded the opinion testimony of an accident reconstructionist where it appears that the "reconstruction" performed is not likely to provide a reliable basis for the opinions proffered. In this regard, the failure to take relevant measurements, or perform relevant tests or calculations, may result in the exclusion of the expert's opinion testimony as unreliable.[1] Experience alone does not render an accident reconstructionist's opinions as to cause reliable, and whatever that experience may be, the expert's opinion must be supported by the facts of the case.[2] Consistent with the general rule that an expert's opinions may not be premised upon mere speculation, courts have rejected the opinion of an accident reconstructionist as to the cause of an

---

730–731, 521 S.E.2d 885, 887 (1999) (inadequate sight distance at intersection located on crest of hill).

[7]Cromer v. Mulkey Enterprises, Inc., 254 Ga. App. 388, 562 S.E.2d 783 (2002).

[8]Cromer v. Mulkey Enterprises, Inc., 254 Ga. App. 388, 562 S.E.2d 783 (2002); cf. Brown v. Hove, 268 Ga. App. 732, 603 S.E.2d 63 (2004), cert. denied, (Jan. 10, 2005).

[Section 10:5]

[1]See, e.g. Drawdy v. Department of Transp., 228 Ga. App. 338, 341, 491 S.E.2d 521, 524 (1997) (observing that the accident reconstructionist's investigation of roadway conditions in an effort to determine the cause of an accident consisted of little more than "eyeballing" the road); see also Johnson v. Knebel, 267 Ga. 853, 858, 485 S.E.2d 451, 455 (1997) (excluding an accident reconstructionist's opinions, in part, because the expert "performed no tests or calculations, but rather simply based his opinion upon his examination of the photographs of the dam-

aged vehicles").

[2]Drawdy v. Department of Transp., 228 Ga. App. 338, 491 S.E.2d 521 (1997). In Drawdy, the plaintiff was injured when her vehicle hydroplaned out of control due to a pool of standing water on the roadway. An accident investigator offered the opinion that the water was allowed to accumulate on the roadway due to lack of maintenance and repair. Specifically, the expert opined that a depression in the roadway had formed over time, thus allowing the water to accumulate on the road's surface. In excluding the expert's testimony, the court observed that the expert had performed only a cursory investigation into the roadway's condition, and could cite no fact in support of his contention that there was a depression, or any defect, which had caused the water to accumulate on the roadway's surface. The court found that the only basis for the expert's conclusion was his experience that roadways tend to settle or deteriorate over time.

accident when it has insufficient factual support.[3] An accident reconstructionist must be able to convey how and in what way his investigation supports his conclusion as to the cause of an accident,[4] and a mere conclusory pronouncement as to the cause of the accident is insufficient.[5] For instance, courts have rejected expert testimony which summarily concluded that a "defect" in the roadway,[6] or a driver's "inattention" or "fatigue,"[7] caused the accident.

An recent example of the detail with which some courts have analyzed the testimony of accident reconstructionists, as well as the difficulty in determining where the line is drawn between testimony which is merely inadmissible speculation and testimony which is based on sufficient facts, may be found in Layfield v. Department of Transportation.[8] There, the plaintiff had run off the road during a heavy rainstorm, but had no recollection of how the accident occurred, and there were no eye-witnesses. However, evidence existed that, two weeks prior to the plaintiff's accident, another driver had lost control of his vehicle on the same stretch of road, and that rain water accumulation on the road had played a causative role in this prior accident. The plaintiff's expert opined that the improper design and mainte-

---

[3]See, e.g. Drawdy v. Department of Transp., 228 Ga. App. 338, 491 S.E.2d 521 (1997). In Rios v. Norsworthy, 266 Ga. App. 469, 597 S.E.2d 421 (2004), a collision occurred after a vehicle attempting to pass a tractor-trailer collided with oncoming traffic. The plaintiff's expert opined that the driver of the tractor-trailer had negligently failed to observe the passing vehicle and move to the right hand lane so as to enable the passing vehicle to avoid oncoming traffic. However, in excluding this testimony, the court observed that there was simply no factual basis in the record for the assertion that the driver had failed to inspect his rear and side view mirrors for passing vehicles. Rios v. Norsworthy, 266 Ga. App. 469, at 473, 597 S.E.2d 421 (2004).

[4]Johnson v. Knebel, 267 Ga. 853, 858, 485 S.E.2d 451, 455 (1997) ("[T]he expert witness must be able to relate the objective means used in applying [his] expert knowledge to determine that the specified injury to the passenger was caused by particular damage to the automobile.").

[5]Rios v. Norsworthy, 266 Ga. App. 469, 597 S.E.2d 421 (2004).

[6]Drawdy v. Department of Transp., 228 Ga. App. 338, 341, 491 S.E.2d 521, 524 (1997) (where expert opined that accident was caused by defect in the construction of a road, but "did not state any facts on which he based his opinion, . . . the opinions stated in his affidavit were mere speculation.").

[7]Rios v. Norsworthy, 266 Ga. App. 469, 597 S.E.2d 421 (2004) (noting that an expert's opinions that a tractor-trailer driver "did not use his mirrors to observe vehicles around him, that he was not attentive and alert, and that he may have been fatigued either have no factual basis or constitute inadmissible speculation and conclusions without probative value.").

[8]Layfield v. Dept. of Transp., 271 Ga. App. 806, 611 S.E.2d 56 (2005), cert. granted, (Nov. 8, 2005) and judgment rev'd, 280 Ga. 848, 632 S.E.2d 135 (2006).

nance of the road had allowed water to accumulate on the roadway's surface, thus causing the plaintiff's vehicle to hydroplane when it crossed this section of the road. In upholding the exclusion of the expert's opinion as "rank speculation," the Court of Appeals found that the expert had made no effort to determine whether and to what extent water accumulation on the roadway played a causative role in the plaintiff's accident.[9] Moreover, the court found that the expert had failed to account for and rule out alternative possible causes of the accident.[10] Finally, despite the expert's reliance on the prior accident for his conclusion that an accumulation of rain water on the roadway had caused the plaintiff's accident, the expert failed to point to any similarities between the two accidents,[11] and had ignored undisputed differ-

---

[9]Layfield v. Dept. of Transp., 271 Ga. App. 806, 807, 611 S.E.2d 56, 58 (2005), cert. granted, (Nov. 8, 2005) and judgment rev'd, 280 Ga. 848, 632 S.E.2d 135 (2006). Specifically, the court observed that the expert had made no effort to determine: 1) the depth of the water at the time of the accident; 2) how long it had been raining; 3) how hard it had been raining; 4) whether the water on the roadway was moving; or 5) whether any accumulated water caused the plaintiff's vehicle to hydroplane, to have a differential friction, or to simply impact the water. Layfield v. Dept. of Transp., 271 Ga. App. 806, at 807–808, 611 S.E.2d 56, 58 (2005) and judgment rev'd, 280 Ga. 848, 632 S.E.2d 135 (2006).

[10]Layfield v. Dept. of Transp., 271 Ga. App. 806, 807–808, 611 S.E.2d 56, 58 (2005), cert. granted, (Nov. 8, 2005) and judgment rev'd, 280 Ga. 848, 632 S.E.2d 135 (2006). In this regard, the court observed that the expert had made no effort to determine: 1) the speed the plaintiff was traveling at the time he lost control; 2) what activities, such as listening to the radio, may have distracted the plaintiff at the time he lost control; 3) whether the plaintiff had driven the road before in the rain; 4) whether an animal may have darted from the woods beside the road; and 5) whether the illegally-low tread on three of the tires on the plaintiff's vehicle had played a role in the loss of control. Layfield v. Dept. of Transp., 271 Ga. App. 806, at 807–808, 611 S.E.2d 56, 58 (2005), cert. granted, (Nov. 8, 2005) and judgment rev'd, 280 Ga. 848, 632 S.E.2d 135 (2006).

[11]Layfield v. Dept. of Transp., 271 Ga. App. 806, 808, 611 S.E.2d 56, 58–59 (2005), cert. granted, (Nov. 8, 2005) and judgment rev'd, 280 Ga. 848, 632 S.E.2d 135 (2006). On this point, the court observed that the expert had merely relied on the fact that both vehicles had lost control on the same stretch of roadway during the rain. The court found it significant that the expert had not consulted with the driver in this prior accident, and had failed to determine the specifics of the prior accident so as to determine what similarities, if any, existed between the two accidents. Specifically, the expert failed to determine, with respect to the prior accident: 1) the depth of water accumulating on the roadway; 2) the amount of rain; 3) the speed of the other vehicle; 4) what role a trailer hitched to the other vehicle may have played in the accident; 5) the effect the deeper tire treads on the other vehicle may have had; and 6) whether the accumulated water had resulted in hydroplaning or differential friction. Layfield v. Dept. of Transp., 271 Ga. App. 806, at 808, 611 S.E.2d 56, 58 (2005), cert. granted, (Nov. 8, 2005) and judgment rev'd, 280 Ga. 848, 632 S.E.2d 135 (2006).

ences between the two accidents.[12] The court characterized the expert's opinion as "nothing more than an impermissible 'res ipsa loquitur' approach: a short-circuited analysis requiring quantum leaps of faith and smacking of rank speculation to link the two accidents together."[13]

Notwithstanding this analysis by the Court of Appeals, Georgia's Supreme Court, in a split decision, reversed the lower appellate court, with the majority finding that the expert's opinion as to the cause of the crash was not speculative.[14] In so holding, the majority emphasized that some degree of speculation in an expert's opinion will not mandate exclusion of the expert's opinion, stating that "the appropriate standard for assessing the admissibility of the opinion of Ms. Layfield's expert is not whether it is speculative or conjectural to some degree, but whether it is wholly so."[15] The Court found that the issue as to whether the expert had "sufficient information from which to reach a probative opinion[]" did not go to the admissibility of his opinion, but rather, presented a jury question as to the expert's credibility and the weight which should be assigned to his opinion.[16] Notably, in arriving at its holding the Supreme Court did not address the admissibility standard of O.C.G.A. § 24–9–67.1 that expert opinion testimony be "based upon sufficient facts or data" in order to be admissible.[17] The three justice dissent strongly critiqued the majority's holding, stating flatly that "[u]nder the majority opinion, summary judgment will never be appropriate so long as a party can find an expert to make a statement supporting that party's case, even if that statement is nothing more than an unsupported conclusion."[18] The dissent agreed with the lower appellate court that the expert's conclusion as to the cause of the accident lacked a sufficient factual basis, and thus, had no probative

---

[12]Layfield v. Dept. of Transp., 271 Ga. App. 806, 809, 611 S.E.2d 56, 59 (2005), cert. granted, (Nov. 8, 2005) and judgment rev'd, 280 Ga. 848, 632 S.E.2d 135 (2006). In this regard, the court observed that, in the prior accident, the vehicle was pulling a fully-loaded trailer which had jack-knifed, contributing to the vehicle's loss of control. By contrast, the plaintiff had not been pulling a trailer. Second, the vehicle in the prior accident had good tread on its tires, whereas the tread on the plaintiff's tires was illegally low. Third, the trailer in the prior accident had begun swerving before the area of the roadway where the water was accumulating.

[13]Layfield v. Dept. of Transp., 271 Ga. App. 806, 809, 611 S.E.2d 56, 59 (2005), cert. granted, (Nov. 8, 2005) and judgment rev'd, 280 Ga. 848, 632 S.E.2d 135 (2006).

[14]Layfield v. Department of Transp., 280 Ga. 848, ____, 632 S.E.2d 135, 137 (2006).

[15]Layfield v. Department of Transp., 280 Ga. 848, ____, 632 S.E.2d 135, 137 (2006).

[16]Layfield v. Department of Transp., 280 Ga. 848, ____, 632 S.E.2d 135, 138 (2006).

[17]See O.C.G.A. § 24–9–67.1(b)(1).

[18]Layfield v. Department of Transp., 280 Ga. 848, ____, 632 S.E.2d

value so as to create an issue of fact sufficient to survive summary judgment.[19]

§ 10:6 Accident reconstruction—Accident reconstruction testimony on the ultimate issue

Experts frequently offer opinions as to how an accident occurred. Courts have generally excluded or limited testimony by an expert as to whether one party was at fault in causing a collision, reasoning that it constitutes a conclusion for which expert testimony is not needed because the jury is able to draw such a conclusion on its own.[1] However, the distinction between what is and what is not permissible opinion testimony can be subtle. For instance, it has been held that, as a general matter, a police officer with proper training and experience in traffic accident investigations may properly opine as to the cause of a motor vehicle accident.[2] However, at the same time, where testimony as to the "cause" of the accident is tantamount to a conclusion that a particular party was at fault in an accident, such testimony may be disallowed.[3]

Perhaps because any discussion of "cause" has the potential to be inculpatory, courts have expressed a preference for limiting expert testimony to a description of how the accident occurred. As explained by one court, a police officer may properly testify as to what he observed at the accident scene and offer an opinion, based upon this evidence, as to how the accident occurred.[4] However, where a police officer is able to do this, the determination as to whether a particular party's conduct was the cause of the collision is a matter which should be left for the jury.[5] At the same time, the courts have recognized that, in the more complex cases, it may be impractical for an expert not to directly address

---

135, 139 (2006) (Sears, J., dissenting).

[19]Layfield v. Department of Transp., 280 Ga. 848, ___, 632 S.E.2d 135, 139–140 (2006) (Sears, J., dissenting).

[Section 10:6]

[1]See, e.g. Baxter v. Melton, 218 Ga. App. 731, 463 S.E.2d 53 (1995); Emory v. Dobson, 206 Ga. App. 482, 426 S.E.2d 50 (1992).

[2]Jefferson Pilot Life Ins. Co. v. Clark, 202 Ga. App. 385, 414 S.E.2d 521 (1991).

[3]McMichen v. Moattar, 221 Ga. App. 230, 230–231, 470 S.E.2d 800, 802 (1996); Smith v. Fee, 197 Ga. App.

483, 483, 398 S.E.2d 801, 802 (1990).

[4]McMichen v. Moattar, 221 Ga. App. 230, 230–231, 470 S.E.2d 800, 802 (1996). See, e.g. Felton v. White, 197 Ga. App. 367, 398 S.E.2d 425 (1990) (where police officer testified as to his observations of physical evidence at accident scene, position of the vehicles, and damage to vehicles, police officer permitted to explain that it was his conclusion that both drivers involved in accident had lost control of their vehicles).

[5]McMichen v. Moattar, 221 Ga. App. 230, 230–231, 470 S.E.2d 800, 802 (1996).

the issue of cause, even though it may have the effect of offering an opinion on the "ultimate issue" to be decided by the jury.[6]

Courts have generally disallowed a police officer's testimony which invokes terms of legal significance, such as "negligence" or "reasonableness," concluding that a jury is able to arrive at such conclusions on its own from the presentation of the evidence. For instance, it has been held that where a police officer had testified fully about what he had observed at the accident scene, and had offered an opinion based on this evidence as to how the collision occurred, the officer should not have been permitted to go one step further and offer the opinion that the defendant was not driving a "reasonably safe" distance behind the plaintiff.[7] Similarly, it has been held that where a police officer has testified as to the speed of the vehicle and the maximum safe speed for vehicles to travel under the existing road conditions, it is error to allow the officer to go the next step and testify that the defendant was traveling "too fast" for conditions.[8]

Police officers are not, of course, the only witnesses bound by these rules. In *Rios v. Norsworthy*, the court upheld the exclusion of a professional engineer's testimony that a tractor-trailer driver was "negligent" in failing to pull to the right so as to allow a vehicle to pass from behind without veering into oncoming traffic, and that the tractor-trailer driver had the "last clear chance" to

---

[6]See, e.g. Deloach v. Deloach, 258 Ga. App. 187, 573 S.E.2d 444 (2002). In *DeLoach,* the court upheld the exclusion of a police officer's testimony that a driver's intoxication was the cause of the collision where the jury had before it evidence that the driver had operated the vehicle while under the influence of alcohol, as well as the driver's testimony to the effect that the fact that the vehicle's accelerator had become "stuck" was the cause of the collision. In so ruling, the court observed that "[a]lthough a complex case may permit the use of expert testimony about the cause of the collision, in more straightforward cases 'jurors are likely able and should be permitted to reach their own conclusions as to who was at fault.'" Deloach v. Deloach, 258 Ga. App. 187, at 188, 573 S.E.2d 444 (2002).

See also Moore v. State, 258 Ga. App. 293, 574 S.E.2d 372 (2002). In *Moore,* the defendant rear-ended a tractor-trailer, killing a passenger in the vehicle. The defendant claimed

that, due to the tractor-trailer's sudden loss of speed, the accident was unavoidable. The court upheld the trial court's refusal to allow the defense to cross the State's expert as to whether the tractor-trailer's loss of speed could have "caused" or "contributed to" the accident, reasoning that the jury could draw this conclusion on its own. However, the court noted that expert testimony on the issue of avoidability, including computations of speed, distance, and human reaction times, were beyond the ken of the jury, and indicated such evidence would have been admissible. Moore v. State, 258 Ga. App. 293, at 295–296, 574 S.E.2d 372 (2002).

[7]Emory v. Dobson, 206 Ga. App. 482, 484, 426 S.E.2d 50, 52 (1992) ("Although police officers may give their opinion as to speed or other causal links in a collision, the officer's opinion may not suggest negligence.").

[8]Baxter v. Melton, 218 Ga. App. 731, 463 S.E.2d 53 (1995).

avoid the ensuing head-on collision between the passing vehicle and oncoming traffic, reasoning that these were conclusions which the jury could draw on its own.[9] The engineer had also offered testimony that the tractor-trailer driver was negligent because he had failed to be "constantly aware" of vehicles attempting to pass, and because the driver had failed to "maintain a constant vigil" while behind the wheel. In upholding the exclusion of this testimony, the court reasoned that not only were these conclusions which the jury could arrive at on its own, they misapplied the correct legal standard by imposing heightened requirements.[10]

§ 10:7 Expert testimony on damages—Establishing injuries were caused by accident

By their nature, motor vehicle accidents are often violent occurrences producing immediate and palpable injuries. Given this fact, it has often been held that where there is no significant lapse of time between the motor vehicle accident and the claimed injury, expert medical testimony is not necessary to establish the motor vehicle accident as the cause of the individual's injuries.[1] However, where the onset of the pain is significantly delayed, or

---

[9]Rios v. Norsworthy, 266 Ga. App. 469, 472, 597 S.E.2d 421, 426 (2004).

[10]Rios v. Norsworthy, 266 Ga. App. 469, 473–474, 597 S.E.2d 421, 426–427 (2004). See also Sotomayor v. TAMA I, LLC, 274 Ga. App. 323, 617 S.E.2d 606 (2005), cert. denied, (Nov. 7, 2005). In *Sotomayor,* a professional engineer with expertise in traffic engineering and accident reconstruction offered testimony that an apartment complex was required, pursuant to "reasonable" design practices, to install "bumper stops" in the parking lot so as prevent vehicles from coming to close to a pedestrian area. However, the expert's testimony was based on standards inapplicable to parking lots, and those standards indicated that such guard devices had a "limited capacity as a shield for pedestrians." Under such circumstances, the court upheld the exclusion of the expert testimony as merely bolstering the plaintiff's theory of the case, reasoning that the jury could conclude on its own, without the assistance of this testimony, whether the failure to install the devices was negligent.

Sotomayor v. TAMA I, LLC, 274 Ga. App. 323, 617 S.E.2d 606 (2005), cert. denied, (Nov. 7, 2005).

[Section 10:7]

[1]See, e.g. Hutcheson v. Daniels, 224 Ga. App. 560, 561, 481 S.E.2d 567, 568–569 (1997) (where plaintiff first noticed problem with wrist a few days following the accident, the court found that expert medical testimony was not required to establish the wrist injury was caused by the motor vehicle accident, as a "lay jury could conclude from common knowledge that a causal connection existed in light of the short lapse between [plaintiff's] accident and his onset of symptoms and receipt of medical treatment."); Madden v. Solomon, 196 Ga. App. 512, 396 S.E.2d 245 (1990) (expert medical testimony not required to establish motor vehicle accident caused plaintiff's pain in neck and extremities where plaintiff began to experience pain within hours of accident and sought continuous treatment for this pain over the course of over one year); Jordan v. Smoot, 191 Ga. App. 74, 380 S.E.2d 714 (1989) (expert medical testimony not required to establish causal nexus between mo-

the connection between the accident and the injury is not of the sort of "common sense deduction" which jurors can be credited with making, expert medical testimony is required to establish a causal nexus between the motor vehicle accident and the claimed injuries.[2]

While courts have found that professional engineers and others with expertise in accident reconstruction are competent to testify as to how a motor vehicle accident occurred, they have sometimes restricted the expert from testifying as to whether an individual's injuries were a result of the motor vehicle accident. For instance, in *Johnson v. Knebel*,[3] the court disallowed a professional engineer's testimony as to which of two collisions in a multi-vehicle accident produced the plaintiff's injuries. The court found that while the engineer's area of expertise likely enabled him to ascertain the course, speed, and points of impact of the vehicles involved in the accident, the determination as to which collision produced the plaintiff's injuries required expertise in human physiology, anatomic structure, biomechanics, and osteology.[4] The court also observed that this determination would require knowledge of the automobile's passenger compartment and the safety devices used.[5] In upholding the exclusion of the engineer's testimony, the court observed that there was no evidence that the expert had any knowledge of these matters, nor any training or experience in deducing the forces exerted on a human body within an automobile's passenger compartment during a collision.[6]

Similarly, in *Cromer v. Mulkey Enterprises*,[7] the court of appeals upheld the exclusion of a biomechanicist's testimony as to which of multiple collisions resulted in the plaintiff's injuries. In so ruling, the court remained unconvinced that the field of biomechanics enabled the expert to make such a determination, observing that there had been limited evidence presented in this

---

tor vehicle accident and injuries where plaintiff experienced pain, and sought treatment for the pain, on the day of the accident).

[2]Lancaster v. USAA Cas. Ins. Co., 232 Ga. App. 805, 502 S.E.2d 752 (1998) (expert medical testimony needed to establish whether motor vehicle accident caused an aggravation of plaintiff's pre-existing fibromyalgia).

[3]Johnson v. Knebel, 267 Ga. 853, 485 S.E.2d 451 (1997).

[4]Johnson v. Knebel, 267 Ga. 853, 858, 485 S.E.2d 451, 455 (1997).

[5]Johnson v. Knebel, 267 Ga. 853, 858, 485 S.E.2d 451, 455 (1997).

[6]Johnson v. Knebel, 267 Ga. 853, 858–859, 485 S.E.2d 451, 455–456 (1997); see also Naimat v. Shelbyville Bottling Co., 240 Ga. App. 693, 524 S.E.2d 749 (1999) (accident reconstructionist not permitted to testify as to which of two impacts caused plaintiff's fatal injuries).

[7]Cromer v. Mulkey Enterprises, Inc., 254 Ga. App. 388, 562 S.E.2d 783 (2002).

regard.[8] By contrast, it has been held that a physician with experience in biomechanics and radiology is competent to opine whether a plaintiff's injuries were likely caused by a specific accident.[9]

§ 10:8 Expert testimony on damages—Evidence of seatbelt use

Prior to 1988, evidence that a motorist was not wearing a seat belt was commonly admitted for the purpose of showing that the defendant's conduct was not the sole cause of the plaintiff's injuries, and that the plaintiff's injuries could have been avoided, in whole or part, had he or she chosen to wear a seat belt.[1] Expert testimony was often employed for these purposes.[2] For instance, in *Bales v. Shelton*, a physician's testimony was offered for the purpose of establishing that the occupant's injuries could have been avoided or minimized had he been wearing a seatbelt during the accident.[3] In 1988, the legislature curtailed this practice by enacting OCGA § 40–7–76.1, which provides that the failure of an occupant to wear a seatbelt shall not be considered as evi-

---

[8]Cromer v. Mulkey Enterprises, Inc., 254 Ga. App. 388, 562 S.E.2d 783 (2002). Specifically, the court found that insufficient evidence had been presented that biomechanics "includes a technique of determining if specific injuries result from specific accidents, let alone that that technique has reached a scientific stage of verifiable certainty." Cromer v. Mulkey Enterprises, Inc., 254 Ga. App. 388, at 393, 562 S.E.2d 783 (2002) The court rejected the notion that "[s]imply mentioning that there have been 'cadaver tests' or that volunteers have been filmed in low-speed accidents" answered the question. *Id.* The court observed that there had been no showing that any scientific studies had been performed which would demonstrate the amount of force and movement needed to herniate a disk or tear a rotator cuff, the two injuries of which the plaintiff complained. *Id.*

[9]Brown v. Hove, 268 Ga. App. 732, 603 S.E.2d 63 (2004), cert. denied, (Jan. 10, 2005). In *Hove*, the court found it significant that the physician, a neuroradiologist, had testified that

tests and experience reported in radiological literature with which he was familiar, had identified "the types of stresses and bodily movements that most likely cause disk herniation." Brown v. Hove, 268 Ga. App. 732, at 735, 603 S.E.2d 63 (2004), cert. denied, (Jan. 10, 2005)

[Section 10:8]

[1]Bales v. Shelton, 197 Ga. App. 522, 399 S.E.2d 78 (1990); Cannon v. Lardner, 185 Ga. App. 194, 363 S.E.2d 574 (1987); Martini v. Nixon, 185 Ga. App. 328, 364 S.E.2d 49 (1987).

[2]See Scott v. Chapman, 203 Ga. App. 58, 59, 416 S.E.2d 111, 112 (1992) (expert testimony that injuries of the type sustained by plaintiff could have been reduced by use of a seatbelt); Bales v. Shelton, 197 Ga. App. 522, 524–25, 399 S.E.2d 78, 81–82 (1990) (expert testimony that seatbelt use would have lessened injuries by preventing occupant from being thrown forward into steering wheel).

[3]Bales v. Shelton, 197 Ga. App. 522, 524–25, 399 S.E.2d 78, 81 (1990).

dence of either negligence or causation, and shall not be used to diminish any recovery of damages.[4]

§ 10:9   Expert testimony on damages—Establishing property damage to vehicle

By statute, expert testimony is not required, and the testimony of a lay witness is competent, to establish the loss of value to a vehicle as a result of a collision. In this regard, O.C.G.A. § 24–9–66 provides:

> Direct testimony as to market value is in the nature of opinion evidence. One need not be an expert or dealer in the article in question but may testify as to its value if he has had an opportunity for forming a correct opinion.[1]

This statute provides an exception to the general rule that lay witnesses are not permitted to offer opinion testimony unless the opinion is based on the witness's personal observations and is necessary for the witness to convey those observations to the jury.[2]

One of two different measures may be used for the purpose of establishing property damage to a vehicle: 1) the difference in the vehicle's value before and after the accident; or 2) the value of reasonably necessary repairs, along with the costs of temporary transportation while the vehicle is being repaired and the value of any permanent impairment following the vehicle's repair, provided that this aggregate amount does not exceed the value of the vehicle prior to the accident.[3] In establishing the property

---

[4]O.C.G.A. § 40–8–76.1(d). See also C.W. Matthews Contracting Co., Inc. v. Gover, 263 Ga. 108, 428 S.E.2d 796 (1993) (O.C.G.A. § 40–8–76.1 constitutional notwithstanding fact that it prevents defendants from introducing evidence that failure to wear seatbelt was the sole proximate cause of the plaintiff's injuries).

[Section 10:9]

[1]O.C.G.A. § 24–9–66.

[2]Compare O.C.G.A. § 24–9–66 with Hines v. State, 276 Ga. 491, 494, 578 S.E.2d 868, 873 (2003); Carnes v. Woodall, 233 Ga. App. 797, 798, 505 S.E.2d 537, 538 (1998).

While lay opinion testimony is the most common means by which to establish a vehicle's lost value, "expert" testimony is occasionally pro-

duced for this purpose. See e.g., Lamar Nash Buick–Pontiac, Inc. v. Crowe, 118 Ga. App. 669, 671, 164 S.E.2d 917, 919 (1968); Olliff v. Howard, 33 Ga. App. 778, 127 S.E. 821, 822 (1925); Lamon v. Perry, 33 Ga. App. 248, 125 S.E. 907 (1924). Expert testimony as to market value may be presented in response to a hypothetical question describing the year, make, and condition of the vehicle and by also showing the bill of sale for the vehicle. Burns v. Brown, 73 Ga. App. 488, 490, 37 S.E.2d 233, 235 (1946). The jury is free to disregard the expert's assessment and consider other evidence as to the vehicle's value. Department of Transp. v. Driggers, 150 Ga. App. 270, 274, 257 S.E.2d 294, 297 (1979).

[3]Canal Ins. Co. v. Tullis, 237 Ga. App. 515, 516, 515 S.E.2d 649, 650

damage sustained by a vehicle during a collision, lay witness testimony has commonly been admitted as to the vehicle's pre-collision market value,[4] the vehicle's post-collision market value,[5] and the vehicle's market value after repair in order to show amount of permanent impairment.[6] Prior to such testimony being admissible, however, a foundation must first be laid showing that the lay witness has acquired reliable information as to the vehicle's market value.[7] The evidentiary threshold for laying such a foundation is not great, and courts have found one or more of the following to constitute a sufficient foundation for purposes of testifying as to value: consultation with automobile dealers;[8] personal experience with buying and selling cars;[9] experience in making car loans;[10] and review of newspaper ads for vehicles of

---

(1999); Knight v. Stevens Logging, Inc., 173 Ga. App. 359, 326 S.E.2d 494, 495 (1985); Archer v. Monroe, 165 Ga. App. 724, 726, 302 S.E.2d 583, 585 (1983); Olliff v. Howard, 33 Ga. App. 778, 127 S.E. 821, 822 (1925); Lamon v. Perry, 33 Ga. App. 248, 125 S.E. 907 (1924). The first measure is used in the case where a plaintiff elects to not make repairs to the vehicle. Standard Guar. Ins. Co. v. Advance Well Services, Inc., 167 Ga. App. 314, 315, 306 S.E.2d 388 (1983).

[4]See e.g., Godowns v. Cantrell, 186 Ga. App. 100, 366 S.E.2d 415, 416 (1988); Dixon v. Williams, 177 Ga. App. 702, 704, 340 S.E.2d 286, 288–89 (1986).

[5]See e.g., Sykes v. Sin, 229 Ga. App. 155, 156, 493 S.E.2d 571, 574 (1997); Standard Guar. Ins. Co. v. Advance Well Services, Inc., 167 Ga. App. 314, 315, 306 S.E.2d 388 (1983).

[6]See e.g., Stone v. Burell, 161 Ga. App. 369, 370, 288 S.E.2d 636, 638 (1982); Apostle v. Prince, 158 Ga. App. 56, 56–57, 279 S.E.2d 304, 305–06 (1981).

[7]Lamb v. R.L. Mathis Certified Dairy Co., 183 Ga. App. 455, 456, 359 S.E.2d 214, 216 (1987); Standard Guar. Ins. Co. v. Advance Well Services, Inc., 167 Ga. App. 314, 306 S.E.2d 388 (1983).

[8]See e.g., Lamb v. R.L. Mathis Certified Dairy Co., 183 Ga. App. 455, 456, 359 S.E.2d 214, 216 (1987) (testimony by plaintiff that he surveyed sales prices offered by dealers); Apostle v. Prince, 158 Ga. App. 56, 56–57, 279 S.E.2d 304, 305–06 (1981) (plaintiff contacted various dealers about the vehicle's worth). See also Godowns v. Cantrell, 186 Ga. App. 100, 366 S.E.2d 415, 416 (1988) (plaintiff testified that he went to used car lots in order to price vehicles of the same age and with the same equipment).

[9]See e.g., Dixon v. Williams, 177 Ga. App. 702, 704, 340 S.E.2d 286, 288–89 (1986) (plaintiff testified he was familiar with the value of automobiles by virtue of having owned a considerable number of automobiles in the past); Stone v. Burell, 161 Ga. App. 369, 370, 288 S.E.2d 636, 638 (1982) (testimony by defendant banker that he had personal experience in buying and selling cars); Apostle v. Prince, 158 Ga. App. 56, 56–57, 279 S.E.2d 304, 305–06 (1981) (plaintiff testified that he had owned and traded cars in the past).

[10]See e.g., Stone v. Burell, 161 Ga. App. 369, 370, 288 S.E.2d 636, 638 (1982) (testimony by defendant banker that he had personal experience in making car loans).

the same make, model, and condition.[11] The fact that the lay witness's opinion is based on hearsay merely goes to the weight such testimony is to be given, not its admissibility.[12]

Where at issue is what damage to the vehicle resulted from the collision, the testimony of lay witnesses is competent to establish that outwardly visible damage was caused by the collision, and "expert" testimony is not needed on this point.[13] However, it has been held that expert testimony is generally required to establish that damages in the nature of internal mechanical or electrical problems were caused by the collision, as these are matters not readily capable of discernment by the average juror.[14]

§ 10:10   Videotaped and computer–animated "reenactments"

Parties in motor vehicle collision cases sometimes seek to use videotaped or computer-animated reenactments of a scene sought to be depicted as a means of conveying a party's expert's version of events or theories of causation. The Georgia Supreme Court has issued a word of caution regarding the use of such evidence,

---

[11]See e.g., Lamb v. R.L. Mathis Certified Dairy Co., 183 Ga. App. 455, 456, 359 S.E.2d 214, 216 (1987). Simply showing that the vehicle's researched were of the same make and model is insufficient for purposes of establishing value; one must also show that the pre-collision condition of the vehicle at issue was the same as the researched vehicles. Sykes v. Sin, 229 Ga. App. 155, 157, 493 S.E.2d 571, 575 (1997); see also Monroe v. Hyundai Motor America, Inc., 270 Ga. App. 477, 479, 606 S.E.2d 894, 897 (2004), cert. denied, (Mar. 28, 2005) (plaintiff failed to establish sufficient foundation in breach of warranty case where, although he researched the market for vehicles of comparable makes and models, he did not research the market for vehicles with the same purported defects).

Expert testimony is generally unnecessary to show the reasonableness of repair costs, as jurors by their own common experience are capable of ascertaining the reasonableness and necessity of the repairs made and the time needed to make such repairs. Stone v. Burell, 161 Ga. App. 369, 370, 288 S.E.2d 636, 638 (1982) ("The na-

ture of the repairs, the length of time required for them, their cost, and the cost of rental vehicles were all matters about which the jurors could be expected to have had some knowledge based on 'everyday experience.' ").

[12]Apostle v. Prince, 158 Ga. App. 56, 57, 279 S.E.2d 304, 306 (1981).

[13]Lamb v. R.L. Mathis Certified Dairy Co., 183 Ga. App. 455, 359 S.E.2d 214, 215 (1987).

[14]Lamb v. R.L. Mathis Certified Dairy Co., 183 Ga. App. 455, 455–56, 359 S.E.2d 214, 215 (1987) (plaintiff's testimony insufficient to establish claim for reimbursement for mechanical work performed on the engine of the car because plaintiff not an expert in the area of engine repairs). See also Ken Thomas of Georgia, Inc. v. Halim, 266 Ga. App. 570, 597 S.E.2d 615 (2004), cert. denied, (Sept. 7, 2004) (finding plaintiff failed to show that defendant's negligence in not repairing left rear knuckle on car caused the accident because defendant introduced unrebutted expert testimony that this defect was unrelated to the car's steering system which allegedly caused the accident).

noting that there is a "particularly great" danger that, due to the "vividness and verisimilitude" of such evidence, a jury may "confuse art with reality."[1]

> The artificial recreation of an event may unduly accentuate certain phases of the happening, and because of the forceful impression made upon the minds of the jurors by this kind of evidence, it should be received with caution. As pointed out in Wigmore, such a portrayal of an event is apt to cause a person to forget that 'it is merely what certain witnesses say was the thing that happened. . . . '[2]

Accordingly, it has been held that where such reenactments are "substantially different" from the facts of the case, and that because of such differences may be prejudicial and misleading, a trial court should not allow the presentation of such evidence to the jury.[3] The proponent of the reenactment bears the burden of showing that it is a fair and accurate depiction of the event sought to be depicted.[4] Such evidence, however, need not achieve the impossible task of being identical in every particular, and need only be "sufficiently similar" such that it is of assistance to the jury.[5] Such a determination is within the discretion of the trial court.[6]

[Section 10:10]

[1]Pickren v. State, 269 Ga. 453, 455–466, 500 S.E.2d 566, 579 (1998). Citing McCormick on Evidence § 241, p. 19 (4th ed. 1992), the Court observed:

> Where videotapes . . . do not portray original facts in controversy, but rather represent one party's staged reproduction of those facts, . . . the extreme vividness and verisimilitude of pictorial evidence is truly a two-edged sword. For not only is the danger that the jury may confuse art with reality particularly great, but the impressions generated by the evidence may prove particularly difficult to limit or, if the film is subsequently deemed inadmissible, to expunge by judicial instruction.

Id.; see also Foster v. State, 275 Ga. 795, 797, 573 S.E.2d 60, 63 (2002).

[2]Pickren v. State, 269 Ga. 453, 455–466, 500 S.E.2d 566, 569 (1998), citing Eiland v. State, 130 Ga. App. 428, 203 S.E.2d 619 (1973), (addressing State's use of video reenactment of a crime).

[3]Foster v. State, 275 Ga. 795, 796, 573 S.E.2d 60, 63 (2002); Pickren v. State, 269 Ga. 453, 455, 500 S.E.2d 566, 569 (1998); Cleveland v. Bryant, 236 Ga. App. 459, 460, 512 S.E.2d 360, 362 (1999).

[4]Eiland v. State, 130 Ga. App. 428, 203 S.E.2d 619 (1973), (addressing State's use of video reenactment of a crime).

Foster v. State, 275 Ga. 795, 797, 573 S.E.2d 60, 63 (2002); Pickren v. State, 269 Ga. 453, 455, 500 S.E.2d 566, 569 (1998).

[5]Doster v. Central of Georgia R. Co., 177 Ga. App. 393, 398, 339 S.E.2d 619, 624 (1985) (addressing experiment designed to measure at what point unlit train at crossing would have been visible to oncoming motorist).

[6]Pickren v. State, 269 Ga. 453, 455, 500 S.E.2d 566, 569 (1998); Cornell v. State, 265 Ga. 904, 905, 463 S.E.2d 702, 703 (1995); Cleveland v. Bryant, 236 Ga. App. 459, 460, 512 S.E.2d 360, 362 (1999); Doster v. Central of Georgia

In *J.B. Hunt Transport v. Brown*,[7] the Court of Appeals addressed the use of such evidence in light of the perhaps inevitable tension between the parties' conflicting versions as to how a motor vehicle accident occurred. There, a party contested an accident reconstructionist's use of a computer-animated video to illustrate *his opinion* as to how the accident occurred, claiming that the video nonetheless accurately reflected how the accident *actually* occurred. In finding that the trial court had not abused its discretion in allowing such evidence to be shown to the jury, the Court of Appeals "decline[d] to apply the evidentiary rule applicable to video-reenactments[,]" i.e., that the proponent must show that it is a true and accurate representation of the event sought to be depicted, instead noting that the animation was being used merely to illustrate the accident reconstructionist's opinion as to how the accident occurred.[8] The court reasoned that items such as photographs, diagrams, charts, and models have long been admitted as a means of "pictorial communication" to illustrate the testimony of a witness, and that where such evidence is used solely to illustrate a witness' testimony, only "minimal authentication" is required.[9] The court found it significant that the video did not "reenact" the accident, that there was little risk that the jury would misconstrue it as such, and that any inaccuracies in the video could be brought out on cross-examination.[10]

In *Cleveland v. Bryant*,[11] the Court of Appeals again addressed the use of an animated videotape illustrating an expert's opinion as to how a motor vehicle accident occurred. In finding no abuse of discretion in the trial court's admission of such evidence despite the opposing party's claim that it did not accurately represent how the collision occurred, the Court of Appeals noted that the expert had visited the accident scene, taken measurements, inspected damage to one of the vehicles and photographs of damage to both vehicles, and had conducted an experiment wherein he observed one of the vehicles traveling on the roadway. The court upheld the admission of such evidence, noting that the animation appeared to be both "sufficiently similar" to the evidence as to how the accident occurred, and an "accurate repre-

R. Co., 177 Ga. App. 393, 398, 339 S.E.2d 619, 624 (1985).

[7]J.B. Hunt Transport, Inc. v. Brown, 236 Ga. App. 634, 512 S.E.2d 34 (1999).

[8]J.B. Hunt Transport, Inc. v. Brown, 236 Ga. App. 634, 635–636, 512 S.E.2d 34, 37 (1999).

[9]J.B. Hunt Transport, Inc. v. Brown, 236 Ga. App. 634, 635, 512 S.E.2d 34, 37 (1999).

[10]J.B. Hunt Transport, Inc. v. Brown, 236 Ga. App. 634, 636, 512 S.E.2d 34, 37 (1999).

[11]Cleveland v. Bryant, 236 Ga. App. 459, 512 S.E.2d 360 (1999).

sentation" of the expert's opinion as to how the accident occurred.[12]

§ 10:11   Commercial motor carriers

Motor vehicle accidents involving tractor-trailers present a host of unique issues in light of the heavy regulation of the commercial motor carrier industry.[1] The Federal Motor Carrier Safety Regulations establish standards for numerous aspects of the trucking industry, including regulations pertaining to the testing of drivers for drug and alcohol use,[2] background and annual investigations required to be performed by employers to ensure a minimum level of driver qualification,[3] and medical evaluations to be performed by employers to ensure the physical fitness of its drivers.[4] These regulations impose standards for the number of hours a driver can operate a tractor-trailer within a given period of time, and impose record keeping requirements upon both the driver and his employer tracking the time spent on-duty.[5] The regulations establish standards for the equipping of tractor-trailers with lighting devices, reflectors, and electrical equipment,[6] braking systems,[7] fuel systems,[8] and devices designed to prevent the shifting of cargo during transport.[9] The regulations further establish standards for the inspection, maintenance, and repair of tractor-trailers.[10] Evidence of the violations of these standards may be used to establish negligent entrustment,[11]

---

[12]Cleveland v. Bryant, 236 Ga. App. 459, 460, 512 S.E.2d 360, 362 (1999).

[Section 10:11]

[1]See O.C.G.A. §§ 46–7–24; O.C.G.A. § 46-7-26; 49 C.F.R. § 325 et seq. through 49 C.F.R. § 399 et seq.

[2]49 C.F.R. Part 40, §§ 40.1 et seq.; 49 C.F.R. Part 382, §§ 382.101 et seq.

[3]49 C.F.R. Part 391, §§ 391.1 et seq.

[4]49 C.F.R. Part 391, §§ 391.41 et seq.

[5]49 C.F.R. Part 395, §§ 395.1 et seq.

[6]49 C.F.R. Part 393, §§ 393.1 et seq.

[7]49 C.F.R. Part 393, §§ 393.40 et seq.

[8]49 C.F.R. Part 393, §§ 393.65 et seq.

[9]49 C.F.R. Part 393, §§ 393.100 et seq.

[10]49 C.F.R. Part 396, §§ 396.1 et seq.

[11]Whidby v. Columbine Carrier, Inc., 182 Ga. App. 638, 356 S.E.2d 709 (1987) (overruled on other grounds by, Pender v. Witcher, 194 Ga. App. 72, 389 S.E.2d 560 (1989)) (noting that a carrier's acknowledgement that it is vicariously liable for a driver may render evidence of its negligent entrustment irrelevant and unduly prejudicial).

negligence per se[12] or conduct sufficient for the imposition of punitive damages.[13]

In order for a violation of the regulations to be relevant, it must be shown that the violation was a proximate cause of the collision at issue.[14] For instance, the regulations limiting the number of hours a driver can operate a tractor-trailer were designed to prevent a driver from operating the tractor-trailer while fatigued, and a violation of these regulations can provide the basis for a charge of negligence per se.[15] However, expert testimony pertaining to the violation of these regulations has been held inadmissible where there was insufficient evidence to establish that the driver was driving in excess of the regulatory time limits at the time of the accident, and insufficient evidence to establish that the driver was in fact fatigued at the time of the accident.[16] Courts have cautioned that the use of expert testimony

---

[12]Minnick v. Lee, 174 Ga. App. 182, 185, 329 S.E.2d 548, 551 (1985) (observing that the regulations must first be properly proved and pled); Reliable Transfer Co. v. Gabriel, 84 Ga. App. 54, 65 S.E.2d 679 (1951) (addressing regulations imposing limitations on a driver's hours of service).

[13]J.B. Hunt Transport, Inc. v. Bentley, 207 Ga. App. 250, 427 S.E.2d 499 (1992) (addressing spoliation of driver logbooks, which would have revealed whether driver operating tractor-trailer within hours of service limitations imposed by regulations and designed to prevent drivers from operating tractor-trailers while fatigued, and spoliation of pre-and post-trip inspection reports required to be maintained by regulations and designed to ensure tractor-trailers were operated in road-worthy condition); see also Glenn McClendon Trucking Co., Inc. v. Williams, 183 Ga. App. 508, 359 S.E.2d 351 (1987) (dispatching tractor-trailer into service despite knowledge that adequate repairs could not be made given tools available, and despite knowledge that risk of failing to adequately repair tractor-trailer was separation of wheels from truck, sufficient to warrant imposition of punitive damages).

[14]Parker v. R & L Carriers, Inc., 253 Ga. App. 628, 560 S.E.2d 114 (2002) (not error for trial court to fail to give jury instruction on regulations imposing limitations on driver's hours of service, where proximate cause of accident was driver's running of red light, a violation of a statutory duty irrespective of whether driver was fatigued); Moore v. State, 258 Ga. App. 293, 574 S.E.2d 372 (2002); cf. Fouts v. Builders Transport, Inc., 222 Ga. App. 568, 474 S.E.2d 746 (1996) (defendant's contention that tractor-trailer brakes working and in compliance with regulatory requirements no defense where tractor-trailer driver violated absolute statutory duty by running red light, irrespective of whether brakes were in working order).

[15]J.B. Hunt Transport, Inc. v. Bentley, 207 Ga. App. 250, 256–257, 427 S.E.2d 499, 504–505 (1992); Reliable Transfer Co. v. Gabriel, 84 Ga. App. 54, 64–65, 65 S.E.2d 679, 686–687 (1951).

[16]Rios v. Norsworthy, 266 Ga. App. 469, 473–474, 597 S.E.2d 421, 426–427 (2004) (noting that the expert's testimony was a mere conclusion devoid of any factual support); cf. J.B. Hunt Transport, Inc. v. Bentley, 207 Ga. App. 250, 427 S.E.2d 499 (1992). In Bentley, the motor carrier had destroyed the driver's logbooks following an investigation into the ac-

is not indicated where the matter addressed is not "beyond the ken" of the jury, and may be irrelevant where the testimony attempts to impose a standard of conduct greater than that imposed by law.[17]

---

cident at issue. Other evidence showed that the carrier had operated a "forced dispatch" system, wherein drivers would be terminated for refusing a load, and had a history of requiring (or permitting) its drivers to operate tractor-trailers while they were in excess of the regulatory hours of service limitations. Observing that the destroyed logbooks would have shown whether the driver was within hours of service limitations at the time of the accident, the court found that "[c]onsidering the destruction [of the logbooks] by Hunt, it was a reasonable presumption that the logbook showed that the driver was compelled by Hunt to driver with insufficient rest. . . . This would be a contributing factor, or cause, of his sustained weaving from lane to lane, failing to slow the fully loaded tractor-trailer from 65 mph despite the warnings of construction ahead and, without braking to avert collision, plowing into a readily visible vehicle parked off the roadway." J.B. Hunt Transport, Inc. v. Bentley, 207 Ga. App. 250, at 256–257, 427 S.E.2d 499 (1992).

[17]Rios v. Norsworthy, 266 Ga. App. 469, 597 S.E.2d 421 (2004). In *Rios*, a case wherein a motorist collided with a tractor-trailer and another vehicle while attempting to pass the tractor-trailer, experts testified that the tractor-trailer driver had failed to "maintain a constant vigil" or use his rear and side-view mirrors so as to be "constantly aware" of the position of other vehicles around him, as allegedly required by regulatory and industry standards. The court found such testimony inadmissible, noting that it imposed a heightened duty beyond ordinary care and was therefore inconsistent with the applicable legal standard and irrelevant. Rios v. Norsworthy, 266 Ga. App. 469, at 473–474, 597 S.E.2d 421 (2004). Moreover, the court held that whether the tractor-trailer driver had acted negligently under the circumstances was not a matter "shrouded in the mystery of professional skill[,]" and that expert testimony on this point was neither helpful to the jury nor admissible. *Id.*

Chapter 11

Personal Injury

> **KeyCite**[R]: Cases and other legal materials listed in KeyCite Scope can be researched through the KeyCite service on Westlaw[R]. Use KeyCite to check citations for form, parallel references, prior and later history, and comprehensive citator information, including citations to other decisions and secondary materials.

§ 11:1   When expert testimony is required to establish causation

The fact that a plaintiff suffers from an injury following a particular accident or event is not, in itself, enough to demonstrate that the accident or event was in fact the cause of the plaintiff's injuries, and a plaintiff has the burden to provide "a reasonable basis for the conclusion that it is more likely than not that the conduct of the defendant was a cause in fact of the result."[1] While expert testimony is often employed for the purpose of establishing the fact that a particular accident or event caused an individual's injuries, it is by no means always required. In some instances, the fact that an event is capable of causing injury is so patently obvious—such as the fact that a stab wound through the heart can lead to death[2]—that no expert testimony as to causation is deemed necessary. Where the issue as to whether an event produced the complained-of injury is one which the jury can

---

[Section 11:1]

[1]Hambrick v. Makuch, 228 Ga. App. 1, 2, 491 S.E.2d 71 (1997) (citing Prosser and Keaton on Torts (5th ed. 1984)); see also Webb v. Thomas Trucking, Inc., 255 Ga. App. 637, 566 S.E.2d 390 (2002).

[2]Jester v. State, 250 Ga. 119, 296 S.E.2d 555 (1982).

ascertain based on common experience, expert testimony is not required to establish the link of causation.[3]

This rule is often employed in the cases such as those involving motor vehicle accidents where it may be said that the fact that the injury resulted from the accident is more-or-less readily understood. In such cases, the determination as to whether expert testimony is required to establish a causal link will often depend on the temporal proximity between the event and injury. In this regard, it has been stated that where "there is no significant lapse of time between the injury sustained and the onset of the physical condition for which the injured party seeks compensation, and the injury sustained is a matter which jurors must be credited with knowing by reason of common knowledge, expert medical testimony is not required in order for a plaintiff to establish a personal injury case[.]"[4]

While there are no hard-and-fast rules as to what constitutes a "significant lapse of time," it has been held that expert testimony is not needed to establish a causal link between a motor vehicle accident and the plaintiff's injuries where the onset of the plaintiff's symptoms occurred on the day of the accident,[5] or within a few days of the accident.[6] By contrast, where the onset of symptoms and the event which is alleged to have produced injuries is separated in time by years, the causal connection between the two is not a matter within the competency of a jury to ascertain on its own.[7]

Similarly, there are no hard-and-fast rules as to when a jury may be credited with being able to ascertain a causal link between an event and an injury by virtue of "common knowledge." In the cases cited above wherein no expert testimony was required, not only did the evidence indicate that the plaintiff's physical symptoms appeared immediately following the accident or within a short period of time thereafter, there was also no evidence that the plaintiff had any preexisting physical symptoms of a similar nature prior to the accident.[8] Where it is shown that the plaintiff has preexisting conditions which the accident or event is alleged to have aggravated, expert testimony has gener-

---

[3]Owens v. General Motors Corp., 272 Ga. App. 842, 847–48, 613 S.E.2d 651, 656 (2005) (fact that plaintiff suffered greater injuries in motor vehicle accident due to failure of seat belt to restrain him and failure of air bag to inflate than he otherwise would have suffered did not require the expertise of a physician or engineer).

[4]Jordan v. Smoot, 191 Ga. App. 74, 75, 380 S.E.2d 714 (1989).

[5]Madden v. Solomon, 196 Ga. App. 512, 396 S.E.2d 245 (1990); Jordan v. Smoot, 191 Ga. App. 74, 380 S.E.2d 714 (1989).

[6]Hutcheson v. Daniels, 224 Ga. App. 560, 481 S.E.2d 567 (1997).

[7]Eberhart v. Morris Brown College, 181 Ga. App. 516, 518, 352 S.E.2d 832 (1987).

[8]Hutcheson v. Daniels, 224 Ga. App. 560, 481 S.E.2d 567 (1997);

ally been required to show that the plaintiff's "new" injuries are attributable to the accident as opposed to an independent and unrelated cause.[9]

Where the event is not of the sort that results in readily apparent trauma, expert testimony is generally required to establish causation.[10] For instance, in cases alleging medical malpractice to be the cause of an injury, expert testimony is usually required to establish that the alleged professional negligence was the cause of the plaintiff's injury, as such a determination is typically beyond the ability of the average juror to ascertain on his or her own.[11] Similarly, in cases alleging that a plaintiff's illness or disease were caused by the plaintiff's exposure to a certain medication or other substance, expert testimony is generally required to establish that the plaintiff's illness or disease were in fact caused by the substance as opposed to some other cause.[12]

Madden v. Solomon, 196 Ga. App. 512, 396 S.E.2d 245 (1990); Jordan v. Smoot, 191 Ga. App. 74, 380 S.E.2d 714 (1989).

[9]Lancaster v. USAA Cas. Ins. Co., 232 Ga. App. 805, 807–808, 502 S.E.2d 752 (1998) (where at issue was not whether neck, back, and knee pain suffered immediately following accident was caused by the accident, but whether the accident aggravated plaintiff's preexisting fibromyalgia, the connection was "not the type of common sense deduction that lay factfinders have been competent to make"); see also Webb v. Thomas Trucking, Inc., 255 Ga. App. 637, 566 S.E.2d 390 (2002) (expert testimony needed to demonstrate that plaintiff's injuries attributable to motor vehicle accident where plaintiff did not seek treatment until five days following collision, and plaintiff had long history of preexisting neck and shoulder problems prior to collision).

[10]Magnan v. Miami Aircraft Support, Inc., 217 Ga. App. 855, 857, 459 S.E.2d 592 (1995) (plaintiff's testimony that eye problems caused by exposure to pesticide insufficient to establish causation, and medical testimony required); see also Lewis v. Smith, 238 Ga. App. 6, 9–10, 517 S.E.2d 538 (1999) (whether defendant's use of medication made it fore-

seeable that defendant would lose consciousness, making it negligent for defendant to operate motor vehicle, presented medical question beyond comprehension of lay person).

[11]See, e.g. Jones v. Orris, 274 Ga. App. 52, 56, 616 S.E.2d 820, 824 (2005), cert. denied, (Oct. 24, 2005) (expert testimony required to show that physician's alleged misdiagnosis caused plaintiff to suffer permanent damage from a ruptured appendix, thereby compromising her fertility); Cherokee County Hosp. Authority v. Beaver, 179 Ga. App. 200, 205, 345 S.E.2d 904, 908 (1986) (expert testimony required to show that plaintiff's symptoms resulted from medical personnel administering injection in a certain part of body); Overstreet v. Nickelsen, 170 Ga. App. 539, 317 S.E.2d 583 (1984) (expert testimony required to show physician's allegedly negligent diagnosis and treatment of cut on plaintiff's finger ultimately caused finger to require amputation). See generally Chapter 10, Medical malpractice.

[12]See, e.g, Lewis v. Smith, 238 Ga. App. 6, 9–10, 517 S.E.2d 538, 542 (1999) (whether individual's ingestion of drug caused him to lose consciousness while driving required expert medical testimony); Magnan v. Miami Aircraft Support, Inc., 217 Ga. App. 855, 857, 459 S.E.2d 592, 595 (1995)

§ 11:2 Causation and physical injuries

The range of experts which may be employed to opine that the plaintiff's personal injuries are attributable to fault on the part of the defendant is as broad as the myriad ways in which individuals may suffer personal injuries. Medical doctors may be offered to opine that a health care provider's conduct fell below the standard of care,[1] engineers may be offered to opine that a product's design or manufacture was defective,[2] accident reconstructionists may be offered to opine as to how a motor vehicle accident occurred.[3] The issue as to how a personal injury occurred, and whether it is attributable to fault on the part of the defendant is beyond the scope of this chapter, and is discussed in the several chapters addressing specific types of cases.

A separate issue arises as to whether the plaintiff's specific injuries were in fact caused by the specific accident or event claimed to have produced the injury. On this issue, medical doctors are commonly employed toward the end of establishing the causal link between an event and the plaintiff's specific injury or injuries.[4] While Georgia courts have expressed a strong preference for the testimony of medical doctors when it comes to establishing this causal link, a medical doctor is not necessarily required to establish the matter of causation. "Georgia law does not mandate that only medical doctors may testify regarding medical issues; others with certain training and experience may testify on issues within the parameters of their expertise."[5] Chiropractors have been held to be qualified to testify as to

---

(expert medical testimony required to show that exposure to pesticides caused plaintiff's eye problems); Morris v. Chandler Exterminators, Inc., 200 Ga. App. 816, 820, 409 S.E.2d 677, 680 (1991), rev'd on other grounds, 262 Ga. 257, 416 S.E.2d 277 (1992) (Andrews. J., dissenting) (whether exposure to pesticides caused plaintiff's physical illness is a medical question necessitating expert testimony). See generally Chapter 7, Toxic torts.

[Section 11:2]

[1]See Chapter 10, Medical malpractice.

[2]See Chapter 6, Products liability.

[3]See Chapter 11, Motor vehicle accidents.

[4]See, e.g. Pennsylvania Threshermen & Farmers Mut. Cas. Ins. Co.

v. Gilliam, 88 Ga. App. 451, 453, 76 S.E.2d 834 (1953) ("The diagnosis and treatment of injury and disease are essentially medical questions to be established by physicians as expert witnesses and not by laymen.").

[5]Cromer v. Mulkey Enterprises, Inc., 254 Ga. App. 388, 392, 562 S.E.2d 783 (2002). In *Cromer*, at issue was whether an expert in biomechanics was qualified to testify that an individual's specific spinal injuries were in fact caused by the accident at issue. The court articulated the analysis as: "whether the ability to determine if a certain accident caused as certain injury has reached a scientific stage of verifiable certainty and 2) whether [the expert] had expertise in that science." Cromer v. Mulkey Enterprises, Inc., 254 Ga. App. 388, 393, 562 S.E.2d 783 (2002) The court excluded the expert's proffered testimony, finding

whether a plaintiff's orthopedic injuries arose out of a motor vehicle accident,[6] and coroners have been held qualified to testify as to whether an individual's injuries were consistent with having been in the driver's seat of an automobile.[7]

Just how far any particular type of expert may go toward the end of establishing causation will necessarily be limited by whether their testimony falls within their area of expertise. "While expert witnesses may give their opinions as to facts, principles and rules involved in the science in which they are learned, they are not, as to questions lying outside the domain of the science, art, or trade in which they are experts, exempt from the restriction of the rule which requires witnesses to state facts and not opinions."[8] For instance, in *Johnson v. Knebel*, an engineer with experience in accident reconstruction was found competent to testify as to the circumstances leading to the multiple vehicle accident, but was not found qualified to provide testimony as to which of the two collisions was the cause of the plaintiff's injuries where there was no evidence that he had knowledge about human physiology, anatomy, biomechanics, or osteology.[9] Similarly, in *Cromer v. Mulkey Enterprises*, the court upheld the trial court's finding that while a physicist with experience in biomechanics may have been permitted to testify as to how a motor vehicle accident occurred and how the plaintiff's body reacted within the cabin, there was insufficient evidence presented that the expert was qualified to testify as to the "next level of conclusion," namely, whether the plaintiff's spinal injuries was in fact caused by the accident.[10] By contrast, in *Brown v. Hove*, the testimony of a neuroradiologist that a plaintiff's disk herniation was not likely caused by a motor vehicle accident was held admissible where evidence was presented that the physician had acquired knowledge in biomechanics in the course of his practice and was familiar with radiological literature identifying

that there was "limited evidence in the record that the field of biomechanics includes a technique of determining if specific injuries result from specific accidents, let alone that that technique has reached a scientific stage of verifiable certainty." *Id.* This analysis came close to the analysis required of O.C.G.A. § 24–9–67.1 even before its enactment.

[6]Madden v. Solomon, 196 Ga. App. 512, 396 S.E.2d 245 (1990).

[7]Sheets v. State, 244 Ga. App. 304, 535 S.E.2d 312 (2000).

[8]Chandler Exterminators, Inc. v. Morris, 262 Ga. 257, 258, 416 S.E.2d 277 (1992) (citing Hammond v. State, 156 Ga. 880, 120 S.E. 539 (1923)).

[9]Johnson v. Knebel, 267 Ga. 853, 858, 485 S.E.2d 451 (1997).

[10]Cromer v. Mulkey Enterprises, Inc., 254 Ga. App. 388, 393, 562 S.E.2d 783 (2002).

the types of stress and body movements likely to cause disk herniation.[11]

The fact that one is a medical doctor does not, of course, enable him or her to testify as to all matters pertaining to the causal link between an event and an injury. As with any expert, a medical doctor can only testify to matters within the domain of his expertise.[12] In some instances, courts have indicated a preference for a certain type of expert in lieu of a medical doctor given the nature of the questions raised in the case. For instance, in toxic tort cases, where at issue is whether a medication is capable of causing a certain condition, courts have recognized that pharmacologists would generally be better qualified to answer such questions than medical doctors.[13]

Expert medical testimony establishing that an accident or event was a possible cause of the plaintiff's specific injuries is, standing alone, insufficient; rather, such testimony must demonstrate that there is a "reasonable probability" that the plaintiff's specific injuries were in fact caused by the accident or event at issue.[14] Nonetheless, medical testimony as to a mere "possibility" of causation may be sufficient where there is other evidence in the record indicating that a causal relation exists between the accident or event and the plaintiff's injuries.[15] "Mere possibility" testimony would not be sufficient, however, where the issue of causation is one which is required to be established by expert medical testimony.[16]

---

[11]Brown v. Hove, 268 Ga. App. 732, 734–735, 603 S.E.2d 63 (2004), cert. denied, (Jan. 10, 2005).

[12]See e.g., Robertson v. State, 225 Ga. App. 389, 484 S.E.2d 18 (1997) (medical doctor not competent to testify that victim shot at close range based on angle of bullet in body because he had no formal training in ballistics); City of Fairburn v. Cook, 188 Ga. App. 58, 372 S.E.2d 245 (1988) (physician not permitted to testify as to the consequences of not wearing a seatbelt absent foundation being laid establishing competence to testify on such matters).

[13]Sinkfield v. Oh, 229 Ga. App. 883, 885, 495 S.E.2d 94, 96 (1997).

[14]Lewis v. Smith, 238 Ga. App. 6, 9–10, 517 S.E.2d 538 (1999); Maurer v. Chyatte, 173 Ga. App. 343, 344–345, 326 S.E.2d 543 (1985). In Maurer, the physician's testimony that a motor vehicle accident was the "most probable" cause of plaintiff's symptoms was admissible where the physician testified that the plaintiff's symptoms would only have arisen from damage to the spinal cord, and that there were no preexisting conditions or any diseases which may have accounted for the plaintiff's symptoms.

[15]Hodson v. Mawson, 227 Ga. App. 490, 492, 489 S.E.2d 855 (1997); Hert v. Gibbs, 191 Ga. App. 471, 472, 382 S.E.2d 191 (1989).

[16]This would be the case where expert testimony is required to establish causation, as in medical malpractice or toxic tort cases. See, e.g. Magnan v. Miami Aircraft Support, Inc., 217 Ga. App. 855, 459 S.E.2d 592 (1995) (where medical testimony did not establish to a reasonable probability that plaintiff's injuries were caused by

§ 11:3   Use of medical records and bills

Historically, the rule in Georgia has been that a physician's opinion testimony which is based solely upon medical records or facts which have not been admitted into evidence is not admissible.[1] "Opinion testimony based merely upon records and case history furnished the witness by other doctors and not a part of the evidence in the case is objectionable."[2] However, where the medical records have in fact been admitted into evidence, a physician providing expert medical testimony may base his opinions on such records.[3] The matter of admitting medical records into evidence will be a relatively simply matter where the records contain only objective, factual data, such as laboratory data, as such records may be admitted under the business records exception to the hearsay rule.[4] By contrast, where the medical records sought to be admitted contain not merely factual data, but diagnostic opinions and conclusions as well, such records are not admissible over objection until a proper foundation has been laid for their admission, to include qualifying the individual forming the opinions and conclusions as an expert and having that individual relate the facts upon which the opinions and conclusions are based.[5] A physician offering opinion testimony is not permit-

exposure to substance, and the only other evidence of record tending to establish causation was plaintiff's own testimony, plaintiff failed to show causation).

[Section 11:3]

[1]Morrison v. Koornick, 201 Ga. App. 367, 369, 411 S.E.2d 105 (1991); Doctors Hosp. of Augusta, Inc. v. Bonner, 195 Ga. App. 152, 159, 392 S.E.2d 897 (1990).

[2]Stouffer Corp. v. Henkel, 170 Ga. App. 383, 386, 317 S.E.2d 222 (1984); see also Buffalo Cab Co., Inc. v. Gurley, 134 Ga. App. 167, 213 S.E.2d 545 (1975).

[3]Morrison v. Koornick, 201 Ga. App. 367, 369, 411 S.E.2d 105 (1991); Doctors Hosp. of Augusta, Inc. v. Bonner, 195 Ga. App. 152, 159, 392 S.E.2d 897 (1990).

[4]Dixon v. State, 227 Ga. App. 533, 535, 489 S.E.2d 532 (1997) (computer printout of laboratory tests contained only factual data, and not opinions or conclusions of physicians about the underlying data; thus, records were admissible as business records without the need for procuring additional foundation testimony from those who may have interpreted or formed conclusions based upon the data); Wilson v. Childers, 174 Ga. App. 179, 329 S.E.2d 503 (1985) (where hospital records custodian laid foundation for hospital laboratory reports as true and accurate copies, unnecessary to offer testimony of personnel who performed laboratory tests and prepared laboratory report as foundation for admitting report); Buffalo Cab Co., Inc. v. Gurley, 134 Ga. App. 167, 213 S.E.2d 545 (1975).

[5]Kohl v. Tirado, 256 Ga. App. 681, 683–684, 569 S.E.2d 576 (2002); Dennis v. Adcock, 138 Ga. App. 425, 226 S.E.2d 292 (1976); see also Moody v. State, 244 Ga. 247, 249, 260 S.E.2d 11 (1979).

ted to act as a mere "conduit" for the opinions of other physicians.[6]

An important qualification has historically existed to these rules. While a physician's opinions cannot be based *solely* on hearsay, a physician's opinions which are based only *in part* upon hearsay—i.e. records or facts which have not been admitted into evidence—are not objectionable.[7] The fact that a physician's opinions are based in part on hearsay goes to the weight of the physician's testimony, not its admissibility.[8] Thus, where a physician forms an opinion regarding a patient's injuries based in part upon his own observations of the patient, his opinion testimony is not inadmissible merely because it is also based in part upon the records or opinions of others which have not been admitted into evidence.[9] It is recognized that a physician's knowledge gained in the course of his education and practice may also provide support for the physician's opinions, even though the sources of this knowledge are not in evidence and would otherwise constitute "hearsay."[10]

It is uncertain how the enactment of O.C.G.A. § 24–9–67.1(a) will impact these historical rules.[11] In pertinent part, this statute provides that "[i]f of a type reasonably relied upon by experts in the particular field in forming opinions or inferences on the subject, the facts or data [upon which an expert bases an opinion or inference] need not be admissible in evidence in order for the opinion or inference to be admitted."[12] This language is identical to the language of Rule 703 of the Federal Rules of Evidence, which was adopted as a rule of convenience based upon the rec-

---

[6]Doctors Hosp. of Augusta, Inc. v. Bonner, 195 Ga. App. 152, 159, 392 S.E.2d 897 (1990); Mallard v. Colonial Life & Acc. Ins. Co., 173 Ga. App. 276, 326 S.E.2d 6 (1985) ("While an expert may base his opinion on facts provided to him by others, he may not simply restate the opinion of another expert.").

[7]Joiner v. Lane, 235 Ga. App. 121, 126, 508 S.E.2d 203 (1998); Bentley v. B.M.W., Inc., 209 Ga. App. 526, 528, 433 S.E.2d 719 (1993) (overruled on other grounds by, Sheriff v. State, 277 Ga. 182, 587 S.E.2d 27 (2003)).

[8]Joiner v. Lane, 235 Ga. App. 121, 126, 508 S.E.2d 203 (1998); Bentley v. B.M.W., Inc., 209 Ga. App. 526, 528, 433 S.E.2d 719 (1993) (overruled on other grounds by, Sheriff v. State, 277 Ga. 182, 587 S.E.2d 27

(2003)); Doctors Hosp. of Augusta, Inc. v. Bonner, 195 Ga. App. 152, 160, 392 S.E.2d 897 (1990);

[9]Joiner v. Lane, 235 Ga. App. 121, 126, 508 S.E.2d 203 (1998); Stephens v. Howard, 221 Ga. App. 469, 471 S.E.2d 898 (1996); Bentley v. B.M.W., Inc., 209 Ga. App. 526, 528, 433 S.E.2d 719 (1993) (overruled on other grounds by, Sheriff v. State, 277 Ga. 182, 587 S.E.2d 27 (2003)); Randall Memorial Mortuary, Inc. v. O'Quinn, 202 Ga. App. 541, 542–543, 414 S.E.2d 744 (1992).

[10]Joiner v. Lane, 235 Ga. App. 121, 126, 508 S.E.2d 203 (1998).

[11]See Chapter 2, § 2:8 for a detailed discussion of this statute and its relationship with Georgia law historically.

[12]O.C.G.A. § 24–9–67.1(a).

ognition that experts frequently rely upon the documents prepared by others, and even the opinions of others, as a matter of course in their routine, day-to-day, professional activities.[13] However, parties may still question the reliability or reasonableness of an expert's testimony which is based entirely on inadmissible hearsay.[14] It may be the case that Georgia's historical distinction between expert testimony which is based only in part upon hearsay, and expert testimony which is based solely or primarily upon hearsay, is carried forward by O.C.G.A. § 24–9–67.1(b), which requires that an expert's opinions be based upon "sufficient facts or data which are or will be admitted into evidence."

O.C.G.A. § 24–7–8 provides that medical records, when certified by a custodian, "need not be identified at the trial and may be used in any manner in which records identified at the trial by the custodian could be used." This statute addresses only the authentication of medical records, providing a means by which such records may be identified absent a custodian appearing at trial.[15] The authentication of medical records pursuant to this statute does not dispense with the need to satisfy other evidentiary requirements. Thus, records which have been authenticated, but which contain the opinions and conclusions of providers who have not testified, are not admissible over a hearsay objection until a proper foundation has been laid for their admission into evidence.[16]

O.C.G.A. § 24–7–9 provides that, in personal injury cases, the

---

[13]Advisory Committee Notes to Rule 703.

[14]See, e.g. Leonard v. State, 269 Ga. 867, 870, 506 S.E.2d 853, 856 (1998). In Leonard, the court observed that:

'[a]n opinion, based mainly on representations out of court, can be no more competent testimony than the representations. If the jury are not informed what the representations were, they do no know upon what hypothesis of facts the opinion rests. If they are informed, they are still left with not evidence of the existence of the facts, except unsworn declarations of a third person out of court, which are not proof in courts of law.'

Leonard v. State, 269 Ga. 867, 870, 506 S.E.2d 853 (1998) (citing Moore v. State, 221 Ga. 636, 146 S.E.2d 895 (1966)); see also In Interest of A.S.M., 214 Ga. App. 668, 671, 448 S.E.2d 703, 706 (1994) ("An expert may five an opinion upon the facts testified to by other witnesses, but not their opinions. A witness' opinion must be his own and he cannot act as a mere conduit for the opinion of others."); Doctors Hosp. of Augusta, Inc. v. Bonner, 195 Ga. App. 152, 159, 392 S.E.2d 897, 903–904 (1990) ("A physician may not base his expert opinion solely on the hearsay opinion of another doctor, thereby acting as a mere conduit for the opinion of the first.").

[15]Moody v. State, 244 Ga. 247, 249, 260 S.E.2d 11 (1979); Dennis v. Adcock, 138 Ga. App. 425, 428, 226 S.E.2d 292 (1976).

[16]Moody v. State, 244 Ga. 247, 249, 260 S.E.2d 11 (1979); Giles v. Taylor, 166 Ga. App. 563, 563, 305 S.E.2d 154 (1983); Dennis v. Adcock, 138 Ga. App. 425, 428, 226 S.E.2d 292 (1976).

patient, the patient's family member, or other person responsible for the care of the patient is competent to identify medical bills incurred in the patient's treatment upon a showing by that witness that the bills were incurred in connection with the treatment of the injuries which are the subject matter of the litigation.[17] The bills must have been received from either a hospital, ambulance service, pharmacy or supplier of therapeutic or orthopedic devices, or a "licensed practicing physician, chiropractor, dentist, orthotist, podiatrist, or psychologist."[18] The bills need not be identified by the medical provider submitting the bill, and it is not necessary for the plaintiff to establish, by way of expert testimony, that the charges reflected in the bills were "reasonable and necessary."[19] This statute, while simplifying the matter of proving the medical expenses a plaintiff has incurred, does not obviate a plaintiff's burden of demonstrating that these medical expenses were causally related to the defendant's conduct, and expert medical testimony may be required in this regard.[20]

O.C.G.A. § 24–3–18 provides that a medical report in "narrative form" which has been signed and dated by certain enumerated types of health care providers[21] who have examined or treated the patient is admissible into evidence "insofar as it purports to represent the history, examination, diagnosis, treatment, prognosis, or interpretation of tests or examinations, including the basis therefore, by the person signing the report, the same as if that person were present at trial and testifying as a witness." The statute requires the party intending to use the

---

[17]O.C.G.A. § 24–7–9(a). This statute does not permit an introduction of a summary of the bills in lieu of the actual bills themselves. Hossain v. Nelson, 234 Ga. App. 792, 507 S.E.2d 243 (1998). In Lester v. S. J. Alexander, Inc., 127 Ga. App. 470, 193 S.E.2d 860 (1972), the court excluded a hospital bill which failed to differentiate between charges directly related to the plaintiff's injuries arising out of an automobile accident and charges for an unrelated procedure. However, in Atlanta Transit System, Inc. v. Smith, 141 Ga. App. 87, 232 S.E.2d 580 (1977), the court allowed the plaintiff to introduce medical bills where, despite the defendant's contention that several of the charges related to a previous unrelated injury, the bills specified the charges and the reasons therefore, and the plaintiff was subject to cross-examination on this matter.

[18]O.C.G.A. § 24–7–9(a).

[19]O.C.G.A. § 24–7–9(b). The statute was "enacted as a pragmatic process to eliminate the necessity of having an expert witness testify that medical expenses incurred for treatment of injuries resulting from the subject of litigation were reasonable and necessary." Glover v. Southern Bell Tel. & Tel. Co., 132 Ga. App. 74, 75, 207 S.E.2d 584 (1974).

[20]Eberhart v. Morris Brown College, 181 Ga. App. 516, 518–519, 352 S.E.2d 832 (1987).

[21]These include licensed medical doctors, dentists, orthodontists, podiatrists, physical or occupational therapists, chiropractors, psychologists, advanced practical nurses, social workers, professional counselors, and marriage or family therapists.

report at trial to produce the report to the adverse party and notify the adverse party of his intention to use the report at least 60 days prior to trial.[22] A statement of the preparer's qualifications may be included with the report, and the preparer may include his opinion as to the cause of the injury or illness as part of the diagnosis.[23] The adverse party has the right to object to the admissibility, other than on the grounds of hearsay, of any portion of the report within 15 days of its receipt, and has the right to cross-examine the preparer and provide rebuttal testimony.[24] The report is to be presented to the jury in the same way as a deposition is read to a jury at trial, but the report does not go out with the jury as original documentary evidence.[25]

This statute, modeled after a similar statute applicable in workers' compensation cases, creates a hearsay exception to medical reports in civil cases involving personal injury.[26] It was designed to "cut down on the time and cost" in personal injury actions by dispensing with the necessity of calling the author of the medical report as a witness at trial.[27] Where an objection to the report is lodged within 15 days of its receipt, the opposing party retains the right to object to the report's admission into evidence, including objections to the effect that the preparer lacked the necessary qualifications to offer the opinions set forth in the report.[28] The statute requires the report to be placed in a narrative form readily understood by lay persons, and medical records which do not meet this requirement are still subject to a hearsay objection.[29]

§ 11:4 Mental and emotional damages

Mental and emotional suffering is often a component of damages in an action for personal injuries, and expert testimony from a mental health professional is frequently employed toward the end establishing that the event in question was a cause of the

---

[22]O.C.G.A. § 24-3-18(a).

[23]O.C.G.A. § 24-3-18(a).

[24]O.C.G.A. § 24-3-18(a).

[25]O.C.G.A. § 24-3-18(b).

[26]Bell v. Austin, 278 Ga. 844, 845, 607 S.E.2d 569 (2005).

[27]Bell v. Austin, 278 Ga. 844, 845, 848, 607 S.E.2d 569 (2005).

[28]Bell v. Austin, 278 Ga. 844, 846, 607 S.E.2d 569 (2005).

[29]Bell v. Austin, 278 Ga. 844, 847, 607 S.E.2d 569 (2005) ("[T]he law authorizes the admission of only those reports which, rather than consisting of unexplicated medical terms and uninterpreted scientific test results, set forth the relevant information in prose language that is more readily understandable to laymen. Other medical records which would require an expert analysis to demonstrate their import are still subject to a hearsay objection.").

individual's emotional injuries,[1] as well as the nature and extent
of the emotional injuries suffered as a result of that event.[2] In actions based on negligence, Georgia's "impact rule" provides that,
in order for a plaintiff to recover for mental and emotional suffering, the plaintiff must have suffered a physical impact which
caused physical injury, and that this physical injury in turn
caused the mental and emotion injuries of which the plaintiff
complains.[3] The requirement of a "physical impact" does not exist
where an action for emotional injuries is premised on a defendant's intentionally tortious conduct.[4] However, in such a case,
the plaintiff's emotional injuries must be so severe that a reasonable person could not be expected to endure them, and expert
testimony as to the severity of the emotional distress suffered

---

[Section 11:4]

[1]See, e.g. Nationwide Mut. Fire Ins. Co. v. Lam, 248 Ga. App. 134, 138, 546 S.E.2d 283, 285 (2001) ("the causal connection between aggravation of an existing mental illness and a traumatic event such as the collision here is at least as susceptible of expert medical proof as many physical soft tissue injuries"); Dickens v. Adams, 137 Ga. App. 564, 224 S.E.2d 468 (1976) (psychiatrist testimony that plaintiff's anxiety and depression caused by involvement in motor vehicle accident).

[2]See, e.g. Norfolk Southern Ry. Co. v. Blackmon, 262 Ga. App. 266, 585 S.E.2d 194 (2003) (psychologist testimony regarding plaintiff's anxiety and depression following train accident); Kane v. Cohen, 182 Ga. App. 485, 356 S.E.2d 94 (1987) (psychiatrist testimony that plaintiff's depression and anxiety due to post-traumatic stress disorder following motor vehicle accident).

[3]Wilson v. Allen, 272 Ga. App. 172, 173–174, 612 S.E.2d 39, 41 (2005), cert. denied, (Sept. 19, 2005) (citing Canberg v. City of Toccoa, 255 Ga. App. 890, 567 S.E.2d 21 (2002)) ("In a claim concerning negligent conduct, a recovery for emotional distress is allowed only where there is some physical impact on the plaintiff, and that impact must be a physical injury. Georgia's current impact rule has three elements: (1) a physical impact to the plaintiff (2) the physical impact causes physical injury to the plaintiff; and (3) the physical injury to the plaintiff causes the plaintiff's mental suffering or emotional distress. The failure to satisfy all three elements has proven fatal to recovery."). Cf. Chambley v. Apple Restaurants, Inc., 233 Ga. App. 498, 504 S.E.2d 551 (1998) (in addressing Georgia's impact rule, a sharply divided court found that the gastric distress suffered by plaintiff after finding an unwrapped condom in her partially-eaten salad was sufficient to allow plaintiff to recover on a claim for negligent infliction of emotional distress, despite the fact that the plaintiff did not come into contact with the condom and the condom was not soiled or otherwise contaminated).

[4]Dodd v. City of Gainesville, 268 Ga. App. 43, 601 S.E.2d 352 (2004). In an action predicated on a defendant's intentional conduct, the conduct must be "extreme and outrageous." Hendrix v. Phillips, 207 Ga. App. 394, 395, 428 S.E.2d 91, 93 (1993). In other words, the conduct must rise to the level of being "atrocious, and utterly intolerable in a civilized community." Turnbull v. Northside Hosp., Inc., 220 Ga. App. 883, 884, 470 S.E.2d 464, 466 (1996). It has been generally noted that this imposes a "stringent" burden upon the plaintiff. Frank v. Fleet Finance, Inc. of Georgia, 238 Ga. App. 316, 318, 518 S.E.2d 717, 720 (1999).

will not necessarily support a recovery where the plaintiff's reaction to an event is exaggerated or objectively unreasonable.[5]

A mental health expert's testimony that an event was a possible cause of the plaintiff's mental or emotional damages is, in itself, insufficient to establish a causal connection between the event and injury.[6] Rather, consistent with the general rule regarding expert testimony on causation, such an expert must be able to testify that there is a reasonable probability that the event at issue caused the plaintiff's mental or emotional damages.[7] However, expert testimony as to a mere possibility that the event at issue was or was not the cause of the plaintiff's mental or emotional injuries is sufficient where there also exists other evidence indicating a causal nexus, or lack thereof, between the event and the plaintiff's injuries.[8]

Prior to 1993, psychologists were deemed incompetent to testify as to the cause of a psychological disorder where it was alleged that the disorder was organic in nature, as this entailed a "medi-

[5]Peoples v. Guthrie, 199 Ga. App. 119, 404 S.E.2d 442 (1991) (psychologist's testimony that plaintiff suffered post traumatic stress disorder as a result of having been accused of cheating on a test insufficient to support plaintiff's recovery). In *Guthrie,* the court observed that "[t]he law intervenes only where the distress inflicted is so severe that no reasonable man could be expected to endure it. It is not the severity of a plaintiff's reaction that controls in these cases: The distress must be reasonable and justified under the circumstances, and there is no liability where the plaintiff has suffered exaggerated and unreasonable emotional distress." Peoples v. Guthrie, 199 Ga. App. 119, at 121–122, 404 S.E.2d 442 (1991); see also Kornegay v. Mundy, 190 Ga. App. 433, 434–435, 379 S.E.2d 14, 16 (1989) (liability "clearly does not extend to mere insults, indignities, threats, annoyances, petty oppressions, and other trivialities. The rough edges of our society are still in need of filing down, and in the meantime plaintiffs must necessarily be expected and required to be hardened to a certain amount of rough language, and to occasional acts that are definitely inconsiderate and unkind. There is no occasion for the law to intervene in every case where someone's feelings are hurt."). However, liability may attach where the defendant is aware of the plaintiff's particular susceptibility to such distress. Peoples v. Guthrie, 199 Ga. App. 119, 122, 404 S.E.2d 442, 444 (1991).

[6]Maurer v. Chyatte, 173 Ga. App. 343, 344–345, 326 S.E.2d 543, 545 (1985).

[7]Maurer v. Chyatte, 173 Ga. App. 343, 344–345, 326 S.E.2d 543, 545 (1985); National Dairy Products Corp. v. Durham, 115 Ga. App. 420, 423, 154 S.E.2d 752, 754 (1967).

[8]Jacobs v. Pilgrim, 186 Ga. App. 260, 262, 367 S.E.2d 49, 51–52 (1988) (although psychologist could not state to a reasonable degree of probability that plaintiff's psychological problems were not caused by head injury, psychologist's testimony, combined with failure of plaintiff to report head injury to treating medical personnel and normal medical tests, sufficient to establish lack of causal nexus between head injury and psychological problems).

cal" determination beyond the scope of a psychologist's expertise.[9] Thus, it was held that a psychologist's testimony that a plaintiff's mental disorder was caused by exposure to a chemical,[10] or a blow to the head,[11] was inadmissible. However, in 1993, O.C.G.A. § 43–39–1 was amended to define the practice of neuropsychology as the "subspecialty of psychology concerned with the relationship between the brain and behavior, including the diagnosis of brain pathology through the use of psychological tests and assessment techniques[,]" and broaden the definition of psychology so as to include "diagnosing and treating mental and nervous disorders and illnesses, rendering opinions concerning diagnoses or mental disorders, including organic brain disorders and brain damage." Consequently, it has been held that a neuropsychologist is competent of rendering opinions as to the cause of a plaintiff's mental or emotional disorder where it is alleged to be of organic origin.[12]

At times, the issue arises as to whether the cause of an individual's mental or emotional suffering was the event at issue in litigation or some other event, such as a preexisting mental illness[13] or other life stressors.[14] Just as expert testimony is employed for the purpose of establishing causation and damages, it is often employed for the purposes of disputing these elements. For instance, in cases wherein lost earnings, past or present, is alleged to be an item of damages caused by the defendant's conduct, expert testimony opining that the plaintiff's inability to work has as its cause a psychological condition unrelated to the defendant's conduct is admissible.[15] Similarly, expert testimony has been admitted for the purpose of showing that a plaintiff's

---

[9]Chandler Exterminators, Inc. v. Morris, 262 Ga. 257, 258, 416 S.E.2d 277, 278 (1992) (noting the distinction between psychiatrists, who are medical doctors, and psychologists, who are not).

[10]Chandler Exterminators, Inc. v. Morris, 262 Ga. 257, 416 S.E.2d 277 (1992).

[11]Handy v. Speth, 210 Ga. App. 155, 435 S.E.2d 623 (1993).

[12]Sinkfield v. Oh, 229 Ga. App. 883, 495 S.E.2d 94 (1997); Drake v. LaRue Const. Co., 215 Ga. App. 453, 451 S.E.2d 792 (1994).

[13]See, e.g. Nationwide Mut. Fire Ins. Co. v. Lam, 248 Ga. App. 134, 546 S.E.2d 283 (2001) (plaintiff suffered from bipolar disorder and various other psychological conditions prior to

motor vehicle accident, which was alleged to have aggravated psychological problems).

[14]See, e.g. Cook v. Partain, 224 Ga. App. 251, 480 S.E.2d 279 (1997) (where plaintiff claimed that she suffered post traumatic stress disorder as a result of defendant's conduct, other lawsuits filed by plaintiff alleging similar damages relevant for purpose of showing plaintiff's mental and emotional injuries were result of events other than defendant's conduct).

[15]See, e.g. Jacobs v. Pilgrim, 186 Ga. App. 260, 367 S.E.2d 49 (1988) (in action for personal injuries and lost future earnings, psychologist's testimony that plaintiff's inability to return to work following motor vehicle accident was due to psychophysiological reaction to stress relevant and admis-

physical injuries are the result of an unrelated psychological condition causing the plaintiff to produce exaggerated reports of his or his or her injuries,[16] or the plaintiff's desire for financial gain.[17] The admission of such testimony has been upheld over the objection that such testimony is an impermissible opinion on the plaintiff's credibility when it has been shown that the condition causing the plaintiff to have or complain of physical symptoms out of proportion to the injury suffered is a recognized psychological or psychiatric disorder.[18]

Of course, the ability of a defendant to discover information from a plaintiff's treating mental health providers toward the end of establishing such defenses is limited by the evidentiary privilege which attaches to communications between a patient and his

sible to counter testimony by another psychologist that plaintiff's inability to return to work was due to organic brain damage, and ensuing depression, caused by motor vehicle accident).

[16]David Jordan Logging Co. v. Sales, 203 Ga. App. 410, 411, 416 S.E.2d 803, 804–805 (1992) (in workers' compensation case for disability benefits, physician's testimony that there was no physical reason for claimant's complaints, and that they were due to "a hysterical reaction to the injury and that psychological factors could be a cause of his continued complaints" relevant and admissible); Wildstein v. Gray, 146 Ga. App. 222, 246 S.E.2d 130 (1978) ("Whether appellant was feigning injury was a relevant inquiry, and expert testimony relative thereto was properly admitted over a relevancy objection.").

[17]Drake v. Shurbutt, 129 Ga. App. 754, 201 S.E.2d 184 (1973); Davis v. Laird, 108 Ga. App. 729, 134 S.E.2d 467 (1963).

[18]Rose v. Figgie Intern., Inc., 229 Ga. App. 848, 495 S.E.2d 77 (1997). In Rose, a plaintiff complained of respiratory problems following exposure to chemicals released by an exploding fire extinguisher. Various treating physicians failed to find any objective medical evidence that the plaintiff's respiratory problems were caused by her exposure to these chemicals, with one opining that the plaintiff "was trying

to make me think that she was actually sicker than she really is." Pursuant to a court-ordered psychiatric evaluation, a psychiatrist and psychologist opined that the plaintiff suffered from "a psychiatric clinical disorder of malingering or somatoform and from a psychiatric narcissistic personality disorder with anti-social features and histrionic traits." The psychiatrist testified that, due to these disorders, the plaintiff: 1) was producing false or exaggerated physical symptoms motivated by financial compensation; 2) often exaggerated or manufactured information "to overcome feelings of inferiority and to inflate her own self importance"; and 3) took advantage of others to achieve her own ends. In finding such testimony admissible, the court observed:

Drs. Davis and Powell do not opine that Rose is lying or not credible. Rather, they diagnose her as suffering from recognized psychiatric disorders that have caused her to have or complain of physical symptoms out of proportion to any injuries she may have experienced. These disorders may explain the testimony of other physicians that her respiratory ailments are sporadic and lack an organic basis, and, if linked to the explosion, have continued over a much longer period of time than would normally be expected. This relates directly to the issue of causation. . . . Such evidence would also relate to damages.

Rose v. Figgie Intern., Inc., 229 Ga. App. 848, at 857, 495 S.E.2d 77 (1997)

or her mental health providers.[19] Applicable to a variety of mental health providers,[20] the privilege protects the communications[21] between a patient and a mental health provider where treatment was given or contemplated.[22] In order for such communications to be subject to discovery, the plaintiff must waive the privilege either expressly or implicitly.[23] The plaintiff's calling of a mental

---

[19]See O.C.G.A. §§ 24–9–21, 43–39–16. In discussing the purpose underlying this evidentiary privilege, the Georgia Supreme Court observed in State v. Herendeen, 279 Ga. 323, 613 S.E.2d 647 (2005):

> Protecting confidential mental health communications from disclosure serves an important private interest and a public interest. Jaffee v. Redmond, 518 U.S. 1, at 10–11, 116 S. Ct. 1923, 135 L. Ed. 2d 337 (1996), *supra*. As far as the individual patient's private interest is concerned, confidentiality is a sine qua non for successful psychotherapeutic treatment since a psychotherapist's ability to help a patient is completely dependent upon the patient's willingness and ability to talk freely, and assurances of confidentiality and privilege foster that psychotherapist's ability to function. Jaffee v. Redmond, 518 U.S. 1, at 10, 116 S. Ct. 1923, 135 L. Ed. 2d 337 (1996). See also Kennestone Hosp. v. Hopson, 273 Ga. 145, at 158, 538 S.E.2d 742 (2000), *supra*, where we observed that " '[t]he purpose of the privilege is to encourage the patient to talk freely without fear of disclosure and embarrassment, thus enabling the psychiatrist to render effective treatment of the patient's emotional or mental disorders.'[Cit.]." Since "[t]he mental health of our citizenry . . . is a public good of transcendent importance[,]" the privilege serves the public interest "by facilitating the provision of appropriate treatment for individuals suffering the effects of a mental or emotional problem." Jaffee v. Redmond, 518 U.S. 1, at 11, 116 S. Ct. 1923, 135 L. Ed. 2d 337 (1996).

Id. at 325–326.

[20]These include psychiatrists, licensed psychologists, licensed clinical social workers, clinical nurse specialists in mental health or psychiatry, licensed marriage and family therapists, and licensed professional counselors. O.C.G.A. § 24–9–21(5–8); see also Kennestone Hosp. v. Hopson, 273 Ga. 145, 148, 538 S.E.2d 742, 744 (2000).

[21]The fact that a patient has received mental health treatment, and the dates of this treatment, are not privileged. State v. Herendeen, 279 Ga. 323, 327, 613 S.E.2d 647, 651 (2005); Plunkett v. Ginsburg, 217 Ga. App. 20, 21, 456 S.E.2d 595, 597 (1995). While a patient's mental health records are not necessarily subject to this privilege, see Dynin v. Hall, 207 Ga. App. 337, 338, 428 S.E.2d 89, 90 (1993), they are to the extent they originate from the communications between a patient and mental health provider. State v. Herendeen, 279 Ga. 323, 327, 613 S.E.2d 647, 650–651 (2005).

[22]State v. Herendeen, 279 Ga. 323, 326, 613 S.E.2d 647, 650 (2005); Wilson v. Bonner, 166 Ga. App. 9, 16, 303 S.E.2d 134, 142 (1983).

[23]Kennestone Hosp. v. Hopson, 273 Ga. 145, 148, 538 S.E.2d 742, 744 (2000). In discussing the implied waiver of the privilege, the Hopson court noted that such a waiver must be shown by "decisive, unequivocal conduct reasonably inferring the intent to waive[,]" and that a plaintiff's failure to object to a discovery request seeking mental health treatment records does not constitute an implied waiver of the privilege. Kennestone Hosp. v. Hopson, 273 Ga. 145, at 148–49, 538 S.E.2d 742 (2000) Similarly, the privilege is not waived where the plaintiff has called the mental health provider to testify in a separate, unrelated matter. Kennestone Hosp. v. Hopson, 273 Ga. 145, at 148, 538 S.E.2d 742 (2000) Bobo v. State, 256 Ga. 357, 349 S.E.2d 690 (1986).

health provider to testify at trial regarding the plaintiff's mental or emotional damages constitutes such an implied waiver.[24] However, the mere fact that a plaintiff puts at issue the cause or extent of his or her mental or emotional damages by filing a lawsuit does not constitute a waiver of the privilege attaching to communications with the mental health providers from whom the plaintiff has sought treatment, despite the fact that such communications are indisputably relevant to the subject matter of the action.[25]

At the same time, the privilege only attaches where the communications occurred in the context of a confidential patient-mental health provider relationship, and where a plaintiff undergoes a court-ordered mental health evaluation, no treatment is either "given or contemplated," and the therapeutic relationship necessary for the privilege to arise does not exist.[26] Pursuant to O.C.G.A. § 9–11–35(a), where the mental condition of a

---

[24]Plunkett v. Ginsburg, 217 Ga. App. 20, 21, 456 S.E.2d 595, 597 (1995); see also Fields v. State, 221 Ga. 307, 309, 144 S.E.2d 339, 342 (1965) (" 'To call a physician to the stand, and examine him as a witness to one's physical condition formerly communicated to him, is a waiver of the privilege in regard to all of his knowledge of the physical condition asked about. No reasoning could maintain the contrary. . . . This rule applies to mental condition as well as to physical. By calling the doctor as his witness and allowing him to testify as to the mental condition of the accused the defense waived the right to object to relevant cross examination of the doctor on the ground that such a matter was a privileged communication between patient and psychiatrist).

[25]Dynin v. Hall, 207 Ga. App. 337, 339, 428 S.E.2d 89, 91 (1993) ("[I]n any action, the actual communications between a psychiatrist and a patient would be relevant to the patient's mental state and would constitute the most objective evidence therefore. Nevertheless, the legislature has clearly expressed its intent that, as a matter of public policy, psychiatrist-patient communications are to be privileged and are to remain privileged even though the patient's 'care and treatment or the nature and extent of

his injuries [have been put] at issue in any civil or criminal proceeding.' "); see also Plunkett v. Ginsburg, 217 Ga. App. 20, 21–22, 456 S.E.2d 595, 597 (1995). In criminal cases, this privilege may yield to a criminal defendant's constitutional right to confront the witnesses against him upon "a showing of necessity, that is, that the evidence in question is critical to his defense and that substantially similar evidence is otherwise unavailable to him." Bobo v. State, 256 Ga. 357, 360, 349 S.E.2d 690, 692 (1986). However, this exception to the privilege is inapplicable in civil cases. Dynin v. Hall, 207 Ga. App. 337, 338, 428 S.E.2d 89, 90 (1993).

[26]State v. Herendeen, 279 Ga. 323, 327, 613 S.E.2d 647, 651 (2005). In *Herendeen*, the court observed:

The requisite professional relationship does not exist when the mental health provider is appointed by the court to conduct a preliminary examination to evaluate a person's mental state because, in such a situation, mental health treatment is not given or contemplated. [Cits.] Similarly, no professional relationship is formed because no mental health treatment is given or contemplated when a court, acting pursuant to O.C.G.A. § 9–11–35, orders a plaintiff in a tort action to undergo a psychiatric examination [cit.], or, invoking O.C.G.A. § 15–11–100, orders persons involved in a pa-

party is in controversy, the trial court may order that person to undergo a mental evaluation upon a showing of "good cause." "A plaintiff in a negligence action who asserts mental or physical injury places that mental or physical injury clearly in controversy and provides the defendant with good cause for an examination to determine the existence and extent of such asserted injury."[27]

§ 11:5 Loss of future income

The loss of future income is a compensable element of damages when an individual's ability to work is compromised or, in the case of death or other catastrophic injury, entirely destroyed.[1] In Georgia, there are three distinct types of recovery for lost future income: 1) diminished capacity to labor; 2) diminished earning capacity; and 3) lost future earnings.[2] The first, diminished capacity to labor, is an element of general damages, and falls under the umbrella of "pain and suffering." This element of damages is often sought where there is little or no evidence from which the plaintiff's future earnings can be determined,[3] as would be the

---

rental rights' termination action to undergo a mental evaluation. [Cits.] In such cases, the lack of mental health treatment or contemplation thereof precludes the existence of the statutory privilege because treatment or contemplation thereof is a prerequisite to the existence of the professional relationship necessary for the privilege. State v. Herendeen, 279 Ga. 323, at 326, 613 S.E.2d 647 (2005) see also Roberts v. Forte Hotels, Inc., 227 Ga. App. 471, 489 S.E.2d 540 (1997).

[27]Crider v. Sneider, 243 Ga. 642, 645, 256 S.E.2d 335, 337 (1979); Roberts v. Forte Hotels, Inc., 227 Ga. App. 471, 475, 489 S.E.2d 540, 543 (1997); Rose v. Figgie Intern., Inc., 229 Ga. App. 848, 858, 495 S.E.2d 77, 86 (1997).

[Section 11:5]
[1]One element of damages in wrongful death actions is the decedent's lost future earnings. O.C.G.A. § 51-4-1; Consolidated Freightways Corp. of Delaware v. Futrell, 201 Ga. App. 233, 233, 410 S.E.2d 751, 752 (1991); Miller v. Jenkins, 201 Ga. App. 825, 826, 412 S.E.2d 555, 566 (1991).

Lost future income is also a recoverable damage where an individual suffers a personal injury which affects his or her ability to be gainfully employed. Alto Park Super Mart, Inc. v. White, 216 Ga. App. 285, 287, 454 S.E.2d 580, 582 (1995); Super Discount Markets, Inc. v. Coney, 210 Ga. App. 659, 659–60, 436 S.E.2d 803, 804 (1993).

[2]Myrick v. Stephanos, 220 Ga. App. 520, 521, 472 S.E.2d 431, 434 (1996); Michaels v. Kroger Co., 172 Ga. App. 280, 283–84, 322 S.E.2d 903, 906–07 (1984); Jones v. Hutchins, 101 Ga. App. 141, 147, 113 S.E.2d 475, 480 (1960).

[3]Wright v. Lail, 219 Ga. 607, 609–10, 135 S.E.2d 418, 420 (1964); Michaels v. Kroger Co., 172 Ga. App. 280, 283–84, 322 S.E.2d 903, 906 (1984); Jones v. Hutchins, 101 Ga. App. 141, 144, 113 S.E.2d 475, 478–79 (1960).

case with a minor,[4] and the amount of such damages is left to the "enlightened conscience" of the jury.[5]

By contrast, both diminished earning capacity and lost future earnings are special damages, and must be proven with reasonable certainty.[6] Recovery for lost future earnings requires a showing of a definite loss of earnings that would have been received but for the plaintiff's injury.[7] Where a plaintiff's diminished earning capacity is at issue, the permanency of the plaintiff's injury, as well as the impact such injury has on the plaintiff's ability to work in the future, must be shown.[8] Relevant to this determination are the following factors: 1) the plaintiff's capabilities both before and after the injury; 2) the nature and extent of the plaintiff's disability; 3) the value of the plaintiff's services prior to the injury; 4) the plaintiff's life expectancy; and 5) the effect medical conditions and aging would likely have on the plaintiff's future earnings.[9]

Future income is, of course, subject to a host of variables such as job availability, economic cycles, desire to work, sickness, old age, necessity for gainful employment, and changing labor requirements, making any calculation of future income inherently uncertain and difficult to ascertain.[10] In light of this recognition, proving lost future earnings with "reasonable certainty"

---

[4]See, e.g. Rubio v. Davis, 231 Ga. App. 425, 428, 500 S.E.2d 367, 371 (1998); Williams v. Worsley, 235 Ga. App. 806, 808, 510 S.E.2d 46, 49 (1998).

[5]Myrick v. Stephanos, 220 Ga. App. 520, 521, 472 S.E.2d 431, 434 (1996); Michaels v. Kroger Co., 172 Ga. App. 280, 283–84, 322 S.E.2d 903, 906–07 (1984).

[6]Cooper Tire & Rubber Co. v. Merritt, 271 Ga. App. 16, 26, 608 S.E.2d 714, 722 (2004), cert. denied, (May 9, 2005); Singleton v. Phillips, 229 Ga. App. 286, 287, 494 S.E.2d 66, 67 (1997); Long v. Serritt, 102 Ga. App. 550, 555, 117 S.E.2d 216, 220 (1960).

[7]Singleton v. Phillips, 229 Ga. App. 286, 287, 494 S.E.2d 66, 67 (1997); Myrick v. Stephanos, 220 Ga. App. 520, 521, 472 S.E.2d 431, 434 (1996).

[8]Schriever v. Maddox, 259 Ga. App. 558, 560, 578 S.E.2d 210, 212 (2003); Olariu v. Marrero, 248 Ga. App. 824, 827, 549 S.E.2d 121, 124

(2001); Myrick v. Stephanos, 220 Ga. App. 520, 521, 472 S.E.2d 431, 434 (1996); Super Discount Markets, Inc. v. Coney, 210 Ga. App. 659, 659–60, 436 S.E.2d 803, 804 (1993).

[9]Wright v. Lail, 219 Ga. 607, 609, 135 S.E.2d 418, 419 (1964); Myrick v. Stephanos, 220 Ga. App. 520, 521, 472 S.E.2d 431, 434 (1996); Michaels v. Kroger Co., 172 Ga. App. 280, 284, 322 S.E.2d 903, 906–07 (1984); Jones v. Hutchins, 101 Ga. App. 141, 149, 113 S.E.2d 475, 481 (1960). See also Schriever v. Maddox, 259 Ga. App. 558, 560, 578 S.E.2d 210, 212 (2003) (proof of the plaintiff's actual earnings before injury is not required to recover for lost earning capacity so long as there is proof, either direct or circumstantial, of the plaintiff's capacity to earn before and after the injury).

[10]Michaels v. Kroger Co., 172 Ga. App. 280, 286, 322 S.E.2d 903, 908 (1984) (quoting Jones v. Hutchins, 101 Ga. App. 141, 148, 113 S.E.2d 475, 481 (1960)). See also Alto Park Super Mart, Inc. v. White, 216 Ga. App. 285, 287, 454 S.E.2d 580, 582 (1995); Super

does not require proof of such earnings with "exactitude,"[11] and recovery is permitted where the evidence enables a jury to estimate or reasonably infer the loss.[12] By contrast, recovery is not permitted when lost future earning is based solely on speculation and guesswork.[13]

While the plaintiff is competent to testify as to his symptoms and how his injuries have affected his ability to work,[14] a lay witness is not competent to testify as to the permanency of an injury.[15] Expert medical testimony is often offered to establish the permanency of the plaintiff's injury, and the effect the injury has on the plaintiff's ability to engage in work-related activities.[16] Additionally, vocational or rehabilitation experts may be employed to offer opinions as to the transferability of the plaintiff's job-related training and skills to other jobs in the

---

Discount Markets, Inc. v. Coney, 210 Ga. App. 659, 659–60, 436 S.E.2d 803, 804 (1993).

[11]Olariu v. Marrero, 248 Ga. App. 824, 827, 549 S.E.2d 121, 124 (2001); Jones v. Hutchins, 101 Ga. App. 141, 144, 113 S.E.2d 475, 478 (1960).

[12]Alto Park Super Mart, Inc. v. White, 216 Ga. App. 285, 287, 454 S.E.2d 580, 582 (1995); Hunter v. Hardnett, 199 Ga. App. 443, 444–45, 405 S.E.2d 286, 288 (1991).

[13]Singleton v. Phillips, 229 Ga. App. 286, 287, 494 S.E.2d 66, 67 (1997); Quiktrip Corp. v. Childs, 220 Ga. App. 463, 467, 469 S.E.2d 763, 768 (1996); Super Discount Markets, Inc. v. Coney, 210 Ga. App. 659, 660, 436 S.E.2d 803, 805 (1993).

[14]Eberhart v. Morris Brown College, 181 Ga. App. 516, 518–19, 352 S.E.2d 832 (1987).d 832, 834 (1987); Everett v. Holmes, 126 Ga. App. 208, 209, 190 S.E.2d 568, 569 (1972).

[15]Guyer v. Mayor and Aldermen of City of Savannah, 162 Ga. App. 598, 601, 292 S.E.2d 445, 448 (1982); Everett v. Holmes, 126 Ga. App. 208, 209, 190 S.E.2d 568, 569 (1972); Ray v. Woods, 93 Ga. App. 763, 765–66, 92 S.E.2d 820, 822 (1956). Indeed, it has been held to be reversible error for a jury to be given a charge on loss of future earnings where no medical evidence exists establishing the permanency of a plaintiff's injuries. See e.g., Ayers v. Bottoms, 136 Ga. App. 46, 47,

220 S.E.2d 134, 135 (1975); McDuffie County v. Rogers, 124 Ga. App. 442, 443, 184 S.E.2d 46, 47 (1971); Lanier v. O'Bear, 101 Ga. App. 667, 670–71, 115 S.E.2d 110, 113 (1960).

[16]See e.g., Olariu v. Marrero, 248 Ga. App. 824, 828, 549 S.E.2d 121, 124 (2001) (physician testified that plaintiff was medically unable to work and suffered a 5% disability); Michaels v. Kroger Co., 172 Ga. App. 280, 281, 322 S.E.2d 903, 904 (1984) (chiropractor testified plaintiff had a 25% disability and could not perform work placing stress on the neck); Northern Freight Lines v. Ledford, 75 Ga. App. 508, 511, 43 S.E.2d 757 (1947) (physicians testified that physical labor medically contraindicated by plaintiff's physical condition). A jury is free to disregard the assessment on the expert's conclusions as to the permanency of injury and the effect it will have on the plaintiff's future income. See, e.g. Great Atlantic & Pacific Tea Co. v. Turner, 180 Ga. App. 533, 535, 349 S.E.2d 537, 540 (1986) (jury could infer permanent injury where plaintiff testified she was physically impaired and unable to completely perform job duties as a nurse); Barker v. Crum Trucking Co., Inc., 137 Ga. App. 435, 436, 224 S.E.2d 53, 54 (1976) (jury could infer permanent injuries where plaintiff testified he continued to suffer pain from his injuries three years after accident at issue).

marketplace, the availability of such jobs, and the education or training required to make the plaintiff a suitable candidate for other type of employment given the plaintiff's injury-related limitations.[17] Such testimony has, however, been excluded as speculative where it failed to take into account factors such as the plaintiff's level of education, the plaintiff's job-related experience, and the availability of suitable jobs in the marketplace given the plaintiff's physical limitations.[18]

Economists are often employed to calculate what the plaintiff's future income would have been but for the injury.[19] In making such calculations, economists typically rely on evidence establishing the plaintiff's pre-injury income, multiplying this figure by the plaintiff's work-life expectancy, making adjustments for future salary increases, and discounting future income to present day value.[20] Provided there exists some evidence in the record that an individual would have continued working but for the injury, an economist may reasonably assume this to be the case in projecting an individual's future earnings.[21] Where an individual's diminished earning capacity is at issue, and economist may rely on an individual's disability rating and other evidence, as proven by others, establishing the degree to which the individual's injury impacts his or her ability to work in making these projections.[22]

---

[17]See, e.g. CGU Ins. Co. v. Sabel Industries, Inc., 255 Ga. App. 236, 564 S.E.2d 836 (2002).

[18]CGU Ins. Co. v. Sabel Industries, Inc., 255 Ga. App. 236, 240, 564 S.E.2d 836, 839 (2002).

[19]See, e.g. Brown v. Macheers, 249 Ga. App. 418, 423, 547 S.E.2d 759, 764 (2001); Southern Ry. Co. v. Montgomery, 192 Ga. App. 308, 311, 384 S.E.2d 907, 909 (1989); Cook v. Seaboard System R.R., Inc., 184 Ga. App. 838, 841, 363 S.E.2d 56, 58 (1987). One need not necessarily be an economist in order to provide such testimony, and others with similar training have been found qualified to testify on such matters. See e.g., CSX Transp., Inc. v. Levant, 200 Ga. App. 856, 859, 410 S.E.2d 299, 303 (1991), rev'd on other grounds, 262 Ga. 313, 417 S.E.2d 320 (1992) (accountant);

Woods v. Andersen, 145 Ga. App. 492, 492–93, 243 S.E.2d 748, 749 (1978) (professor of finance); Henry Grady Hotel Corp. v. Watts, 119 Ga. App. 251, 167 S.E.2d 205, 207 (1969) (actuary).

[20]See, e.g. Cooper Tire & Rubber Co. v. Merritt, 271 Ga. App. 16, 608 S.E.2d 714 (2004), cert. denied, (May 9, 2005) (see Barnes, J., dissent, for general explanation of methodology); Henry Grady Hotel Corp. v. Watts, 119 Ga. App. 251, 167 S.E.2d 205 (1969).

[21]Southern Ry. Co. v. Montgomery, 192 Ga. App. 308, 384 S.E.2d 907 (1989).

[22]See, e.g. Central of Georgia R. Co. v. Mock, 231 Ga. App. 586, 499 S.E.2d 673 (1998); Cook v. Seaboard System R.R., Inc., 184 Ga. App. 838, 363 S.E.2d 56 (1987).

The fact that a person does not have a steady history of earnings or employment does not preclude proof of future earnings.[23] Tax returns or an employer's wage statement is not required to establish past earnings for purposes of providing a basis for the calculation of future earnings.[24] In the case of children without any employment history whatsoever, statistical studies of average incomes, taking into account matters such as education level, occupation, and age, have been held to provide a reliable basis for projections of future income.[25]

In figuring an individual's work-life expectancy, certain mortality tables are, by statute, admissible for purposes of "computing the value of the life of a decedent in wrongful death cases or of determining the present value of future earnings or amounts in cases involving permanent personal injuries."[26] Such tables do not, however, conclusively establish what an individual's work-life expectancy will be, as specific health and life conditions may, of course, influence an individual's life and work expectancy.[27] The use of past inflationary trends to project future cost of living

---

[23]Michaels v. Kroger Co., 172 Ga. App. 280, 322 S.E.2d 903 (1984). In *Michaels,* at issue was whether an individual with an intermittent work history as a model and other odd jobs could show past earnings so as to make any projection of her future earnings reasonably certain. In finding that the plaintiff's intermittent work history did not preclude such proof, the court observed:

> The general rule that the amount of damages must be proved with a reasonable degree of certainty and cannot be based on guesswork does not mean that only a plaintiff who works on an everyday basis and on the date of the injury can prove a diminished earning capacity. . . . Nor does the rule mean that one who works intermittently cannot recover for diminished earning capacity, i.e. an artist, sculptor, professional athlete, author, actor, dancer, singer, musician, or even a lawyer.

Michaels v. Kroger Co., 172 Ga. App. 280, at 285–286, 322 S.E.2d 903 (1984) See also Robert & Co. Associates v. Tigner, 180 Ga. App. 836, 351 S.E.2d 82 (1986) (plaintiff, former musician who had historically been paid in cash and who could not produce tax returns to establish past income, permitted to rely on wage rate for job he had recently taken with airline for purposes

of calculating lost future wages as result of injury).

[24]Robert & Co. Associates v. Tigner, 180 Ga. App. 836, 351 S.E.2d 82 (1986); Michaels v. Kroger Co., 172 Ga. App. 280, 322 S.E.2d 903 (1984).

[25]See, e.g. Woods v. Andersen, 145 Ga. App. 492, 243 S.E.2d 748 (1978); Henry Grady Hotel Corp. v. Watts, 119 Ga. App. 251, 167 S.E.2d 205 (1969).

[26]O.C.G.A. § 24–4–45(a). These mortality tables are: 1) The Commissioners 1958 Standard Ordinary Mortality Table; and 2) Annuity Table for 1949, Ultimate. While these two tables are recognized as admissible, they do not constitute the exclusive means by which an individual's life expectancy may be shown. O.C.G.A. § 24–4–45(b) and (c).

[27]See e.g., Taylor v. RaceTrac Petroleum, Inc., 238 Ga. App. 761, 762–63, 519 S.E.2d 282, 284 (1999) (anecdotal evidence of decedent's prior drug and alcohol use inadmissible where no expert testimony as to effect drug and alcohol use would have had on the decedent's life expectancy); Henslee v. MARTA, 142 Ga. App. 821, 822, 237 S.E.2d 225, 226 (1977) (mortality tables useful, but not conclusive,

increases has been held to provide a reliable basis for determining the likely increases in an individual's salary.[28] By statute, a 5% per annum rate is to be used to discount future earnings to present day value.[29] An expert's testimony as to how a plaintiff may profitably invest any award, as well as the yields from such an investment, is not admissible as potentially confusing and antithetical to the application of this statutory discount rate.[30]

§ 11:6 Future pain and suffering and medical expenses

A plaintiff may, of course, testify as to the injuries he has suffered and how such injuries have affected him, including the pain and suffering he has experienced as a result of such injuries.[1] Similarly, other lay witnesses who have personally observed the plaintiff may testify as to how the plaintiff's injuries have affected him.[2] However, lay witnesses, including the plaintiff, are not competent to opine as to the permanency of the plaintiff's injuries,[3] or whether the plaintiff will continue to experience pain and suffering in the future as a result of such injuries.[4] Such

---

and jury may consider other evidence as to individual's life expectancy); Isom v. Schettino, 129 Ga. App. 73, 79, 199 S.E.2d 89, 95 (1973) (no error in charging jury that it could take into consideration the health, habits, manner of living, and surroundings of decedent in determine life expectancy).

[28]Woods v. Andersen, 145 Ga. App. 492, 243 S.E.2d 748 (1978); see also Cook v. Seaboard System R.R., Inc., 184 Ga. App. 838, 841, 363 S.E.2d 56, 58 (1987); Georgia Southern & F. Ry. Co. v. Odom, 152 Ga. App. 664, 666, 263 S.E.2d 469, 472 (1979).

[29]O.C.G.A. § 51-12-13; Barnes v. Wall, 201 Ga. App. 228, 411 S.E.2d 270, 271 (1991); Piggly–Wiggly Southern, Inc. v. Tucker, 139 Ga. App. 873, 877, 229 S.E.2d 804, 807 (1976).

[30]Barnes v. Wall, 201 Ga. App. 228, 411 S.E.2d 270 (1991); CSX Transp., Inc. v. Levant, 200 Ga. App. 856, 410 S.E.2d 299 (1991), rev'd on other grounds, 262 Ga. 313, 417 S.E.2d 320 (1992).

[Section 11:6]

[1]Everett v. Holmes, 126 Ga. App. 208, 209, 190 S.E.2d 568, 569 (1972).

While a plaintiff may testify as to the pain he has experienced, and how such pain has affected his daily activities, he may not place a dollar figure on the value of such damages. Graham v. Clark, 114 Ga. App. 825, 831, 152 S.E.2d 789, 793 (1966); Hardwick v. Price, 114 Ga. App. 817, 820, 152 S.E.2d 905, 908 (1966).

[2]Central of Georgia R. Co. v. Swindle, 194 Ga. App. 24, 26, 389 S.E.2d 779, 781 (1989), rev'd on other grounds, 260 Ga. 685, 398 S.E.2d 365 (1990); Kirby v. State, 145 Ga. App. 813, 814, 245 S.E.2d 43, 44 (1978); Redd v. Peters, 100 Ga. App. 316, 322, 111 S.E.2d 132, 136 (1959).

[3]Everett v. Holmes, 126 Ga. App. 208, 208, 190 S.E.2d 568, 569 (1972); U.S. Fidelity & Guaranty Co. v. Wilson, 103 Ga. App. 674, 675, 120 S.E.2d 198, 199 (1961).

[4]Ray v. Woods, 93 Ga. App. 763, 766, 92 S.E.2d 820, 822 (1956); Goodrum v. Jenkins, 91 Ga. App. 377, 379, 85 S.E.2d 633, 634 (1955).

matters are medical questions and must be addressed by competent medical testimony.[5]

Having said this, expert testimony is not required to establish future pain and suffering as an element of general damages where the nature and extent of the plaintiff's injuries and condition at the time of trial enable a jury to reasonably infer that the injuries will continue into the future.[6] For instance, continued physical pain without improvement over a period of time is sufficient to enable a jury to infer that the plaintiff will continue to experience pain into the future without supporting medical testimony.[7] As an element of general damages, the pain and suffering a plaintiff will suffer in the future is a matter for the jury's determination,[8] and there exists no precise "yardstick" by which such damages are to be measured.[9] While there must be some evidence that the plaintiff's pain will continue into the future,[10] it has been held that "slight" evidence on this point is sufficient.[11]

Future medical expenses are an item of special damages and, as such, must be proven with reasonable certainty.[12] Proof of this item of damages entails a two-stepped process: first, a showing that future medical treatment will be required for the injury which is the subject matter of the action; and second, a showing of the cost of this future medical treatment.[13] The testimony of a physician that a plaintiff will experience future pain and suffering as a result of an injury, while sufficient to authorize an award

---

[5]Hunnicutt v. Hunnicutt, 237 Ga. 497, 228 S.E.2d 881 (1976); Eberhart v. Morris Brown College, 181 Ga. App. 516, 352 S.E.2d 832 (1987).

[6]Super Discount Markets, Inc. v. Coney, 210 Ga. App. 659, 436 S.E.2d 803 (1993).

[7]Rigdon v. Williams, 132 Ga. App. 176, 178, 207 S.E.2d 591, 593 (1974); National Upholstery Co. v. Padgett, 111 Ga. App. 842, 846, 143 S.E.2d 494, 498 (1965); Redd v. Peters, 100 Ga. App. 316, 322, 111 S.E.2d 132, 136 (1959). Where the plaintiff suffers from a disfigurement, such as a scar, at the time of trial, a jury may reasonably infer that such disfigurement will be permanent. Malcolm v. Cotton, 128 Ga. App. 699, 701, 197 S.E.2d 760, 763 (1973); Manees v. Scicchitano, 122 Ga. App. 591, 593, 178 S.E.2d 262, 264 (1970).

[8]AT Systems Southeast, Inc. v. Carnes, 272 Ga. App. 671, 672, 613 S.E.2d 150, 152 (2005); Department of

Human Resources v. Johnson, 264 Ga. App. 730, 738, 592 S.E.2d 124, 131 (2003), cert. granted, (Mar. 8, 2004) and cert. denied, (Mar. 8, 2004).

[9]Smith v. Crump, 223 Ga. App. 52, 57, 476 S.E.2d 817, 821 (1996); see also AT Systems Southeast, Inc. v. Carnes, 272 Ga. App. 671, 672, 613 S.E.2d 150, 152 (2005); Redd v. Peters, 100 Ga. App. 316, 318, 111 S.E.2d 132, 134 (1959).

[10]See Daniel v. Smith, 266 Ga. App. 637, 644–45, 597 S.E.2d 432, 439–40 (2004), cert. denied, (Sept. 7, 2004); Hardwick v. Price, 114 Ga. App. 817, 821, 152 S.E.2d 905, 908 (1966).

[11]Daniel v. Smith, 266 Ga. App. 637, 643, 597 S.E.2d 432, 439 (2004), cert. denied, (Sept. 7, 2004).

[12]Whitley v. Ditta, 209 Ga. App. 553, 554, 434 S.E.2d 108, 110 (1993).

[13]Wayco Enterprises, Inc. v. Crews, 155 Ga. App. 775, 776, 272 S.E.2d 745, 747 (1980).

for future pain and suffering as an element of general damages, is in itself insufficient to authorize an award for future medical expenses as an element of special damages.[14] There must be evidence that the pain and suffering, or other medical condition from which the plaintiff suffers, will in fact require future medical treatment in order for an award of future medical expenses to be a recoverable item of special damages.[15] Evidence that the plaintiff's condition will require future medical attention must be based on more than mere speculation and conjecture, and expert testimony as to the mere possibility that the plaintiff's condition will require such attention is insufficient to authorize an award for future medical treatment.[16] That an injury or other condition will require future medical treatment must be established with reasonable certainty.[17]

Evidence of an injury or condition requiring future medical treatment is not, standing alone, sufficient to authorize a charge for future medical expenses as an element of special damages.[18] Rather, in addition to showing that an injury or condition will require future medical treatment, a plaintiff must also produce evidence as to the cost of such future treatment such that the jury has a basis to calculate what these damages will be.[19] While

[14]Clayton County Bd. of Ed. v. Hooper, 128 Ga. App. 817, 198 S.E.2d 373 (1973).

[15]Gusky v. Candler General Hosp., Inc., 192 Ga. App. 521, 524, 385 S.E.2d 698, 702 (1989) ("To warrant future medical expenses, there must be evidence that the injury will require that future medical attention."); on Clayton County Bd. of Ed. v. Hooper, 128 Ga. App. 817, 198 S.E.2d 373 (1973) (physician's testimony, while sufficient to establish that plaintiff would likely experience future pain and suffering as result of injury, insufficient to establish that plaintiff's condition would require future hospitalization); Daugherty v. Vick, 127 Ga. App. 767, 195 S.E.2d 208 (1972) (evidence that plaintiff's injuries were of a permanent nature insufficient in itself to establish that plaintiff would incur future medical expenses as a result of such injuries).

[16]Bridges Farm, Inc. v. Blue, 221 Ga. App. 773, 774–775, 472 S.E.2d 465, 466 (1996), rev'd in part on other grounds, 225 Ga. App. 786, 488 S.E.2d 130 (1997) (physician's testimony plaintiff would likely develop arthritic condition as result of injury insufficient to authorize charge for future medical expenses where physician could only state that future medical attention for arthritic condition was a possibility); Womack v. Burgess, 200 Ga. App. 347, 347–348, 408 S.E.2d 159, 159–160 (1991) (physician's testimony that there was a 50% chance that plaintiff would require future surgery, depending on how and whether plaintiff's condition progressed or deteriorated, insufficient to authorize charge for cost of future surgery).

[17]Whitley v. Ditta, 209 Ga. App. 553, 554, 434 S.E.2d 108, 110 (1993); Bennett v. Haley, 132 Ga. App. 512, 515, 208 S.E.2d 302, 306 (1974).

[18]Hughes v. Brown, 109 Ga. App. 578, 136 S.E.2d 403 (1964).

[19]Southern Airways, Inc. v. Dross, 162 Ga. App. 572, 291 S.E.2d 93 (1982).

such expenses must be proven with reasonable certainty,[20] "mathematical certainty" is not required.[21] A physician's testimony as to the current costs of such treatment,[22] or estimation as to the future costs of such treatment,[23] is sufficient to meet this standard.

[20]Whitley v. Ditta, 209 Ga. App. 553, 554, 434 S.E.2d 108, 110 (1993).

[21]Pruitt v. Pierce, 100 Ga. App. 808, 809, 112 S.E.2d 327, 329 (1959).

[22]Massie v. Ross, 211 Ga. App. 354, 439 S.E.2d 3 (1993); CSX Transp., Inc. v. Barnett, 199 Ga. App. 611, 405 S.E.2d 506 (1991).

[23]White v. Jensen, 257 Ga. App. 560, 571 S.E.2d 544 (2002); Food Lion, Inc. v. Williams, 219 Ga. App. 352, 464 S.E.2d 913 (1995); Harris v. Hardman, 133 Ga. App. 941, 212 S.E.2d 883 (1975).

Chapter 12

Expert Testimony In Commercial and Business–Related Disputes

> **KeyCite®:** Cases and other legal materials listed in KeyCite Scope can be researched through the KeyCite service on Westlaw®. Use KeyCite to check citations for form, parallel references, prior and later history, and comprehensive citator information, including citations to other decisions and secondary materials.

§ 12:1   Overview

Experts are often used both to comment upon industry practices that are alleged to have harmed commercial interests and to present testimony about resultant economic damages. The type of individual who may be called in commercial disputes to testify as an expert is quite varied. Typically, parties proffer as experts economists, accountants, or statisticians; by no means, however, does the fact that a witness carries such a designation guarantee that the witness may in fact give opinion testimony. Whether offering testimony about practices or damages, all witnesses who are offered to give opinions must, regardless of professional title, first demonstrate the requisite qualifications to be deemed an expert.

Traditionally, Georgia has favored the admission of relevant opinion testimony.[1] This expansive view of admitting expert testimony is evident in several commercial disputes wherein the witness's qualifications were at issue. For example, in a suit brought by a builder to recover amounts owing on an express contract to build a hotel, the court qualified a plaintiff's witness as an expert and allowed his testimony on cost estimates.[2] The fact that the witness, a registered architect, lacked prior personal experience in estimating costs involving hotels–the subject of the lawsuit—was deemed a matter bearing on credibility rather than admissibility.[3] Moreover, in a case involving a dispute over real estate fees, a plaintiff real estate broker was allowed to testify as an expert regarding the fair market value of his services despite admitting during his testimony that he was "no expert on the subject."[4]

This same openness to expert testimony appears in cases in which the market value of property has been at issue. Georgia has traditionally followed the rule that "one need not be an expert or dealer in the article in question but may testify as to its value if he has had an opportunity for forming a correct opinion."[5]

§ 12:2   The new Georgia rules

Georgia's adoption of Federal Rule of Evidence 702 and the *Daubert* line of cases marked a dramatic change in the admissibility of expert testimony in Georgia in commercial disputes.[1] In Moran v. Kia Motors America, Inc.,[2] the Georgia Court of Appeals upheld the trial court's decision to exclude plaintiff's expert

---

[Section 12:1]

[1]See Home Depot U.S.A., Inc. v. Tvrdeich, 268 Ga. App. 579, 580, 602 S.E.2d 297, 300 (2004), cert. denied, (Oct. 25, 2004).

[2]See Hardin v. Hunter, 174 Ga. App. 756, 756, 331 S.E.2d 83, 84 (1985).

[3]See Hardin, 174 Ga. App. at 756, 331 S.E.2d at 84–85.

[4]Taylor v. Smith, 159 Ga. App. 797, 799, 285 S.E.2d 200, 202 (1981).

[5]Community Bank v. Handy Auto Parts, Inc., 270 Ga. App. 640, 648, 607 S.E.2d 241, 244 (2004) (in suit alleging breach of contract, conversion, and property damage, property owner qualified to state opinion as to value if based upon a foundation that the witness has some knowledge, experience, or familiarity with the value and testifies as to reasoning for value), see also First of Georgia Ins. Co. v. Worthington, 165 Ga. App. 303, 307–308, 299 S.E.2d 567, 572 (1983) (proprietor of retail establishment with many years experience qualified to opine as to value of his inventory in dispute with insurer over coverage of inventory damage); Shipman v. Horizon Corp., 151 Ga. App. 242, 243, 259 S.E.2d 221, 223 (1979), rev'd on other grounds, 245 Ga. 808, 267 S.E.2d 244 (1980) (in suit against seller of real estate, defendant's assistant to vice president of sales permitted to opine as to value of property).

[Section 12:2]

[1]O.C.G.A. § 24–9–67.1.

[2]Moran v. Kia Motors America, Inc., 276 Ga. App. 96, 622 S.E.2d 439

witness on damages in a breach of warranty case concerning an allegedly defective car. Using a *Daubert-like* analysis, the trial court excluded the plaintiff's expert because the court determined that the expert's methodology for determining damages had not been used by others in the automotive industry, had not been reviewed by other qualified experts and did not have a known error rate.[3] This exclusion came despite the expert's having been qualified to present similar testimony in several other Georgia courts.[4]

§ 12:3 Qualification of experts

Historically in Georgia, mere affiliation with the party is not enough to qualify a witness to offer opinion testimony.[1] In *Georgia Kraft*, for example, an employer sued a union for tortious interference and in support of its claim, proffered an employee's opinion.[2] But several factors disqualified the employer's witness including the fact that she had been with the company only four and one-half months at the time of the strike, and her previous strike experience was limited to one strike in a completely unrelated industry in another state.[3] Georgia courts have also limited opinion testimony in commercial disputes where the witness's testimony would exceed his or her credentials. This was seen in a fraud suit against a mortgage assignee and closing attorney where the trial court disqualified the plaintiff's non-lawyer "expert" who would have characterize various relationships among the parties involved in the mortgage transaction as to whether they were in the nature of attorney-client relationships.[4] Although the proffered witness was by experience qualified as an expert in lending practices, nonetheless, his disqualification was upheld because his opinion about the attorney-client relationship

---

(2005), cert. denied, (Mar. 27, 2006).

[3]Moran v. Kia Motors America, Inc., 276 Ga. App. 96, 622 S.E.2d 439 (2005), cert. denied, (Mar. 27, 2006).

[4]Moran v. Kia Motors America, Inc., 276 Ga. App. 96, 622 S.E.2d 439 (2005), cert. denied, (Mar. 27, 2006).

[Section 12:3]

[1]See, e.g., Zhou v. LaGrange Academy, Inc., 266 Ga. App. 445, 450, 597 S.E.2d 522, 525 (2004) (school board member who would have testified for plaintiff in breach of employment contract case not qualified as an expert); Georgia Kraft Co., Woodkraft Div. v. Laborers' Intern. Union of North America, Local Union 246 (AFL-CIO), 170 Ga. App. 581, 583–84, 317 S.E.2d 602, 606 (1984) (employee not qualified to opine as to how many workers would have returned to work absent violence in employer's action against union for tortious interference with business).

[2]See 170 Ga. App. at 583–84, 317 S.E.2d at 606.

[3]See 170 Ga. App. at 583–84, 317 S.E.2d at 606.

[4]See Garrett v. Fleet Finance, Inc. of Georgia., 252 Ga. App. 47, 52, 556 S.E.2d 140, 145 (2001).

was "beyond the education, skill, and knowledge of a non-lawyer."[5]

In looking to federal authority, at the outset, it is important to note the distinction which federal courts have emphasized between the qualification of a witness to offer opinion testimony and the inquiry into the basis of that opinion.[6] As a matter of fact, the Eleventh Circuit has stressed this, stating that "although there is some overlap among the inquiries into an expert's qualifications, the reliability of his proffered opinion and the helpfulness of that opinion, these are distinct concepts that courts and litigants must take care not to conflate."[7] In *Quiet Technology*, the plaintiff's challenge to the defendant's expert's qualifications failed because his alleged shortcomings were not directed at the witness's credentials but rather were couched in terms of how he had conducted his analysis.[8]

In some respects, the analysis of expert qualifications in commercial disputes undertaken in federal courts has not been unlike that historically conducted by Georgia courts. In particular, Georgia and federal courts have reached similar conclusions about the qualifications of witnesses who are affiliated with a party.[9] In the *LifeWise* case, for example, a lending company's CEO was not qualified as an expert in damages analysis or in any of the techniques used to create the damages model about which he would testify.[10] The CEO's shortcomings were borne out in his testimony when he admitted that he had never used the methods used to create the damages model, and even confessed that "I am not a [damages] modeler . . . I am not an accountant and I'm not an academic . . . I'm not an expert on regression

[5]Garrett, 252 Ga. App. at 52, 556 S.E.2d at 145.

[6]See Quiet Technology DC–8, Inc. v. Hurel–Dubois UK Ltd., 326 F.3d 1333, 1341 (11th Cir. 2003) (suit involving dispute between companies involved in the development of noise reduction technology for aircraft engines); see also Infinity Products, Inc. v. Premier Plastics, LLC, 2002 WL 1608229 at, *1, 2 (D. Minn. 2002), aff'd, 93 Fed. Appx. 90 (8th Cir. 2004) (defendant in contract dispute could not use objection stating only "lack of foundation" to challenge witness's methodology where made after testimony about his qualification but before he described his methodology for his damages calculation).

[7]Quiet Technology DC–8., 326 F.3d at 1341.

[8]See Quiet Technology, 326 F.3d at 1342.

[9]See, e.g., Lifewise Master Funding v. Telebank, 374 F.3d 917, 921 (10th Cir. 2004)(CEO offered as damages expert in breach of contract suit brought by lending company against its loan financer); TK–7 Corp. v. Estate of Barbouti, 993 F.2d 722, 723, 727–29 (10th Cir. 1993) (company president offered lost profits testimony for securities clearing firm that brought action against corporation for failure to register stock certificate).

[10]See LifeWise Master Funding, 374 F.3d at 921, 928.

analysis."[11] In upholding the trial court's exclusion of this testimony, the Tenth Circuit stated that "[g]iven [the CEO's] utter lack of any familiarity, knowledge, or experience with damages analysis, the district court did not abuse its discretion in ruling that he cold not testify as an expert regarding such a complex subject matter as LifeWise's . . . damages model."[12] In another case, *TK–7 Corp.*, the plaintiff's president did not demonstrate that he had any familiarity with the structure of the market for which he was making a forecast; he was thus not qualified as an expert and thereby prohibited from giving opinion testimony on lost profits.[13] Hence, the mere fact that a witness is an officer, director, or employee of a party will likely continue, absent other germane credentials, to be an insufficient basis to qualify the witness to give opinion testimony.

On first blush, this principal may seem at odds with recognized trends permitting business officials to testify about lost profits. This trend was recognized when Federal Rule of Evidence 702 was amended in 2000; then, the advisory committee noted that

> most courts have permitted the owner or officer of a business to testify to the value of projected profits of the business, without the necessity of qualifying the witness as an accountant, appraiser, or similar expert. Such opinion testimony is admitted not because of experience, training or specialized knowledge within the realm of an expert, but because of the particularized knowledge that the witness has by virtue of his or her position in the business."[14]

The distinction between this general trend cited by the Advisory committee and the line of cases wherein an official of a business was prohibited from giving opinion testimony appears to lie in the complexity of the issue about which the witness seeks to testify. In *LifeWise*, for example, the damages about which the CEO sought to testify had been calculated using regression analysis, a complex subject in which the CEO admittedly had no expertise.[15] And in *TK–7 Corp.*, the company's president sought to testify about likely profits from foreign markets; but his foreign marketing experience was limited to one country (Israel) and he had no knowledge of the laws or governmental regulations or distributions systems of the country about which he sought to testify (Venezuela).[16]

Another factor considered in the qualifications inquiry by both federal and Georgia courts is the degree of precision that the

---

[11]LifeWise Master Funding, 374 F.3d at 928.

[12]LifeWise, 374 F.3d at 928.

[13]See TK–7 Corp., 993 F.2d at 723, 727–28.

[14]Fed. R. Evid. 702 Advisory Committee's Notes to 2000 Amendments. (internal citation omitted).

[15]See 374 F.3d at 928.

[16]See 993 F.2d at 728.

witness's credentials must coincide with the facts at issue in the case. In other words, courts weigh whether the witness's particular credentials qualify him to give particular opinion testimony. Rather than amounting to an absolute "in-or-out" as to a witness's testimony, this factor will dictate the extent of permissible opinion testimony. The question of an "expert's" qualifications is usually not an all-or-nothing matter.[17]

A good example of this is seen in *City of Tuscaloosa,* which was an anti-trust action decided before *Kumho*[18] that was initiated by Alabama cities against distributors of repackaged chlorine.[19] In *City of Tuscaloosa*, the district court *sua sponte* excluded an accountant's testimony about costs borne and profits garnered by defendants in the Alabama chlorine market without benefit of a *Daubert* hearing and simply stated that the plaintiff's CPA was "no more qualified than [plaintiffs' other statistician expert] to testify on opinions based on economic theory."[20] But this was reversed on appeal; the witness held a C.P.A. license and had experience analyzing the books of companies that participate in allegedly collusive markets; this qualified him to testify about costs and profits at issue in the case.[21] The plaintiff's statistician was also qualified by virtue of the fact that he held a Ph.D. in statistics and had considerable experience in the analysis of markets alleged to be collusive.[22] His testimony, however, would be limited because parts of it "concern[ed] issues . . . outside [his] areas of competence as a statistician."[23]The statistician could opine about market shares, provided this was based on reliably complied data but could not characterize certain conduct as

---

[17]See, e.g., City of Tuscaloosa v. Harcros Chemicals, Inc., 158 F.3d 548 (11th Cir. 1998) (district court abused its discretion by barring all testimony of plaintiff's CPA and statistician where each was qualified to give some testimony); Morse/Diesel, Inc. v. Trinity Industries, Inc., 67 F.3d 435, 444 (2d Cir. 1995) (trial court erred in excluding all testimony of CPA expert for defendant in damages action where the CPA was not qualified to testify about inclusion of certain work in opposing expert's calculations but was qualified to testify about accounting methods); In re Polypropylene Carpet Antitrust Litigation, 93 F. Supp. 2d 1348, 1358–60 (N.D. Ga. 2000) (in carpet antitrust litigation, plaintiff's econometrician qualified to testify about economic model estimating competitive pricing but not to offer opinions on the types of evidence that economists identify as indicia of collusive activity).

[18]Kumho Tire Co., Ltd. v. Carmichael, 526 U.S. 137, 119 S. Ct. 1167, 143 L. Ed. 2d 238 (1999).

[19]See 158 F.3d at 553, 563.

[20]158 F.3d at 553, 563.

[21]See City of Tuscaloosa, 158 F.3d at 563.

[22]See City of Tuscaloosa, 158 F.3d at 564 n.20.

[23]City of Tuscaloosa, 158 F.3d at 564.

"signals" of a conspiracy between companies to inflate market prices.[24]

On the other hand, some federal courts have taken a narrower view of case issues and witness credentials and thereby completely excluded the testimony of a witness whose qualifications are deemed too general to fit the specific issues of the case.[25] By the same token, where a witness may lack a professional title, this fact will not automatically disqualify the witness as an expert where his background is closely tied to the facts at issue in the case.[26]

A good example of this is seen in the *Montgomery* case, where the defendant sought to introduce testimony of a witness who had knowledge and experience in the development, marketing,

---

[24]See City of Tuscaloosa, 158 F.3d at 565–66.

[25]See, e.g., Montgomery v. Noga, 168 F.3d 1282, 1286–87 (11th Cir. 1999) (software "expert" not qualified to testify in copyright infringement case brought by holder of a copyright in a computer software utility program); Sun Ins. Marketing Network, Inc. v. AIG Life Ins. Co., 254 F. Supp. 2d 1239, 1245 (M.D. Fla. 2003) (forensic accountant not qualified to testify in beach of contract action); O.L. McLendon v. Georgia Kaolin Co., Inc., 841 F. Supp. 415, 417 (M.D. Ga. 1994) (in fraudulent concealment case, economic geologist not qualified to testify at all where his education did not include any study of kaolin, the mineral at issue in the case, and he had minimal work experience with kaolin); see also Jinro America Inc. v. Secure Investments, Inc., 266 F.3d 993, 1002–1005 (9th Cir. 2001) (professional commercial investigator not qualified as expert on Korean business practices and culture where testimony based on his background would include generalizations about Korean business as opposed to the practices of the defendant company); Broadcort Capital Corp. v. Summa Medical Corp., 972 F.2d 1183, 1194–95 (10th Cir. 1992) (in case brought by securities clearing firm against corporation, attorney with "general" securities law education and training but no experience representing large brokerage houses, clearing

corporations, or transfer agents not qualified as an expert in securities area involved in the case); Baker v. Urban Outfitters, Inc., 254 F. Supp. 2d 346, 353–54 (S.D. N.Y. 2003) (photographer's agent not qualified to testify on damages from alleged infringement of copyright in stock photograph where her experience was limited to commissioned work as factors applicable to pricing licenses of stock photographs involved in the case differed from factors applicable to pricing commissioned work); Berlyn, Inc. v. Gazette Newspapers, Inc., 214 F. Supp. 2d 530, 533–37 (D. Md. 2002) (in antitrust suit involving newspapers witness with longtime newspaper business experience who had performed predatory pricing analysis for major national newspapers not qualified to offer opinion on complicated antitrust issues such as defining relevant markets where he was not an economist, had almost no knowledge of antitrust economics, and had never performed a relevant market analysis).

[26]See Infinity Products, Inc. v. Premier Plastics, LLC, 2002 WL 1608229, at *2 (D. Minn. 2002), aff'd, 93 Fed. Appx. 90 (8th Cir. 2004) (witness who was not a certified public accountant nonetheless qualified as damages expert where he had an M.B.A. and a Ph.D., many years experience with companies in financial distress, and had particular knowledge of plaintiff's business practices).

and licensing of commercial software used by banks.[27] Although the topic of software licensing and distribution of software was at issue in the case, bank software was not.[28] Rather, the software at issue was a utility program.[29] Thus the witness was barred from testifying because the court found that the two fields were "totally distinguishable" and therefore his experience was "not germane to the issues involved in the case."[30] Further, in *Sun Ins. Mktg.*, an insurance agency proffered testimony about the value of its business through a forensic accountant who had audited insurance companies, valued them and valued blocks of insurance business but had not valued particular agencies such as that of the plaintiff's.[31] The plaintiff agency sold only one particular type of product—long-term care insurance.[32] The accountant was deemed not qualified to testify "in the areas of business valuations for insurance agencies" because he was "not a business appraiser[,] . . . [did] not have any background information on the long term care insurance industry[,] . . . [had done] no work in the long term care industry in the [previous] ten years[,] . . . [and had] only read some articles his staff pulled from the internet."[33] Perhaps, the outcome of these cases cast some doubt on the continued precedential value of Georgia cases such as *Hardin v. Hunter*[34] following the institution of the new rules for admissibility of expert testimony.

At the same time, there does appear to be some divergence in the way that courts view a witness's credentials for their "fit" in the case. Indeed, some courts have not taken this "laser-beam" approach to matching a witness's credentials to the issues in the case.[35] In the *Maiz* case, for example, a group of Mexican citizens alleged that certain individuals and companies solicited their investment in a Georgia real estate venture only to defraud

---

[27] 168 F.3d at 1302.

[28] See Montgomery, 168 F.3d at 1302–1303.

[29] See Montgomery, 168 F.3d at 1302–1303.

[30] Montgomery, 168 F.3d at 1302, 1303.

[31] See 168 F. Supp. 2d at 1245.

[32] See Sun Ins. Mktg., 168 F. Supp. 2d at 1241.

[33] Sun Ins. Mktg., 168 F. Supp. 2d at 1245.

[34] See 174 Ga. App. at 756, 331 S.E.2d at 83.

[35] See, e.g., Maiz v. Virani, 253 F.3d 641, 650–51 (11th Cir. 2001); Main

Street Mortgage, Inc. v. Main Street Bancorp., Inc., 158 F. Supp. 2d 510, 513 (E.D. Pa. 2001) (in unfair competition suit, accountant sufficiently qualified as damages expert despite fact that instant case was first time he worked on a case concerning mortgage industry because "proposed witness does not have to be the best qualified or possess the most appropriate qualifications"); see also Southern Cement Co., Division of Martin-Marietta Corp. v. Sproul, 378 F.2d 48, 49–50 (5th Cir. 1967) (in a case before the federal adoption of Fed. R. Evid. 702 witness qualified to testify in case involving limestone mining despite fact that his mining experience had not included limestone mining).

them.[36] As evidence of their lost value damages, the plaintiffs offered the opinion of an economist who possessed a Ph.D. in economics from Yale, extensive experience as a professional economist, and a substantial background in estimating damages.[37] Defendants challenged the qualification of the economist to offer an opinion regarding lost value damages because he had no real estate development experience; but given the witness's credentials, the testimony was properly admitted because "[t]he subject matter of his testimony–calculating the economic losses suffered by the plaintiffs as a result of defendants' conduct was sufficiently within his expertise."[38] The court took the same approach with challenges to the testimony of a forensic accountant and an immigration expert.[39] The accountant, a partner at Arthur Anderson, had been qualified as a forensic accounting expert with an expertise in detecting and tracing the misappropriation of funds in complex financial transactions.[40] Defendants argued that the accountant was not qualified to testify as an expert regarding the meaning of the parties' contracts, that he repeatedly offered "legal" opinions regarding the effect of disputed provisions of the contracts, and as a non-lawyer was not qualified to opinion on the legal effect of the agreements.[41] But his testimony was also properly admitted because he was "certainly qualified to opine on forensic accounting issues, and as part of that process he was entitled to state reasonable assumptions regarding the requirements of the applicable contracts in order to put his opinions in context . . . to the extent he spoke of the contracts, he generally did so in the context of setting forth or explaining reasonable assumptions he was asked to make by counsel."[42] Furthermore, even if some small portion of the testimony should have been excluded, the defendants were not entitled to a new trial in large part because they had "ample opportunity to cross-examine [the accountant] vigorously about the sources and content of his assumptions" and the trial court had repeatedly instructed the jury about the witness's role in the trial.[43] Likewise the plaintiff's immigration expert was qualified to testify about the passport-stamping practices of Mexican immigration officials, and opined about those practices as they related to one of the defendants, de-

---

[36]See 253 F.3d at 650–51.

[37]See Maiz, 253 F.3d at 662, 665.

[38]Maiz, 253 F.3d at 665. (emphasis added).

[39]See Maiz, 253 F.3d at 666–69.

[40]See Maiz, 253 F.3d at 666.

[41]See Maiz, 253 F.3d at 666.

[42]Maiz, 253 F.3d at 667.

[43]Maiz, 253 F.3d at 667.

spite the fact that he had no experience with Monterrey (place of entry at issue at trial) as opposed to Mexico generally.[44]

In another example, a suit brought by the owner of a racquetball club against its insurance company, a "roofing expert" was deemed qualified to offer opinion testimony as to the cause of roof damage despite the fact that he had no engineering background.[45] In this case, the witness's "general expertise in the broad subject of roofing [was] enough to qualify him as an expert . . . and [his] lack of specialization in the specific aspect of what causes roof damage [went] to the weight of his testimony, but . . . [did] not necessarily entail engineering and aerodynamic principals (sic) beyond his expertise."[46]

Thus the fact remains that there appears to be two schools of thought with respect to evaluating an expert's qualifications. There is precedent for the view that credentials must narrowly coincide with the circumstances in the case. At the same time, other courts look for the expert's testimony to be "sufficiently within his expertise."

Another aspect of the issue of the expert qualifications entails the question of what subject matter a party may explore in challenging the witness's qualifications. An interesting case, involving a challenge to the witnesses general credibility that touched on the witness's credentials, that is instructive in this regard is *Ad-vantage Telephone Directory Consultants, Inc. v. G.T.E. Directories, Corp.*[47] In this case, the plaintiff offered expert testimony on lost profits through a witness who was both a CPA and a lawyer.[48] After trial, the Eleventh reversed and remanded to the trial court for a new trial finding that the trial court erred in allowing the defendant to cross examine the witness on three particular areas where the defendant sought to discredit the witness's testimony.[49] These areas were: 1) a personal bankruptcy; 2) disciplinary proceedings against him by the Florida Bar and the American and Florida Institutes of Certified Public Accounts neither which resulted in sanctions, and 3) his censure

---

[44]See Maiz, 253 F.3d at 668–69.

[45]See Spearman Industries, Inc. v. St. Paul Fire and Marine Ins. Co., 138 F. Supp. 2d 1088, 1096 (N.D. Ill. 2001).

[46]Spearman Indus., 138 F.Supp.2d at 1096.

[47]See Ad-Vantage Telephone Directory Consultants, Inc. v. GTE Directories Corp., 37 F.3d 1460 (11th Cir. 1994) (seller of yellow pages ad-

vertising sued publisher for interference with advantageous business relationships, federal and state antitrust violations).

[48]See Ad-vantage Telephone Directory Consultants, 37 F.3d at 1462.

[49]See Ad-vantage Telephone Directory Consultants, 37 F.3d at 1464.

by the Florida Board of accountancy almost 25 years prior to the trial.[50]

§ 12:4 Methodology employed by experts

Although in some cases an expert's qualifications may be apparent, this is rarely the case when it comes to the methodology utilized to arrive at the conclusions and opinions that comprise an expert's testimony. Heretofore, once a witness has been qualified, Georgia courts have appeared to be somewhat open to allowing expert testimony on various issues arising in commercial disputes. In these types of cases the courts have appeared to have undertaken little structured analysis of the expert's methodology and instead allowed the opinion testimony with only some limitation.[1]

As set forth in previous chapters, the new rules regarding the admissibility of expert testimony in Georgia establish the tripartite test of Federal Rule 702 for evaluating the substance of expert testimony in commercial and business related disputes:

1. Is the testimony based upon sufficient facts or data?

2. Is the testimony the product of reliable principles and methods?

3. Did the witness apply the principles and methods reliably to the facts of the case?[2]

The analysis of these factors by federal courts has not necessarily entailed a "pigeon-hole" approach, evaluating each factor independently, but rather courts have evaluated putative expert methodology based on the interplay of these factors as they bear on the particular testimony at issue. That being said, each of these factors is isolated below to show how federal courts have considered each one in evaluating the methodology of expert testimony in the context of commercial disputes.

---

[50]See Ad-vantage Telephone Directory Consultants, 37 F.3d at 1464.

[Section 12:4]

[1]See, e.g., T.C. Property Management, Inc. v. Tsai, 267 Ga. App. 740, 600 S.E.2d 770 (2004) (allowing expert testimony on damages in action for breach of fiduciary duty, fraud and breach of contract where both parties' experts relied upon same documents in forming opinion); Dan Gurney Industries, Inc. v. Southeastern Wheels, Inc., 168 Ga. App. 504, 506, 308 S.E.2d 637, 639 (1983) (in action on account testimony allowed on industry practices showing diminution in value upon discontinuation of a product line); but see Williams Tile & Marble Co., Inc. v. Ra–Lin & Associates, Inc., 206 Ga. App. 750, 751, 426 S.E.2d 598, 599 (1992) (in breach of contract suit upholding trial court's exclusion of "expert" testimony amounting to the personal interpretation of a contractual provision by a stranger to the contract).

[2]See O.C.G.A. § 24-9-67.1(b); Fed. R. Evid. 702.

§ 12:5   Methodology employed by experts—Basis of the testimony (sufficient facts or data)

An expert's conclusions and opinions have little worth if they are not, from the start, based on appropriate information, otherwise the expert's work amounts to nothing more than "garbage-in-garbage-out."[1] Nonetheless, where a particular methodology has had widespread use in the relevant industry, an expert's testimony may be admitted despite the fact that his calculations may have been based upon some inaccurate or incomplete data.[2] This is because "[t]he identification of such flaws in generally reliable scientific evidence is precisely the role of cross-examination."[3] However, "the Federal Rules of Evidence require that expert testimony pass the threshold of admissibility independent of mechanisms which may aid the jury in weighing such testimony at trial."[4] Indeed, while cross examination and rebuttal testimony, as opposed to wholesale exclusion, are appropriate safeguards, the basis of expert testimony must nonetheless meet the standards of Federal Rule of Evidence 702,

---

[Section 12:5]

[1]See Quiet Technology DC–8, Inc. v. Hurel–Dubois UK Ltd., 326 F.3d 1333, 1341 (11th Cir. 2003) (suit involving dispute between companies involved in the development of noise reduction technology for aircraft engines).

[2]See Quiet Technology, 326 F.3d at 1343–45 (engineer's incorrect calculations in computational flow dynamics model not a basis to exclude his testimony where the inaccuracies involved only an ideal condition as opposed to the purported actual conditions at issue); Main Street Mortgage, Inc. v. Main Street Bancorp., Inc., 158 F. Supp. 2d 510, 515 (E.D. Pa. 2001) (plaintiff's damages expert permitted to testify despite exclusion of one year's figures from historical trend used to calculate lost profit); see also Micro Chemical, Inc. v. Lextron, Inc., 317 F.3d 1387, 1392 (Fed. Cir. 2003) ("not the role of the trial court to evaluate the correctness of facts underlying one expert's testimony").

[3]Quiet Technology, 326 F.3d at 1345 (internal citations omitted); see also; In re TMI Litigation, 193 F.3d 613, 692 (3d Cir. 1999) (so long as the expert's testimony rests upon "good grounds," it should be tested by the adversary process—competing expert testimony and active cross-examination—rather than excluded from jurors' scrutiny for fear that they will not grasp its complexities or satisfactorily weigh its inadequacies); Firestone Tire and Rubber Co. v. Pearson, 769 F.2d 1471, 1482–83 (10th Cir. 1985) (in suit for breach of warehouse agreement, admission of expert testimony not abuse of discretion despite fact that expert may have based opinion on "speculation derived from incomplete data" where such inadequacies were fully disclosed and subject to cross examination).

[4]Lithuanian Commerce Corp., Ltd. v. Sara Lee Hosiery, 179 F.R.D. 450, 458–59 (D.N.J. 1998) (reversing magistrate's admission based on availability of measures available at trial of "shaky but admissible" expert testimony)

otherwise "[t]o conclude that evidence is admissible because it is subject to such safeguards is . . . circular."[5]

Where reliable methods are used, the court will often take a detailed analysis of the factors and variables that form the basis for an expert's conclusions. A particularly good example of this is seen in the price-fixing case of *In re Polypropylene Carpet Antitrust Litigation*.[6] wherein the District Court for the Northern District of Georgia undertook a thoughtful analysis of the factors and variables used by a plaintiff's statistician who developed a multiple regression model to forecast competitive prices during the relevant time period in the case. The court considered the factors used by the statistician and the facts not used; in particular, the statistician had not used "firm-specific" data but instead had used industry wide indices, a practice challenged by the defendants.[7] After a detailed analysis of the defendant's specific cost accounting practices and the concepts of cost accounting in general, the court found that the expert's decision not to use defendant's internal cost was "reasonable and grounded in the knowledge of econometrics."[8]

In evaluating what data is reasonable for an expert to include or exclude in reaching his conclusions about damages, it is important to courts that the expert has not overlook important financial factors.[9] In *City of Tuscaloosa*, for example, the plaintiff's damages expert, an accountant, was allowed to testify because he had analyzed costs, revenues, and profits and verified data compiled by economist, he had also considered material costs, labor costs, overhead costs, transportation costs, depreciation costs, insurance costs, and a host of other costs and had not appeared to have overlooked any important factor.[10] By contrast, in *Sun Ins. Mktg.*, an accountant's lost profits projection was excluded because in valuing the plaintiff insurance agency, he did not consider all possible approaches to arriving at a value, he did not discuss the various factors that bear on the value, he ignored risk factors and based his projections on assumptions that were "not grounded on known facts, but speculation and

---

[5]Lithuanian Commerce Corp., Ltd., 179 F.R.D. at 458.

[6]See In re Polypropylene Carpet Antitrust Litigation, 93 F. Supp. 2d 1348, 1359–70 (N.D. Ga. 2000).

[7]See In re Polypropylene Carpet Antitrust Litigation, 93 F. Supp. 2d at 1367–68.

[8]In re Polypropylene Carpet Antitrust Litig., 93 F. Supp. 2d at 1370.

[9]See, City of Tuscaloosa v. Harcros Chemicals, Inc., 158 F.3d 548, 563 (11th Cir. 1998).

[10]See 158 F.3d at 563.

conjecture."[11] In particular, one assumption that was not credible was that the projection was based on a time horizon of ten years; the agreement between the parties was, however, terminable at any time.[12] Likewise, in *MTX Communications*, a start-up retailer of telecommunications services brought an action against its provider to recover damages allegedly caused by complications with the provider's services.[13] The plaintiff sought to prove damages with expert testimony about the growth and value that MTX would have achieved but for the alleged complications with WorldCom's services.[14] In reaching his valuation, the expert did not review the plaintiff's financial statements, and, in particular, he failed to consider the amount of money actually received from its billings and instead based his projections on gross billings alone.[15] According to the court, "financials and quality of management–particularly of a start-up company–must be considered in valuing a company and its probability of success."[16] Because of the "expert's" failure to consider these factors, his valuation was deemed unreliable.[17]

Statistics which have been generated based upon public sources have been found reliable so as to be admitted into evidence.[18] For instance, census data, even if containing some inaccuracies, "is the type of data reasonably relied upon by economists."[19] However, the extent of the inaccuracies in the census data may limit the scope of an expert's testimony. This was the case in *In re Polypropylene Carpet Antitrust Litig.*, where the census data at issue failed to accurately reflect the defendants' carpet sales.[20] While the census data was proper support for a general picture of the polypropylene carpet market, it could not support a "detailed analysis of the data to determine changes in market shares over time or whether defendants restricted output" as the defendants had alleged; and thus the expert was precluded from testifying

---

[11]61 F.Supp.2d at 1245, 1247.

[12]See Sun Ins. Mktg., 61 F. Supp.2d at 1248.

[13]See 132 F.Supp.2d at 290.

[14]See MTX Communications, 132 F.Supp.2d at 290.

[15]See MTX Communications, 132 F.Supp.2d at 292.

[16]MTX Communications, 132 F.Supp.2d at 292.

[17]See MTX Communications, 132 F.Supp.2d at 292.

[18]See City of Tuscaloosa, 158 F.3d at 565–66 (plaintiff's statistician allowed to testify where his statistics were in part generated through "simple compilation of data from . . . public sources"); Webster v. Fulton County, Georgia, 85 F. Supp. 2d 1375, 1377 (N.D. Ga. 2000) (statistics based upon data from county records and public sources reliable).

[19]In re Polypropylene Carpet Antitrust Litig., 93 F. Supp. 2d at 1355.

[20]See 93 F.Supp.2d at 1356.

about these issues.[21] Also data from noted industry publications has also been found to be a reasonable basis for expert analysis and opinion.[22] Further, in one circumstance, calculation of damages based on the performance of an REIT (real estate investment trust) index has been found to be an appropriate benchmark for gauging the Plaintiff's damages in the form of lost profits on monies which plaintiffs had invested with defendants but were allegedly pilfered thereby.[23] In *Maiz*, the plaintiffs had, in fact, invested in the U.S. real estate market and the index was not "too risky" or "too speculative" a basis because the defendants had expressly stated in their documents that no return could be guaranteed on the venture involving the plaintiffs.[24]

Another indicator of reliability of data is that it is derived from an opposing party's internal records.[25] But it is also appropriate for an account, acting as a damages expert, to review the business and financial records of the plaintiff.[26]

However, the expert must be careful to properly verify information where facts suggest the information may be flawed and the expert should not base his opinions on too optimistic of a forecast for his client.[27] In *JMJ Enters.*, a distributor brought suit against a maker of Italian water ice for breach of contract, detrimental reliance and intentional interference with contractual

---

[21]In re Polypropylene Carpet Antitrust Litig., 93 F. Supp. 2d at 1356.

[22]See Allapattah Servs, Inc. v. Exxon Corp., 61 F. Supp. 2d at 1349 (expert's pricing analysis reasonably based on publicly available posted prices from Lundberg, Inc.).

[23]See Maiz v. Virani, 253 F.3d 641, 662–66 (11th Cir. 2001).

[24]See Maiz, 253 F.3d at 665.

[25]See City of Tuscaloosa, 158 F.3d at 565–66 (plaintiff's statistician allowed to testify where his statistics were in part generated through "simple compilation of data from the . . . the defendants through discovery"); Allapattah Servs, Inc., 61 F.Supp.2d at 1349 (plaintiff's expert's economic opinions "well-grounded on [defendant's] own documents and actions"); Cf. De Saracho v. Custom Food Machinery, Inc., 206 F.3d 874, 879 (9th Cir. 2000) (in action against seller of food processing equipment for fraud

and breach of fiduciary duty, appropriate for plaintiff's damages expert to rely on bank loan agreements and promissory notes on which plaintiff defaulted).

[26]See International Adhesive Coating Co., Inc. v. Bolton Emerson Intern., Inc., 851 F.2d 540, 545 (1st Cir. 1988) (plaintiff's business and financial records and interviews with company personnel are sources of information normally and reasonably relied upon by accountants); see also Total Control, Inc. v. Danaher Corp., 338 F. Supp. 2d 566, 569 (E.D. Pa. 2004) (in breach of contract action plaintiff's expert's opinion based on sufficient facts or data despite arguably excessive reliance on business records provided by plaintiff).

[27]See, e.g., JMJ Enterprises, Inc. v. Via Veneto Italian Ice, Inc., 1998 WL 175888, at *1 (E.D. Pa. 1998), judgment aff'd, 178 F.3d 1279 (3d Cir. 1999).

relations.[28] The plaintiffs sought to prove damages through the testimony of their expert, a CPA, who, to determine lost profit, had reviewed the distributor's tax return, accounting, payroll and sales records, and the deposition testimony in the case.[29] Despite the distributors' admission that their tax returns were inaccurate, the expert had done nothing to verify the information contained therein.[30] Moreover, in calculating the sales projection that was the "linchpin" of his testimony, he ignored data for some of the time that the distributor was in business and he ignored certain expenses.[31] The court found that the expert's "success story" was pure speculation and excluded it.[32]

Similarly, in cases involving market issues, an expert must use the proper market definition; particularly, the expert should not use a definition that derives from an "eye toward litigation."[33]

This "eye toward litigation" problem was also seen in other contexts, for example, in *Rowe Entertainment, Inc. v. William Morris Agency, Inc.,* concert promoters brought action against booking agencies alleging race discrimination and sought to prove this through expert testimony.[34] The testimony was, however, excluded because the conclusion of plaintiffs' expert was not based on an independent study but solely on material provided by the plaintiffs.[35] In yet another case, a civil RICO action, expert opinion on damages allegedly suffered by plaintiff from alleged kickbacks was excluded because the accountant had relied on statements made by witnesses for the plaintiff "under circumstances which could reasonably be construed to be of financial

---

[28]See JMJ Enterprises, Inc. v. Via Veneto Italian Ice, Inc., 1998 WL 175888, at *1 (E.D. Pa. 1998), judgment aff'd, 178 F.3d 1279 (3d Cir. 1999).

[29]See JMJ Enterprises, Inc. v. Via Veneto Italian Ice, Inc., 1998 WL 175888, at *4, 6 (E.D. Pa. 1998), judgment aff'd, 178 F.3d 1279 (3d Cir. 1999).

[30]See JMJ Enterprises, Inc. v. Via Veneto Italian Ice, Inc., 1998 WL 175888, at *7 (E.D. Pa. 1998), judgment aff'd, 178 F.3d 1279 (3d Cir. 1999).

[31]See JMJ Enterprises, Inc. v. Via Veneto Italian Ice, Inc., 1998 WL 175888, at *7, 9–10 (E.D. Pa. 1998), judgment aff'd, 178 F.3d 1279 (3d Cir. 1999).

[32]See JMJ Enterprises, Inc. v. Via Veneto Italian Ice, Inc., 1998 WL 175888, at *11 (E.D. Pa. 1998), judgment aff'd, 178 F.3d 1279 (3d Cir. 1999).

[33]City of Tuscaloosa v. Harcros Chemicals, Inc., 158 F.3d 548, 567 n.27 (11th Cir. 1998); see also Bailey v. Allgas, Inc., 284 F.3d 1237 (11th Cir. 2002) (in price discrimination and tortious interference suit plaintiff's expert improperly determined the relevant geographic market to be based upon a radius surrounding the plaintiff's intended service area).

[34]See Rowe Entertainment, Inc. v. William Morris Agency, Inc., 2003 WL 22124991, at *1 (S.D. N.Y. 2003).

[35]See Rowe Entertainment, Inc. v. William Morris Agency, Inc., 2003 WL 22124991, at *2–4 (S.D. N.Y. 2003).

benefit to the [witnesses] who gave the statement."[36] The *De Jager Constr.* court found that the hearsay statements given under such circumstances would not be the type of facts upon which a certified public accountant would rely when giving damages assessments.[37]

Finally, expert testimony is completely undermined when it is based on information which is unsupported by evidence.[38] For instance, in the *Tyger* case, a contract dispute among parties to a joint venture in a highway bridge project, the trial court allowed the defendant to present mitigating testimony from an expert in the areas of construction methods and assessment of cost overruns.[39] Specifically, the expert was allowed to testify about increased costs caused by time delays associated with a lack of sand.[40] But the appellate court found that the trial court abused its discretion in admitting this testimony because the uncontroverted evidence was that a sand stockpile existed during the relevant period and that the sand operation was delayed for reasons other than the plaintiff's actions.[41] Further, in *DSU Medical*, the plaintiff's damages expert was prohibited from testifying to damages based upon a market reconstruction theory based unsound economic data terms of a hypothetical contract that were so divorced from reality as to be speculative.[42] Indeed, the evidence showed that theorized contract terms had been rejected by the defendant in previous negotiations.[43]

§ 12:6 Methodology employed by experts—Reliable principles and methods

In assessing the reliability of the proffered expert evidence, federal courts have, of course, relied upon the "non-exclusive" *Daubert* factors.[1] Some courts have noted, however, that these factors "may be particularly inapplicable when evaluating expert

---

[36]De Jager Const., Inc. v. Schleininger, 938 F. Supp. 446, 450, 452 (W.D. Mich. 1996).

[37]See 938 F.Supp. at 453.

[38]See, e.g., Tyger Const. Co. Inc. v. Pensacola Const. Co., 29 F.3d 137 (4th Cir. 1994); Cary Oil Co., Inc. v. MG Refining & Marketing, Inc., 2003 WL 1878246, at *8 (S.D. N.Y. 2003) (retired fuel marketer precluded from testifying for plaintiffs in contract dispute where his opinion that plaintiffs could have obtained financing to purchase full contract volumes of petroleum unsupported by facts and counterintuitive); DSU Medical Corp. v. JMS Co., Ltd., 296 F. Supp. 2d 1140, 1145, 1150–58 (N.D. Cal. 2003).

[39]See Tyger, 29 F.3d at 138, 140.

[40]See Tyger, 29 F.3d at 142.

[41]See Tyger, 29 F.3d at 143.

[42]See DSU Medical, 296 F. Supp. 2d at 1145, 1150–58.

[43]See DSU Medical, 296 F. Supp. 2d at 1145, 1150–58.

[Section 12:6]

[1]See DSU Medical Corp. v. JMS Co., Ltd., 296 F. Supp. 2d 1140, 1147 (N.D. Cal. 2003).

testimony on business transactions."[2] Instead, courts may consider other factors pertinent to the case.

In many commercial disputes the type of experts who will be proffered will be economic and statistical experts. Because these experts will be testifying about very fact-specific circumstances and issues, the inquiry into the reliability of their testimony will in turn be a very case-specific one. This was noted by the Eleventh Circuit in *City of Tuscaloosa*, an antitrust action, in which the court discussed the proper inquiry regarding the reliability of the methodologies implemented by these type experts in the *Daubert* context. The court pointed out that although

> [e]conomic or statistical analysis of markets alleged to be collusive . . . cannot readily be repeatedly tested, because each such case is widely different from other such cases and because such cases cannot be made the subject of repeated experiments. The proper inquiry regarding the reliability of the methodologies implemented by economic and statistical experts in this context is not whether other experts, faced with substantially similar facts, have repeatedly reached the same conclusions (because there will be few or no cases that have presented substantially similar facts). Instead, the proper inquiry is whether the techniques utilized by the experts are reliable in light of the factors (other than testability) identified in *Daubert* and in light of other factors bearing on the reliability of the methodologies.[3]

Where a particular methodology has had widespread use in the relevant industry, an expert's use of that methodology may be deemed reliable despite the fact that he may have used inaccurate calculations; this is true of a discipline known as computational flow dynamics (CFD), a method "rooted in real science."[4] Econometric and regression analyses have also been

---

[2]DSU Medical, 296 F.Supp.2d at 1147 citing ProtoComm Corp. v. Novell Advanced Services, Inc., 171 F. Supp. 2d 473, 477 (E.D. Pa. 2001) (noting that the Daubert factors "do not easily apply in the context of testing the reliability of opinions concerning complicated business transactions").

[3]158 F.3d at 566 n.25 (internal citations and quotations omitted); see also In re Aluminum Phosphide Antitrust Litigation, 893 F. Supp. 1497, 1506 (D. Kan. 1995) ("To the extent that Daubert factors are relevant to its determination [whether an economist's methodologies are reli-

able], the Court considers them along with any other relevant factors[;] . . . [t]he inquiry is a flexible one, with the overarching subject being the evidentiary relevance and reliability of the principles that underlie a proposed submission.").

[4]Quiet Technology, 326 F.3d at 1346, 1343–44 (CFD repeatedly used to assess internal flow, evaluated in peer-reviewed articles, has a low rate of error, widespread use in the aviation industry, and U.S. Defense Department lists CFD as a critical technology of top priority).

deemed to be reliable disciplines, readily accepted by courts.[5] At the same time, where a methodology has wide spread use in a particular industry, the industry standards will be used to evaluate whether the expert followed them in reaching his conclusions and where an expert deviates from those standards his testimony will be excluded.[6] For instance, a "concept survey" is a type of market survey widely used in the survey industry and for which standards and protocols have been established for their conduct.[7] In *Albert*, a plaintiff employed an expert who conducted a concept survey to calculate damages in a fraud action but the survey he conducted failed to conform to these established protocols.[8] In particular, the "expert" had used a sample size so small as to preclude the calculation of confidence intervals; thus no margin of error could be demonstrated.[9] This being so, the court found that the expert's "survey methodology so flawed as to be an archetypical example of the kind of 'junky' science that *Daubert* commands be excluded from the jury's realm."[10]

Can an expert's methodology be deemed reliable just because he says so? Of course, it is a given that "[n]othing in either *Daubert* or the Federal Rules of Evidence requires a district court to admit opinion evidence that is connected to existing data only by the *ipse dixit* of the expert."[11] Nonetheless, this may be a factor considered by the court in assessing the reliability of an expert's methodology.[12] In *Maiz*, the defendants challenged the methods used by the plaintiff's economist as unreliable in part because he was unfamiliar with the individual plaintiffs.[13] In dismissing this challenge, the court seemed to rely on the *ipse dixit* of the expert when he stated that "most economists would not . . . have interviewed individual plaintiffs to evaluate what those parties would have done with the pilfered funds, given the high risk that their responses would be distorted by hindsight."[14] However, the expert must demonstrate some methodology other

---

[5]See City of Tuscaloosa, 158 F.3d at 566; Petruzzi's IGA Supermarkets, Inc. v. Darling–Delaware Co., Inc., 998 F.2d 1224, 1238 (3d Cir. 1993); In re Polypropylene Carpet Antitrust Litig., 93 F.Supp.2d at 1359; Webster, 85 F. Supp. 2d at 1377–78; Allapattah Servs, Inc., 61 F. Supp. 2d at 1347.

[6]See Albert v. Warner–Lambert Co., 234 F. Supp. 2d 101, 105, 106 (D. Mass. 2002).

[7]See Albert, 234 F. Supp. 2d at 105.

[8]See Albert, 234 F. Supp. 2d at 105.

[9]See Albert, 234 F. Supp. 2d at 106.

[10]Albert, 234 F. Supp. 2d at 106–107.

[11]Allapattah Servs., 61 F. Supp. 2d at 1340 citing Kumho Tire Co., Ltd. v. Carmichael, 526 U.S. 137, 119 S. Ct. 1167, 1179, 143 L. Ed. 2d 238 (1999).

[12]See, e.g., Maiz, 253 F.3d at 665–66.

[13]See 253 F.3d at 665.

[14]Maiz, 253 F.3d at 666.

than his own expertise that would typically be used in the circumstances of the case.[15] For example, in *Zenith Elecs.*, where a San Juan broadcaster sued a manufacture of set-top converter boxes alleged to be defective, the broadcaster sought to prove lost profit damages through the testimony of an "expert" who, projected the plaintiff's growth without looking at other markets or using regression analysis to account for market variables.[16] The "expert" explained the methods he had used to generate his projections as "my expertise" and "my awareness" and "my curriculum vitae."[17] The court found that this meant that he was merely "relying on intuition, which won't do."[18]

Finally, as a fundamental principle, an expert must employ methods which follow the laws of the state. For instance, "to recover lost profit damages in Georgia, one must show the probable gain with great specificity as well as expenses incurred in realizing such profit."[19] Indeed, lost profit damages are available in

---

[15]See Moran v. Kia Motors America, Inc., 276 Ga. App. 96, 622 S.E.2d 439 (2005), cert. denied, (Mar. 27, 2006) (court excludes ecpert testimony in a warranty case in part because no other auto industry experts had relied upon or conducted peer review of the methodology for damages developed by the expert); DSU Medical, 296 F. Supp. 2d at 1158 (opinion of damages expert based upon hypothetical contract terms so divorced from reality as to be speculative deemed "classic ipse dixit"); LinkCo, Inc. v. Fujitsu Ltd., 2002 WL 1585551, at *4 (S.D. N.Y. 2002) (in misappropriation of trade secrets case court unable to assess reliability of damages expert's conclusions where he supported opinions only with references to his experience); Zenith Electronics Corp. v. WH–TV Broadcasting Corp., 395 F.3d 416, 419 (7th Cir. 2005), cert. denied, 125 S. Ct. 2978, 162 L. Ed. 2d 890 (U.S. 2005) ("witness who invokes 'my expertise' rather than analytic strategies widely used by specialists is not an expert as Rule 702 defines that term").

[16]See 395 F.3d at 418–19.

[17]Zenith Elec., 395 F.3d at 418.

[18]Zenith Elec., 395 F.3d at 418.

[19]Club Car, Inc. v. Club Car (Quebec) Import, Inc., 362 F.3d 775, 780 (11th Cir. 2004), cert. denied, 543 U.S. 1002, 125 S. Ct. 618, 160 L. Ed. 2d 461 (2004) (internal citations and quotations omitted) (excluding accountant's damages testimony where contrary to governing law, his estimate omitted expenses and was based only on gross sales and profits); see also TK–7 Corp. v. Estate of Barbouti, 993 F.2d 722, 733 (10th Cir. 1993) (testimony of putative expert excluded in corporation's civil conspiracy case where testimony did not meet requirement under Oklahoma law that the plaintiff show lost profit damages with reasonable certainty); G.T. Laboratories, Inc. v. Cooper Companies, Inc., 1998 WL 704302, at * 4–6 (N.D. Ill. 1998) (excluding expert testimony on lost profits where expert did not consider variable costs where controlling state law required that variable costs be included in lost profit calculation); Interstate Development Services of Lake Park, Georgia, Inc. v. Patel, 218 Ga. App. 898, 898, 463 S.E.2d 516, 517 (1995) (lost profit damages only available if the business has a proven track record of profitability).

Georgia only where a business has a proven track record of profitability.[20]

§ 12:7 Methodology employed by experts—Application to the facts of the case

"[M]erely using an appropriate methodology does not ensure reliability in terms of its application."[1] For example, experts must be certain that the model they utilize to develop their conclusions conforms to the geographic circumstances of the case.[2] In *City of Tuscaloosa*, part of a statistician's testimony was excluded because in constructing his database, he had included information regarding chlorine sales in the Florida panhandle but the conspiracy alleged in the suit was limited to the state of Alabama.[3]

In addition, as noted above, there is often interplay between the evaluating factors of case application, or "fit" and qualifications. Where a witness's background does not "fit" the particular context of the case then their testimony would not be reliable because it could not apply to the case. These "lack of fit" exclusions are seen in many cases, including, for example, those where a software expert's testimony was inadmissible because he did not have experience with the particular type of software at issue in the case, and where a geologist was precluded from testifying because he did not have experience with the one particular type of mineral that was the subject of the case.[4]

Similarly, there is interplay between the case application fac-

---

[20]See Interstate Development Services of Lake Park, Georgia Inc., 218 Ga. App. at 898, 463 S.E.2d at 517.

[Section 12:7]

[1]Allapattah Servs., 61 F. Supp. 2d at 1347.

[2]See City of Tuscaloosa, 158 F.3d at 566–67.

[3]See 158 F.3d at 566.

[4]See, e.g., Montgomery v. Noga, 168 F.3d 1282, 1286–87 (11th Cir. 1999) (software "expert" not qualified to testify in copyright infringement case brought by holder of a copyright in a computer software utility program); Sun Ins. Marketing Network, Inc. v. AIG Life Ins. Co., 254 F. Supp. 2d 1239, 1245 (M.D. Fla. 2003) (forensic accountant not qualified to testify in beach of contract action because of lack of familiarity with plaintiff's specific type of business and the product at issue); O.L. McLendon v. Georgia Kaolin Co., Inc., 841 F. Supp. 415, 417 (M.D. Ga. 1994) (in fraudulent concealment case, economic geologist not qualified to testify at all where his education did not include any study of kaolin, the mineral at issue in the case, and he had minimal work experience with kaolin); see also Jinro America Inc. v. Secure Investments, Inc., 266 F.3d 993, 1002–1005 (9th Cir. 2001) (professional commercial investigator not qualified as expert on Korean business practices and culture where testimony based on his background would include generalizations about Korean business as opposed to the practices of the defendant company); Broadcort Capital Corp. v. Summa Medical Corp., 972 F.2d 1183, 1194–95 (10th Cir. 1992) (in case brought by securities clearing firm against corpo-

tor and the inquiry into the expert's principles and methods. This was the case in *In re Polypropylene Carpet Antitrust Litig.*, where the plaintiff's expert, in defining the relevant market, used census data that failed to accurately reflect the defendants' carpet sales.[5] While the census data was proper support for a general picture of the polypropylene carpet market, it could not support a "detailed analysis of the data to determine changes in market shares over time or whether defendants restricted output" as defendants had alleged; thus testimony based upon this information did not fit the facts of the case.[6]

Finally, there is also interplay between the case application factor, or "fit," and the requirement that expert testimony assist the trier of fact. A good example of this is the contractual dispute case of *Lake Michigan Contractors.*[7] In this case, the plaintiff's expert had concluded that the parties agreed on a fixed price for the subject work when, in fact, they had agreed on a unit price, what's more, his conclusions assumed facts contrary to rulings by the court.[8] Thus his opinions did not "fit" the facts of the case, as such would not assist the trier of fact, and were therefore excluded.[9] Another example of this is seen in the *BioCore* case, where a medical R & D company brought action against former employees for disclosure of confidential information; the plaintiff sought to prove lost profit damages through an expert's extrapolation of sales.[10] The company's all-time high historical sales increase for the relevant period was 87.6%, yet the expert, in

---

ration, attorney with "general" securities law education and training but no experience representing large brokerage houses, clearing corporations, or transfer agents not qualified as an expert in securities area involved in the case); Baker v. Urban Outfitters, Inc., 254 F. Supp. 2d 346, 353–54 (S.D. N.Y. 2003) (photographer's agent not qualified to testify on damages from alleged infringement of copyright in stock photograph where her experience was limited to commissioned work as factors applicable to pricing licenses of stock photographs involved in the case differed from factors applicable to pricing commissioned work); Berlyn, Inc. v. Gazette Newspapers, Inc., 214 F. Supp. 2d 530, 533–37 (D. Md. 2002) (in antitrust suit involving newspapers witness with longtime newspaper business experi-

ence who had performed predatory pricing analysis for major national newspapers not qualified to offer opinion on complicated antitrust issues such as defining relevant markets where he was not an economist, had almost no knowledge of antitrust economics, and had never performed a relevant market analysis).

[5]See 93 F. Supp. 2d at 1356.

[6]In re Polypropylene Carpet Antitrust Litig., 93 F. Supp. 2d at 1356.

[7]See 225 F. Supp. 2d at 796.

[8]See 225 F. Supp. 2d at 796.

[9]See Lake Michigan Contractors, 225 F. Supp. 2d at 796–97.

[10]See BioCore, Inc. v. Khosrowshahi, 183 F.R.D. 695, 700 (D. Kan. 1998).

calculating damages, had assumed an increase of 558.7%.[11] Because the basis of the expert's opinion did not fit the facts of the case, it would thus not assist the jury, and was therefore excluded.[12]

§ 12:8 Methodology employed by experts—A note about "dueling experts"

Parties to an action will frequently proffer experts to both support their respective positions and to undercut those of opposing experts. In these cases where the opposing experts have utilized the same methodologies and recognized or used the same data, challenges have, for the most part, been unsuccessful; it appears that where well qualified experts who have used sound methods disagree, the court will typically permit both to testify.[1] However, there are some limitations. For while an expert may criticize the opinions of an opposing expert, he may not, in so doing and to prove his point, testify about assumptions that are outside his area of expertise.[2]

Allapattah Servs., is a good example of a "complex mini trial" in which the court undertook to address "dueling experts" and noted that "[m]erely because two qualified experts reach directly opposite conclusions using similar, if not identical, data bases, or disagree over which data to use or the manner in which the data should be evaluated, does not necessarily mean that, under *Daubert*, one opinion is *per se* unreliable."[3] In this case, gasoline dealers brought a class action against Exxon for breach of contract alleging that Exxon had failed to reduce wholesale prices of gasoline to offset credit card charges incurred by the dealers.[4] It is noteworthy that this case "[did] not lack in analysis" in that both experts filed volumes of supporting documentation with the court.[5] Each party introduced expert testimony on the issue of damages and each party challenged the admission of the opposing expert

---

[11]See BioCore, Inc., 183 F.R.D. at 700.

[12]See BioCore, Inc., 183 F.R.D. at 700.

[Section 12:8]

[1]See Webster, 85 F. Supp. 2d at 1377–78; Allapattah Servs., 61 F. Supp. 2d at 1353–54 (experts of each party used defendant's internal pricing data).

[2]See KW Plastics v. U.S. Can Co., 199 F.R.D. 687, 692 (M.D. Ala. 2000) (in breach of contract action defendant's expert may not testify in rebuttal of damages estimates as to what plaintiff's would have done absent defendant's actions); Cf. De Jager Constr., 938 F. Supp. at 449 (in civil RICO action expert accountant precluded from testifying about conclusion that defendants had engaged in wrongful acts as alleged).

[3]61 F. Supp. 2d at 1341, 1346.

[4]See Allapattah Servs., 61 F. Supp. 2d.

[5]Allapattah Servs., 61 F. Supp. 2d at 1341 n.10.

testimony.[6] Both experts had used regression analysis as part of their methodology but the court did not stop there and, instead, took a more refined view of the methods and data used, looking at the analysis of retail margin of Exxon dealers and how the experts had compared wholesale prices to the net average wholesale prices of competitors.[7] The court admitted the testimony of both experts, apparently persuaded by the fact that each expert had relied upon the defendant's internal price data in conducting analysis and reaching conclusions and found "similar use of the data, methodologies and statistical techniques" by both experts.[8]

§ 12:9   Testimony must be helpful to the trier of fact

"The ultimate touchstone in evaluating admissibility of **expert** testimony is helpfulness to the trier of fact."[1] The requirement that the testimony "**assist** the **trier** of **fact**" means the evidence must be relevant.[2]

§ 12.10   Testimony must be helpful to the trier of fact— Expert testimony helpful

Where the context of the litigation is itself complex, expert testimony will help the trier of fact to understand the issues involving the actions of the parties in the particular economic context of the case.[1]

Expert testimony about corporate governance principles and

---

[6]See Allapattah Servs., 61 F. Supp. 2d at 1336.

[7]See Allapattah Servs., 61 F. Supp. 2d at 1346–53.

[8]Allapattah Servs., 61 F. Supp. 2d at 1353–54.

[Section 12:9]

[1]Total Control, Inc. v. Danaher Corp., 338 F. Supp. 2d 566, 569 (E.D. Pa. 2004) (internal citations and quotations omitted); BioCore, Inc. v. Khosrowshahi, 183 F.R.D. 695, 699 (D. Kan. 1998).

[2]Daubert v. Merrell Dow Pharmaceuticals, Inc., 509 U.S. 579, 591, 113 S. Ct. 2786, 125 L. Ed. 2d 469 (1993); see also Biocore, Inc, 183 F.R.D. at 699.

[Section 12.10]

[1]See, e.g., Cary Oil Co., Inc. v. MG Refining & Marketing, Inc., 2003 WL 1878246, at *4 (S.D. N.Y. 2003) (in contractual dispute between supplier and marketers of petroleum products expert testimony offering a general overview of derivative instruments, the Commodity Futures Trading Commission, its regulation of futures trading, and other general economic background would help the jury understand the nature of the contracts and the regulatory scheme that structures such contracts); ProtoComm Corp. v. Novell Advanced Services, Inc., 171 F. Supp. 2d 473, 478, 481 (E.D. Pa. 2001) (specialized knowledge of investment banker/attorney and accountant/fraud examiner would help trier of fact determine relevant issues such as the characterization of complex business transactions and fraudulent conveyances); Vaulting & Cash Services, Inc. v. Diebold Inc., 1998 WL 726070, at *1 (E.D. La. 1998), aff'd, 199 F.3d 440 (5th Cir. 1999) (testimony of plaintiff's chief operating officer found an expert in ATM and

the concept of veil-piercing, where it is limited to general explanations of principles and is based on analysis of objective facts, such as the composition of a board of directors, will not impermissibly invade the province of the jury and is therefore helpful.[2]

Although juries do not need technical assistance with such fundamentals as addition or multiplication, financial analysts, testifying as experts, can be assist a jury because of their ability to present a vast quantity of calculations derived from disparate sources in an understandable format.[3] For instance, in one antitrust case, *City of Tuscaloosa*, the court found that the plaintiff's expert's calculation and explanation of costs borne and profits enjoyed by defendants during the period of the alleged conspiracy would aid the jury's determination whether, for purposes of the antitrust claims, the defendants acted in a consciously parallel fashion and whether, for purposes of the fraud claims, defendants' costs impelled price increases.[4]

§ 12.11   Testimony must be helpful to the trier of fact— Expert testimony not helpful

Juries do not need technical assistance with the law applicable in a case. As such, expert testimony that addresses legal issues, such as the measure of damages to be applied, has been held to be inadmissible because it is is not helpful to the trier of fact.[1]

Juries also do not need assistance with issues that are within common understanding or which simply recount information already contained in the record.[2]

Nor do triers of fact, whether the jury or the court, need expert

---

banking industry helpful to jury in understanding technical aspects of ATMs).

[2]See Cary Oil Co., Inc. v. MG Refining & Marketing, Inc., 2003 WL 1878246, at *5–6 (S.D. N.Y. 2003).

[3]See Total Control, 338 F. Supp. 2d at 569; see also City of Tuscaloosa v. Harcros Chemicals, Inc., 158 F.3d 548, 563–64 (11th Cir. 1998); Atkinson Warehousing and Distribution, Inc. v. Ecolab, Inc., 99 F. Supp. 2d 665, 669 (D. Md. 2000) (in breach of contract action defendant's expert, an accountant, had "specialized knowledge which would assist the jury to determine the facts in issue, namely the damages asserted by plaintiff); KW Plastics v. U.S. Can Co., 199 F.R.D. 687, 692 (M.D. Ala. 2000) (in breach of contract action defendant's expert

could testify to flaws inherent in plaintiff's damages report as this would help the jury evaluate the plaintiffs' damages expert's assessment).

[4]See 158 F.3d at 563–64 (the trial court had abused its discretion by excluding this testimony).

[Section 12.11]

[1]See LinkCo, Inc. v. Fujitsu Ltd., 2002 WL 1585551, at *3 (S.D. N.Y. 2002) (in case alleging misappropriation of trade secrets, testimony of plaintiff's damages expert not helpful where he sought to instruct the jury on the measure of damages–reasonable royalties–as opposed to the amount of damages).

[2]See LinkCo, Inc. v. Fujitsu Ltd., 2002 WL 1585551, at *3 (S.D. N.Y.

assistance in determining the intentions of the parties.[3] In *Vaulting & Cash Servs.*, for example, the plaintiffs in a breach of contract action proffered their Chief Operating Officer to testify as an expert on defendant's intentions in terminating the subject agreement early.[4] Although deemed an expert in the ATM and banking industries, his specialized knowledge would not assist the court in ascertaining Diebold's intentions in terminating the subject agreement.[5]

Where an otherwise qualified expert does not employ sound methodology in reaching his conclusions, his testimony is not helpful to the trier of fact.[6]

Further, where an expert's analysis has confused the application of governing legal principles, such testimony will not help the trier of fact.[7] For example, in *Williamson Oil Co., Inc. v. Phillip Morris U.S.A.*, wholesalers of cigarettes brought an antitrust action against manufacturers and proffered expert testimony about the activities of the manufacturers in the market place in order to show that their activities went beyond

---

2002). (opinion of plaintiff's expert was merely recounting of record evidence); S.E.C. v. Lipson, 46 F. Supp. 2d 758, 763 (N.D. Ill. 1998) ("Expert testimony may not be used merely to repeat or summarize what the jury independently has the ability to understand"); see also Media Sport & Arts s.r.l. v. Kinney Shoe Corp., 1999 WL 946354, at *3 (S.D. N.Y. 1999) ("secondhand knowledge unnecessary for the edification of the jury"). But see U.S. v. Hamaker, 455 F.3d 1316 (11th Cir. 2006)(In bank fraud case, court permitted FBI financial analyst to testify even though his testimony ultimately depended only upon basic math).

[3]See Vaulting & Cash Services, Inc. v. Diebold Inc., 1998 WL 726070, at *1 (E.D. La. 1998), aff'd, 199 F.3d 440 (5th Cir. 1999).

[4]See Vaulting & Cash Services, Inc. v. Diebold Inc., 1998 WL 726070, at *1 (E.D. La. 1998), aff'd, 199 F.3d 440 (5th Cir. 1999).

[5]See Vaulting & Cash Services, Inc. v. Diebold Inc., 1998 WL 726070, at *1 (E.D. La. 1998), aff'd, 199 F.3d 440 (5th Cir. 1999) citing In re Air Crash Disaster at New Orleans, La., 795 F.2d 1230, 1233 (5th Cir. 1986) (expert must "bring to the jury more

than the lawyers can offer in argument").

[6]See Zenith Electronics Corp. v. WH–TV Broadcasting Corp., 395 F.3d 416, 419 (7th Cir. 2005), cert. denied, 125 S. Ct. 2978, 162 L. Ed. 2d 890 (U.S. 2005) (method such as "expert intuition" which is "neither normal among social scientists nor testable . . . [isn't] worth much to . . . the judiciary"); Elder v. Tanner, 205 F.R.D. 190, 194 (E.D. Tex. 2001) (plaintiff's experts, though qualified, precluded from testifying in patent infringement action where their reports failed to elaborate the reasoning or thought process by which they reached their ultimate opinion regarding infringement and as such would not assist the trier of fact).

[7]See, e.g., Williamson Oil Co., Inc. v. Philip Morris USA, 346 F.3d 1287, 1321–23 (11th Cir. 2003); City of Tuscaloosa., 158 F.3d at 565 (statistician could not characterize certain evidence as "signals" of a conspiracy between companies to inflate market prices "because the trier of fact is entirely capable of determining whether or not to draw such conclusions without any technical assistance).

permissible behavior (conscious parallelism) and instead amounted to impermissible collusive price fixing.[8] Because the expert had defined collusion to include conscious parallelism this evidence did not tend to make it any more probable that the defendants were (or were not) engaged in a price fixing conspiracy.[9] Thus this evidence was irrelevant and therefore of no use to the fact finder who had to determine whether manufacturer's behavior was or was not legal.[10]

The same is true for an expert's use of evidence; that is, where an expert has not correctly understood and used the evidence in the case, his conclusions will therefore be unhelpful.[11] By the same token, where an expert's proffered opinion is so divorced from reality, it is not relevant and thus will not assist the trier of fact.[12] Indeed, courts have rejected testimony where the "expert's" conclusions are "so far afield that one familiar with the facts in [the] case would be compelled to wonder after reading the report whether it was prepared for a different case."[13] The case of *Lake Michigan Contractors*, a contractual dispute, is a good example of expert testimony found to be "so divorced from reality" as to be unhelpful.[14] In this case, the plaintiff's expert had concluded that the parties agreed on a fixed price for the subject work when, in fact, they had agreed on a unit price; and what's more, his conclu-

---

[8]See 346 F.3d at 1321–22.

[9]See Williamson Oil Co., Inc. v. Philip Morris USA, 346 F.3d 1287, 1321–23 (11th Cir. 2003).

[10]See Williamson Oil Co., Inc. v. Philip Morris USA, 346 F.3d 1287, 1323 (11th Cir. 2003).

[11]See Holiday Wholesale Grocery Co. v. Philip Morris Inc., 231 F. Supp. 2d 1253, 1288 (N.D. Ga. 2002), aff'd, 346 F.3d 1287 (11th Cir. 2003) (expert testimony regarding institution of permanent allocation systems was premised on an erroneous understanding of the evidence and thus inadmissible).

[12]See, e.g., Craftsmen Limousine, Inc. v. Ford Motor Co., 363 F.3d 761, 777 (8th Cir. 2004) (in anti-conspiracy suit by limousine manufacturer against competitors and base vehicle manufacturer testimony of plaintiff's damages expert did not sufficiently aid the jury in determining whether there was an "unreasonable" restraint on trade as his opinion failed to "incorpo-

rate all aspects of the economic reality") citing Concord Boat Corp. v. Brunswick Corp., 207 F.3d 1039, 1057 (8th Cir. 2000); DSU Medical Corp. v. JMS Co., Ltd., 296 F. Supp. 2d 1140, 1150–58 (N.D. Cal. 2003) (expert's opinion excluded where based on assumptions so divorced from reality as to be speculative because juries are told that they cannot decide damages by speculation); Baker v. Urban Outfitters, Inc., 254 F. Supp. 2d 346, 353–54 (S.D. N.Y. 2003) (photographer's agent not permitted to testify because of her "apples and oranges comparison" where her starting point for calculating damages was plaintiff's fee for commissioned work as opposed to his fee for a stock photograph which was type of photograph at issue in the infringement case); BioCore, Inc., 183 F.R.D. at 700.

[13]Lake Michigan Contractors, Inc. v. Manitowoc Co., Inc., 225 F. Supp. 2d 791, 796 (W.D. Mich. 2002).

[14]See 225 F. Supp. 2d at 796.

sions assumed facts contrary to rulings by the court.[15] Thus his opinions did not "fit" the facts of the case, were therefore irrelevant and thus would not assist the trier of fact.[16] Another example of this is seen in *BioCore*, where a medical R & D company brought action against former employees for disclosure of confidential information; the plaintiff sought to prove lost profit damages through an expert's extrapolation of sales.[17] The company's all-time high historical sales increase for the relevant period was 87.6%, yet the expert, in calculating damages, had assumed an increase of 558.7%.[18] Because the basis of the expert's opinion was without evidentiary support it would not assist the jury in understanding the evidence or in determining the amount of damages and was thus excluded.[19]

---

[15]See 225 F. Supp. 2d at 796.

[16]See Lake Michigan Contractors, 225 F. Supp. 2d at 796–97.

[17]See 183 F.R.D. at 700.

[18]See BioCore, Inc., 183 F.R.D. at 700.

[19]See BioCore, Inc., 183 F.R.D. at 700.

APPENDICES

APPENDIX A

Expert Testimony Check List

1. Is the subject or topic of testimony beyond the comprehension or experience of the average juror?

2. Is the expert qualified by experience, education and/or training? How?

3. Do the expert's qualifications fit the facts of this case?

4. What facts are relied on by the expert?

5. Which facts relied on by the expert are admissible?

6. Is the expert's testimony based on "sufficient" facts or data that are or will be admitted into evidence?

7. Is the expert relying on other experts? (Is the expert a "mere conduit" for other experts?)

8. Is the expert's opinion helpful to the jury?

a. Does the opinion add something more than just what the parties or lawyers would argue at closing?

b. Is the opinion so complex as to be unintelligible?

9. Is the expert's opinion "reliable"?

a. Has the expert's theory or technique been tested? (can it be tested?)

b. Has the theory or technique been subject to peer review or publication?

c. What is the known error rate (and what did the expert do to rule in or out other theories or explanations for causation or damages?)

d. Do standards exist regarding this topic of testimony? (If so, did the expert take those standards into consideration?)

e. Has the theory or technique been generally accepted in the relevant scientific community?

10. Has the expert's opinion been reasonably applied to the facts of the case?

a. Does an analytical gap exist between the data and the conclusion? (i.e., did the expert miss a step?)

b. Did the expert apply the same intellectual rigor in the courtroom as employed by other experts in the field?

c. Has the expert relied too much on anecdotal evidence?

d. Are studies or research used by the expert relevant and reliable?

e. Has the expert changed his or her opinion or shaped it in an effort to shape testimony for trial?

11. Do general grounds exist to impeach the expert?

a. What percentage of the expert's annual income is derived from work as an expert (testifying or non-testifying?)

b. How is the expert's work divided between plaintiffs and defendants? (Between companies and individuals? Between doctors and patients?)

c. How much is the expert being paid in this case? (How does that compare to work outside work as an expert witness?)

d. How may times has the expert testified in court or in a deposition? (How many times does the expert testify, on average, in a given year?)

e. Has any court ever ruled that the expert's testimony was admissible? (or not admissible?)

f. Has the expert ever been fired or asked to leave a job?

g. Has the expert ever been sued?

h. Has the expert ever been refused admission to a professional society or organization?

i. Has the expert ever been arrested or convicted of a crime?

12. Procedural matters.

a. Did the parties request in discovery the identity of all testifying experts and the facts upon which the experts rely and the conclusions the experts will offer at trial?

b. Did the party challenging introduction of the expert's testimony make a motion to exclude the testimony pretrial? (If not, motion is untimely.)

c. Will the court hold a pretrial hearing to consider the motion to exclude expert testimony? (If so, will the court permit or require the expert to appear and give testimony?)

d. Is the motion to exclude expert testimony filed with a summary judgment motion? (If so, will exclusion of the expert result in the granting of a summary judgment motion?)

e. If the expert's testimony is excluded, will the party who offered the expert be permitted to offer another expert?

13. Special Considerations for Professional Malpractice Actions.

a. Was the expert licensed by an appropriate regulatory agency to practice his or her profession in the state in which the expert was practicing or teaching?

b. If this is a medical negligence case, does the expert have actual professional knowledge and experience in the area in which the opinion is to be given?

c. If this is a medical negligence case, has the expert actually practiced in the area of specialty of his or her opinion for at least three of the past five years immediately preceding the allegedly negligent act or omission with sufficient frequency to have adequate knowledge regarding the performance of the medical procedure, diagnosis of the condition, or treatment that was alleged to be negligent?–or–Has the expert taught for at least three of the last five years immediately preceding the allegedly negligent act or omission as an employed member of the faculty of an educational institution accredited in the teaching of such profession, with sufficient frequency to establish an appropriate level of knowledge (as set forth above)?

d. If this is a medical negligence case, is the expert:

- A member of the same profession?
- A medical doctor testifying about a doctor of osteopathy or a doctor of osteopathy testifying about a medical doctor?
- A physician testifying about nurses, physician's assistants or other non-physician medical personnel where the physician would have regularly supervised such medical personnel for at least three of the past five years immediately preceding the act or omission alleged to be negligent?

APPENDIX B

Sample Deposition Duces Tecum for Expert

IN THE STATE COURT OF FULTON COUNTY
STATE OF GEORGIA

Mr. and Mrs. Smith, Individually,   :
and on Behalf of the Estate of   :
Son Smith,   :
                                           :
                          Plaintiff,   :   CIVIL ACTION FILE
                                           :   NO. _____ _____
                                           :
vs.   :
                                           :
XYZ Company, and Mr. Jones,   :
                                           :
                        Defendants.   :
                                           :

NOTICE OF DEPOSITION DUCES TECUM FOR EXPERT WITNESS

TO: **[OPPOSING ATTORNEY]**

PLEASE TAKE NOTICE that, pursuant to the provisions of O.C.G.A. § 9–11–30, the deposition of **[MEDICAL EXPERT]** will be taken on _____, beginning at _____a.m./p.m., (Eastern Time) at **[insert doctor's address]**.

This deposition will be taken for purposes of discovery, cross-examination and for all other purposes permitted under the Georgia Civil Practice Act before an officer authorized by law to administer oaths. Said deposition will continue from day to day until the examination is complete.

Pursuant to the provisions of O.C.G.A. §§ 9–11–30(b) (5) and 9–11–34, this notice requires you to produce those documents and tangible things set forth in Schedule A accompanying this notice. It is specifically requested that you bring those documents and materials set forth in Schedule A with you to your deposition to be made available for inspection and copying.

This _____ day of _____, 2007.

[Attorney's Name, Address and bar information]

SCHEDULE A

1. A copy of your current curriculum vitae.

2. A copy of the retainer, fee agreement, contract, or other such document between you or your office and **[Plaintiff's or Defendant's]** counsel or their office relating to the provision of your services in this case.

3. All correspondence (whether by way of letter, fax, or e-mail) *from you* or your office *to [Plaintiff's counsel or Defendant's counsel]* or their office which relates to your opinions in this case.

4. All correspondence (whether by way of letter, fax, or e-mail) *from [Plaintiff's counsel or Defendant's counsel]* or their office *to you* or your office which relates to your opinions in this case.

5. The most recent Rule 26(a) (2) (B) report you have prepared, executed, or signed in conjunction with cases pending in federal court.

6. Any and all memoranda, summaries, synopses, correspondence, statements, depositions, or any other documents of any kind provided to you by **[Plaintiffs or Plaintiff's attorneys or Defendant's or Defendant's attorneys]** which form a basis for your opinions in this case.

7. Any and all memoranda, summaries, synopses, correspondence, statements, depositions, or any other documents of any kind which you have provided to Plaintiffs or Plaintiffs' attorneys which form a basis for your opinions in this case.

8. Copies of all _drafts_ of the affidavits (whether reduced to printed form or in a word processor or computer) which you have signed in this case.

9. All medical records, depositions, documents, photographs, or other documents which you have reviewed in conjunction with this case.

10. All notes you have created in conjunction with your review of this case.

11. Copies of any documents which evidence the identity of (identified by the case style and court where the action was or is pending) any action in which you have provided trial or deposition testimony in the last four (4) years.

12. Copies of any and all depositions, sworn statements, and/or affidavits given by you in the past four (4) years in cases which you have provided trial or deposition testimony or testimony by

affidavit. (The party seeking these documents will pay for reasonable copying and mailing costs.)

13. Copies of any and all records of time you have spent on this matter and invoices that you have prepared in conjunction with your work in this case.

14. Documents which evidence the following:*

a) Your income derived from serving as a consulting or testifying expert over the past four (4) years;

b) The percentage of your total income derived from serving as a consulting or testifying expert over the past four (4) years; and

c) The percentage of cases over the past four (4) years in which you have served as a consulting or testifying expert on behalf of Plaintiffs, and the percentage of cases in which you have served as a consulting or testifying expert on behalf on Defendants.

---

*Note: Courts will rarely allow parties to obtain tax returns or other tax records relating to the expert's income. Most Courts will require the expert to testify as to the percentage of total income derived from serving as an expert witness and the relative distribution of income between cases on behalf of Plaintiffs and Defendants.

APPENDIX C

Sample Scheduling Order (State Court) for Motions to Exclude Expert Testimony

IN THE STATE COURT OF FULTON COUNTY STATE OF GEORGIA

Mr. and Mrs. Smith, Individually, and on Behalf of the Estate of Son Smith,	:	
	:	
	:	
Plaintiff,	:	CIVIL ACTION FILE NO. _____
	:	
vs.	:	
	:	
XYZ Company, and Mr. Jones,	:	
	:	
Defendant.	:	

CASE MANAGEMENT AND SCHEDULING ORDER

The parties are hereby directed as follows:

(a) Within 30 days of the case being stipulated to the trial calendar, or upon such other earlier date as may be ordered by the Court, each party shall file with the Court any exceptions to the opposing party's expert witness testimony pursuant to O.C.G.A. § 24–9–67. Such exceptions shall specifically delineate:

(1) The name of the expert;

(2) The specific testimony objected to;

(3) The reasons for the objection and a citation to the statute or applicable case authority to support the objection;

(4) Copies of pertinent deposition transcripts, or other sworn testimony, and/or other competent evidence in support of the motion;

(5) Certification that the parties have conferred in good faith to attempt to resolve the issues and that a good faith dispute remains.

(b) Each party shall have 30 days to respond to an opposing

parties' motion. A reply brief may be filed within 5 days of any response.

(c) After conferring with the parties, the Court will schedule an evidentiary hearing to consider such motions. Parties will be entitled to present live witnesses on the issues raised and make argument to the Court. Deposition or other sworn testimony may also be tendered.

(d) After the hearing, the Court will enter an order on the objections to expert testimony and thereafter, the case will be set for trial.

(e) The parties will be ordered to participate in mediation after the Court enters an Order on the objections to expert testimony and before trial.

(f) For any motion in limine other than a motion pursuant to O.C.G.A.§ 24–9–67, the parties shall confer in good faith to attempt to resolve the issue by stipulation and shall only file motions pertaining to issues that remain in dispute. The parties shall certify same to the Court. All motions in limine shall be filed no later than _____, 200____.

(g) A pre-trial conference is scheduled to be held on _____, 200____ at _____:00 a/p.m. before Judge Susan B. Forsling in Courtroom 2–F in the State Court of Fulton County. All motions in limine and any issue pertaining to the proposed pre-trial consolidated order will be taken up at this time by the Court.

(h) This case is specifically set for trial beginning _____, 200____ at _____:00 a/p.m. before Judge Susan B. Forsling in Courtroom 2–F in the State Court of Fulton County.

(i) Prior to trial, each party shall mark and exchange as marked all exhibits which are listed on the pre-trial order and/or demonstrative aids that the parties expect to show the jury. Such exhibits and demonstrative aids shall be so marked and exchanged no later than the day before trial.

(j) Prior to trial each party shall submit to the Court a list of all exhibits and demonstrative aids with corresponding exhibit numbers on a chart in a form substantially similar to Exhibit A attached hereto (not included). This list shall be filed at the time of filing Requests to Charge but not later than the day the trial commences.

(k) The parties shall submit Requests to Charge which shall be numbered and which shall have the following notations, in addition to relevant case authority, at the end of the charge:

Charge Given: _____
Charge Refused: _____
Change Modified & Given: _____

Included in General Charge: _____
Withdrawn: _____

Parties are not required to submit verbatim request to charge from Suggested Pattern Jury Instructions, but may request such charge by number only.

The requirements of this Order shall be in addition to and shall not supercede any requirements set forth in the Pre–Trial Order or any statutory requirement pertaining to exhibits or Requests to Charge.

SO ORDERED, this _____ day of _____, 200____.

_____

Susan B. Forsling
Judge, State Court of Fulton County
Copies to:

APPENDIX D

Sample Motion to Exclude Expert Testimony

IN THE UNITED STATES DISTRICT COURT
NORTHERN DISTRICT OF GEORGIA

Mr. and Mrs. Smith, Individually,	)	
and on Behalf of the Estate	)	
of Son Smith,	)	
Plaintiff,	)	
	)	Civil Action No.:
vs.	)	
	)	
XYZ Company, Mr. Jones	)	**DEFENDANTS' MOTION TO**
	)	**EXCLUDE EXPERT**
	)	**TESTIMONY OF ALEX**
	)	**WHITE AND REQUEST**
	)	**FOR ORAL ARGUMENT**
Defendants.	)	

TO: ATTORNEYS FOR PLAINTIFFS:

COME NOW Defendants in the above-styled case, by and through their attorneys of record, and pursuant to Rules 104 and 703 of the Federal Rules of Evidence, hereby move this Court to exclude the testimony of Plaintiffs' expert, Alex White, in whole or in part. In support of this Motion, Defendants hereby submit their Memorandum of Law, filed contemporaneously herewith. Defendants rely upon all evidence of record, and any other such matter which may be considered by this Court.

Defendants request that Oral Argument be granted in this matter.

Respectfully submitted this_____day of _____, _____.

APPENDIX E

Sample Memorandum in Support of Motion to Exclude Expert Testimony

IN THE UNITED STATES DISTRICT COURT
NORTHERN DISTRICT OF GEORGIA

Mr. and Mrs. Smith, Individually	)	
and on Behalf of the Estate of	)	
Son Smith	)	
Plaintiffs,	)	
	)	Civil Action No.:
vs.	)	**DEFENDANTS'**
XYZ Company, and Mr. Driver Jones	)	**MEMORANDUM OF LAW**
	)	**IN SUPPORT OF MOTION**
	)	**TO EXCLUDE TESTIMONY**
	)	**OF ACCIDENT**
	)	**RECONSTRUCTIONIST,**
	)	**ALEX WHITE**
Defendants.	)	

COME NOW the Defendants in the above-styled action, by and through their undersigned attorneys, and file this Memorandum of Law in Support of Motion to Exclude the Expert Testimony of Expert Witness, Alex White, showing this Court as follows:

I. Introduction

This lawsuit arises out of Son Smith's loss of control of his vehicle and collision with a guardrail while driving along Interstate 85 at 2:00 a.m. on _____, 200____. Following this collision, which destroyed the rear of Mr. Smith' car, Mr. Smith's vehicle was thrown 350 feet forward until it came to rest in the middle of the nighttime roadway without any rear lights available to warn of its positioning to oncoming southbound traffic, such as Mr. Jones. Mr. Smith' vehicle remained masked in the roadway for at least 2 to 3 minutes without any effort on the part of Mr. Smith to extricate himself—leading the pathologist who performed an autopsy on Mr. Smith to conclude that he very well may have died as a result of this initial collision. Approximately 2 to 3 minutes later, a tractor-trailer driven by Defendant, Mr. Jones, came upon the Smith vehicle, but Mr. Jones was unable to see it in enough time to avoid colliding with it. The Smith vehicle exploded on impact.

Expert Witness, White, is Plaintiffs' accident reconstructionist in this litigation. Globally, Mr. White's opinions can be broken down into two overarching categories. First, Mr. White has offered an opinion on the circumstances of Son Smith's collision with the guardrail—the collision which caused the Smith vehicle to become stranded in the middle of the nighttime roadway. See White report, p. 4, attached hereto as Exhibit 9. Based on assumptions founded upon assumptions, Mr. White has concluded that the deceleration, or "Delta V," of the Smith vehicle as it impacted with the guardrail was 20 miles per hour, and the principle direction of force acting upon the Smith vehicle was in a rearward, or a "6 o' clock," direction. White report, p. 4. Presumably, Mr. White's calculations in this regard have been made for the benefit of another of plaintiff's experts, Dr. Christmas, who has opined that the forces in this impact were insufficient to render a lethal blow to Mr. Smith.

Mr. White's opinions regarding the force of the initial impact are unreliable. Mr. White admitted that he did not know, or alternatively, failed to take into account, several factors relevant to this determination. Mr. White did not know the initial speed at which the Smith vehicle was traveling, nor did he have sufficient information to determine the speed of the Smith vehicle when it impacted with the guardrail. Mr. White did not know the angle at which the Smith vehicle impacted with the guardrail, or the deceleration of the Smith vehicle as a result of its impact with the guardrail. Mr. White did not know the damage suffered by the Smith vehicle as a result of this impact, or the amount of force exerted upon the vehicle or Mr. Smith himself. Without this admittedly relevant information, Mr. White's opinions regarding the initial collision constitute nothing more than speculation.

Second, Mr. White has offered an opinion as to the cause of Mr. Jones' collision with the Smith vehicle once it had come to rest in the middle of the nighttime roadway—opining that the cause of this second accident was Mr. Jones' "failure to maintain a proper lookout." White report, p. 3. In support of this opinion, Mr. White has assumed that Mr. Jones had "minutes" of advanced CB radio notice of a disabled vehicle in the roadway. White report, p. 2, para. 4, and p. 3. Mr. White also claims that the Smith vehicle "should have been visible for 500 to as much as 1000 feet[,]" and that Mr. Jones would have had sufficient time to perceive and react to the stranded vehicle so as to avoid it had he been paying attention. White report, pp. 3, 4.

Mr. White's opinions regarding the cause of this second collision are unreliable for a variety of reasons. First, the undisputed eye-witness testimony unequivocally demonstrates that the Smith vehicle was not visible under cover of darkness, and that it could not have been seen in time for Mr. Jones to avoid it. Mr. White's opinions regarding the distance at which the Smith vehicle could be seen are untested, and constitute nothing more than the *ipse dixit* of Mr. White. While Mr. White has assumed Mr. Jones received CB radio notice of the disabled vehicle "minutes" before the collision, the undisputed evidence show this notice occurred only a few seconds before impact. Finally, Mr. White's opinions regarding the time it would have taken Mr. Jones to react to the Smith vehicle are untested and unsupported, and nothing more than a guess that is nothing beyond what could be determined by lay observation.

For these reasons, set forth in greater detail below, Mr. White's testimony should be excluded.

II. Factual Background

A. The August 1, 2000 accident.

At around 2:00 a.m. on _____, Son Smith lost control of his vehicle while traveling southbound on I–85, and collided with a guardrail while approaching the Blue River bridge. See Trooper depo., p. 49, attached hereto as Exhibit 1. Son Smith's vehicle rebounded off the guardrail, and came to rest over 350 feet from the initial point of impact in the right hand lane of the Blue River bridge. Trooper depo., p. 56. The impact with the guardrail was of such force that the rear bumper was torn from the Smith car, the license plate from the Smith car was wrapped around the post of the guardrail, and the tail-lights of the Smith car were shattered. Trooper depo., p. 49.

At the time of this initial collision, the roads were wet, and it was, of course, dark outside. See witness depo., p. 11, attached hereto as Exhibit 2. There were no streetlights over the highway, and no moonlight so as to illuminate the Smith vehicle. See witness depo., p. 63, attached hereto as Exhibit 3. While the headlights of the Smith vehicle appear to have survived the initial impact, the Smith vehicle had come to rest in a position such that the headlights were pointed away from southbound traffic. Witness depo., p. 52.

At around 2:00 a.m., Mr. Jones was also traveling southbound in the right hand lane of I–85, a little north of where the Smith vehicle had come to rest. See Mr. Jones depo., p. 163, attached hereto as Exhibit 4. Mr. Jones was traveling in his tractor-trailer at between 60 to 65 m.p.h., and the posted speed limit was 70 m.p.h. Jones depo., p. 176; Page depo., p. 64. Mr. Jones was not tired at the time, and had only been driving for three to four hours since the time he had taken a three or four hour nap in the sleeping berth of his tractor-trailer. Jones depo., p. 185. The evening before, Mr. Jones had slept for eight hours. Jones depo., p. 214.

The Smith vehicle was not within Mr. Jones' sight at the time it collided with the guardrail, and Mr. Jones could not see the Smith vehicle, or any lights coming from the Smith vehicle, as he approached it. Jones depo., pp. 164–165, 182. Mr. Jones described the moments before the collision, and his inability of the Smith vehicle, as follows:

A: . . . [D]own at the bottom of the hill, right around the bridge area, my headlights picked up a dark object in the road and within a split second, I went from a dark object to knowing it was a car. . . .

Q: From the time you realized there was an object in front of you, the dark object as you call it, until the time of impact, how much time passed?

A: Oh, split second, split second or two, just—it was like instant.

Jones depo., p. 165.

The one eye-witness who observed the Smith vehicle from both the north and south before the collision confirms that while the Smith vehicle could be observed from the south on account of its headlights, it could not be seen from the north. Another trucker witness was a northbound tractor-trailer driver who first saw the Smith vehicle headlights, which were pointed toward him in a southbound direction, when he reached the base of the bridge on which the Smith vehicle was situated. Upon passing the Smith vehicle, Mr. Trucker looked behind him to see whether the vehicle was visible to southbound traffic. Mr. Trucker testified that he was not able to see the car despite the fact that he knew its precise location. At his deposition, Mr. Trucker testified as follows:

Q: Could you see—after you passed the car, could you see the headlights?

A: No.

Q: Could you see taillights?

A: No.

Q: Could you see anything reflecting on the car?

A: No.

See Trucker depo., pp. 24–25, attached hereto as Exhibit 5. Recounting the Smith vehicle's utter invisibility, Mr. Trucker went on to testify:

when I looked back in my rear view mirror, it was just pitch dark. I mean, there was no—there was no—there was nothing shining in my rear view mirror to even see a car that was—you know, that was back there. I mean, *there was just nothing but darkness.*

Trucker depo., pp. 30–31.

Other northbound tractor-trailer drivers who had seen the Smith vehicle recognized the danger the Smith vehicle posed to southbound drivers, and issued CB radio warnings regarding the Smith vehicle. Witness depo., p. 15; Witness—2 depo., pp. 52–53. Other eye-witnesses to the accident have testified that they heard a varying number of warnings about the "spun-out" Smith vehicle in the moments before the accident. Trucker Two, a northbound driver, has testified that he heard one warning of a "spin out" approximately two (2) to three (3) minutes before the collision, a second warning approximately one (1) minute later, and a third warning some time shortly thereafter. Trucker Two depo., pp. 29–30. Trucker Three, a southbound driver behind the tractor-trailer operated by Mr. Jones, recalls hearing only two (2) warnings over the CB prior to the accident. Trucker Three depo., pp. 7–8.

While Mr. Jones had his CB turned on prior to the accident, the volume was "turned way down low" and the "squelch" turned up such that he was not able to receive transmissions from drivers a quarter of a mile distance from him, and probably less. Jones depo., pp. 170–171.[1] At his deposition, Mr. Jones could not recall hearing any CB warnings regarding the spun-out Smith vehicle prior to the accident. Jones depo., p. 169. However, various post-accident investigations indicate that Mr. Jones heard the last of these CB warnings just as his headlights hit the Smith vehicle. Miss Investigator, an accident scene investigator who interviewed Mr. Jones in the hours following the accident, testified that Mr. Jones reported to her that he "heard over the CB that a car was in the right lane *just as he saw the car in the right lane*." See Investigator depo., pp. 162–163, attached hereto as Exhibit 6. An investigative note created by Corporate Defendant's safety director—noted that Mr. Jones heard this CB warning "*just a few seconds*" before "his headlights came upon a car in his lane of travel," providing him with "*no time to miss the vehicle*." See Safety Director depo., p. 321–322, attached hereto as Exhibit 7; Post-accident notes of Mr. Jones interview, attached hereto as Exhibit 8.

---

[1]"Squelch" is a setting on a CB radio which monitors the distance at which transmissions from other CB radios can be received. When "squelch" is turned to the "high" position, the distance at which other CB radio transmissions can be received is one-quarter of a mile or less. See also Smith depo., pp. 13–15.

In recounting his observations of the accident, Witness, a northbound driver who witnessed the accident from the south, testified as follows.

> . . . [W]hen you got traffic running between 70 and 80 miles an hour and you run up on someone doing half that speed, even when they're just doing half the speed you're doing, you have to spot it pretty soon to avoid running into the back of them[.] . . . And as far [a vehicle] being stopped, . . . you have to spot that danger a lot further away to avoid it.

Witness depo., p. 46. Mr. Witness went on to testify:

> Q: In response to a question as to why you stayed at the accident scene, you responded in part, "I didn't want them to think that this truck driver had just run up on this car going down the road and run over it. I wanted it to be known that the car was sitting dead in the road."
>
> Do you see that?
>
> A: Yes.
>
> Q: And tell me what you meant by that statement?
>
> A: Like I was saying a while ago, you could run up on someone going the minimum speed of 45, when you run over someone that's moving at minimum speed and you run over them, then, you know, I didn't want them to think something like that happened. I mean, I wanted them to know that the car was stopped in the road.
>
> Q: Okay. Why did you believe that to be an important point?
>
> A: Because it happens, you know, especially if there's no one around to say different. Like I say, I've been driving a long time and I heard stories of truckers getting blamed for things that's not their fault, and I just wanted to let it be known that this truck just didn't come along and run over a slow moving vehicle.
>
> Witness depo., pp. 66–67.

Similarly, Witness Two, a southbound driver who witnessed the accident from the north, testified as follows:

> At night, at night if he had his—-if there were no lights on the Smith car and the XYZ Company driver was in the right lane, if he was in the right lane—and I, and I assume he was—by the time he seen the car in the dark, whether it's light or no light, moon shining or not, time you see, you don't. It's too late.

Witness Two depo., pp. 52–53. Witness Two further testified that but for the fact that he had actually heard two CB transmissions when he did, he too would have hit the Smith vehicle had he been driving in front of Mr. Jones. Witness Two depo., pp. 53. Finally, consistent with his opinion as to the Smith vehicle's utter invisibility from the north, Trucker testified that he did not "feel like [Mr. Jones] could have had time to see the vehicle" so as to avoid the collision. Smith depo., p. 32.

B. **Expert Witness' opinions.**

1. **The Smith' vehicle's collision with the guardrail.**

For purposes of his "reconstruction," Mr. White inspected the accident scene on three occasions: 1) June 4, _____—nearly a year after the August 1, _____ accidents; 2) December 18, _____—over 2 years after the August 1, _____ accidents; and 3) May 31, _____—nearly 3 years after the August 1, 2000 accidents. White report, p. 1. The reason for these several visits was that Mr. White initially assumed that the Smith vehicle had struck the bridge over a river, as opposed to the guardrail leading up to the bridge. See Alex White depo., pp. 135, attached hereto as Exhibit 10. It was only on his last site visit—nearly 3 years after the subject accidents—that Mr. White inspected the area in which Mr. Smith had collided with the guardrail. White depo., p. 207. Mr. White never personally inspected the damage to the guardrail caused by the Smith vehicle, as the guardrail had been repaired by this time. White depo., pp. 135–136.

Mr. White attempted to calculate the speed and angle at which the Smith vehicle collided with the guardrail to come to his ultimate conclusion that "[t]he Delta V, or total speed change relative to the [guardrail,] was 20 miles per hour from a 6 o' clock direction." White report, p. 4. With respect to the speed, Mr. White admitted that _he did not know_ the speed the Smith vehicle had initially been traveling down the roadway. White depo., pp. 184–185. For purposes of his "reconstruction," however, he _assumed_ that it was traveling at 70 m.p.h. White depo., p. 184.

Mr. White then attempted to "reconstruct" where on the roadway the Smith vehicle first lost control by searching for "yaw" marks. Mr. White claimed, initially, that while he could not identify any yaw marks on the roadway during his various site inspections, he was able to identify yaw marks left by the Smith vehicle by inspecting photographs taken by Defendant's accident reconstructionist, taken the day after the August 1, 2000 accident. White depo., p. 177. Mr. White retracted this statement by claiming that on his last site visit—nearly 3 years after the subject collision—he was able to identify yaw marks which he attributed to the Smith vehicle, although he did not take any photographs of these alleged yaw marks. White depo., pp. 207, 240. Mr. White measured the path of these phantom yaw marks to conclude that the Smith vehicle had "probably" traveled 105 feet from where it first lost control in the roadway to the guardrail. White depo., p. 232. Mr. White admitted, however, that he was not able to conclusively determine this. White depo., pp. 236–237.

To "determine" the speed the Smith vehicle impacted with the guardrail, Mr. White assumed that the vehicle would have decelerated from the point where it "probably" lost control (traveling at the assumed initial speed of 70 m.p.h.) to the point of its impact with the guardrail. In this regard, Mr. White observed that the vehicle had spun out (it was the rear of the vehicle which hit the guardrail), but admitted that did not know how many times it had spun. White depo., p. 243. To account for the friction that would be operating to decelerate the Smith vehicle as it spun across the roadway, Mr. White assigned a "drag factor," or coefficient of friction, of 0.5 to the Smith vehicle. White depo., p. 208. Mr. White admitted that the friction, or drag factor, operating on the vehicle would be less than this arbitrarily-assigned value if the road was wet. White depo., pp. 196–197, 249. Mr. White did not have any knowledge as to whether the road was wet or dry, but assigned this value to the drag factor nonetheless. White depo., pp. 194, 255. Mr. White did this because he believed that it would have been difficult for the yaw marks which he "observed" to appear on a wet road. White depo., p. 195. Mr. White did not take into account the reduction of resistance in the down gradient slope upon which the Smith vehicle was traveling in assigned this 0.5 value to his drag factor, commenting that "this is a non-precision calculation anyway." White depo., p. 208.

From these assumptions, Mr. White concluded that the Smith vehicle was traveling at 58 m.p.h. at the time it impacted with the guardrail. White depo., pp. 208–209. Mr. White also "approximated" the angle at which the Smith vehicle impacted with the guardrail to be 20 degrees. White depo., p. 208. Utilizing the speed and angle at which the Smith vehicle collided with the guardrail, Mr. White concluded that "[t]he Delta V, or total speed change relative to the [guardrail,] was 20 miles per hour from a 6 o' clock direction." White report, p. 4. According to Mr. White, the "principle direction of force" operating on both the Smith vehicle and Mr. Smith as a result of this impact was such that Mr. Smith would have been thrown directly back into his seat at 20 m.p.h. White depo., pp. 309–312. While not set forth in his initial report, Mr. White asserted at his deposition that Mr. Smith would not likely have received a "life-threatening" injury from such an impact. White depo., p. 402.

However, Mr. White admitted that he did not know the actual angle of impact, and that this would have a bearing upon the direction of force exerted on Mr. Smith body within the car. White depo., pp. 313, 410–411. Mr. White did not know at what speed the Smith vehicle was rotating when it impacted with the guardrail, and was unable to state at what angle the vehicle rebounded off the guardrail following this impact. White depo., p. 238, 271. Mr. White did not have any knowledge as to the deceleration of the Smith vehicle as a result of its impact with the guardrail, and was unable to calculate the speed of the Smith vehicle following the impact with the guardrail. White depo., pp. 243, 246. Mr. White did not know the force exerted upon the Smith vehicle as a result of the impact with the guardrail, and did not know the force exerted upon the body of Mr. Smith as a result of the impact with the guardrail. White depo., pp. 247, 265. Mr. White did not have any knowledge as to the damage to the Smith vehicle as a result of the impact with the guardrail. White depo., p. 213.

2. **Mr. Jones' collision with the Smith vehicle.**

Mr. White was requested to identify each and every basis for his opinion that the cause of the second collision was Mr. Jones' "failure to maintain a proper lookout." First, Mr. White stated that the headlights on the Smith vehicle were on. White depo., p. 316. Second, Mr. White opined that Mr. Jones heard CB warnings regarding the Smith vehicle. White depo., pp. 316–317. Third, the Smith vehicle would have been visible from between 500 and 1,000 feet due to the reflective nature of the taillight assembly on the Smith vehicle. White depo., p. 317. Fourth, it was dark and there was no artificial lighting in the area. White depo., pp. 318–319. Fifth, and finally, Mr. White stated that the fact that Mr. Jones actually collided with the Smith vehicle "without apparently making any evasive maneuvers," supports his opinion that Mr. Jones was not keeping a proper lookout. White depo., p. 321.

a. **Mr. White's opinions as to the visibility of the Smith vehicle are unsupported by any testing or data.**

The evidence of this case demonstrates that the Smith vehicle taillights were significantly damaged during the rearward impact with the guardrail. Trooper depo., p. 49. However, Mr. White stated that due to the reflective nature of taillight lenses, the taillight assembly of the Smith vehicle would have "start[ed] to become visible at about 1,000 feet." White depo., pp. 47, 322. According to Mr. White, the headlights from the Smith vehicle, pointing in a southbound direction and away from Mr. Jones, "may have been" visible beyond 1,000 feet. White depo., p. 322. According to Mr. White, at 500 feet away, the taillight assembly "should be quite prominent." White depo., p. 323.

Significantly, Mr. White did absolutely no testing to confirm whether light reflecting from a Son Smith's car taillight assembly could in fact be seen at night from distances of 1000 feet, 500 feet, or even 300 feet. White depo., pp. 323–324, 383. While Mr. White claims to base his knowledge on generalized studies he has performed in the past, these studies have never been published or peer-reviewed. White depo., p. 385, 388. Mr. White could not identify any literature which supports his opinion that light reflecting from a 1993 J30 Infinity could be identified at a distance of 1000 feet. White depo., p. 389. Mr. White had no knowledge regarding Mr. Jones' visual acuity, and could identify no known error rate in his studies. White depo., pp. 383, 388.

Mr. White did not know what portion, if any, of the taillight assembly remained on the Smith vehicle following its impact with the guardrail, and was not able to determine this based upon his inspection of the photographs taken by another expert. White depo., pp. 361, 365. Mr. White conceded that the untested and unpublished figures quoted above would be reduced if the taillight assembly had been destroyed. Under such a scenario, Mr. White admitted that the Smith vehicle would not have become visible until 400 to 500 feet, and that a driver would not be able to recognize the car as a "threat" for which some evasive action was required until 400 feet. White depo., pp. 92, 97.

Mr. White opined that the Smith vehicle taillight assembly would still have reflective properties even if the headlights had been destroyed on account of the fact that the taillight casing had a silverized, reflective backing. White depo., p. 47. However, Mr. White admitted that in order to determine whether Son Smith's car was equipped with such a silverized, reflective backing, one would need to remove the taillight lenses. White depo., p. 52. This Mr. White admittedly did not do. White depo., pp. 49–50.

For purposes of his visibility "calculations," Mr. White assumed that the Smith vehicle was directly in line with the southbound roadway, as opposed to an angle to the left or to the right. White depo., p. 324. Mr. White admitted the basic physical principle that the angle at which an oncoming light source hits the taillight assembly would impact the angle at which that light will reflect off the taillights. White depo., p. 53. However, Mr. White claimed that, in this case, the angle at which the Smith vehicle was situated in the roadway would not matter in terms of taillight visibility to an on-coming driver, as the taillights would reflect an equal amount of light back to the oncoming light source whatever the angle of the taillights. White depo., pp. 57–58, 325.

b. **Mr. White's opinions on perception and reaction time are unreliable.**

As recognized by Mr. White, even after an individual is able to actually see the taillights or headlights of a stationary car in the middle of the roadway, it will take some time for the individual to perceive and recognize that the car is a threat that must be responded to. White depo., p. 98. Mr. White identified this principle as "perception and reaction time," explaining it as follows:

> Perception and reaction time in a driving situation basically is that second or two from when something becomes visible or noticeable to you, you need a second or two. In other words, everybody takes a moment or two to necessarily recognize that it's there and basically have a recognition, see it, realize it's there, decide to take some kind of action or not take some action depending upon what it is.

White depo., p. 104. Mr. White recognized that a variety of both physiological and psychological factors play an important role in determining an individual's ability to perceive and react, but could not list what any of those factors were. White depo., pp. 105, 108–109. Mr. White was not able to account for how he arrived at his value of 1 to 2 seconds for perception and reaction time. White depo., p. 105.

c. Mr. White's opinion that Mr. Jones heard a CB warning regarding the Smith vehicle 2 minutes before the collision is without evidentiary support.

Mr. White recognized that when an object is more difficult to perceive in the first instance, the time it will take to react to it will be greater. White depo., p. 105. Mr. White also recognized that perception and reaction is made more difficult, and more time-consuming, when an individual "would not reasonably expect" the object to be present, such as a dark object in the roadway. White depo., pp. 105, 111.

Notwithstanding the fact that the Smith vehicle was stationary in the middle of an interstate highway without its taillights, Mr. White felt at liberty to discount the time it should take Mr. Jones to perceive and react to the Smith vehicle. Mr. White did this by assuming that Mr. Jones had received meaningful advanced notice of the positioning of the Smith vehicle. White depo., p. 327. Ignoring Mr. Jones' statement that he heard a CB warning regarding the Smith vehicle only seconds before the collision—as the Smith vehicle appeared in his headlights—Mr. White assumed Mr. Jones heard this CB radio warning approximately 2 minutes prior to the collision because other tractor-trailer drivers stated that this was when they first heard the CB warnings. White depo., pp. 327–329.

Mr. White conceded that there is a critical distinction between the transmission of a CB message and the hearing of a CB message. White depo., p. 331. Mr. White noted that reasons for this can include: 1) the volume of the CB radio; 2) the decibel levels within the cab of the vehicle; 3) whether the AM/FM radio is on and at what volume; 4) whether the squelch on the CB radio is turned up; and 5) the effect of the terrain upon the reception of CB transmissions. White depo., pp. 332–335. Mr. White was either unaware of any of these factors bearing upon Mr. Jones' ability to hear a CB transmission, or decided not to consider them in his "analysis."

d. **Mr. White's opinion on the time it would have taken Mr. Jones to perceive and react to the Smith vehicle by making a lane change is unreliable.**

According to Mr. White, perception and reaction time entails an individual "see[ing an object], realiz[ing] it's there, [and then] decid[ing] to take some kind of action or not take some action depending upon what it is." White depo., p. 104. Of course, following this, the person must execute the action they have decided to take. Mr. White opined that it should have taken Mr. Jones 2 to 3 seconds to execute a lane change in his tractor-trailer while moving at 65 mph along the interstate. White depo., p. 366. Mr. White offered this opinion despite the fact that he has never been employed as a tractor-trailer driver, has no commercial driver's license, and has never driven a tractor-trailer on an interstate. White depo., pp. 26–27.

Mr. White purported to have arrived at this "estimate" through admittedly "informal" studies, wherein he took a stopwatch while driving down the road and timed tractor-trailers as they made lane changes. White depo., pp. 378–379. Mr. White has never consulted with any of these tractor-trailer drivers to find out when in fact they first decided to execute their lane change. White depo., p. 381. None of these "studies" have ever been published or peer-reviewed, and Mr. White has never documented any of his findings. White depo., pp. 381–382.

III. **Argument and Citation of Authority.**

Rule 702 of the Federal Rules of evidence governs the admissibility of expert testimony, providing that:

> If scientific, technical, or other specialized knowledge will assist the trier of fact to understand the evidence or to determine a fact in issue, a witness qualified as an expert by knowledge, skill, experience, training, or education, may testify thereto in the form of an opinion or otherwise, if (1) the testimony is based upon sufficient facts or data, (2) the testimony is the product of reliable principles and methods, and (3) the witness has applied the principles and methods reliably to the facts of the case.

Pursuant to Rule 702, the trial court has a duty to act as a "gatekeeper" to screen expert testimony: "[T]he trial judge must ensure that any and all scientific testimony or evidence admitted is not only relevant, *but reliable.*" Daubert v. Merrell Dow Pharmaceuticals, Inc., 509 U.S. 579, 589, 113 S.Ct. 2786 (1993) (emphasis supplied). As stated by the Daubert Court:

> The adjective "scientific" implies a grounding in the methods and procedures of science. Similarly, the word "knowledge" connotes more than subjective belief or unsupported speculation. . . . [I]n order to qualify as "scientific knowledge" an inference or assertion must be derived by the scientific method. Proposed testimony must be supported by appropriate validation—i.e. "good grounds," based on what is known.

Id. at 590. In Kumho Tire Co. v. Carmichael, 526 U.S. 137, 141, 119 S.Ct. 1167 (1999), the United States Supreme Court made it clear that this gate keeping requirement exists not only for expert testimony that is "scientific" in nature, but for *all* expert testimony, whether based upon "scientific," "technical," or "other specialized" knowledge.

The trial court has a responsibility to ensure that only properly admitted evidence is considered by the jury. The "Supreme Court deemed this USS objectionable thus, dumping a barrage of questionable scientific evidence on a juror, who would be likely less equipped then the judge to make reliability and relevance determinations." Allison v. McGhan, 184 F.3d 1300 (11th Cir. 1999). The objective of the trial court's gate keeping role is to ensure that an expert "employs in the courtroom the same level of intellectual rigor that characterizes the practice of an expert in the relevant field." Kumho, 526 U.S. at 152.

A. **Mr. White's "reconstruction" of the Smith vehicle's impact with the guardrail is unreliable.**

1. **Mr. White's opinions regarding the force of the Smith vehicle's impact with the guardrail is unreliable because it is premised upon mere assumptions.**

An expert opinion must have an adequate basis in fact, and expert testimony is admissible only if the expert is in possession of such facts as would enable him to express a reasonably accurate conclusion as distinguished from mere conjecture. See Hall v. United Ins. Co. of America, 367 F.3d 1255, 1261–62 (11th Cir. 2004). Moreover, Georgia law now requires that an expert's opinion be based upon sufficient facts or data that are admissible in evidence. O.C.G.A.§ 24–9–67.1.

Courts have consistently excluded purported "expert" testimony where the expert has been unable to demonstrate that he has a sufficient factual basis for his opinions, as an opinion without sufficient factual basis is nothing more than speculation on the part of the expert. For instance, in Oglesby v. General Motors Corp., 190 F.3d 244 (4th Cir. 1999), a mechanical engineer attempted to opine that a component part of a radiator hose failed because it was defective, thereby causing the plaintiff's injuries. The engineer made a variety of assumptions about the shape, composition, and stress resistance of the component part, as well as the actual stress exerted upon the component part when it failed. In excluding the engineer's testimony, the Fourth Circuit found that the engineer "had none of the necessary data and therefore could not make any such calculations for the part in this case. He could only speculate as to a possibility which was no more likely than other available possibilities." Id. at 252; see also Collier v. Varco–Pruden Buildings, 911 F.Supp. 189, 192 (D.S.C. 1995).

Here, Mr. White performed "[a]n analysis of Son Smith's automobile . . . to determine the speed with which it collided with the guardrail and the resultant Delta V (speed change at impact)." White report, p. 4. Mr. White concluded that the speed at which the Smith vehicle impacted the guardrail was 58 m.p.h. White report, p. 4. This conclusion, however, was admittedly built upon assumption after assumption. First, Mr. White admitted that he did not have any knowledge as to the initial speed at which the Smith vehicle was traveling, and merely "assumed" that it would have been traveling at 70 m.p.h. along the interstate. White depo., pp. 184–185. Second, Mr. White asserted that the Smith vehicle would have lost speed as it "spun out" on the interstate towards the guardrail. In calculating this deceleration, Mr. White stated that it was his belief that the point at which the Smith vehicle "probably" went into the spin was 105 feet from the guardrail. White depo., p. 232. Mr. White was not, however, able to conclusively determine this. White depo., pp. 236–237.

Third, to account for the friction that would have been operating on the Smith vehicle so as to reduce its speed as it spun across the roadway, Mr. White utilized a coefficient of friction, or drag factor, of 0.5. White depo., p. 208. Mr. White admitted that he had no knowledge as to whether the road was wet or dry, and conceded that the friction operating on the Smith vehicle would be less, resulting in a lower drag factor, if the road were in fact wet. White depo., pp. 194, 196–197, 248, 255.

The import of these "convenient" assumptions cannot be understated. Mr. White's assumptions as to: 1) the Smith vehicle's initial speed; 2) the point at which it lost control and went into a "spin out;" and 3) the wetness of the road, all go to Mr. White's conclusion that the Smith vehicle impacted with the guardrail at a speed of 58 m.p.h., and the resulting force exerted upon the Smith vehicle and Mr. Smith himself. However, Mr. White's conclusion in this regard is built upon assumptions, and is not founded upon the methodology which courts deem either reliable or admissible.

2. Mr. White's opinions regarding the force of the Smith vehicle's impact with the guardrail is unreliable because it is inconsistent with the underlying facts and fails to take into account relevant data.

Just as an expert's opinion is not reliable when it is premised upon mere assumptions, an expert's opinion which is premised upon faulty assumptions is all the more unreliable. Courts properly exclude such testimony as likely to mislead the jury, noting the danger that the jury may accept as fact not just the faulty assumptions on which the expert relied, but may also accept the conclusions that are drawn through his use of these assumptions. Tyger Construction Co. v. Pensacola Construction Co., 29 F.3d 137, 144 (4th Cir. 1994) (where expert testimony as to cause of economic damages contrary to evidence, testimony excluded); J.B. Hunt Transport, Inc. v. General Motors Corp., 243 F.3d 441 (8th Cir. 2001) (where damages expert assumed that plaintiff's vehicle had been impacted only three times, and evidence demonstrated that plaintiff's vehicle had been impacted four times, testimony excluded).

Here, not only is Mr. White's calculation as to drag factor premised upon an assumption that the road was dry, it runs contrary to the overwhelming evidence in this case. Mr. White based his assumption as to the drag factor on the fact that while "one person said that [he] thought it was wet," all other witnesses said it was dry. White depo., p. 195. Mr. White also based his assumption on the testimony of the investigating officer, Mr. Page, who reported finding visible yaw marks on the roadway. White depo., p. 195. Mr. White observed that it is "more difficult" for yaw marks to appear on a wet roadway, and concluded "that the road was probably dry." White depo., p. 195.

However, whereas one witness *could not recall* whether the roads were wet or dry, all other witnesses recall that, while it was not raining at the time, the roads *were* in fact wet. Trucker depo., p. 75; Jones depo., p. 162; Witness depo., p. 63; Witness depo., p. 11; Trooper depo., p. 23. Moreover, the investigating officer testified that the yaw marks that he found were "faint" *precisely because* the roads were wet at the time of the Smith vehicle spin out. Trooper depo., p. 24. It is significant to note that Mr. White never bothered to inspect the area around the guardrail until nearly 3 years after the subject collision. White depo.,

p. 207.[2] By contrast, Mr. Expert, an accident reconstructionist retained by Defendants, investigated the accident scene the day after the collision, and identified "cleaning marks" leading directly into the point of the Smith vehicles impact with the guardrail. Tyner depo., p. 90. Cleaning marks are formed where tires sliding across a roadway heat *water* on the roadway. Tyner depo., p. 91.

The unreliability of Mr. White's calculation does not stop there, as Mr. White either did not know, or failed to consider, other factors admittedly pertinent to the friction that would have been operating upon the Smith vehicle as it slid across the highway. As noted by the United States Supreme Court in General Elec. Co. v. Joiner, 522 U.S. 136 (1997):

> Trained experts commonly extrapolate from existing data. But nothing in either Daubert or the Federal Rules of Evidence requires a district court to admit opinion evidence that is connected to existing data only by the *ipse dixit* of the expert. A court may conclude that there is simply too great an analytical gap between the data and the opinion proffered.

Id. at 146. Indeed, the methodology employed by Mr. White in reaching his conclusions is similar to that of an expert whose testimony was held inadmissible in Adams v. Pro Transportation, Inc., 2002 WL 801911 (D. Neb. 2002). There, an expert proposed to offer testimony as to the cause of a tractor-trailer accident. The court held that the methodology the expert had employed in arriving at his conclusion was unreliable because the expert either did not know, or did not take into account, specific characteristics of the collision at issue, include the grade of the slope on which the vehicle was traveling and the vehicle's speed. Id. at *7.

Here, Mr. White had no knowledge as to how many times the Smith vehicle spun, but admitted that the number of times the

---

[2]While Mr. White did not personally observe any of these yaw marks on his first 2 site visits, Mr. White claims that on his third site visit he was in fact able to identify the presence of yaw marks which can be attributed to the Smith vehicle. White depo., p. 207. Mr. White did not, however, bother to photograph any of these yaw marks, which he claims to be associated with the Smith vehicles' impact with the guardrail. White depo., p. 240. Mr. White's assertion strains credibility, and his decision not to photograph these yaw marks is revealing. Apart from the fact that the guardrail had been repaired at the time of this third visit, the third visit occurred nearly three years after the collision, and after countless vehicles had passed through the area. According to Mr. Trooper, the yaw marks were "faint" only hours after the accident, and according to Mr. Defense Expert, the yaw marks were barely perceptible the day after the collision. Trooper depo., p. 24; Defense Expert depo., p. 212–213, attached hereto as Exhibit 11. Mr. Defense Expert noted that Mr. White would not have been able to identify any yaw marks from the Smith vehicle during this site visit, a point which even Plaintiff's counsel conceded. Defense Expert depo., p. 212.

Smith vehicle spun would be something "I'd want to look at" for purposes of calculating a drag factor. White depo., p. 242. While Mr. White acknowledged that there was a down gradient slope to the roadway which would, like the wet roadway surface, operate to reduce the friction operating on the Smith vehicle, he did not take this slope into account when calculating his drag factor. White depo., p. 208. Mr. White admitted that the condition of the Smith vehicle tires-i.e. whether worn or with new tread—could have an effect on the friction generated on the vehicle as it slid along the roadway, but did not take this into account when arriving at his estimate of drag factor. White depo., p. 257. While Mr. White admitted that the relative smoothness or coarseness of a roadway bears upon the drag factor calculation, Mr. White merely took an "approximated" figure for his drag factor. White depo., pp. 248, 258. Mr. White took into account none of these factors, reasoning that his calculation of the friction operating on the Smith vehicle was "a non-precision calculation anyway." White depo., p. 208.

Mr. White's opinion as to the speed the Smith vehicle impacted with the guardrail, and the resulting Delta V, is unreliable as failing to take into account several factors which are admittedly important in making such calculations. Mr. White's opinions are premised upon nothing more than guesswork and speculation, and constitute nothing more than inadmissible *ipse dixit* testimony of an expert.

3. Mr. White's opinions regarding the Smith vehicle's angle of impact with the guardrail, and the amount and direction of force exerted upon the Smith vehicle and Mr. Smith himself, are unreliable.

While an expert's opinions may be premised generally upon scientific principles, where the expert is without sufficient data to apply those principles to the specific case, the expert's methodology is unreliable. For instance, in Phelan v. Synthes, 35 Fed. Appx. 102 (4th Cir. 2002), the plaintiff was injured after a "tibial nail" surgically implanted in her fractured, and proferred expert testimony that the tibial nail was defective. The expert, however, had not conducted any tests or performed any calculations with regard to the nail in question. Moreover, the expert was not able to identify extent of the stress or force that would have been placed on the nail under similar circumstances. In upholding the trial court's exclusion of the expert's testimony, the Fourth Circuit noted that the expert's opinion "was based largely on extrapolation from a simple principle of engineering without quantitative or otherwise specific examination of the properties of the Synthes nail itself." Id. The court went on to observe that [m]issing from [the expert's] proffer . . . was any basis for believing that this nail broke because of the stresses he suggested would have been placed on it in the position it was in, or for eliminating equally plausible causes for the nail's breaking[.] Id.

Here, Mr. White utilized the speed (58 m.p.h.) and angle at which the Smith vehicle collided with the guardrail to arrive at his conclusion that "[t]he Delta V, or total speed change relative to the [guardrail,] was 20 miles per hour from a 6 o'clock direction." White report, p. 4. Stated another way, according to Mr. White there was a rearward, or 6 o'clock, principle direction of force operating on Mr. Smith such that Mr. Smith would have been thrown directly back into his seat at 20 m.p.h upon impact with the guardrail. White depo., pp. 309–312. While not set forth in his initial report, Mr. White asserted at his deposition that Doug Smith would not likely have received a "life-threatening" injury "from a 20 mile per hour rear impact." White depo., p. 402. Citing support for this proposition, Mr. White stated: "I think both my engineering training as well as common sense tells you that very few people would be killed from a 20 mile per hour impact." White depo., p. 403.

Mr. White would create the impression that Mr. Smith' impact with the guardrail would have been, at most, "unpleasant," much like being thrown too hard on grandma's feather bed during overly-spirited horseplay. However, Mr. White's conclusion that Mr. Smith suffered a 20 m.p.h. impact that would have thrown him directly into his seat back is merely an assumption without factual basis, and the methodology he employed to arrive at this conclusion fails to take into account admittedly relevant data. First, Mr. White was only able to "approximate" the angle at which the Smith vehicle impacted with the guardrail—an angle which he determined to be 20 degrees. White depo., p. 208. Mr. White was not able to arrive at this "approximation" based upon personal observation or field testing. White depo., pp. 135, 176–177. Instead, Mr. White utilized the *photographs taken by Mr. Defense Expert*, who inspected the scene the day following the impact. White depo., p. 136; Defense Expert depo., p. 86. However, based upon actual scene inspection and field testing, Mr. Defense Expert concluded that while the angle of impact could not be precisely determined, the angle of impact fell within the range of 24 to 31 degrees. Defense Expert depo., Exhibit 7. Mr. White admitted that he did not know the actual angle of impact, and conceded that this knowledge would be relevant for purposes of determining the actual direction of force exerted on Mr. Smith' body within the car. White depo., pp. 313, 410–411.

Moreover, while Mr. White acknowledged that the rotational speed of the Smith vehicle at the point of impact with the guardrail would be relevant for purposes of determining the direction of forces acting upon Mr. Smith, Mr. White conceded that he did not make these calculations. White depo., p. 271. While Mr. White would create the impression that the Smith vehicle gingerly kissed the guardrail so as to be gently eased back into its lane of travel, Mr. White was unable to state at what angle the Smith vehicle rebounded off the guardrail following this impact. White depo., p. 238, 271.

Further still, Mr. White did not have any knowledge as to the deceleration of the Smith vehicle as a result of its impact with the guardrail. White depo., p. 243. Similarly, Mr. White was unable to calculate the resultant speed of the Smith vehicle following its impact with the guardrail. White depo., pp. 246–247. Mr. White did not know the force exerted upon the Smith vehicle as a result of the impact with the guardrail. White depo., pp. 247–248. Mr. White did not have any knowledge as to the damage to the Smith vehicle as a result of the impact with the guardrail. White depo., p. 213. Finally, Mr. White did not know the amount of force exerted upon the *body* of Mr. Smith as a result of the impact with the guardrail, and did not perform any tests to determine the principle direction of this force. White depo., pp. 265, 408.

An expert's opinion must be based on something more than the *ipse dixit* of the expert, i.e. "it is so because I say it is so." See Dukes v. Georgia, 428 F.Supp. 1298, 1314 (N.D. Ga. 2006). An expert may not arrive at an admissible conclusion absent sufficient factual data, and may not simply chose to consider and examine only certain pieces of evidence to the exclusion of other relevant data. Rather, an expert must consider all relevant data in order to show that he had formed an opinion based on the facts of the particular incident rather than making an 'opinion' judgment based entirely on what he considers to be his experience. Id. at 1314. Here, Mr. White did not know, or failed to consider, admittedly relevant data. The methodology employed by Mr. White in arriving at his conclusion as to the force of the impact with the guardrail and the direction of those forces is not only dubious, it is essentially non-existent. For these, reasons, Mr. White's opinions would neither be reliable nor helpful to the trier of fact, and should be excluded.

B. Mr. White's opinion that the cause of the accident was "Mr. Jones' failure to maintain a proper lookout" is unreliable.

1. Mr. White's opinion that the Smith vehicle was detectible and could have been avoided is contradicted by the undisputed testimony of eyewitnesses.

An expert's opinion which assumes facts that run contrary to eyewitness testimony is nothing more than unreliable speculation. For instance, in <u>Newman</u> v. <u>Hy–Way Heat Systems, Inc.</u>, 789 F.2d 269 (4th Cir. 1986), the plaintiff was injured when an asphalt strainer sprayed hot asphalt on him, and the plaintiff's expert opined that the only way the accident could have happened was for someone to have entered into the control room and turn the motor of the asphalt strainer on in reverse. However, the eyewitness testimony demonstrated that no one had been in the control room, and that the asphalt strainer was never operated in reverse. In upholding the trial court's exclusion of the expert's testimony, the Fourth Circuit held that the expert's opinions as to the cause of the accident were speculative—not only were they without factual support, they ran contrary to the facts of the case. <u>Id.</u> at 270; <u>Guidroz-Brault v. Missouri Pacific R.R. Co.</u>, 254 F.3d 825 (9th Cir. 2001) (expert testimony that cause of train derailment was railroad engineer's failure to keep a proper lookout and discover defect in rail excluded where eyewitness testimony demonstrated that defect in rail was not visible).

Here, Mr. White has opined that the collision between the tractor-trailer operated by Mr. Jones and the Smith vehicle was caused by Mr. Jones' "failure to maintain a proper lookout." Having *assumed* the taillight assembly of the Smith vehicle was intact, Mr. White opined that Mr. Jones would have "started to see" the taillight assembly at 1,000 feet, and that the taillight assembly would have become "quite prominent" at 500 feet away. White depo., pp. 47, 322–323. Mr. White also opined that the headlights of the Smith vehicle, while obscured by the Smith vehicle itself and pointing away from Mr. Jones, "may have been" visible beyond 1,000 feet. White depo., p. 322. Mr. White's opinion as to the distance at which Mr. Jones was able to perceive the fact that there was a disabled vehicle in his lane of travel is, of course, critical to his opinion that Mr. Jones would have been able to timely react.

The facts upon which Mr. White bases his opinion are, however, directly contradicted by all eye-witness accounts. Mr. White conveniently ignores the testimony of Mr. Jones, who testified as to when he was able to see the Smith vehicle as follows:

A: . . . [D]own at the bottom of the hill, right around the bridge area, my headlights picked up a dark object in the road and within a split second, I went from a dark object to knowing it was a car. . . .

Q: From the time you realized there was an object in front of you, the dark object as you call it, until the time of impact, how much time passed?

A: Oh, split second, split second or two, just—it was like instant.

Jones depo., p. 165. Mr. White also conveniently ignores the testimony of Trucker, a northbound tractor-trailer driver who was able to see the headlights of the Smith vehicle, on account of the fact that they were pointed in a southbound direction, as he approached the base of the bridge. Even though Mr. Trucker had seen the Smith headlights of the Smith vehicle from the south, Mr. Trucker confirmed that the Smith vehicle could not be seen once he had passed the vehicle to the north:

Q: Could you see—after you passed the car, could you see the headlights?

A: No.

Q: Could you see taillights?

A: No.

Q: Could you see anything reflecting on the car?

A: No.

Trucker depo., pp. 24–25. Indeed, every eye-witness has stated that the Smith vehicle was not visible in sufficient time for Mr. Jones to have given Mr. Jones an opportunity to react. Trucker depo., p. 32; Witness depo., pp. 66–67; Witness depo., pp. 52–53.

Mr. White's utter disregard of eyewitness testimony regarding the visibility of the Smith vehicle in the middle of the nighttime roadway is revealing. Mr. White sees fit to opine that, notwithstanding all eyewitness testimony to the contrary, the Smith vehicle *really was* visible to Mr. Jones at such a distance that he could have successfully evaded the Smith vehicle. Mr. White's opinions are not only rank speculation, but are directly contradicted by the facts of the case.

2. Mr. White's assumption as to when Mr. Jones heard the CB warning is contrary to the evidence.

As repeatedly stated before, an expert's opinion should be excluded when it is based on assumptions which are speculative and are not supported by the record. Here, notwithstanding the fact that the Smith vehicle was situated in the middle of the nighttime highway, Mr. White has assumed that Mr. Jones received meaningful advanced notice of the presence of the Smith vehicle by way of CB warnings. White depo., p. 327. Mr. White has based this assumption upon the testimony of other tractor-trailer drivers who reported hearing CB reports of a "spun out" vehicle in the right hand lane of I–85 southbound. White depo., pp. 327–329. For instance, one northbound driver testified that he heard one warning of a "spin out" approximately two (2) minutes before the collision, a second warning approximately one (1) minute later, and possibly a third warning some time shortly before the collision. Witness depo., pp. 29–30.

Mr. White's contention is that because other drivers heard various numbers of CB warnings at various times prior to the collision, Mr. Jones *necessarily must have* heard a CB warning "minutes" before the collision. Mr. White's assumption is without basis, and is directly contradicted by the evidence in this case. Although Mr. Jones, at his deposition, could not recall hearing any CB warnings regarding the spun-out Smith vehicle prior to the accident, Mr. Jones agreed that his CB radio would have been on prior to the accident. Jones depo., p. 170. Mr. Jones testified that he customarily drove with the volume of his CB "turned way down low" and the "squelch" turned up such that he was not receive CB transmissions from sources farther than a quarter of a mile distance from him, and probably less. Jones depo., pp. 170–171. Various post-accident investigations indicate that Mr. Jones heard only the last of these CB warnings—just as his headlights hit the Smith vehicle. A note by Martha Williams, indicates that Mr. Jones "heard over the CB that a car was in the right lane *just as he saw the car in the right lane.*" Inspector depo., pp. 162–163. An investigative note created by Company Safety Director—noted that Mr. Jones heard this CB warning "*just a few seconds*" before "his headlights came upon a car in his lane of travel," providing him with "*no time to miss the vehicle.*" Safety Director depo., p. 321–322; Post-accident notes of Mr. Jones interview.

As even Mr. White concedes, there is a critical distinction between the *transmission* of a CB message and the *hearing* of a CB message. White depo., p. 331. Mr. White admitted that reasons for this include: 1) the volume of the CB radio; 2) the decibel levels within the cab of the vehicle; 3) whether the AM/FM radio is on and at what volume; 4) whether the squelch on the CB radio is turned up; and 5) the effect of the terrain upon the reception of CB transmissions. White depo., pp. 332–335.

At bottom, Mr. White's opinion that Mr. Jones heard a CB warning regarding the Smith vehicle at any time other than when Mr. Jones was able to see the vehicle in his headlights is rank speculation and contradicted by the evidence of record.

3. Mr. White's opinions as to: a) the distance at which Mr. Jones would be able to see illumination from the Smith vehicle headlights (which were pointed away from him); b) the distance at which Mr. Jones would be able to see reflecting light from the Smith vehicle taillights (assuming there was some piece of the taillight assembly still intact following the impact with the guardrail); and c) the time it would take for Mr. Jones to execute a lane change are unsupported by any testing or literature, and are unreliable.

In <u>Daubert</u>, the United States Supreme Court noted that a "key question" to be answered in determining whether an expert's methodology is reliable is whether it can be, and has been, tested by the expert. <u>Daubert</u>, 509 U.S. at 593. As explained by the Court in <u>Daubert</u>: " '[s]cientific methodology today is based on generating hypotheses and testing them to see if they can be falsified; indeed, this methodology is what distinguishes science from other fields of human inquiry.' " <u>Id.</u>

Here, despite all evidence to the contrary, Mr. White opined that the Smith vehicle would have been visible to Mr. Jones based upon his bald and conclusory statements that: 1) due to the reflective nature of taillight lenses, the taillight assembly of the Smith vehicle would have "start[ed] to become visible at about 1,000 feet"; 2) at 500 feet away, the taillight assembly should have become "quite prominent"; and 3) the headlights from the Smith vehicle, pointing in a southbound direction and away from Mr. Jones, "may have been" visible beyond 1,000 feet. White depo., pp. 47, 322–323.

With respect to the visibility of the Smith vehicle, Mr. White did absolutely no testing to confirm whether light reflecting from a car taillight assembly such as the make and model driven by Son Smith could in fact be seen at night from distances of 1000 feet, 500 feet, or even 300 feet. White depo., pp. 323–324, 383. While Mr. White claims to base his knowledge on generalized studies he has performed in the past, these studies have never been published or peer-reviewed. White depo., p. 385, 388. Mr. White could not identify any literature which supports his opinion that light reflecting from this particular make and model car could be identified at a distance of 1000 feet. White depo., p. 389. Mr. White had no knowledge regarding the visual acuity of Mr. Jones' eyesight, and could identify no known error rate in these studies. White depo., pp. 383, 388.

It is significant to note that untested and unpublished figures quoted above were premised upon an assumption that the taillights were intact (a fact which is contradicted by the evidence of record). Mr. White conceded that did not know what portion, if any, of the taillight assembly remained on the Smith vehicle following its impact with the guardrail. White depo., pp. 361, 365. Mr. White opined that if the taillight assembly had been destroyed, the Smith vehicle would not have become visible until 400 to 500 feet, and that Mr. Jones would not be able to recognize the car as a "threat" for which some evasive action was required until 400 feet. White depo., pp. 92, 97.

Mr. White opined that the Smith vehicle taillight assembly would still have reflective properties even if the headlights had been destroyed on account of the fact that the taillight casing had a silverized, reflective backing. White depo., p. 47. However, Mr. White admitted that in order to determine whether this particular car make and model was equipped with such a silverized, reflective backing, one would need to remove the taillight lenses. White depo., p. 52. This Mr. White admittedly did not do. White depo., pp. 49–50.

Mr. White recognized that once an individual can physically see an object such as a stationary vehicle in the middle of the road way, it will take time for the individual to realize that there is a threat which needs to be reacted to, and to formulate a plan of response. White depo., p. 104. Mr. White stated that this time—commonly referred to as "perception and reaction" time—would be approximately 1 to 2 seconds. White depo., p. 105. Mr. White was not, however, able to account as to how he arrived at this approximation, and although he recognized that a variety of physiological and psychological factors play an important role in determining an individual's ability to perceive and react, he could not identify any of these. White depo., pp. 105, 108–109.

Mr. White recognized that once an individual has perceived a threat and formulated a response, the individual must then execute the action they have decided to take. Mr. White opined that it should have taken Mr. Jones 2 to 3 seconds to execute a lane change in his tractor-trailer while moving at 65 mph along the interstate. White depo., pp. 366. Mr. White offered this opinion despite the fact that he has never been employed as a tractor-trailer driver, has no commercial driver's license, and has never driven a tractor-trailer on an interstate. White depo., pp. 26–27. Mr. White purported to have arrived at this "estimate" through admittedly "informal" studies, *wherein he took a stopwatch while driving down the road and timed tractor-trailers as they made lane changes.* White depo., pp. 378–379. Mr. White has never consulted with any of these tractor-trailer drivers to find out when in fact they first decided to execute their lane change. White depo., p. 381. None of these "studies" have ever been published or peer-reviewed, and Mr. White has never documented any of his findings. White depo., pp. 381–382. Mr. White's opinions constitute nothing more than the "lay" observations of an "expert," and offer nothing beyond the ken of the average juror. See, e.g. Dukes v. Georgia, 428 F.Supp.2d 1298, 1310 (N.D. Ga. 2006) (excluding expert's opinion as being nothing more than what lawyers and parties can argue in closing.)

Mr. White's opinions regarding the essential issue in this case—whether Mr. Jones had time to perceive the threat posed by the disabled Smith vehicle in the middle of the roadway—are not premised upon a reliable methodology. He has performed no tests to confirm his conclusions as to when Mr. Jones would have been able to see the Smith vehicle, perceive it as a threat (i.e. a stationary vehicle in his lane of travel), formulate a response, and execute this plan of action. Mr. White has cited to no authoritative literature which supports his propositions, and was unable to account for any rate of error in his time estimates. Mr. White's conclusions are unsupportable speculation, and nothing more than the *ipse dixit* of an expert. Because Mr. White's conclusions lack any reliability whatsoever, Mr. White's testimony should be excluded.

IV. Conclusion.

For the foregoing reasons, Defendants respectfully request that Mr. White's testimony be excluded as unreliable.

APPENDIX F

O.C.G.A. § 24–9–67

Experts; opinions admissible, when:

The opinions of experts on any question of science, skill, trade, or like questions shall always be admissible; and such opinions may be given on the facts as proved by other witnesses.

Formerly Code 1863, § 3792; Code 1868, § 3812; Code 1873, § 3868; Code 1882, § 3868; Civil Code 1895, § 5287; Penal Code 1895, § 1022; Civil Code 1910, § 5876; Penal Code 1910, § 1048; code 1933, § 38–1710.

APPENDIX G

O.C.G.A. § 24-9-67.1

O.C.G.A. § 24-9-67.1:

(a) The provisions of this Code section shall apply in all civil actions. The opinion of a witness qualified as an expert under this Code section may be given on the facts as proved by other witnesses. The facts or data in the particular case upon which an expert bases an opinion or inference may be those perceived by or made known to the expert at or before the hearing or trial. If of a type reasonably relied upon by experts in the particular field in forming opinions or inferences upon the subject, the facts or data need not be admissible in evidence in order for the opinion or inference to be admitted. Facts or data that are otherwise inadmissible shall not be disclosed to the jury by the proponent of the opinion or inference unless the court determines that their probative value in assisting the jury to evaluate the expert's opinion substantially outweighs their prejudicial effect.

(b) If scientific, technical, or other specialized knowledge will assist the trier of fact in any cause of action to understand the evidence or to determine a fact in issue, a witness qualified as an expert by knowledge, skill, experience, training, or education may testify thereto in the form of an opinion or otherwise, if:

(1) The testimony is based upon sufficient facts or data which are or will be admitted into evidence at the hearing or trial;

(2) The testimony is the product of reliable principles and methods; and

(3) The witness has applied the principles and methods reliably to the facts of the case.

(c) Notwithstanding the provisions of subsection (b) of this Code section and any other provision of law which might be construed to the contrary, in professional malpractice actions, the opinions of an expert, who is otherwise qualified as to the acceptable standard of conduct of the professional whose conduct is at issue, shall be admissible only if, at the time the act or omission is alleged to have occurred, such expert:

(1) Was licensed by an appropriate regulatory agency to practice his or her profession in the state which such expert was practicing or teaching in the profession at such time; and

(2) In the case of a medical malpractice action, had actual

professional knowledge and experience in the area of practice or specialty in which the opinion is to be given as the result of having been regularly engaged in:

A) The active practice of such area of specialty of his or her profession for at least three of the last five years, with sufficient frequency to establish an appropriate level of knowledge, as determined by the judge, in performing the procedure, diagnosing the condition, or rendering the treatment which is alleged to have been performed or rendered negligently by the defendant whose conduct is at issue; or

B) The teaching of his or her profession for at least three of the last five years as an employed member of the faculty of an educational institution accredited in the teaching of such profession, with sufficient frequency to establish an appropriate level of knowledge, as determined by the judge, in teaching others how to perform the procedure, diagnose the condition, or render the treatment which is alleged to have been performed or rendered negligently by the defendant whose conduct is at issue; and

C) Except as provided in subparagraph D) of this paragraph:

(i) Is a member of the same profession;

(ii) Is a medical doctor testifying as to the standard of care of a defendant who is a doctor of osteopathy; or

(iii) Is a doctor of osteopathy testifying as to the standard of care of a defendant who is a medical doctor; and

D) Notwithstanding any other provision of this Code section, an expert who is a physician and, as a result of having, during at least three of the last five years immediately preceding the time the act or omission is alleged to have occurred, supervised, taught, or instructed nurses, nurse practitioners, certified registered nurse anesthetists, nurse midwives, physician's assistants, physical therapists, occupational therapist, or medical support staff, has knowledge of the standard of care of that health care provider under the circumstances at issue shall be competent to testify as to the standard of care of that health care provider. However, a nurse, nurse practitioner, certified registered nurse anesthetist, nurse midwife, physician's assistant, physical therapist, occupational therapist, or medical support staff shall not be competent to testify as to the standard of care of a physician.

(d) Upon motion of a party, the court may hold a pretrial hearing to determine whether the witness qualifies as an expert and whether the expert's testimony satisfies the requirements of subsections (a) and (b) of this Code section. Such hearing and ruling shall be completed no later than the final pretrial conference contemplated under Code Section 9–11–16.

(e) An affiant must meet the requirements of this Code section in order to be deemed qualified to testify as an expert by means of the affidavit required under Code Section 9–11–9.1.

(f) It is the intent of the legislature that, in all civil cases, the courts of the State of Georgia not be viewed as open to expert evidence that would not be admissible in other states. Therefore, in interpreting and applying this Code section, the courts of this state may draw from the opinions of the United States Supreme Court in Daubert v. Merrell Dow Pharmaceuticals, Inc., 509 U.S. 579 (1993); General Electric Co. v. Joiner, 522 U.S. 136 (1997); Kumho Tire Co., Ltd. v. Carmichael, 526 U.S. 137 (1999); and other cases in federal courts applying the standards announced by the United States Supreme Court in these cases.

APPENDIX H

Federal Rules of Evidence, Rules 702, 703

FEDERAL RULES OF EVIDENCE, RULES 702 and 703

RULE 702. TESTIMONY BY EXPERTS

If scientific, technical, or other specialized knowledge will assist the trier of fact to understand the evidence or to determine a fact in issue, a witness qualified as an expert by knowledge, skill, experience, training, or education, may testify thereto in the form of an opinion or otherwise, if (1) the testimony is based upon sufficient facts or data, (2) the testimony is the product of reliable principles and methods, and (3) the witness has applied the principles and methods reliably to the facts of the case.

[Amended April 17, 2000, effective December 1, 2000.]

RULE 703. BASES OF OPINION TESTIMONY BY EXPERTS

The facts or data in the particular case upon which an expert bases an opinion or inference may be those perceived by or made known to the expert at or before the hearing. If of a type reasonably relied upon by experts in the particular field in forming opinions or inferences upon the subject, the facts or data need not be admissible in evidence in order for the opinion or inference to be admitted. Facts or data that are otherwise inadmissible shall not be disclosed to the jury by the proponent of the opinion or inference unless the court determines that their probative value in assisting the jury to evaluate the expert's opinion substantially outweighs their prejudicial effect.

[Amended March 2, 1987, effective October 1, 1987; April 17, 2000, effective December 1, 2000.]

APPENDIX I

Federal Rules of Civil Procedure, Rule 26(a)(2)

FEDERAL RULES OF CIVIL PROCEDURE

RULE 26(a)(2):

(2) *Disclosure of Expert Testimony*

(A) In addition to the disclosures required by paragraph (1), a party shall disclose to other parties the identity of any person who may be used at trial to present evidence under Rules 702, 703, or 705 of the Federal Rules of Evidence.

(B) Except as otherwise stipulated or directed by the court, this disclosure shall, with respect to a witness who is retained or specially employed to provide expert testimony in the case or whose duties as an employee of the party regularly involve giving expert testimony, be accompanied by a written report prepared and signed by the witness. The report shall contain a complete statement of all opinions to be expressed and the basis and reasons therefore; the data or other information considered by the witness in forming the opinions; any exhibits to be used as a summary of or support for the opinions; the qualifications of the witness, including a list of all publications authored by the witness within the preceding ten years; the compensation to be paid for the study and testimony; and a listing of any other cases in which the witness has testified as an expert at trial or by deposition within the preceding our years.

(C) These disclosures shall be made at the times and in the sequence directed by the court. In the absence of other directions from the court or stipulation by the parties, the disclosures shall be made at least 90 days before the trial date or the date the case is to be ready for trial or, if the evidence is intended solely to contradict or rebut evidence on the same subject matter identified by another party under paragraph (2)(B), within 30 days after the disclosure made by the other party. The parties shall supplement these disclosures when required under subdivision (e)(1).

APPENDIX J

Federal Rules of Civil Procedure, Rule 26(a)(4)

FEDERAL RULES OF CIVIL PROCEDURE

RULE 26(a)(4):

(4) *Trial Preparation: Experts.*

(A) A party may depose any person who has been identified as an expert whose opinions may be presented at trial. If a report from the expert is required under subdivision (a)(2)(B), the deposition shall not be conducted until after the report is provided.

(B) A party may, through interrogatories or by deposition, discover facts known or opinions held by an expert who has been retained or specially employed by another party in anticipation of litigation or preparation for trial and who is not expected to be called as a witness at trial only as provided in Rule 35(b) or upon a showing of exceptional circumstances under which it is impracticable for the party seeking discovery to obtain facts or opinion on the same subject by other means.

(C) Unless manifest injustice would result, (i) the court shall require that the party seeking discovery pay the expert a reasonable fee for time spent in responding to discovery under this subdivision; and (ii) with respect to discovery obtained under subdivision (b)(4)(B) of this rule the court shall require the party seeking discovery to pay the other party a fair portion of the fess and expenses reasonably incurred by the latter party in obtaining facts and opinions from the expert.

APPENDIX K

Local Rule 26.2(c) for the Northern District of Georgia

LOCAL RULES FOR THE U.S. DISTRICT COURT, NORTHERN DISTRICT OF GEORGIA

N.D.Ga.L.R. 26.2(C)

C. Expert Witnesses. Any party who desires to use the testimony of an expert witness shall designate the expert sufficiently early in the discovery period to permit the opposing party the opportunity to depose the expert and, if desired, to name its own expert witness sufficiently in advance of the close of discovery so that a similar discovery deposition of the second expert might also be conducted prior to the close of discovery.

Any party who does not comply with the provisions of the foregoing paragraph shall not be permitted to offer the testimony of the party's expert, unless expressly authorized by court order based upon a showing that the failure to comply was justified.

Any party objecting to an expert's testimony based upon *Daubert v. Merrell Dow Pharms., Inc.,* 509 U.S. 579, 113 S.Ct. 2786 (1993) shall file a motion no later than the date that the proposed pretrial order is submitted. Otherwise, such objections will be waived, unless expressly authorized by court order based upon a showing that the failure to comply was justified.

[Effective April 15, 1997; amended effective January 1, 2001; May 1, 2001; June 1, 2002.]

Table of Laws and Rules

UNITED STATES CODE ANNOTATED

42 U.S.C.A. Sec.   **Sec.**
9201 .... 7:5 n.10

CODE OF FEDERAL REGULATIONS

49 C.F.R. Sec.	Sec.	49 C.F.R. Sec.	Sec.
40.1	10:11 n.2	393.65	10:11 n.8
325	10:11 n.1	393.100	10:11 n.9
382.101	10:11 n.2	395.1	10:11 n.5
391.1	10:11 n.3, 7	396.1	10:11 n.10
391.41	10:11 n.4	399	10:11 n.1
393.1	10:11 n.6		

FEDERAL RULES OF CIVIL PROCEDURE

Rule	Sec.	Rule	Sec.
26	4:6	26(a)(2)(B)	4:6
26(a)(2)(B)	4:6 n.25	104(a)	4:6 n.7

FEDERAL RULES OF EVIDENCE

Rule	Sec.	Rule	Sec.
104	1:12		3:3 n.8, 11; 3:7; 3:8 n.10; 3:9 n.1;
104(a)	4:6 n.1, 2		5:1; 5:3 n.6; 5:8 n.11; 6:2; 12:2;
403	1:3		12:3 n.14, 35; 12:4 n.2; 12:5;
702 . 1:1; 1:3; 1:5; 1:6 n.1, 3, 4, 5, 6, 7,			12:6 n.15
8, 9, 10, 11, 12, 13, 14, 15, 16,		703 .. 1:3 n.26; 1:7 n.1, 2, 3, 4, 5, 6, 7,	
17, 18, 19, 20, 21, 22, 23; 1:7		8, 9; 1:11; 2:8 n.5, 11, 18, 19, 20;	
n.10, 11, 12; 1:8; 1:10; 2:9 n.1;		9:15 n.8, 12; 11:3 n.13	
2:10; 2:11; 2:12; 3:1; 3:2 n.7, 12;			

GEORGIA CODE

GEORGIA CODE—Continued

Table of Cases

H

Hailey v. Blalock, 209 Ga. App. 345, 433 S.E.2d 337 (1993)—§§ 4:5 n.1; 9:14 n.12, 14

Hall v. Harris, 239 Ga. App. 812, 521 S.E.2d 638 (1999)—§§ 7:6 n.3, 4; 7:8 n.22; 7:9 n.1

Hall v. Scott USA, Ltd., 198 Ga. App. 197, 400 S.E.2d 700 (1990)—§ 5:11 n.1

Hall v. State, 255 Ga. App. 631, 566 S.E.2d 374 (2002)—§§ 2:1 n.6, 11; 8:3 n.8

Hall v. State, 261 Ga. 778, 415 S.E.2d 158 (1991)—§ 2:4 n.1

Hall v. State, 196 Ga. App. 523, 396 S.E.2d 271 (1990)—§ 8:3 n.3

Hall v. United Ins. Co. of America, 367 F.3d 1255, 64 Fed. R. Evid. Serv. 76 (11th Cir. 2004)—§§ 3:2 n.10; 3:7 n.6

Hamblin v. City Of Albany, 272 Ga. App. 246, 612 S.E.2d 69 (2005)—§ 7:2 n.2

Hambrick v. Makuch, 228 Ga. App. 1, 491 S.E.2d 71 (1997)—§ 11:1 n.1

Hammond v. State, 156 Ga. 880, 120 S.E. 539 (1923)—§ 11:2 n.8

Hammond v. City of Warner Robins, 224 Ga. App. 684, 482 S.E.2d 422 (1997)—§§ 7:5 n.2, 7, 13, 17, 18, 19

Hancock v. State, 277 Ga. 835, 596 S.E.2d 127 (2004)—§§ 8:8 n.13, 14

Handy v. Speth, 210 Ga. App. 155, 435 S.E.2d 623 (1993)—§ 11:4 n.11

Hardeman v. Spires, 232 Ga. App. 694, 503 S.E.2d 588 (1998)—§ 7:3 n.2

Hardin v. Hunter, 174 Ga. App. 756, 331 S.E.2d 83 (1985)—§ 12:1 n.2

Hardwick v. Price, 114 Ga. App. 817, 152 S.E.2d 905 (1966)—§§ 11:6 n.1, 10

Harper v. Patterson, 270 Ga. App. 437, 606 S.E.2d 887, 194 Ed. Law Rep. 1016 (2004)—§§ 2:7 n.9; 8:3 n.13

Harper v. State, 249 Ga. 519, 292 S.E.2d 389 (1982)—§§ 1:1 n.13; 1:8 n.1, 2, 3, 5; 6:2 n.2; 8:7 n.22

Harrell v. Lusk, 263 Ga. 895, 439 S.E.2d 896 (1994)—§ 4:2 n.1

Harris v. Hardman, 133 Ga. App. 941, 212 S.E.2d 883 (1975)—§ 11:6 n.23

Harris v. Leader, 231 Ga. App. 709, 499 S.E.2d 374 (1998)—§ 9:10 n.15

Harris v. State, 256 Ga. 350, 349 S.E.2d 374 (1986)—§§ 8:8 n.3, 14

Harris v. State, 168 Ga. App. 458, 309 S.E.2d 431 (1983)—§§ 8:7 n.20, 21

Harvey v. Kidney Center of Cent. Georgia, Inc., 213 Ga. App. 319, 444 S.E.2d 590 (1994)—§§ 4:4 n.3, 6

Hashwani v. Barbar, 822 F.2d 1038 (11th Cir. 1987)—§ 4:6 n.13

Hayes v. Brown, 108 Ga. App. 360, 133 S.E.2d 102 (1963)—§§ 9:1 n.9; 9:7 n.3

HCA Health Services of Georgia, Inc. v. Hampshire, 206 Ga. App. 108, 424 S.E.2d 293 (1992)—§ 4:3 n.24

Heller v. Shaw Industries, Inc., 167 F.3d 146, 50 Fed. R. Evid. Serv. 1393 (3d Cir. 1999)—§§ 1:6 n.21, 22

H. Elton Thompson & Associates, P.C. v. Williams, 164 Ga. App. 571, 298 S.E.2d 539 (1982)—§§ 7:7 n.2, 3, 4, 9; 7:8 n.6

Hendrix v. Phillips, 207 Ga. App. 394, 428 S.E.2d 91, 82 Ed. Law Rep. 259 (1993)—§ 11:4 n.4

Henry Grady Hotel Corp. v. Watts, 119 Ga. App. 251, 167 S.E.2d 205 (1969)—§§ 11:5 n.19, 20, 25

Henslee v. MARTA, 142 Ga. App. 821, 237 S.E.2d 225 (1977)—§ 11:5 n.27

J

Johnson v. State, 271 Ga. 375, 519 S.E.2d 221 (1999)—§ 8:6 n.9

Johnson v. State, 236 Ga. App. 252, 511 S.E.2d 603 (1999)—§ 8:6 n.9

Johnson v. State, 266 Ga. 624, 469 S.E.2d 152 (1996)—§§ 2:3 n.14; 8:2 n.1, 6, 8, 18, 19; 8:5 n.4, 11

Johnson v. Wills Memorial Hosp. & Nursing Home, 178 Ga. App. 459, 343 S.E.2d 700 (1986)—§§ 9:8 n.6; 9:11 n.10

Joiner v. Lane, 235 Ga. App. 121, 508 S.E.2d 203 (1998)—§§ 2:8 n.9; 11:3 n.7, 8, 9, 10

Jones v. Amazing Products, Inc., 231 F. Supp. 2d 1228 (N.D. Ga. 2002)— § 5:5 n.6

Jones v. Bates, 261 Ga. 240, 403 S.E.2d 804 (1991)—§§ 9:8 n.1, 3, 4, 7

Jones v. Chatham County Bd. of Tax Assessors, 270 Ga. App. 483, 606 S.E.2d 673 (2004)—§ 1:8 n.6

Jones v. City of Columbus, Ga., 120 F.3d 248, 38 Fed. R. Serv. 3d 746 (11th Cir. 1997)—§ 4:6 n.11

Jones v. Hutchins, 101 Ga. App. 141, 113 S.E.2d 475 (1960)—§§ 11:5 n.2, 3, 9, 10, 11

Jones v. NordicTrack, Inc., 274 Ga. 115, 550 S.E.2d 101 (2001)—§§ 5:1 n.7; 5:5 n.5

Jones v. Orris, 274 Ga. App. 52, 616 S.E.2d 820 (2005)—§§ 9:13 n.3, 10; 11:1 n.11

Jones v. Sofamor S.N.C., 1999 WL 1062103 (N.D. Ga. 1999)—§§ 5:8 n.1, 2, 3, 4

Jones v. State, 273 Ga. 213, 539 S.E.2d 143 (2000)—§ 8:6 n.10

Jones v. State, 191 Ga. App. 561, 382 S.E.2d 612 (1989)—§ 8:8 n.12

Jones v. State, 232 Ga. 762, 208 S.E.2d 850 (1974)—§§ 8:6 n.7, 8, 14

Jordan v. Georgia Power Co., 219 Ga. App. 690, 466 S.E.2d 601 (1995)— §§ 1:8 n.6; 6:1 n.9; 6:2 n.1, 3; 6:4 n.8, 9; 7:5 n.9, 24, 25

Jordan v. Santa Fe Engineering, Inc., 198 Ga. App. 600, 402 S.E.2d 304 (1991)—§§ 6:3 n.2, 3, 4, 6, 9, 12, 13

Jordan v. Smoot, 191 Ga. App. 74, 380 S.E.2d 714 (1989)—§§ 10:7 n.1; 11:1 n.4, 5, 8

Jordan, Jones & Goulding, Inc. v. Wilson, 197 Ga. App. 354, 398 S.E.2d 385 (1990)—§ 7:7 n.5

K

Kane v. Cohen, 182 Ga. App. 485, 356 S.E.2d 94 (1987)—§ 11:4 n.2

Kapsch v. Stowers, 209 Ga. App. 767, 434 S.E.2d 539 (1993)—§§ 2:6 n.13; 9:7 n.2

Karoly v. Kawasaki Motors Corp., U.S.A., 259 Ga. App. 225, 576 S.E.2d 625 (2003)—§ 5:6 n.5

Kellogg, In re, 197 F.3d 1116 (11th Cir. 1999)—§ 4:6 n.14

Kennedy v. State, 274 Ga. 396, 554 S.E.2d 178 (2001)—§§ 8:5 n.3, 9

Kennestone Hosp. v. Hopson, 273 Ga. 145, 538 S.E.2d 742 (2000)— §§ 11:4 n.19, 20, 23

Kenney v. Piedmont Hospital, 136 Ga. App. 660, 222 S.E.2d 162 (1975)— § 9:11 n.1

Ken Thomas of Georgia, Inc. v. Halim, 266 Ga. App. 570, 597 S.E.2d 615 (2004)—§ 10:9 n.14

Ketchup v. Howard, 247 Ga. App. 54, 543 S.E.2d 371 (2000)—§§ 2:3 n.6; 9:7 n.1; 9:10 n.9, 10, 11, 12, 13, 14, 15, 16

McCorkle v. Department of Transp., 257 Ga. App. 397, 571 S.E.2d 160 (2002)—§ 1:1 n.2

McCorvey v. Baxter Healthcare Corp., 298 F.3d 1253, 59 Fed. R. Evid. Serv. 856 (11th Cir. 2002)—§§ 3:1 n.10; 3:4 n.13; 5:3 n.6, 7, 8, 9

McCrickard v. State, 249 Ga. App. 715, 549 S.E.2d 505 (2001)—§ 8:3 n.13

McCurley v. Ludwig, 215 Ga. App. 798, 452 S.E.2d 554 (1994)—§ 7:8 n.20

McDaniel v. Hendrix, 260 Ga. 857, 401 S.E.2d 260 (1991)—§ 9:11 n.9

McDowell v. Brown, 392 F.3d 1283 (11th Cir. 2004)—§§ 3:1 n.16; 3:2 n.11, 15; 3:7 n.9; 3:9 n.12

McDuffie County v. Rogers, 124 Ga. App. 442, 184 S.E.2d 46 (1971)—§ 11:5 n.15

McElmurray v. Augusta-Richmond County, 274 Ga. App. 605, 618 S.E.2d 59 (2005)—§§ 7:5 n.6, 14, 15

McEver v. Worrell Enterprises, 223 Ga. App. 627, 478 S.E.2d 445 (1996)—§§ 1:11 n.3; 2:8 n.7, 12

McGee v. Evenflo Co., Inc., 2003 WL 23350439 (M.D. Ga. 2003)—§§ 3:1 n.16; 3:3 n.11; 3:4 n.7, 9, 10, 14, 15; 3:5 n.9; 3:7 n.3, 6; 5:8 n.5, 6, 7, 8, 9, 10, 11; 5:12 n.3, 4, 5, 6, 7

McGee v. Evenflo Co., Inc., 2003 W.L. 2335049 (M.D. Ga. 2003)—§§ 3:8 n.6, 9, 10

MCG Health, Inc. v. Casey, 269 Ga. App. 125, 603 S.E.2d 438 (2004)—§§ 4:3 n.11; 4:4 n.13; 9:10 n.17

M.C.J., In re, 242 Ga. App. 852, 531 S.E.2d 404 (2000)—§§ 4:7 n.26, 27

McLendon v. Georgia Kaolin Co., Inc., 841 F. Supp. 415 (M.D. Ga. 1994)—§§ 3:2 n.10; 12:3 n.25; 12:7 n.4

McMichen v. Moattar, 221 Ga. App. 230, 470 S.E.2d 800 (1996)—§§ 2:5 n.22; 2:6 n.9; 10:6 n.3, 4, 5

McNabb v. Landis, 223 Ga. App. 894, 479 S.E.2d 194 (1996)—§§ 2:3 n.9; 9:11 n.2, 3

McNeal v. Days Inn of America, Inc., 230 Ga. App. 786, 498 S.E.2d 294 (1998)—§§ 7:4 n.4, 9, 10

Media Sport & Arts s.r.l. v. Kinney Shoe Corp., 52 Fed. R. Evid. Serv. 1338 (S.D. N.Y. 1999)—§ 12.11 n.2

Medlock v. State, 263 Ga. 246, 430 S.E.2d 754 (1993)—§§ 2:6 n.11; 2:7 n.10

Mendoza v. Pennington, 239 Ga. App. 300, 519 S.E.2d 715 (1999)—§ 4:4 n.12

Metropolitan Life Ins. Co. v. Saul, 189 Ga. 1, 5 S.E.2d 214 (1939)—§§ 1:1 n.5; 2:5 n.4

Michaels v. Kroger Co., 172 Ga. App. 280, 322 S.E.2d 903 (1984)—§§ 11:5 n.2, 3, 5, 9, 10, 16, 23, 24

Michigan Millers Mut. Ins. Corp. v. Benfield, 140 F.3d 915, 49 Fed. R. Evid. Serv. 549 (11th Cir. 1998)—§ 3:8 n.6

Micro Chemical, Inc. v. Lextron, Inc., 317 F.3d 1387, 60 Fed. R. Evid. Serv. 794 (Fed. Cir. 2003)—§ 12:5 n.2

Milanowicz v. The Raymond Corp., 148 F. Supp. 2d 525, 57 Fed. R. Evid. Serv. 395 (D.N.J. 2001)—§§ 3:4 n.9; 5:8 n.7

Millar Elevator Service Co. v. O'Shields, 222 Ga. App. 456, 475 S.E.2d 188 (1996)—§ 7:3 n.3

Q

Rosen v. Ciba-Geigy Corp., 78 F.3d 316, 43 Fed. R. Evid. Serv. 836 (7th Cir. 1996)—§§ 3:1 n.9; 3:2 n.15; 3:6 n.18; 3:7 n.3

Ross v. Chatham County Hosp. Authority, 200 Ga. App. 448, 408 S.E.2d 490 (1991)—§ 9:11 n.7

Rouse v. Fussell, 106 Ga. App. 259, 126 S.E.2d 830 (1962)—§ 10:4 n.3

Rowe Entertainment, Inc. v. William Morris Agency, Inc., 2003 WL 22124991 (S.D. N.Y. 2003)—§§ 12:5 n.34, 35

Rubio v. Davis, 231 Ga. App. 425, 500 S.E.2d 367 (1998)—§ 11:5 n.4

Ruiz-Troche v. Pepsi Cola of Puerto Rico Bottling Co., 161 F.3d 77, 50 Fed. R. Evid. Serv. 984 (1st Cir. 1998)—§ 1:6 n.22

S

Salisbury v. State, 221 Ga. 718, 146 S.E.2d 776 (1966)—§ 8:7 n.5

Samuelson v. Lord, Aeck & Sergeant, Inc., 205 Ga. App. 568, 423 S.E.2d 268 (1992)—§ 7:7 n.8

Sanders v. Ramo, 203 Ga. App. 43, 416 S.E.2d 333 (1992)—§§ 9:12 n.1; 9:14 n.8

Sanders v. State, 251 Ga. 70, 303 S.E.2d 13 (1983)—§§ 8:4 n.9, 10, 11

Sandford v. Howard, 161 Ga. App. 495, 288 S.E.2d 739 (1982)—§§ 9:5 n.8, 9, 10, 14

Satterwhite v. State, 212 Ga. App. 543, 442 S.E.2d 5 (1994)—§ 2:7 n.8

Savannah Valley Production Credit Ass'n v. Cheek, 248 Ga. 745, 285 S.E.2d 689 (1982)—§§ 2:6 n.13; 9:7 n.2

Sawyers v. State, 211 Ga. App. 668, 440 S.E.2d 256 (1994)—§ 8:6 n.9

Schriever v. Maddox, 259 Ga. App. 558, 578 S.E.2d 210 (2003)—§§ 11:5 n.8, 9

Scott v. Chapman, 203 Ga. App. 58, 416 S.E.2d 111 (1992)—§ 10:8 n.2

Seaboard Air Line Ry. v. Bradley, 125 Ga. 193, 54 S.E. 69 (1906)—§ 4:7 n.3

Seaboard Coast Line R. Co. v. Clark, 122 Ga. App. 237, 176 S.E.2d 596 (1970)—§ 5:6 n.1

S.E.C. v. Lipson, 46 F. Supp. 2d 758, 51 Fed. R. Evid. Serv. 1383 (N.D. Ill. 1998)—§ 12.11 n.2

Seely v. Loyd H. Johnson Const. Co., Inc., 220 Ga. App. 719, 470 S.E.2d 283 (1996)—§§ 4:2 n.1; 7:8 n.19, 20

Self v. Executive Committee of Georgia Baptist Convention of Georgia, Inc., 245 Ga. 548, 266 S.E.2d 168 (1980)—§§ 7:2 n.3; 9:7 n.1; 9:8 n.2

Sembler Atlanta Development I, LLC v. URS/Dames & Moore, Inc., 268 Ga. App. 7, 601 S.E.2d 397 (2004)—§§ 4:2 n.4; 4:3 n.20; 7:7 n.7; 7:9 n.3

Shannon v. Kaylor, 133 Ga. App. 514, 211 S.E.2d 368 (1974)—§§ 4:7 n.12, 15

Shea v. Phillips, 213 Ga. App. 269, 98 S.E.2d 552 (1957)—§§ 9:1 n.7; 9:7 n.1, 5; 9:9 n.2, 3, 8, 11

Sheehan v. Daily Racing Form, Inc., 104 F.3d 940 (7th Cir. 1997)—§ 1:6 n.18

Sheets v. State, 244 Ga. App. 304, 535 S.E.2d 312 (2000)—§ 11:2 n.7

Shepherd v. Michelin Tire Corp., 6 F. Supp. 2d 1307 (N.D. Ala. 1997)—§§ 5:10 n.3, 4, 5, 6

Shipman v. Horizon Corp., 151 Ga. App. 242, 259 S.E.2d 221 (1979)—§ 12:1 n.5

Tysinger v. Smisson, 176 Ga. App. 604, 337 S.E.2d 49 (1985)—§ 9:12 n.1

U

Ultima-Trimble, Ltd. v. Department of Transp., 214 Ga. App. 607, 448 S.E.2d 498 (1994)—§ 2:6 n.15

Union Carbide Corp. v. Holton, 136 Ga. App. 726, 222 S.E.2d 105 (1975)—§ 5:11 n.6

Uniroyal Goodrich Tire Co. v. Ford, 218 Ga. App. 248, 461 S.E.2d 877 (1995)—§ 5:6 n.4

Upson County Hosp., Inc. v. Head, 246 Ga. App. 386, 540 S.E.2d 626 (2000)—§ 9:14 n.7

U.S. v. Abreu, 406 F.3d 1304, 67 Fed. R. Evid. Serv. 17 (11th Cir. 2005)—§§ 3:6 n.5, 15

U.S. v. Ambriz-Vasquez, 34 Fed. Appx. 356 (9th Cir. 2002)—§ 4:6 n.6

U.S. v. Bennett, 368 F.3d 1343 (11th Cir. 2004)—§ 3:2 n.5

U.S. v. Brown, 415 F.3d 1257, 67 Fed. R. Evid. Serv. 816 (11th Cir. 2005)—§§ 3:1 n.11, 12; 3:2 n.2, 10; 3:3 n.8; 3:4 n.19; 3:5 n.2; 3:6 n.5

U.S. v. Duque, 176 F.R.D. 691 (N.D. Ga. 1998)—§§ 3:2 n.10; 3:6 n.11, 12

U.S. v. 14.38 Acres of Land, More or Less Situated in Leflore County, State of Miss., 80 F.3d 1074, 44 Fed. R. Evid. Serv. 103 (5th Cir. 1996)—§ 1:6 n.23

U.S. v. Frazier, 387 F.3d 1244, 65 Fed. R. Evid. Serv. 675 (11th Cir. 2004)—§§ 1:6 n.2; 3:1 n.2, 4, 10; 3:2 n.4, 6, 12, 13; 3:4 n.9; 3:7 n.5; 3:8 n.10; 3:9 n.2, 3

U.S. v. Gilliard, 133 F.3d 809, 48 Fed. R. Evid. Serv. 832 (11th Cir. 1998)—§§ 3:4 n.19; 3:5 n.7

U.S. v. Great Lakes Dredge & Dock Co., 259 F.3d 1300 (11th Cir. 2001)—§ 3:5 n.5

U.S. v. Hamaker, 455 F.3d 1316, 70 Fed. R. Evid. Serv. 722 (11th Cir. 2006)—§ 12.11 n.2

U.S. v. Hansen, 262 F.3d 1217, 57 Fed. R. Evid. Serv. 121 (11th Cir. 2001)—§§ 1:6 n.2; 3:1 n.2; 4:6 n.8

U.S. v. Henderson, 409 F.3d 1293, 67 Fed. R. Evid. Serv. 350 (11th Cir. 2005)—§§ 3:4 n.16, 17, 18, 20, 21, 22

U.S. v. Lauder, 409 F.3d 1254, 67 Fed. R. Evid. Serv. 486 (10th Cir. 2005)—§ 4:6 n.6

U.S. v. 2.61 Acres of Land, More or Less, Situated in Mariposa County, State of Cal., 791 F.2d 666 (9th Cir. 1985)—§ 4:6 n.13

U.S. v. Waters, 194 F.3d 926, 52 Fed. R. Evid. Serv. 1574 (8th Cir. 1999)—§ 4:6 n.6

U.S. Fidelity & Guaranty Co. v. Wilson, 103 Ga. App. 674, 120 S.E.2d 198 (1961)—§ 11:6 n.3

U.S. Fidelity & Guar. Co. v. J. I. Case Co., 209 Ga. App. 61, 432 S.E.2d 654 (1993)—§ 5:1 n.10

V

Val D'Aosta Co. v. Cross, 241 Ga. App. 583, 526 S.E.2d 580 (1999)—§§ 7:3 n.8, 9, 10

Vaughn v. Protective Ins. Co., 243 Ga. App. 79, 532 S.E.2d 159 (2000)—§ 2:3 n.2

Index